WHERE SADNESS BREATHES

a true-crime novel
by Jack Earl

Jack Earl Publishing
Roseburg, Oregon 97470

Third Printing November 2013

All photographs and documents are from the author's private collection except where noted. Those exceptions were originally published in *The Sacramento Union* newspaper and are republished courtesy of the Library Special Collections Department of the University of California at Davis.

Interior design and formatting – Gail Hanson
Cover design – Caroline Gober

ISBN 1-934 332-10-0

Printed in The United States of America

Table of Contents

This is a true story.
No names have been changed or pertinent information altered in its creation. This book has been compiled from physical evidence, personal interviews, newspaper and other media reports, police reports, legal documents, court transcripts, and available facts. Portions of the dialogue between some individuals depicted herein have been extrapolated or created by the same means.

Jack Earl

FOREWORD.

We met the way Gretzler and Steelman did, by accident, kismet, or design; depending on the way you see stuff like this. Simple as the ringing of my old black landline. Weaver Barkman, feisty Pima County homicide detective that I'd done a magazine profile on, screeched. "Greenie, I got someone in this office right now who can't wait to bend your ear." And with that he handed the phone to Jack Earl.

That was twenty years ago. And in our first conversation I sorta tossed Jack a slight curve: That there was a small documentary about Steelman and Gretzler in the works. That a law clerk who met Gretzler at 23, 24, and later became a juvenile court judge, hungered to write a book about him. How a born again woman wanted me to pen the story of Willie Steelman's alleged death row religious conversion.

After a few minutes, I could hear the release of Jack's long sigh, his expression of disappointment. He'd said he thought he was the only one chasing the Steelman/Gretzler murder spree when out of nowhere Barkman springs me on him.

At the time I was the Features Editor for the local city magazine and I'd already forged a close relationship with Douglas Gretzler going on four years. I was Gretzler's confidante. He was my friend, a prison source, a subject of fascination. For ten years we exchanged letters and tapes.

Jack and I met in late spring. And in July we drove the Phoenix freeways that steamed from the summer heat, with the Superstition Mountains our backdrop. We talked about his rocky marriage, his print shop business, his two grown children and of course, the murders. He had always played by the rules. Done the right thing. And was infinitely curious how people could move from ordinary and turn cold and dark. Like Willie and Doug.

After the hour drive, we landed in Florence, home to Arizona's death row.

I remember the three of us sitting in the over painted visitation room. At first it was just tip-toe talk across Radio Shack plastic phones as I noticed beads of moisture pop like a rash across Gretzler's forehead. I'd spent hours in visits with him and I'd never seen him break a sweat. We crossed the easy terrain of Led Zeppelin (Gretzler's favorite rock group), weather (fry an egg hot) and he sweated more.

I brought up the violence, my filter turned off, cut through the polite play of words. *Talk about the spree, Doug*. He danced around the edges of those 17 days and 17 victims back in the fall of 1973. At one point Gretzler apologized to Jack; said *I'm so sorry for what I did to your family*. He seemed especially concerned about Jack's grandmother. His sorry ended up buried in a hail of cross talk and questions. I think for years Jack either didn't remember it or didn't really think it was a true apology.

I don't know if one can appropriately apologize for annihilating a family. The deed is done, the words ring hollow. Regardless of any remorse or guilt, Gretzler had punched his ticket.

After the visit Jack and I grabbed some Thirstbusters on the way out of town. He talked about seeing Gretzler for the first time in 1973 on a small black & white TV after he'd been captured. Jack thought they must've had the wrong guy – he sure didn't look like a killer. Skinny kid with a deer caught in the headlights atmosphere. The face of a college kid or accountant. He looked a bit like Jack felt. The following day after Jack's private visit, he said to me, a little surprised, – "Laura, I know more about what happened than he does."

Jack had caught the fever. In the last twenty years we've spent hundreds of hours talking about Steelman, about Gretzler, and the crimes that took the lives of 17 people, including Jack's Uncle Richard, Aunt Wanda, and their two kids, his teenage cousins, Ricky and Debbie.

While his obsession was still in the early stages, he latched onto one of the victims in particular. The young adventurous boy who had the bad fortune of getting picked up hitchhiking by Willie and Doug. Steve Loughran had just turned 18 and Jack wanted to chart the landscape of his short life.

Jack sat at a picnic table outside the sheriff's office in Pinal County, armed with play-by-play police reports. He was better at sniffing out official documents, any stray memo, than most professional reporters I've known. I'd tease him about playing the victim card, because people were often more willing to talk to him than me. And he was kind enough to give me copies of the small library he'd collected. We were friends with a touch of healthy competition thrown in.

He'd sit with old cops who remained territorial over a twenty-year-old solved mass murder and listen to them practically reprimand him for his interest, while hiding crime scene photographs they were sure would "upset" him. After they invariably took a restroom break, Jack, the guy who always played by the rules, would slip the duplicates, the triplicate records into his briefcase, strolling out the door with a smile. His good looking, friendly face could outsmart the most seasoned cop. And they never saw it coming.

Jack's a man that can't be figured out easily or stuffed into a neat stereotype. He does not give up or give in, no matter the obstacle. Comes from a gene pool that would make a model proud. Strong and bright blue eyes, features more symmetrical than not. When we first met he favored baseball hats. As the hair wore off, he shaved it cue ball smooth and hip.

The years marched on. Jack divorced, remarried, had another family. I got married, moved, stopped writing for a spell. But we always kept in touch, even with the big spaces between, when one or the other was knee deep in writing and there was always another question to be asked.

Sometimes we wondered out loud about what happened that savage drizzly night in the orchards of Victor. Why didn't the men fight back? They were young and strong. Thick with muscle. I think we asked that question partly because we project what we hope we'd do if ever faced with mortal danger. Because to think otherwise was to put ourselves in that walk-in closet, with the nightmare on perpetual repeat.

In March 1998, Jack sat in my Tucson living room with a draft of his book. At that point I think it weighed in at more than 1100 pages. He read parts to me, then admitted "I'm the historian and collector of Steelman/Gretzler memorabilia."

I agree with him. While I've always considered myself Gretzler's archivist, Jack is a puzzle solver. Just like the old Ford Mustangs he'd buy and reassemble, Jack was able to take the thousands of pieces, with so many different angles you'd need a spread sheet, and break the puzzle down into not only something manageable, but infinitely readable. The fever burned bright in him and carried him through.

As they say in the world of writing, this baby has narrative drive – I couldn't wait to turn the page, and you won't be able to either.

Laura Ann Greenberg
2012

PROLOGUE.

Collecting the lives of strangers.
Wednesday, November 7, 1973.

On this day, the front page story in the afternoon edition of the Antioch *Daily Ledger* was brief and careful with details. There were no names given, let alone how or why it happened. The paper simply reported that nine people – two entire families – had been found murdered in farmhouse near Lodi. All had been shot, including two small children.

The location startled me. Lodi was less than an hour from where I lived and we had relatives there. As it was, just a week earlier we had driven over to visit an aunt and uncle, and there had been plenty of trips as a kid for big weekend get-togethers. As I read, I remembered muttering something about these being such crazy times, because Lodi was the last place on earth I would have ever expected anything like this to happen.

And it was at that moment when the phone rang. It was my mother, and although she usually waited until the weekend, for some reason the call didn't seem out of place, except that she was crying.

"Jackie…?" She always calls me that when she is upset. "Jackie. I have some very bad news."

My heart sank. My father had been away on business. I was certain there must have been an accident, and so I braced myself. But before I could speak, she continued. "It's your Uncle Richard…and Aunt Wanda," she sputtered. "Ricky and Debbie too."

And in that instant, it all fell into place; the newspaper story, the phone call, and now this sick, gut wrenching feeling that indeed something horrible had happened. Mom told me all she knew, which was not much, including the obvious, Why?

She didn't know. No one knew.

Decades later, the images of that evening are still crystal clear in my mind. I remember hanging up the phone, trembling. I was barely 22, but a husband, and a father of a 3 year old boy. What's more, I had the same last name as my aunt and uncle, and what my Uncle Richard could have done to make someone angry enough to kill him, I had no idea. But I was terrified. Who knows? Maybe we were next! I double locked the windows and doors, gave my son and wife an extra kiss, and put a softball bat next to my bed. It all seems so crazy now, perhaps even a bit silly, but I never closed my eyes that night. To this day, it was the only time in my life I had wished I owned a gun.

The family began arriving in Lodi the next day, and the one thing I remember is the phone rang constantly as new reports and even more questions came in. And there always seemed to be a sheriff deputy standing around somewhere, ordered by his boss to protect us from only God knows what. What skimpy details they provided were carefully worded, as if to somehow calm us, knowing the truth would be difficult to handle. I remember a deputy taking my father aside, cupping his hand over his mouth and explaining, "Each had a single bullet. We assure you they felt no pain." We would soon discover otherwise.

By now, a mere 24 hours after the bodies were discovered, authorities confirmed they already knew who they were looking for; a local by the name of Willie Steelman, and his partner from New York, Douglas Gretzler. In fact, it was on the front page of the newspaper that morning when I first saw Willie – a mug shot taken years earlier – a photo that would soon become his undoing. And while this smothering sense of dread made the time seem so much longer, before the day was over our family hovered around the TV and watched Steelman being captured 40 miles north in Sacramento. Gretzler, who was arrested minutes earlier at a dingy downtown hotel, had told the cops where they could find him.

So for many, it was finished. And yet to me, this whole picture seemed very wrong. I guess I wasn't quite sure what to expect, really. I imagined the killer being some old con like you see in the movies, but these guys were my age! I kept waiting for a correction to be made, but it never came. And before the weekend was over, Willie Steelman and Douglas Gretzler admitted to not only these murders, but to a staggering month-long killing rampage of horrific porportion. During that weekend, it seemed as if bodies were being uncovered almost hourly throughout Arizona and California. When the search finally came to an end late Sunday, the count had climbed to 17. While we were all shocked at this string of killings, I was absolutely astounded at the pair who now had confessed to committing them.

We buried Richard, Wanda, Debbie and Ricky the following Monday, afterwhich our families returned home with this vain attempt to sort it all out. Over the coming years, death took others, so we all found new reasons to mourn, and I'm sure for some of us, those few foggy days in November so many years before, simply faded away.

But not for me. I could never get it out of my head. I kept thinking back to that house on Orchard Road and all those people; two entire families, plus a young man and woman with dreams of starting a family of their own. Men, women and children tied up and executed with not one bullet, but one after another, after another, after another, to a number unthinkable. I remember someone telling me that when they removed Debbie's body, a Kleenex was clutched tightly in her hand. That last picture I had of her in my head drenched me in sadness, and I could not for one minute imagine the horror as they watched the one next to them die; a father, a son, a wife, a daughter, knowing their turn was coming, knowing these were final seconds of their lives.

It also haunted me, that while I knew my aunt, uncle and cousins so well, I knew nothing about the two men who, in the blink of an eye, changed everything forever. I remember thinking over that November weekend, when all this was swirling around us, that one day someone would have to explain it to me, because nothing made sense. There would have to be a book, a movie, or a story that would lay it all out so I could see it, touch it, and maybe somehow understand it. And so I waited.

But two decades passed and the story never came. There was never anything written that explained how or why it happened. There was never a big trial where the truth could be exposed, let alone a reasonable explanation given to satisfy this unsettling feeling of loss felt by so many. Eventually, Willie and Doug disappeared, and their words, their story, vanished along with them. To this day, it remains one of the single most terrifying killing sprees in American history, and yet, through all those years, this story remained a secret. The names of Willie Steelman and Douglas Gretzler are not found in any book anywhere, except volumes of legal ones their cases would help write.

And so it was, that this murder of my family, along with thirteen other people I never knew, tormented me for years, and honestly, the lives of the two men responsible troubled me equally as much. Then there came this winter day almost twenty years after the killings when I realized that if this story were to be told, it would be up to me to do it. Until this moment I had lived my life within the white lines. I had never once known the other side – the secrets and deeds of the evil and wayward souls, who until now were only found in books and movies, but never on my doorstep. I had spent 40 years trying to be good, to be responsible, to always do the right thing. Yes, I was afraid of the dark. Or at the very least, in awe of it. Despite being a child of the 60's, I had never once tasted what it was like to drop out, give in, give up, or flirt with the unknown, let alone dance with the devil. In every good sense of the word I had lived a very sheltered life. I had never been a part of death. I had no idea what was on the other side, no clue about dysfunctional families, a child's world absent of love, the crippling dispair that had a way of wrapping its arms around an unfortunate few, or what ugliness could slither amongst us, even in places like Lodi. I never knew hatred could dwell so long in so many, or that anger could fuel careers. I would have never believed how swift and how unforgiving could come a young man's fall. Nor could I have ever imagined a father who didn't love me. And yet before this story could be completed I would witness the depth of a father's heartache my words would forever fail to express. I will be the first to admit I was naive as to what I was about to stumble into, but what would surprise me the most was that these people, in many ways, were not that much different than you and I. This I'm certain. The experience changed me. For better or for worse, I'm still not sure. But I do know that years later I would come out on the other side of this journey divided. Even today, I view my existent on this planet as two different men living two different lives. Before, and after, my search for Willie and Doug.

Because if it wasn't me to do this, then who? It was as if Debbie's life and that of her family, as well as all the others, would be wasted if you did not have the opportunity to know them like I did. Sadly, she had become a mere statistic, a paragraph in the newspaper, a footnote in a law review. She lived. She died. She was gone. Forever. The sudden, tragic ending to her brief life ate at me, nor could I explain why I had become so obsessed with the lives of Willie and Doug, or the lives of all the people they affected, or ended, in the autumn of 1973.

Obsessed. That was putting it mildly.

This journey began in early 1992, almost twenty years after the killings, when I was shown the original crime reports from Apache Junction, Arizona where Willie and Doug's spree began. These police reports written two weeks before Lodi, detailed the initial investigation into a double homicide east of Phoenix. These turned out not to be the first victims, I would soon learn, but those reports had a chilling effect on me as I turned the pages and reconstructed this crime. I realized that as the two Arizona detectives investigated these killings, my family was still very much alive. Of course they had no way of knowing that as the minutes and hours clicked away in these reports, their lives were drawing to a close as well.

I wanted to jump into those pages and warn them! I wanted to go back in time and change everything, to tell them what fate already knew. I wanted to rewrite the words that had long before been written, feeling an overwhelming sense of helplessness as I read. It came to the point where I knew I had to do everything I could to relive those days, and retrace the steps of the men who forced their way into the house on Orchard Road, and eventually into my life.

So for the next several years I traveled thousands of miles throughout the West, gathering material, pouring over endless spools of microfilm, digging through musty newspapers and court documents, collecting volumes of binders bursting with police reports and interrogation transcripts. I began collecting the lives of strangers, pieces to my puzzle, although I had no idea what this picture was supposed to look like. I scoured phone books for names uncovered in my search, just to see if the people were still alive and could remember those days so long ago. I interviewed hundreds of people; cops, witnesses, reporters, family members and friends of both the killers and their victims, lawyers and prosecutors, judges and jurists; anybody who would talk to me. I read the words of the killers, and listened to their confession tapes, cursing and indifferent, nonchalantly admitting these unspeakable acts.

I spread it all out in front of me, making intricate notes, detailing each minute, every hour, the directions taken, the phone calls not returned, those little twists of fate clustered around that precise moment when Willie felt compelled to take this deadly road, and Doug made the decision to blindly follow. I had to find out, at any time, at any place, if anyone could have changed the outcome? Was there a time when one of those little insignificant details could have kept the killers out of that house on Orchard Road? It crushed me to find several.

I retraced Willie and Doug's path from California and New York to the Denver crash pad where they met, to the deserts of Arizona and the shallow bogs of inland California where they left their dead. I was obsessed with little things in people's lives that have such huge, catastrophic consequences; worthless little events that sometime dictate life and death.

I was obsessed with the people they met, what was said, where they stayed and why they left. I drove their route and walked the sleazy motel strip of East Van Buren in Phoenix where they kidnapped their first two victims and justified the first of many killings. I had a beer in a Tucson bar while a stranger told me about how Willie sat right where I was sitting and offered his killing services to a small time drug dealer. He said the following night Willie murdered a young Mexican kid for sixty bucks, a belt buckle and a good laugh. So that same night I found that small piece of desert outside of town and let the ghosts of twenty years dance around me. I was obsessed.

I was obsessed with a man my age, who grew up in my time, and lived, in essence, a life parallel to mine. We graduated from high school the same year, found joy in working on cars and listening to the same rock music, got married about the same time, and unknowingly even gave our daughters the same name. And while in many cases our lives were so similar, he found he could somehow put a gun to a child's head, pull the trigger, and not feel one sliver of guilt, shame, or remorse. I became obsessed with how some people rejoice in their life, and some just drown.

There would come a time in my travels when I would sit not three feet away from this man, look him in the eye and realize that I had a choice to forgive him, or not. The decision was mine and mine alone; a decision I knew would most certainly place much of my own family against me. But I didn't care. That's how consumed I was in his life. That's how obsessed I had become in his story; how much I cared about him, and how little, it seemed, I cared about me. I know now what a huge a price I paid to write this, and during those years of selfish wandering, I often wondered whether I had become another of Willie and Doug's victims. Sometimes I still do.

A reporter, who would later play a key role in these events, once called it, "The Greatest Murder Story *Never* Told" and I believe that to be true.

I also believe that to many, especially those of us whose lives were so greatly affected, it will forever be considered a true American tragedy.

When all that's left to do,
is to reflect on what's been done.
This is where sadness breathes.
The sadness of everyone.

Book 1

THE KILLINGS.

1
Willie.

In the summer of 1935, Lester Steelman, his wife Ethel and their four-year-old daughter, left behind the swirling winds and an Oklahoma sky darkened by the scattering earth. There was nothing left for them there, so they relented and headed west, joining the plodding trains of Model A Fords with tattered remnants of households roped to the running boards.

California. Where it was told a hardworking man like Lester could find a job and feed his family, for farming was the only thing Lester knew. Some of the migrants stayed to work the newly irrigated deserts of the Imperial Valley, while others were lucky enough to get a factory job in Los Angeles. Still others, like Lester, continued north over the Tehachapi Mountains and up Highway 99 to the Central Valley, where thick green orchards, rich fields of tall corn, and lush sugary vineyards offered a man as much work as he could ever hope for.

You can smell it, taste it, especially in the early morning; from the very moment Highway 99 drops down out of the Grapevine Pass and stretches north out into the flatlands, it rushes in and overwhelms you, hanging in the air, whirling in the dirt clouds behind a tractor, the smell of earth, and cool water bubbling from the irrigation pumps, fertilizers sprayed on a newly planted field, and diesel fumes bellowing from the long haul trucks grinding gears in the distance. The spicy smell of freshly picked tomatoes, the yellow, stinging singe of crop dust, the stench of a man's sweat embedded in his soiled denim shirt, and the pungent aroma of fruit rotting on the ground. From the first sprouts of an early spring, to the last golden days of an October harvest; it is the smell that has lingered for the better part of a century. It was the smell Lester relished that morning; the comforting fragrance of his life's work.

But the family continued up the highway, finally settling in the small San Joaquin Valley town of Lodi. While Lester dreamed of having a little place of his own one day, he was resigned to his fate as a sharecropper. John Dougherty, who not only ran his own farm, but also leased more acreage around the area, was always in need of good help and hired him on. He saw Lester as honest and hard working, and soon made him his foreman, guaranteeing him year-round work. Lester rewarded his employer with long hours and fierce loyalty. Dougherty soon became part of the Steelman family and the two would work together for the rest of Lester's days.

And when John hired Lester, he hired the whole family, really, for everyone was expected to help – picking, hoeing, canning – anything that needed to be done, was done by all. Even young Frances, and now her little brother Gary, spent many weekends and summers working for Dougherty, although their payment was a usually nothing more than an appreciative nod, for this was not an easy life, or one well rewarded. Three or four dollars a day was a man's wage. A woman, or even her children, might manage a nickel a bin for picking grapes. Yet the Steelman family seldom went hungry and felt fortunate to have a place to call home.

In the early spring of 1945 the third Steelman child was born. They named him Willie, but because it took both Lester's strong back and his wife's helping hand just to earn enough to scrape by, the job of raising the baby fell to 14 year old Frances. When he was old enough to speak, he would call her mommy, and would do so for the rest of his life.

"He was the most precious little thing," she reminisced. "Bill had the most beautiful head of curly blond hair, and his eyes, my goodness, they were the prettiest blue you'd ever seen. He was just an angel!"

Being the baby of the family, he was naturally the center of attention. Little Willie learned to love the spotlight, not only from his own family, but also with farmhands and laborers who were regulars at the Steelman place. Problem was, hanging around the rough and tumble field workers taught Bill the vocabulary normally associated with a sailor.

"Oh Lordy, the mouth on that child!" Frances declared. "The men who worked with dad got a big kick out of teachin' him every cuss word they knew. I would hear all this laughin' and commotion goin' on outside, and go to lookin' for Billy and there he'd be, not four or five years old, standin' in the middle of a bunch of men, cussin' a blue streak! Course they'd be just splittin' their sides laughin', teachin' him more naughty words! Needless to say, daddy wasn't around when this was goin' on, but more than once Bill rattled him with one of his new words! Oh that Billy! He really loved bein' the show-off!"

Truth be told, Lester wasn't around much at all those days. His work kept him away from the house from sun up to sundown – seven days a week most of the year – but there were no complaints. He lived for hard work, knowing it was expected of him, equating his long hours of toil with his value as a man. So while his days were devoted to the soil, his nights were spent lubricating the aches and pains that came with the job, so there was little time for anything, or anyone else. Frances could not remember ever getting a hug or a kiss from her father, or hearing him tell her he loved her. There was no affection of any kind for any of the children, and yet they all still loved him, and no one more than little Willie.

In 1950, Willie started school at Live Oak Elementary in Acampo, the next small town up Highway 99 from Lodi. Once again it was Frances who nudged him awake, packed his lunch, ironed his shirt and made sure he got to school on time. She was the also one they called when he wasn't feeling well, or for the rare reprimand from his teacher. Frances would often laugh, recanting Willie's final day of kindergarten, when a small graduation ceremony had been planned. When the teacher finished the speech and said she looked forward to seeing them all again next year, Willie turned around and stared up at Frances with a puzzled face. "Why do I gotta come back?" he asked, thinking one year was all anyone needed. "I did aready gadruated."

During his days at school, Willie had plenty of friends and always found ways to stay busy, and while it was too early for him to stand out, his sixth grade teacher could remember only that he was 'a little plugger', a term of affection given to a lot of young boys.

"He was a quiet kid. Handsome, clean, always well dressed, never in trouble," Mr. Chappell recalled many years later, crushed to hear what his former star pupil had done.

Willie was ten when he finally learned what the rest of family had known for years. There were a lot more trips into town to see the family doctor these days, and his father stayed home from work more often, which Willie liked, but did not quite understand. Some of the grownups tried to explain it to him, but most of the time they just told Willie to hush up while he was in the house, or better yet, go outside for the afternoon. His father was sick. Willie knew that much.

As a child, Lester was crippled with Scarlet Fever, advancing to a stage where he had to learn how to even walk again. Although he somehow managed to survive, the illness left his heart leaking and enlarged. Even at that young age, he knew the disease would one day kill him. But as an adult, his pain seldom shortened his days in the field; he would not allow that, despite the repeated warnings from his doctor. Working hard was all he knew, so he decided to do the best he could for as long as his heart would let him. Still, there were many days when he had barely enough strength to roll out of bed, let alone toss twenty-foot lengths of irrigation pipe onto a flatbed truck.

By the early summer of 1958, Lester knew his time was short. The pain in his chest was crippling and his voice was no more than a raspy whisper. These days were difficult for Willie and his lonliness showed. His older brother Gary was still home, but they were brothers in name only. What was worse, Frances was gone, married now, living in Denver, expecting a child of her own, and it had pained Willie no end to let her go. In their years together they had created their own small family – they loved and understood each other – he was her child, her baby, and she was the only comfort he had ever known. When Frances moved away, Willie was left with a mother he barely knew, and a father he worshiped but could not get close to.

The grownups wouldn't let him. They made it perfectly clear that something as innocent as slamming a door, or a stern note sent home from a teacher might be all it would take to end his daddy's life. "You go on now. Don't you be creatin' such commotion," they snipped. And it was then when Willie knew his father's life was in his hands, certain that when the time came, he would somehow be responsible, so Willie could only sit and watch his father die. Sometimes when he tried to talk to him, Lester screamed, allowing the pain in his chest to overcome the love he still had in his heart. Frightened, Willie ran to his mother, sobbing, "What did I do? Why is daddy so mad at me?" As hard as she tried, there was no explanation she could offer that would take away the hurt.

When they buried his father on that warm September day in 1958, Willie was certain he had lost the only person in his family who really loved him. With his sister gone, and now his father, he felt he had no family left. Frances believed with all her heart that Willie – her precious little Willie – spent a great deal of his adult life trying to piece together another family to replace the one he had lost.

Ethel Steelman was incomplete without a man around to take care of her. She was a tiny slip of a woman, and never mind how hard he worked while he was alive; Lester had left her with very little. When he knew his time was short, he told her it would make it easier on him if he knew she was going to be taken care of after he was gone. He suggested Lee Mize, a family friend with an ample income but no wife, might be just that man. Love probably had little to do with it, but less than a year after her husband passed away, Ethel remarried.

By now there was not a soul around who hadn't noticed the big change in Willie, and no one more than she. Guilty about having so little to do in his upbringing, she overcompensated, coddled him, treating him like the little boy she still remembered, but whose life she had never been a part of. Problem was she hardly recognized the hateful young man who stood before her. Willie was now a skinny, miserable, vicious-tongued teenager, and if he was angry with his father being taken from him, he was absolutely livid about his mother remarrying so soon.

Ethel knew she had failed him. Willie was never a planned child – two young mouths to feed were plenty at the time – and while she didn't resent him, she never saw him in the same light Frances did. Now it was too late. Willie hated her and told her so, calling her a tramp for what she had done to his father's memory. The harder Ethel tried, the more Willie pulled away.

And she did try, but instead of being firm, she caved in. Lee Mize did his best to stay out of it, but soon even his patience was tested. He couldn't stand by and watch his woman be threatened, even if it was only her 15-year-old son, so he would kick the ungrateful punk out of his house more times than he cared to remember. It was his house, he was quick to remind Willie, but Ethel would always go looking for him, bring him back home and forgive him, until the next day, or the next week, or the next time Willie went into one of his fits of rage.

Still, for the next few years, Ethel stood by her son. She begged him to go back to school, (He had dropped out in the eight grade, the year of his father's death), encouraged him to join the Navy, (He enlisted at seventeen, but got booted out a few months later), or help him get a job, (He could get one, he just couldn't keep one). In the beginning she was there to support him in whatever he wanted, which usually included her giving him money. Now she worried about him hurting her if she refused. Mize told her, that if given half a chance, Willie would kill her for a lousy four-bits.

In the fall of 1963, exasperated, Ethel put Willie on the bus to Denver to live with Frances, hoping maybe she could help him. Several weeks later Frances sent him back, telling her mother she didn't recognize her brother anymore, and that he scared her and the children.

Throughout his teenage years Willie went looking for trouble. Usually petty things like stealing tires and car batteries, if for nothing more that a lark and some cigarette money. But at nineteen he had his first serious run in with the law after he forged a name on some stolen checks and passed them around town.

"I apologize," Willie said, attempting to charm the court. "I honestly don't know why I did it, but I've learned my lesson, you can be sure." His apology, along with the $200 his mother managed to come up with to cover the bad checks, persuaded the judge to dismiss the charges, and Willie promised to stay out of trouble.

But he didn't. Soon he was at it again, writing stolen checks all over town; $500 worth, it was determined, even though he had less than five dollars on him when he was caught. When his mother asked what he had done with all the money, he broke down and cried, admitting that he had spent it all on alcohol. She held him tight, patting him gently, promising that everything would be okay. But on a cold and foggy morning during the first week of 1965, Willie was turned over to the California Youth Authority and sent the Pine Grove Work Camp. It would be the first of many such incarcerations. Willie was not yet twenty years old.

He served nearly seven months, and was released shortly after turning on the charm and convincing everyone he had just made a youthful mistake and was ready to get on with his life. A parole report prepared in July 1965 prior to his release stated:

> *"Ward began the work program earning good grades and has continued above average. He gets along well with both staff and other wards, and in view of his resentfulness toward authority as indicated (by the report) it is now felt that he has made an excellent adjustment to the camp program and that he had developed some understanding of his problem."*

The report recommended Willie for parole, which was granted. He was back home in Lodi by the middle of the month and promptly got a job as a field hand. He worked hard – up at five am, followed by ten hours a day – all for a buck-twenty five an hour.

One night in August, he met a young girl named Sharon and a month later, with her parent's permission, they went to Reno and got married. He was twenty and Sharon just fifteen.

By the time his parole agent caught up with him, Willie seemed well on his way to straightening out his life, so the officer wrote a glowing report about his manners, his enthusiasm and cooperation. Within two weeks time, however, it had all crumbled.

Sharon now complained he would just run off and never say where he was going or when he might be back. He, on the other hand, accused her of cheating on him. He had quit his good job, so they lived off the few dollars his mother gave him or what little money Willie could sponge from his ever-dwindling circle of friends. Having nowhere else to go, Ethel took them in for a while. Other times home was a rundown $25 a month house trailer with an eviction notice forever thumb tacked to the door. Sometimes they just lived in his old car, which seldom ran anyway.

On what seemed like a weekly basis, Sharon would leave him and go back home, where her mother would call Willie's parole officer and complain about how her daughter was being mistreated 'by this convict'. Each time, before the parole agent could catch up to him, Willie somehow convinced Sharon he had changed his ways and couldn't live without her, at which time she would give in long enough to stall the parole officer, only to have the cycle repeat itself before the week was out.

All this madness transpired within a whirlwind 90 days, and yet the parole report dated December 1, 1965 painted another glowing picture of Willie and his young bride.

> *"Ward now reports relationship with wife and mother-in-law somewhat better. Ward now living with wife's parents and wants to conduct himself differently."*

Two weeks later the Lodi Police were again looking for Willie Steelman. After swiping checks from an ex-boss, he went on another spree. On December 11th, he bought a $25 dollar car battery with a $45 dollar check. He got his change, but never bothered to pick up the battery. The service station owner got suspicious and called police.

When the check came back from the bank, the cops knew exactly who was responsible and issued a warrant. On December 30th Willie phoned the police and promised to turn himself in the next day. He never showed. A few days into the New Year, while trying to cash another bad check at the Lakewood Sporting Goods store, Willie was arrested.

A second forgery conviction was bad enough, but he violated parole as well. It was not looking good for Willie as he was booked into County Jail in Stockton and on the night of January 5th, he attempted suicide. The method was not reported, and it apparently wasn't a serious attempt because he was never removed from jail and was back in court the next day, pleading guilty to the recent charges while explaining what happened last night "I just couldn't take it all no more. No money, no regular house, my wife's old lady hassling me, that's why I lost those jobs, man, she kept calling my work and hassling me and my boss. Shit! Now my wife says she's P.G. – and if she is, well, you tell me, cuz they told me I was sterile!"

In the meantime, Willie sat. Rumor was Sharon had suffered a miscarriage, but in any event, her parents had the marriage annulled and she was not heard from again.

During this time Willie was interviewed by members of both the legal and medical profession, and each time he came off a different person. At times, he was quiet and remorseful, apologizing for his actions and the problems he had caused. It was also not uncommon for him to cry; sobbing unashamedly at the mere mention of his family, or at the suggestion that he was more than likely going to do time for his latest crimes. He was a pathetic figure, a stick-boy of a man, swimming in his institution-orange overalls, weeping out loud, nervous, pale, frightened, stammering for the right word to show how scared he was, how sorry he was about what he had done.

One such interview stuck out above all the rest, and his parole officer made special note of it in his report.

> *"Steelman indicates that he needs 'help' and seems to feel that he may hurt somebody someday unless 'I get help'. He reportedly loses his temper quite easily, make threats, and has, in fact, struck his wife, so he says."*

Yet, the next day he was defiant and loud, pacing the room, pounding the wall, demanding he be given a release date because, "I don't want no fuckin' down time!"

During these sessions his imagination ran wild and he told outlandish stories of the things he had done, crimes he had gotten away with, and people he knew who would be there for him when he got out.

While Willie waited, his mother visited him as often as she could talk her husband into driving her the twelve miles from their Lodi home to the jail in Stockton. She had become increasingly worried about her son and how disturbed he seemed when they talked. She pleaded with officials to send him to the state hospital for help instead of prison for punishment.

No one listened. On February 7th, the Parole Board notified him his parole had been revoked and Willie now knew he was looking at two to three years at least. Once again, he thought he had the answer. That night, from the soles of his county-issued size eleven shoes, he carefully removed a dozen tiny nails and swallowed them, calmly signaling his suicide attempt by feigning unconsciousness in his cell.

They took him to Stockton State Hospital for observation, but when they could find nothing physically wrong, they hauled him back to county lock-up three days later.

But again, on the night of his return, realizing his last attempt had not convinced anyone, Willie did it again. This time he tried to end his life by swallowing a few checkers he had melted down into a small plastic glob.

Back to the hospital he went, but this time he stayed. His actions, along with the nonstop badgering by his mother, finally got someone's attention. On February 21, 1966, his criminal case was suspended and he became a patient of the California Department of Mental Hygiene. He was sent to Atascadero State Hospital for evaluation where he spent his 21st birthday, quickly becoming a pro at working not only the system, but also the good intentions of the people he came in contact with. It was at Atascadero where Willie found out how to fit in and tell them exactly what they wanted to hear. He began group psychotherapy sessions, often the most willing and animated participant of all. Staff members bubbled about his quick turnaround and prepared bulging files proclaiming his remarkable progress. It was at this time when he was first prescribed the antidepressant, Thoramine.

While he was still classified as mentally ill (due to his suicide attempts) he had been placed in a treatment ward with very little supervision. According to the records, Steelman "soon responded by overcoming any evidence of depression" and was a standout success story with the hospital, popular with staff and patients as well. In his group sessions he often took over the role of counselor, quick to offer his opinions or even a specific diagnosis of another patient. He held long, intense discussions with the staff about anything and everything, surprising them with at not only his intelligence, but with his conservative slant as well. At one such session he announced his solution to the growing drug problem on the streets – a harsh, get tough approach to users and dealers alike.

By now his dependency on his prescribed medication was snowballing and he had already managed to get his dosage upped dramatically. Because of his 'remarkable progress', he was transferred back to Stockton State Hospital so he could be closer to home. Five days after having been given ground privileges, and while on one of his breaks for fresh air, Willie just kept walking, right off the hospital grounds and into the streets of town.

When it was clear to all that he wasn't coming back, they labeled his departure an unauthorized absence, and then went one step further by giving him a written discharge and his classification was changed to "Not Mentally Ill." If that wasn't enough, they issued a "Certificate of Competency" to Willie Luther Steelman.

But despite this apparent good fortune, his problems were far from over. While he might not be in the Nut House, as he jokingly referred to it, he was certain to be in the Big House shortly, unless he could convince the court he had overcome his marital problems and therefore his financial problems, which in turn created this need to forge his name to other people's checks.

In June, several correctional counselors reviewed his file, giving special attention to his brief stay in the state mental institution. One of those reports stated:

> *"Steelman appears to be a rather passive dependent, an emotionally hungry individual who had many feelings of inadequacy, particularly in relation with his sexuality, and who is given to self-destructive episodes when depressed. He appears to feel safe within an institution and therefore recovers quickly from the depression which is often noted in a free society. Since his emotional problems are obviously of long-standing, it is not felt that they would be responsive to short term treatment".*

The report suggested, that regardless of whether he was granted probation or incarcerated, Willie Steelman needed help, and not for just a few sessions, but for an extended period of time. Speaking before the court, Willie admitted his need for psychotherapy. "But I prefer probation," he countered, "and I am very willing to cooperate by going through therapy if probation is granted."

While he wasn't in the hospital, he was still in jail, having been taken there shortly after he strolled off the grounds. On July 21st he was released pending the court's decision.

But his freedom was short-lived. Three weeks later the court ruled that Steelman had already been given his one chance and blew it, therefore probation was out of the question. For his second forgery conviction, for pocketing twenty dollars and some change in the bogus battery deal, Willie was sentenced to 14 years in prison at the San Luis Obispo Men's Colony.

He served two.

On September 16, 1968, after doing his time and being an exceptional inmate, even obtaining his G.E.D., Willie was paroled and returned home. As promised as a condition of his release, he got a job working as a shipping clerk at the Gibson Discount Center in Lodi, and told everyone they were looking at a new Willie Steelman.

But he was soon up to his old tricks. He started smoking dope and drinking, hanging around with kids much younger than he. At twenty three he seldom acted his age and could usually be found Friday nights, cruising the gut on Lodi Avenue, yelling obscenities at passing cars, buying beer for kids, trying to impress them, hoping they would look up to him.

Two weeks into December, he and a friend rented a room at the COZY U MOTEL, scored some LSD, and invited a couple of 16 year old girls to join them. On a tip from the night manager, the cops busted in and Willie was right back at county jail.

He spent Christmas and New Year's Day there. It wasn't until late January 1969 when he finally went to court, where he was convicted of two counts of Contributing to a Minor. The drug charges were dropped, so he was sentenced only to the 43 days he had served and fined $625. Relieved at the surprisingly light punishment, he readily agreed to pay the fine back at $100 per month, although he didn't say how. He had lost his job when he was arrested.

It was during those days in jail when Ronnie, his partner in the motel episode and now a cell partner as well, introduced Willie to his girlfriend, a young woman named Kathy Stone. She had made regular visits to the jail and soon realized Willie was always in the middle of her and Ronnie's conversations. But instead of being upset, she felt sorry for him. He seemed so lonely. He never had any visitors of his own, so it wasn't long before Kathy found herself talking to him as much as her own boyfriend. Before long he was all she could think about.

Kathy wasn't even twenty, but had already been on her own for a couple of years. She knew exactly what Willie meant when he talked about not having any kind of family. It was all she could do to keep a part time job and scrape together $35 a month for a tiny cabin in an alley off of Central Avenue in Lodi. She knew Willie would be getting out soon and wondered if she would ever see him again. One day after work she came home and was shocked to find him sitting on her bed.

Willie said he was sorry for scaring her, claiming it was Ronnie who insisted she wouldn't mind him staying there for a few days until he got back on his feet. He even gave him a key to get in. They picked up where they had left off and talked well into the next morning. He said she was the only person he had ever met who seemed to understand the pain of not having a real family. She shared that emptiness, offering the compassion no one else would, feeling sorry for him, consoling him, comforting him.

For the next several weeks, Willie helped out a little, making sure there was always food and cigarettes in the house. A couple of times he even took her along when he went to see his mother; visits with the sole intent of getting a few bucks. Although privately Willie cursed his mom and complained about how she had disgraced his dead father, Kathy could tell that down deep he really loved her, he just didn't know how to show it. "I remember going over one time to see her and Bill was so anxious to get there. When we walked up and she opened the door, his face lit all up and he tried to give her a hug. But she turned away. All she could do was run him down, comparing him to his brother Gary, asking him why he couldn't be more like his brother. Bill just walked away with his head down. I know he was embarrassed, but I also know he was sad. He was down for several days and would hardly even talk to me."

"You know, all Bill wanted was a family. He kind of acted like we were a family. . .he told me a lot that I was his family." Kathy was smart enough to realize Bill Steelman was not the man of her dreams – he was a bit too weird sexually for her – but she had very few friends in Lodi. Bill seemed like a good friend, and that was enough for her.

"Bill would never let you down if you were his friend, but it was hard knowing if you were really his friend or not. One night Bill and I were out, a show or something, and some guy made a dirty remark about me. It was nothing serious, guys do it all the time, but one minute Bill is laughing and joking, then all of a sudden he tears into this guy. He just went crazy! I started tugging and grabbing at Bill, trying to get him off this guy. He was scarin' me! I knew if I didn't pull him away he was gonna kill him! But Bill jumped up and looked right in my face. My blood ran cold! His eyes, they were evil."

Kathy shuddered as she remembered that moment. "Bill had the eyes of the devil himself."

2

Richard and Wally.

It was that smile. That cautious uncertain smile, now frozen on this young man's face, trapped for the ages in the photograph pasted on the black vellum pages of a tattered family album. The colors surrounding him had faded over the years; now mere washes of Kodachrome, a reminder of just how long it had been since the camera last clicked. A birthday. A sleepy Christmas morning. A Disneyland summer. A Halloween dance. A new house. A new car. A young man, chest out, with his new baby girl. And always that smile. It might be said that as he got older he learned to hide behind that smile, to disguise what was really on his mind. People often remarked that he had a Steve McQueen kind of cool about him, and he liked that.

And he had this uneasy laugh as well. A quick laugh. Sharp, yet guarded. A bit forced. An easy substitute, maybe, for what he truly felt. And yet, when he laughed, I mean really laughed, well, his eyes – the brightest, clearest aqua blue you could ever imagine – warmed the room like a September sky. But if he was upset, those same eyes focused in like a laser beam, and you would swear, Jesus God Almighty, they were going to burn a hole right through you.

Fortunately for Richard, at least during the early summer of 1973, it seemed like he had every reason in the world to laugh and smile. Thirty-seven years young, he had all a man could ask for; a beautiful wife, two great kids, and a brand new home outside of Lodi; a house he built himself, mind you. Even his health was better these days. An out of control thyroid a few years back had caused him to question whether he would even reach forty, and now he bragged he would retire by then.

Richard Allen Earl was 11 years old when his parents packed up all Indiana had allowed them and headed west for the California Promise. He walked out of the sad excuse for the only home he had ever known and never once looked back. Stuck between six sisters in the back seat of a 1940 Chevrolet Sedan, for days on end they crossed America's emptiness on Highway 40. It was the summer of '47, a hot suffering wind blowing through an open window, with their last meager possessions strapped to the small trailer that bounced along behind them. They were certain their dream, their rainbow, was waiting for them in California. Or maybe even over the next hill, or just beyond the water mirage that never left the black ribbon of asphalt that stretched out forever in front of them.

They weren't leaving much behind. Richard's family never had much to begin with, except kids. Lots of kids. Even for their neighborhood – even for the times– they were considered poor. Two room homemade house kind of poor. A privy out back poor. Six kids to a bed sort of poor. A father, defeated by the beer and the burden of all he had created, kind of poor. He was only eleven, but Richard knew enough to understand there had to be something better, something more, somewhere else, and that was terribly exciting. He believed his mother when she told him the streets in California were paved with gold. The very idea made his skin tingle.

Along with those sisters, he had a brother nine years older who was already gone. He had joined the Coast Guard near the end of the war, claiming he wanted to see the world, but truth was he didn't want to be around for the responsibilities forced on the oldest of eight. He told his little brother one thing before he left home. A man does not have to live this way, he said, and Richard never forgot those words.

Wanda Jean Cummings came from a large family as well, who had also come west a few years earlier. Following the harvests from Oklahoma to California, they soon realized it was easier to feed a family with a regular job in the city than bent over in the fields, so the Cummings settled in the East Bay industrial sprawl of Richmond and squeezed into a trailer park on 13th Street.

Wanda soon became friends with Richard's sister, Barbara, and it was one day after school when she first met him. It was easy to see why he went nuts over her; barely 14, she was quite a beauty even then. Shapely and stylishly thin, with dark hair and soft eyes, she contrasted sharply with Richard's short build, wavy blond hair and fair skin. Although her family could never afford much, Wanda somehow managed to follow the latest fashions; tight petal pushers and a snug sweater with a scarf tied around her neck. Soon she began calling him Richie, and wrote him long, melting love letters pledging herself to him forever.

In 1954, after several years of courtship, and a few off and on interruptions in their young romance, Richard and Wanda were married. He was just eighteen, she a year younger.

True to his spirit, Richard was determined to get a quick start. Debbie was born the next year, followed in 1958 with Richard Jr. During the days Richard worked construction with his brother in law, and at night he pumped gas at a filling station downtown. To him just making ends meet wasn't enough.

His hard work paid off, and shortly after his 21st birthday, they bought their first home. But not one to just sit back, Richard decided he also wanted his own business. So with what little money he managed to save, along with a big note, he took over a neighborhood gas station. It was not an easy way to make a living, but he promised Wanda that it was just a matter of time before he would be able to give her everything she ever wanted.

He opened and closed the station, spending long hours waiting for someone to pull in for a couple bucks worth of gas. Every night Wanda delivered his dinner in a casserole dish and they would tell each other about their day, talk about the kids, and what dreams lay ahead. Within a few years Richard's hard work provided them with a larger station on a busier street where more traffic meant more sales, and of course, more money. More money meant more goals, of which he never seemed to run out of. Then, in 1964, without any notice whatsoever, he sold the house, sold the station, and announced they were moving to Lodi, a throwback little town in the San Joaquin Valley two hours east. It was early fall when Richard settled his family into an old brick house on the highway just outside of Lodi, barely a half mile from a spot in the road known as Victor. The perfect place to raise his family, he decided.

The house was surrounded by acres of grapes, and it was Richard's job as part of the agreement when he rented the house to watch over the vineyard. He knew nothing of growing grapes, but he took it seriously, walking the acreage, little Ricky in tow, inspecting the crop, examining the grapes. It was under the trees bordering the rear of the property where he taught his son how to shoot a rifle. Convinced the blackbirds were ruining the fruit, Richard offered his son a nickel for every bird he could hit.

On the weekends, his family walked the short distance up the road to Victor. It wasn't much of a town; a few packing sheds, a two pump filling station, a hardware store and a market. Far more than just a country store, the United Market was their town hall; a gathering place to discuss the stories of the day or gossip about who was up to what. Old friends met as their carts crossed paths in the tiny isles or as they loaded groceries into their station wagons out front. The bulletin board inside was a collage of thumb tacked notices announcing the annual pancake breakfast at the Grange or a yard sale planned rain or shine. Young men found their first job on that board, while teenage girls offered babysitting for 35 cents an hour. Outside, Richard and Wanda shared a soda, nodding hello to their neighbors, struggling to remember names, promising each other they needed to find the time to get to know all of them better. And after the harvest was in, when windfall grapes rotting on the ground left a sweet vinegary smell in the autumn air, Richard once again wandered the property. As he walked, he told himself that one day he would have his own place just like this one.

But it wasn't long before Richard again became restless and moved the family out of the old house and into Lodi, where he got back to what he knew best, operating a large and successful Douglas Service Station downtown.

As the years passed and the kids got older, the Earl family spent a lot of time together. Richard bought a ski boat, and there were picnics at Lodi Lake and an occasional trip up to Tahoe, and even if it was simply just watching Ricky's skating lessons, or attending one of Debbie's functions with Rainbow Girls, they made an effort to do everything as a family. The kids were growing quickly and Richard wished there was a way to slow life down. Their times in Lodi were good ones, and Richard, still only in his mid 30's, hadn't lost the drive and enthusiasm that had got him to this place. As 1971 approached, he reminded himself there was still just one thing missing. He had never recaptured the life they had enjoyed out at the old place in Victor.

Richard had heard about a 20 acre vineyard for sale not far from where they once lived, so he snapped it up and soon he and Wanda were building the home they had long talked about. It was a showplace really, sitting right on the edge of their property at the corner of Orchard and Dustin Road, overlooking vineyards in every direction – theirs and an adjacent 20 acres that Richard boasted he would soon own. "When I do, then I'll retire," he announced, and not a soul doubted him.

He was building the house himself, and gave tours for family and friends who came to visit, proudly displaying each day's progress. When they moved in the following year, the house at 7536 Orchard Road became the focal point of the rural Victor neighborhood. But by autumn of 1973, while the grapes were again ready for harvest and the tart smell he so fondly remembered lingered in the air, Richard wondered if he wasn't in over his head.

The hot dry summer had been perfect and the grapes were bountiful. Rumor had it the crop might bring as much as $10,000 from the wineries. But Richard was also in some very serious financial trouble and knew he would need every penny he could get his hands on if he was going to pull through. As November approached, Richard's world had become as unsettling as the weather. What started off as one of his best years, was fast crumbling down around him.

The house had never really been finished. Inside, the little final touches loomed large and nagged this perfectionist, reminding him of his failure as a builder. There were ongoing arguments with subcontractors that had reached a point where, damn it, somebody was going to sue somebody soon. The construction money borrowed for their home had run out, and with it, their income. Bills were piling up, liens were filed, collection notices began arriving, property taxes were due, and there was not one extra dime to pay any of them.

After an especially exasperating weekend, the first one in November of '73, Richard gave in and picked up the phone. "Mom, I don't know what to do," he lamented. "I made all these plans about taking it easy, and now the car is broke, the washer and dryer is broke, the tractor's broke. . .and I'm broke." Certainly his mother had no money to offer him, nor was Richard's call a cry for help. But it was, in fact, the first time she could ever remember her son letting on about his worries.

There was no way for Richard to know that his real troubles had not found him yet. Within a matter of a few days, hours really, all of the problems he struggled with tonight would not matter in the slightest.

The owners of The United Market in Victor were a young couple named Wally and Joanne Parkin, and their store had long been considered the focal point of the small town. There was never any doubt amongst the locals that the real reason the United Market was so busy and so successful was simply because of the Parkin family who ran it.

Everyone knew Wally, and everyone liked him. He had graduated from Lodi High in 1958 after excelling at very little except having plenty of friends. He never stood out, and at barely five and a half feet tall, he certainly didn't stand above many of the other graduates either. He got through school like most of his buddies – he studied and passed – but his real enthusiasm was saved for sports, and all the boating and fishing that was never more than a few miles away.

It was at Lodi High where he met Joanne Bettger. She wasn't quite as sociable or outgoing as he, so she seldom protested when he left her for a pick up game of basketball, or an outing up at the lake. "She's kinda artsy," Wally explained to his friends who were always questioning his choice in girls. "And I like that about her."

Even after they graduated, they continued seeing each other while attending a nearby junior college. There they spent hours designing houses in the drafting class they shared; Wally explaining all the details and features, Joanne putting them on paper. Dream houses, they called them – drawings of the home they knew that somehow, someway, they would one day build together.

Besides that, however, they appeared to have very little else in common. Wally was happy and loud, positive and boisterous, with tons of friends always hanging around. Joanne, on the other hand, was far more reserved and selective, content with what little time Wally might have left over for her. Their differences could not have been more apparent, and maybe that's why everyone was a bit taken back, when on June 18, 1960, they got married.

Wally hooked on at the local Safeway, learning a little about every aspect of the grocery business. It was a good job and the union scale helped them get started. Wally would have been the first to admit that he was never going to be the brightest man on the payroll, so he made an all out effort to be the most enthusiastic. His coworkers watched as he stood back and analyzed the situation for a minute, then jumped feet first, no matter what size the project, staying with it until he got it done.

The only problem with his job at Safeway was it didn't allow him enough free time – his time – the time he needed to do all the things he wanted to do; softball games after work in the summer, basketball in the fall, bowling league on Tuesday nights. Seemed like work always got in the way, and being the new guy, he got the weekend work schedule, so it was tough for him to watch his friends head off waterskiing while he had to pull a Saturday afternoon shift.

Yet Wally stayed with Safeway for a couple of years, and in January 1962, their daughter Lisa was born. It was later that year when, along with a partner, they took a chance and bought a run down little market east of town. Because there was no money left to fix the place up, Wally provided the hard work of repairing the broken equipment, while Joanne stayed busy with a bucket and brush. They even spent Thanksgiving Day fixing the coolers and painting the counters, so the new United Market could open for business bright and early Friday morning.

In their dress-white aprons, they greeted each and every customer that day, and continued to do so every day for the next eleven years. From the day they took over, there was never a time when a member of the Parkin family wasn't there, because soon Wally's parents, even his younger brother, Norm, had joined in. But the United Market became more than just another grocery store, it became an extension of the Parkin family, and they in turn became a big part of small town life in Victor. Their reputation stretched the few miles back to Lodi and it was not uncommon for people to drive all the way out there simply to have the butcher remember their favorite cut of meat, or hear the checker call them by name.

A year later their second child, Bobbie, was born, and with his arrival, Joanne spent even less time in the store and more time at home. There was still no Dream House yet, just a dream, so their home remained a cramped single wide parked behind the market, although they did manage to move into a rented duplex shortly after Bobbie arrived.

Wally was always big on holidays, no matter what the occasion. And no occasion meant as much to him as New Year's Eve, so each one became a big effort to outdo the previous. One year, while still living in the duplex, Wally realized it was much too small to hold a party of the magnitude he was planning, so on the spur of the moment, he and a friend tore out two walls and created a large dance floor. It didn't seem to matter that it took away the living room and one of the bedrooms to build it, Wally was determined to make it the biggest party ever. That New Year's Eve went down as one of Wally's best, and the town talked about The Big Bash for years to come.

On his rare off day he was either waterskiing or playing basketball with some buddies. His brother, Norman, could only remember one instance when Wally was too sick to work.

"We had a softball game one evening and he came by to pick me up. When I answered the door, I couldn't believe my eyes! Wally was standing there, swaying back and forth, white as a sheet and you could just see he was deathly ill. I mean you could see it in his eyes! He was so sick it scared me."

Norman tried talking his brother out of playing. "It's just a game, man. You should be home in bed!"

To no avail. After the game, Wally finally went home. Joanne panicked when she saw him come through the door, and she rushed him to the hospital. That's where he remained for several days, stricken with hepatitis.

"He played the whole game though," Norman remembered with a grin. "And as I remember, he went four for four."

When he wasn't at the store, Wally was always in the middle of some event in town and Joanne was right there with him. He coached Little League and became a volunteer fireman while she taught a Sunday morning class at the Methodist Church. When the children started school, she helped out there as well. When a social event was planned in Victor, the Parkins could be counted on to bring something extra special to the potluck. "If you asked him for a hand," a friend once admitted, "he would give you his arm."

That became his policy at the store as well, and it wasn't long before the United Market became the informal Bank of Victor; always ready to cash a paycheck or carry a small account for a customer temporarily down on their luck. During the busy fall harvests there were lots of checks to be cashed, and the amounts could be rather large, so it was not uncommon for Wally to make a trip every day to his bank in Lodi, just so they would have plenty of money on hand for customers.

"You could go in there and get three or four hundred dollars anytime of the day, and not even make a dent," a customer told police later. "I know for a fact that he had thousands and thousands of dollars in there most of the time. I thought it was unsafe for them to do that, and I told Wally and his father that more than once, but they never seemed to worry about it."

He was right. Wally didn't worry. As he reminded all the doomsayers, he had never been robbed or even threatened in all the years of running the store, and the day's deposits always rode home with him on the front seat of his pickup, right next to "Duke", the family's German Shepard. "If there's ever a problem," Wally joked, "Duke'll git 'em!"

Just to be safe though, Wally got a permit to carry a gun; a .38 revolver he picked up at a shop in Stockton. Still, he thought the whole damn thing was ridiculous – this big idea that he needed to protect himself. "From who? From what?" he asked. "I know every single soul in this town and everyone of them I consider a friend of mine."

Wally and Joanne eventually got around to building their Dream Home. The market was doing well, and there was finally enough money, so once again they sketched out their ideas. She wanted the kids to have their own room and he wanted a large family room, big enough for a pool table. She wanted a nice big kitchen and he wanted extra guest rooms for when company stayed. Together they agreed on a massive stone fireplace and living room walls paneled in dark woods. And of course they just had to have a big swimming pool and patio, because Wally could already picture his now legendary parties continuing at their new place In 1972 work began on their acreage on Orchard Road, just a couple of miles from the market. It was country lane of older homes, although the Earls had almost finished their new place at the other end of the road, all of which made Wally even more anxious to get started on his.

Never at a loss for friends to help out, the house was completed quickly. They moved in the spring of 1973 and christened their new home with a big party on Easter Sunday. Afterwards, Wally and Joanne reminded each other how good their life was. A new home in a nice town, a good business and plenty of friends.

It was true. Everyone in Victor knew Wally and Joanne Parkin, and there didn't seem to be a person for miles around who didn't absolutely think the world of them.

3
Denise.

Denise Machell was still a high school senior when her best friend, Kathy Stone, introduced her to Willie Steelman. Despite being raised in a straight-laced Christian family, Denise had a bit of a wild streak; sneaking a smoke on the way home from school, hanging out with an older crowd, or even cutting class once in awhile, all of which Denise, for the most part at least, managed to hide from her parents. She could rap about good weed, rock music and motorcycles with the best of them, then attend church with her folks on Sunday. But while she was good at talking trouble, most of her friends agreed that she went out of her way to avoid it. All that changed in March of 1969 when she met Willie.

At first Denise was flattered that a man his age would even be the slightest bit interested in her. Because her parents were so strict, she had to come up with ways to sneak out of the house to see him, so they met at Kathy's place, at a party, or even at Lodi High where Denise would show him off to her girlfriends. It did not take long, however, for the real Willie to surface.

Soon after they first met, the two of them sat in his car out front of a record store in Lodi, wrapped up in the front seat, hugging and kissing, wrestling around, unaware that inside the store, the manager had gathered everyone by the window to watch. When the couple finally came up for air and noticed the crowd, Denise was embarrassed and laughed it off, but Willie went berserk and stormed inside, threatening to kill each and every one of them.

Startled by a rage she had never seen before, Denise chased after him. Willie had picked up an iron pipe, and acted every bit like he was ready to use it. His eyes were glazed over and had a completely blank stare to them. She screamed at him to stop; to put the pipe down and come outside, but he ignored her. For some reason, just as quickly as it had exploded, his anger cooled and Denise managed to get him back to the car, where he eventually calmed down.

Later that night, when Denise found the courage to ask what happened, Willie swore he couldn't remember any of it; especially the part about picking up the pipe. He even accused her of lying about the whole thing and said he never wanted to discuss it again. She could see that he was upset, but shuttered to think what would happen if he ever got that mad at her. He seemed such a contradiction. She had seen the anger explode inside him and yet he confessed to her that he prayed for peace and how sad it was that people couldn't get along. He once told her that his father had tried to teach him how to hunt, but the whole idea troubled him. "I tried to miss on purpose," he admitted, "because I just couldn't imagine killing anything."

Soon after the record store incident, Willie had to settle some unfinished business with the Lodi Police. When he failed to make even one of the promised $100 a month payments on his fine for the Cozy-U Motel incident, the cops picked him up again. Realizing now that he had neither the money nor the inclination to pay, they sent him back to county jail.

Denise said she would wait for him, and he wrote to her often, claiming he expected her to marry him after she graduated. She couldn't tell if he was serious or not because he never really asked her, he just told her, like there was no use in discussing it. She visited him when she was able, but usually left more mixed up than when she had arrived. Sometimes she couldn't wait until the day he was released, yet more often than not, she felt safe knowing exactly where he was. She couldn't make sense of this confusion, or decide how she honestly felt about him. She didn't know if she really wanted to marry him, but he just knew she couldn't stand the idea of hurting him. It was during one of her visits when she mentioned a $2,000 gift her aunt was giving her after she turned 18 and graduated from high school. Willie lit up, and for the next several visits, the two grand was all he could talk about. He promised her it would be more than enough to get a place of their own and start a family. He had a way of wrapping words around her and clinging to her, telling her she was the only one he wanted. He wanted her and a family. A real family. His family.

He got out May 16th, but only three days later Lodi P.D. busted him again. This time the charge was armed robbery, but when they couldn't get the needed evidence to make it stick, the charges were dropped and Willie was released. Word around town was that Steelman had threatened the victim would be killed if he didn't back off. The episode upped his standing in the small circle he ran with, and it was the first time anyone heard Bill Steelman talk about "his people" and the power they wielded in the community.

Soon after, Denise mustered the courage to take him home to meet her parents. She was surprised how well it went, and how courteous and well mannered Bill acted. He said all the right things – even her mother seemed to like him – and Mrs. Machell was not an easy sell. Denise felt relieved and very uncomfortable all at the same time. She couldn't put her finger on it, but something still bothered her about Bill. And yet, during those final weeks of spring, Denise was either busy counting the dwindling days of school, or she was with him. He never let her out of his sight, and when he wasn't with her, he wanted to know where she was going and with who. His jealousy was starting to show, and on occasion, he became violently angry when she gave the wrong answer.

When Denise reminded him that her parents expected her to go to college in the fall, Willie brightened. "You go to school. I'm gonna get a little job and help out and maybe I can even take a night class or two. You know I been telling you about learning nursing and helping people." She was moved. Here he was talking about working in a hospital and taking care of her and people who needed his help. Maybe Bill was a little pushy, a little hard to understand, but he had finally convinced her. Just a few weeks after he was released from jail, Denise graduated from Lodi High. She turned 18 the next day, and they drove to Carson City, Nevada that weekend. Her parents had made it clear how they felt about the trip, but she was an adult now and there was nothing they could do to stop it.

On the night of June 15th, Mrs. Machell answered the phone, pleased to hear her daughter on the other end. But her heart soon sank when, in a tearful, trembling voice, Denise confessed, "Mom, I've just made a terrible mistake."

Bill Steelman wouldn't have been their first choice as a son-in-law, but at times they too saw his child-like innocence and his eagerness to please. He was exceptionally polite, and maybe just a bit too shy, but they realized that was to be expected around his new family. Not long after the young couple returned to Lodi, and after the shock of the marriage had worn off, Mrs. Machell decided that it was time to make the best of it and plan a wedding shower for the couple, and she asked Bill to invite his family.

"They won't come," he announced. "Besides I really don't have any family anyways."

A few weeks later, in the evening shade of the Machell backyard patio, some friends from high school and a few aunts and uncles got together to celebrate the marriage while Mr. Machell scurried around, snapping pictures, encouraging everyone to smile.

Everyone did. Everyone except Willie. He stood apart from the rest, his wavy hair neatly combed, his stark white shirt a little rumpled, a long thin necktie that only made him appear more gaunt. He said very little, smiled weakly when spoken to, but only after being encouraged by his new bride to do so. He looked horribly uncomfortable, hopelessly shy and helplessly out of place.

His mother-in-law watched him that evening. His loneliness tugged at her. He seemed so sad. She felt terrible. Here he was at his own wedding party and not even one member of his family bothered to show up. She could feel his embarrassment. That night, after the party was over and everyone had gone home, all Mrs. Machell wanted to do was to sit down and cry.

The couple found a small apartment in town. Denise got a job at Lodi Fab, a manufacturing plant in town where her parents worked, while Willie kicked around a few odd jobs, realizing that everything he knew of as work bored him. The $2,000 was disappearing fast.

In the fall they moved to Sacramento, where Denise honored her parents wishes by enrolling in a junior college. Again, Willie went through the motions of helping out, but it was clear to everyone, especially the Machells, that he wasn't holding up his end of the marriage. While Denise attended classes and worked part-time, Willie was hanging out with friends. He always managed to have a few bucks on him, although never enough to pay any of the bills.

Denise knew he was spending his money smoking dope, deciding he was probably dealing a little as well. Willie claimed he always hid his dirty work from her. "I would come home with a $500 stereo," he once bragged, "and she wouldn't even ask me where I got it. She just figured I was out workin', but I never told her shit about what I did, and she was smart enough not to ask."

Six months into their marriage and it was all Denise could do to keep it together. There was school and work and cleaning house during the week, then trying to follow Willie around town on the weekend as he partied. Denise was no prude, and she still enjoyed having fun and going out with Bill and their friends. He was always the center of attention and she liked that, so she continued to tell herself that she just needed to give it more time, and that Bill and the marriage would come around.

She heard of a job near Mountain View, which was a couple hours away, and she talked him into moving, hoping that getting him out of Lodi might straighten him up. While he agreed to go, the change of scenery offered no help. Denise worked, Willie screwed off. Her meager paycheck was gone before she knew it, and disappearing with it was her husband, who seldom stayed home long enough for Denise to argue about the hopeless situation she had found herself in. Finally, on one of her many weekend trips back home to Lodi, she broke down and confided to her parents the obvious; she was miserable, broke, worn out and hungry. There would be no money for at least another week, she admitted, and their rent and all the other bills were going unpaid. She said that the only thing in the house to eat was a bag of uncooked popcorn. It was that bad.

It all became too much. Denise gave up, moved back to Lodi with Willie following close behind. And he continued his downward spiral, so during 1970 and 1971 he was busted for everything from forgery to driving without a license. He even got caught with a small bag of pot at a New Year's Eve party, but in most cases the charges were either dropped, or he was given a small fine.

The most serious of the arrests was the marijuana bust, and in March of 1972 Willie appeared in court fully expecting to do time. For whatever the reasons, the judge sentenced him to six months in jail and a $250 fine, then suspended both. Once again, Willie walked.

But Denise could see that this latest situation bothered Willie, and for the two months prior to his court appearance, he sweated out what surely was going to be more time in jail. He swore to God he was going to kick his habit and turn his life back around once and for all. Even after he got off, Willie still promised everyone that this time it was for real.

So once again he was welcomed back into his in-laws home, where he and Mrs. Machell would stay up well past midnight discussing the rewards of a Christian life and the remarkable changes it could offer him. "Give your life to the Lord," she begged. "Learn the meaning of a true Christian love." Willie, with sincerity spilling over and outstretched hands joining her across the kitchen table in prayer, promised he truly believed His way was the only way out of this terrible life he was living. But Willie's new lust for this life was brief. The good fortune he felt from the lenient sentence was forgotten before the week was out and he lost his religion just as quick.

While 1972 certainly could have been his turn-around year, as he so promised, it actually became his point of no return. He never could rid himself of his drug addiction totally, managing only to slow down for awhile, limiting himself to a daily joint or two. But before the year was over, it was back up again, and he had now added heroin to his arsenal. For a short time that year, it was widely rumored that Lodi's only connection to the drug ran through Willie. Somehow he managed to impress the head of a small time Mexican drug family with, and they agreed to let him be their shuttle. The only problem was, Willie became his own best customer, and there was seldom any left to sell.

It was about this same time, not long after his court date in March, when Denise got a phone call that Willie had fallen on a sidewalk outside Macy's department store in Stockton. The accident was serious enough to keep him in the hospital for a few days of observation, and even after Denise took him back home, he complained of tremendous headaches and blackouts. He swore that nothing would relieve the pain, so he consumed even larger quantities of dope, including every prescription drug he could convince a doctor into offering.

Which might explain his renewed interest in nursing and medicine. That spring, after he was back on his feet, he proudly announced his new job – an orderly at the Vista Ray Convalescent Hospital in Lodi. It was part time, but it satisfied Denise and her family enough to get them off his back for a while.The job also helped his habit. His friendly manner soon won over supervisors, co-workers and even patients, and before long Willie had free run of the storeroom. If it looked like a pill, or was in a pill bottle, he swiped it, often downing it before his shift ended. He also had access to an endless supply of prescription pads, and his old forgery skills again came in handy. He became an expert in duplicating the scrawl of many of the doctors who had patients at Vista Ray, so he never lacked for a "pain reliever" after that. And he was generous with others, so writing prescriptions became his connection to a renewed popularity among those who just months earlier were trying to find ways to ditch him. Once again he was on the inside, and those who flocked around him and his Rx pad, affectionately referred to him as "Doctor Bill".

But on the other side, Willie's initial months at Vista Ray were also filled with hope for him, as well as praise from bosses and the new friends he had made on staff. Outgoing and friendly, most people quickly grew attached to Willie, even though they laughed at his quirky dress and new afro hair style. He was often at the center of the coffee room discussions, either being in the middle of them when he was there, or the subject of them when he was not. He was certainly a hardworking employee, willing to take on the most unsettling of tasks, or stay late to help out without complaint. More than once he remained long after his shift was over simply to push a wheelchair patient on a leisurely stroll around the grounds. He could be found sitting at a table in the cafeteria, or at a bedside, talking with one of the many elderly patients. He was one of the few employees who would take the time to listen to those whose only wish was to have someone to talk to. For his efforts, Willie made $320 a month.

He made new friends, like Carol Jenkins, an adventurous seventeen year old who never could quite figure out Bill Steelman, but took the time to try anyway. Not long after Willie started, the two of them became the hot topic of the coffee room rumor mill. More than one fellow worker thought the friendship was getting carried away. "Bill and Carol had something going on, I tell you. I don't care what anyone says, it was a love affair. I saw it with my own two eyes!"

Carol, of course, denied it, but the alleged affair followed her long after Bill Steelman left the Vista Ray.

By now his "Jeckel and Hyde" routine was getting old, not only to Denise, but to the others who knew him. After the prescription pad con was discovered, his friends were once again scraping together excuses to avoid him. He was invited to hang out and get high with much less frequency than before. His circle again became smaller and it was apparent, even to him, that he was becoming more and more alone. He continued to try and buy his friends, so it was not uncommon for him to give away what little he had, or what Denise had earned, just to please some stranger at a party. He was constantly broke, but would refuse money for a drug buy just to impress someone he barely knew.

In April of 1972, Willie talked himself into another part time job at Bowis Service, a small gas station next to the United Market in Victor. Before his first week was over, the owner fired him for stealing gas, cigarettes, and money. Oddly enough, even as broke as he was, he wasn't stealing for himself. The goods went to a couple of high school kids named Mike and Duff, who were joyriding around due to Willie's generosity.

When Mr. Bowis cut him loose, Willie glared down on him and vowed to 'get him', a threat Bowis would shudder about soon enough.

Willie even offered to help out people he barely knew. One afternoon at the convalescent home, he walked into a lunchroom conversation between two co-workers. It seemed one was having problems with a troublesome relative. As nonchalant as could be, Willie interrupted just long enough to offer his help. "I can do him for you if you want," he said.

They both looked up, stunned at what they had heard. Willie just stared down at one, then the other, then repeated his offer. "Did a guy in Denver once. Was easy. Just lemme know if you need some help." And he walked away.

By early 1973 Willie and Denise had split. She returned to her parent's home on Eureka Street, while Willie crashed where ever anyone would let him. By this time the management at the Vista Ray had caught on to his act and dismissed him, only to hire him back within the week. Several days later he called in sick, then came back for one day of work, then stayed away for days without even a phone call. They took as much of Willie as they could, then like all the others, tired of his endless string of excuses, fired him a second time. Even as he was letting him go, his boss confessed, "I really like you Willie. I just can't depend on you anymore."

Willie's drug consumption was now at an all time high. He was strung out on a mind-boggling mixture of heroin, speed, hash and a medicine chest full of prescription drugs. He had the hallow look of a junkie, with eyes sunk further back into his head. They were huge globes, bugged out and piercing with massive areas of yellow-white with constantly dilated pupils. He seldom ate. Or cared to. His six foot frame carried less than 150 pounds and his clothes hung like sheets around him. His mustache was small, pathetic, and had a mind of its own. His tall, thin head, perched on an even skinner neck, was overwhelmed by a huge Adam's Apple knot at his throat. He was paranoid. Kept there by the speed, fearful of cops, and strangers he insisted were cops. Sleep was rare. He could have overdosed at any moment and would have probably welcomed the relief, but he didn't have the guts and he knew it. Suicide looked good that summer, and he thought it might not be a bad out. If nothing else, maybe Denise would finally realize his troubles were more serious than she was willing to believe. Killing himself would prove to her that he was more than just a junkie. It would show how much he loved her, and that there really was a good man deep down inside him. A good man dying to get out.

In the spring of 1973, at the insistence of Mrs. Machell, he contacted Pastor Fischer of the Temple Baptist Church in Lodi. On two occasions, Willie went to him for help and prayed with the pastor, admitting his life was wrong, asking for forgiveness. After which he would disappear for several weeks, only to return and repeat the process. When Fischer could find him, he managed to keep Willie in Bible study classes along with regular Sunday service, and even a weekly prayer session Wednesday night. As late as July, the pastor felt Willie might be turning the corner. Willie would even show up at the Lodi House – a crisis center for young people – seeking help with his heroin addiction, only to slip away after a visit or two.

In between church meetings, Willie was injecting, smoking, and swallowing whatever he could find. He admitted stealing purses, not only for what little money he could find, but for whatever amber plastic bottles might be hiding in the bottom. His desperation reached so low at one point he emptied a fancy plastic prescription wheel of tablets, downing them all in one mouthful. When they failed to alter his state of mind, he showed the plastic case to an equally strung out friend, asking if he knew what it was, and why it didn't work.

"Shit, Bill, you just did a whole month's worth of fuckin' birth control pills!" He laughed in Willie's face. "Least you don't gotta worry 'bout gettin' knocked up!"

They had been separated since the first of the year. Denise said it was over, but Willie still held out hope. She had run out of patience with him. She was tired. Tired, she told him, of his excuses and his scams. Tired of being broke and being evicted. Tired of working long shifts and longer weeks, only to turn over her meager check to a man who, without giving it another thought, would swap it for a needle full of peace. She told him she was tired of the cops cruising by her parents house looking for him, and tired of the endless deluge of phone calls and registered mail from the courts. She was tired of his callous approach to her emotions, tired of his not remembering, tired of his attitude, and tired of not knowing what Bill Steelman might show up next. Just plain tired.

So after just four years of marriage, with countless separations, Denise told him it was over for good. She again had found sanctuary at her parents house in Lodi. The same small home where she had grown up, where she had first met Willie, and where in the summer shade of the small backyard she had celebrated her marriage to him only a few years earlier. Mrs. Machell told Willie that he was not welcome in their home anymore.

It was then when Willie learned that Denise had been seen around town with a guy named Ivan. Willie knew who he was, a so-called badass biker, and he imagined his Denise all leathered out, riding on the back, hanging on tight. The very idea of her with Ivan tortured him no end.

So the summer of 1973 found Willie Steelman at his lowest point ever. He had no place to live, no job, no money and really no friends – Ronnie Bretbenner was about it – and all they really had in common was drugs and their days together in county jail. Willie had no home, no wife, or a halfway honest way to make a buck. His friends avoided him and his connections no longer trusted him, or his promise to pay.

He had kissed off his latest "last chance" with the courts. In June he missed a meeting with his parole officer, who immediately notified authorities, who in turn sent a warrant out for his arrest. He was now a wanted man, but not in the way he wished. So maybe it was odd, that of all people, it was Ronnie who tried to get Willie back on track again.

Each summer the local wineries hired on extra workers to get ready for the busy fall harvest. Ronnie managed to get on at a winery near Victor and arranged to get Willie a job there as well. Willie gave in and started in the middle of August. But it didn't last long. Soon he and Ronnie were back to their old ways, showing up for work stoned, laughing, bullshitting, wasting time, spending their day making jokes, pissing everyone off.

Although Willie had worked only a few days, he knew it was over for him. His job. His marriage. His shambles of a family. His sanity. His life.

On one side of the winery were giant vats of fermenting grapes. Over each was a large chalkboard where notes about the contents of the barrels were recorded. On the morning of August 21st, as high as he could get from whatever drug he could find, Willie showed up late for work, screwed around, cussed people out, and before they got the chance to fire him, he walked over to the three blackboards and scrawled as big as he could on each.

FUCK YOU LODI!

He left town that day. No one noticed. No one cared.

He would return soon enough, only to change everything forever.

4

Doug.

In Casper, Wyoming, that very same summer, June 28th to be exact, Sheriff Officer Ken Lindbloom began his late evening patrol. Part of his routine, and one of his first duties each night, was to check around the Platte River on the outskirts of town for kids breaking curfew.

It was just before midnight when he drove by a park near the river and noticed a sports car about twenty feet off the road. In the moonlight he could make out the silhouettes of two people huddled on the ground next to a tent. It was not unusual, especially in the summer months, to see hippies on their way to Yellowstone, camping out in the park. But such activity was forbidden, and Lindbloom spent much of his time explaining the rules.

The kid was young and tattered, but polite, and apologized for breaking any law. Lindbloom ran a check on his license and the plates on the car while quizzing him about what he was doing in Casper. After dispatch reported no wants on either, and because of the late hour, he decided to let the couple stay the night. He warned them he would back by when his shift ended at 7 a.m. and advised them to be up and gone by then, which they were.

Several nights later Lindbloom was again doing security in an industrial park on the north side of town. He guided his blue and white Dodge Polara quietly through the empty streets, lights off, windows down, scanning and listening. The area had seen a rash of burglaries lately and the Sheriff's Office had upped its drive bys.

As he pulled onto C Street, he was surprised to see the dark blue sports car from the other night. He stayed back and watched it slowly roll through a stop sign as it turned the corner. Lindbloom hit his lights and pulled the MGB over.

Once again he called in the plate number and his location. This time he figured he had their burglar, and was upset at himself for not settling this a few nights earlier. He took his spotlight and lit up the suspect's vehicle, blinding the driver, while ordering him to step out with his hands up where he could see them. Sure enough, it was the same guy.

"I was just driving around. I haven't done anything," he explained.

Lindbloom had drawn his Smith & Wesson just in case, but the kid repeated his innocence, a statement the officer had a hard time believing. There was nothing innocent about him. His blond hair was long and stringy, and hung down well over his eyes. His jeans were ripped and dirty, his jacket greasy, his tall frame rail thin, all of which screamed guilty. Lindbloom had nailed a hundred guys just like him, and experience told him this guy was up to no good.

"Then you won't mind if I check out your car?" he asked.

"No sir, go right ahead."

Lindbloom sprayed his flashlight around the front seat, but could see only fast food wrappers, wadded up newspapers and empty cigarette packs littered throughout. He popped the trunk. Inside was a big set of tools - burglar tools, he quickly decided.

"I'm a mechanic. Those are mine."

By now back up had arrived, allowing Lindbloom more freedom to check out the guy's story. He figured this time if he held him long enough, something would have to show up on his record. But once again dispatch radioed back that there was nothing. Lindbloom refused to believe it, so he took his only shot.

"Got any money on you?"

"No, not really."

"Well, then I'm going to have to take you in for running this stop sign. And because you aren't a resident, and have no way to pay the fine, I'm going to add a vagrancy charge to it."

Lindbloom knew it was a bad rap, but the guy didn't offer a single word of protest. As he put the cuffs on, he prayed his supervisor, or the judge tomorrow, for that matter, wouldn't take him down a couple of notches for such a bogus charge. But he just had this gut feeling that if he could just hold the guy overnight, something would just have to come up.

It was well after midnight before he got him booked in and locked down, yet the guy was still so polite and understanding that Lindbloom started feeling really embarrassed about the whole thing. "Hey, tell you what. You get a good night's sleep," he said as he shut the cell door. "Because they're gonna come and get you up pretty early in the morning to see the judge."

His guilt was getting the best of him and he couldn't shut up. "You know, look at it this way, at least you'll get a good breakfast out of all of this."

The prisoner grinned. "Yeah, that's right. Thanks"

Lindbloom walked away shaking his head. That was the first time he ever had anyone thank him for getting popped.

At nine the next morning, the accused stood before Judge Bishop as the charges were read. Lindbloom still had not been able to get anything on the guy. A speeding ticket in Miami years back. Big deal. There wasn't so much as a DUI. He couldn't figure it out. Somewhere, somehow, he was missing something. The guy had to be guilty of something someplace. He just had that look about him.

With nothing else to hang on him, Bishop set the fine at $70 for the traffic ticket and vagrancy charge, and knowing he couldn't pay, suspended it and let him go.

The guy was even polite to the judge, thanking him repeatedly as he walked out of the courtroom. Lindbloom decided he must have left Casper right after that because he never saw him again.

But it wasn't even six months later that he read about what Douglas Gretzler had done. He couldn't believe it. He had been this close to stopping the guy before any of this happened. The magnitude of his failure made him sick to his stomach.

A year earlier, home for Doug was a fifth floor apartment in the Bronx, not far from the upscale suburb of Tuckahoe where he was raised. He had a wife, and a baby, but damn little beyond that. He had been married only a short time, most of which had been spent arguing about his immaturity and inability to support his family. Arguments that usually led to him walking out, because he couldn't stand the lectures. As he had pointed out to his wife on countless occasions, he had a lot of jobs. He was a good worker, he reminded her, it was just that he couldn't handle people telling him he *had* to do something, and that included her.

So he would quit, or get fired, or simply walk away, but in any event, he couldn't quite find his calling. So it was left up to Judy to support them with her $125 a week job at a nearby bank. Doug went through times when he acted like he was working, or at least that's what he told her. He got up early and came home late, yet he seldom brought a paycheck home with him. Judy wanted to believe him, but when she asked anything about his job, he would clam up and go hide.

Which he often did. He couldn't stand all the yelling, so he locked himself in the bathroom while Judy stood outside and cried. There was no doubt Judy loved Doug, maybe even worshipped him to some degree. Both were just eighteen when they got married and Doug had not grown up enough to face the responsibilities he had helped create. Most of his friends were no older or no more mature than he, so Judy stood by and watched as they hung out together and did kid's stuff like shooting BB guns and goofing around with Doug's car.

However, after their daughter Jessica was born, Judy was pleased to see Doug act a bit more serious. If he was still not quite the breadwinner she had hoped for, at least he was turning out to be a good father, and always seemed anxious to watch the baby while she worked. Her problem, she began to realize, was that she depended on Doug too much. She was now the head of their small household, and yet she couldn't make even the simplest of decisions without consulting him. Doug told a friend once his wife actually bugged him for over an hour one night about whether she should clip her toenails or file them. It drove him crazy. He couldn't make his own decisions, and he had no desire to make hers, so the arguments and hassles continued.

As one might expect, most of Doug's problems revolved around drugs. He had been doing one form or another since he was thirteen, and for the past several years they ruled his life. The more he took, the more Judy lectured, so the more he took. The more they argued, the more he wanted to disappear, so he found his hiding place in every illegal pharmaceutical he could get his hands on. The spiral continued to the point, where to avoid the bickering, he just wouldn't come home at all.

On his 21st birthday, in the spring of 1972, Doug received a trust fund of several thousand dollars from a relative. His father loudly protested the gift, saying he didn't deserve it; that he would just blow it on dope, but there was nothing he could do to stop it. Judy was relieved, knowing how much they could use the help. Her job alone was never enough to support them, so she welcomed this unexpected windfall.

She never got a penny of it. Doug went out and bought an MGB sports car, then proceeded to drop the rest of money into fixing it up. He spent the summer either buying something for it, working on it, or driving it around. He loaded it up with the nicest eight-track stereo and the biggest speakers he could shove into it. Top down, stereo cranked, you could hear Doug coming a block away.

The car and his music became the center of his life, along with the daily high of course, but after a while, negotiating New York City streets, or the occasional turnpike, didn't seem quite enough. He dreamed of the day when he could really get in the car and drive. No particular place, just turn the wheel and hit it. Drive until you ran out of road. Hit the highway and disappear once and for all.

But being a husband and father, and holding on to that thread of responsibility, he knew he couldn't leave. He hated everything about his life. Each day he dreamed about what he really wanted to do, struggled with what he had to do, and continued to lock himself in the bathroom whenever the voices got too loud.

That fall, hounded by his wife and now by his father to find a job, Doug gave in and started work at a concrete factory in Tuckahoe. Surprisingly, he acted as if he even enjoyed it, and for the next few months things were looking up.

Like before, it didn't last. When his father discovered Doug had quit yet another job, he marched down to the plant and talked to the owner himself, trying to find out just what in God's name Doug's problem was. They couldn't explain it either. Everything was going fine, they said. Everyone liked him. He was a good worker. A nice guy to have around. But one day he just didn't bother to show up. Didn't call. No message. Nothing. They never saw him again. He didn't even bother to come in and collect the few bucks the company still owed him.

Mr. Gretzler was livid, and he tracked his son down and told him so; told him what a no-good bum he was and how embarrassed he was having him for a son. "You have never done one good thing in your life," he screamed, "and I'm through with you! I don't want to see you crawling back home the next time you need something. In fact, I'm tired of seeing your face, so don't bother coming around at all!"

Doug did not tell Judy. He continued to lie about going to work just so he wouldn't have to be around her. It wasn't that he didn't love her, because he really didn't know for sure. He didn't know about all of those feelings regular people had, nor did he care to know. He was best at hiding everything, masking it all with drugs and depression and escape, and he realized he felt better when he didn't feel anything at all.

Doug knew the marriage-thing smothered him, that much he was certain. The responsibilities, the demands, the money, the family pressure, it was all much too much. He thought about a divorce, but knew he didn't have the guts or the energy to go through with it. He knew Judy would just cry, his father would give him a load of shit, and it would start all over again.

So Doug decided that if he just wasn't around – as in gone for good – then Judy could get an uncontested divorce, find someone who could take care of her and the baby, and get on with her life. If he was gone, then he wouldn't even have to think about all the crap that went along with breaking up a marriage. He started dreaming again about hitting the road.

Somehow the Gretzler family found a way to sweep everything under the rug long enough to spend Christmas together. Doug, Judy and the baby went there for the holiday and they all managed to act civil to each other for one day.

The next morning, back in their apartment, Judy got up, got ready, said good bye, and left for her job at the bank, taking Jessica with her to the babysitter, leaving Doug home alone like she had most days of late.

After she was gone, he threw some clothes in a duffel bag and left. Jumped in his car and just split. No note. No explanation. No phone call. No nothing. Gone.

He headed west. Just as fast and as far as the hundred bucks he had stashed would take him. It was snowing hard, and he dreamed of the beaches. It was gray and cold and he pictured himself in the sun. California. The Promised Land. The Pacific Ocean and the Redwoods. He imagined himself riding that cable car in the Rice-a-Roni commercial. He knew they were all just gonna shit, but he had to get away.

Far enough away to live a different life in a different world, because he had already seen enough of who he was and where he was from, and he just wanted to stop being Douglas Gretzler and having to deal with his asshole father and his nagging wife and the crying baby, and the endless hassles and the forever string of bills and all the other shit he had left behind – driving, dreaming, free and reckless, wipers slapping the high beam glare, hiding well into the night, wet asphalt as far as he could see, eight track rolling straight into the wild, wild west, coming up for air as someone else, somewhere else, somebody nobody would ever know. Just go. Just drive. Just disappear.

Twenty-four hours later and he had got as far as Casper, Wyoming.

So he bummed around there during the first half of 1973. He had car troubles but no money, so he took a few odd jobs; farm hand on a sheep ranch, truck driver, oil field worker, even played a couple of gigs in a bowling alley bar sitting in for the drummer. He cleaned 55 gallon barrels for a roughneck oil crew. Nothing lasted. He earned just enough to fix his car and stay high. He got into a few scrapes, made a few friends, even a couple of enemies, and that was about it. When he got arrested around the Fourth of July, Doug decided it was time to move on.

He had met a guy named David Beckner, who had been on him to come on down to Denver and hang out for a while. There's plenty of good dope and good people, David promised, and not so many damn rednecks. Which was fine by Doug, who had his share of run-ins with the locals.

Casper really didn't take kindly to hippies and Doug stuck out like a sore thumb, which only made his existence there that much more unbearable. One night, back when he was working on the ranch, some of the boys got liquored up, and when Doug fell asleep, they took out a knife and gave him a free haircut. When he woke up and saw them standing around with the knife, laughing their asses off, Doug figured Casper wasn't the end of his road after all.

So after the arrest he stayed low, spending the rest of the summer trying to collect some back wages so he would have some money to get out of town. He finally gave up and drove down to Denver to try and find David.

Other than the crap he had to put up with in Casper, Doug got a real high being out west. Living in New York City, with the crowds and the traffic and the garbage and the stink, this was indeed a trip. Wide open spaces and scenery he had seen only in picture books. It was so different, so immense. He felt so insignificant, so good, so far away from everything and everyone. Out here nothing touched and he felt like driving forever.

But he stopped in Denver and found David. There was a little place over off of Broadway in the south part of town, David told him, where things were cool and there was always a loaded bong or a roach clip being passed around, so he brought Doug over to meet everybody the moment he hit town.

And it was there, one afternoon in late summer, when Doug first met Willie Steelman.

5

August 1973.

Frances would not have been any more surprised if it had been the Devil himself standing on her front porch.

"Good heavens, Bill! What in the world you doing here?"

"Just thought I'd come out and see ya. Surprised?"

Indeed she was! Frances had left but for a few minutes, running an errand or something, and when she got home, there he was, big as life. He gave her a hug hello, helped carry her packages in, giving his nephews and nieces a playful swat as they poured out of the car and ran into the house. However, Frances soon learned her brother had not come to Denver for a vacation. He was in trouble, and he wasted no time in telling her just how much. They sat for the better part of the afternoon and talked.

It was just weeks earlier when Frances and the kids drove out to Lodi for a family visit. There were times when years would pass without her seeing Willie, and now, Good Lord, here it was, twice in one month! She talked with him only a few times during her stay in California. She knew about the drugs, and she could tell the toll they had taken, and although she didn't like seeing him like this, she was never much for lecturing. One afternoon while she was there in Lodi, they went out for Chinese food and he told her about his bad marriage, his troubles with the law, and everything else hanging over his head. He felt like he could talk to her. Talk to her like nobody else. Talk to her like old times, when it was just the two of them. He told her about how screwed up his life was. How out of control things were. About how hopeless it all seemed.

Of course Frances had not seen him in quite some time, and she was sick at just how far down he had tumbled. She knew about his mental problems as a teenager, and she worried that day he might try to kill himself. It was that bad. And yet, just when she thought he had hit rock bottom, he would brighten up and gush about how he planned to go back to Delta College in the fall and take up nursing again.

He frightened her, all this back and forth talk, and for the first time in her life she didn't know what to say to him. She no longer had the words to make everything better. Her brother had changed. Her precious little Bill. There were times that day in Lodi when she didn't know if she should hold on to him for dear, sweet life, or get up from the table and swear to God never to see his face again.

And now here he was, a month later, sitting in her living room.

During his first week in Denver they got along fine. Willie told her he had made up his mind to trash the drugs, and she wanted to believe him. There was a little pot, but he said that didn't count. He promised to help out around the house and watch the kids when she was at work.

One of them, Terry, the oldest, looked up to her uncle. She was a teenager, and bit of a handful herself, so it was hard for Frances to watch her idolize Willie; with his tall tales of seeming adventure and his careless attitude about life. Willie slept upstairs in the unfinished area of the house, a place he called his crash pad, and Terry spent a lot of time up there rapping with him, bringing her friends over to meet him, and he would hold their attention for hours with his stories, earning their admiration, becoming the guy you went to when you had a problem, needed someone to talk, or somebody just to hang out with.

Somewhere along the line a young girl named Marsha Renslow stopped by. She was a tiny little thing – eighty pounds, maybe, and not even close to five feet tall – barely seventeen but a self-proclaimed wild child. Her mother was handicapped – crutches and a wheelchair kind of handicapped – so she had a tough time getting around, and even a harder time chasing her only daughter all over town. Marsha had three older brothers who were always in and out of trouble, so she had become quite a tomboy, and Mrs. Renslow had her hands full with all of them

One day after she had got to know him better, Marsha told Willie that she was just ten when her real father died. He hadn't been around much when she was little, she remembered, but the day he did come home, after promising to be a better dad and a better husband, he fell over dead in the bathroom. Aneurysm, they told her. Whatever the hell that was. Young Marsha was devastated, thinking it was somehow her fault. From there on she was frightened of the power men seemed to hold over her and she swore never to get close to another one again. Willie listened. He said he really understood. She said he was the only one who did.

So she kind of dug Willie. Not in any sexual way – she had decided her preference a couple of years earlier – but she liked his style, and the way people flocked to him. She stopped by the house on Ellsworth almost everyday just to see him.

Frances had been having her own problems, even before her brother showed up, and other than the simple chores he did on occasion, Willie offered little help. She had lost her first husband a few years back, and the new man in her life did little more than get drunk and threaten her and the kids. Willie had already had words with him over it, telling him where the line would be drawn, but Frances told her brother not get involved in her personal affairs. Money was her biggest problem. She had a meager job and a rather large family to support, and Willie gave her nothing. By the first of September, and realizing another payment could not be made, Frances told him that the bank was probably going to take the house back. She didn't ask him for any help, and he didn't offer any.

It hadn't taken Willie long to slip back into his old ways. Other than trying to figure out how to get loaded everyday and be the center of attention, he had no plans. No talk about finding a job, and the one and only time Frances casually asked when he might be heading back to Lodi, he became angry. He glared at her with this hateful silence, like she had insulted him.

"When I fucking feel like it! How does that sound?" he screamed.

Frances was so hurt, and so scared, she decided not to bring the subject up again. For the next several days she made sure to not say anything to cross him. Willie, on the other hand, acted as if nothing had ever happened.

Although one night not long after that, Willie seemed especially distraught. Frances asked what was wrong, and he started in about Denise, and why she had left him. They sat on the sofa and talked, while Frances tried to console him, saying maybe there was still a way to get her back.

"No, it's over. I know it is," Willie said.

"Now why would say that? You don't know for sure."

"I know because I hit her, sis. I got so mad I dragged her out to the car and hit her hard."

He was now cuddled up with his sister, confessing sins he would never dare tell anyone else. He was crying, and she was holding on to him, rocking gently back and forth.

"I'm really afraid," he cried. "I was out of control like I've never been. I could of hurt her. I was so scared after it was over, I was just shaking."

A newcomer stopped by the house on Ellsworth one day in early September. Just another one of the endless faces that came in and out of the place while Willie was there. But this guy was different somehow. He was quiet, polite, and before he left that day, he took the time to say hello to Frances. None of the others even acknowledged this was her house they were living and partying in, so his manners surprised and impressed her. He was tall, and amazingly thin, considering he was always scavenging for food; something in very short supply in the house as of late. His hair fell across his face and over his thick wire frame glasses, and he had a habit of jerking his head to one side to keep it out of his eyes; eyes that set back deep in a long thin face. He had a few scrawny hairs on his chin and upper lip, but not much anywhere else. It was scruff that would never make it to a full beard. He had too much baby skin for that.

But he had a car. The only one in the group who did, so he became their chauffeur. He had been coming by for over a week before Frances even learned his name.

One day he offered his hand to her and introduced himself as Doug.

6

September 1973.

The house on Ellsworth sat not a block off Broadway in the south part of town. It was a small two story home, brick, like a thousand others in town, and it appeared to have been painted once, although there was no telling how long ago that might have been. In an older neighborhood, where few cared about keeping up with anybody, Frances' house was nothing special, other than it was her's. At least for a while, anyway.

Next to the house was a large building; a nondescript warehouse of some sort that blocked out the morning sun, along with their view to the busy boulevard beyond. Next to that, on the corner of Ellsworth and Broadway, was American Jewelry. Willie would walk down to the corner almost everyday just to look in the window and tell himself what an easy score it would be.

Broadway actually began a few miles north near the center of town, and at one time, long before the highways and interstates began to circle Denver, it was considered a main drag and given the designation State Highway 25, South it traveled, well past Ellsworth, for miles and miles, straight as an arrow, into the exploding suburbs and far beyond. In its heyday, most of the major department stores and five and dimes had a location on Broadway, and for years it remained one of Denver's busiest streets.

Around the corner from Frances' house was the Mayan Theatre; an impressive old movie palace, with its towering 1920's era Egyptian facade and krieglight beams inviting people from all over town. There was a pharmacy on one corner, a bakery on another, fine clothing stores were found everywhere and auto dealerships abounded during the splendid years when being on Broadway meant something.

But by the time Willie and Doug arrived, those days were over. Broadway was now a third rate part of town, and not a place one would have wished to call home. The buildings were still there, but the businesses were gone, replaced by second hand stores and discount waterbed warehouses that filled up some of the big spaces, while head shops and bars took over the smaller ones. The Mayan stayed open, but no one cared much anymore. And although the American Jewelry store remained, for the past several years they would only put inexpensive costume jewelry in the windows. The cops from District 3 were being called to that area more often now, for Broadway had become a major hub for drug activity. Denver Police guessed that half the dope being peddled in the city either came in or out of that part of town, which was just fine by Willie.

At first, drugs were the only common bond between he and the new guy. Of course, they were the reason any of them stopped by the house in the first place. They even had their own drug-man who came by daily to see what kind of high they all wanted. The house on Ellsworth just happened to be on his route, like the milkman twenty years earlier. But now Willie had met his match. Until Doug arrived on the scene, Willie was king. No one dared keep up with him, or were as experienced or as daring with chemicals, as was he.

However Doug had a head start. As a teenager his first thrills were smoking cheap weed in the basement, and soon he was into pills and good hash. As a senior in high school, Doug was The Man; dealing acid, STP, or any other high his classmates desired. His buddies would haul him down to the train station and away he went, deep into the Bronx to his connections. They called him Tuckahoe's Pied Piper of Drugs, and he was barely 17. When he got married he was shooting speed every day for as long as he could go, and cocaine was pretty cheap, so he did as much as he could afford. Even Doug had to agree with those who considered him nothing more than a human garbage pail, for there was no end to what he would try for a high. So it was no surprise that by the time he got to Denver there wasn't a whole lot Willie Steelman could teach him about dope, and Willie respected him for that.

They stayed loaded all night, revved up on speed, rapping nonstop about everything. Willie loved talking politics, world religion, or the war in Vietnam, and could go on forever. Doug talked music, because that's what he knew. It was during these sessions when a connection developed between them. Willie found someone intelligent enough to converse with, while Doug finally had someone who listened to him, respected his opinions, and didn't put him down like his old man always did.

The scene at the house was growing and now there was something happening almost around the clock. Besides Willie and Doug, and of course Frances and her kids, someone was always stopping by, crashing in, hanging out, or even living there. First there was Terry, Frances' oldest, who was becoming more and more attracted to Doug. Then there was Gypsy, a biker whose background impressed Willie, although not for long. Gypsy's lady, Suzanne, hung out there too and soon had a thing going on with Willie, as did a young woman named Charlys. David Beckner, who had brought Doug along, was a regular, as was his sister. They called her Little Red, and her long auburn hair was the reason. She was a familiar face at the house, and although she lived nearby with her mother, they didn't get along, so she spent her days and nights on Ellsworth, having given up on school years earlier. She could not have been more than fifteen.

A guy named Loser hung out there, and although he had a semi-regular job moving furniture, he was still somewhat of a fixture at the house. He had known Marsha for a year or two and took it upon himself to watch over her, simply because no one else did. He claimed to be a boxer, and he was a huge man – half black, half Indian – with massive scars across his chest credited to a mountain lion he claimed to have wrestled once.

He worried about Marsha and fretted over the long hours she was spending at the house. Yet despite his size and tough demeanor, Loser was a gentle man, at least with his feelings, and he cared deeply about Marsha and her brothers.

Loser was also interested in music, so he and Doug had something to talk about as well. One day he brought over his old electric bass guitar to show Doug, but Willie somehow talked Loser into selling it, then managed to get his hands on the money to buy more dope. That was the final straw for Loser. He was tired of the scene, said he was in training for an upcoming fight, and stopped hanging out on Ellsworth.

Marsha was there all the time now, finding Willie terribly exciting, never quite getting enough of his stories. Willie viewed her intentions as sexual, although everyone knew Marsha had very little interest in men. Of course, Willie decided that was only because she was so young and had never been with an older man. He was certain, that with a little time, he could set her straight.

One night, when she was shit-faced on red wine and passed out on the bed, Willie attempted to seduce her. Too drunk to fight him off or to remember much of what happened, Marsha figured he did what he wanted to do. It hurt her, even pissed her off a little, that he would do such a thing, because by now, she thought he was her friend. It was the only time anything like that happened between them, unless you asked Willie, who would brag otherwise.

Marsha's brothers became regulars on Ellsworth too. Jake claimed he was there only to look after his little sister, but Doug showed him how to stick a needle in his arm and thereby change Jake's life forever. Russ, who of all the brothers was undoubtedly the closest to his sister, spent his young life in an elusive search for simply a place to belong. He hung out at the house because he couldn't get enough of Willie Steelman. He would do anything Willie asked, regardless of how dangerous or stupid that might be, and Willie was quick to take advantage of such loyalty.

The people Willie surrounded himself with; the ones he was so eager to impress, were usually younger than he, and it was no different at the house on Ellsworth. Of the regulars, Doug was the oldest, and even he was a half dozen years younger than Willie. Some of them, like Little Red or even Marsha, were barely sixteen or seventeen. And the age thing was important to Willie, not so much in years, but in attitude and experience, because it gave him the upper hand, and no one dared question him or his decisions. So all activity now orbited around Willie, and these people became his family and looked to him for the dope, the answers, and the next move.

There were others who lived there, some with no name at all, maybe only to stop by once and never be seen again. One day a kid showed up, best guess he was twenty, and everybody figured he was just somebody's friend. But before long he had his suitcase unpacked and was living at the house. He came and went as he pleased, and had been there for the better part of a week before the others started talking about him, realizing that they didn't know anything about this guy, not even a name. No one really gave it too much thought up until then because there were no real rules or anything, and everybody was trippin' all the time anyway, so any rational thinking had long since disappeared.

This kid was different, and soon the whole idea of him hanging out there got on Willie's nerves. Every morning the kid got up and got dressed, even going so far to put on a tie, which really freaked Willie out, so he figured this guy had to be a narc.

One day, while the kid was out, Willie decided the house could not take a chance on anyone infiltrating their scene. The kid was bad news, he told the others, and they had to get rid of him. Of course Willie said he would handle it, and he bet everyone that when the kid came back that night, he could take him out with just one punch. One punch, right in the face, he said, and the guy would go down. They took his bet.

Later on when the kid walked in, Willie faced him down. "Nice tie," he said.

"Thanks."

Then Willie hit him, and the kid hit the floor. Willie turned around and looked at them. "What did I tell ya?"

He wasn't done. While the kid was down, Willie kicked him in the back a few times, then a couple more to his gut for good measure. The expression on Willie's face was of a man possessed, and it frightened Marsha. By now the kid had stopped moving, so Willie ended his attack, picked him up, took him to his room and laid him on the bed.

For the next few days Willie hovered over the kid with no name, nursing him back to health, going so far as to shove a tube into his lungs and suck out all the fluids resulting from his injuries – a procedure learned from his days at the Vista Ray. When the kid recovered enough to get up, he was told to get out.

Late September found Willie with woman problems, which was another reason he was on such a power trip. Suzanne, Gypsy's lady, was now wrapped up in the Steelman mystique, leaving no doubt she was ready and willing to do whatever Willie wanted, including, according to him, lots of dope and sex. While the combination excited Willie no end, it did not do much to improve Gypsy's reputation as a bad ass. For a biker to lose his woman was a major blow, and when Suzanne started lying to Gypsy about why she was spending so much time at the house, Willie let it be known that Gypsy wasn't welcome anymore. "If he doesn't have the balls to protect what's his, then he's shit, and I don't want any shit in my house."

Willie told the others that Gypsy was banished.

Charlys also liked Willie, and that's where the problems began. He had to juggle both, usually leaving Doug to run interference for him. When Willie and Suzanne were upstairs, doing whatever, and Charlys would stop by unexpectedly, asking for him. Doug's rehearsed line was that Willie was out, or not feeling well, or whatever he could think of to get rid of her. It was hard for him to do because Doug cared for Charlys and hated lying.

Although both Suzanne and Charlys wanted Willie, his main interest was still Marsha, the girl everyone was now calling Short Shit. He confided to Doug his intent to get closer to her, and more and more he was making up excuses for the three of them to hang out together. Many nights they would all get ripped and drive around in the MGB, laughing and squealing tires. When Willie and Doug hit a bar, Marsha sat patiently on the curb.

Short Shit was a whirlwind and sometimes difficult for Willie to keep up with. When she saw Doug shooting up, she insisted he teach her how to do it. But Willie was reluctant, and only agreed to it if he was around to help her. Before long she became a pro and could tie off a vein with the best of them. Willie called her 'a little scooter tramp', because she loved motorcycles, and probably knew more about them than he could ever hope to. She told him she was building her own bike, which impressed Willie big time. She even convinced he and Doug into going out and stealing parts for her, which Willie was more than happy to do. Willie was always talking about starting a cycle gang, and because Marsha almost had a bike, (although it was no more than a pile of parts in her bedroom); it was enough of an excuse to have a club. So the three of them formed a biker gang, and after he insisted, made Willie president.

It was also about this time, towards the end of September, when Willie and Doug started talking about getting some money together. When Doug first arrived in Denver he looked for a job just to keep him in gas, food and drugs, but after he fell in with Willie, that did not seem quite so important. But getting high was expensive and Willie was running out of people in the house to sucker.

Besides the jewelry store on the corner that he brushed aside, claiming it was much too easy, Willie told Doug about all of his Denver connections, and all the opportunities available to them. He boasted about being on the inside of a local drug family. "It's kinda like a Mafia thing," he said, claiming to know exactly where their money drops were and when they took place. There was also a Western Union office in town with $10,000 in the safe at all times. "A straight rip," he said. "Just walk in and take it, cuz there ain't nobody in there gonna give you shit with a gun in their face."

But they didn't have any guns, and Willie said he was working on that, but in the meantime they needed some daily cash, so Willie schooled Doug in the fine art of snatching purses. "Three things you can find in a purse," he said, "cash, a checkbook and sometimes a prescription bottle with who knows what kind of pills."

All three were cool, Willie continued, but the checkbook is the best because it created the most opportunities for money. The best place to find one is in a store. "One that's just laying there, because there's no hassles that way. Now if that's not possible, then look for an easy mark, a woman who isn't likely to scream or chase you down. Then scout your territory, plan your route, and figure out beforehand how you can disappear quickly."

Doug had never done anything like this, although he was not opposed to the idea, so one afternoon soon there after, Willie pointed out a woman he thought would be an easy target. Walking a short distance behind her, he gave Doug the sign to go for it.

Doug ran up, bumped the woman and grabbed for the bag. When he did, she tripped and began to fall. Doug had the purse and was on his way gone, when she cried out for help. Thinking he had hurt her, he stopped dead in his tracks and turned around. "Are you okay?" he asked. The woman was still screaming. Willie couldn't believe it. "Run you asshole!" he yelled. "Run!"

With his first purse snatching now behind him, Doug was more receptive to bigger jobs. Willie told him the best money out there, the easiest money, was drug money. If you ripped off a dealer, Willie proposed, who were they going to spill to? Certainly not the cops, so there was a certain safety in that. Problem was again the lack of weapons. No weapons, no rips. And with no money to buy a gun, Willie had to figure out away to get one fast.

One day Russ Renslow was at the house, hanging out and hanging onto every word from Willie's mouth, when the subject of guns came up. Willie was going on about how he needed one to protect himself from some blacks that had been threatening him and everyone who lived in the house. Russ jumped in and said he knew a couple of guys who had some shotguns and he might be able to talk them into selling one of them.

Willie perked up. "You go get us one. Let us see it, and if we like it, we'll give you the money.

So Russ, eager to please, did exactly as Willie asked. Later that night he walked back into the house with the shotgun. Thinking he would be welcomed with open arms, Russ began bragging about how he got it and who he got it from. The owner, Russ said, was a guy named Ted, who was a big deal in a little motorcycle gang in the south part of Denver. Ted told Russ to take it, but he damn well better be back the next day with $60. Russ agreed, knowing Willie would be pleased.

Instead, Willie went into a rage; slapping Russ around, screaming about what a idiot he was for bringing this bad karma into the house. Willie said he didn't want to owe no biker club money for some chintzy piece a shit shotgun. He had screwed up big time, Willie said, and now he was going to have to suffer for it. So he and Doug took Russ out behind the building next door and beat the hell out of him. They took an ax handle to his knees, then took the shotgun.

"This is ours now, man," Willie told him. "And it's up to you to figure out how to pay your little friend."

Russ hobbled back home and told Marsha he had fallen off a motor scooter.

Now that they had some firepower, Willie and Doug got down to business. It was then when they first discussed what they later referred to as The Pact. According to Willie, any scam, any heist, any rip, needed a team to pull it off, and in order for it to go down smooth, there needed to be an agreement; a pact, and that each member of the team had to agree to back the other's play, regardless of the situation or the consequences. There had to be someone who called the shots, planned the deals, and made sure they followed them through.

Willie said that this being Denver and the West and all, it was only natural that he be that man. He knew how things worked out here, he told Doug, who was who more than content to follow along. "Now if we were in New York" Willie offered, "you would be the guy with the plan, and I would listen to what you had to say." It was like a military thing, he continued, where once in battle, there was just one leader. No matter what was said, or what went down, despite everything else, you backed the other guy's play. It was the only way to guarantee their success, he assured him.

It made sense to Doug, who was always willing to let someone else make the decisions anyway. It gave him more time to do what he wanted to do, like staying loaded.

So not much came of The Pact initially. Whatever rips Willie planned usually fell through, but Doug didn't blame him for that because Willie always had a good excuse. When it happened – if it happened – Doug told himself he would be ready.

Frances was in trouble. Willie had been there for over a month now, and not only had he stopped helping her out around the house, he was constantly trying to con her out of what little money she managed to scrape together. As of late, she went out of her way to avoid him, allowing he and all the others to have the run of the second floor if they promised to leave her and her family alone downstairs.

To make matters worse, Art, the guy in her life, was a drunk, and like all the others in the house, did little more than sponge off what little she had. Short of leaving town, Frances had no idea in the world how to get rid of him. To add to her misery, Frances was now several payments behind on the house and worried about losing it to the bank. Autumn was settling in and the Denver weather had turned bone cold, with morning temperatures below freezing. Adding insult to injury, the furnace went out.

Willie was no help, even though he could complain like hell about being cold. The only hope France had in staying warm and keeping the house was to try and borrow some money. She learned quickly no one would even talk to her without some kind of collateral. In frustration, she mentioned all of this to Doug one day, never expecting he could do anything more than just listen.

"Why don't you put up my car for the loan?" he offered.

Frances was taken back by his generosity. "Doug, I couldn't do that!"

"Why not? We need the heat, and you need the money." Without saying another word, he went out to the car, came back in and handed her the title. Somewhat reluctantly, Frances put it in her purse, thanking him from the bottom of her heart. She had $200 to her name. That might be enough to keep the bank happy, and now with Doug's help, maybe she could get a small loan to fix the furnace too.

Not an hour later, Willie and Doug stood at the front door and watched her get into her car to go down to the bank. Before pulling away, she remembered leaving something in the house and ran back inside. When she returned to the car only minutes later, her purse was gone. Along with it, her last few dollars, her checkbook, the car title, and any hopes she had of struggling through this mess. She was frantic, and searched everywhere; although she knew good and well she had left the purse on the backseat of the car, in plain sight.

It was obvious the purse had been stolen. All she could do was go back inside and have a good cry. Later that night, she decided to just give the house back to the bank. She was done trying. While she never said so, she could not help but wonder if Bill took the purse. She didn't want to believe for one moment he had sunk that low, but who else? Not Doug. Especially after he gave her the title and offered his help. That left only her brother, and it made her sick to think he would do such a rotten thing.

Art Wallen came over later that night, drunk as usual, and she told him what happened. "It's that no-good piece of shit brother of yours!" he slurred. "He did it. I know for a goddamn fact it was him!"

Regardless of what she thought, she didn't like Art or anyone else talking about Bill that way. The argument got nasty. He told her she was trash, no better than that asshole brother of hers, or any of the others in this goddamn house, for that matter. He gave her an ultimatum. Either her brother and all his friends go, or he would.

Frances knew she had no guts, but regardless of what she thought of Bill, he was family, and she could no sooner kick him out of her house than she could one of her own kids. She gathered all of the courage she could muster and told Art exactly that. He made good on his threat, packed his stuff, and left.

The next morning Frances told the bank of her intentions. It did not really matter, she rationalized, she had become a stranger in her own house anyway. It was now ruled by her brother, and there was seldom any privacy or a moment's peace. She found a little apartment about a mile away, and for the next few days she began moving her things out. Doug was the only one who offered to help.

She didn't even bother with the big stuff; leaving the refrigerator and stove, even some furniture too big to squeeze into her station wagon. On the last day of September she left for good, and as she walked out, Bill leaned on the front porch and watched her go.

"You're welcome to stay," Frances said. "I figure the bank will be by soon to kick you out, but you can stay 'til they do."

She had no idea what to think of her brother these days. He had changed so much she hardly recognized him anymore. She didn't want to blame him for what happened to the purse, or what happened to her house, for that matter, but she had a hard time liking who he had become. She still loved him, of course, but she certainly did not like him. She thought about that for a minute. How odd that seemed. She remembered the little boy she loved so much and took such good care of, and how sweet he was, and how he would run to her, grab on to her leg and bury his face into the pleats of her skirt, telling her he was hiding from the bogeyman. She gave up much of her youth to mother him all those years ago, never once giving it a second thought, never once blaming him for those lost years, and this is how he repaid her.

She was at the end of her ropes, but he acted like he couldn't wait for her to leave. "So, it's all yours," she sighed.

Bill could only stare down at her with the most hateful glare she had ever felt.

Good Lord, he frightened her! It was the look of a monster, a man gone mad, and she had to fight to just catch her breath. Willie didn't say a word, just stared; his eyes burning a hole clean through her. It was the look of the devil, she was certain.

She stepped away; afraid to turn her back on him, worried what he might do. She kept retreating until she reached the safety of her car, and it wasn't until she turned the corner and lost herself in the traffic on Broadway that she could even breathe.

She never saw her brother again.

Later that day, Willie went out and passed a few bad checks. That night he threw a big party at his house on Ellsworth.

7

Saturday, October 6, 1973 | 1:30 pm.

Charlys Frazier wanted desperately to please Willie. This afternoon she got her chance.

She could see what was going on. She knew he was avoiding her; using Doug to make up phony excuses why he wasn't home or why he couldn't come to the phone, yet she had no idea why she found herself so attracted to him. Certainly it was not his looks or his money, because he had neither. Maybe it was because he just seemed so vulnerable, so hurt, like a little lost boy. Sure, he talked tough – stories about his wild past and all the important people he knew – but she didn't believe them. When they were alone, which was not very often as of late, she saw another Willie; an intelligent man, anxious to tell her about his childhood and how he never really had much of a family, especially after his father died. When his mother remarried, he said, there just wasn't any room left for him. He told her he married his childhood sweetheart a few years back, but found her in bed with another man, so he left town, and here he was, alone again.

"The only family I have now is that lady in the other room," Willie once told her. "She's all I got left in the world."

Charlys crumpled. He seemed so sad. She just knew he would be a good father. He was so patient and loving with his sister's kids, even helping his nephew throw a paper route a couple of afternoons. And it was clear to see the kids loved their Uncle Bill, who was always ready with piggyback rides and Hide-n-Seek out in the yard. He might be fooling the others with all his tough talk, but he wasn't fooling her. She knew if Willie understood how much she cared for him, maybe it could make a difference in his life.

By appearance alone, Charlys was just the type of woman Willie should be attracted to; blonde, just tough enough, and kind of a biker chick look. In fact, he told Doug she reminded him of his ex-wife. She wasn't into the drug scene, and she knew the house on Ellsworth offered too many temptations for Willie. She did her best to get him to leave, and more than once she asked him to move in with her; promising no strings if he did. She even offered to work and support them both, yet Willie refused. He was already getting tired of her hanging around and hassling him, and it didn't take long before he was avoiding her altogether. The closer Charlys tried to get, the more Willie backed off. The more frequent her visits, the more times Doug said he wasn't around. When she called, he was always gone. Tired of the rejection, her trips to the house became less often, and while she wasn't quite ready to give up on him yet, he was slowly becoming a smaller part of her life.

So she was surprised, and a bit excited, when he called her earlier that week asking for help. He told her, "Some blacks are after us, threatening all of us in the house. What I need is a piece. You know, just something to protect us with."

A gun was the last thing she wanted to buy him, but she also realized this might be her only chance to show how much she cared. Charlys knew all about the rough crowd hanging around the house – there were times in her not-so-innocent life when she had been involved with these people as well – so she believed Willie when he said he was worried. Of course, he said nothing about already having a shotgun.

"Don't need nothin' big," he said. "Just something to have close by, you know, just in case."

So Saturday afternoon, October 6th, Charlys drove over to the Woolco department store on the corner of West 72nd and Federal Boulevard. She tried making sense of all the guns, in particular the .22s Willie requested. She picked out the cheapest one, a Japanese built Fie Model R-6 .22, with a long blue steel barrel and a plastic imitation wood stock. She filled out the paperwork, including the required Federal Firearms Transaction Record, using her driver's license as identification. She paid cash; $15.88 for the rifle, another 79 cents for a box of shells.

She went straight over to the house, anxious to surprise Willie, praying this would please him, fingers crossed this might help get them back on track.

Willie was like a kid at Christmas, thanking her a hundred times while he ran his hand up the barrel, admiring it, showing it to all the others. He never asked how much it cost, or offered to pay her back, but that didn't matter to Charlys, who was pleased he was so happy. She hung around for a while, but soon the afternoon faded away, and Willie did as well, so Charlys realized it was time to go. Willie said he would call, promising they would get together the first part of the week. When she left, he was still going on about the rifle, and that's all she cared about.

He never called. She never saw him again. And in fact, almost a month went by before she heard anyone even mention his name. But this time it was the cops who were asking about Willie Steelman. More importantly, they wanted to know all about the rifle with her name on it.

Doug spent Sunday morning modifying the .22, just as he had done with the shotgun; shortening the blue steel barrel and the plastic stock. The entire length of the weapon was now less than 18 inches. Willie instructed him to file the serial number off it so it couldn't be traced. When he was finished, Doug tossed the remains of the rifle, along with his tools, into the trunk of his car. A few days later he built a carrying case for the weapon, using an old gray Samsonite briefcase swiped from a second hand store on Broadway.

Willie called it his long gun. It did not matter that it was nothing more than a $15 rabbit rifle, it was now his pirate pistol and he thought it looked pretty damn good stretched out at the end of his arm. He liked the feel, caressing the shortened barrel, aiming it around the room, slowly squeezing the trigger, his tongue making popping noises as the imaginary bullets exploded towards their target. Their pact could now proceed. Each had their own weapon, and no excuse not to back the other's play.

By now the Colorado summer had all but faded away. Hidden in the shade of tall trees, as well as from the large building next door, the house on Ellsworth stayed cold during the day, and near freezing at night. Fall was now firmly settled in, the Denver winter close behind, and Willie wanted no part of either. He had no idea how long before the bank would come to kick them out. And then where would they be? Shit out on the street, that's where. He decided the time had come to move on.

Marsha stopped by that afternoon and Willie brought his new toy out for her to admire. She got excited at just about everything, and was enough of a tomboy to appreciate its uniqueness. She handled it, under Willie's watchful eye of course, before announcing it as 'fucking cool'. She smoked some weed with the others as they came and went, and when Willie mentioned that they were thinking about leaving Denver for someplace warmer, Marsha lit up. "Where 'bouts?" she asked.

"I don't know," Willie answered. "Maybe Phoenix. Got some people down there who owe me. They've been talking about setting me up with some shit to unload – about a hundred pounds of some pretty righteous Mexican – and we been thinking about it."

Phoenix! Marsha knew she just had to go with them. That's where Yahfah had moved, and she could not get her out of her mind. Yahfah had promised to send for her soon, but it was only words on paper. She was dying to see her. "Jesus, Bill, I really wanna go with you guys!"

Willie was silent. He hadn't really thought about taking anybody with them, nor did he know anything about this Yahfah chick Short Shit kept blabbering about. But he knew he wasn't ready to say goodbye to her yet. He was really into her. "Marsha's cool," he told Doug one day. "She's into bikes, and gettin' high and shit. Ain't nothing but a little scooter tramp, just like me." He could see the two of them together. She was a handful, all right, and Willie guessed he liked that most of all. She was just tough enough, just cold enough to make him work a little harder to get closer to her. What in the hell did she know about men, anyway? She had never been with a man. Not a real one. It was obvious to Willie and everyone else she looked up to him, counted on him, so if she was that hot to see this Yahfah chick again, then he would make sure he was the one who delivered Marsha to her doorstop.

"Yeah, sure," he said. "Why not?"

She couldn't believe it. She was actually going to see Yahfah again! Oddly enough, Marsha thought she should tell her mom what she was up to. Until now, she had pretty much come and gone as she pleased, answering to no one, and that included her mother, so even Marsha was surprised that she thought she needed to ask her mom. She had always done as she damn well pleased – shit, she was never home – so even Willie and Doug thought it strange she would bother telling her mom what she was up to. Both had met Mrs. Renslow, even claimed to have got high with her a time or two. Doug thought her especially cool – the kind of parent he would have liked to have had - but it was still weird. Marsha never asked her mom for anything, except maybe money, and here the three of them were going to try and get her permission.

Mary Renslow's life, or her role as mother, would ever be used as an example for others. Her fragile health, her crippling handicap, being a single parent, all interfered with her ability to keep her kids on the straight and narrow. She had her own problems, and her life was as tangled as that of her children. She figured her three boys were old enough to fend for themselves, but she just prayed they would keep an eye on their sister, because Marsha was the one she worried about the most.

By late Sunday afternoon, the few people who still hung out at the house had learned Willie and Doug were leaving, and that included Russ.

The shotgun episode settled nothing. He still looked up to Willie more than he did his own brothers. Forget the recent ass kicking; Russ would still do anything Willie said. Now he felt left behind. He told Willie he wanted to go to Arizona too.

Much to his surprise, Willie said yes. Might be a good idea to have someone keep an eye on Marsha, he said. There was a catch though; everyone would have to pay their own way. He told Russ he needed to have $50 to make the trip. Russ didn't have a dime. He was still trying to come up with a way to get the money to Ted for the shotgun. While Russ scrambled out to find some cash, Willie and Doug took Marsha to talk to her mom, who was in the hospital, her ongoing misery now complicated by cancer surgery performed days earlier. Marsha knew she would be in no condition to argue.

But she did. She said there was no way her daughter was going all the way to Arizona with anyone. Nothing personal, she said. In fact, she liked Doug, who was the only one who asked how she was doing; the only one who acted as if he cared about her, and that included her own kids. But Marsha's request was just a formality, because she had already made up her mind. She was going to see Yahfah again, and no one, including her mother, was going to stop her. "I'll be gone less than a week," she pleaded.

"Marsha. No."

"Come on. I'll be O.K. It's just for a week."

Willie figured it was time for him to step in. "Mary, you know Russ is going along with us."

Mrs. Renslow perked up. Marsha shot Willie a look of surprise. "Russell is going?" Mary sparked. "Why didn't you say that, Marsha? I feel better knowing your brother will be there to look after you."

So it was settled. Willie talked a little about the trip, reassuring Mrs. Renslow they would be careful. Doug asked again about the surgery, while Mary did her best to explain all the troublesome complications.

They dropped Marsha back at her apartment on Sherman Street then headed to the house. Doug said it was going to be pretty crowded in the car, and Willie asked him what he was talking about. "You know, now with Russ going too."

Willie laughed. "Shit, man, don't worry about that. Russ ain't goin' nowhere."

8

Monday, October 8, 1973.

Frances hadn't been out of the house for more than a week before Willie emptied it. The stove, refrigerator, sofa, all the things she planned on coming back for, were sold for just enough cash to keep he and Doug loaded.

Art Wallen came by and jimmied the back door open, figuring it was his duty to check up on Willie and his piece-a-shit friends. When he discovered everything gone, he went right over and told Frances what her brother had done. He said if Willie could take the stuff in the house and sell it, then he certainly could have swiped her purse. "He's stealin' you blind and you don't even care!"

France listened to his words, but ignored the message, acting as if she could care less about any of them now. While it hurt her to think he could have done such a thing, in her heart she knew she was finished with him. She could remember a time not that long ago when he was her whole world, her precious little Billy, but those days were gone for good.

For as far back as he could remember, Doug had never felt the connection Willie and Frances once had. There was nothing, not even the simplest of feelings connecting him to the resemblance of a real life; of being close to someone who cared about him. He wanted to believe that maybe his wife cared. She married him, didn't she? But he never felt anything back. Years of drugs had removed him from feeling anything at all. So it wasn't that he felt good about being around Willie; he really didn't know how good was supposed to feel. All he could come up with was somehow this was the place he was meant to be.

Doug had an older brother once, and two younger sisters, so while growing up he just kind of hid out in the middle. He wasn't the smartest, or the cutest, or anyone's favorite – especially his father's – so he was just there, always in trouble, and always feeling like an embarrassment. When Doug was ten, his best friend was a kid named Paul, and the two of them sat next to each other on the school bus, then goofed off together on the weekend. Paul lived a block away, so after school they would stop by Doug's house first. One day Doug told Paul he was anxious to show his father a good grade he had got on a report card. Paul watched as Mr. Gretzler looked it over, then, without even the slightest smile, told his son he expected him to do better next time.

Doug even went so far as to work in the school cafeteria; a job no self-respecting kid would even think about doing. When Paul asked him if he was nuts, he just shrugged and said he was only doing it because of his father. Right then Paul realized Doug would do just about anything to please him. Everyday after school, Doug had to knock on the front door just to try and get in his own house. Paul could hear the Gretzlers inside talking, but they never answered the door, so Doug just tossed his schoolbooks on the porch and waited. He eventually admitted to Paul that his parents locked him out on purpose, and he wasn't allowed in until they called him for supper.

Dinnertime at the Gretzler's was a formal affair and all the children were required to be prompt and to bring something to add to the conversation. Doug said it was like they were all being tested. Typically the talk got around to what brilliant things his older brother Mark had done that day, and there was little attention given to what Doug or his sisters had to say. Before long, Paul could see that Doug had stopped trying to please his father, and was looking for ways now to spite him, which he did on a regular basis.

Years later, Doug realized he didn't belong in his marriage either. After the newness wore off and reality set in, he was a miserable husband as well. There was always some chore to be done, some rule to follow, some problem to deal with, some decision to be made, some place he had to be. Like work, for example. He knew he was a good worker, a hard worker, and it wasn't that he was opposed to working, it was just that he was *supposed* to work, *required* to work, like it was his duty as a man to have a steady job. That's what bugged him; someone telling him it had to be done. 'Don't push me,' became his trademark phrase, and it simply meant that he was done listening to whatever was being said.

So it was Willie who finally made Doug feel liked he belonged somewhere. Willie gave him money, gave him drugs, didn't hassle him, didn't lecture him, made few demands on his time, didn't even require him to think. All Willie wanted Doug to do was listen and pay attention to what he said needed to be done. Which was easy for Doug, because he always considered himself an excellent listener. He figured the only reason Willie kept him around was to have somebody who would listen to him talk.

Marsha did not know Doug very well, at least not like she knew Bill. Doug never said anything about his life and his past like Bill did. Shit! Bill wouldn't shut up! But Doug was real quiet, and Marsha wondered if maybe he felt like he didn't quite fit in either. And if that was so, then she could certainly understand, because she had felt that way most of her life. It wasn't until she started getting high or getting drunk, that she started coming out of her shell.

Marsha believed there was no place for her in this world. No one could possibly know how she felt. She too was quiet, and always considered herself different from everyone else. She didn't like school, nor was she very good in it, so she quit. She never had many friends, and the few she did have she just got in trouble with, so maybe they weren't really friends after all. Her mother made sure to remind her of that as often as she could.

She couldn't talk to her mom. Not like she wanted. She tried, but her mother would only listen to the easy stuff. She knew her brothers wouldn't understand either, so while she ran around town with goof-offs like herself, acting reckless and stupid, she still felt terribly alone on the inside.

Then one day her entire world changed. She wasn't even sixteen when she first set eyes on Yahfah. The attraction was instant, overwhelming, and she knew at that very moment what she truly wanted in life, and where she was meant to be. Yahfah was sitting on the lawn in front of her house when Marsha first saw her. She looked so peaceful, so tranquil and spiritual, so beautiful in the soft flowing dress that gathered in layers at her bare feet. She was alone, yet Marsha was afraid to approach her, certain she would stumble on her words and embarrass herself in front of someone so special.

But Marsha somehow found the courage, and to her relief, Yahfah was warm and welcoming, and invited Marsha inside where they continued talking and getting to know each other. Over the next few days, she introduced Marsha to health foods and natural healing, along with hash and psychedelic mushrooms. All the while, incense burned and folk music floated from the stereo. It was as perfect as Marsha could have ever imagined. She knew Yahfah had to be much older than her, but still, her only disappointment that afternoon came when Yahfah mentioned the name of the boyfriend who lived with her.

But even that did not matter for long because Marsha was smitten. She spent as much time as she could at Yahfah's, finding any excuse to stop by. Everyday she promised herself she would come out and tell her how she really felt, but everyday she lost her courage. Despite her honest and intimate desires, Yahfah had become Marsha's first real female friend, and she certainly did not want to jeopardize that. Still, for the next several weeks, Marsha was on top of the world.

Then one day she came by and found Yahfah packing her suitcase. She said jobs were better in Phoenix; so she and a few friends were heading down to check it out. Crushed, and feeling more alone than ever, Marsha said goodbye and watched Yahfah drive away. They kept in touch as promised, writing often, and Marsha couldn't wait until the next letter arrived. When it did, and before she read even a word, she pulled the pages close to her face and lingered in the patchouli oil Yahfah had dabbed on each one. Her heart was broken, and she wondered if she would ever see her again.

Marsha came by the house on Ellsworth Monday night and said the cops had stopped by her mom's apartment that afternoon looking for Russ. She didn't know anything about the shotgun, or the money, so she asked Bill why the cops would have it out for her brother? Bill acted like he didn't have a clue, but came down on Russell for being such fool. "I got no idea. But I'll tell you what, that brother of yours needs to get his shit together. I'm not taken any heat with me to Phoenix. He ain't going nowhere with me."

Marsha said she really didn't care if Russ went or not, as long as she did.

"Yeah, all right," Willie said. "We'll take off tomorrow. You just be sure you're ready to go, cuz we ain't waitin' for nobody."

Less than two miles south of Denver's city center, The South Platte River and South Santa Fe Drive merge. During the Flood of 1965, the South Platte crested at an historic high. Spilling over its banks during those wet slate days, the river ran wild down South Santa Fe Drive, devouring all in its wake. Cars and homes were washed away, factories destroyed, buildings damaged beyond repair, silt rings marking the river's crest two stories up their sides.

After the waters resided, many of those who lived or worked on South Santa Fe merely walked away, and eight years later the damage was still visible. Up and down the street were empty lots and vacant buildings, with mud the color of mocha still caked to their deserted shells, the remnants of plywood and cardboard still sucked up tight against the cyclone fences that ringed abandoned warehouses and barren parking lots. By 1973, rundown motels and boarded up motor courts were all that remained on South Santa Fe. This was now the home to nowhere men and women who spent their days in a blur of whatever they could swallow, shoot, snort, smoke or sniff.

So it was only natural that Willie Steelman found his way to South Santa Fe Drive. He and Doug had checked it out a few weeks earlier after they heard they might be able to score some heroin there, or maybe some crank, which they easily did.

So it made sense that Willie decided to go back there to see if he could put together one final deal before heading to Arizona. After screwing around Tuesday trying to get things together, Willie, Doug and Marsha arrived at the J.B. Motel late Wednesday afternoon, October 10th. Marsha complained it was pretty stupid to go only a couple of miles from home and spend money on a room, especially when they were so tight for cash, but Willie bragged that he could take their $80 bankroll and triple it. And that, he assured her, would be all the money they would need for Arizona.

Mrs. Settlers remembered them well because Willie and Doug had stayed at her motel several weeks earlier. She didn't trust them then, and she didn't trust them now, so even after they filled out the guest card and paid cash up front for two nights, she still looked outside to double check license numbers. The plates on the blue sport scar didn't match the one they had written down, so she made a note of the discrepancy, but didn't say anything more about it. The motel was an older, single story building that sat close to the road. Day and night, the traffic pulsed, engines revved, trucks roared, and horns honked. There was no way to shut it out, so the motel offered its guests little privacy and even less solitude.

Regardless, the trio hung around the room for most of the day. Willie said he was going out for a while, but Marsha peeked out the window and saw him get only as far as the pay phone by the office, where he talked for almost an hour. Doug did nothing except stay stoned, almost to the point of comatose, so he was very little company to Marsha, who was incredibly bored. By Thursday afternoon, it was clear that Willie's boasts of big deals weren't happening. Frustrated, he announced they would stay one more night, but no matter what, they would leave for Arizona in the morning.

The television stayed on, although not nearly loud enough to cover the sounds of the street. Marsha sprawled across the bed, while Willie sat on its edge, edgy, a Marlboro constantly dangling from his lips. Doug couldn't seem to get enough of the sawed off shotgun. During his rare times of being amongst the living, he was content to sit in the chair and fondle the weapon. He aimed it at the TV, or at the ceiling, and made believe he was firing away.

All of which got on Willie's nerves, who more than once told him to give it a rest. Things were not going as planned, and Doug's screwing around just pissed him off. "Will you put that fuckin' thing away?" he barked. "Jesus! That's all you been doin'!"

Doug acted as if he wasn't listening. Marsha looked at him, then at Willie, wondering who was going to make the first move. The shotgun fascinated her, and scared the shit out of her, all at the same time.

"Besides," Willie continued, "that goddamn thing might be loaded for all you know."

"Not loaded," Doug snapped back.

Willie shook his head and turned away. Doug felt the need to prove his point, so he aimed the shotgun over Willie's head and pulled the trigger.

BLAM!

The shell, that wasn't supposed to be in the chamber, exploded, blasting out through the window and into the traffic beyond. Glass shattered onto the walkway. The recoil threw Doug back, his eyes as big as golf balls as his chair tipped over backwards.

"Fucking A!" Willie screamed. He heard commotion out on the street. He was certain Doug had hit something. "You just fuckin' nailed a truck, man!" He jumped up and scrambled for his things. "Let's get the hell outta here!"

Within seconds, the room was cleared. They looked around outside, but nothing seemed damaged, and no one appeared hurt. In fact, they could see no one who seemed to have even noticed the blast. But they took no chances. The MGB squealed out of the parking lot, weaved between a couple of cars, then quickly blended into traffic.

They laughed all the way to the city limits. Marsha rolled a few joints and they laughed some more. They were far out of Denver by sundown. So far south, the lights of the city had long since disappeared behind them. They crossed into New Mexico just before midnight. The MGB was having trouble and Doug watched the dash lights flicker on and off. Eventually the taillights went out as well. Despite how much they wanted to keep going, they knew busted taillights were a cop's bread and butter, so Doug pulled off the highway.

Shit faced stoned, they spent their first night on the road sleeping under a big black bowl of southwestern stars.

9

Friday, October 12, 1973 | 7 am.

Doug was up before the others, trying to get the lights on the cars fixed. Announcing his repairs a success, they were soon back on the road.

The MGB could hardly be considered a rolling drug lab, as Marsha often joked, but it did leave Denver with a substantial mixture of dope. Some pot, an assortment of pills for Doug, a little speed and a few tabs of acid, of which Willie begged off. *Don't like trippin', man. Don't like the way it makes you feel.* And if there was any heroin, like Willie boasted, then Marsha didn't see it. But there was plenty to get them to Phoenix, and that's all any of them cared about.

Regardless, Doug was a contented man. He had finally found his place; living the adventure he had dreamed about when he left New York. The West. It was huge. It seemed forever. It felt as if he could disappear here. The desert and its endless landscape could shelter him, conceal him, forgive him. So he drank it in, overwhelmed by its magnitude. Its enormity made him feel small and insignificant, which made him feel good. Very good. As good as he felt in a long, long time.

Fall had arrived in the desert and the morning was cool. He remained wrapped up in his leather bomber jacket, the only gift from his father he ever cared about. But by mid morning, the sun was warm enough for him to shed the coat and even put the top down.

They pulled into a roadside diner. They had no idea where they were; some out of the way place well off the highway. It was late morning, and if there ever was a rush at the restaurant, it was long gone, because only two cars occupied the gravel lot. The dingy little whitewashed building stood alone, smack dab in the middle of Nowhere, New Mexico.

As they walked up to the door, Willie said that if it was real quiet inside, it would be a good place to pull a rip. While they found just one old guy sitting at the counter and a skinny young waitress leaning over him, Willie didn't say another word about robbing anybody. They walked in laughing, already stoned, already deciding out loud what they were going to eat.

The waitress smiled, shook her head and grabbed some menus. Over the years she had seen plenty just like them wander in off the desert. She was cool. She laughed along. She knew they were high, joking with them about 'how good it is to have a little smoke before breakfast'. Willie decided right off that she was his kind of people.

They tumbled into a booth, and she brought over her smirk and her coffee pot, forgetting about the old regular spilling over his stool at the counter. He was already whimpering about not getting his refill. She ignored him. She arranged the silverware and began pouring, asking the usual questions. Where they all were from? Denver, New York, California, came the reply. And where they were heading? Phoenix.

Willie asked if she wanted to go too. She looked through the window at the little sports car parked outside. "And just where in the hell would you put me?"

He told her they was plenty of room, right on top of him. He did his best to tempt her, talking about all the drugs they had stashed out in the car. She could only laugh and remind him to keep it down; she still had a customer, and a job, to worry about. When they were ready to leave, Willie asked one more time if she was coming along, or at least she could go out to the car and get high with them. He rattled off all the they had to offer, none of which seemed to impress her.

"You guys ever done peyote?" she asked.

They all just looked at each other and grinned.

The regular was in no hurry to leave his perch, so the waitress went over and hustled him out. "Listen, honey, it's kind of an emergency. We gotta close up now." She was pulling plates and coffee cups out from under him, tossing them in a big plastic tub under the counter.

"But. . .it ain't even lunchtime yet!" he whined. "You never close up this early!"

"Well, something has come up. You can just come on back tomorrow and have your coffee." She scooted him out the door, locked it behind him, and flipped the CLOSED sign around.

"Come on," she said, motioning for them to follow her out the back. "You're gonna like this."

They walked out into shade behind the restaurant and she began pulling peyote buttons from a wrinkled paper sack, passing them out like gumdrops. "Got 'em from my boyfriend," she confessed.

The buttons were foul tasting; rubbery, like eating tar or chewing tobacco, but when they kicked in, the desert caught fire.

Incoherent babble, like talk in alien tongue, rose up from beneath them, splitting the sand. Their thoughts were sucked from their brains and reappeared as written words that floated up through the cracks in the earth, only to explode like fireworks just inches off the ground. The world spun around them, kalidescoping into a hundred shades of white, as scrub brush took human form, but in fluorescent neons, and it hissed at them like snakes.

Doug wandered away from the others, but could still hear them. Their voices were radio static; like sounds from a broken speaker. The sky had turned a deep denim blue, and his skin, blood red. He could see his veins pulsating in the most brilliant purple he ever imagined. He yelled out to the others that he was floating over them, and was watching them all die.

Later, when the sun bleached the drug from their senses, they knew it was time to leave. The waitress gave them some more for the road. "When you get into Arizona," she instructed, "take them at the Painted Desert. It's such a trip. Just a fucking mindblower!"

So they again headed west, into the blaze of an southwestern afternoon sunset. Seventy. Seventy-five. Who cares? Just roll.

Somewhere along the road in New Mexico, Marsha decided that she had been here before. During those brief periods when she was actually in school long enough to ditch class, she took off into the mountains around Denver. After a few days, she would usually manage to find her way home, where she would catch hell from her mom, only to leave again whenever the urge hit her.

Shortly before her fifteenth birthday, Marsha and a friend hitchhiked to California, bumming and panhandling along the way. They got sidetracked somewhere in New Mexico, (hence the uneasy feeling) but finally made it to their original destination; the Wheeler Ranch commune in Southern California, where the hippies who ran it took them both in.

Bikers sold the hippies their drugs and guarded the dirt road leading into the ranch, protecting those already inside and hassling any newcomer who dared approach. It was a strange relationship between the two groups, but Marsha discovered she liked them both. She spent the night getting high up on the ranch, and her days at the front gate talking about motorcycles, begging a ride from anyone who would listen. She hung out for almost three months before she got bored and hitched a ride back to Denver. But even then she didn't go right home. Nor did she bother to call to let anyone know she was okay. She just wandered the streets of south Denver, looking for trouble.

Russ spotted her one afternoon sitting in the back of a van swigging wine from a gallon jug. He grabbed her by the neck and dragged her home, all the way threatening to beat the ever-lovin' crap out of her for the worry she had brought upon their mom. For her punishment, Mrs. Renslow kept the Runaway Pick Up report out on her daughter, which meant that if Marsha was ever picked up for any reason, it would mean an instant trip to Juvenile Hall.

But even that wasn't enough to keep her home. Days later Marsha was back on the streets. Her new thing was motorcycles and she bugged everyone she saw for a ride. She would even ask a stranger at a stop light if she could hop on the back, and very few said no. One night some guy dumped his with her on it, sending Marsha to the hospital.

Her first visitors were the police, and armed with the Pickup Report, proceeded to shackle her wrists and ankles to the bed. Being so tiny, though, she had almost managed to free herself (visions of a quick escape on her one good leg urging her on) before the cops came back into the room and rearranged her plans.

So Marsha looked for some kind of landmark there along the road in New Mexico. Something to jog her memory, knowing she had come this way before.

Staying loaded, they crossed the state on Highway 40, racing along intermittent stretches of freeway, interrupted by long spells of narrow two-lane road, all cutting through the high desert. Sometimes, just for the hell of it, Doug would pull off the pavement and take off through the low brush. Busting with laughter, they bucked and bounced in the front seat, Doug doing donuts in the clearing, kicking up sand and dirt in huge rooster tails. Back on the road, jammed tight in the MGB, Willie and Marsha dared him to do it again, and eventually he would.

They crossed over the Arizona state line somewhere around midnight, but the off road adventures had taken their toll; a rear tire blew out and Doug was too ripped to fix it. He pulled over, crawled out and crashed right next to the car. Willie and Marsha smoked some dope and wandered out into the desert, trying to count the stars above them one at a time.

They were in Indian Country now, Willie said. Right in the middle of the mighty Navajo Reservation. As they roamed the nighttime desert, Willie told her about the Navajo people, and about how the white man had cheated them out of everything they ever had. He seemed very angry. Off on another one of his rampages, Marsha realized, knowing now how quickly he could change his mood. Almost scary, was her reaction the first time she experienced one of these explosions. She was exceptionally stoned, but tried to follow along when Bill talked about how the white man had ripped off the Indians. No wonder they wanted to kill all of us back then, he concluded, although he eventually calmed down long enough to light up another joint.

But Marsha, knowing she was finally in Arizona, could care less about any of his tormented rambling. All she could think about how close she was to Yahfah. Maybe even today, she comforted herself; maybe today she would finally see her again.

So Marsha and Willie wandered around and talked for a while before finding their way back to the car. Willie got out a bedroll and they finally crashed out on the sand.

10

Saturday, October 13, 1973.

"Right here," he told her. "All this is Apache Country."

He stretched his arms wide to encompass the vista, hoping she could somehow grasp such huge boundaries. "You know, Fort Apache and all. You heard of Fort Apache, right?"

She didn't know. Yeah, maybe. Maybe on TV or something. It was the Navajos, right? That's what he said last night, wasn't it? She tried to pay attention. She really did. But here it was barely sun up, and Bill was back at it again, going on and on about something she really couldn't give two shits about. Too much like school, she thought. She acted as if she cared. She looked like she was listening, but just so he wouldn't get all mad again.

Doug had hitched a ride to the nearest town to have the flat fixed, so Marsha and Bill were back to roaming the desert, killing time.

"And Cochise, a very famous, very righteous Indian chief. . .well, he. . .you know, this was all his." He spun his body in a three-sixty, arms out wide. "He and his Apache warriors held off the fuckin' white soldiers right here…Well, around here anyway."

"No lie? Shit! That's pretty cool!" Marsha found herself getting into the story. The Cowboy and Indian angle had got her attention.

"Oh, shit yeah!" Willie went on. "A very, very brave man. You heard of the Cochise Stronghold, right?"

Marsha couldn't really say she had. She had to take his word for it. She had no idea if he was telling the truth, or making it all up, but either way, she decided right then and there, that Bill was a pretty smart sonafabitch.

Doug got back, changed the tire, and they hit the road.

All things considered, it was a good trip. Even the problems with the car didn't bother Doug that much. He enjoyed the company of the guy who gave him a lift. They rapped for a while. Pretty nice dude, actually. Good talker. Just part of the adventure, he decided.

An hour down the road, they pulled into a gas station / trading post just off the highway. They had almost no money left for gas, let alone to eat. Willie jumped out and said he would handle it. He walked inside and loitered around the big white enamel cooler, like he was picking out a soda. When things got quiet, he walked to the counter and eyed the register. But he had waited too long. The attendant came back and asked if he needed any help.

Back at the car, Doug and Marsha got an earful. Not only did he have to pay for the gas, Willie fumed, but the Cokes as well. He promised success a little further down the road.

Until now they had been doing the drug that fit their surroundings. First thing in the morning, a little weed. On the long stretches of open road, it was yellow poppers and downers. They listened to the waitress and finished the peyote in the Painted Desert. She was right. Later, Doug and Marsha dropped a few tabs of acid when they went through the Petrified Forest. South at Holbrook to Show Low, Willie said they would be in Phoenix before dark. On the highway outside of Globe, he spotted a big white Cadillac parked off the side of the road. "Hey! Jesus, look at that! Pull over!"

Whoever drove the Cad had money, Willie promised, said he planned on taking it. He grabbed the .22 and told to Doug to get the shotgun. They threw jackets over the weapons and marched down the bank into the ravine. But when they spotted the car's owner, Willie busted out laughing. It was a young guy and his girlfriend, butt naked, sunbathing in the nude.

Startled, the couple jumped up and fumbled for their clothes. Willie tried not to laugh as he uncovered his weapon and announced the reason for their visit. "Really hate to bother you two, but we're out of money and out of gas."

The guy, more embarrassed than scared, reached for his pants and wallet, while his girlfriend, shielding herself behind him, shadowed his every move. He handed over everything he pulled out; several wadded up bills totaling maybe $20. Willie looked it over, kept a five and tossed the rest back on the blanket at the guy's feet. "Check this out. I want you to know I'm not the type to take all a dude's money."

He turned and headed back up the hill, Marsha and Doug in his wake. Willie stopped laughing long enough to offer some final advice. "I recommend you two stay here for awhile. And try being a little bit more careful from now on."

Just to be safe, Doug popped the hood on the Caddy, yanked the distributor cap and threw it as far as he could down into the canyon.

Highway 60 drops down out of the Salt River Canyon, through the copper mines at Globe and Miami, then into the Valley of the Sun. At Florence Junction it splits, heading northwest through the desert, past the Superstition Mountains and into the trailer park sprawl of the Phoenix suburbs. The highway continues through Apache Junction, Mesa, Tempe and eventually into the city, becoming the main street of each town.

Except for Marsha, no one knew what they were looking for, and no one knew where they were heading or where they would stay. They just kept driving towards the city. The five dollars worth of gas was long gone. Willie talked about ripping off a motel – there were hundreds of them on both sides of the road – but decided it was too early, and too risky.

In Tempe, after crossing the old bridge that spanned the dry bed of the Salt River, Willie spotted a hitchhiker; thumb out, heading the other way. In the fading sunlight, Willie caught the gleam of a large ring on the man's finger. He didn't have to say anything, he just nodded in the guy's direction and Doug turned the car around.

Willie insisted the guy was a fag, so this one would be easy. It was the way he was dressed, he said, the way he stood, limp wrist, begging for a ride. Willie made it clear he had no use for queer dudes, and this dude was just asking to have the shit kicked out of him. He told Marsha this one was her's. She sucked it up and nodded, then Willie took a minute to school her in the art of being an asshole. A *chick* asshole. With a gun. Which was definitely the worst kind, he reminded her.

She was the man-hating dyke, he explained, and he was the good guy who was trying to hold her back. The dude is a fruit, so he wouldn't put up a fight, he promised. At the very least they would get that ring off his finger, which had to be good for a few bucks. Anything else would be a bonus.

Doug pulled up next to the hitchhiker and Marsha hopped up on Willie's lap, opening a tight spot in the middle. Marsha gave him her best practice scowl. The MGB headed back towards Tempe. There were a few miles of small talk.

Willie changed the subject. "You're a queer, aren't cha?"

The man paused, then nodded.

Marsha took a deep breath. Willie was right on cue. "She fuckin' hates fags, man!"

Realizing now what he had gotten himself into, the guy struggled to get out of the moving car. Marsha pulled out a handgun, a worthless little tear gas pistol she carried around, but he couldn't tell the difference. She tore into her role, placing the gun at his head, screaming obscenities. Doug pulled into the cover of an orange grove.

"She is one man-hating dyke!" Willie yelled. "I think she wants that ring of yours."

They pulled him out of the car and dragged him into the orchard. Willie was fully into the scene now, like an animal hovering over his kill. He turned to Marsha and gave his okay. "He ain't gettin' it. Fuck him then. Waste him!"

The guy was hauled to the base of a tree, squirming, still unwilling to part with the ring. Doug joined in, pulling his knife from the sheath on his belt. He threatened to slice the whole finger off if he had to. Finally the hitchhiker relented and slipped the ring off.

But it wasn't enough for Willie. He grabbed the gun from Marsha and pointed it at the guy's head. "Gimme your wallet!"

He didn't balk this time. He handed it over and Willie pulled two bills from it. "You got any more on you?"

He answered that he didn't.

"Well, let's see about that. Take your clothes off!"

The man peeled off his boots, pants and shirt. Willie rifled through them looking for more. In the pants pocket he found a twenty. He went berserk. "Don't you fucking dare hold out on me! I'll fucking kill you myself!"

He smashed the pistol across the man's face; hitting him so hard the plastic handle broke off and flew into the darkness. Willie knew this rage. He felt comfortable within it, so he hit him again. And again.

Using the guy's own clothes, Doug tied him to a tree. Willie still wailed out of control. The man stopped moving. Willie stopped hitting. He calmed down. His worry now was the missing pistol handle and he told at the others to help him look for it.

They warned the guy not to leave. If he told anyone what happened, they would come back, find him and kill him. On the way to the car they threw his shoes in a creek, just for the hell of it.

They headed back towards town. Willie was laughing, congratulating Marsha on how good she was, how so totally cool she had been. Marsha was shaking like a leaf. It was her first real holdup, and she had this nervous feeling she liked it.

Within a few minutes their victim freed himself, gathered his clothes and hurried across the street to a garage. From a pay phone he called the police, promising them the thieves would suffer in hell for what they had done.

The ring brought $60 at a downtown Phoenix pawnshop. They turned around and headed back down East Van Buren, pulling into a run down old motor court called the Stone Motel.

It was well after seven when they checked in. The Stone had its cast of regulars. So much so, the clerk was suspicious of any new arrivals. He trusted no one, so he walked out to the parking lot to verify the license number given on the registration slip. Willie identified himself on the form as W.L. Steal from San Francisco, and that he was driving a Ford. The desk clerk could have sworn he saw them get out of a red, late model Chevy pickup, so he went out to have a look. Even though nothing matched, he didn't say a word, just took the money and handed over the key to the room.

It had been a long day. Nerves were shot. Drugs didn't help. In fact, Willie was really tired of Doug's nonstop self-inflicted coma. They hadn't been in the room two minutes before Doug started shooting up, and he was now sprawled flat out on the bed.

But it was Saturday night and Willie felt good, so he talked Marsha into going out with him. They walked down the busy boulevard, checking out the hustlers, playing a game of who was buying and who was selling. Willie was high. They both were. It was a good high. Willie said he felt like dancing.

At a nearby hotel nightclub, they bullshitted the bouncers into letting them in, and then conned the waitress into serving Marsha. She barely looked fifteen, and there was no fake id, but Willie convinced her to let them both stay.

The place was crowded with hotel guests and plenty of locals. Willie was having a great time. He never missed a beat all night; never missed a song, and Marsha had to admit he was a very good dancer. Soon he was the star of the show and everyone else was content to just stand back and watch. Marsha quickly caved into the half dozen Tequila Sunrises and did her very best to keep up with him. There were times that night when she looked at Willie and could only shake her head. She didn't recognize him. Here he was smiling, laughing and jumping around, when just hours earlier he was a crazy fucking lunatic willing to kill a guy for some shitty ring. She decided from here on she wasn't going to try and figure him out. But she knew she liked being around him, if nothing more for the scene he created and the pressure he put on her to try and keep up.

Willie and Marsha closed the place down, embracing for the last slow dance. As they walked back to the motel in Sunday's early hours, he held her hand and told her that was the most fun he had had in a long, long time.

In Yahfah's final letter to Marsha, she wrote she would be moving soon and her new place would be hard to find. She would leave her new address with two guys she knew in Phoenix named Ken and Mike. That's all the directions Marsha had to go on. Yahfah put in her letter that Ken Unrein and Michael Adshade lived on 18th Street in Phoenix. It was a duplex. Ken lived on one side, Mike on the other.

Yahfah and her new roommate Bob Robbins had spent Saturday moving from their trashy downtown motel apartment to a nice new trailer park in Apache Junction. Without knowing it, Marsha had passed within a mile of Yahfah's place late Saturday afternoon. She told herself the next time she saw Yahfah she would tell her how she really felt. She knew she couldn't go another day without Yahfah knowing the truth.

At about nine o'clock Sunday morning, an anxious Marsha finally managed to get Willie and Doug out of the room. The morning was warm and the top stayed down. As they drove back down East Van Buren, they kept an eye out for 18th Street, while Marsha had plenty to say about this Ken guy, none of which was very nice. Willie listened, but told her this Yahfah trip better be quick because he had some important business to take care of.

They found the street and the duplex. They went up to the door and Ken and Mike acted as if they were expecting them. Fueled by what Marsha had to say, Willie decided he didn't like Ken either. They sat around for an hour, talking about Denver, watching TV, listening to the stereo and smoking dope. Willie kept bugging Ken to sell him some weed, but he couldn't show the cash, so there was no deal. Every time Marsha pressed Ken about Yahfah, he changed the subject, acting like he wasn't going to tell her anything about where she had moved, or how to find her. Ken's lack of cooperation pissed Willie off and he said they had come for one reason; Yahfah's address. He started in, saying he didn't like being jacked around, reminding Ken that he, *'had fucked some people up before and would do it again if he had to'*.

Of course, such talk was as much for Marsha as it was for Ken. In any event, Ken either got the message, or just tired of Willie, because he finally gave in and wrote Yahfah's address down for Marsha. *Vista Grande Mobile Home Park. 11425 E. University #133.* That was it. No town. No directions. No clue where it was, or even how far away. Sorry, he offered, but that's all he had. He hadn't been out there yet either, so they were on their own.

Remembering a street called University, Doug headed back the way they had driven in yesterday afternoon. Past the orange grove and beyond. Way beyond. Without knowing how far East University really went, they found themselves further and further from town. A half hour later they were miles and miles out in the country. There was an occasional house trailer parked in a clump of brush, but they had yet to come across an address even close to 11425, let alone a mobile home park. Willie decided there was no way anyone they knew would be living out this far. He felt stupid, and cursed that weasel Ken for lying to them, and for giving them the wrong address on purpose.

He told Doug to screw it. Turn around and head back to town. They would go back and pay another visit to Ken and Mike, and one way or another; he would get the right address this time. He promised a very disappointed Marsha that he would find her friend. But for now, Yahfah would have to wait. They had wasted too much time already and Willie had other more important business to tend to.

The rest of Sunday was spent in pursuit of a man Willie called Preacher.

Marsha remembered him talking about the guy, and even Doug claimed to have heard about a Preacher back on the East Coast. Willie assured him it was the same dude. Preacher was a hit man for the Kappa Family, who ran a syndicate in California and handled a lot of dope in Arizona. Problem was, Willie said, the Preacher's own brother was skimming cash off the top of the family's lucrative business activities, so they told Preacher to get his brother out of the way. Remove him. Permanently.

Willie never bothered to explain just how he had met Preacher. He was on the phone a lot, and both Doug and Marsha figured that's what the conversations were all about. Although neither was ever close enough to hear exactly what was being said, Willie claimed all the calls were with the Preacher about setting up the hit. For his help, he would be given a piece of the Arizona action, and if he pulled it off, Willie boasted he would be a very influential man in Phoenix.

When they got back into town, and after several more phone calls, Willie gave Doug the address of a condominium complex they needed to scope out. It was where the hit was going to come down. They eventually found the place; a new development of condos just off University Avenue near Tempe. It was a quiet Sunday, and the grounds were deserted, so they made themselves at home. They found a big rec room with a pool table, so Marsha and Doug kept occupied while Willie went to have a look around.

He was gone no more than a half hour, and said nothing upon his return. He didn't appear to be in any hurry to leave, or seem worried about being spotted at this soon-to-be murder scene. They even played a few more games of pool before heading back to town. Willie said he was told to stay at the Coronet, a motel on Central in downtown Phoenix. He would receive his next instructions there.

It was early afternoon when Willie signed in at the Coronet Ramada and this time he was Will McSteal from San Francisco driving a 1959 Ford. He carried no luggage, so the manager made him pay for the two nights in advance. They hung around the room, while Willie fidgeted and made several trips to the pay phone. When darkness fell, Willie and Doug left Marsha upstairs and walked out to the street. Willie spotted a woman sitting alone in a pickup, and he approached her through the open window. He place the .22 on her cheek and told her to hand over her purse.

Back in the room, he told Marsha they found it in the front seat of a car in the parking lot. The car was unlocked so they just swiped it. Twenty dollars and a checkbook.

Flush with new found cash, they walked down the street to a Big Boy for dinner. On the way back from the restaurant they noticed some cops in the parking lot talking with the woman from the truck. Willie managed to get them back to the room without being spotted. The woman had filed a report with the Phoenix Police, giving a detailed description of her assailant.

Later, Willie pulled the curtains back from the window of their third floor room and looked down at the parking lot below. He told the others that it was time. "He's here. It's Preacher"

Doug peeked out and saw a guy get out of a black Ford sedan and walk into the hotel. Willie headed downstairs. He was to meet Preacher in the bar. A few minutes later he returned to the room, grabbed his briefcase with the rifle, and hurried out again. Doug waited, then looked out the window. The black Ford had never left the parking lot.

Marsha claimed it was a half hour, Doug said no more than twenty minutes, but in either case, Willie returned to the room. They both agreed on one thing. At the very least, Willie had been in a scuffle. At the very worst, a gunfight. His shirt was torn and there was a small amount of blood on his side. He was going off on how much pain he was in. Doug said it looked like he got grazed by some buckshot. His belt buckle was smashed, like it had taken most of the hit. Marsha helped clean him up while he explained what went wrong.

Willie claimed they went to the house; he, the Preacher, and some guy named Larry. Preacher was the one who was supposed to do the actual number, and Willie and Larry were just back up. Preacher knocked on the door, but hesitated for a split second as it opened. His brother, apparently tipped off to the hit, was waiting and unloaded his shotgun as the door opened.

Preacher was killed instantly by the blast, Willie claimed, but he and Larry finished the brother off before he could nail them too. "After Preacher went down, I stepped in the doorway and blew his brother away. Larry went after an associate with an ice pick. He got the guy in the neck and killed him. Broke the handle off doing it."

Willie said Larry brought him back to the room, then went back for Preacher, his bother and the other guy. Larry promised to take the bodies out into the desert and bury them.

With Preacher now dead, there would be no piece of the Arizona action, and Willie complained he was now just shit out of luck. His take, he told Doug and Marsha, was to be a hundred pounds of grass. But instead they were just stuck in Phoenix with no connections, no money and no dope.

Willie said he was too hot to leave the room. The Feds would be snooping around soon, and because he and the Preacher had last been seen together in the hotel bar, they would connect him to the killing. They would lay low in their room at the Coronet for another day or so, then they would pay Ken and Mike another visit.

The three bodies would never be found. Nor was the man known as Larry ever heard from again. There was never a call to the police. No gunshots heard. No report ever filed.

Other than Doug and Marsha's separate recollection of that evening weeks later, and their agreement as to the details surrounding it, there was no reason for anyone to believe Willie's story about the man called Preacher, or the murders he claimed to have been responsible for.

11

Tuesday, October 16, 1973 | 11 am.

The three had spent Monday at the Coronet; Willie recuperating, Doug vegetating, Marsha complaining. The room was paid for and Willie said he wanted the streets to cool down before he went back out. If he said it once, he said it a hundred times; he was a wanted man in Phoenix, and not just by the cops. His life, maybe their lives too, were in danger. They had to be very careful from here on.

The Tahiti Motel sat at the corner of 29th and East Van Buren, several miles from the downtown, and in its heyday, which was years earlier, visitors to the Valley of the Sun got a big kick out the palm trees, bamboo fencing, tiki torches and all its other tacky Polynesian touches. But today, like most of its neighbors on this seedy street, few vacationers dared even step foot in the Tahiti.

Doug stayed with the car while Marsha followed Willie into the office. As usual, the manager requested payment in advance, made a couple of standard, 'watch the noise and the pool closes at ten' announcements, before handing over the key to room 208. At $8.40 a night, Willie was again low on cash.

The next few hours were spent watching TV and doing some dope. But it was another hot afternoon, so they eventually hit the pool; swimming in their Levis and soaking up the sun. It was either the swimming or the grass, or maybe because they hadn't eaten all day, but hunger soon set in, and again they looked to Willie, so he and Marsha walked across the street to the corner store with ideas of a nice big meal paid for with some bad paper. Problem was the store didn't take checks so Willie was forced to hand over what little money he had left. He slumped back to the room carrying only a small sack. Lunch that afternoon was peanut butter and jelly sandwiches.

Realizing Doug's car was all they had left that was worth anything, Willie decided to sell it. Later that evening, with Marsha's help, he smudged cigarette ashes under his eye to make it look like he had been in a fight, stuffed wads of toilet paper in his cheeks to puff them out, mussed up his hair, ripped the top button off his shirt, then walked back down to the motel office.

Mrs. Weld had not been on duty when they checked in earlier in the day, but remembered seeing the couple around the pool that afternoon. Willie told her he had just been beat up right outside the motel and his wallet, cash and credit cards had been stolen. They had hoped to stay one more night, he said, and they needed something to eat, then asked if she could loan them $25 until the banks opened tomorrow morning. He could offer their car as collateral until then.

Whether she believed him, or decided $25 for a shot at owning a nice little sports car was a deal she couldn't pass up, she called her husband to the front desk. After listening to the story, he opened the register and handed over the money, then agreed to let them stay another night. (The $25, along with the receipts for the two nights were never included in the daily totals, and remained with the Welds when they were fired as managers of the Tahiti a week later.)

"Where's the title?" Weld asked as he was handed the keys.

Willie looked at Marsha, then paused. "Oh. . .uh. . .it was stolen too. In the robbery." He reached over on the counter and picked a business card. "Let me get your address and I'll mail it to you when I get another one."

Willie walked out, quite proud of himself for this latest piece of work. Tomorrow he would figure out a way to get some money and talk the guy into selling the car back. Might even add a few bucks just to sweeten the deal.

"Here's dinner!" he proclaimed, walking back into the room waving the cash. Marsha was right on his heels and her grin was equally as wide. Willie explained how the manager loaned it to them and all he did was put the car up for security. Tomorrow they would just go out and get some money, then buy it back. Doug didn't even blink.

But it bought hamburgers from a restaurant down the street. Afterwards, as they walked back to the motel, Willie's anger towards Ken and Mike about this Yahfah deal resurfaced. "Those dudes know where she lives and they're just fuckin' with us. I think it's time we make 'em talk."

Willie was ready. He hailed a cab back to the Tahiti and told the driver to wait. He and Doug went upstairs and grabbed the guns, and the more Willie thought about the impending confrontation, the more excited he became. The taxi dropped them off at the corner of 18th and Van Buren, and they walked the remaining few blocks. Willie knew Ken had made him look bad in front of Marsha. He didn't like that. He didn't know what Ken's trip was, or why he was trying to keep them from this Yahfah chick, but he marched towards the duplex intent on settling the score.

In February of that year, Ken and Mike, along with a young woman by the name of Rendy Soller, moved from Denver to Arizona. Along with them was a friend, Michael Bland, who knew a guy in Phoenix named Donald who had offered them a place to crash for a couple of weeks until they got settled in.

Don's roommate was a 21-year-old junkie and part time masseuse/part time prostitute named Yahfah Hacohen.

Known as Katherine Mestities in her hometown of Albany, New York, she came west to start a new life with a new name. Originally settling in Denver in early 1972, she moved south to Phoenix later that year, finding her niche in the plentiful massage parlors, and the spin-off second incomes of prostitution and drugs. But her passion was the occult, feeling its mystery complimented her new identity. One day, not long after they all had moved in together, she casually mentioned to the others that she was a witch. They laughed at her. While she had mastered the tarot cards and learned enough about the supposed magic of numbers and candles to bring it up in conversation, for all the darkness she wrapped herself in, Yahfah was pleasant, friendly, and seemingly well liked by just about everyone who knew her. Always wearing a smile, Yahfah thought of herself as a white witch, quick to point out she did only good deeds with her powers. But for the few who found themselves on her bad side, Yahfah could be relentless in her scorn. It was a fate Ken Unrein would feel before the year was over.

It didn't take Yahfah long to grow tired of the company she now found herself in, so towards the end 1972 she packed up and returned to Denver. The following spring she met Marsha, and was surprised at how much she cared for the young girl, because the only thing they seemed to share was an interest in getting high. Yahfah viewed it as a big sister thing, so she decided it was her job to look after Marsha and to teach her the ways of the world. By appearance alone, the two had little in common. Yahfah was always in flowing granny dresses; her soft, dark hair pulled back, skin smelling of patchouli oil. She played the sex game only because that's where the easy money could be found.

Marsha, on the other hand, wore jeans and a t-shirt. She was the tomboy, showing absolutely no interest in men, unless it was for a ride on their motorcycle or some of their weed or wine. She once confided to Yahfah about how the only two men she ever tried getting close to had died, and now men only made her feel uncomfortable. She explained how her father, who had left the family years earlier, had died suddenly, just as she was getting to know him again. Then there was her boyfriend in high school, who was killed right after she agreed to marry him. Marsha took both events as a bad sign.

But Yahfah said no, this was all good. Two was the number of woman and wickedness, of evil and deceit. All women, Yahfah maintained, get their way by persuasion and seduction, and the idea that two men who loved her had died, made perfect sense. The twisted logic made a lasting impression on Marsha.

But much to her heartache, Yahfah's stay in Denver was brief, and in July of 1973 she returned to Phoenix, this time moving in with Ken Unrein. Both had more than just a recreational approach to drugs; both buying and selling to pay the bills and support their habit. However, Ken was not at all happy about Yahfah's occupation. She had taken a new job at the Soft Touch Massage Parlor in North Phoenix and it was clear she enjoyed her work, and even more so the side money it offered. Hardly an evening went by when Ken didn't return home to find Yahfah earning a little extra income in their bed. It took less than a month for his patience, along with his pride, to wear out. One night he came home to find her entertaining yet another customer, so he threw her out. Literally. He slammed her through the window of the kitchen door, and cut her hand so badly, she required a trip to the hospital.

Needless to say, Yahfah was out of the massage business for a while. She swore to Ken that she would even the score. She left him, but because they shared so many friends, they often found themselves in the same room, but could barely tolerate each other from that point on.

Yahfah rebounded quickly, moving in with a newcomer to the group, a young kid named Bob Robbins. Bob had grown up just a few miles away, but because of continuing conflicts with his parents, he left home and wound up with the low life on East Van Buren. His association with drugs had long ago consumed him, and of all those in his new circle, Robbins was clearly the heaviest abuser, reportedly even heroin, which no one else in the group would even consider. Reddish-blond hair fell across his forehead and over the collar of his trademark flannel shirt. Dirty Levis and brown high top boots completed his Beach Boy-Gone-Bad-wardrobe. His motivation for anything other than getting loaded had long ago left him, and he was satisfied with what was thrown to him, or left over from others. It was rumored that he worked in landscaping once, but there was no record of any employment or income. If he did work, it was short lived, because everyone remembered Bob Robbins as forever just hanging out, night or day, getting high, staying mellow.

Yahfah felt Bob's easy going style made him the perfect roommate – no hassles and no lectures – so the two rented a rundown apartment behind the derelict Silver Spur Motel on East Van Buren. Yahfah continued working nights at the massage parlor, and entertaining afterwards, while Bob did whatever it was he did.

Flush with new income, they rented a mobile home miles away in a new park in Apache Junction, and had moved their few belongings in on Saturday, October 13th. On Monday, Yahfah began a job at the Playful Kitten Parlor near their new home, content to pay all the bills, including Robbins ever-increasing drug habit. Bob was, of course, content to let her.

After he and Yahfah split, Ken and Mike teamed up again, renting both sides of an older duplex on North 18th, just off East Van Buren. Ken got on driving for Yellow Cab, and Mike worked sporadically at odd jobs through a temp agency. Both enjoyed their smoke, selling a little on the side to make ends meet, which often required them to go back to Denver on business. Their friendship was solid and it was uncommon to see one without the other. And now their money allowed them the luxury of a car. From the guy who supplied them some of their dope, they got a white 1961 VW Bus, that looked like the last of the hippie vans. Contact paper resembling stained glass lined the rear windows, and a psychedelic tapestry separated the front from the back, offering more privacy when desired. Someone had gone to the trouble of cutting out magazine photos and pasting them to the dash. There was only one problem with the van. It wasn't really theirs.

It still belonged to Robert Peters, a man well known by the police in San Diego, Los Angeles, and Phoenix, for narcotics trafficking. Peters had served time in California at Lompoc and carried an extensive rap sheet. While he probably wasn't involved in Ken or Mike's daily activities, it did a lot to explain their constant supply of easy weed.

The lights were on in both sides of the duplex. Willie, Doug and Marsha stood on the sidewalk and removed the rifles from the cases, hiding them under their coats. Ken flipped the porch light on and answered the door. As soon as he stepped inside, Willie pulled the .22 out and held it in the air. "You guys have been fuckin' with us about Yahfah! This shit is gonna stop, now!"

He pointed the rifle at each of them to show he was serious, and Doug joined in by waving the shotgun as his partner did the talking. "Now you are going to show us, or else. And this time we're taking your van."

Ken got behind the wheel and Willie sat up front, resting the .22 across his knee, barrel aimed at the driver, repeating about how he had killed before and wouldn't hesitate to do it again. To make his point, he slapped Ken upside the head more than once.

When they finally arrived at Vista Grande, it was no wonder that they couldn't find it on their own. The trailer park was nearly thirty miles outside of Phoenix, and there were a few nervous times in the desert darkness when Willie and Doug felt it was they who were being taken for a ride. But once there, Marsha and Yahfah were ecstatic to see each other. While Willie wasn't looking, Ken and Mike quietly slipped out and returned to Phoenix in the van.

The trailer was actually quite nice; sparse, but pleasantly furnished. When Willie and Doug walked in, Bob Robbins freaked out. He didn't have a clue as to who these two dudes with guns were, but had every chemical reason in the world to be paranoid. But soon even he warmed up, and as protocol would dictate, welcomed them into his home, then offered them his stash. For a short time the five acted like old friends.

They had been there about thirty minutes when Willie said that he and Doug needed a ride back to town to get their stuff, and despite the distance, Bob was more than anxious to oblige. Willie promised Marsha they would be back in an hour. Other than the guns, they had taken nothing else from the room at the Tahiti.

Bob fired up the blue Chevy convertible that set out on the driveway slab. It made a horrendous noise even while idling, and it was remarkable the car ran at all. The interior was in shreds, the seats and floor were littered with trash, and the windshield was smashed. Fortunately, the night was still quite warm, because the blue wreck was permanently a convertible; the top never came up, and there was a question if there was even a top on it at all. But the Chevy rolled, and that was all Bob ever cared about.

It was on the ride back when Willie decided to have Doug remain at the motel, offering some excuse that somebody had to stay and protect their belongings. It was well after midnight when they pulled into the lot, and while they all went upstairs, only Bob and Willie came back down.

If the Chevy did anything, it begged to be pulled over. It was so loud and so thrashed; whoever was in it must be guilty of something. Robbins had been stopped many times, usually resulting in a fix-it ticket for one of the convertible's endless violations. So at 2:05 Wednesday morning, on East University Avenue outside of Mesa, a county patrol car hit the lights and pulled the convertible over to the side of the road. Robbins gave the usual answers, and although he surely looked guilty of something, the officer had nothing, and let him off with merely a glare.

As procedure required, his passenger was also questioned and was asked to produce some ID. The man gave his name as Bill Bender from Denver, but he was sorry, he had left his wallet back at the house. The sheriff deputy shined his flashlight on him, making note of their ragged appearance; the unusual afro, the dirty jeans, and his fake leather jacket. Back at his car, he recorded this info on a field interview card, then allowed the Chevy to leave.

Nothing out of the ordinary happened on the deputy's watch that night and the two men in the convertible were quickly lost among the names and faces of hundreds of others just like them. Bob Robbins and the bad luck Chevy would be stopped again within a few days, but it would be more than a week before his name, and his tragic fate, become known to authorities serving east Maricopa County.

12

Wednesday, October 17, 1973 | 6 pm.

To the west, the downtown twilight flickered, catching hold as darkness fell upon the city. Behind the skyline silhouette, an orangeade sky sprayed a sunset wash of starfire pink and brilliant crimson, while candy purple blended with deep lunar cobalt. The horizon, like a struck match, flared, exploding into a nuclear fireball of color. Then, as suddenly as it appeared, it all gently faded away. The heavens above them now, the blackest of blue, welcomed the coming night, as it had done so many times in the autumn summers of the southwest.

But here, in the midst of these hot fairground days of mid October, the winter of Douglas Gretzler's young life was upon him. The cold truth was, that until this moment, his actions were reversible. The confusion could be reconciled. Apologies offered, and possibly accepted. And maybe somehow who he had become and what he had done, explained, overlooked, or ignored. Nothing so terrible had been done that could not be lied away, or simply forgotten. This was true turning point in his life – and it was now less than twenty-four hours away – for after that there would be no going back, no retreat, no return to the quiet lost soul most would remember him as. Ironically, as he lay comatose, spread eagle on the motel bed, Doug Gretzler's life was not unlike the glorious sunset that blazed above him; a fiery supernova, streaking towards its eventual, and soon irreversible demise.

Willie and Doug had spent the day apart for the first time since they met nearly six weeks earlier. Willie hung out at the trailer in Apache Junction, smoking dope and shootin' the shit; screen doors open wide to feel the 90 degree day, a couple of women to impress and some dude who would believe any stupid story he told. It was a perfect afternoon for Willie – bright, loud, breezy– which was just the way he liked it.

At the Tahiti Motel, Doug never left the drape drawn darkness of 208. The whirl of the air conditioner fought the television game show chatter that consumed the room. Downers kept him gray and groggy, and he slipped in and out of consciousness, which was just where he liked to be.

So when Doug answered the door and squinted into the glare of an exploding sky, he might have been surprised how late it was, and maybe how hot it still was, but he was not at all surprised at who it was.

"Come on man, let's go." Willie barked as he walked into the room. He glanced around, quick to gather what few items remained. "We got the van," he snapped. "Time to go."

Ken went to work as usual that Wednesday, pulling his regular shift at Yellow Cab. He was off at four-thirty and home before five, sharing his customary joint with Mike. Ken had told everyone at work about all that went down last night, emphasizing just how serious it could have been. "They're a couple of bikers from Denver, and they are fuckin' crazy." Yet no one seemed overly concerned about his apparent close call. In their line of work they had all met their share of whackos. It just came with the territory. But even Ken had to figure the worst was over. Now that Marsha had found Yahfah, and this Bill Steelman dude had done his job in getting her there, Ken had no reason in the world to believe he would ever cross his path again.

Earlier in the day, as they hung around the trailer, Yahfah confided in Willie her stormy relationship with Ken Unrein. These were just the kind of stories he loved to hear; a woman in distress. Before she was even finished, Willie decided her plight was somehow his responsibility.

A month earlier, Frances had discovered firsthand this need Willie had to solve other people's problems. Her relationship with Art Wallen had always been an ugly one – he abused the bottle, then abused her – and when Willie arrived unannounced in August, he interrupted their ongoing battle. One day, while in another drunken rage, Art took the back of his hand to Frances' youngest boy. Until now she had bit her lip, but she could control herself no longer. She broke down, cursing Wallen just as Willie walked into the room. Willie looked at her, sat down and wrapped his arms around his still whimpering nephew, then watched as Art stormed out the front door.

"I wish he was dead!" Frances wailed. "I wish he would just go away. Just leave us alone! I wish I had the guts to kill him myself!"

Willie said nothing. He cradled the boy in his arms and carried him upstairs, listening to his sister's sobs. She eventually calmed down, wishing she hadn't made such a spectacle of herself in front of her brother and child.

A bit later, Willie came back down and got right in his sister's face. "You serious about this? Cuz if you're serious, I know a way we can do it and no one will ever find out."

She didn't quite understand, and her puzzled look forced Willie to back up and explain. "If you want Art done, I'll do it, and no one will ever find out."

Frances was speechless. Her brother was dead serious.

"There's a drug – we would have to forge a prescription – but just a needle full of this stuff will stop a man just like that." Willie snapped his fingers. "Next time he gets drunk and passes out, we just stick him right between his toes. No one will ever know. They'll just think it was a heart attack. That's the beauty of this stuff, it looks just like a heart attack."

He was perfectly calm as he spoke, pleased to have solved his sister's dilemma.

"Bill, are you joking? Kill him? You mean kill Art?"

"That's what you wanted, wasn't it?"

"Well. . .I. . .I didn't mean. . .I didn't think. . ."

"I'll do it. I'll take care of everything. You don't even have to be in on it."

Frances was dumbfounded. "Bill, for god sakes, don't be silly!" It was her conscience talking now, because so many times later, after so many more of his slaps to her head, she would second guess her answer to her brother that day. "No, Bill. Don't talk crazy. Absolutely not!"

He shrugged, not quite sure why she refused his offer, but he said nothing more about it and slipped back upstairs.

So Yahfah's lament that afternoon was directed at someone who did not take such talk lightly. While she complained about her struggles with Ken - the broken window and trip to the emergency room - she was at best only half serious about what evil things she wished upon him.

Despite her harsh talk to Willie, Yahfah was in a good mood and spent most of the day relishing old memories with Marsha. Yahfah brewed tea and they relived those days in Denver when they had first met. For Marsha it was a bittersweet afternoon. It was easy for her to see just how much Yahfah had changed. She was crude, harder, nastier. And yet Marsha, so happy to simply be near her again, refused to concede the obvious.

And Marsha was different too when she was around Yahfah. Gone was the defiant, smart ass little tomboy, replaced by a slight, delicate young woman, more confused than ever about her place in this world – Yahfah's world, she was certain – and she struggled with these flood of emotions. She wanted so badly to tell Yahfah how she felt, but she didn't. She just couldn't.

All of which explained why Marsha was so oblivious to anything Bill did that afternoon. She only remembered them passing around a couple of joints and him saying something about going back into town to get Doug, and promising to be back soon. Marsha barely paid any attention to him as he walked out.

Bob returned to the trailer a couple of hours later, alone. Marsha was a little concerned at first, but knowing Bill, she figured he was just up to some of his tricks and would show up sooner or later.

The two women spent the next few days hanging around the pool or inside the house. Yahfah took her clothes shopping, Marsha having only what little she had shoved in her backpack. Bob gladly handled the chauffeur's duties behind the wheel of the noisy blue convertible. They drove to town, laughing and yelling to be heard above the Chevy racket, the wind hopelessly tangling their hair.

At first there was no reason to worry about Bill and Doug's disappearance, but after a couple of days Marsha realized she was stuck with no way back to Denver. She had already been gone longer than expected, and now Yahfah seemed bothered by her lengthy stay as well. By Friday she was ready to send Marsha back home, and told her so.

Marsha knew she needed to get back, but she was hurt at how quickly Yahfah's mood had changed. Yahfah told her if Bill and Doug weren't back by Saturday, then Marsha would be on the next flight to Denver.

Saturday came and went and no Willie. Yahfah bought Marsha a plane ticket for Sunday morning. They had a little going-away party that night and wound up oversleeping, thereby missing the plane. The next flight was early Monday morning and Yahfah was adamant about Marsha being on it.

She was.

While Yahfah and Marsha lounged about the trailer last Wednesday afternoon, Willie arrived at Ken and Mike's place unannounced. Carrying the briefcase with the .22, he told Robbins to drop him off down the street from the duplex, cautious that Ken or Mike might hear the convertible coming. Whatever Willie's excuse was for being there, their departure was quick, and at gunpoint. Lights were left on and uneaten food remained on the counter. Even Ken's cat was left inside. The front door was shut, but unlocked, and it appeared that Ken and Mike left with only the clothes on their back. He never told Doug what he said to Ken and Mike that afternoon to get them and their car, he just showed up back at the Tahiti Motel late that afternoon and rustled him awake.

"Come on, we got the van. Let's go."

So they headed to California. Doug drove. Ken and Mike huddled in the back with only the tapestry curtain between them. Tonight it was pulled back so Willie would have a clear view. He told them this wasn't some kind of joyride, and both guns were kept in sight as a reminder for everyone to stay cool. He spent hours recanting his wild and violent past, assuring them he would not hesitate to kill them if he had to. Neither was tied up, and if they were ever willing to test Willie's threats, they had plenty of chances. There were even long stretches of freeway when Mike drove under Willie's watchful eye.

It was 2 am and they were on the other side of Los Angeles, with the VW straining to climb the Tehachapi Mountains. Willie told Doug to pull into a rest area. He warned them he never really slept, so there was no use thinking about going anywhere.

13

Thursday, October 18, 1973 | 9 am.

Willie pulled the newspaper from the rack and glanced at the headlines. Like every paper everywhere, the *L.A. Times* ran with Nixon's latest troubles splashed huge across the front page. He flipped through the sections of the paper as he walked back to the VW. The others had waited in the van while he went into the store, then watched as he emerged with what would pass for breakfast. He tossed the small bag at them and followed it in, more interested in the front page than in the food.

Back on the road, the Volkswagen wound its way through the Tehachapis, their stark range covered in its fall coat of tan and gray suede. By mid morning the overcast skies peeled away and blue skies again poured through.

"Well, what's gonna happen?" Ken asked for the hundredth time. "Where are we going? What are you gonna do to us?"

Willie gave them shit for their whining. It was driving him crazy. "Why don't you two just shut the fuck up and stop actin' like a couple of little babies?"

"Well, you ain't thinking about killin' us, are you?" Mike asked.

The thought had crossed Willie's mind. The idea fascinated him. He talked about it, boasted about doing it, lied about the number of victims, even visualized himself pulling the trigger, although he never had.

Doug didn't know that. He figured Bill was who he said he was. A hundred times he heard Willie brag about offing his wife, ("Had to. The hit was ordered by my people") or killing two people in Stockton in a bad drug deal, ("Gun fucked up. Wound up having to slit their throats") and most recently the Preacher in Phoenix ("Still don't know what went wrong on that one. . .just fucking gunfire everywhere") Not to mention the countless he claimed to have killed in Nam.

("Really man, what's the difference between killing some gook over there, or wasting someone over here? Either way, it's a war.")

Doug had seen the rage and anger erupt inside of him, so it was easy to make the connection, easy to see him pull the trigger. He never questioned his story, never doubted his sincerity. Of course Doug Gretzler took everyone at their word. 'I go on feelings,' he once said. 'They motivate me to make a decision.' He never believed people would have any reason to lie to him, especially his partner, especially now. So he mimicked Bill rather than argue with him, evading any possible confrontation. More than anything, he hated confrontation.

But if Willie had any kind of plan that afternoon – if he honestly knew what he was going to do with Ken and Mike – he wasn't telling. Ideas swirled in his head. Lots of ideas. But he didn't have a concrete plan. But the time to act was drawing near. They would be in Lodi within the hour, and it was certain he didn't want to be dragging these two around with him when he pulled into town.

He had just three things on his mind. First, he needed the van. Secondly, he would have to come up with a way to get rid of the two guys whimpering in the back. And finally, he needed some money. More than just swiping some old lady's purse kind of money. He needed real money. Big money.

The sea level sameness of California's San Joaquin Valley changes rapidly east of the towns like Merced, Modesto, Manteca and the list of others along Highway 99. The vineyards, orchards and dairy land soon unfold into the big oak foothills, an area referred to simply as Calaveras. Here are huge tracts of rolling land, dotted occasionally with massive, companionless oak trees, land used for little more than open range grazing. Here, years ago, the wild rivers flowing down out of the Sierra Nevada were dammed and reservoirs built to hold water for irrigating the Valley. As a result, hundreds of dry creek beds and gullies now filled with water only when the winter rains come, becoming little more than shallow ponds where only reeds and cattails thrive. Narrow bridges carry roadways that ford nothing more than indentations in the earth, muddy crevices and shallow bogs where the grazing cattle search for a mere lick of moisture.

This area between the farmland in the foothills and the Sierra is cattle country. Ranches often consume thousands of acres of rolling terrain. County roads connect the ranches to the towns below, but much of the traveling is on the private roads that weave in and out of the hillside; sometimes graveled, but in most cases merely ruts made by the rancher's trucks. Hundreds of miles of dirt roads; so isolated they might have company but only a few times a year. Seldom marked or named, these roads lead in circles to nowhere, created only to allow the cattleman to keep an eye on his wandering herd. All of this is less than 30 or 40 miles from Highway 99, and yet so remote a man could get lost in their maze, and many times did.

Besides the rancher or maybe his hired help, hunters knew these roads best. In the autumn months they drove as far out as they could, and ignoring the posted signs, crawled under a barbed wire fence and walked the hills looking for dove, pheasant or duck hiding in the occasional watersheds. Land, quiet and remote, but in the fall the air above it crackles with the sound from the hunter's rifle.

As a teenager, especially in the first few years following the death of his father, he also walked these fields, alone. He shot at quail and ground squirrels, but mostly he just walked, discovering the seclusion of these hills only a few miles from his aunt's house in Modesto. He disappeared here often, so he knew this land. He knew its vastness and its ability to hide both people and their feelings. And now Willie decided he needed this land to hide Ken and Mike.

At his instructions, the Volkswagen pulled off Highway 99 and headed east onto Highway 120 towards the towns of Escalon and then Oakdale. At a small store on the eastern edge of town, Willie got a couple of beers for Ken and Mike, a Pepsi for Doug and a bottle of apple cider for himself.

Not a word was said as they drove, Willie simply peered out the window, scanning the countryside, deep in thought, as if he was looking for something, or someone. Eventually he turned around and instructed the two in the back to get down on the floor of the van. They did as he said, and Doug continued driving in the directions Willie gave. Still struggling with the loose ends, Willie decided it was time to get some help.

Terry Morgan had headed west too, or so he believed. Her last conversation with him indicated she was tired with her life in Denver and she was going to Modesto to live with her grandmother. Terry's father was from this area, and from a big family as well. The phone book was loaded with Morgans. He hoped he could find her.

During one of their late night conversations at the house on Ellsworth, Willie told her that if he ever went back to California, he would need some help; what kind of help he didn't say, but whatever it was, Terry agreed to be there for him. He promised to call her when he got to California and suggested they meet at the Orange Blossom Bar, an old hangout well out in the country, and away from anyone who might recognize him.

Willie and Doug spent the better part of an hour driving up and down these remote stretches of road looking for the Orange Blossom. He reminded Ken and Mike to keep down, threatening to drag them out of the car and blow their brains out if they as much as peeked out the window. They obeyed. He eventually found the tavern. Doug pulled up near the front door and Willie walked inside.

Lucillia Plante was a thirty-ish woman on the pleasant side of plump. She tended bar part-time at the Orange Blossom and had for years. She knew just about everyone who stopped in and she was sharp enough to remember a face and the brand of beer that went with it. But she had never seen this man before and later remembered him only by his jeans. She couldn't recall ever seeing any rancher around these parts wearing skintight Levis with silver medallions up the side. Eyeing those in the room as if he was looking for someone, the stranger headed for the bar. He pulled out a large black billfold and took out a single dollar bill, which he placed on the bar.

He was polite, almost shy, as he spoke. "I. . .ah, I guess I'll have an Oly."

Lucillia poured him a draft and set it in front of him. He picked up the glass and took a small swig. "I'm supposed to meet someone here, my niece, her name's Terry. You don't know her, do you? She's about 20. About this tall."

Lucillia thought for a moment and shook her head.

"Her name is Morgan," he continued. "Terry Morgan."

Sorry, she apologized, that name didn't ring a bell.

"I'm from out of town and I'm supposed to meet her here." He pulled a slip of paper from his shirt pocket, suggesting maybe he could call her, and Lucillia pointed to the pay phone on the other side of the room. He stayed at the phone for several minutes, but Lucilla didn't notice him talking to anyone, and he never came back to finish his beer.

Doug had the radio up loud as he waited for Willie to come out. Loud enough to earn a scornful look from some of the regulars who had pulled up along side him in the parking lot.

Willie climbed in. "Shit, I'm hot! No one wants to touch me. None of my people will have anything to do with me. Fuck! Lemme think here! What the fuck we gonna do?"

He told Doug how he hoped some of 'his people' would have the balls to help him out in this jam and, "stay with him until things cooled down." It was the least they could do, he said, especially after all he had done for them. Doug had no idea what jam he was referring to.

Willie made Doug drive around the country roads again for nearly an hour. After which it was clear the van had made at least one complete circle and they were now right back where they had started, a point made by the driver. During that time they had crossed the same covered bridge twice, and stopped again back in Oakdale where Willie made yet another phone call. The sun was setting. It would be dark soon and a somber thin blanket covered the late afternoon sky. The Volkswagen turned onto old Sonora Road and Willie studied the landscape on both sides of the two-lane road. It seemed to Doug they were retracing their steps for a third time, but before he could say anything, Willie told him to pull over.

The small concrete bridge crossing Littlejohn's Creek had been built over a half-century earlier and still boasted the bronze plaque naming the county supervisors who were responsible for its construction back in 1917. On the other side of the bridge was a wide spot just off the road where Doug pulled and parked. Willie grabbed the sawed off .22 and jumped out of the van.

"Out! Both ya. Get out!"

Willie, and with Doug on his heels, marched the pair to a nearby trail sloping down to the creek below. At the bottom of the trail, just above the marsh, Willie told them this was far enough.

In the small ravine where they stopped, the earth was moist and the cool air smelled of stagnant water and manure. Cattle were once crowded in this hollow spot of earth and the remnants of those days; rusted steel posts and broken concrete pilings sprouted old and twisted from the ground. Willie pointed to a cement block and ordered them to sit. Dressed only in the t-shirts they left Arizona in 24 hours earlier, they shivered from the cold, as well as the uncertainty of the moment. Willie paced in front of them and thought hard about what to do next. He rolled a joint and passed it around. They talked as they smoked and Willie danced around the reason for them being here.

"What's gonna happen man?" one of them asked.

"Yeah, Jesus, it's gettin' cold," said the other.

Willie gave the signal. Doug had taken a microphone cord and some small pieces of rope from the van, and he circled behind the two while they sat focused on Willie. Ken and Mike tried to keep one eye on Willie, who was holding the gun, and one on Doug who was coming at their backs.

"Get up!" Willie yelled. "Now, I'll tell you two what's gonna' happen. Douglas is gonna tie you up and we're gonna leave you here for a while. Then you guys are gonna give us an hour before you try to take off. We might be way the fuck outta here, or we might be just over that little hill there with our guns fuckin' ready to blow you away! See? You won't know."

While Willie talked, Doug cinched their hands tight behind them. They squirmed and fidgeted, which only angered Willie even more. God, he hated to see men act this way! It pissed him off no end.

"Remember, one hour. Then you can do whatever you want."

Ken and Mike watched as they walked back up the trail and disappeared from view.

As they approached the van, Willie stopped and reached for Doug. "Hold it. This ain't comin' down right. They're witnesses man and I don't need any more people on my ass right now." They stood in silence for a moment before Willie made his move.

"We gotta go back. We can't leave them, you know, they're witnesses to the whole thing." He turned around. As he walked back down the trail he laid out his new plan.

Surprised to see them return so soon, Ken was hopeful as Willie pulled him to his feet, even though they were walking away from the others and closer to the bog's edge. Ken stumbled forward a few steps ahead of Willie. The gag in his mouth prevented him from talking, from asking once again what was going on. He felt Willie's cold hands around his neck and a knee suddenly shoved into his back as he lay face down in the mud.

When Willie was through, he returned to the clearing, making sure his partner had done his part as well. He hadn't, so together they finished the job.

It made Doug sick to his stomach; disgusted by the sight and sounds of it all. It had this slow motion feel to it. He thought it would never end. He was breathing hard. He was afraid he had enjoyed it.

When it was finally over he said not a single word. He helped Willie clean up, and then climbed back up the hill to the van.

Doug turned the Volkswagen around and headed back the way they had come earlier. He raced through the gears, feeling the need to get as far away as possible. As they drove back down Sonora Road, Willie rolled down the window and began throwing stuff out. Red corduroy pants, soiled shirts, new brown boots. Finally, he reached down and grabbed the long handled knife that rested in his lap. He heaved it as far as he could, unable to see it land. He rolled the window up to brave off the chill. He sat back in silence, which was so unlike him.

He was barely 5 years old, so the story went, when Frances gave him a chicken. A rooster actually. The scrawniest little rooster anyone had ever seen.

"Now Billy," she instructed, "if you take care of him, and he grows a bit, soon he'll crow just like all the other roosters in the pen. But you've got to promise me you'll watch over him." The curly blond haired boy nodded, and promised to take extra special care of his new friend.

"Do you have a name for him yet?" she asked.

He looked at her for a moment and nodded his head yes. "I tink I weil call him Char-wee."

So Charlie the Rooster became a common sight around the house in Acampo. He followed Billy everywhere, eating from his hand, getting fatter, and eventually crowing. Billy had even taught Charlie to sit on the top of his head as he wandered the yard. The little boy balanced the rooster atop his mop of curls and strutted the yard, entertaining the hired hands.

At night, Billy cried when he had to leave Charlie outside with the other chickens, and was quick to race out the next morning with breakfast scraps for his buddy.

One day John Dougherty stopped by the house and noticed this chicken perched upon the little boy's head, nesting in the bushy blond curls.

"Billy!" Dougherty laughed. "What in tarnation are you doing with that chicken?"

He looked up and answered. "Nuttin'."

"Well then, what are you *going* to do with him?" The big man smiled as Billy paused to ponder the question.

"I weil jus love him," he replied with a shy grin. Dougherty grabbed the rooster off Billy's head.

"Well, you know what you're *supposed* to do, don't you?" He put his hands around Charlie's neck and pretended to tug.

"You ring their necks and cook 'em!" His loud laugh filled the air, and he tossed the bird at the child's feet. "You cook 'em and eat 'em!!" he bellowed as he walked away, still laughing from the sight of those two.

Frances was inside the house when she heard the god-awful screeching coming from the front yard. Knowing Billy was out there, she raced to the door. As she opened the screen, he tore by her into the house, screaming at the top of his lungs.

"Char-wee. . .Char-wee. . .Char-wee!!!"

Frances looked at him and then out front. There in the yard was Charlie the Rooster flopping around in the dirt, an ear piercing squawk shot through the air. Billy had listened carefully to Mr. Dougherty, and as soon as the man disappeared around back, he picked up Charlie and put his tiny hands around the rooster's neck and snapped it. Just like the man showed him.

And the devil now danced in this angel's head.

The Volkswagen crept the back roads north. It was late, nearly 10:30, when they turned off the highway and found the place. They pulled in between the old man's pickup and a Cadillac Willie didn't recognize. Doug stayed put as Willie got out and started towards the door of the house on Clown's Alley. Cliff heard the noise and turned on the porch light and peered out front to see who the late night intruders were.

Cliff Wardrobe's house sat barely a block off Highway 88 in Clements, a little town about a dozen miles east of Lodi. It could hardly be considered a town. Nothing more than a cluster of old buildings and boarded up businesses, so small the listings in the phone book had trouble filling up a couple of pages. In fact, Clements was known solely for the A & W Drive Inn resting along the highway.

The directions to the Wardrobe place were simple. Turn at the A & W. That's it. If you could manage to find a place to stand amidst the sea of junk and trash in the yard, you could probably take one of the old paint cans lying around and hit the orange and brown root beer sign not a hundred feet away.

Cliff was one of Willie's old partners, and the story was they ran pot from Santa Cruz and Mendocino back to Lodi. Willie called the shots and the younger Wardrobe followed along. Cliff wore huge coke bottles glasses, so heavy they were constantly sliding down his nose and he was forever pushing them back up again. He slumped. Willie called him his stooge, and there was a time when Cliff would do anything Willie asked.

But then Willie went sideways, got messed up bad and dropped out of sight. Cliff hadn't heard from him in almost a year. He was relieved. He still got caught doing dumb stuff, but he could see now how Willie had made him look so stupid.

"Hey Cliffy! How ya doin?"

Cliff squinted into the darkness. He couldn't see him, but the voice was unmistakable. His gut turned over. His reply was nervous and automatic. "Bill? Jesus, I heard you were on the run! Whatcha doin' back?"

"Here for just a day or so, Cliffy. Gotta deal we're gonna do and thought I might stop by and see what you're up to."

Cliff walked out to the van and Willie clasped his hand tight and gave his a slight hug. Willie hadn't noticed them at first, but the people who were in the Cad were now out and had boosted themselves up on the hood to see what was going on. Willie recognized one as Cliff's old girlfriend Diana and he knew the others only as Terry and Lester. Willie lit a number and passed it around while he and Cliff made small talk. They breezed through names of the crowd they ran with and what each had been up to since Willie took off in August.

"Greg Flattery just got outta CRC," Cliff offered. "You knew he was in, right?"

Willie laughed. Hell yes, he remembered Greg! Didn't know he had gotten popped, but remembered just how much he used to like hanging around with Flattery. Really liked running around in his car. Greg drove a blue Corvair and Willie was flat out convinced the Corvair was just about the best car ever built. ("You put the goddamn engine in the back where you get the most traction," he used to yell at Greg over the sputtering. "Air cooled, fuckin' great mileage. Shit! Chevy was nuts to stop makin' 'em.") He reminded himself to try and find Greg while he was in town.

But Willie had not come all the way out here to hang around and talk. He had come for some business. He gave those sitting on the Caddy the look to get lost, and they did. Willie turned around, looked at Wardrobe and got serious. "We been to Mexico, Cliffy, and we just came back to make some money. Some easy money, man. Righteous money. You interested in making some eeeeasy money?"

That kind of talk scared Clifford. Seems like he had been in trouble all of his life and he was now trying to stay clean. He knew better than to tell Willie that, so he laughed, but his nervousness showed. "You know me, man, I can always use the dough."

That's all Willie needed. "We're gonna do the United Market."

Clifford broke a tiny grin. He felt better. He hoped Bill couldn't see it. There was no need to worry. Over the years Willie had worn that idea into the ground. He knew Steelman well enough to know he could never find the guts to pull it off. But before he could say a word, Willie repeated his pitch. "We're gonna get the United Market and we want you in it with us."

"Jesus, Bill, you been talkin' about hittin' that place for as long as I've known you!" He was quick to give his old partner the brush off. "Naw, I just got out Bill and I don't wanna go back in. Sorry man, not interested."

"Wait a minute man. Hear me out now. I just want you to go in and look around, you know, look around and then lemme know if we should come in."

"I'm not gonna do it Bill."

Steelman wasn't taking no for an answer. "Christ, Cliff, don't worry so much! I wouldn't get you involved or anything, because there won't be nobody else there, you know, like witnesses and shit. But if there was, then I wouldn't come in. I would only come in if you told me he was in there alone."

Cliff knew the "he" Steelman was referring to was Wally Parkin. Bill always seemed to have it out for the guy.

"Now all you have to do is go in, buy a beer or something, look around, see who's in the check stand, then walk back outside and signal me. If you say it's ok, then we walk in and you just sit in the van and keep it runnin'. That's it."

Cliff shut up, but Willie wanted to make sure he heard. "If he's alone, then signal me," he repeated. "That's all."

Diana, Terry and Lester returned and Willie changed the subject. He reached behind Cliff and pulled something from inside the van. "Oh, by the way," Willie said, handing it to Cliff, "why don't you get rid of this for me?"

Wardrobe held it up to the light and looked it over. It was some kind of twisted cord. "What in the hell is this, and just what exactly do you want me to do with it?"

"We just robbed a couple of dudes," laughed Willie. "We tied them up with it."

Cliff shook his head and shoved the cord in his pocket. Bill was always pulling some stupid stunt like this. It made Cliff twitchy. He wasn't so sure they weren't laughing at him. He didn't like to hear it and he started towards the Caddy. "I'm leavin'. I'm outta here. I'm not gonna stick around here in front of my old man's house with all this shit going on."

"My place is open," Lester offered.

"Then let's go!" Willie said. "Cliff, you can ride with Doug and me."

Lester, who had stayed silent to this point, walked up and looked into the Volkswagen. He stepped back and rubbed his hand along the side. "You wanna sell it?" he asked Willie.

"Yeah, I'll let you have it."

"How much?"

"Fifty bucks," Willie replied, pulling a figure out of the air as he moved around to the driver's side with Lester close behind.

"It any good?"

"It should be," Willie said. "We just got back from Arizona in it."

Lester looked over at Cliff, and then at Steelman. "Thought I heard you say you just got back from Mexico?" Willie ignored him, turned around and climbed in the van to drive. He waved at Doug to get out and let Clifford sit between them. Willie backed up and waited for the Cadillac to pull out, then followed it down the highway to Lester's place.

Lockeford sits about halfway back to Victor, where the highway becomes the main street of this little town. When things got too hot in Lodi for Willie, Wardrobe and all the others, they headed to Lockeford. No one ever bothered them here. It was common knowledge you could buy any drug, in any amount, any time of the day or night, right in the middle of town. Underneath the old neon sign of the Lockeford Liquor Store, or around the corner in the parking lot, was where most of the drug deals went down. Sometimes it might be across the street at the Dalton Bar, or in broad daylight in the narrow alley behind, but they were deals done with a boldness not found anywhere in Lodi.

"You know Cliff," Willie said as the van headed towards Lockford, "there's a dude in Arizona who is willing to pay some tremendous money, some outrageous money, to hit Parkin."

Cliff didn't understand the connection. He knew Bill had this thing about robbing the market in Victor, but what Wally Parkin had to do with it confused him. He told Willie he didn't get it.

"Parkin is dirty!" Willie shot back. He lit another Marlboro and let it dangle between his lips as he spoke. "He's in it up to his little neck and my people down south will pay big to take him out."

Cliff listened but didn't say a word. After all the time they had spent together, it finally dawned on him that Bill was a real asshole. He wondered if he had always been that way and he just didn't notice before. Cliff hoped that he could figure out a way to cut the evening short. He fingered the cord in his pocket and as Bill babbled on, he quietly pulled it out and flipped it into the back of the van. Bill said nothing more about Parkin or the market. Cliff relaxed.

On the street behind the Dalton Club were three small houses. Lester lived in the middle one, along with whoever needed a place to crash. Willie beat the Cadillac to the house and the three walked in and made themselves at home. Doug felt better taking his briefcase in with him.

"Pool cue," he explained when asked. "I make a few bucks shootin' pool."

"He's good, man," Willie butted in. "Damn good."

Within a couple of minutes Lester and the others arrived, walking in on Steelman and Wardrobe's conversation. They swore they heard the word "killing", and didn't really care to hear any more, so for the rest of the night they stayed away from Bill and Cliff and the talk that was coming from the tiny living room.

Chuck Shipley showed up later. He lived in the house too and his bed was in the kitchen. As usual, Chuck was shit faced stoned, but sober enough to recognize Steelman. Bill had been his dealer a couple years back, because when he returned from Vietnam, he brought back with him to Lodi a piss poor attitude and a white-knuckle addiction to opium and hashish. In 1970, he met Steelman, who became his connection, and it was during this time when Willie was dabbling in heroin. Dealing in small amounts, but enough to satisfy Shipley's needs as he tried to transfer his habit to something a little easier to come by in the states. Shipley traded Thai sticks he had smuggled back from Nam to Willie for the smack he was hustling for the Mexicans.

Like Steelman, Chuck had lived his entire life around Lodi, but the two had never met until drugs brought them together. Other than the dope, Shipley didn't have much use for Steelman, and in all honesty, was more than a little freaked out by this strange dude with the bushy white man's afro and pierced ears. From the moment he first met him, Shipley took Willie's drugs, then laughed at him behind his back. Chuck had the mountain-man, greasy Levi look, while Bill paraded around with goofy looking hair standing high on top of his head, wearing bright polyester slacks and an open shirt with huge collars. Shipley admitted he was outright embarrassed to be seen with him, even if it was only to buy his dope.

Willie, on the other hand, was fascinated with Shipley's time in Vietnam and bragged that he too had served in the Navy, and did a tour in Southeast Asia during the war.

"I know he's lying," Shipley told the others. "Shit! He names off a city or base, a place he was supposedly stationed, and he can't even tell you where 'bouts it was. Can't even fuckin' pronounce it! A couple a times I even came right out and told him that he was full of shit, that he had never been to Nam. He never called me on it or even got mad. He just sat there. I never felt sorry for anyone in my life. Hell with 'em. But I kinda feel sorry for him. It's like he just wants to be noticed."

For all the badass he portrayed, Shipley had a soft spot for Willie Steelman and he wasn't too big to admit that to the others. He somehow managed to look inside him and see the weakness and insecurity Willie tried so hard to hide. Shipley didn't have to give Willie the time of day, but over the few months he knew him, he kind of took a liking to the strange guy. "You know, I think he's good people," Chuck admitted to some friends when the conversation got around to Willie. "But honest to God, sometimes he scares the shit outta me."

Doug was minding his own business in the kitchen while tall tales flew from the other room. Shipley walked in and sat down across from him. Doug was quiet, but true to form, Chuck made an effort to strike up a conversation with him, even as drunk as he was.

"Whaddaya play?" Shipley slurred, thinking the case held some kind of instrument.

"Violin."

Shipley wasn't so ripped that he believed him. Nobody plays the violin, for chisssakes. Not around here, anyway. Doug was acting a little cocky, and despite Shipley's constant prodding to get a straight answer, Gretzler wasn't giving in easy.

"No, straight up, man. What's in the case?"

Doug paused for a moment without responding, then reached down, picked up the case and placed it on his lap. He turned it around so Shipley could get a good look and opened the lid.

"I told you," he deadpanned. "It's my violin."

Shipley's jaw dropped when he caught a look at the dull blue steel of the shotgun.

"Now," Doug asked with a sneer, "wanna hear me play a tune?"

Willie and Doug had wore out their welcome. It was nearly 3 in the morning when the party broke up. No one encouraged him to stay, but Clifford tossed him a sleeping bag, a sign it was time to go. He said nothing about getting together again. He wanted nothing more to do with Bill Steelman.

They left the cabin in Lockeford and headed west towards Lodi. Willie knew of a spot on the other side of town where they could lay low for the night. As they sped down Highway 12, he pointed out the United Market in Victor. Doug didn't know what to expect, but for as much as Bill talked about robbing the place, he was a bit surprised. Willie made it sound like a big supermarket, but it was a dinky little country store at best. Willie wouldn't shut up about all the money in there and how easy it would be to just walk right in and take it, so Doug just nodded and listened.

Willie felt good. Around here all the others were stuck with their measly little lives in these measly little towns, doing whatever stupid little things they could to stay alive. But he had been places, been a part of big deals and had returned to tell about it. Tonight they all knew about his busted parole and the way he quit the job at the winery last summer. They knew about Denver, how big a man he was there, and how they all waited for his return.

He told them about the fag in the orchard and the gun battle along side the Preacher. They heard tales about Arizona and down Mexico way, and the nonstop high from endless amount of drugs available at their leisure. Willie bragged about the cons and scams and thievery and robbery performed along the way. He said nothing about Ken and Mike.

He had made it clear he was better than any of them, far more exciting and important than they could ever imagine being. More dangerous, more decisive, more powerful. He felt that good. A huge weight had been lifted off him. The words he spoke and the pictures in his head were now real. What he had dreamed of and bragged about had finally come true, and his truth tonight rested face deep in the runoff, hidden amongst the reeds, the cattails, and the mud.

14

Friday, October 19, 1973 | 10 am.

That painful day in September years earlier, the day they buried his father, was to be Willie's first day of junior high school. When he finally came back to class, he struggled to keep up, to concentrate, and to just get along. Once a good kid and a good student, he now raged battle after battle against any teacher or authority figure that got in his way. His attitude had become such a problem that a year later, after arguing with a teacher about his repeated tardiness, he got up and walked out.

But he returned later that afternoon with a gas can and a Zippo lighter. He set the teacher's desk on fire, and left Needham Intermediate School for good, his formal education over.

In that first year following his father's passing, Willie had turned quiet and moody. Cute was long gone, and his once small delicate body was now lanky and gaunt. His blond curls had turned dark and wild; his boyish enthusiasm suddenly sour and cold. The bright blue eyes that at one time captivated his sister, seemed distant, haunting, menacing. A stark look of pain ruled his face and insecurity was evident in his every move. A teenager now, he was too much for his mother to handle. Sometimes Gary intervened and attempted to set his brother straight, usually with a harsh word and a slap upside the head, but it only served to make Willie hate him more.

Ethel Steelman was terrified of her son, afraid to turn her back on him, fearful of what he might do with his red-hot temper that could erupt without warning. Their battles were well known to the family and the neighbors, and hardly a day went by that wasn't accompanied by one of their screaming matches. She had resorted to hiding her purse and what little money she had in it, so Willie threatened her on a daily basis. "Gimme a dollar, you bitch!" She had little choice but to cave in to his demands. And yet sometimes, maybe only a few minutes later, he could be cuddling up next to her on the sofa, whimpering, "I love you, mommy. Please don't be mad at me."

At first Lee Mize knew well enough to stay out of it, but eventually he too was dragged into the melee. His efforts brought only physical confrontations with his stepson, after which he would kick Willie out of his house, and he could be gone for two days, two weeks, or two months.

It was during these times away when Willie began his first major attempt at crime. A stolen tire could get him a buck or two, a car battery even more. He stole produce from nearby farms, and hubcaps and radios from the cars left in their driveways. Lee had a hunch what Willie was up to – he had not only been stealing money from them, but from their neighbors as well – so he tracked Willie down and beat the devil out of him, just to let him know he wasn't getting away with anything.

Willie never strayed far. Less than a mile down Dustin Road were the Billingsley boys, Wayne and Jack. They lived with their grandparents, who made them sleep in an old bunkhouse out back, so Willie moved in with them, and soon he and Wayne had developed a two man wrecking crew, breaking into just about every house and shed within a couple miles. They never lacked for a little pocket cash after that. Once in awhile, usually at his mother's tearful pleading, Willie came back home, but the reunions were brief, and before long he and Mize would be back at each other. "You're only a guest here, mister!" he reminded Willie. So most of the time he stayed away. He decided it was better to be on his own and live in a shed, than to be in a house where he didn't belong.

Willie continued swiping stuff around the area without getting caught, and he was almost seventeen before he had his first real run in with the law. With the bunkhouse now his home, he and Wayne decided to hit the road, hitchhiking up Highway 99 to Sacramento. They were gone for a couple of days before the police caught them stealing food. Ethel didn't even know he had left until authorities told her she needed to pick him up at the county juvenile center. They warned her that charges of an Out of Control Youth would be handed down if she couldn't show some improvements in his attitude and day-to-day activity. Lee Mize scolded his wife at the lack of responsibility in raising her son. "What this boy needs is a firm hand and a daily regimen."

Ethel agreed. But how?

"He needs to join the Navy," Mize decided.

Willie had little to say in the matter. The judge was either going to send him to work camp, or Mize was going to send him into the Navy. So, on the morning of March 22, 1962, the day following his seventeenth birthday, Willie boarded a bus to San Diego to begin a four-year stint.

He lasted three months before the Navy got tired of his act and sent him back to Lodi. During his few weeks in boot camp, Seaman Recruit Steelman bucked and resisted, complained and argued, ignored every command and fought every word from every officer above him. He was sent to the infirmary at least four times, anguishing over every supposed illness and pain imaginable. Out of the first three months, records showed he was in sickbay almost six weeks. "I swear there's something wrong with me," he pleaded, although they weren't about to listen, or care. While he was still in the base hospital (records are unclear if it was the mental ward, as some suggested) the Navy presented him with an Honorable Discharge just to get rid of him. The report indicated, "He lacks maturity" and "failed to grasp even the most simple commands". Steelman, according to them, was untrainable.

So he returned to a life of misery in the Mize household, hiding in his room most of the time. He had no friends and no interests. Nor did he even have the enthusiasm to argue with his stepfather, who was now suffering from very poor health himself and remained as quiet as Willie. Even Ethel appeared resigned and tried hard to distance herself from her son.

There was, however, an elderly lady next door who took time to spend with Willie. She enjoyed his company, actually, and they spent many afternoons talking about everything and anything. She loaned him books and National Geographic magazines, and he would in turn help do her dishes and small chores around the house. She wasn't blind to his shortcomings, including reports of his thievery, but she accepted Willie for who he was; a troubled young man simply wanting someone to be with. Her husband liked having him around as well and treated him like his own son. Even Willie's mother noticed he seemed much happier than he had been in quite awhile, although Willie spent most of his day at the neighbors or locked in his room.

One day an ambulance was called next door and Willie raced over to see what was happening. The old man was taken away, and within a couple of weeks the neighbor lady moved out as well. Once again Willie was alone, and it wasn't long before he returned into his darkness.

In November of 1963, Ethel suggested Willie go to Denver to be with his sister. Terribly frustrated, she hoped the change of scenery might help, knowing how well the two of them used to get along. But when he arrived, Frances barely recognized him. The little boy was long gone, along with the funny little voice that squealed with delight whenever he saw her. His eyes, once the brightest blue, that danced at the silliest of things, were now evil and dark. His cheeks were sunken and hollow and he looked much older than his eighteen years. One moment he could happy and excited, the next, menacing and angry. His moods could change in a moment's notice. There were times when he would be rolling around on the floor, wrestling and giggling with her children, and others when Frances was afraid to even be around her brother, uncertain what terrible things he might be capable of.

Willie had been in Denver only a few weeks, but their time together had been difficult and tense. One afternoon, shortly before he left to return home, she sat next to him on the sofa, consoling him, his eyes fixed on the television set, watching him sob uncontrollably. It suddenly hit her how much he had changed and how fragile he had become. She held him in her arms, comforting him as she had done many years earlier when he was her little boy. "Bill, come on now. It's going to be alright," she soothed. "Don't you worry. Everything is going to be okay."

Willie and Doug were up early Friday morning, the cold autumn air being their alarm clock. They had stayed all night in the van, out near the old town of Woodbridge at a place called the Ice House. They snorted a few lines of coke for breakfast, then Willie grabbed a smoke, and they headed back to town. He fought the urge to call Denise. He wanted so much to hear her voice and imagined her caving in, begging for him to come back home. But he didn't, knowing just as easily she might turn him in, as would his brother Gary if given a chance. He figured his mom might still be around, but he decided not to call her either. He wouldn't know what to do if she started giving him shit about taking off. So there was no one, with the exception of Clifford, who knew Willie had even left Lodi, or cared that he had returned.

He wanted to see Cliff again, and was at a pay phone out front of a Westside market trying to reach him when he spotted an old friend. He hung up the receiver and walked over to where she was loading groceries into the trunk of her car. "Hey, remember me?" he asked.

It took her awhile. He had startled her, and had to give him a long slow look before realizing who he was. But yes, she remembered. Goodness! He was so skinny now. Dirty and scroungy, and she had never seen him with his afro, which this morning stuck out in every direction possible. His face was pock mocked and unshaven. A pierced ear was adjourned with a small marijuana leaf. His worn out Levis fit tight to his stick legs and the jeans were slit up the side, decorated with silver medallions.

He was so thin, so frightening, so unlike she remembered him years earlier when they had been friends. Even in the bright sunlight and the crowded parking lot, his presence caused her to gasp for the next breath. Sure, she remembered him. But she recalled back then a softer man who carried with him a painful sadness; a much more gentle soul, despite the reputation that followed him around back in those days. Her recollection was not of this unsightly beggar in front of her, but of a friend who always offered to baby-sit, then helped her pin freshly washed diapers on the clothesline to dry in the blue sky afternoon, all the time talking about his plans, clearly making them up as he went. She smiled. She had a photo somewhere. Bill Steelman bouncing her baby boy on his lap. She remembered him that way, not this. For a minute she wondered how she could have ever enjoyed his company, let alone allow him to watch over her child. She recalled how she had lost his friendship; something about a silly motorcycle deal between him and her husband.

"Bill!" she stammered. "My, it's been a long time!"

He asked how everyone was; like nothing ever happened, like nothing had changed. She made small talk. Eventually he said goodbye, suggesting they all get together soon. That night she told her husband about seeing Bill Steelman, about how much he had changed and how he frightened her. He reminded her of the deal gone bad, and that Steelman was a no good low life. So good riddance to him, he said.

The van crisscrossed through Lodi side streets and his old neighborhoods. Every so often he would point out a house that he and Denise once lived in and he would think about her again. On the way out Highway 12 to Victor, Willie showed Doug the United Market and how it looked in daylight.

The landlord of the house in Lockeford had told Cliff, and whoever else living there, to be out by sundown. Doug pulled up and they watched Cliff and the others haul boxes out and put them into the cavernous trunk of the Cadillac. Wardrobe hoped to be gone before Willie came back. He had told Diana he wanted no part of him, or his crazy talk, but it was too late. They walked out of the house and were greeted by Willie and Doug. Steelman sent Diana down to the store, handing her a wadded up dollar for a pack of Marlboros.

"Headin' back to Arizona man, wish you were goin' with us."

"Naw Bill, don't think so. Gotta start my new job today."

"You know, Doug and me were talkin'. We're gonna go back down south and come back in a few weeks with a shit load of pot. You think you and Lester can move some of it for me?"

Cliff tried to remain uncommitted, knowing Bill had a way of sucking you in. "Hell, Bill, you know, there's always someone lookin' for a little smoke."

"Shit! No lie man. Always!"

Within a few minutes Diana returned to interrupt the conversation. She handed Bill the cigarettes and stood next to Cliff signaling the meeting was over. Those who lived in the house were on their way out. Cliff offered to let them stay until the landlord came by that night, and Willie took him up on it. Now that it was clear he couldn't count on Cliff's help, and wasn't bold enough to do it alone, he decided to put off the United Market for awhile. He was willing to wait because he was sure of one thing now. When it went down - and it would go down - then Cliff and everyone else would realize Bill Steelman wasn't just a lot of talk.

He and Doug went back into Lodi that night. Willie treated Doug at his old hangout; the Texas Burger Drive-in across from the Tokay Bowl on Cherokee Lane. And he apparently caught up with Greg Flahtery too, because he was spotted riding around later in the blue Corvair.

15

Saturday, October 20, 1973 | 10 am.

It was a perfect Saturday. That seamless day that somehow separates summer and fall in California. It was a drive-to-town dime store kind of Saturday. A blue jean and sweatshirt Saturday of raking leaves and front lawn football. A Saturday morning of yard sales and the family station wagon in the driveway with the hood up. At the Hollywood Cafe, customers continued their weekend ritual of eggs, coffee and conversation. The overnight dew had evaporated quickly, and the autumn chill of daybreak was replaced by the warmth of the morning sun that filtered through the trees; massive, majestic trees of yellow and gold, amber and orange, that towered over the busy streets of town. And behind them now, on this perfect, brilliant Saturday, all of this hustle and bustle, all of this sense of connection and community, all of this which was Lodi, disappeared in the rearview mirror.

The Volkswagen labored west on Highway 12, passing fruit stands, flatbed trailers, and small stuccoed houses standing guard over a sea of smooth chocolate colored earth. They crossed through farmland and over the bridges that span the twisting waterways of the delta; Rio Vista, Suisun City, and storefront crossroads without a name. Downshifting and sputtering over even the smallest of hills, the van managed the speed limit but no more, and was eventually passed by cars in even more of a hurry. To the coast the van was headed; Sonoma, Mendocino, Bodega Bay and the luring prospects of a drug buy. Willie knew the area well because this was where the dope was. The north coast of California had always been one of the most fertile areas for weed, and if it wasn't being grown in the coastal forests, then it was being unloaded from small boats in the privacy of hidden harbors. Concealed as fishing boats, they made clandestine trips to Mexico and back, sneaking in under the cover of the forever fog and low overcast. Willie knew the connections here, or so he claimed, and he hoped they could trade some of their coke for a bigger stash of grass. Or better yet, maybe convince an old associate to let them have some on consignment, with the promise of big appetites and bigger dollars in Arizona. Such talk excited Doug, for he carried an insatiable taste for all things dope.

As the morning turned to afternoon, they continued to drive, leaving the blue skies behind, for ahead of them was a blanket of huge charcoal-gray clouds, and as they turned up Highway 101, giant drops began hitting the windshield, and soon the Volkswagen descended into the gathering rain.

When Doug walked out on his wife and baby back in December, he had no map, no plan, he just headed west. He pointed the M.G. to the coast he had heard so much about and took off. Nonstop, all the way to the Pacific Ocean, he thought, just so he could feel it for himself. Now he was almost there. It was nearly dusk and the dark skies had cut the daylight hours even further. The highway twisted and curved, following the river's path to the ocean, so close now he could even smell the salt air as it poured over the hillsides that separated them from the sea.

They had stopped several times that afternoon when Willie needed a pay phone. He was always talking, but there was no word yet of any deal, so they kept driving. Doug followed Willie's directions but the van was running rough. "Points," Doug was quick to say, noticing out loud the problem was getting worse with every mile. But he was good at babying the engine. He considered it an art, a touch, a talent that could not be taught. He was master of riding the clutch, and when it sounded like the van was about to stall, he gently kissed the gas and brought the engine back to life. It barely made each grade – coughing and misfiring every time he shifted gears – but Doug took pride in overtaking and conquering each small hill. Willie knew they would need to either fix it, or swipe another car soon. "Burnt points," Doug repeated. Willie knew little about cars or what was wrong when they didn't run. It was the one area his partner had over him, so Doug was, for the first time today, vocal and animated. When they pulled off of Highway 116 and onto the Coast Highway 1, Doug saw the black sheet of ocean out ahead of him. At the exact same time the Volkswagen died, and Doug managed to muscle the van over onto the shoulder of the road.

"It's the fucking points," he repeated.

It was raining now, steady and cold. The wind off the ocean knifed through them as them climbed out to take a look. Doug lifted the lid up on the engine compartment, but it was dark and the faint glow from Willie's lighter was little help. To make matters worse, there were no tools in the van, so Doug fumbled around with makeshift screwdrivers using keys and coins.

For nearly two hours they huddled over the rear of the bus, the rear window up to ward off the rain. But it was no use. The wind blew the rain sideways and into their faces. Cars passed by but Willie was cautious about flagging one down. Highway 1 was a well traveled road and he would feel better about their situation if they were in a more out of the way place.

When it was clear they weren't going to get the van running, Willie decided to leave it. They removed the firearms from their cases, then tossed the cases over the side of the road and into the shrubbery. Doug wiped the car down while Willie waited. He pulled his brown leather jacket tight around him, as much to hide the .22 as to protect him from the cold.

A Sonoma County Sheriff cruiser whisked by, but didn't stop. Deputy Carr spotted the two men walking near the van and made a mental note to return later. Normally, given the late hour and the inclement weather, he would have stopped to check it out, or at least offer them a ride, but he was on a call and couldn't be delayed. He did however jot down the license number for future reference if needed.

Willie and Doug headed back north, crossing the bridge over the Russian River just before it spills into the sea, and then east on Highway 116 towards the resort communities that dot the river. The closest town was at least 7 or 8 miles away and the rain was not about to let up. In front of them the saw headlights from a car stopped up ahead. As it started towards them again, Willie jumped out into the road and waved his arms for them to stop.

Tonight was the first time, and the last, that Jim Fulkerson ever went out with Eilleen Hallock. He wasn't much of the dating kind, but she seemed different – a little younger and a little wild – which was more to his liking than most of the girls he knew.

Eilleen was only 17 and still in high school, but she had heard about Jim. He had a reputation of being a bit excessive and sometimes even stupid in the things he got himself into. But despite that, or because of it, she agreed to go out with him, but just this once. There were no plans, just drive around and talk, Jim told her, but he decided to go all out anyway and borrow his grandmother's bright yellow '67 Chevy Nova two door. There was only one drawback to the car. It had no license plates, front or rear. A minor concern, Jim decided. He stopped by to get Eilleen, found someone to buy him a six-pack, and headed towards the coast.

Jim was used to picking up hitchhikers. Most of the time he was the one by the side of the road, waiting for the kindness of a stranger. The area was full of young people, out on adventure, hitching to nowhere, and in no particular hurry to get there. Even with a date and the pressure to impress her, Jim didn't give it a second thought when he saw someone standing by the side of the road up ahead.

A young woman stranded with car trouble. She climbed into the front seat with Jim and Eilleen and the Nova continued on. But no more than 50 yards down the highway; their headlights hit the outline of a man standing in the middle of the road, his arms signaling madly for them to pull over.

Jim did so, but also noticed another man, who until they got closer, had been out of view. He rolled the window down and heard the greeting from the hitchhikers standing in the murky drizzle.

"Car broke down. Need a ride to a station."

Jim said they were going only as far as Jenner, a couple of miles up the road. The young woman with no name said there was a station right across the street from her house. Jim was certain that any place in town would be closed, it being almost 10 pm, and he didn't want to spend his one evening with Eilleen looking for a garage. He hedged for a moment before deciding he could at least get them to town. He leaned forward, pulled the seat with him and Willie and Doug slipped into the back.

They dropped the woman off at her house, but as Jim suspected, the station was closed. He felt sorry for the two men and offered them a ride back to Monte Rio. Surely they could find help there. Once more they retraced their steps back down Highway 116, Willie making his usual small talk from the backseat as he pulled the .22 out from under his coat.

"Hey, could you pull over?" Willie asked. "I think I lost my wallet around here."

Jim agreed, still trying to be of assistance, but as he pulled off the road, Willie placed the gun on the back of his head.

"Now you listen. If you give us any shit, we'll blow you away just like we did the CHP pig!" Eilleen turned around to see the shape of the gun and she let out a gasp. Jim felt the gun, too scared to turn around to face it. Doug now had his shotgun out and pointed at the girl. "You're our way out," Willie continued, "and you're gonna take us to Santa Clara and do exactly as we say, or else!"

After the initial shock, Jim decided to play cool and go along with them. "No problem," he said, trying to sound as calm as he could with a gun in his ear. He didn't know much about guns, but this thing felt like a cannon. "We'll take you anywhere you wanna go."

Willie didn't flinch or remove the .22 from Jim's head. He was thinking furiously, desperate to figure out his next move.

Jim, on the other hand, was talking. He was talking a lot, jabbering because he was scared, but not wanting to let it show. His only concern was what Eilleen thought of him, embarrassed to have gotten her in such trouble. He wanted to come up with something smart to say, something that would make these two think twice about what they were doing, but managed to blurt out the only thing he could think of that could possibly make a difference to the men in back.

"I gotta tell ya right now, there aren't no license plates on this car. None. If you killed a cop, there's gonna be CHP everywhere. They're gonna stop us."

Without missing a beat Willie responded. "If they do, hit the floorboards. I'll fuckin' blow them away!"

Shut up and drive, he barked, and take all the back roads until the Golden Gate Bridge. Jim knew the country well, but the guy in the back seemed lost. Jim turned the car around and decided to take the Coast Highway down. There were plenty of lightly traveled roads he could take from there. The pistol was no longer at his head, but rested on the seat, still aimed at him. The Chevy crossed back south over the bridge at Russian River, and Willie pointed up the road. "There's our van."

Jim looked over and spotted a Volkswagen bus in the headlights.

"Fuckin' highway patrol stopped us and tried to search it," Willie spat, "so we shot him, put him back in his car and ran it over the cliff."

Jim cringed at such talk. He looked again at the van as they drove by.

"See the blood?" Willie pointed out. "See the blood all over the side of it? That's his fucking blood all over the side of that thing!"

Jim looked hard but couldn't see what the guy was talking about. But just in case, he realized he had better get on these guys' good side, so he rummaged around for things to talk about.

"Listen, might as well tell you who we are. My name's Jim and this is Eilleen."

Surprisingly, the gunman responded. "I'm Bill and this here Doug. We call him Loki."

"Well, Bill, we got no problem taking you to Santa Clara, or wherever it is you guys need to go. No problem at all." Eilleen looked over at Jim as he spoke, nodding in agreement. "I don't know much about guns," he continued. "What kind you got there?"

Willie paused for a moment, looked at the pistol, then again aimed it straight ahead, staring one-eyed down the barrel and pointed directly at the radio in the middle of the dash.

"This here is a .44 Magnum," he answered in his best Dirty Harry, "and if fired right now, it would blow a hole right through to the engine and stop it dead."

"Man!" Jim exclaimed, feigning excitement, "that's some kinda gun!"

He continued driving south through Oceanview and Bodega Bay, where the highway leaves the water and heads inland. The two in the backseat had pulled the guns away and were now just whispering between themselves. Sometimes Willie laughed out loud, pointing the pistol out the side window, pretending to shoot at a target somewhere in the darkness. He had loosened up considerably now; downright chatty, actually, offering his opinions on music and politics and what dope gave the best high. Even Doug, who seldom spoke at all to strangers, talked about his life back in New York and his recent travels to Wyoming. Willie rolled a joint and passed it around, but he made Jim toss the beer out, afraid that if they got stopped an open container charge could bust them. But the dope flowed, and Willie rolled another one. The four grew more comfortable with each other, even singing to a Kris Kristopherson song on the radio. "Lord help me Jesus, I'm wasted. . ."

And they laughed and got stoned while Willie told them all about Phoenix and the good dope found down there. They were going back too, he promised, if nothing more than to get out of this shitty rain.

It had been almost an hour and they were coming into Petaluma, Eilleen's hometown. She wished she could just get out and run as fast as she could, but she said nothing about living there. Even though things had calmed down, she was still afraid about what was going to happen to them. Jim was nervous too, but felt his plan might be working. The guys in the back acted a lot more relaxed than before.

Back onto 101, from Petaluma south towards San Francisco, but the traffic made Willie nervous, and he wasn't nearly as friendly now. He stared over to the other side of the highway, watched cars sail by the other way, and saw the huge screen of the Midway Drive In. He decided this Jim guy was trying to pull a fast one. "Thought I told you to take only back roads! You got us out in the middle of a fucking freeway! Turn off here."

Jim started to protest, to explain that there just weren't anymore back roads to the City, but he decided against it. He just did as he was told, pulling off on

San Antonio Road and heading east into the rolling foothills on what became barely a two lane road. It was dark and desolate, and once again Jim panicked. The weed wasn't strong enough to make that go away.

Up ahead was a sign that read *Marshall.* Willie told Jim to pull over. They were out in the middle of nowhere.

"Okay, both of you, out!" Willie yelled. He nudged at Eilleen too, and they opened the doors.

"We decided to tie the both of you up and leave you right here. No more screwing around. Then we're gonna take your car to the airport." He grabbed Jim by the arm and led him back away from the car while he looked at Eileen. "First we're gonna fix up your boyfriend, so you stay right here where we can see you. I'll be watching you, and if you move I swear I'll blow your head off. Understand?"

She nodded.

Yanking his arm, Willie dragged Jim to the graveled edge of the road where Doug yanked his wrists up behind him and tied them with a small piece of cord. They marched him up the hill. It had stopped raining now, but the earth was soft and damp. At the crest of the hill Jim could see a lone oak tree in the distance, but could no longer see Eilleen or the car she was told to stand next to. They continued to poke him with their guns, and Jim finally gave into his fear about what was coming.

"Hold it right here!" Willie barked. "Sit down and take your boots off."

He obeyed and the two men knelt down beside him. Doug pulled a large knife from the sheath on his belt and Jim swallowed hard. Doug pulled the toes of his socks away from his feet and slit them up the side. He twisted and tied them together, firmly binding Jim's ankles. Willie yelled at him to kneel down and not look up. Again Doug came up behind him and fastened his belt around Jim's shoulders, cinching it tight. Jim bowed his head, the cool mud only inches from his face. He closed his eyes, knowing deep inside what was coming next.

When he was sixteen, Jim claimed to have had what he later said was a religious experience, and it temporarily guided him to a somewhat more righteous lifestyle. Even at sixteen, he had fully experimented with alcohol and drugs, and because school was a drag, getting smashed and driving fast was infinitely more fun. And yet, for a short time after this experience, he managed to steer clear of all of that. It surprised him that he was really trying to do the right thing. He even prayed. He didn't really know how, he thought, but he could talk to God like he could talk to a friend. It was just that easy, and he was certain that either God was tugging at him, or Jim was seeking Him out. He was never sure, but his soul ached for something true and real. There were times he was so close to God he felt like he could touch him, let Him wrap His arms around him so tight he could never get away.

But He did. Jim felt God leave, so it wasn't long before he was back to his old tricks, and for the past several years he carried the guilt of giving up on Him. He had denied the Lord, he was certain, and he wondered if he would ever get another chance. And now this. The only thing he could think of was, that if he could have only stayed straight he wouldn't be in this jam. So he laid there in the mud and waited for the worse to happen, for God's wrath to finally be revealed, knowing it was all his fault.

As his body buckled down, waiting for the end, a surprising calm overcame him. Even as he felt the barrel of the gun on the back of his head, he wasn't scared. There was an awkward joy to this moment and a wicked little smile came to him, although he was careful not to let it show. He squeezed his eyelids tight, knowing the end would come quickly, and for that he was thankful.

"Where's Efrem and the FBI when you need them?" he joked to himself, picturing the TV star racing in out of the darkness to his rescue. That stupid image, he figured, would be his last thought.

The gun rested at the base of his skull for what seemed like forever. But he never heard a shot. Never felt the impact of the bullet, although he was curious about what it was going to feel like, and if it would hurt. He was breathing rapidly, but he remained silent, never once pleading for his life, never begging. His strength surprised him and he was proud of how he was handling this. *So where's the bullet?* he asked himself.

Finally he spoke, but moved not an inch, his eyes still squeezed tight, and almost with a wince he asked. "I know I don't have much say in this, but please don't hurt Eilleen, okay? Please, don't hurt her."

The gun was pulled back and he heard the guy who was at the end of it walk away. There was more muttering in the background. Jim relaxed, took a deep breath and remembered his short-lived conversion a few years back. He had nothing to lose. *You know, God,* he whispered to himself, *I haven't talked to you in quite awhile, but it looks like I'll be coming to see you real soon. I hope you have room for me.*

At which time the gunman returned and stood over him, announcing somewhat dejectedly, "I don't know why I can't do it. I had every intention of blowing your fucking head off." He reached down and untied him. He helped Jim to his feet while Doug stood by, glaring at the both of them.

"My friend here says we should still cut your throat." And Jim believed every word. They walked back down to the car, leaving Jim's boots on top of the hill. But the initial sense of relief turned to panic! They had been gone a long time. What if Eilleen had left? They would certainly kill him then! He didn't want her hurt, but he prayed again to God that she be standing at the car as she had been told.

As they came down off the hill, he saw her silhouette in the darkness, arms folded, shivering in the cold. He thought how so incredibly beautiful she looked standing there. He had never been so happy to see someone in his entire life. She looked at his bare feet, then right into his eyes, but had the sense not to ask any questions.

They climbed back in the Chevy. This time Jim stayed on the back roads as much as possible, not wanting to chance his good fortune. However, they could only get as far as Novato before he had to get back onto Highway 101, and he warned Willie of this.

The more Willie thought about the episode on the hilltop, the more it bothered him. This guy was strong, he thought. Too righteous for his own good. Either he was too stoned to care, or he was one brave dude. Then again, maybe he had something up his sleeve. Willie thought it over hard, wondering if he was the man he believed himself to be. He wondered what Doug thought about him. They were back on the highway again but it was well after midnight and traffic was light. He handed a roach clip to Jim, who accepted and took a hit. "You're a little too brave, man." Willie said. "You're gonna try something, aren't cha?"

"No way!" Jim replied. "No way, man. I told you we would take you anywhere you wanna go. Just tell us where.

"Turn here."

Again the yellow Nova pulled off the highway and into the parking lot of a Holiday Inn. Jim hit the brakes and stopped the car behind a tall hedge hiding them from the traffic racing by. Once again Willie ordered him out of the car. "Gimme the keys," he demanded.

Jim handed them over and Willie went around and opened the trunk. He told him to get in, and Jim knew better than to resist. Willie slammed the lid closed, then got behind the wheel, with Eilleen safely between he and Doug. Back on 101, they drove south, crossing the Golden Gate and through downtown San Francisco. Doug had arrived, with all the sights he had dreamed about out in front of him; the lights outlining the high rises and those that framed the western avenues as they narrowed and disappeared towards the ocean. He looked out the window, but didn't say anything.

Eilleen relaxed a bit, figuring they couldn't hurt her or Jim as long as they were driving. It seemed Bill was now more familiar with where he was. He pointed out street names and places he had been. He told her stories about landmarks and cities with Spanish names, and with each, taking the time to explain what their names meant in English.

They got to Santa Clara about two in the morning, and pulled beneath an overpass. He told Eilleen to get out. She was startled by his quick turn around and the anger now evident in his voice. He walked to the back of the car, the shotgun in his right hand. He grabbed Eilleen. "You and me are gonna take a little walk and you're gonna give me whatever I ask for. Got it?"

Eilleen twisted her arm away to resist his advance. Jim heard her start to argue and so badly wanted to tell her to shut up and go along, certain Bill was having second thoughts about letting him live.

"Hey!" he heard Bill growl. "You'll do what I want or I'll blow a sonofabitchin' hole in the fuckin' trunk!"

"No, wait a minute!" she relented, tugging at his arm. "Don't hurt us, I'll do what you want."

Doug waited for them in the car as Willie pulled Eilleen into the shrubbery. He knew what was going on; the sick shit in his partner's head. He wasn't into that. It didn't turn him on like it did Bill. He never saw the excitement in it. Couldn't imagine being that strong or that horny. He figured it was him that was the twisted one because most guys he knew seemed to get off on the control freak rough stuff. It was the one thing that made him feel less about Bill, although he never told him so.

He heard rustling in the bushes, but it had only been a few minutes. He knew Bill hadn't performed. Doug was smug, and lowered his eyes to avoid looking at them as they slid back into the front seat. Willie said nothing as he gunned the engine and tore away.

A few minutes later he stopped in a parking lot and let Jim out of the trunk. Not more than a couple hundred feet away, Jim saw two police cars parked right next to each other, engines running, headlights beaming out into the night.

Willie stared at them too, uttering not a single word. He pulled the .22 to his side, as if daring them to try something.

16

Sunday, October 21, 1973 | 3 am.

Three am on a Sunday. It didn't get much worse than this. They had been kidnapped, robbed, tied up, had a gun shoved in their ear, locked in the trunk of a car, into the bushes to be raped and dragged up a hill to die. Yet somehow they were still alive. Jim had no idea what was being said up front - all he heard was mumbling - but he worried about Eilleen and how she was doing without him.

Before his mood spun around and he yanked her from the car, Eilleen had asked Bill how he knew where he was going. He said he used to live nearby in Palo Alto, and that he worked the state mental hospital there. "I know you ain't gonna believe me, but I'm a registered nurse. I like helping people, especially older ones."

Eilleen thought that odd, and decided he was right, she didn't believe him. From the very start she had a hard time figuring out when he was lying to her, and when he wasn't.

She recognized Doug's accent. "New York," he answered. "Born and raised on the east coast. Only been out west for less than a year." Both he and Willie bragged about serving time in prison, although they never said what for, and she wasn't sure she would believe them anyway, regardless of what they claimed.

After Jim was released from the trunk, he and Eilleen sat in the back while Willie drove, to nowhere, really, for what seemed like hours. One time they even stopped under an overpass to try and take a nap, without success, so Willie drove some more. The sun came up. There were more people out on the road. Paranoia was setting in again. He skirted away from the main highway, hiding on the side streets and frontage roads, looking without success for another car to steal. Frustrated, he swung back onto Highway 101 and headed south.

Then it hit him. He knew right where he could get a car – a new car – and all he had to do was walk in and take it. He turned back up over the highway and found the street in Mountain View where Denise used to work.

In 1970, when he and Denise lived in Santa Clara for a few months, she was employed at a business called Cirtel; one of the hundreds of small electronic companies springing up overnight in what was being called the Silicon Valley. She worked and Willie loafed, smoked dope, buying and selling on the side, wasting the day driving around. What little money she brought home, Willie took, and the two lived those months in poverty. Willie dropped her off at work, and then spent the day acting like he was looking for a job.

Cirtel was located in the middle of a large industrial park and built over a small underground garage. Willie found the place and drove down into the darkness. The cars were still there, and if he remembered correctly, the keys would be right inside the back door. Willie rifled through Jim and Eilleen's wallets, looking for money and credit cards. He removed photos, asking who they were, getting names and phone numbers of friends and relatives. When he was finished he tossed the wallets into the back seat and threatened them. "Now, I've got the names of your friends and I know where you guys live. If you tell any of this to the pigs, I swear to you that I will make one phone call and have my people kill both of you. Do you understand me?"

He got out and disappeared inside. Moments later the sound of breaking glass signaled he had found what he was looking for. He grabbed the keys, rustled without luck through a desk drawer looking for cash, and when he returned, Doug got out and helped him put their guns and backpacks into the trunk of a large brown Ford sedan parked next to them. Willie repeated his warning. "Now you remember what I said. We're taking this car and it's gonna be hot in a few hours. You wait here for a while before you even think about leaving. Got it? Because I want you to know I could be sitting right up there at the corner watching the both of you."

He turned to walk away, then stopped and stuck his head back in the open window and smirked, "Oh yeah. You two be careful now."

The Ford pulled away and Jim waited a several minutes before finding the courage to leave the basement garage. Out onto the main road, Jim noticed the gas gauge was on empty and every dime they had was gone. At 10:30 Sunday morning, not a mile from where Willie had left them, at the top of a busy overpass, the Nova ran out of gas.

Traffic quickly backed up behind them and Jim got out to wave everyone around, wondering what else could possibly go wrong. A car pulled up and stopped, and a well-dressed black man got out. Jim tossed his hands up in exasperation. "Out of gas," he apologized, but he said nothing of what they had been through. The stranger offered him a ride to a nearby station and Jim answered they had no money. He told Jim to get in, he would pay for the gas. After returning to the car, Jim extended his hand along with a sincere thank you. The man put his hand out as well, and in it was the $15 left over from the gas.

"We just got back from church, son, and we just had a nice big breakfast. I want you two to enjoy the same. Take the money and good luck." The man walked back to his car and waited to make sure the kid had the car running again.

Desperate to get at far away as possible, Jim and Eilleen hit the 101 north, not daring to stop until they got back to San Francisco. At the Hippopotamus Restaurant on Van Ness they spent the money on lunch and agreed not to tell anyone what happened. No one was hurt, nothing much was taken, and the risk of calling the cops was far too great, and it was early afternoon when Jim dropped Eileen off at her house in Petaluma, which was, coincidently, right across the street from the police station.

But at 2 o'clock Jim got a phone call from a very frantic Eilleen. When her parents jumped on her for being out all night, she broke down and told them the story, trying her best to convince them all this madness had actually happened. If this is true, they said, then she had to go to tell the police. Seeing this as the only way out of a jam with her folks, Eilleen tearfully gave in.

Initially, thinking she was just another promiscuous teenager trying to cover her tracks, the police didn't buy her story, but she managed to convince them to at least call her friend and find out for themselves. When Jim gave the same account, they reconsidered. Also realizing this was out of their jurisdiction, they called Sonoma County Sheriff's office in Santa Rosa and made arrangements for someone to transport Miss Hallock to their office. Jim was instructed to be there as well.

Arriving at 2:30 accompanied by Deputy Washburn, Eilleen was introduced to Detective Robert Nelson. He listened to her story and a few minutes later to Jim Fulkerson's as well. It sounded a little too wild to believe, but what did concern Nelson was the part about the two suspects bragging they had killed a Highway Patrolman. While there had been nothing reported about any missing officer in their area, he broke away long enough to have dispatch start counting heads, not only among their staff, but Santa Rosa Police and CHP officers as well. Ultimately, everyone was accounted for.

Nelson felt it all began with the van. If it was where the two kids indicated, then they could work on the rest of the story. Coincidently, his call to verify the location of the vehicle went directly to Deputy Carr, the same officer who had noticed it the night before. He indeed recalled the Volkswagen, as well as two men walking away from it.

Within thirty minutes, word came back the van in question was still parked along Highway 1. Within the hour, it was impounded and towed to Noonan's Garage in Guerneville; a small town along the Russian River. Because it was Sunday, getting a search warrant for the vehicle would be difficult, so Nelson decided any evidence inside the Volkswagen would have to stay there, a delay, he admitted, that could prove costly. He ran the license number and found the registered owner to be a Robert Peters of Phoenix. The two kids said the men claimed to be from Arizona, so after a call was placed there, officers in Arizona promised to check out the listed address and get back to him. For the time being, Peters became his number one suspect.

Earlier, during the course of the interrogation with Eilleen Hallock, Deputy

Washburn never asked, nor was he told about any sexual assault. However, later Sunday evening, while he and Nelson were reviewing the case, Nelson mentioned the young woman claimed she had been raped. Officer Washburn was sick. Nelson had assumed incorrectly that Washburn knew of the attack and had made the necessary arrangements for an exam. Now it was too late. Eileen had been allowed to return home and had certainly bathed, so any search for fluid or hair samples would be useless, and without the examination, rape charges would not hold up. That left only a kidnap charge, and knowing what he had found out about both kid's wild streak, even that one might be tough to prove.

But regardless of the setback, it was now official. Sonoma County Sheriff Detective Robert Nelson would lead the first team of law enforcement officers to search in earnest for Willie Steelman and Douglas Gretzler.

There was a time when football was Steve Loughran's first love. Everything else came in a distant second.

And he was good at it. In the fall of 1972 he lettered as a senior, making First Team Varsity, and for years to come, Coach Zimmerman remembered Loughran as one of the best defensive backs to ever play for him. But the following February, and with the season now over, he obtained the minimum credits needed in order to graduate and quit school. After that, his life began a slow crumble; a series of attitudes and circumstances that had brought him to the place he was today; eight months later, lost, broke, tired, shivering in the pouring rain of the Monterey Bay, hoping someone would give him a ride somewhere, anywhere other than where he was right now.

Steve grew up in the Marysville/Yuba City area of northern California; fertile farm country less than an hour north of Sacramento. Other than the brief time in his sophomore and junior year when his family moved to Santa Barbara, he had lived there all his life. But he returned in 1972 to do what he had long dreamed about, play varsity football for Marysville High.

And he had the size to go along with the game. By the time he was seventeen, Loughran stood over six feet and weighed at over 180 pounds. His wavy brown hair, dark eyes and broad smile, along with his status as a jock on campus, made him popular with the girls who battled for the opportunity to hook their arm through his as he walked the halls between classes. Although it had taken him over a year to grow them, he now sported big mutton-chop sideburns and he kept his hair as long as Coach Zimmerman would allow. He joined the Block M CLUB and was elected sergeant-at-arms, anxious to get involved in school activities, knowing it would look good on his application to San Diego State, where this coming autumn he would play football, he was certain.

The Loughran family had split up. Steve lived with his father across the river in Yuba City while his two younger sisters stayed with their mother outside of town. After playing his last game at Marysville, and leaving school early, Steve was on his own. He decided to take it easy that spring and summer, maybe do a little exploring, a little hitchhiking to see the countryside before having to get serious again about school. He kicked back and started roaming around.

Whether it was during this time, or while he was still in school like some of his friends believed, Steve became acquainted with marijuana. It was certainly nothing unusual, considering the times, but these days smoking dope had become a big part of his day-to-day life. His attitude changed, goals shifted, his choice of company was different. Spring and summer came and went, and in the fall Steve had still not registered at San Diego State.

His independence often took him out on the road. There was a girl near Santa Barbara worth the hassle of hitchhiking several hundred miles to see. Sometimes Steve would be gone for a week or two, maybe longer, and while his family worried, they knew their Steve was a big guy, certainly capable of taking care of himself. They didn't know about the drugs, or the circles one needed to run in to obtain them, or they would have had far more to worry about.

Steve turned 18 on October 9th and he spent that day, and several more after, at home with his family. But soon the itch to take off got the best of him and he once more headed south. On Saturday, October 20th, a friend gave him a ride to Berkeley where he spent the night. Early Sunday morning he got a lift as far as Monterey. He knew no one there, and although the weather was terrible, he decided to keep going, figuring Highway 1 down the coast to Santa Barbara was his best shot. Cold rain whipped off the Monterey Bay that afternoon, and fell so hard at times, it bounced off the pavement. Steve stood near the Mission, where the tourist traffic would give him a better chance at catching a ride. He pulled the collar of his coat up around his ears to brave off the wind and rain, his duffel bag at his feet. He thought about taking a bus, but his funds were limited. Winter would be upon them soon and Steve knew he would either have to get a car, or at least make up his mind about where he wanted to be and what he wanted to do. He had missed the fall term, but there was still plenty of time to think about the next one. There were days like these, nasty and crazy cold, when home sounded good to him again.

He spotted a brown Ford up ahead that looked promising. It slowed down and pulled over. The passenger door opened and a young blond guy with glasses waved at him to get in.

And like so many times before, Steve Allen Loughran disappeared. This time forever.

When Willie and Doug left the underground garage, there was little doubt they were heading back to Arizona. Come tomorrow morning the owners of the car would discover it missing and report it stolen, and despite his threats, he also knew the two kids would eventually go to the cops, if they hadn't done so already, so he figured he had maybe 24 hours to get back to the trailer before they would be really hot.

Their trip to the north coast had been a bust, but Willie still hoped to put together something before going back to Yahfah's. It would not look good to return empty handed, so he decided to give Santa Cruz one last shot, the place he had made so many deals with Cliff Wardrobe over the past couple of years. Hopefully he could roust a few of his old contacts and talk them into helping him out. But by early afternoon he had again come up empty. Lots of calls and nothing to show for it. It was getting late and Phoenix was who knew how far away. He would try one more time in Monterey, where he told Doug there was a guy who owed him big time.

But Willie claimed his phone calls had gone unanswered and conceded he was out of ideas. As they drove the loop near the Mission, he planned to cut over to Interstate 5 south and then from Los Angeles, east across the desert. They had very little money and the huge Ford sucked gas. What they needed was some help with expenses and Willie was now willing to use force if necessary to get it. It was important they be back at the trailer before sun up, so Willie told Doug to look for someone with a thumb out, and it wasn't long before they found him. They were well down the road before Willie bothered to ask a name and where he was headed.

"Steve" came the reply, along with, "South." But that he would ride along as far as they would take him, happy to just get out of the miserable weather. Willie passed a joint to the back seat and announced they were going to Arizona. They could take him as far as L.A. if he wanted.

Steve asked what they did for a living, and Willie laughed and replied that he and Doug work for some people in Arizona who paid them very well to handle important business matters for them. He told Doug to roll another joint. "Plenty more where that came from," Willie promised, explaining it was just one of the fringe benefits of the job. Arizona was wide open, Willie announced.

Steve said he had relatives there; a grandmother he hadn't seen in awhile, and after Willie explained how great the weather was and how much dope was around, Steve decided Arizona would be a nice detour. He asked if he could go down there with them for a while.

Willie said that would be cool and even offered him a place to stay. "If things work out," Willie offered, "I might be able to stake you to a large, rather righteous quantity of drugs."

Steve was sold. He pitched in what money he had for gas and food, and even drove some of the time. Doug slept while the other two talked. Willie never lacked for something to say, but when Steve got on the subject of football, and wouldn't shut up about it, he started getting on Willie's nerves. A couple of times Willie thought about just kicking him out of the car in the goddamn middle of nowhere.

But the big brown Ford continued to roll. Eventually Steve got quiet and fell asleep, and Willie woke Doug up to drive so he could do the same. The nighttime skies cleared over Southern California and the stars were extra large as they crossed the Colorado River and slipped back into Arizona. Soon a huge orange sun rose on the horizon, and as the sky turned pink and the desert earth violet, they hit the edge of town, creeping back through the streets of Phoenix towards the trailer on the other side of the valley.

Detective Nelson was back in his office early Monday morning to work on the Hallock-Fulkerson case. He meet with Deputy Carr to go over what he could remember about Saturday night and hopefully get a description of the two men. But the deputy wasn't much help; pretty thin, rather tall, both six feet maybe, he remembered, dark clothing, that's about it. When Nelson gave him the victim's description of the suspects, Carr shrugged and said they could indeed be the same guys he saw.

Another check to dispatch confirmed the Volkswagen had been impounded and was waiting in Guerneville. Nelson called the garage to let them know the car was involved in a possible kidnapping and was not to be touched. He also asked if they could see anything unusual about the vehicle, any blood or markings on the outside. "No. It's just a regular looking old hippie bus," came the reply.

Nelson got help preparing the search warrant, hoping to serve it that afternoon. He also called and left a message for Jim Fulkerson, requesting he bring the Nova down to the station so they could fingerprint it.

Pressing business from other cases pulled Nelson off this one for the rest of the day. The warrant was delayed as well and would have to be put off until at least tomorrow, but just before noon, Nelson did call the Phoenix Police Department to discuss the van, and its registered owner; the man known as Peters. Phoenix P.D. said they had sent a car by the address shown on the registration, but Robert Peters no longer lived there. After checking further, they learned that he not only had an extensive rap sheet in their city, but in Los Angeles and San Diego as well. According to their records Peters was heavily involved in narcotics and had served time in California for trafficking. But being 33 years of age and only 5' 9", Nelson felt Peters didn't quite fit the description given by the victims. Phoenix said they would send a photo along with his rap sheet and promised to do some follow up to see if there was any record of Peters working with an accomplice at any time. Nelson checked with DMV and got two possible addresses of Peters' current residence, both of those in Southern California. Another photo, and his driving record, was on their way. Doubt was setting in, but until he could get the pictures and run a photo lineup by the victims, he still had to figure Robert Peters was his man..

The brown LTD crossed through the downtown and retraced the path they had taken several times before, past the motels they had stayed and eventually the very street where Ken and Mike had lived.

At 30th and Van Buren, Larry Williams was trying to get a ride to work early that morning when the Ford stopped to let him in. Williams said he was heading to work in Mesa, and Willie replied they would be going right by there and there was no problem giving him a lift. They spent the next twenty minutes talking about nothing in particular and as they got closer to the place where he worked, Larry told Doug to just let him off up ahead on the corner of Extension Road and University Avenue. The place looked familiar to Willie and Doug. It was there where they had stopped a week before; the orange grove where they had let off another hitchhiker that Saturday night.

They continued on to Vista Grande and pulled in next to the trailer. The blue Chevy was gone and there was no answer at the door. The morning was bright and the sun bounced off the mobile home, warming them as they sat on the step, waiting for Bob and Yahfah to return.

Which they did within an hour. Yahfah showed surprise in seeing them, but not disappointed. Willie looked around and asked where Marsha was, and Yahfah told him they had waited as long as they could, but finally had to send her back to Denver. That's where they had been that morning, at the airport, getting her on a plane.

Willie introduced Steve, claiming he was a friend from California, although he was already tired of his company. Bob admired the new wheels they had arrived in, and Willie hinted that if things worked out right he could probably let Bob and Yahfah have the car real cheap.

Willie wanted to make sure Marsha was okay and he asked again what happened to her. He was sorry she was gone, but relieved she wasn't around in case things got heavy about Ken and Mike. He took Yahfah aside. "Now you won't have to worry about Ken giving you anymore trouble," Willie said with a wry smile. She nodded.

The rest of the day was spent laying around, listening to music and talking. Bob was proud of his stereo room, which was simply the small middle bedroom of the trailer that had all his stuff crammed into it. He and Steve got along well, which bothered Willie. Steve made a few references to the drugs Willie had talked about, and that pissed him off too. He realized that picking this kid up had been a big mistake.

It was not uncommon for some of the neighbor kids to drop by the trailer. Brinda Lee Lowery was a 15-year-old junior high student who lived nearby and had met Bob and Yahfah soon after they moved into the park a week earlier. That afternoon, on her way home from school, Brinda saw a different car in Yahfah's driveway and the sliding door wide open. She stopped in to say hi and Yahfah introduced Brinda to her friends from California.

Just before four that afternoon, Yahfah arrived for work at the Playful Kitten Massage Parlor. She seemed in a good mood, telling her boss, Barbara, that friends from California arrived that morning and were going to be in town for a few days. There was more good news, Yahfah announced. These guys have a really nice Ford, almost brand new, and that she and Bob were going to buy it off them real cheap.

But when she got off work that night, Yahfah acted disappointed it was only Bob picking her up, and that he was driving that shitty old convertible.

Willie, Doug and Steve waited back at the trailer for their return. When they did, the five of them partied well until the early morning hours.

17

Tuesday, October 23, 1973 | 12 noon.

Life inside the trailer did not resume until the day was nearly half over. Steve Loughran's life ended just a few short hours after that.

It was Bob and Yahfah's habit to sleep in late. Their evenings did not begin until after he picked her up from work, usually about eleven. Back home, they would share a little wine, sometimes cook a simple meal and always get exceptionally loaded. On occasion a new friend from the trailer park would join them.

Until recently, Yahfah seemed content with a little pot and some hash, maybe some psychedelic mushrooms, if she was so lucky. But now she craved the variety of hard stuff Bob was bringing into their home. The kitchen counter was now littered with spoons and syringes, vials of prescription drugs dispensed to a Katherine Mestites for a variety of supposed ailments. There were dozens of baby food jars, each partially filled with powders and substances unknown. Bamboo pipes and bongs rested on the living room tables along with huge glass ashtrays full of cigarette butts and spent matches.

Yahfah, who spoke of only health foods and natural healing to the impressionable Marsha back in Colorado, had taken a hard turn of late. Marsha cared only to remember the fragrance of incense and patchouli oil, but she had seen firsthand the change during the brief time she was there. The living room of the trailer was the scene of a different lifestyle. Pink matchbooks and snappy new business cards advertising the "Playful Kitten" were strewn about, along with numerous pornographic photos of Yahfah in various positions and countless expressions, but all with the same large pouting lips. Dark amber beer bottles loaded with stems and seeds were scattered among the piles of books and men's magazines.

Roach clips and rolling papers were always within arms reach. A heavy stale odor hung in the air – a mixture of herbs and weeds and chemicals – so it was not uncommon to find the sliding door open during much of the day.

Once soft spoken and agreeable, Yahfah had become vulgar and harsh. Bob Robbins may have gotten used to Yahfah's smart-ass scorn and ridicule, but Willie had not. It didn't take him long to get his fill of her astrological cosmic crap. She spent much of her time and energy droning on about her immortality and life in the hereafter, and Willie mocked her behind her back. *I've got your immortality, bitch,* he muttered, now imaging what it would be like to kill a woman. *Let's just see if you've got another life in that bag a tricks of yours.*

Today everybody and everything angered Willie. He stood back and watched the others as they moved about the trailer, hating their habits, despising their talk, even the very way they looked. It pissed him off, every last little thing, and he could sense the rage building inside him again.

Steve Loughran wasn't helping matters any. He barraged Willie with the promise made about all the drugs. "Shit, what gives man?" Steve questioned. He was putting Steelman on the spot, making him look bad in front of the others.

Bob took Yahfah to work around three-thirty, and when they left, Willie's hassle with Loughran came to blows. He had an inch or two on Willie, and at least thirty pounds, so when push came to shove, he stood up and met Willie head on. They started arguing and yelling, but Steelman was not about to duke it out with this guy, and he disappeared into the back room. Grabbing his .22, and Bob's sleeping bag, he walked to the front room and stared down at Loughran. He pointed the gun in Steve's face, yanked him up off the sofa and marched him outside.

From the front window of the trailer you could look east over the low block wall surrounding the Vista Grande and across the empty field adjoining it. Directly in front of you are the Superstition Mountains, and just a few miles from Bob and Yahfah's rented single wide, the cliffs rose straight up from the desert floor. The spell of the mountain had lured people for centuries, and today it was Willie Steelman who could not resist.

He never hesitated, as if the force of the Superstitions themselves pulled him. Steve bucked and kicked, but with a gun in his ear, could only stumble out towards the Ford, where Doug pushed him hard into the back seat.

Straight down University they drove until they ran out of road. They crossed the highway, and then up the rutted dirt trails that cut and weaved up through the rugged foothills, past the quiet Mining Camp Restaurant and its Texas-sized dirt parking lot. Empty this afternoon, it looked very much like the ghost town it tried so hard to emulate. Dust billowed from the Ford as it twisted its way to the base of the mountain. When they eventually ran out of road, the car stopped, and Willie again ordered everyone out.

He marched Steve Loughran to the edge of a fence and pointed him down into a small gully. They staggered along the wash another two or three hundred feet. Steve, then Willie, then Doug, who in the late afternoon of 90 degree day, carried the sleeping bag, stumbling along, trying to keep up.

At the bottom of the wash, Willie and Steve turned and faced each other. Willie wasted no time. He exploded; cursing and slapping Steve across the head, the .22 pointed at his face. He demanded his wallet, and Steve handed it over. Willie fanned through it and then tossed it back to his partner. He was on fire now. His eyes burned and his temples throbbed. He strutted about, Doug watching, mimicking his moves, dancing around the perimeter like a prizefighter. The more Steve flinched and whimpered, the more powerful and important Willie felt. He could no longer contain himself. He snatched the sleeping bag and tossed it down at Loughran' s feet. "Get in!" he demanded.

"What?"

"Get the fuck in!" Willie screamed. "Head first. . .GET IN!"

Steve fumbled and found the opening. He pulled it down over his head, overwhelmed from the heat, smothered by the lack of air, but he crawled all the way in, standing upright, where only his brown shoes showed at the bottom of the bag. He cussed Willie, but his words were only a murmur.

Willie spun him around and Loughran rocked like a blindfolded drunk. Willie kept his hand on the top of the bag, groping wildly for Steve's head, and when he found it, he grabbed hold, like he was palming a basketball. He placed the barrel of the .22 next to his outstretched hand. The wash went silent. The hot dusty wind quieted. No one spoke. No one breathed. Willie could wait no more, and squeezed the trigger.

The pistol snapped and jerked. Willie held on long enough to feel the warmth of the blood ooze out upon his hand. He heard the gush of the last breath exit from the body, and its life sigh as the bag crumpled and the body collapsed in the welcome shade of a small Palo Verde tree.

It felt good. God, it felt good! So good that he would soon forget the name, but never the rush of the moment. But the rage departed quickly, and when it did, Willie looked up and walked away, Doug shadowing close behind. They retraced their path back to the highway as Doug fumbled again through the wallet. When they hit the main road, he tossed it out the window, only a few dollars richer for the effort.

Back onto University, and not more than a half mile from the Vista Grande, the right rear tire blew out, a victim of the rugged path taken up the mountain. For the next few minutes they stood along side the car, wondering if they should fix it or just screw it. As traffic brushed by them, Willie decided it was just too risky to be standing out there in the open, so they limped back to the trailer on the rim.

Within a few minutes he had the hubcap off and the ass end of the big Ford up on a jack. But it was too much work, so he tossed the handle on the driveway and went back inside the trailer.

Randy Zimmer stopped by. He was one of Bob's friends and Robbins proudly showed him the new car he was going to buy. As the two of them looked over the vehicle, flat tire and all, Willie strolled out to offer his two cents. "Fucker's got bullet-proof glass all around," he bragged. Randy looked over at him. Willie was staring down at the side of it, pointing at the fender. "Reinforced panels too. Here's where we took a 12 gauge to it to try it out." He rubbed his hand over a big section covered in gray bondo.

Randy left and Willie and Doug spent the rest of the evening with Bob. When

Yahfah get home, they stayed up most of the night. Willie said nothing about Steve, and nobody asked.

Just before eight o'clock that same evening, Mrs. Pat Johnson, a friend of Ken and Mike, called the Phoenix Police. No one had seen either one of them for almost a week and she had an awful feeling something terrible had happened. She and her husband, Vic, had gone over to the boy's place earlier to take another look and this time Pat got the nerve to go inside.

It was obvious they had left in a hurry. The front door was unlocked and Ken's kitten cried to be fed. Yet nothing appeared missing and even their clothing and travel items had not been taken.

Officer Cortez responded to the call and discovered a note from Ken's brother left on the counter, also expressing concern over their disappearance.

Two missing person reports were filed that night, one on each man. Vic Johnson said he had heard Ken talk about two bikers from Colorado who had followed them down to Phoenix and were threatening them. Now certain these guys were somehow involved, he told the officer there was a massage parlor on Perry Lane in Tempe and a girl who worked there who called herself Yahfah. He didn't know her real name, but she was supposedly Ken's girlfriend once, so maybe she knew something.

Cortez asked Tempe Police to send a car by the massage parlor. Perry Lane was in an unincorporated industrial area of Tempe, its rutted gravel street lined with old metal buildings and trashy trailers. Tempe Police knew the place well; seemed like every night a call came in about a drunk being knifed or a prostitute getting beat up. They found the massage parlor easy enough, but nobody inside was willing to cough up anything on anyone named Yahfah.

18

Wednesday, October 24, 1973 | 9 am.

When Randy Zimmer drove over to the Vista Grande about five o'clock the night before to see Bob Robbins, he had noticed a brown Ford with a flat tire pulled off the side of the road not far from the entrance to the trailer park. So needless to say he was a bit surprised to see the same car an hour later jacked up in the driveway at Bob and Yahfah's place.

There was another thing he thought was strange. He was sure that one of the guys standing next to the car out on University was Robbins. When he went over to see Bob later that night, he asked him about it. Bob acted as if he had no idea what Randy was talking about. Their conversation was interrupted when the owner of the car came out and started talking about all the bulletproof glass and shotguns and stuff. Randy asked Bob again about it later, but he never did get a straight answer.

He never would. Bob Robbins would be dead before the day was over.

Eight hundred miles away in Santa Rosa, Sheriff Detective Nelson, loaded with a backlog of other cases, decided to call in some help on his kidnapping investigation. One of those who answered the call was Officer Butch Carlstedt, who this morning had obtained the warrant to search the Volkswagen. By now the van had been moved again, this time to the protected garage of the Sheriff's building downtown.

But before the van's contents were examined, the Mountain View Police notified Carlstedt they had reached the owner of the business where the victims were left and the Ford stolen. Carlstedt drove down to Mountain View and was introduced to Mr. Wod of Circuit Technologies Inc. Of the four businesses located in the building, only his had been broken into, and even then, only the cabinet holding the car keys and a desk drawer was disturbed. The car taken bore no markings linking it to Cirtel, so Carlstedt was confident whoever stole the car, and kidnapped the young couple as well, had to have prior knowledge and access to the business.

Mr. Wod supplied them with a list of employees and several ex-employees he felt were the most likely suspects. They soon whittled that down to a single candidate, a man who Mountain View Police had already located and were in the process of questioning. Carlstedt scanned the sheet. This was not their guy. The man in question stood only about 5'5" and was Oriental, hardly fitting either suspect's description.

The search stopped there, and Mountain View and Sonoma authorities parted company. On Wednesday, the 24th, three days after the crime, the city police department finally placed an APB on the stolen Ford and the two suspects, promising to advise Sonoma County if they got anything.

Back in Santa Rosa, Carlstedt picked up the warrant that made their search of the van a legal one. While an I.D. officer snapped pictures, he removed and tagged items found inside. There wasn't anything that deserved much attention: a small jar and an empty gallon jug, gym shorts and a red nylon windbreaker, a straw hat and a bumper sticker from a radio station, along with some of the usual fast food wrappers. The only real items of interest were a map of Denver, and a *Los Angeles Times* newspaper dated October 18, 1973. There were no weapons, no blood, no names, not a lead, not a clue, not even a scrap of incriminating evidence. Just the same, the van and its contents were dusted for prints and the items booked into the property room for storage.

Sonoma authorities continued to look at the teletype, follow up on calls from other jurisdictions, but their investigation into the kidnapping and assault of Jim Fulkerson and Eilleen Hallock hit a dead end Wednesday afternoon.

It was yet another ninety-degree day in Phoenix and no one took the brunt of it more than the sheet metal houses at the Vista Grande. The swamp coolers strained to keep up, swirling an artificial cool down upon those inside space 133.

But Willie's high was on this new sense of power, a trip that even he was amazed with. He was in complete control. He was now the one who decided who would live and who would die. It was so simple. A single word, a mere look, even a bad attitude could help him determine who might be next. There would be others, that much he knew.

Willie sat back and watched Bob and Yahfah, sizing them up, gauging their value. Ken and Mike had been worthless to him, and so was the kid in the sleeping bag yesterday. And now this afternoon, as he watched Bob and Yahfah act out their stupid little lives, he realized they had little value to him either.

Bob is the biggest joke of all, Willie decided. He's nothing more than her flunky. He scoots around like he's cleaning the house while she's out turning tricks. He takes her to work, then picks her up when she's finished screwing every guy with a twenty dollar bill in his hand. Yahfah earns the bread and Bob damn well better have everything straightened up by the time she gets home, or else. And then he sits next to her, listening to the endless stream of cosmic babble that spews from her lips. Hell, Bob has to wait until Yahfah is out of the room before he dares to have an original thought, or her safely at work before he dares dip into her stash. Bob Robbins is nothing more than her boy, Willie decided, and the first time he gets out of line, she's going to cast some kind of stupid spell on him. So Bob goes along, trading his manhood for a roof and a constant supply of her dope.

Did he want to keep hanging out with a chump like this?

No.

Could he stand even one more night of watching this guy sucker up to Yahfah?

Absolutely not.

Pathetic, really. No man should have to live like this. So today Willie decided that Bob Robbins would not.

But he was also paranoid that Bob knew what happened to Ken and Mike, and to the kid yesterday for that matter. He knew Bob was no different than every other junkie, and would sell his very soul if it guaranteed his next fix. He told Doug that if push came to shove, Bob Robbins would turn on them in a heartbeat, and they just couldn't take that chance.

So the two of them sat around the pool Wednesday afternoon and devised the plan. It would have to be done that night, Willie said, before Yahfah got back from work. But this time, he said it was Doug's turn to do it.

They would tell Yahfah there was talk going around about a drug bust that went down last night not far from the Vista Grande and Bob was freaking out about all the narcs snooping around, so they took him out of town to lay low for a few days, just until things cooled down. Knowing her attitude about Robbin's do-nothing life, Willie knew she would buy it.

Willie also said no guns. They couldn't chance the neighbors hearing any shots, so Bob would have to be done by hand, just like Ken and Mike. It was just too risky otherwise.

Brinda Lowery saw them sitting by the pool and walked over to say hello. They were a bit older than the guys she hung around with, but they seemed friendly enough. Bill, with his afro and long sideburns, was so different from anyone she had seen around Apache Junction. She told him that she liked the silver marijuana leaf earring that pierced his ear, and Willie started to pull it off to give to her. Brinda declined, knowing what her mother would do if she caught her wearing such a thing.

Doug was different, a little more her own age. He reminded her of a kid at school with his oversized glasses, his long stringy blond hair and scraggily goatee. Doug never said much, and Brinda thought maybe he was just shy, because he would only speak after Bill did, and then it was only to copy him. Like when Bill said he played in a rock band, Doug did too, like he was trying to be just as important. He was quiet, and she kind of liked that about him.

Brinda saw her friend Monique walk by and she waved for her to join them. The guys were introduced as friends of Bob and Yahfah's and Brinda made sure to point out that they played in a rock group, news Monique found terribly exciting. She had never met a real rock star before.

"The band is called Mountain", Bill said, and Monique had no reason to doubt him. Doug blew on a harmonica as they talked.

Bob showed up, said he was going swimming and jumped in, making as much noise as he possibly could. Willie ignored him. He told the girls that he and Doug could only stick around tonight because tomorrow they had to head back to San Francisco on business. "Yeah, we got a concert to do Friday night up there, then we'll probably come back. Tell you what; maybe we'll throw a big party when we do. You two wanna come?"

There was no question they did.

Doug told Willie that it was almost six o'clock, and that they had better get moving if they were going to meet their deadline. Willie looked over at Bob who was still floating around in the pool, and agreed. "Yeah, we only got five hours left."

The sun was already down by the time Bob Robbins returned to the trailer. Willie and Doug sat in the shadows of the front room as Bob walked back to his room to change out of his wet clothes. When he came out to the living room, Doug slipped up behind him and wrapped an electrical cord around his neck and cinched it tight. Bob's head jerked back and his hands went to his throat as Doug yanked and twisted the cord, his size and the rush of adrenaline pulling the smaller man completely off the floor. Robbin's legs dangled, then kicked madly, flailing and twisting in mid air. Both men grunted. Doug continued to knot the cord as Bob fought off the attack. He clawed at the cord, trying to get his fingers under it. But lacking the strength to do so, his arms fell to his side. Other than his gasps for air, and the gurgling sound he made as his windpipe was crushed, the trailer was silent.

Doug let go, and Bob Robbins slumped to the floor. Willie never got up. Never said a word or left the chair where he had witnessed the struggle. Doug lifted Bob up by his arms and asked Willie to help him get the body into the back.

They dragged him into his own room, where Robbins continued to twitch and emit air from his lungs. This movement from the dead man either frightened Doug or aroused him, because he grabbed Willie's gun, and breaking the agreement they had made earlier, rolled the body over and put a bullet into the back of his head, once and for all silencing the reflexes that had annoyed him.

The body lay face down, the head resting on a crumpled arm as blood trickled from the wound. They lifted the mattress that had been his bed and threw it on top of him, not even bothering to completely cover him up.

They picked Yahfah up in the old Chevy later that night, disappointing her, hoping she would get to ride in the nice new Ford one day. "Flat tire," Willie said. "I'll fix it tomorrow." Yahfah perked up when she heard about them taking Bob out of the area for a few days. She said he was getting on her nerves just lying around all day. "He's nothing but a leech, and I'm getting tired of taking care of him."

So Yahfah was in a good mood again that night and all she talked about was partying when they got home Willie and Doug obliged, trying to make sure they kept her out of Bob's room. Willie went so far as to agree to spend the night in her bed, just so he could keep an eye on her.

19

Thursday, October 25, 1973 | 12 noon.

On what was to be the last day of her twenty-one years, Yahfah slept in. Her line of work demanded late nights, and typically her days were half over by the time she got up anyway, but that she and her guests partied until almost five in the morning probably had something to do with her late awakening as well.

As she rolled out of bed, Yahfah could hear voices in the other room and was anxious to join them. Bill shared her bed last night, but nothing more. And although it bothered her a little he hadn't come on to her, she decided it was drugs and wine responsible for his lack of performance. Besides, what difference did it make anyway? She wasn't all that interested in him either.

And starting today things were going to be different. Until now she worked and Bob stayed stoned. But those days were over, and if he didn't like it, well, he could just stay gone. It was her turn now, and so before she even got out of bed, Yahfah decided to call in sick, just so she could stay home and kick back.

As she dressed, she caught a glimpse of herself in the mirror. The lean look of high school was gone – she reminded herself again that all the guys wanted her back then – but these last few years had been hard ones and it showed in the woman who stared back at her. Her once lissome figure, thin to the point of boyish, was now puffy and pale. She leaned closer to examinee the dark circles under her eyes, the price paid for the path she had taken. An attempted smile brought only a dingy reflection and teeth on the edge of decay. She sighed as she pulled away from her disappointment and got dressed, tugging on a pair of bell-bottoms and slipping into a red and white pullover sweater. She ran a quick brush through her brown hair, fumbled with a silver barrette to hold it in place, and with her new found freedom, and a junkie's eye for a good time, she opened her bedroom door to meet the new day.

The others were already up. Bill slouched on a chair near the front door, the first cigarette of the day dangling from his lips, his eyes mere slits from the smoke circling his head, while Doug rambled through the kitchen, opening cabinets two at a time in his ongoing search for food.

"Won't find much," Yahfah announced as she entered the room, helping herself to one of Bill's Marlboros. "We're gonna hafta go to the store."

She had no sooner sat down when she noticed two of the neighbor kids peeking through the open screen door. She yelled at them to come on in. Usually it was the sisters, Tarnyn and Teresa Sexton who were inseparable, but today it was just Tarnyn and her older brother, Melvin.

"Hey, how you guys doin'?" Yahfah asked between drags. "Where's sis?"

"Home," Tarnyn answered.

"She's still home." Melvin echoed.

They glanced over at the two strangers, halfway expecting to see Bob lying around somewhere. The girls were 13 and 14, Melvin slightly older, but all of them old enough to know what went on at Yahfah's. Just about everyone at Vista Grande liked Yahfah, except many of the parents, who put the place off-limits, which naturally gave them even more reason to hang out there.

Yahfah introduced Doug and Bill, friends from California.

"Yeah, came back in last night,' Willie started in. "Doug and Bob and me got chased across the desert by the cops. Lost 'em on the other side a town. Good thing they didn't catch us. I would have had a hard time explaining the eight hundred bucks I had on me." He went on, oblivious to the fact that those he was seemingly so desperate to impress were just a couple of kids.

Yahfah changed the subject and asked about the girl's recent trip to Oklahoma. "When did you guys get back?"

"Day before yesterday. Kinda late." Melvin answered.

"Where 'bouts in Oklahoma?" Willie butted in. "Cause I was born in Oklahoma City, but really I'm from New York. . ."

Yahfah interupted again, lifting herself from the sofa. "Hey, we gotta split guys. We're gonna go get something to eat."

Melvin backed up, clearing a path to the screen door. He looked at the guy who had been doing all the talking. "That your car. . .the brown one?" he asked, nodding towards the open door.

"Yeah, it's mine."

"Gotta flat."

"Yeah, shit I know," Willie admitted. "Musta got it last night ditchin' the fuckin' pigs!"

A few minutes later the roar of the Chevy's exhaust rumbled through the trailer park. Doug sat behind the wheel and Willie rode shotgun, one arm stretched out over the seat and the other resting on the door. In the back,Yahfah started in about finally having a little space, and how good it felt to have Bob out of her hair for a few days. She directed the way down University Avenue, then crossing back over to the main desert drag, Apache Trail Boulevard, all the while babbling nonstop. She threw her arms up skyward. She said she loved the sun. She moaned about needing to do some coke really bad. She had big plans for tonight, she promised, a special service; a circle of candles, and a reading to direct her future, now that both Ken and Bob were out of her life. Jesus! She really needed that coke! Willie just rolled his eyes.

Doug found the store. They followed her inside and wandered around while she shopped. Back out to the Chevy and Yahfah pointed to the A & W just a short distance away. But as Doug pulled out onto Apache Trail Boulevard, he glanced back in the rear view and saw the flashing lights.

Earlier in the week, Monday, according to the date on his report, Officer Preston of Maricopa County Sheriff Department stopped at a nearby Circle K Market for his morning coffee. Working out of the east county substation, Preston was a familiar sight on Apache Trail, especially at this particular market he frequented around break time.

When he stepped up to the counter that morning, the clerk pointed to a ratty Chevy ragtop that appeared abandoned in front of the store. The deputy did a quick registration check, but there was no report of the vehicle being stolen, learning only that the legal owner was a Charles Wiley of Phoenix. Preston looked over the open interior of the car and made a note of the worn upholstery and trash littering the inside, taking special interest in a matchbook advertising The Playful Kitten, an establishment he was familiar with, being just a few miles down the road. Other than that, he took no further action, and he couldn't remember if it was later on that day, or possibly the next, but eventually the Chevy was gone and he gave the matter no further thought.

Until today. On routine patrol, Preston was heading west on University when the convertible once again crossed his path. It pulled out from the Vista Grande directly in front on him with the roar from a worn out muffler. But most of all it was merely his cop curiosity that told him to follow the car just to see where it was headed. He stayed back and called dispatch.

Again, nothing unusual. He continued to follow, hoping the driver would make a mistake, but the convertible obeyed all the laws and eventually stopped at a small grocery store on Apache Trail. Preston went up another block, then circled back around and waited on a side street next to the store. When the people got back in the Chevy, they headed east on Apache Trail. It was there where Preston hit the lights and pulled them over in front of the A & W.

Doug had noticed the cop behind him soon after they left the trailer park, motioning to Willie to check it out, who in turn suggested to Yahfah that the cops must still have it out for Bob. Good thing they had gotten him out of the trailer when they did, he said. They all breathed a sigh of relief when the cop kept going after they stopped at the store.

But it didn't last long. They no sooner got back on the road when Doug saw the lights and pulled over on the gravel shoulder. "Stay cool," Willie warned.

Doug stepped out, met the officer halfway, and offered his New York driver's license. When asked whose car it was, he explained that his friend, Bill Knickerbocker, had bought it but was having trouble getting the title because the previous owner had left the state. Preston still felt something had to be out of order, so he gave the convertible a quick once over, nodding hello to the man and woman who had remained in the car. He jotted down their description and features, making note that the woman was "pregnant looking" and that both of the men wore simulated leather jackets, even though the temperature did not call for such clothing. He handed the license back to the driver, who asked about the time limit for new residents to obtain an Arizona license. When Preston asked where he was staying, and for how long, Doug replied without hesitation, "Vista Grande Trailer Park, Space one thirty-three."

Resigned that everything seemed in order, the officer allowed the young man to go on his way. An Arizona D.P.S. vehicle arrived as backup just as Doug got into the car and detonated the engine, roaring away, dusting the sheriff patrolman and the DPS agent standing at the side of the road.

The three went back to the trailer and shared a few lines of coke, just to settle the nerves, while Yahfah continued to compliment Doug on how well he took care of what could have really turned out to be a bad scene. They hung around the trailer for the rest of the afternoon, Willie and Doug jumping up to intercept Yahfah everytime she headed down the hall. And now she had announced that she wasn't going to work tonight, so there was no way they were going to get Bob out of the trailer. And as hard as he tried Willie could not convince her to change her mind. Bob was going to be back in a day or so, she reminded him, and then it would be life as usual. Besides it was already after four and she would be late anyway. Might as well call in and make it official. "Ligthen up," she joked as she left to use the pay phone at the rec hall. "It's gonna be a really good night."

Her boss answered the phone. Barbara had a problem calling her Yahfah – the name didn't seem to fit – so she just called her Katie. It wasn't uncommon for the girls to call in sick occasionally. Most of the time they didn't even bother to call, and that's one of the things she liked about Katie; very responsible. All of them worked on commission anyway, so it was no big deal. Barbara wasn't even twenty-five yet, so she acted more like a friend than a boss. She took a liking to Katie, always enjoying her smile and her spirit. This kind of work had a habit of trashing young women, making them hard and bitter, but not Katie. She never complained, never refused a client, never gave any indication that her life was anything but rosy. She knew about Bob, assumed he was a junkie, figured he sponged off Katie like most of the boyfriends did, but had only met him once or twice, so she really could say much about him.

But she sure as hell didn't like the new guy; the one who picked Katie up last night. The minute she met him she didn't like him. Maybe it was more like she didn't trust him. He was scrawny, with an earring and an afro. Dirty too, and his complexion dark, so at first she thought he was a black dude, which seemed out of place in Apache Junction. She couldn't remember his name, but she was now sure who had put Katie up to it. "Take care of yourself," she told Katie and reminded her she still had $40 coming in wages. The voice assured Barbara she would feel better tomorrow and would get the money then.

As she walked back to the trailer, Yahfah passed by the Sexton place and Tarnyn raced out to intercept her. "Hey, wait!" she yelled. "What happened today? Melvin and me saw the cops pull you guys over by the A & W."

Yahfah turned around and shrugged it off. "Oh shit, the cops followed us today looking for Bob, but we got him hiding out. Gonna leave him there another couple nights, at least 'til things calm down. Hey! Don't sweat it. Everything's cool."

This was exciting stuff, and Tarnyn pretended to share Yahfah's distain for the cops. *Yeah, pigs,* she said. *They're always hassling someone.* The conversation was cut short by Mrs. Sexton yelling that dinner was ready, so Tarnyn scurried inside, resigned she would have to wait until later to hear more.

The sun was gone, but the sky was still ablaze, and the park was blanketed in early evening dusk. The red sky radiated the simple beauty of Indian summer and the trailer's metal siding reflected the sunset's fiery brilliance. Yahfah's shadow was long and it reached the trailer door before she did. She hesitated for a moment, as if to remind herself the vow she took to enjoy everything, including sunsets, even as the final minutes of her life were burning away.

Darkness settled inside the trailer as well, and Yahfah went about transforming the blonde end table in the corner of the living room into her altar. As the candles flickered, the doors were shut and the drapes drawn, the holy objects of her worship carefully placed around the small table. Despite her encouragement, both men ignored her, so she proceeded alone, softly singing unintelligible verses as she gently touched each candle. A stack of tarot cards lay close to her right hand, while in the dim light, a nude woman gracing the cover of *OUI* magazine gazed back at her, an item Yahfah had overlooked, and now the photo took center stage on the makeshift pyre. Yahfah continued in whispers, but made sure she could be heard across the room. Kneeling down on a small pillow, she faced the corner of the room, her back to the others. She hovered over the table and continued her chant.

Seeing her consumed in this trance, Willie pulled the .22 from under his coat and wrapped a towel around the barrel as he crept up behind her. He placed the gun at the back of her head and stared down upon her. He paused, then jerked the trigger.

For that first moment, Yahfah did not flinch, did not move, and then blood began its slow trickle from her open mouth, her eyes rolled back in her head, and her body collapsed into a small bundle, knees still resting on the floor. Her chanting had ceased, and the room was again dead still.

Willie stood over her and watched the blood flow blacken the carpet. "Gimme a hand," he said.

They pulled at her now limp body, half lifting her, half dragging her down the hall and into her bedroom, while Yahfah continued to twitch and expel her final gasps of air. It was a now familiar, yet uncomfortable sound to Doug, who, after laying her out on the floor, grabbed the gun and placed another slug into her forehead. They dropped her face up, arms stretched out just as they had carried her, her bloodied head tilted to one side, and that's how they left her.

Monique Jered was surprised to see Bill and Doug later that night at the rec hall, especially after they told her they were leaving for California earlier that morning. But it was seven o'clock and they were still here.

A half hour later Monique watched as the brown Ford pulled out of the park with a flat tire. It was making a god awful noise and the tire wiggled around like it was ready to fall off. She couldn't believe how some supposedly famous rock star could be so stupid. They weren't going very fast, and apparently not very far, because a few minutes later she watched them return, and Bill and Doug went back inside Yahfah's trailer.

Willie told Doug they would go south down to Tucson where their chances of setting up some kind of deal would be better. He had never been there, but word back in Denver was that Tucson was wide open and all the dope coming out of Mexico went through there. They would lay low tonight, then leave before the sun came up. It was too risky, he said, to try and move the bodies. They would have to stay right where they were. They cleaned the place up a little, taking a cloth to the carpet where Yahfah dropped. Willie scoured the trailer for the money, even turning Yahfah's pocket inside out for a couple of extra dollars. They kept the lights on, the stereo low, and the curtains closed. Then they heard a pounding on the front door.

Willie froze. The front door to the trailer was a large glass slider and the drapes were drawn across it, so he had no idea who might be on the other side. He moved the small end table over to cover the stains still visible on the carpet, then walked over to the small window near the front door and peered out. He took a moment to check the room, then pulled the drapes back and slid the door open. Staring back up at him were the Sexton girls.

"Hey, whaddya guys doin'?" he asked, relieved at who he saw.

"Oh, nothin'. Yahfah home?" Tarnyn asked.

"Nah. We went and picked up Bob, took them both to town. They should be back in a couple a minutes, though."

The girls remained on the wooden step, silhouetted in the dirty yellow glow of the porch light, while Willie guarded the entrance to the trailer. Tarnyn turned and pointed out in the driveway at the Ford. "That yours?" she asked.

"Yeah. Brought it over from California to give to Bob and Yahfah."

"Just give it to them?"

"Hell yeah! Listen, you guys wanna come in for a minute?" The girls stepped inside. They were uncomfortable in the darkness, but more worried what might happen if their parents caught them there. Tarnyn sat on a wicker chair near Bill and Teresea on the floor in line with the hall. He offered them a cigarette.

"We're gonna be leaving here in a couple of hours," Willie announced. "Just waiting for Bob and Yahfah to get back."

"Where you goin'?"

"California. Got a concert to do. But we'll be back in two weeks, and when do we're gonna throw a big party!"

"Far out!" Teresea exclaimed.

But the longer they stayed, the more the girls worried. They looked over at each other from time to time, letting the other know just how much trouble they would be in if they didn't get home before their parents returned, although they didn't dare say anything, not wanting to look like a couple of little kids. Teresea heard a noise at the end of the dark hallway and recognized the shadow as Doug, who was just coming out of the back bedroom. He said hello and sat on a stool at the kitchen bar.

Then there was noise outside and both girl's jumped. "It's mommy and daddy!" Teresea whispered. She bolted for the hallway to hide, Tarnyn close behind. Doug intercepted them and blocked their entrance to the room where Bob was. "Don't go in there!" he warned.

"But if mommy and daddy find us. . .!"

Doug couldn't stop both girls and it was Tarnyn who reached around him and opened the door. The room was pitch black. The pair pushed Doug ahead of them, back into the darkness, and he was now all that stood between them and the body only partially hidden under the mattress at their feet.

Willie headed towards the room, not knowing what the girls had discovered. If they had seen too much, he knew what would have to be done. "Hey, c'mon out," he said.

"No, they'll see us!" The voices could still be heard outside, calling their names. The girls refused to leave the room.

Doug finally managed to push them back out into the hall. He closed the door behind him. The four now stood in the narrow hallway. Finally the voice outside faded away.

"We'll go out the back door," Tarnyn whispered, and headed that way. Afraid they might again try to hide, this time in Yahfah's room, Willie put his arm out and blocked their path. There would be no close calls in that room. "NO!" he barked. He grabbed Tarnyn and pushed both girls back towards the front room. "Go out this way. You'll be okay."

They hesitated for a moment, but Willie slid the door open and guided the girls out. "You guys take care. You'll be okay."

Tarnyn and Teresea tiptoed around the front of the trailer and disappeared into the night. Willie closed the door and exhaled. He looked at Doug, standing at the edge of the hallway, still clutching the .22 hidden beneath his jacket.

Willie Steelman, 21

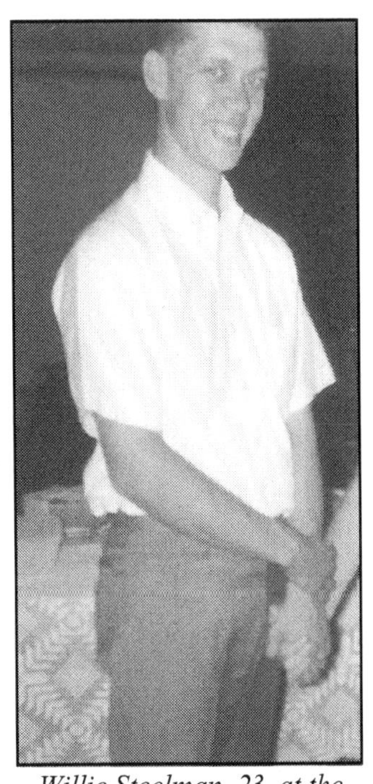

Willie Steelman, 23, at the wedding reception held at the Machell home in June 1968.

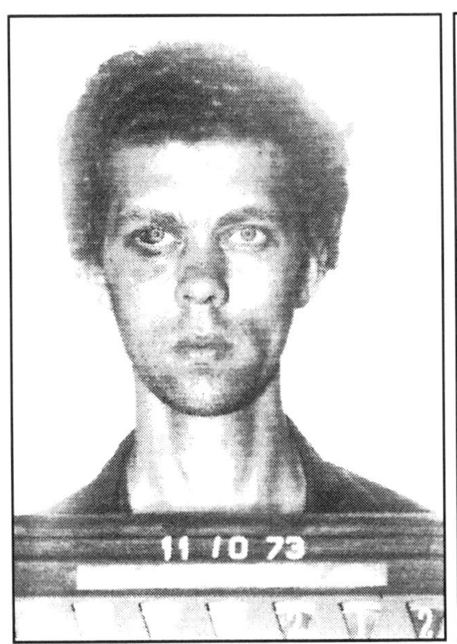

Willie Steelman
His right eye still damaged from the fight in Tucson.

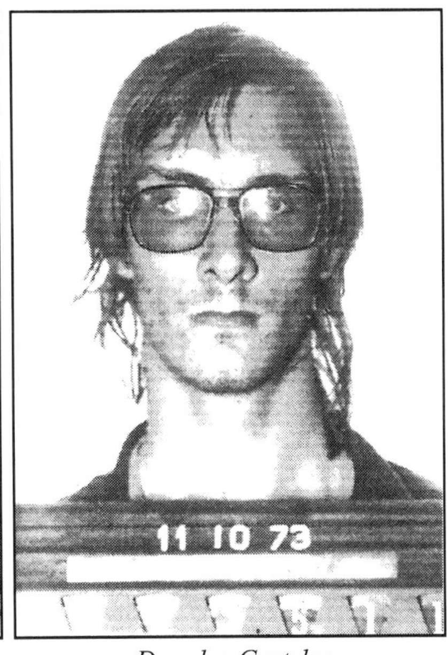

Douglas Gretzler
Stockton, California
November 1973

Marsha Renslow, 16
Denver, Colorado

Marsha Renslow 1973

The house on Ellsworth – Denver, Colorado

Ken Unrein

Mike Adshade
July 1973

Steve Loughran
Marysville, California
High School 1972

Steve
Loughran
High
School
Photo
1972

Kathy Mestites
1973 – 21 years old

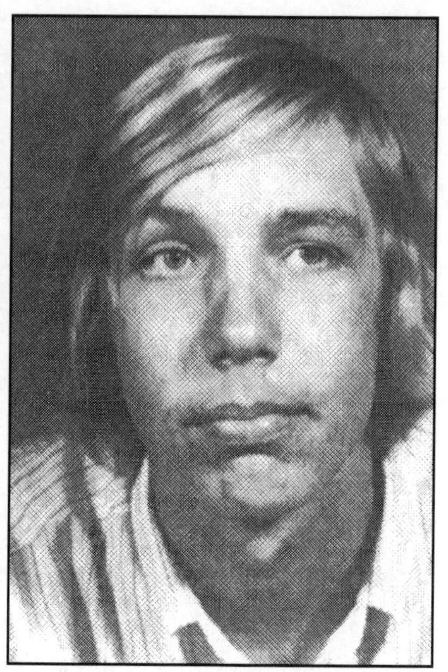

Bob Robbins

The mobile home at the Vista Grande in Apache Junction.

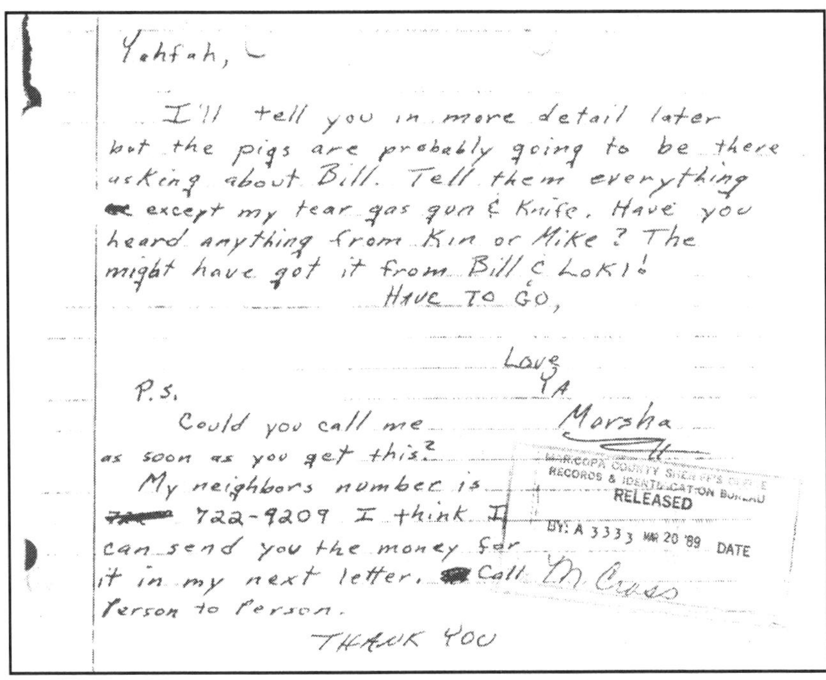

Yahfah,

I'll tell you in more detail later but the pigs are probably going to be there asking about Bill. Tell them everything except my tear gas gun & Knife. Have you heard anything from Kim or Mike? The might have got it from Bill & Loki!

Have to go,

Love Ya
Marsha

P.S.
Could you call me as soon as you get this? My neighbors number is 722-9209 I think I can send you the money for it in my next letter. Call Person to Person.
THANK YOU

MARICOPA COUNTY SHERIFF'S OFFICE
RECORDS & IDENTIFICATION BUREAU
RELEASED
BY: A 3333 MAR 20 '89 DATE
M. Cross

The letter from Marsha to Yahfah.

The table where Yahfah conducted her last worship.

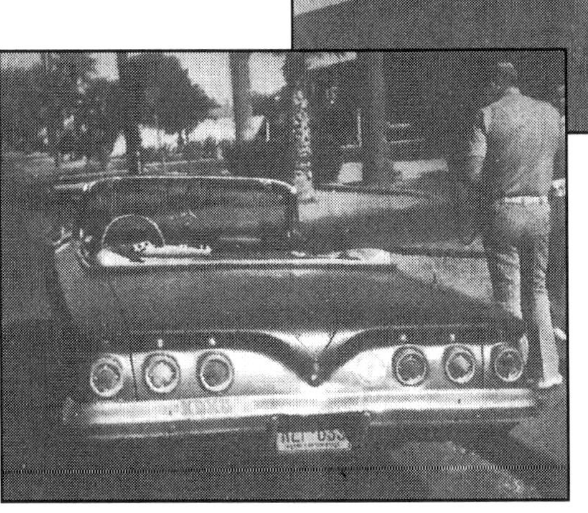

Phoenix Police discover Bob Robbins' Chevy convertible on a side street off East Van Buren.

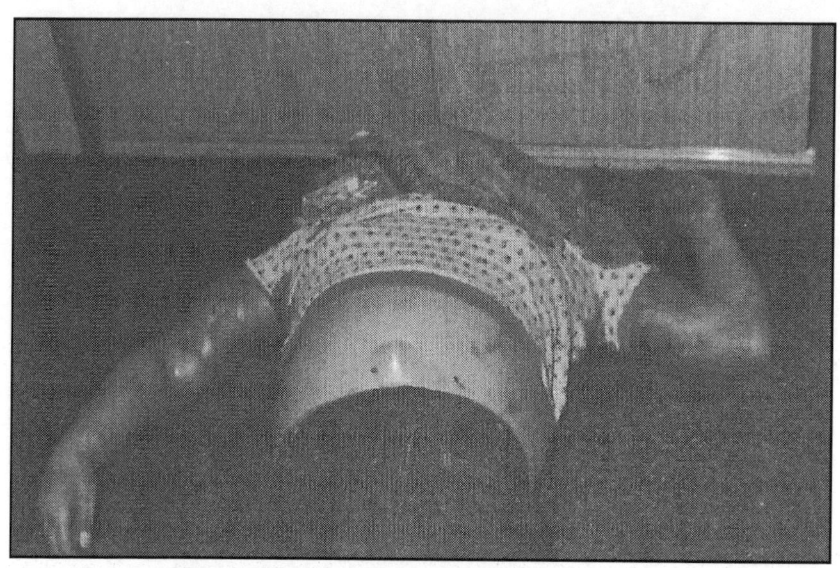

Kathy Mestites "Yahfah"
Photo taken by Maricopa County Sheriff

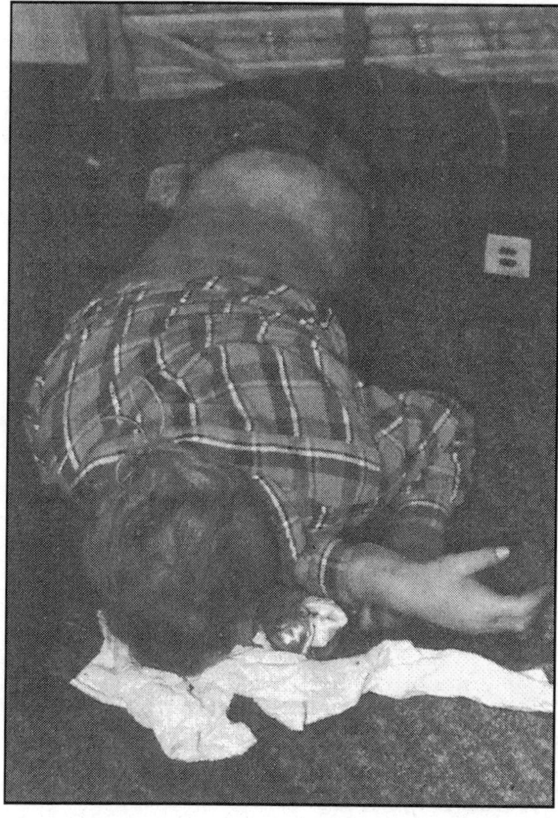

Bob Robbins

Photo taken by Maricopa County Sheriff

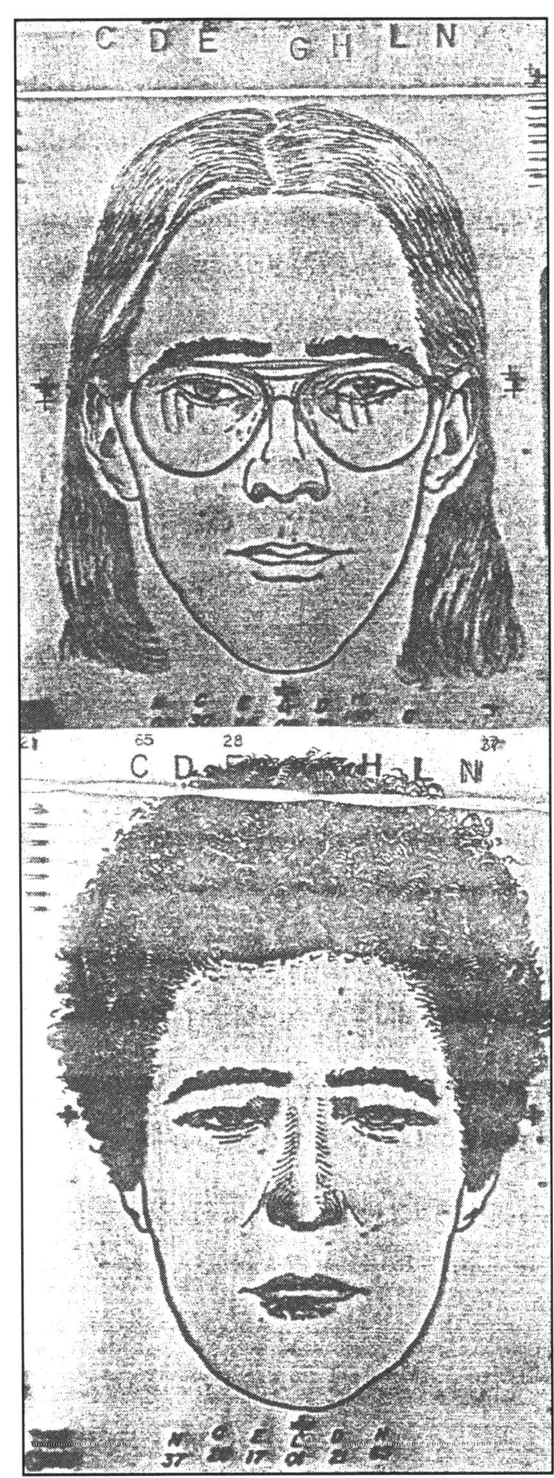

Composite drawing of Gretzler and Steelman, created with the help of Monique Jered in Arizona.

20

Friday, October 26, 1973 | 5 am.

Each had dozed off for only a few minutes, Doug a few more than Willie, but beyond that there had been little sleep. Willie claimed he never needed much anyway. Sharper without it, he boasted. But this whole Bob and Yahfah thing was messed up. The desert. That's where the two of them should be right now, but Yahfah screwed that up, and Willie blamed her for what happened. Killing her wasn't a big deal. It had to be done. He told Doug from the beginning, no witnesses, and sticking to that was their only shot at getting out of all this. These people needed to be dealt with. And they were.

Doug's self-assigned task was to wipe the place down for prints. He tried to retrace his steps and recall every spot he had stood during those last few days. He wiped it all down, but he was not satisfied, so he went back and did it again. Willie went about his work amidst the bodies in the back rooms. He emptied out his and Doug's knapsacks, folding the few shirts and pants they carried and placing them in amongst Bob's clothing. If the time came when someone tried to describe what he and Doug were wearing, the cops would never even think to look for it right under their noses. Willie congratulated himself on this clear thinking, exactly the kind of thing they would need to survive. He scrambled through the drawers and closets, shoving the extra clothing into one of Bob's knapsacks. The trailer park would be awake soon and he planned on being long gone by then. Tucson first. Hell, maybe even Mexico, if they were lucky.

He took the few steps down the hall to the room where Yahfah lay. The blood around her head had soaked into the green carpet and matted her hair. He grabbed some towels from the bathroom and placed them over her face. The blood was still slightly moist and it soaked in. The heat trapped inside the room had kept her body warm. Willie stood back and thought to himself that at least she would look a little better when they found her.

He told Doug to help him look for the money he insisted was hidden somewhere in the trailer. It had to be here, he promised. With the kind of cash Yahfah brought home each night, and with the little bit of dealing she and Bob did on the side, there just had to be something stashed around here somewhere. But what little they found, no more than a hundred bucks, was tucked inside Yahfah's purse. Willie grabbed her tarot cards and placement cloth. He looked over a couple of the books she had stacked on the counter, picked two that looked interesting and squeezed them into the knapsack. A last look around, then Doug slid the trailer door open.

They tossed their meager belongings in the trunk of the convertible. In the distance, the low roar of a truck shifting gears was the only sound. Doug hesitated even starting the car, knowing the havoc it would create, certain the clatter would wake every last person in the park. He sank down low as he got behind the wheel. Closed his eyes and turned the key, knowing the racket he was about to ignite. The engine cranked and moaned, fired, then roared to life.

Willie was just closing the trunk when he spotted someone walking out of the shadows towards them. He froze. The guy said, "Hey man, thought you guys had already split."

It was Rick Baugh, a kid from the park they met earlier. Willie tried to hide his panic. He had no idea what this guy was doing up so early. "Got tied up," came his excuse. "Just runnin' late, that's all." Willie talked in whispers. Rick didn't.

"San Francisco, right?" he asked.

"Yeah. Gotta gig this weekend." Willie had told that lie so many times even he believed it.

"Shit, that thing ain't gonna getcha there," the kid popped back, giving a nod to the car rumbling in front of him.

"We got another one out in the desert. Cadillac. Nice big Eldorado. Black one. Gonna switch 'em." With that Willie shut the trunk and moved around to the passenger side while Doug revved the motor impatiently. He slid in and looked up at the kid. "Listen, I gotta warn ya. Bob and Yahfah are still gone and the narcs have an eye on the trailer. You better tell everyone to stay away."

Rick nodded he understood, and was ready to ask about this party he had heard about, but before he could, Doug dropped it into drive, hit the gas and the Chevy lurched forward. Willie was still staring up at the kid as they pulled away. He seemed to look him for the longest time, even straining his head around to do so. As the blue Chevy disappeared, Rick saw Willie turn and say something to Doug and laugh.

They headed back towards Phoenix. East University Avenue stretches for miles and miles from Apache Junction west to Tempe. It's as straight as a rifle shot, from a narrow two-lane country road, it widens to a comfortable four-lane boulevard as it passes through Mesa. It was still dark but Doug had a sense that he had passed this way before. When? He didn't know. Five days ago? Five weeks? Five bodies? He didn't know. It was all just a blur. It had no meaning. There had been no past. The time was always now. He was not a participant in any of this anyway, he decided, merely an observer.

They passed Arizona State University, crossing the old narrow bridge spanning the dry bed of the Salt River, and within a few minutes they were amongst the lights of East Van Buren. One by one, the cool motel neon flashed blues and greens, brilliant oranges and yellows, while bright red 'vacancy' signs sputtered as the Chevy rolled by.

Although he hadn't been asked, Doug voted to get rid of the car, and tried to convince Willie of that. They were getting closer to downtown and all the cops, he said, and two guys driving a beat up old car at this hour was asking for trouble. He said they had gone far enough, pressed their luck to the limit. He told Willie they should just ditch it and take a cab to the bus station.

"Jesus! Then pull the fuck over then," Willie shot back, angry that he wasn't doing all the thinking. Doug hit the brakes and rolled off the main drag.

The Tropics Motel stood at 19th Street and Van Buren. Doug pulled onto the side street near the motel and shut the Chevy down, anxious for the quiet. Willie scanned his surroundings. This would do fine. The motel traffic might disguise the vehicle for a few days, and there was some kind of hospital next door, so nobody was going to pay much attention to a parked car. He saw a pay phone near the motel lobby and told Doug to get their stuff out of the trunk, he was going to get them a cab. Doug had everything on the sidewalk and had wiped the car down before Willie got back.

The pair had come full circle. They were only a few blocks from Ken and Mike's house. They had traveled thousands of miles, only to return to the place where it all began. These days had taken their toll, but the big scores and big cash Willie promised never came. Doug remembered planning how he would spend all the money they were going to make down here, and he told Bill they needed to get a clipboard and keep a ledger, just to keep all the cash straight. He could retire then, and maybe even enjoy life for once. That seemed so stupid now. He had nothing except for more of Willie's promises. That was all he had to go on. Promises. And Willie was all he had left.

Once downtown, Willie checked the area for cops. Satisfied, they climbed out of the Yellow Cab the moment it pulled up in front of the Continental Bus Station. Then it hit him. Nobody was looking for them. No one even knew what they had done. He relaxed and slowed his pace, sliding inside the terminal with Doug on his heels.

"One way to Tucson. Two of 'em." Willie tossed Yahfah's money on the counter. He knew they wouldn't be coming back this way again, at least not on a bus. Tucson was looking better all the time. He had heard some pretty far out stories about that town, and the drugs, and the wide-open feel to the whole scene. There was a guy back in Denver, Willie told Doug, who said how they store all the dope down there; all the dope going anywhere on the west coast was just sitting in these warehouses waiting to be had. Just crash in and take your share, Willie claimed. Even got some names and numbers in the book, he added, patting at his knapsack. So it ain't going to take us long, he promised. Least not like Phoenix. Willie was angry with himself for not going to Tucson to begin with. Phoenix was a real downer, a lot of bullshit and two-bit junkies.

He had wasted his time in Phoenix, and he was totally convinced Tucson was the place.

The bus station was quiet, with only a handful of people sprawled about, most waiting for the same bus they were. They found a bench over on the far side of the room and sat backs to the wall, the entire terminal in full view. Willie did his best to stay inconspicuous. He placed the knapsack safely at his feet.

But before long Doug was up, scrambling for change, making a display, mumbling something about the coffee machine. The whole thing was making Willie nervous. He grunted and zipped open the bag for some quarters to shut him up. He fumbled around, tugged a bit, and then yanked out a small satchel. To his surprise, another box came with it, and in that split second he realized the consequences of what he had just done. He and Doug's eyes locked, as if to warn the other about what was going to happen next.

It was the box of .22 shells, and as the lid came off in mid air, the tiny brass casings seemed to explode out of it, each bouncing off the shiny tile floor, dozens upon dozens of bullets, ringing the room with an incriminating, heart-stopping sound. Willie wanted to run and hide, but instinct told him to start gathering them up, and he tried in vain to catch each one before it the floor again. He dove head first, arms flailing, hands scooping, eyes as big as fists, while the metal-on-tile symphony he had created played out like a xylophone on acid. Heads turned as the two men scrambled around on all fours, gathering as many as they could in one motion. The bullets bounced and twirled, spinning far from the immediate reach of the panic stricken pair, some disappearing under nearby benches or coming to rest at the feet of those people who strained to see what the sudden commotion was all about. While it most likely seemed longer, within a matter of seconds all of the shells in plain view had been rounded up and pocketed. Willie never looked up, not even after he had sat back down and hurried to put the casings back into the knapsack. The gawkers eventually turned away. Silence returned. Willie could breathe again. Doug got his coffee.

The bus climbed on the freeway and merged with the morning commute. Willie closed his eyes while Doug stared out the window, watching the cars pass by, wondering who was in them, where they were going, and what dark secrets they too held. They passed the Red Rock and South Mountain, and soon there was only the desert surrounding them. The sun was low and bright, painting the barren land lavender and pink. Doug feel asleep.

Two hours later and the driver slowed down a final time. Tucson, he announced, and wheeled the bus off the Congress Street exit and headed left back towards town. All the passengers were awake now, looking out the windows at the office buildings and downtown department stores. The Continental Trailways station was on the corner of 5th and Broadway, and much smaller than the busy Greyhound terminal just across the street. It was snug fit, but the driver squeezed the big bus into a narrow slot, opened the door and thanked everyone as they walked down the steps.

Willie and Doug broke away from the others, wandered out into the side street, and squinted into the bright sky. Blue. Everywhere blue. They walked across Broadway for a better look at where they were. Willie got the attention of a guy carrying a package into the terminal. "Hey! You think you might be able to tell us where we could get a beer and something to eat around here?"

The man stopped for a moment and sized the two up. With the way these guys looked he didn't hesitate. He turned and pointed to the nearby railroad tracks. "See that street, and the tunnel going under the tracks? Just go through there."

Willie nodded that he understood, but the man wasn't finished.

"Go up a coupla blocks and you'll come to a little place called Ray and Red's. It's right on 4th Avenue. I think it's just what you're looking for."

21

Saturday, October 27, 1973

"Tucson is a crime city," Pima County Attorney Steven Neely once admitted. "Despite its peaceful veneer, Tucson has more rapes and robberies, assaults, burglaries, thefts and homicides than any of its American counterparts."

By the early seventies, the statistics were proving Neely correct. The sleepy Old Pueblo was becoming a more dangerous and turbulent place to live. Just two years earlier it ranked seventh in the nation for overall crime in a city its size, and everyday it seemed determined to climb further up that list

For decades Tucson had been known as one of the top spots for dope smuggling, earning the nickname "Heroin Port" from the enormous shipments coming in daily from Mexico. Loose borders, along with a lack of manpower to guard them, allowed a constant flow of marijuana, cocaine and heroin to hit the streets of the city. It was a traffic so tempting financially, even a member of the Pima County D. A.'s office was caught smuggling cocaine, and there was seldom a crime committed that didn't have a drug connection to it.

"People hooked on drugs are desperate enough to do just about anything for it," reported Sheriff Lt. John Lyons. Even his own department was racked with scandal 5 years earlier in 1968, when Sheriff Waldon Burr and several aides came under fire for corruption. Sixty-seven counts of misconduct, including payoffs from the prostitution racket, drug rings, and links to underworld figures, were filed by the Grand Jury, only to be dismissed, reinstated, then dismissed again.

But even with his office in turmoil, Burr still refused to resign, and finally in September of 1971 the charges were reapplied and the case went to court. A no-nonsense judge from Apache County named Dick Greer, who's direct, down home style of running a courtroom was well known throughout the state, was all set to begin the proceedings, when Burr was suddenly hospitalized with a serious illness. The very same day, his attorney, H. Earl Rogge, disappeared. When his body was discovered several days later in the desert, the cause of death was quickly ruled a suicide. Eventually Burr, his Under Sheriff and a Captain, along with three deputies, resigned. But the Sheriff's Department was hanging by a thread, demoralized, and working understaffed trying to keep up with the trouble on the street.

Tucson's crime problem was linked to not only to its famous weather and close proximity to Mexico, but to its rapid growth as well. In the twenty years from 1950 to 1970, the population more than quadrupled; from less than 50,000 to almost 250,000 people; expanding at a nervous rate, rolling towards the Catalina Mountains as fast as construction teams could level the sand, leaving in its wake an empty downtown and tattered neighborhoods ripe for crime.

One of those areas was 4th Avenue. At one time it anchored a pleasant, prosperous neighborhood of neatly kept homes and a street chock full of businesses catering to the people living nearby. A trolley ran its six block length, and visitors to Tucson flocked to the stores and restaurants lining the street. Although 4th Avenue's western edge bordered the hustle and bustle of downtown, it seemed so remote, so unique and so inviting.

Later that connection became its undoing. When the suburbs began sucking the life out of the downtown area in the mid 1960's, the Avenue started its decline. The railroad station was only a few hundred yards away, along with two bus stations, so the area soon attracted the lowlife, drifters, hippies and transients looking for warm winters and cheap dope. By 1970, and with no law on the books against loitering or vagrancy, 4th Avenue had become a cop's worst nightmare, with the bars, drugs and the crime that went along with it. In the spring of that year, 500 young people, mostly non-students from the Avenue area, battled 400 cops on the University grounds. And again in January of '72 a three-day riot resulted in the arrest of 146 people. In both cases, authorities pointed to 4th Avenue as the problem.

The following February, the legitimate business owners there were so upset at what was taking place on their street, they urged the city to impose tougher restrictions on loitering, as well as more police presence in their neighborhood. The problem was the legitimate business owners were now greatly outnumbered. 'Storefronts of Doom' they called them. These new businesses, which specialized in beads, bongs, intricate roach clips, pipes and paraphernalia, sprouted like weeds. Most lasted only a few months, but were quickly replaced by one just like it.

And there was a sea of bars on 4th. Like Choo Choo's; a rowdy, dank place where the cops were constantly making a bust. For entertainment, people sat in their lawn chairs on the roof across the street, tapped a keg, and watched bouncers toss drunks head first out on the Avenue.

Then there was the Balcony Bar, where the upper class pleasure seekers, including professors, lawyers and even an occasional judge, came looking to score. Story was told that hometown girl Linda Ronstadt got her start singing at the Balcony.

Ray and Red's was Arizona's first bar opened after Prohibition, and forty years later, twenty-five cents would still buy a 16 ounce glass of A-1 Brand Beer. *Possum Piss* was what they called it, but the locals chugged it by the keg full. Ray and Red's was an unruly, god-awful place, where the smell of stale beer and urine spilled out onto the Avenue, and where even a newcomer could score some easy dope. Speed, coke, LSD, an onslaught of pills, as well as grass, was always on sale, and transactions were made openly around the bar or outback in one of the vacant buildings. The sign out front said it was "A Poor Man's Bar", and it certainly was one of the most popular hangouts on 4th Avenue.

Down the street, closer to the tracks and bus stations, was the Shanty Bar. Owned by the same family for decades, it had a famous copper bar and a shaded outdoor patio. It tried hard to stay clean, but always appeared to be swimming against the tide. Across the street was a broken down tavern called JuJu's, along with the old Coronado Hotel, which these days was little more than a flophouse. Next door to the Shanty was a non-descript faded pink box building with a sign out front that simply said, 'Rooms'.

So 4th Avenue was a place for hippies, college kids on a lark, and young businessmen looking for a little adventure. Once a week, just like clockwork, the cops rolled down the street in an unmarked van and snatched up anyone who even looked guilty. They got tossed in the van, frisked, asked a bunch of questions, maybe even slapped around a little. After which they were thrown back out on the Avenue with a warning that if they knew what was good for them, they would find a different place to hang out.

So when Willie and Doug arrived yesterday afternoon, they took the stranger's advice and soon found themselves in the crowd of people ready for a wild, destructive Friday night on 4th Avenue.

Before the day was over they had scored some crank and made their acquaintance with the woman who sold it to them. Willie tossed his name and his street rap around, and with the help of their new friend, they got somewhere to stash their stuff and later even a place to crash; a room upstairs in the building next to the Shanty. Ten hours in Tucson and they were right at home.

Doug Gretzler was the first to admit he grew up in a nice house in a nice neighborhood and went to good schools in a good town. His father had a respectable job, while his mother stayed home and cooked ambitious meals for the family, although sometimes they piled in the car and went out to dinner at their favorite restaurant, or down to the YMCA to swim.

While there weren't many of them, the friends he had were good ones; buddies from school, kids from around the block with whom Saturdays were spent building tree forts and exploring the nearby woods. Doug always played the television hero; dressed as Davy Crockett with his coonskin cap, and later masquerading as Superman, or in the black cape of Zorro.

He spent hours alone in the garage creating little gadgets, proud to show his father what he had done. He was fascinated with animals, constantly bringing home a wounded bird, putting its damaged wing in a splint, nursing it until it either died or could fly away. Never interested in regular pets, Doug either had a snake, an iguana or a pet alligator living in cage somewhere in the house. His life, at least up until the time he became a teenager, was, as he once put it, about as close to *"Leave It To Beaver"* as you could come, and he had no reason to think it would ever change.

But he was wrong. While the family didn't change, how Doug came to view them did. His parents, his older brother, his sisters, they all had problems, but it was *his* difference that suddenly stood out the most. Now thirteen, Doug didn't see the happy family he once saw. It was all a big joke. His father yelled, his mother cowered, his bother and sisters went along quietly to avoid the wrath. But Doug refused, and his father did not at all appreciate his son's new found independence.

Norton Gretzler was a big man; 6' 4", well over 200 pounds, and with his size and stern demeanor, he towered over his family with a strict code of conduct he expected them all to adhere to. Good children, good manners, good students, good grades. That was all he asked of his four offspring.

Mark was first, then two years later, Doug, and two years after that, Joanne. Several years later, the baby Dianne was born. Being the oldest, Mark was quick to understand what was necessary to please their father, and up to now he had succeeded at the highest level. By the time he reached high school, he routinely got straight A's, and they came so easy he still had room left for the band and a host of school activities. When it came time for the college exams, Mark breezed through those as well, with some of highest scores recorded in New York state.

Needless to say, Mr. Gretzler was proud. Now serving as the President of the Tuckahoe Board of Education, he held Mark's lofty achievements as goals for his other children to follow. But none of that came as easy to Doug, who by the time he became a teenager had already experienced enough of 'Mark did this and Mark did that' to last a lifetime. He was as far removed from his older brother as a kid could get, and while he didn't hate him, he just had nothing in common with him. So as Mark nonchalantly got Honors and A's, Doug struggled with C's and D's. Other than English class, he was bored with school and refused to do any homework. When his father became concerned about Doug's grades, he had him tested for aptitude and it was clear Doug was a bright kid, but just didn't care. The more Mark excelled, the more his father held him up as his shining son, and in turn, the more Doug withdrew.

He had also discovered pot at about this time, and it wasn't long before his father became suspicious. Thinking it could be the reason for Doug's failure as a student, Mr. Gretzler didn't say anything, but placed a bug on his phone, hoping to catch his son in the act. But Doug found the microphone first and hid it from his father. When Norton discovered it missing, he confronted his son by grabbing him by the shirt collar and pushing him up against the bedroom wall. With the senior Gretzler's size and strength he crashed right through and landed in the next room, still wrestling around with Doug on the bathroom floor.

By the age of 15, Doug was well into his dope smoking days. It was the quickest way to escape, because when he was high, he didn't care, and Doug found that life was much easier to face when he didn't give a shit. Day after day, he sat alone in the basement, playing his drums, talking on the phone and smoking hash.

He found other ways to stand out, and by the time he was a sophomore in high school he was letting his hair grow and wearing odd outfits to school. Bell bottom blue jeans, cowboy boots, flowery mod shirts and funny hats, all of which laughed in the face of the established dress code. But with his pull on the School Board, and to avoid embarrassment, Mr. Gretzler found a way to fix it so his number two son could stay in class.

Embarrassment. That was probably as good a word as any to describe Mr. Gretzler's feeling about Doug. His defiance at home, his poor school work, his loud music and obnoxious dress embarrassed Norton Gretzler, and he took every opportunity to let Doug know of his utter disappointment.

It was also around this time when Doug and his parents began family counseling. For two years he attended regularly, every Tuesday night, but hated every minute of it. The psychologists seemed to side with Doug, and tried to get his parents to see their son as an individual and not to expect the same level of achievement from him as the did from his older brother. But according to Joanne, her father refused to listen, and even shoved one of the counselors when it was insinuated that it was he who might be to blame for the defiant personality of his son.

While Doug wouldn't admit it, during all of this time he truly did look up to Mark, a little in awe that one person could be and do so much. Everything came so easy to him and he was always on his father's good side. While Doug told everyone that Mark was way too square, he was impressed how his brother could do anything he set his mind to.

Mark was far from perfect, however. During the last days of school in 1966, Mark stole the Regent's Exams. The same tests he had sailed through, were not quite so easy for some of his friends, so on a lark, he swiped them. When the others all got surprisingly good grades, the suspicious finger was pointed at Mark, who admitted what he had done. But what punishment the school handed down was nothing compared to how disappointed Mr. Gretzler was. It was the first time Doug could ever remember Mark letting their father down, and the subsequent lecturing and scolding was relentless. "How could he do this to me?" Mr. Gretzler lamented.

The school decided Mark could not participate in any activities for his upcoming senior year. He could not be in clubs, go on field trips, be in the band or go to prom. He would also be banned from his own graduation ceremonies the following year. He couldn't even eat in the school cafeteria. But as bad as that was, Mark knew he still had to deal with his father. Mr. Gretzler promised his own punishment for the deed and dangled it over his head, saying it would be a family retribution, for Mark had disgraced them all. For weeks it was all that was heard in the Gretzler home.

In August, as the summer of 1966 was winding down and fall classes were to begin, Mr. Gretzler called the family to dinner one night to discuss the punishment Mark would receive. Doug was late getting to the table as usual, scolded again by his father for his tardiness. Doug shot back that Mark wasn't there yet either, and tired of waiting, Mr. Gretzler walked upstairs to personally usher his son to the dinner meeting. There was commotion from Mark's room and Mr. Gretzler yelled for someone to call an ambulance. Doug and his sister raced upstairs, only to be blocked by their father who ordered them to go to their rooms, close the door and not come out until instructed to do so.

In the confusion of the next few minutes, Doug slipped back into his brother's room. On the bed, swimming in a pool of blood, was Mark. With a borrowed gun, he had ended his life, as well as the demanding days of being the oldest and the fairest of the Gretzler children. Numb from what he witnessed, Doug went in and told his sister what Mark had done. Doug was as white as a ghost, but he wasn't crying and hysterical like all the others. Joanne watched him sit there on her bed, repeating over and over, "I didn't think he could do it. I just didn't think he could do it."

Later that night, for some sad reason, Mr. Gretzler left Mark's suicide note on the dining room table for everyone to read. In it he thanked his aunt for loaning him the gun, but said not a single word on why he decided his life had become too much to handle. Doug was sure it was because of the pressure from their father, but Joanne disagreed, believing Mark just could not stand the idea of being banned from his senior year activities.

But regardless of why, the damage had been done, and yet Mr. Gretzler refused to believe he was to blame. He kept Mark's bedroom as a shrine, not moving a single thing since the day the trigger was pulled. He locked the room up tight, going so far as to place a hair across the door to be able to tell if anyone had trespassed into the now sacred ground. Doug watched his father go into the room late at night, and then seal the door back as he left. Sometimes Doug would sneak into the room and just sit and look around, sometimes just to mock his father, sometimes wondering why he wasn't sad like the others, or why he had to fake the tears at the funeral. The only thing he did feel was an odd sense of pride and envy, and for months afterward he could be heard mumbling to himself how he never thought Mark had the guts to carry it out. "He did it. . . he really did it," he repeated.

Joanne said Doug was never the same after that. Maybe he was just frightened about now being the oldest and having to fill Mark's shoes, or knowing his father would now demand more from him. But in any event, Doug withdrew further, used more drugs, did worse in school, and alienated his father even more. Norton Gretzler spent more time in his basement office, locked inside with a bottle, grieving over the loss of his beloved son. One night he stumbled out of his hideaway and looked his remaining son straight in the eye and asked why it had been Mark, and not him, who had killed himself.

Doug still thought a lot about those days. He knew this much. He hated his father for how he treated all of them, as much as he envied Mark for how he got back at him. He knew he didn't have the guts to kill himself like his brother did, but that didn't keep him from wanting to die.

So Doug found an odd comfort in where he was and what he had done. Regardless of what Willie said about running and getting away, he realized his life was finished. For what he had been part of, and what he was apparently still willing to do, he knew these days would eventually become his undoing, and therefore achieve the same results as did his brother Mark.

22

Sunday, October 28, 1973 | 3:30 pm.

Even for Arizona this was hot. Here it was the end of October and the mercury was still hovering around ninety. Thanksgiving was less than a month away, and holiday decorations were already showing up in the department stores, but outside it still felt like summer. Today even the snowbirds wondered whether they had arrived too early. Hiding under umbrellas and canopies, seeking relief from the very sun they had come thousands of miles to worship, they were thinking maybe that snow back east wasn't so bad after all. Day after October day, ninety plus, and the weatherman was guessing there was no change in sight.

And as if that wasn't bad enough, there had been no rain for over a hundred days. The monsoons that normally drenched the valley in late summer never came. No drizzle, no showers, not even a drop. This year it seemed like summer had never left, and while the desert barely noticed the unusual heat and dry weather, its people always did.

So when Dave Arellanes went out to pick up the Sunday morning paper off the porch, he wasn't interested in the news or even what football games were on the tube that day. Instead, Dave went straight to the weather page. Sunny. Hot. Dry. All week. Same story. He let out a sigh, put the paper down, walked outside and turned the sprinklers on. Two things that can't take the heat, he decided a long time ago, were lawns and people. Hot weather brings out the worst in both.

Arellanes knew what he was talking about. He was a rare breed in Arizona; a real, honest to goodness native. Not a transplant or some snowbird who decided to stay, he had spent his entire life here, growing up not far from the small tract house in West Phoenix that he and his family called home. Sure, he was used to warm weather, but even for a native, this October was unusual. So much so, that for years to come, the first thing he would mention about this particular Sunday was how hot it was. And he would remember this Sunday for as long as he lived.

Dave Arellanes was a cop. A sheriff detective, to be precise, and ever since he was a kid, that's all he ever wanted to be. He was a twelve-year veteran with the Maricopa County Sheriff's Department in Phoenix and for the past several years he worked strictly homicide cases. Around the office they called him "Number 1", not just because he had been there the longest, but because they all considered Dave a product of the old school; long hours, a strict attention to detail, and the belief many criminals wind up catching themselves.

But that didn't mean it was an easy job, or an easy place to work. Maricopa County sprawls across Arizona, encompassing over 9,000 square miles. From the edge of the city to the barren deserts hours away, Dave's territory was mind boggling, and just four men, two teams, were responsible for piecing together the clues left from the murderous minds of others.

The job was complicated by not only the immense geographical area and ever expanding population, but now by simply the times in which they lived. Dave decided that in just the past five years things had become a lot different. People were meaner now it seemed, and with all the dope out there, they were more apt to commit crimes unthinkable just a decade earlier. All of which made Dave's work more difficult, and the poor excuse for people he dealt with daily much uglier and harder to understand.

It may have been 1973, but this was Arizona, and Dave's beat was still the Wild Wild West. He had a huge task in a huge area, and yet Dave came within about a hundred yards of never becoming involved with Willie and Doug at all. The biggest case of his career was ultimately decided by just a few hundred feet. When the radio connecting Dave with the office downtown squealed on this simmering Sunday, it meant only that it was time to go to work. Someone somewhere had found a body.

The dispatcher informed Dave that one of their officers had responded to a call in an unincorporated area of East Mesa and discovered not one, but two victims. The deputy felt there was no question it was a multiple 187 and requested a team out there immediately.

And it really was out there. The East Mesa-Apache Junction area was completely on the other side of the valley and Dave let the office know it would take him almost an hour to be on scene. He told dispatch to notify his partner and to let him know he would be there in a few minutes to pick him up.

Michael Bland was worried. It had been over a week now and there had been no word from Ken or Mike. Michael thought maybe those guys from Denver who had been hanging around could have something to do with it. Of course it was just a hunch, because other than the wild story Ken was tossing around at work, Bland had no proof Ken and Mike were even in trouble. But this morning Bland and Mike Adshade's brother John, decided to drive out and find where Yahfah had moved. Michael remembered Ken telling everyone how they were forced to take these guys out to find her, so maybe she knew where they were. While searching through Ken's apartment that morning, Bland discovered a slip of paper with Yahfah's new address. The apartment looked deserted, like Ken and Mike just up and disappeared. There were no other clues to their surprising disappearance.

Making the trip to Apache Junction with Bland and Adshade was Vic Johnson, who had reported the disappearance earlier in the week. They got started about noon, and one hour and fifty miles later, they finally found the Vista Ray Mobile Home Park.

"We're looking for some friends," Michael yelled at the first person he saw.

There wasn't an immediate response. The man just stared back at the car, but it soon became clear he knew exactly who they were talking about.

"You friends of Bob and Yahfah?" he finally asked. "Cuz if you are, they ain't home."

"Can you show us where they live? Where's number one thirty three?"

The man motioned them to follow and began walking towards the far side of the park. Most of the mobile homes were new and there were many empty spaces. Standing alone near the edge of the park was a tan and white single wide facing a low block wall, and beyond it, an empty field. A late model brown Ford sedan with a flat tire was in the dirt area close to the mobile, but neither Mike Adshade's VW or Bob's old convertible were anywhere in sight.

Michael admitted this did not look like any place Bob Robbins or even Yahfah would live. It was too nice, and he was hesitant to disturb anyone who might be inside. He didn't recognize the brown Ford, but this was indeed space 133, for it was clearly painted on the asphalt in front of them. Now he began to question himself. He really had no idea if the slip of paper even had anything to do with Ken and Mike at all, and for the first time he felt like maybe he had led everyone on a wild goose chase.

He and the others had been circling the trailer, carefully keeping their distance, looking for an excuse to knock on the door, while people who lived nearby began peeking out their doors and windows, wondering what was going on. "You sure this is where they live?" Michael asked the guy who had just moments earlier brought them here.

"Yep, that's it. But like I said, they ain't home."

Michael and the others had to agree. The place was closed up tight. Not even an open window. It looked empty.

But there was something in the air surrounding the trailer. It was faint, but sickly sweet, and overpowering. Everyone seemed to notice at the same time. It wasn't garbage; it was much too strong for that. Michael went to the sliding glass door and knocked. There was no reply. The smell seemed to ooze from the cracks around the door. He knocked again. "Anybody home?" he yelled through the closed door. "Hey! Anyone in there?" There was no answer.

Now there was every reason to worry. Several of the onlookers were brave enough to peer through a window. The drapes and curtains were drawn tight and the trailer gave no clue as to who or what was inside. Both doors were locked. Michael glanced over at the Ford with the flat. He picked up a jack handle and began to pry open a window on the front of the trailer. The fragile aluminum frame gave way and he pulled the window open towards him. The hot, stale air from inside the sealed trailer poured out all over him. With it came the full effect of the foul, horrid odor that is attributed to only one thing.

There was no longer any doubt as to what they would find inside the trailer. It was now only a question of whom.

It was a family barbeque keeping Bill Miller busy early Sunday afternoon. He was refilling his drink, making sure the coals were hot and the guests were hungry, when the call came. As was usually the case in the life of a cop, you could always count on being interrupted at the worse possible time. The radio from downtown caught Detective Miller just as it had his partner a few minutes earlier. Not today, he thought. Not now. But it was too late for that. Dispatch told him Arellanes was already on his way to pick him up. He apologized to his dinner guests, but there was no need. This was not the first time, and they all knew what he did for a living. Several minutes later Bill was in the car with his partner and on their way to the trailer in Apache Junction.

At 2:30 in the afternoon, the sheriff substation in Mesa received a call from a young male adult, extremely animated, excited, panicky, rambling, asking for help at the Vista Grande Trailer Park on University Ave. The dispatcher managed to stop him and ask that he slow down and start from the beginning, wondering now if she had heard correctly the first time. The caller paused, identified himself as Michael Bland, then repeated his story. He had found two people inside a trailer. They were his friends, and they had been murdered.

Sergeant Gardner and Deputy L.B. Briscoe were at the station when the call came in. Seeing there was now little reason to rush, the officers took a few moments to discuss the course of action, then proceeded to the address given; a drive of about 15 minutes. In route, Gardner radioed back in requesting an I.D. Technician and a homicide detective be sent to the trailer park. Judge Coombs should be notified as well, he advised. His help would be required later, if for nothing more than giving his permission to remove the bodies.

Upon hearing this radio chatter, every patrol car cruising the eastern edge of Maricopa County on that lazy afternoon responded. Within minutes of Briscoe and Gardner's arrival, the narrow streets of the trailer park were thick with county sedans, and by now, dozens of curious onlookers as well.

Deputy Bell, only a few blocks away when he heard the reports, was first on the scene. He was greeted by Bland, who approached the officer's car before it even pulled to stop, all the time talking about what was inside. When Bell stepped out of the car, the stench overwhelmed him. The smell had escaped the trailer and now consumed the carport and the dirt lot next to it. Neighbors who lived close by ringed the area, most of whom had their hands to their face in an effort to shield themselves. Bell winced and blinked hard as he walked towards the trailer, guided by the man who never stopped talking. He opened the sliding door, covered his nose with a handkerchief, and cautiously stepped inside.

It was almost too much to endure. The rancid, moist air felt as if it was seeping into his uniform. It gagged him. He had come across dead animals before and was familiar with the odor, but this was a thousand times worse. For a moment he wondered if he was going to pass out, or at the very least, throw up.

They walked down the hallway and Bland showed him where to look. "We closed the doors", he said, "just like we found them."

Bell slowly pushed the first one open. On the floor, protruding from underneath a box spring mattress, a blood-matted head rested on a towel. Although he was told the bodies were of a man and woman, he guessed this was the one identified as Bob. He closed the door and took a few steps to the third bedroom, but this time there was nothing to hide the grim sight. The body of a woman lay near the wall, one arm at her side, the other twisted up over her head. The body was huge and bloated, as if ready to explode. Towels, now brown from dried blood, covered her head and blisters welted on her arms. Bell had worked homicides, but had never seen anything as bad as this. He was relieved this stuff was out of his league. He walked back out into the daylight, filled his lungs with air, and waited for the backup he prayed would arrive soon.

Gardner and Briscoe pulled in and Bell verified the report. Two bodies. Cause of death appears to be unnatural. And as if the stench didn't already tell them, both had been dead for quite some time. Sergeant Gardner assumed control of the crime scene, asking Briscoe to start taking names. More officers arrived, and he got them busy as well; setting up barriers, sealing the area surrounding the trailer, making sure nothing was touched or moved.

In addition to the ever-increasing number of sheriff officers present, space 133 was teeming with people from the park, all of whom wondered what was going on. Word filtered through the crowd that the two dead people were the new tenants; the young couple known only as Bob and Yahfah. Rumors flew. Some said they had heard gunshots several days before, and yet those who lived only a few feet away said they had heard nothing at all. Some reported cars and strangers and people coming and going at all hours. A few proudly stated they always minded their own business. Some boasted they could have told you, that with all the low life moving in, something like this was bound to happen sooner or later. Most of the adults had paid little attention to the coming and goings at space 133 and were of no help. But the young people, those who had met Bob and Yahfah, and their so-called friends, knew immediately what had happened, and who was responsible.

Deputy Briscoe pulled Michael Bland aside and took notes as Bland explained how he had been looking for two other friends – guys named Ken and Mike – who had been missing for well over a week. Ken, Mike, Bob and Yahfah had been friends and Bland thought that Yahfah might know what happened. When he went to Ken's house in Phoenix, he found a slip of paper on the counter with Yahfah's address; 11425 University #133. Bland said that the moment he got here he knew there was something wrong. He could smell it. When there was no answer at the door, they broke in, smashing a window, fearing the worst. Expecting to find their friends inside, they discovered Bob and Yahfah instead. There was no sign of Ken or Mike, but he was still worried. If Bob and Yahfah had been murdered, he was now certain Ken and Mike had been too. What's more, he explained to the deputy, he was pretty sure he knew who killed all of them.

As Bland and the others were being interviewed, Briscoe talked to the neighbors who looked on. While opinions varied, one thing remained constant. The murdered couple had visitors this past week; a young woman named Marsha, who had not been seen in awhile, and two men, strangers actually, who had been here up until just a few days ago. Their descriptions differed just slightly, but all agreed on one thing. Everyone knew the names. The older one was Bill, and his friend was called Doug.

The drive from their west side homes was a long and quiet one for the detectives. Dave was nearly ten years older than his partner, and other than their profession, they had little in common. Dave had been around awhile – a cop for almost 18 years – and his job these days was not only to solve murders, but to train Bill Miller how to as well.

On the way to the scene, they chatted about the usual stuff, none of which involved the situation they were about to find themselves in. Dave made a practice of not pre-thinking anything, or trying to guess about matters he had yet to view firsthand. Trying to get a jump-start on an investigation, he explained to Miller, only complicated matters later on. Dave wanted a clear head, so he and Bill struggled for other subjects to talk about, eventually getting around to the unusual weather.

Bill Miller was pleased to be Dave's partner. He had been on the force less than five years, all as a patrolman, and although he was in his early thirties, he was still considered somewhat of a rookie when it came to the kind of crimes Dave specialized in. Yeah, Arellanes could be a little full of himself, Bill decided, a bit of a know it all, but he also knew how fortunate he was to be in a position to learn what Arellanes already knew.

Dave had studied hundreds of killings over the years. He had stood over numerous bodies and examined them with the skill and expertise of a surgeon. He had patiently walked dozens of murder scenes, piecing together the bits of information that ultimately led him to the person responsible for the crime. In fact, he was only a teenager when he came across his first dead man, and it was then when Dave realized his passion for detective work.

The victim was lying in one of the many irrigation canals that ran through the cotton fields of west Phoenix where Dave and his family lived. He never would forget the sight of the body lying broken and twisted, face down in that ditch. Nor could he believe, let alone forgive, the backwards, bumbling county sheriff who quickly and callously decided it was all just an accident. Dave refused to believe him, and even at his young age, he knew in his heart the sheriff was wrong, or worse yet, just plain lazy. He was amazed at how little work the sheriff did, and how many things he ignored or overlooked.

So Dave took it upon himself to reenact the victim's last steps, talking to relatives and friends about the dead man's habits and daily rituals. Before the body was removed, Dave found the courage to study it, and then carefully retrieve the many clues that scattered the scene. His findings differed from those of the sheriff. This was not an accident, as he had proclaimed, but a killing, most likely by a hit and run driver.

Dave was angry, not only at what had happened and who the person was, but how little was done to find out why, or even who might be responsible. Through his rage, and later his tears, Dave resolved he would one day change the antiquated ways law enforcement handled what were obviously cases of murder.

Dave kept that promise, and years later joined the Maricopa County Sheriff's Office, the same department that had ignored him and brushed aside his conclusions to what really happened in that ditch years earlier. He never forgot those days; the sight of the dead man, or the lessons he learned from it. Without knowing it then, the man in the ditch became the single reason Dave became a homicide detective.

The dead man was Dave's father.

Jack Gilchrist and Herb Wissman, detectives also assigned to the East Mesa substation, were waiting for Arellanes and Miller when they arrived. Although not officially considered members of the homicide team, Gilchrist and Wissman worked closely with their associates from downtown on other cases. They knew the east county area well, including the countless characters, both good and bad, that made up the sparse population of Apache Junction.

They walked the carport slab and the dirt lot adjacent to it, making notes of their findings. Discoveries seemingly as insignificant as a penny or a brass button were recorded for future use. Even the debris from a vacuum cleaner bag, dumped near the front of the trailer, was logged and collected as evidence. Nothing was left to chance by either detective.

Sergeant Ed Calles made his presence known as well. Officially credited as a coordinating supervisor with the department, he and Arellanes never seemed to hit it off, and this case would prove no different. Dave always had the feeling Calles was never willing to share the credit or acknowledge a job well done, regardless of who was on the case. A glory hog was how Dave saw him. Ironically, these were the same views Calles had of Arellanes, so there was always this friction between the two. It was Calles, however, who briefed Miller and Arellanes when they arrived, although the smell alone gave it all away, and Dave realized he had been here too many times before.

He figured there must have been at least a hundred bodies he had come across in his work. Some had been dead only minutes, others so long only their sun-bleached skeletons remained; their fleshed having been picked apart by coyotes and scavengers who roamed the desert where the bodies had been dumped. What was left was usually all Arellanes had to work with. The dead were his clients. He was the only one left to represent them, even when they were found less than perfect, so Dave always referred to them as *'dead human beings'* in his typed reports, still treating them with the respect and dignity he felt they deserved, regardless of who they were, or how they got here.

The first thing Dave learned was that it didn't take long for a body to decay. The odor accompanying decomposition began almost immediately. He also had made a couple of other unscientific findings during his years of investigating murder scenes. The first one was that dead women always seemed to smell worse than dead men, why he never learned, and two, a little Vicks Vaporub smeared under the nose went a long way in getting through the tedious investigation of either one. Dave reached for his tube of mentholatum as Calles showed he and Bill Miller into the trailer.

It was suffocating. Even though it had been opened occasionally during the last couple of hours, there was no immediate way to rid the trailer of its smell. Arellanes noticed the condition of the living area and kitchen. It was fairly neat, with no outward signs of a struggle or quick departure; a telltale sign the victims probably knew their killer. The furnishings were secondhand and ordinary, nothing noticeably out of place. Calles pointed out the stains on the blue green carpet. There was little question it was blood, as were the stains leading from the front room down the narrow hallway.

The doors to the rooms had remained closed, but Calles now opened the first one to reveal the body partially exposed beneath the mattress. Arellanes backed out of the room without disturbing it. He and Miller were then led to the back room and shown the body of the second victim, the woman with the towels wrapped about her head.

Arellanes decided no further steps would be taken inside the trailer until Wissman and Gilchrist could finish their work outside. Daylight was fading fast and they would need every minute available. Arellanes and Miller retraced the other detective's steps, retrieving items found in their earlier search. I.D. Technician Edwards followed them around, taking pictures as they gathered and marked potential evidence.

It was now six o'clock and getting dark, so Arellanes took the murder investigation back inside. Nothing had been moved, nothing altered, and when one deputy suggested earlier they turn on the swamp cooler in the trailer, and hopefully remove some of the stagnant air along with it, Arellanes denied the request. He wanted everything as they found it. The doors to the house had stayed shut. Dave pointed to Edwards the shots he wanted.

Maricopa County Sheriff Paul Blubaum, who had been elected along with other Republicans in the 1972 Nixon landslide, made his appearance at the trailer in the late afternoon. Running on a platform of research, long range planning, and creating innovative police programs, he had spent most of his law enforcement years behind a desk. What he hadn't done during his tenure was to face the absolute lowest level in the crime food chain; multiple murder victims left to rot inside a tightly sealed tomb of a trailer.

Making sure the photographer was still clicking away, Blubaum told Sgt. Calles he was going inside, positive he could be of some assistance in the investigation. Calles was in no position to argue with his boss, although Arellanes was dead set against it and said so. This wasn't a show, and he didn't think Blubaum was prepared for what he was about to see. But with a handkerchief covering his nose and mouth, Sheriff Blubaum followed them in. As Arellanes pointed out the victims, the sheriff nodded to indicate he was listening, but he soon turned around and scurried from the trailer. His car left the Vista Grande moments later.

The four detectives remained inside for nearly four hours. Their inquiry would not be rushed. Bodies were marked, distances measured, blood stains sampled, evidence seized. The mattress was finally pulled off the man's body and for the first time they saw the electrical cord wrapped around his neck. The towels around the woman's face were carefully removed, cautious not to pull away any of the delicate flesh that stuck to the fabric. Her face was now revealed, and at first glance it appeared as if she had been beaten, although it was difficult to be certain, her face and head were so swollen and misshapen.

Dave's initial question during an investigation was always why, and yet there was no obvious answer here. Both victims had their pockets turned inside out, so the killers were most likely in search of money, yet nothing else in the house seemed disturbed.

The patrolmen who continued to interrogate the neighbors briefed Arellanes and Miller. The consensus was it had been at least several days since the victims had last been seen, and that there had been visitors to the trailer last week; a young girl who had left about a week ago, and two men who were seen in the park no later than Thursday evening. Dave's best guess was they had been dead for at least 3 days, maybe longer. The suspects, the two men now known as Bill and Doug, had one helluva head start.

The bodies were soft, bloated, blistered, and very fragile. Arellanes filled out the Red Tags that would accompany the bodies downtown to the office of the Medical Examiner. Then, when the mortuary was finally allowed in, he stood guard, demanding extreme care as the bodies were placed in the zippered black bags.

Everyone else had left. The October night air was warm and quiet, but the stench still lingered. Bill Miller placed the coroner's seal on the window, then closed the trailer door behind him. He and Arellanes remained a few extra minutes, long enough to make they had not overlooked anything. It was ten thirty before they dropped back into their county sedan, exhausted, but buzzing from the strong adrenaline rush only a murder scene could offer.

Dave pulled up to entrance of the Vista Grande. He looked down the county road and pointed it out to Miller. The sign marking the Pinal County line was no more than a hundred yards away. In a territory of thousands and thousands of square miles, that's how close they came to not even being called out on this one. No more than a few hundred feet.

23

Monday, October 29, 1973 | 9 am.

He had found his calling. The Hitman. The Enforcer. The first one called when nothing else worked and the shit was flying. Damn right he could collect the money, make the threats, call the shots, get it done. Just say when and where. This was his moment. This was who he was. A bad dude with a bad attitude.

Sue Harlan decided she needed someone like Bill the moment she met him at Ray and Red's Friday afternoon. He looked the part. He talked the talk. He told her about the work he did back home. Just the kind of stuff she was knee deep in. He dropped a few names. Said she probably had heard of them. She nodded that she had. He offered to do some piecework. Money shouldn't be a problem, he said. Maybe she could help them get settled in. You know, a favor, and he would do her a favor in return. Show her how he handled himself. Take the rest from there. See how they worked together. She said yeah.

Sue was nickel and dime, but even drug punks have trouble collecting, plus she admitted she could never trust any of the others to do it right. But Bill seemed different. A little more in control. Not so strung out. She liked the sound of his voice; slow and methodical, punctuated with just enough bad ass whenever he talked about his experience doing the very thing she needed done. Shithole apartments lined the second floor of almost every building on 4th Avenue. Converted garages and crash pad shacks ran up the alleys of all the side streets. Sue told Willie that living in just about every one of them was someone who owed her something. Maybe it was only twenty bucks, but it added up. It was business, she said, and Willie said hell yes it was! HIS business. "Just tell me where I can find them and how much they're into you for, then you just let me take care of the rest."

He and Doug spent the weekend hanging out, laying low. There was no telling when the cops would be all over them, but most of the time they gave no thought to what they had done. Like maybe it had never happened, or that it didn't matter, or that no one really cared. Willie told Doug they needed to rest before they started out again. Sue got them a room upstairs at the place next door to The Shanty, staked them to a little stash, and said she would be in touch.

The boarding house held a mixture of odd and interesting characters, and like The Avenue itself, it attracted quite an assortment; from the university cast-offs and dropouts, to transients, hitchhikers and burnt out old hippies who stumbled into Tucson for the winter. Most of the occupants held onto some kind of sad, twisted life full of problems and struggles, always of someone else's making. A simple nod hello was usually followed with a long painful story of how they managed to get screwed out of what was rightfully their's; whether it be a child, money, drugs, the love of another, or the happiness that forever eluded them. They wouldn't tell you their real name, but they were always willing to explain, for the thousandth time, the tragic reasons of how they fell head first onto the Avenue – down right anxious for you to know how they got to be so mixed up, fucked over, unlucky and unloved.

There was a woman, hooked on heroin, who escaped to Tucson but never her addiction. She lived there, as did a young guitar player from Wisconsin, who spent every night playing across the street at JuJu's, every day dreaming of a better gig, where pay was more than a cold bean burro and a warm beer.

In another room two college dropouts toiled to create the perfect socialist government and passed out mimeographed fliers announcing rallies for various causes, all carrying the headline of 'people's something or another' and their handiwork could be seen stapled to the telephone poles around the neighborhood. There were several drunks who lived there. A few junkies. Some of which who went so far as to have a regular job in an attempt at a semi-regular life.

Downstairs was a huge black man named Nelson, who Willie clashed with the first time their eyes met. He wore brown rust colored bell-bottoms and big flowered shirts. Word was, back in the Sixties, he was a fairly righteous militant dude. Now he was content to just rob liquor stores. His wife lived on the other side of town, hiding out, trying to resume her life as a nurse. He never let her be, always hassling and threatening her along the little boy he claimed was his. Nelson usually had company, either one of his brothers in the robbery deal, or a hard looking white woman with stringy bleached blonde hair. The first time Willie saw Nelson, he was out front of the building beating the shit of out her. True to form, Willie stepped in and told him to cool it; he had no business hitting a woman. But Nelson, it seems, didn't appreciate the interference and let it be known that from now on he damn well better stay out of his way.

Across the hall from them lived a beatnik. Doug thought it was cool to have this guy, the last of his breed, like some kind of dinosaur, living right there in the building. The old guy sold marijuana cigarettes one at a time to pay his rent, and had a habit of saying 'wow' at the beginning and end of every sentence. He quoted Ginsberg and Ferlinghetti, as if he expected Doug to know who he was talking about. Just the same, Doug was mesmerized by the guy, and wished he could have spent a little more time hanging out with him.

Willie and Doug completed the scene at the rooming house, but during the first few days spent little time there. Usually they were across the street at JuJu's listening to music, next door at The Shanty, or on a stool at Ray and Red's. But today, however, Willie had to go to work.

Sue told him this first job was going to be a piece of cake. This guy named Rudy had stiffed her and then had managed to avoid her for several weeks now. She said Rudy had some things that were her's and she wanted them back. "You go see him and get my stuff. Rudy knows what he has is mine. He stole it from me. He won't give you any shit if you show him you mean business."

So armed with Rudy's address, and the .22 under a jacket, Willie and Doug showed up at Rudy's place and announced the reason for their visit. Willie was in his element and gave his best *'give me one good reason not to waste you'* speech, but before Rudy could say a word, Willie smashed him across the face with the butt end of the gun. After a few kicks to the ribs, Rudy finally was allowed to tell his side of the story. In the end, Willie walked away empty handed and had to explain what happened to his boss later that night. It seemed the items in question weren't stolen at all, but taken by Sue's own sister. She in turn sold them to an unsuspecting Rudy, who wound up getting the shit kicked out of him as a bonus.

Sue and her sister, Joanne, another prize on 4th Avenue, had long waged this sibling war of 'You have, I want'. Sue was a businesswoman and demanded respect around the area. She had a house, a car, a fairly good income, and of course lots of the very thing her sister coveted the most. Dope. Joanne had nothing, except for a nasty heroin habit and a full time hatred for her older sister. Now, in less than 72 hours, they had managed to get Willie involved in their family feud. It was his first go around into the gun for hire profession he had long dreamed about – a twenty dollar beef between two conniving sisters – but Willie was quick to retell the story about his hit on Rudy every chance he got, and each time it became larger and more vivid.

"I took my Magnum and shoved it in his mouth," he droned on to anyone within earshot. "The money or your fucking worthless life, I said. I don't really care which one I walk outta here with."

The autopsies on Katherine Mestites and Robert Robbins began before dawn Monday morning, and by 11 am Dr. Heinz Karnitschnig, the County Medical Examiner in Phoenix, had confirmed what everyone suspected. The cause of death of both victims was attributed to a gunshot wound. The cord wrapped around Robbins neck had been left in place for the examination, but it was never mentioned in the report submitted later that afternoon. The .22 slugs causing the damage were recovered and turned over to the Sheriff's Department. Although Mestites' body revealed two gunshot wounds, only one bullet was found so Detectives Gilchrist and Wissman decided to try and find the other slug, and they returned to the trailer late that morning with a lab technician from the State Department of Public Safety.

The detectives met up with Arellanes and Miller who had arrived several hours earlier. The smell inside was still overpowering, even though the windows were now open and the swamp cooler left to labor all night. But the odor had permeated the carpet, the furniture, even in the curtains still drawn tight across the windows. Tests were performed on the blood-discolored carpet and spots found on the walls and doors, and the results noted. Gilchrist conferred with Sgt. Calles regarding the missing bullet, being advised that the autopsy showed that it passed completely through the body of Katherine Mestites and therefore was most likely still imbedded in the carpet under where the victim was found.

Upon closer examination, a small hole was discovered in the carpet and the padding beneath it, but no bullet was found. However, squares of carpet were cut out and placed into evidence just the same. Before leaving, Gilchrist filled two more cardboard boxes with Kathy's books and letters, hoping they could supply a name of a friend or customer, someone who might have a reason for wanting her dead.

The list of those claiming to know something about either the victims or the suspects was lengthy and comprised several pages of handwritten notes taken yesterday afternoon. When Miller and Arellanes returned to the trailer Monday morning they began knocking on the screen doors of the nearby trailers, looking for anyone who might have something else to add. The two people who seemed to know the most about the suspects, and apparently the last to see them alive, were the two young girls named Monique and Brinda, so naturally they were the ones that Dave wanted to talk to first.

Brinda was in school, but Monique Jered was home, and to Arellanes delight, supplied a windfall of information. It was Monique who not only offered up the names of the suspects, but detailed descriptions of them as well. Monique explained how she first met the two men, and how they all had hung around the pool last Wednesday night, and she remembered seeing Bob there as well. It was the last time she saw him, or Yahfah, for that matter. She thought Bill and Doug were leaving for San Francisco, but the following night they were still there, although she didn't speak with either one. "Brinda would know more", she said, "because I saw her walking with them the next night."

Monique gave a detailed account of her visits with Bill and Doug, offering precise times and details of conversations. Her manner was exact and unwavering. She even wrote down all the things she remembered and handed in over to Arellanes when he came to interview her. She recalled fake leather jackets with torn sleeves, a brown Ford with a flat tire, and the sound it made as it left the trailer park. She remembered the songs Bill and Doug played as they sat in the rec center, and the color of the car that Bill said was waiting for them in Mesa. "Black," she recalled, "and they were taking it to a big concert in San Francisco." The 17 year old had given the best description of the two suspects thus far, so before he left, Dave arranged for her to come downtown later in the afternoon to help put together a composite drawing.

Arellanes and Miller set up shop in the recreation center of the park, and talked with people throughout the morning and well into the afternoon. All of those they spoke with offered tiny bits of information, that when connected, gave a much clearer picture of what had unfolded the previous week at the Vista Grande. But what Arellanes really wanted to know was when the two suspects had actually left the trailer park and how much of a head start they had.

The info he was looking for came from one of the last people he talked to that day. A kid named Randy told how he had seen them loading stuff into Bob's old blue convertible early last Friday morning. "I think I startled 'em though cuz they were tryin' to be real quiet."

"What time Friday morning was this?" Dave inquired.

"Oh. . .'bout three."

"Three? You mean you saw them leave at three in the morning?" Arellanes asked again, wondering if he had heard correctly.

"Yeah, 'bout then."

"What did they say?"

"They just told me to stay away from the trailer."

While the interviews were continuing at the Vista Grande, Wissman and Gilchrist stopped in at the Playful Kitten to talk to Yahfah's boss and co-workers, who had already heard the terrible news.

None had much to offer. They hadn't known Yahfah very long, but Barbara remembered her as always in a good mood. When asked about anyone else staying with her, Barbara said yes, she was told they were some friends and had even met one of the men. She couldn't remember his name, but gave a description that closely matched the one given by Monique; a white man with negro features, she said, and very polite. The last time she saw Katie was Wednesday night when they worked together. Katie called in sick on Thursday and she never heard from her again, figuring she just up and quit like most of the girls do sooner or later.

Wissman and Gilchrist went back over to the Vista Grande and interviewed Brinda Lowery. Brinda said she first met Yahfah and Bob the weekend they moved in. Then, about a week later, she was introduced to a girl from Denver named Marsha who had came to visit. Marsha was Bill's woman, or at least that's what she had heard, but Marsha left before Bill came back, and as far as she knew, Marsha had returned to Denver a week ago.

When asked the last time she remembered seeing either of the victims, she thought for a minute and said it was Thursday. She saw Yahfah that afternoon talking on the phone at the rec hall. After Yahfah got off the phone, she and Brinda chatted for a few minutes and Yahfah said she had gotten mad at Bob and sent him to stay with some friends in Chandler for a few days. She said Yahfah was wearing blue jeans and a red-stripped mid-riff sweater, the same clothes she was wearing when they found her. So as it was, Brinda Lowery was the last person to see both of them alive, even though it was a day apart.

Later, when the detectives relayed this information to Arellanes, they began to question whether the two had even been killed at the same time. Bob Robbins disappeared at least 24 hours before Yahfah, and she even talked to others about him "leaving for a few days". Yet he never left at all. Clearly, Bob Robbins was killed inside the trailer, and they wondered how that could be without Yahfah knowing about it. The initial speculation Monday was that it was quite possible Yahfah was killed simply because she discovered Robbin's body, and knew who had murdered him.

Miller and his partner returned downtown late in the afternoon. Without a photo, the next best tool was the composite drawing; a scientific sketch made from the best recollection of witnesses. A certain nose, or chin, big earlobes or sunken cheeks, features when placed together give a fairly accurate portrait of a suspect. They were one-dimensional sketches on a clear Mylar, and when placed on top of the others, created a close resemblance of any given suspect. It was called the Iden-ti-kit. Each forehead or mustache was given a number, and everybody in the world, every face you have ever encountered, could come out of that box. Everyone was just a series of numbers. The hairstyle and shape could be an H-61 or an H-152, but it had a number, as does every feature on your face.

That task would fall to Monique, who arrived on time, and Dave was waiting with the black box full of lips, cheeks and hairdos. For the next hour he and the teenager built the faces of the two men who had visited the trailer park last week. She described a nose, and Dave pulled out 3 or 4 that might match, then Monique pointed to the one that looked the closest and Dave would place it on the outline. Eventually the faces took a familiar form, and it was at that moment when the young girl shuddered, knowing what they had created. Willie and Doug. Dark hair, Afro, H-55. Long blond hair, parted in the middle, H-160. Noses. . .N-37 and N-03. Lips. . .L-01 and L-09. When it was finished, Monique felt confident these were the two men. For the first time, Arellanes had a much better idea of who he was looking for.

It had been a little more than 24 hours since they had first been called to the trailer to view the bodies, bodies that could have been there at least three or four days. They had names, but a cold trail. California still seemed a good bet and Dave made a note to do some checking tomorrow morning with authorities there. The brown Ford had California plates and was most likely stolen, but there had been no word back from the registered owner; a leasing company in Los Angeles. The suspects were last seen in the blue convertible early Friday morning, a car most witnesses admitted wouldn't get them very far. Dave hoped it would show up soon to help give a better idea the direction the suspects took. They had more than enough to keep them busy tonight, and plenty of leads to follow up on tomorrow, but Dave knew that unless he and Miller caught a break on this one, and fast, the killers would probably make the next move.

Arellanes understood the Catch-22. If Willie and Doug were heard from again, his guess was their names would be followed by more crime reports, along with details of their latest victims.

24

Tuesday, October 30, 1973 | 7 am.

If nothing else, Francis Jaramillo was a man of routine. Each morning at seven sharp, in the cool chrome brilliance of a new day, he arrived at his job just north of the boulevard.

It was always seven because each morning he crossed the same streets and passed the same houses at exactly the same time. He could set his watch to his travel. He could remember the name of every person he greeted on his walk to work and what they talked about. He had memorized every lawn he mowed, every hedge he clipped, precisely how long each task would take, and exactly how it was supposed to look when he was finished. Francis was a gardener, and the numbered streets that crossed East Van Buren was where he performed his duties each day.

His routine became so orderly that he grew suspicious of even the slightest change, so when he first noticed the blue convertible last Friday, he knew only that it did not belong there. His curiosity got the best of him, so he cautiously approached the car that morning and stared down into it, thinking he might find out whom it belonged to. A woman's purse lay on the floor behind the passenger seat and he started to grab for it, but then realized that was not such a good idea. He would never want someone to accuse him of stealing.

So Francis returned to work, but as he trimmed the lawn around the parking lot and pool area of the motel, he kept glancing over at the Chevy, thinking that the next time he looked over the car would be gone.

But it was still there Monday morning. The purse was still on the floor of the backseat and he could tell it had not been touched. He thought that was strange considering the neighborhood, but he did nothing more about the car that day, except look at it from time to time. That night Francis watched the TV news about two people who had been found murdered in a trailer in Apache Junction. The report said the police were looking for a blue Chevrolet convertible that could be involved.

But this could not possibly be the same car they were looking for, Francis thought, because they certainly would have discovered it by now. It was only a few feet off of East Van Buren and he knew there must be a hundred police cars pass right by there each day. No, he decided, this must be a different Chevrolet. Still, he could not stop thinking about the car that night, and several times he came close to calling the police, just to ease his mind.

The Tropics Motel stood at the corner of 19th and East Van Buren, its perimeter dotted with tall palms. Early Tuesday morning, Dave Arellanes got the call from Phoenix P.D. saying they had found the Chevy parked next to the motel.

Police Officer Woods was on routine patrol Tuesday morning, and as he pulled around the corner off East Van Buren, it jumped out at him. He was positive it was the car from the trailer.

Mr. Jarmillo was working close by, and saw the officer get out to look at the convertible. Francis put down his rake, walked over, introduced himself, and told him the car had been there since last Friday. Jarmillo pointed at the purse and Woods picked it up, combing through it for a name. At the bottom of the purse was a gold colored key. He yanked open the passenger door and leaned in to see if it fit the ignition. It didn't. Reminding himself the vehicle was wanted in a homicide, Woods backed off to wait until the sheriff unit arrived.

The convertible had not even on the morning's list of stolen cars. Monday had been a blur, and it had slipped through the cracks. Between trips to the trailer, interviewing witnesses and rehashing notes, Arellanes and Miller had not been able to tend to every detail. So although most of the Sheriff deputies knew about the Volkswagen bus in Califonia, and the blue Chevy, Arellanes had failed to officially notify other agencies around the valley about the wanted vehicles until Tuesday morning.

Dave had no specific details about the convertible until he got a call from Deputy Preston just before noon on Monday. Preston told him about his encounter with three people in a blue Chevrolet a week earlier in Apache Junction, just a couple of miles from the murder scene. But he said his registration check that day listed someone other than either of the two victims as the owner; info that troubled Dave, who now worried there may be another body somewhere. He asked Preston to try and track down the registered owner, and added he wanted him to hear the man's voice for himself, just to make sure he was okay.

So first thing Tuesday morning, Dave took the license and VIN number he got from Preston and phoned it in. By 9 am the Chevy entered the National Crime Information Computer as stolen. It was also listed on the daily bulletin given to the patrol officers at the Sheriff's office, then sent to other law enforcement agencies in Arizona.

Less than an hour later, Phoenix Police Officer Woods called in to report he had the car. Minutes later Arellanes and Miller were on their way, and it was deemed such a big break in the case that Sergeant Calles, Lieutenant Hill, Wissman and Gilchrist came along as well. As they drove to the location, Dave realized there was the possibility the two suspects were still somewhere in the area. He radioed to those already on the scene to checkout the rooms at the motel along with the neighborhoods surrounding it.

Before they even turned off East Van Buren, Dave could see the car, along with several officers milling around it. It was in plain view, not fifty feet off the main drag. There did not appear to have been any attempt to hide the car, and by its looks alone, Dave wondered if it hadn't just died there.

For the next couple of hours he and the others worked the car, noting every scrap inside it, logging each item, but removing nothing. While several items linked Yahfah to the Chevy, there was little else to link it to any crime. There were no bloodstains, no weapons, no bullets, only bits of trash; like a book of matches from the Playful Kitten and wrappers from Jack in the Box.

Jaramillo said Friday morning at seven was the first time he noticed the car, and Dave remembered the witness at the trailer park telling them he had seen two men leave Yahfah's place at about 3 o'clock Friday morning in Bob's blue Chevy, so that much fit.

The detectives went through the purse found on the floor of the back seat, but it yielded nothing. Dave took a few Polaroids, then called for a tow truck. The Chevy was hauled to the Sheriff's garage downtown, and that afternoon the lab went over it with their fine toothcomb. It gave up very little. I.D Technician Ness dusted the car from bumper to bumper, inside and out, but managed to lift just six prints, and most of those below average quality. It was joked around the garage that the only thing anyone ever bothered to clean off that piece of shit car was their fingerprints.

Later, the victim's prints taken during the autopsy and what little they got off the car were compared, and Ness spent the rest of the day trying to come up with something positive he could give Arellanes. But it was hopeless. The only prints he could match up belonged to Bob Robbins.

By the time Arellanes got back to the office, Preston's report of the traffic stop was sitting on top of a tall stack of paperwork on his desk. It was frustrating to read how his department had his two suspects just a week earlier, and let them go. Dave admitted maybe no one had been killed yet – certainly not Yahfah, who apparently was in the back seat – but it was crystal clear the suspect Preston interviewed on Apache Trail was Doug Gretzler.

In Tucson, Nelson Erskine had taken all he cared to from the skinny-ass white dude upstairs. When Willie came strolling down Tuesday night, Nelson and four of his men were waiting for him in the street. Before he could turn and run, Willie was in the middle of it and getting beat up badly. Nelson hit him across the face and he fell to the pavement while the others kicked him. Doug, who was only moments behind his partner, heard the commotion and ran down to help. He found Willie on the ground but still swinging. Doug could only do what they had agreed; try and back him up. So he got into the fight as well, knowing he and Willie were overmatched.

Before it was over, Willie had a huge swollen eye, along with cuts on his face and arms. Doug claimed to have been stabbed in the side, although the injury was slight. Both had taken more punishment than they had given, but that was not the worse part of the fight.

Nelson took both their weapons, so Willie and Doug hid out in their room for the rest of the night, not sure if Nelson was coming back or not.

25

Wednesday, October 31, 1973 | 4:30 pm.

The long southwestern summer in Arizona had never ended. Only the calendar could confirm what day of the year this was. Nightfall came earlier, but the air did not snap with the sensation fall weather usually brings. The natural signs of autumn were nowhere to be seen here in the desert, and yet the final day of October was upon the people of the Vista Grande.

For the past several days the park manager, Fred Quimby, had gone door to door trying to get the residents together for a Halloween party this night at the rec center. He found little interest. The events of the past week had cast a pall upon the young neighborhood, and the Coroner's Seal posted on the trailer at Space 133 seemed much more horrifying than any cardboard skeleton or witch hanging in a nearby window. The smell was gone, but not their memories or their imagination. The children now believed the trailer was haunted, and took great delight in showing other kids from around Apache Junction where the killings took place. The residents at the Vista Grande spent these past few days magnifying their own close calls with the two killers. Killers who, they reminded each other, were still out there somewhere; a feeling that jarred their already jangled nerves.

To some cops, this was the part of the job they hated. But not Dave Arellanes. He enjoyed interviewing witnesses. He believed he was good at it. No. He *knew* he was *great* at it. He was glad to have them. Hell, he would take all he could get. But to pick through dozens of interviews, and figure out who is telling the truth and who is conning you, well, even Dave agreed that was tough. Ten different people would tell twenty different stories. The ones who knew the most, told the least, and the ones who didn't know shit wouldn't shut up. But, as Arellanes said many times, and as he reminded his partner today, a good cop had to be a good listener "Open your ears, and these people will tell you all you need to know."

But of all the people they talked to, only one could give the detectives a clue about where to begin looking. It was Michael Bland who had said the two suspects had come down from Denver, so a call was placed to the police there, hoping the names Bill Steelman or Douglas Gretzler had surfaced recently. If either of them had been arrested, maybe Denver had some background, or better yet, a mug shot. He had also given names of a few people who Yahfah hung out with up there, so their main focus was a girl now identified only as Marsha Renslow. It wasn't much to go on, but they gave the leads to Denver P.D. and waited. Wednesday afternoon the call came back.

"Yeah, this is Bill Miller."

"Bill, this is Captain Hinds, Denver Police. We spoke about your request regarding a couple of people up here. First off let me introduce Sergeant Walsh – he's here on the other line – he did some checking and has a little bit of good news."

"Detective Miller? Walsh here. Listen, a couple of your leads checked out. We did find this Marsha Renslow and we talked to her early this afternoon. She said she knew a couple of guys by those names you gave us – the Bill you mentioned is Bill Steelman and the other a Douglas Gritzler. That's correct, isn't it?"

"That's Gretzler, we think, with an 'E'," Miller answered. "Did you tell her anything about the victims? We heard one of them was her friend. We haven't officially released that information yet."

"No, didn't mention a thing. Just said these two men were connected to a crime and we wanted to talk to them. I got to tell you though, this Marsha girl, she's just a little bitty thing, but a real smartass."

Denver relayed information gathered during their brief talk with Marsha. She spoke of a blue MGB convertible and a rock group named Mountain. She wasn't positive about Doug's last name, but said his nickname was Loki. She said that Bill said he was born in Los Angeles. They also said they didn't think she was being totally up front with them.

"You indicated this Marsha girl was in Phoenix with the suspects a few weeks ago. Are we right on that?" Walsh asked.

"That's what we were told," Miller answered. "Witnesses said she even stayed at the house where the victims were found."

"Well then, I think we're going to need to follow up on that angle with her again."

"Why's that?"

"Well, she says the last time she saw the suspects was on the 6th or 7th of October, and they said they were heading to a place called Modesto, California. She says she was never in Phoenix"

"She lying," Miller shot back. He told Denver to expect two detectives from their department in Denver by midnight.

It was now three in the afternoon and Marsha was freaking out. Yahfah didn't have a phone, but she desperately needed to contact her, so the minute the cops left her apartment, she grabbed a piece of lined notebook paper, tore it in half and wrote a quick note, desperate to warn her friend about what was coming down. Instructed by the cops not to leave her house, she asked her brother Jake to run down to the post office and mail the letter for her. *Special Delivery,* she told him, *and hurry!* She looked it over one last time before sealing it in the envelope.

> *Yahfah*
> *I'll tell you in more detail later but the pigs are probably going to be there asking about Bill. Tell them everything except my tear gas gun & knife. Have you heard anything from Ken? or Mike? They might have got it from Bill & Loki.*
> *P.S. Could you call me as soon as you get this? My neighbor's number is 722-9209. I think I can send you the money for it in my next letter. Call person to person.*
> *Love ya*
> *Marsha*

She just knew Bill was going to try something stupid one day. He was always talking about 'doing someone' and how much he hated Ken, and when Bill didn't come back to the trailer that day, well, she just had this hunch. She knew she should have warned Yahfah while she was there, but couldn't stand the thought of making her angry, knowing how upset she would be with her for bringing Bill down there in the first place. She hated the idea that she had now gotten Yahfah involved in all this, so it was the last thing Marsha wanted, the cops hanging around Yahfah's asking a bunch of questions.

It was a little after four o'clock when he watched his car accelerate up Mission Road and disappear. He remembered because it was the last time Gregorio Sierra saw his brother alive.

Greg had agreed to let him use his car to get to work Wednesday because Gilbert Sierra had a hard time holding a job. He had only been on this new one for a couple days and he was already finding excuses why he couldn't go. Making excuses was one of the few things Gilbert Sierra was really good at. That and getting loaded. Still, Greg agreed to meet his little brother that afternoon to give him the keys.

The elder Sierra had already finished his day and was now working on his first beer, kicking back on the lawn at Kennedy Park in south Tucson. Gregorio and his roommate shared a little place at the Golden Spur Trailer Park nearby. It wasn't much, except hot, so the two spent their leisure time elsewhere, usually stretched out in a shady spot at Kennedy, drinking and killing time. Now that Gilbert had a job, the two agreed to let him move in with them – something he said he would get around doing by the weekend, for Gilbert had few possessions. These days he cared only about drinking and smoking dope, and all his energy and money went into that. But every once in awhile he allowed his conscience to get the best of him and he would promise himself, and his family, that he was going to change; he was going to find a job and a place to stay, and he was going to stop screwing around and finally make something of himself. All of which he would do - for a few days, at least - or just long enough to get another loan from his mother, money he would quickly party away. After which he would then lose his job, and the process would repeat itself all over again.

Gilbert was young, male, and Mexican-American. He grew up in Morenci, northeast of Tucson, and even though the town was small, the mining pits were huge. Morenci was the home of Phelps Dodge copper mines and the canyons carved out of the earth were among the largest in the world, so opportunity for work was just as big. Unlike many of the others in Morenci, Gilbert had graduated from high school, and even thought about attending a community college in the fall of '72, but the chance to make $36.60 a day as a smelter was just too good to pass up.

To his credit, Gilbert worked at Phelps Dodge for almost a year, and as his income rose, so did his intake of alcohol and pot. He had a long list of close calls, but somehow always managed to keep his job there. His problem was not just the drugs and alcohol, but the manner in which he acted when using them. Even Gregorio, who shared some of Gilbert's habits, said his brother could be a real asshole when he was drinking.

So it became almost inevitable that Gilbert would one day get fired from Phelps Dodge, which he eventually did in late summer of 1973. Reasons why varied, but on his application at a different company several weeks later, he admitted 'being absent for 28 days' at his old job. By now Gilbert had enough of little Morenci and saw this as a good excuse to head down to Tucson. So at 19 years of age, and with a loan from his family, Gilbert packed a few clothes and said goodbye.

Tucson was only about an hour away and Gilbert had spent lots of time there visiting his brother and cousins who had left Morenci for the big city years ago. He moved in with a cousin, Lorenzo, but was asked to leave before the week was out. One night, while hanging out at one of the many bars up and down the old Nogales Highway, he started drinking with an airman stationed at the nearby Davis/Monthan Air Force Base. Upon hearing Gilbert's hard luck story, the guy offered to let him stay his place, but that didn't last long either. Where Gilbert called home these last few weeks was anyone's guess, so Gregorio offered him a bed in his cramped trailer, just so he could keep an eye on him. Gilbert had no money, no car, nothing. Even his driver's license had been revoked after five DUIs in less than a year, but he promised his family he would soon be back on his feet and then he would find a place of his own.

On Friday, October 26th, Gilbert hitched a ride to the offices of Magna Copper in San Manuel, where he filled out the employment application. He wrote down a couple of names of current employees who might put in a good word for him. He listed his job at Phelps Dodge Mines, cautiously avoiding the reason he left. He said he had never been convicted of any crime, although his rap sheet, even in a brief 19 years, was already nearly a page long. He also claimed to have a valid driver's license. Much to his surprise and relief, the company never checked out those statements. He listed his past experience and wages, and noted he was willing to start anytime and work any shift. On the last line of the application Gilbert wrote, "I want to live here and make my living here." Magna

Copper desperately needed laborers, so he was hired that afternoon and told to start Monday. It was during the company required physical at the San Manuel Hospital later that day when Gilbert met Peter Arredondo, another hew hire and they agreed to car pool from Tucson. Gilbert was relieved at the arrangement, because it allowed him a little time to work out his car problem. Although he had the job, he wondered how he would even get to work on his first day.

Big Red's, Steve's, The Blue Note, The Body Shop, Sierra hit all his spots on Saturday and Sunday as he spent the weekend in his usual stupor. But he did find enough time to call his grandmother in Morenci and tell her the good news about the job. He hinted about his money problems and she promised to send him a check to hold him over.

Gilbert's first couple of days at Magna Copper passed without difficulty, although getting to and from work was going to be a big problem. Without a car, he couldn't hold up his share of the car pool and now Peter Arredondo had quit after Monday's shift for the very same reason. Gilbert could have used the same excuse, but decided to tough it out, at least through the week. Gregorio offered his car at a last resort, just to help his brother. The $100 check from his grandmother arrived as promised on Tuesday. He scored a small bag of grass, then proceeded to The Cabaret Bar on Speedway to celebrate his windfall. Somehow Gilbert managed to get to his job that night without a problem. Two days in a row.

On Wednesday, October 31st, Sierra slept in late. Working a swing shift cramped his lifestyle, but the benefits were not having to worry about an alarm clock. He told Gregorio that he needed his car today to get to work and to Gilbert's surprise, he didn't complain. "Meet me at Kennedy Park about three-thirty. You can take it then."

Gregorio loved his car, his pride and joy; a 1972 Dodge Charger, and that he allowed his brother to borrow it surprised even him. A tank full of cheap 98 octane brought the powerful Hemi to life under the mile long hood, and you heard the car coming a block away. Gregorio remembered adding the chrome wheels, but not the dent on the right front fender, the obvious result of a late night journey home, so he knew that somewhere in Tucson there was a post or guardrail, maybe even a Ford, sporting a touch of Mopar Hemi Orange paint.

But on Wednesday afternoon the Charger sat silent at Kennedy Park while its owner kicked back in the shade nearby nursing a cold one. As soon as he saw him, Greg waved and motioned him over to where he and his roommate Ned were sitting. It didn't take long for him to see Gilbert was very drunk.

"Little brother!" Gregorio greeted him and held up the brown bag. The two brothers shared many of the same features; both short and stocky, although Greg probably had another thirty pounds on his little brother. He was also ten years older, and that showed as well. They spent the next few minutes drinking and talking until Gilbert said he had some things to do before going to work and he didn't want to be late.

"Tonight then? You moving in tonight? Gregorio asked, wondering how he was going to get his car back.

"Probably be too late, man," Gilbert answered. "Maybe tomorrow."

Greg shrugged, as if to say that would be fine, then tossed him the keys. Gilbert started to walk away, but then turned around and reached in his pocket. He pulled out an envelope and handed it to his brother. "Keep this for me until tomorrow. I don't want to get busted with it." It was what was left of the pot Gilbert had bought yesterday. Gregorio laughed. His brother was usually not so trusting. A few minutes later he heard the low rumble of his Charger, then eventually fade away, heading north on Mission Road, back towards downtown Tucson.

Gilbert had reached his crossroads. He had his brother's car, a fat wallet and the urge. Unfortunately, he also had a job, and even he was smart enough to realize this might be his last shot at getting back on track. so as he sped towards town, he had already decided he could always get another job, but opportunities like this didn't come around everyday. What he needed was a drink, and someone to help him enjoy the evening.

Fortunately, Carmen, an old friend, was still at work when Gilbert knocked on her door late Wednesday afternoon. His polite rap became a pounding when he realized she wasn't home. Neighbors heard him slam his fist against the door and scream obscenities at her. They also saw the Dodge Charger fishtail away from the curb and roar up the street moments later.

Gilbert figured screw it, and drove the 40 miles to the mines at San Manuel for his third night on the job. But it was difficult for him to concentrate and he constantly checked his Timex, fidgeting, as the hands crawled towards the end of his shift. He was already making big plans about where he was going; the bars would still be open when he got off at midnight, and still rowdy with all the Halloween craziness. Gilbert could barely stand the wait.

It was well after eleven when the Frontier Airlines jet taxied to the terminal at Stapleton Airport in Denver. The first thing they noticed was how much colder it was here, a reminder that while Phoenix held on tight to their long Indian summers, the rest of the world was already bracing for winter. Wissman and Gilchrist grabbed their suitcases and hurried into the city for their appointment with Marsha Renslow. Denver P.D. told her earlier two officers from Arizona would be arriving later that night and insisted on meeting with her the moment they got to town, regardless of the hour. So Marsha stayed home, dreading the call she knew would come sooner or later.

Wissman and Gilchrist had little idea what they would find in Denver. All they had to go on were the names of their two suspects and whatever they could drag out of Renslow. She had lied about her involvement – and they were going to catch her in that – but what else? For all the detectives knew, their suspects may have already come back to Denver for the protection of people, like Marsha, who were apparently willing to lie for them.

In a small apartment just off 4th Ave in Tucson, Willie nursed his wounds and replayed the fight from the night before. With him were a few people he had met over the past couple of days; a guy named Michael Marsh, his girlfriend Joanne, and two other women known only as Shawnee and Cathy. Willie made it clear it was not a fair fight, trying to avoid the embarrassment of not only losing the battle, but their weapons as well. He started in with his storytelling and he eventually got around to his favorite; the one where he was hired to kill his own wife in a family-ordered hit. "Shit, I didn't know she was even the target until the very last minute, and by then it was too late. It was either her or me, so I did what I had to do." He left the ending hanging right there for effect. Man, he loved telling that one! He waited for a gasp, or a comment, or at least a little sympathy, but there was nothing.

Doug sat in the corner, paying little attention to Bill. He believed him, but he had heard the story before. Noticing Doug's lack of enthusiasm, Willie leaned over and whispered to Joanne, his eyes still on his partner.

"You know, I usually don't like killing women. I let Doug take care of them because that shit just doesn't bother him."

He waited a moment to let what he had just said sink in. "And Joanne, I want you to know that I never, ever, leave any witnesses."

26

Thursday, November 1, 1973 | 1 am.

The interrogation of Marsha Renslow had begun. Denver Police picked her up at her mom's apartment on Sherman Street shortly after midnight, brought her downtown and up to the third floor offices of Homicide where Herb Wissman and Jack Gilchrist were waiting. Because she was barely 17, as well as the difficulty bringing her handicapped mother in with her, Detective Cantwell received permission from Mrs. Renslow to take Marsha in alone. Angered her daughter was again in trouble, she readily agreed to his request.

Anyone who met Marsha first noticed her size. Or better yet, lack of it. She was tiny thing, under 5 feet, and her long brown hair seemed much too long for her body. It hung straight down, well past her shoulders, and she purposely let it cover her face, her dark eyes hiding behind it. She was all tomboy; in her walk, her dress, even the vulgar movement of her arm as she wiped the snot from her dainty nose with the sleeve of her flannel shirt. She coughed repeatedly. Loud. On purpose. Out of a small but nasty mouth, and from behind an old and vile tongue. She turned up her nose to the offer of coffee, then jerked her elbow away as Cantwell attempted to guide her into the room. He stepped back and laughed. With a sarcastic bow and a royal sweep of his arm, he invited her inside. There was a gray metal table, four chairs, and nothing more, and it was the last time Cantwell showed her any kindness.

However, Wissman began politely, telling her they were here from Phoenix, investigating the possible murder of two people in Arizona, and that her name had come up. He said nothing about the victims nor did he offer any additional details. He let her know that she wasn't under arrest, at least not yet, and they were just looking for a little information.

But Marsha wasn't buying. Believing this was about Ken and Mike, she just stared back and sneered. She was damned sure not going to give up Bill and Doug over those two pricks, so she decided to play hard-ass. "Listen," she slouched, "I ain't givin' you people shit. Besides, I really don't know where you guys are comin' from. I don't know nothin' about no murders."

That was all it took. Cantwell exploded. He snatched the two Polaroids from Gilchrist's hands and leaped towards the table. "Well then, let me tell you something!" he spewed right in her face. "We got some pictures of your little friend here. Lemme just show those to you!"

He tossed the two snapshots onto the table in front of her. Marsha looked down to see the bloated, disfigured and very dead body of her dear sweet Yahfah lying before her. She screamed and jerked away. She shrieked and wailed, shaking her head, daring not to look again, pulling at her hair in disbelief.

Cantwell continued his attack. "There! How's that?" he screamed "What do you think of your friends now? How do you like what they did to your poor little what's-her-name?" He laughed at her outright stupidity. "And you sit here protecting them. Shit! They would have killed you too. Hell, you'd be on the floor right next to your little friend there!"

Marsha collapsed. She couldn't believe what Bill had done! He knew how she felt about Yahfah! How could he do this to her? She wept and moaned, and while it might have seemed like forever, it was mere moments later, when she finally caught her breath as the spit and defiance left her body. She broke down and agreed to tell them what she knew, but they had to believe her, she pleaded. She didn't know anything about anyone getting killed.

But she still held back, knowing she was mixed up in it too, explaining how she first met them and how they hung out together, But one day Bill said they were going to Phoenix to buy a hundred pounds of marijuana then bring it back to Denver to sell it. She begged them to let her go, just so she could see Yahfah again. They all squeezed into Doug's car and it took 2 or 3 days to get there. She admitted Bill and Doug pulled a couple robberies along the way, but nothing real big. Just for gas money. She said one of them was some people who were sunbathing way out in the middle of nowhere, around a place called Globe maybe, and they robbed them before they ever got to Phoenix, but no one was hurt or anything.

She said they couldn't find Yahfah's house and finally Ken and Mike took them out there. After staying overnight at the trailer with Yahfah and Bob, Bill went back to town and she never saw him or Doug again. She waited at Yahfah's for days, hoping Bill would return, but he never did. Yahfah finally bought her a plane ticket back to Denver, and she had been home for over a week and hadn't spoken to anyone since, nor did she know anything about any of this until yesterday afternoon when the cops came by. Sure, she lied to them about it at first, but only because she had been in trouble with the cops before. She gave them names of people in Denver who hung out at the house – people who might offer more help – but didn't say a word about the letter she had mailed a few hours earlier. She shut up and sobbed.

There was one more question Wissman needed to ask. "Do you think if Bill and Doug came back to Denver they might try and contact you?"

Marsha wasn't paying attention. Her mind was still on Yahfah. She eventually looked up from the photos. "What? Yeah, maybe. Maybe Bill would."

"Do you think they're in Denver now?"

She shuttered. "Oh God, I hope not." She paused to consider the consequences if she was wrong. "Am I going to get protection?" she asked.

Cantwell wasn't altogether buying her scared little girl act. He was still pretty sure he didn't like her, certain he didn't trust her, and still pissed off by her shitty attitude, so he laughed. "Yeah sure. Maybe we'll have a car drive by your place every once in awhile."

In California, Detective Nelson arrived at the office long before the others, if nothing more than to shuffle through reports, looking for anything to get him off the dime. It had been a week since Butch Carlstedt issued the APB on their suspects and the stolen brown Ford, yet nothing had come from their Stop and Hold. They had the names Bill and Doug, along with a Ronald Peters who owned the Volkswagen, but that was it.

Objects in the van had given up a half dozen prints. But from whom? Without any other names, the prints held little or no promise. Nelson and Carlstedt agreed that if they couldn't find this Bill or Doug, then the next best thing was locating the car they were last seen driving.

It was about eight o'clock Thursday morning when Nelson finally got some good news. A teletype from Arizona claimed the Ford had been found. The sheriff's department in Phoenix had located it at the scene of a double homicide they were investigating. Nelson groaned, realizing their case was now going to take a back seat to murder.

He phoned Maricopa County and was turned over to Sergeant Calles, who admitted they hadn't found their suspects yet, but said they were looking for two guys – William Steelman and Douglas E. Gretzler – and that he had two of his detectives on it there, and two more who would be returning soon from Denver where there was some connection. Nelson told him his department had impounded a green VW van apparently driven by the same two men.

Calles sounded excited. "We're also looking into another kidnapping. Seems that van you have belonged to a couple of young men who have been reported missing, and we think our guys had a hand in that one as well."

"What's the names of the victims?" Nelson asked.

"A Ken Unrein and a Michael Adshade. Both white male, early twenties. Been missing about two weeks."

Nelson sat back to put the pieces together. Calles said that Unrein and Adshade were last seen on October 17th after some sort of beef with two guys from Colorado, most likely this Steelman and Gretzler pair. A *Los Angeles Times* newspaper, dated the 18th, was found in the van, so it appeared they passed through there on their way north. There was also a pair of gym shorts with the name 'Ken Unrein', along with maps from Colorado, possibly explaining the Denver connection. The incident in Sonoma took place on the 20th and the Ford was stolen the next day. According to Calles, Steelman and Gretzler were seen back in the Phoenix area by Monday the 22nd, and the bodies were discovered in Apache Junction a week later. It all seemed to fit, but now Nelson had even more reason to worry. Chances were good the two men Arizona was looking for were dead. Even worse, he had a sick suspicion he knew where to find them.

The area where the Fulkerson/Hallock kidnapping occurred, the Russian River, was a well known dumping ground. There was hardly a year that went by when his department didn't have to go out there to dig up a body. Nelson remembered a case he worked on almost a year ago to the day. A hand was seen rising from the muddy ground along the river near the town of Guerneville. When they uncovered the rest of the torso, they found the hand belonged to young man wearing a Marine Corp tunic. It appeared a shotgun blast had killed him, after which the head was severed from the body, just to be sure. He was identified as twenty six year old James Willet, an ex-Marine from Los Angeles, and three days later his car was found parked in front of a house in Stockton. When police stormed the home, they arrested two men and three women. They also uncovered another murder victim, nineteen year old Lauren Willet, shot once in the head then buried in the basement. It appeared she was killed shortly after her husband.

It was soon learned those arrested for the murders had strong ties to the Manson Family. One of those was Lynette "Squeaky" Fromme. A highly visible face during the Manson trial just a few years earlier, she proclaimed herself leader defacto of the Family, now that Charlie was behind bars. Surprisingly, while the others were sent to prison for the Willet murders, Fromme was released, only to surface again years later for trying to kill President Ford.

So Nelson remembered the Willet case very well, and he knew the Russian River area like the back of his hand. Now having been told of the murders in Arizona, and knowing two more victims could very well be hidden in the underbrush and deep forests there, he was almost afraid to wonder whether this apparent murder spree could not be compared to that of Charles Manson. It was a boast Willie himself would utter soon enough.

Both Miller and Arellanes were back in the office early Thursday morning, anticipating the news from Denver. Much like what happened to the blue Chevy, Dave had failed to get the information about the brown Ford out over the wire. That problem was solved late last night, and while the response from Sonoma County came in mid morning, Calles said nothing to Arellanes about it until much later in the day.

Herb Wissman called to report Marsha Renslow had talked, and it was now up to Arellanes and Miller to verify her story. He gave them names of some places in Phoenix where Marsha said they had stayed, along with information regarding a couple of robberies they committed there. If any of the crimes had been reported, and the descriptions even remotely matched, then Wissman felt they had at least enough for an armed robbery complaint against the two.

Marsha gave up the name Janet Runyon. She said she remembered seeing it on a checkbook stolen by Steelman. (Although she said nothing about being the one who passed the bad check at the Tahiti) So maybe there was a paper trail, Wissman offered. There were few more people in Denver to talk to, so they would be there at least through Friday, but promised to call back later with an update.

Knowing they couldn't follow up on all the leads before the end of the day, Dave asked another detective for help while he and Bill headed nearly thirty blocks up East Van Buren to the Tahiti Motel to check out Marsha Renslow's story. They asked to see the guest records of October, specifically the 15th or 16th. The manager said he had only been there for a week, and the people they really needed to talk to were the previous managers named Weld. They had been let go last Saturday, but they might know more about the people Arellanes was asking about. However, the motel guest log did show someone by the name of STEAL had registered on the morning of the 16th, but no receipt could be found to verify it. Renslow had said Bill Steelman had given the motel manager Doug's blue sports car in lieu of another night's stay. When Arellanes asked about that, the young man said he did remember a car like that the Welds took with them when they left. Maybe that might explain the lack of a receipt, and possibly the very reason the Welds were dismissed in the first place, he offered. They were now staying at the Stone Motel down the street. They could find them there. The Stone was coincidently one of the stops on Dave's list, having been mentioned by Renslow as the first place they stayed after getting into town. The Welds were now out of a job and just living at the motel, not managing it.

Bill Weld didn't seem one bit surprised to hear the cops were looking for the man he knew only as Will Steal, or the young woman with him, for that matter. The first night they were there, Weld remembered, Steal came into the office and said that he had just been robbed, and offered to sell him the MGB for $25 and another night's stay. When Weld asked about the title, Steal said it was taken in the robbery and he would have to send him a new one. The next morning, the young woman who was with him asked if she could cash a small check. She filled it out for $40 and signed it JANET RUNYON. He gave her the money and that was the last time he saw either of them.

But Weld said he got suspicious and decided maybe he had been cheated, so he called the police, who showed up that afternoon and ran a check on the car. Weld was now positive it had been stolen, but Phoenix PD reported no problem and left.

Still not satisfied, Weld called back the next day, Thursday the 18th. This time the cops decided to examine the car more closely. Opening the trunk, they discovered another set of New York plates and a sawed off rifle barrel. He also overheard one of the officers say they had found lots of marijuana stems and seeds, but didn't seem overly concerned one way or another. Weld said he didn't touch the car after that and removed only an insurance identification card from it, and although he was sure he still had the card somewhere, he had sold the car a few days later. A hundred bucks, he said, to a person he didn't know and who's name he couldn't remember.

Arellanes asked him to try and find the card, they would be in touch, then he and Miller went back to the motel office. The record book indicated that sometime in the early evening of October 13th, a person by the name of STEAL, and another man whose name was unknown, registered at the motel. The manager noted in the log that W.L. STEAL claimed to be from San Francisco and wrote down that he was driving a Ford with California plates.

While they were still downtown, Dave decided to head back to the office and see if Detective Falls had any luck. He had sent Falls over to the Coronet Ramada Hotel on Central, just a few blocks north of the station. According to Wissman, Marsha said they left the Stone Motel on October 14th and checked in at the Coronet later in the day. Fall said he contacted the manager, Frank Madison, who showed him the record book of the date in question. A WILL McSTEAL of San Francisco, who was again driving a 1959 Ford, made out the registration card for room #308. But the card was filled out very poorly, almost in an effort to obliterate the information. McSTEAL was listed as a 'walk-in' – a person who has no luggage and is required to pay in advance – which he did. Mr. Madison admitted he was not on duty when the suspects checked in, but Mr. Stamets, the desk clerk, and Mrs. Dykes, a housekeeper, were. They both remembered quite clearly the people in question, and gave a detailed description of all three. While Falls was relaying his success at the Coronet, Arellanes got a call from Bill Weld. He had found the insurance card taken from the sports car.

Dave knew the card was an important link. So far everything they had uncovered matched the story Renslow told in Denver – the sequence of events and the descriptions of the suspects – so there was little doubt Steelman and Renslow had stayed at these motels. But there was nothing that proved Gretzler was with them. While some witnesses did report someone matching his description, there was no hard evidence he was ever there; evidence they certainly needed to carry their case to the D.A.

That problem was solved, however, when they caught up with Weld. Remarkably, in just the few hours since they had left him at the Stone, Weld and his wife had moved again. This time to another low-end motel, the El Ray, just around the corner on North 21st Street. Weld greeted his guests like old friends and reached for the card on the table. It was a New York State insurance identification card, typed out to a Douglas Gretzler, 1522 Beach Avenue, Bronx, New York. It applied to a 1967 MGB convertible. Along with the card was the missing motel receipt dated October 16th, listing the name STEAL. The I.D. card placed Douglas Gretzler in Phoenix with Steelman during the times the robberies were reported. It was enough to get a warrant for their arrest, and Bill Miller wasted no time getting started.

While Wissman and Gilchrist were in Denver, Jack Cantwell and Dale Lawless were their hosts – Cantwell out of Homicide, Lawless from Robbery – and even though the murders were in Arizona, and up to now, no evidence found that a crime had even been committed in Denver, they felt this was as much their case as anyone's. Wissman and Gilchrist were in Denver's jurisdiction and could not make any move on their own. Cantwell knew only what Wissman and Gilchrist had told him about what happened down in Arizona, but he knew the suspects had been in his town recently, and that they had killed at least two people somewhere. It didn't matter where; he now made it his job to help find them, so he and Lawless were at their service.

Cantwell explained the layout of Denver. Police headquarters sat a couple blocks north of the center of town, and just south of there was Broadway Avenue. Broadway, and the neighborhoods around it, was an area of town on the skids; full of drug addicts and low lifes who kept them busy. Most of the older two story homes had been divided into cheap apartments and crash pads where everyone had a nickname, an angle, a habit, and if anyone had any money on them, you could bet it wasn't their's. So because of that, the District 3 cops who were responsible for the Broadway area, happened to know most of the people who hung out around there. It was with this knowledge that when Marsha began dropping a few names, Cantwell and Lawless knew just where to look.

The man Renslow had referred to as "Loser" was one of them. His real name was Mahalon Joseph Anthony Frilot, and he was the first person they went looking for Thursday afternoon.

They caught up with him at work. A place called People Furniture. He knew the police had interrogated Marsha and he agreed to go downtown to do the same. He said had known Marsha for about two years, but had only just met Bill and Doug recently. It was around the first part of September when they blew into town, and it was over at a house on Ellsworth where he met them. He just assumed they lived there with the woman named Frances, supposedly the sister of one of the guys, but he never knew which one. There was always a party going on at the place, Frilot said, with lots of acid and speed. While Bill was loud and obnoxious, Doug seemed more quiet and stayed to himself. Over the next month, he noticed Bill and Doug were hanging out together more, until they became almost inseparable. Then one day they were gone and someone said Marsha left with them.

When Wissman asked what happened during these parties, Frilot answered, "You know, the usual stuff. But I'll tell ya, somebody was always taking pictures of what was going on, and I thought that was kinda funny."

Wissman perked up.

"Do you remember if Bill or Doug were in any of them?"

"Yeah, I'm sure they were."

"Who has these photos?" Wissman asked, worried they could be just about anywhere now.

"Well, I've got a few."

Cantwell and Lawless wasted no time. They drove Frilot back to his apartment down on Broadway and found the photos. "I'd like these back," Frilot said, half asking, half demanding.

It was going on five when Dave got the news. The photos were an unexpected plus. Four days into the investigation and they had the suspect's names, and now pictures of them as well. It was just one big jigsaw puzzle – a million pieces scattered all over their desks – but now slowly, one by one, the pieces were starting to fit, and the more pieces that fell into place, the easier the big picture was to see. Dave was certain they had solved part of the puzzle – that Steelman and Gretzler were the men responsible – but that was the easy part. It appeared the killing of Bob Robbins and Katherine Mestites was nothing more than a thrill kill, and Arellanes knew in his gut those responsible would likely do it again. Maybe they already had, and that was what ate at him the most.

Miller worked on the robbery warrant, but it was getting late in the day. He hurried through the reports, attached the evidence, and then rushed them into court for review. Within a half hour, Deputy Attorney Martin issued the felony warrants for the arrest of William L. Steelman and Douglas E. Gretzler. Judge Jennings signed the paperwork and the first hurdle in arresting the suspected killers of Robert Robbins and Katherine Mestites was complete. Over the Teletype, the information and physical descriptions of Steelman and Gretzler, along with their suspected crimes, was sent to law enforcement agencies across the country:

Willie L Steelman and Douglas E. Gretzler
Wanted in Maricopa County, Arizona – Suspicion of Armed Robbery.
Considered Armed and Dangerous.

All in all, it had been a good day, yet Arellanes didn't feel much like celebrating. In fact, the more he wrapped himself up in this more the whole thing gnawed at him. He fidgeted. Chewed Rolaids for his persistent sour stomach. Breathed rapidly, like he couldn't catch it. He hadn't eaten much lately, or very well when he did, so maybe that was it. They had known for days who they were looking for, and soon he would know what they looked like. But he had no idea in the world were to start looking, and that gnawed at him the most.

He did know this, however. Wherever Steelman and Gretzler were tonight, those who were with them were in grave danger.

Willie and Doug were now staying at Shawnee's place in the Executive Apartments on 9th Street, just a few blocks up from the rooming house from where they had been chased after the fight with Nelson. Willie had convinced her of his need for a weapon, and she had given him a small handgun earlier that day. With it, Willie promised protection from not only Nelson, but all the others he swore were out there waiting to finish what they had started. That list now included several members of a powerful Denver drug family who Willie claimed were on his tail. "They have made it clear that if they caught up with me, they'd fuckin' waste me."

There were others who stayed at the apartment, including a rather quiet guy everyone called Georgia Bob. Joanne McPeek and her boyfriend Michael Marsh were there more now, hoping Willie might be the answer to their immediate needs. McPeek's heroin habit had chased her out of California to Tucson where she was hiding from a felony drug rap. Marsh was a registered nurse who managed to work only on rare occasion, but nursing was something he had in common with Willie. He spent most of his time battling booze and pills, and just two days earlier Marsh had been arrested on a DWI and a concealed weapon rap. He was positive he was going to do time for the charge, and was giving much thought about leaving town before it all came down. Both he and Joanne figured Willie might help them out of their immediate jam, although Marsh was somewhat shy and said very little, content to leave all the talking to his loud and boisterous girlfriend.

Through her sister, Sue Harlan, Joanne had met Willie and Doug earlier in the week. Joanne was the one who caused all the hassle with Rudy, and that's how she got involved with Willie in the first place. When things calmed down though, Joanne decided it was better to have Willie on her side than Sue's, so she invited he and Doug to stay at her friend's apartment. Joanne wasted no time in making Willie another offer. She told him Sue always had a lot of dope stashed in her house, and with no one to protect her, an easier score would be hard to find. Always one to consider a sure thing, Willie said they would talk more about it later.

So Joanne felt she had Willie in her pocket and told Michael as much, bragging about how Willie would do anything for her now. But Joanne was obnoxious and brash, and Michael realized how dangerous that could be. He pleaded with her to stay cool when they were around Willie, but Joanne didn't hesitate for one minute to yell bullshit when she thought Willie was lying. "That's so fuckin' stupid," he scolded her. "You don't know nothing about this guy, or what he's done. What if he's tellin' the truth?"

But Joanne shined him on. "He's a bullshitter, Mike. He's just talk, nothing else." But closer to the truth, Joanne didn't want to lose Willie, knowing how sweet the revenge would be in getting him to take care of her sister once and for all.

So sitting around the apartment Thursday afternoon, the four of them kicked around their next move, and it was fairly unanimous that getting out of Tucson was the best plan. Willie decided traveling in a group was a good idea, but it was about the last thing they all agreed on. He wanted to go to California because he knew his way around there, but Joanne didn't like going back to where she had run from. Marsh said Chicago. Hometown, he said, and always plenty of good drugs, which pleased Doug, but Willie didn't like the idea of being cold and he said no way. Let's just get a car, he suggested, take care of this Sue thing for some traveling money, then figure out where we're heading.

It was about six when he and Doug left the apartment and started walking east, soon disappearing amongst the crowds and traffic milling around the University. Getting a car was the easy part, he assured Doug. Once that was done, and they pulled off this Sue rip, then Willie promised Michael and Joanne would be history, and the two of them would be back on track.

Gilbert Sierra thought about going into work that night, but by now he was already late and already drunk, so it really didn't matter much anyway. He lifted himself off the barstool and went in to take a leak. When he came back, he ordered another round. Other than when he passed out earlier that morning, he hadn't stopped drinking since getting off work last night. He hung around the bar for another hour or so, drinking alone but arguing with anyone who came within earshot. He soon wore out his welcome and was asked to leave. *Fine,* he slurred, and staggered outside.

Minutes later, he pulled the Charger into the Hudson Gas Station at the corner of 6th and Michigan in South Tucson, and Gilbert made a beeline for the restroom. But the door was locked and he rattled it and cursed. Coincidently, a friend of Gregorio, Albert Munguia, watched him make a scene. At first he believed the guy pounding on the door was Greg because he recognized the car, but he soon realized it was his little brother Gilbert and that he was very drunk. Munguia watched him pace back and forth for a few minutes, scream obscenities at the door, then climb back in the Dodge and peel away, heading north towards the university.

It was the last time anyone who knew Gilbert Sierra ever saw him alive.

Park Avenue borders the western edge of the University of Arizona and runs north-south almost the entire length of Tucson. The street was loaded with taverns, fast food joints, book stores and head shops, all catering to the students living in nearby dorms, frat houses, apartments and run-down houses that surrounded the campus. Willie and Doug walked the half dozen blocks to Park Avenue and melted in with the horde of students and transients hanging around on a warm autumn night.

They hadn't been there long, maybe 20 minutes, waiting with their thumbs out, when Willie spotted a Mexican kid in a white car cruise by and pull over. He waved him down while fumbling for the gun tucked in his waistband. Willie broke into a trot, reaching the car just as Sierra leaned over to unlock the door. "Hey man, we need a ride," Willie said.

It wasn't a request, but a demand, and he pointed the gun at Gilbert through the open window. Sierra said nothing. By this time Doug had caught up with Willie and stood next to him while Sierra's eyes shifted back and forth between them. There wasn't so much fear in his stare, as there was defiance.

"We need a ride," Willie repeated. "Need a car. Your car."

"Ees nah my fuking car," Gilbert said, spitting out the words.

Smart-ass spic! Willie felt like finishing this guy right here on damn sidewalk. He hated the way the guy looked, and the greasy sound of his voice. He felt this rage return, and he wanted so badly to just squeeze the trigger, but instead just told the guy to shut the hell up and get in the back seat.

The gun followed Gilbert as he obeyed, and he mumbled in Spanish as he did. Willie nodded at Doug to drive and soon the car pulled from the curb and back into traffic. Willie toyed with Sierra, like a cat with a moth, playing with him, acting friendly, then threatening to put a bullet in his forehead if he didn't shape up, using his 'hit-man for the syndicate' routine, none of which Gilbert seemed to understand. "Just wasted a cop," Willie boasted. Sierra gave him a blank stare.

Man, he couldn't wait to pop this piece of shit, and he as much as told him so to his face. But all they found was asphalt and more buildings. What he needed was some desert to do the deed. This whole city was surrounded by desert, and Doug couldn't find even one speck of sand, so Willie caved in. "To hell with it," he said. "Turn around and go back to the apartment."

Doug wheeled the Charger down Speedway to 4th Avenue, turned on 9th, where Willie told him to pull over, directly across from the Shanty Bar. Willie pointed the .22 at Sierra and ordered him out of the car. He grabbed the keys, then walked around and opened the trunk. "Get in," he growled. Sierra hesitated for a moment, then climbed in, cursing something unintelligible as he did. Willie slammed the lid shut and they drove the few blocks up 9th to the apartment.

Joanne and Shawnee were just coming out of the Shanty when they saw Willie getting back in the car and drive away, so they hurried back to the apartment to see if it was really him with the cool car. Mike and Georgia Bob heard them pull up so they went downstairs to check it out. They looked in the windows and ran their fingers along the shiny paint, before Doug stepped between them and told them not to get fingerprints all over it. Willie was back with the stories. "See, I got the car," he said, "just like I said I would." But of course it was now much bigger than that. It was now all part of big rip off gone bad. "Yeah, couple a dudes went down. Just a couple a pigs, though. Shit! Had to leave $800 back there, so we gotta go back and finish it."

Joanne said now that they had a car, they could go take care of her sister, and Willie felt accommodating. Get in, he said, let's go take a look at the situation. Nothing was said about what was in the trunk. They piled in the car and went for a ride.

They found the house and parked down the street. Willie walked up alone and they could see Sue come to the door. They stood on the porch for a moment, then she went in the house, and came out and handed something to Willie. He turned and walked back around to the car.

"Shit, Joanne! It ain't gonna happen. Not the way you said. Not tonight. This whole thing with you and your sister is fucked up!" Willie scolded her, and she wanted so badly to argue, but Michael nudged at her for silence.

After they had drove around the South Side for a few minutes, Willie popped open the glove box and pulled out a wallet. He rummaged through it, holding it up to the light at the window for a better look. "We got a dude in the trunk," Willie announced, "and he's a fuckin' narc!"

"Yeah, like shit you do!" Joanne snapped back, still pissed off about Willie giving up back at her sister's.

Willie held the wallet up near his face and yelled. "Hey, your name Gilbert?"

From behind the back seat came a muffled reply. "Yeah."

"Fuckin' A!" Joanne squealed. But Willie stayed his cool. He scanned the wallet and pulled out some cash, holding it up so everyone could see. He turned around and looked at Michael. "How do we get to the desert? I'm gonna kill this sonofabitch."

Joanne now went deadly quiet. She looked at Mike as if to say, 'this guy can't be serious'. But now Doug got into the act and begged Willie to let him do this one. Afraid of what might happen to them if they didn't go along, Marsh hedged at first, but after Willie asked again, he pointed them west towards the foothills. Soon there were no buildings and no light, except that from the moon that hung at the very top of the sky. The road narrowed and they drove into the quiet silhouette of small hills, ravines, and tall saguaro. Willie told Doug to stop, he had found his desert. Mike stayed silent in the back seat, very much like whoever it was in the trunk behind him. Doug and Willie argued about who had the privilege of this one, while Joanne claimed they were both full of shit and didn't have the guts to do anybody.

Willie yanked the .22 from his waistband. "Everyone out," he barked.

Doug turned the engine off, ran around to the trunk and fumbled with the lock. The lid popped open and Gilbert Sierra glared up at them. Willie pointed the revolver at him. "Out, motherfucker!"

Again, Gilbert defied Willie. Willie reached in and grabbed him. "OUT!" he repeated.

Mike and Joanne cowered on the far side of the car, as Doug jumped and danced around behind his partner, echoing his threats, acting itchy to get in the middle of all of this.

Sierra was now out of the trunk and had walked a few steps from the car, as if he thought they were going to leave him there. But Willie began yelling and cursing him, calling a pig and a narc. Each time Sierra shook his head to deny it, answering only with a broken, *'No, No, No'*.

But with each word spoken, Willie could feel the hatred burn and the blood race through his head. He knew what was going to happen. He saw it pass before his eyes, like a movie. "Joanne! Gimme your blouse!" he demanded. "Take your shirt off and give it to me! Willie never looked at her, still staring down Sierra as he screamed.

But Joanne refused. Instinct, most certainly, because she must have understood by now what the consequences of saying no could be. This new side of Willie frightened her and all she and Mike were worried about now was what was going to happen to them when he was finished doing whatever he was going to do to this Mexican kid. Marsh, even more than Joanne, coward close to the car.

To their relief, Willie didn't ask again, but he turned to Sierra and made the same demand, shoving him as he did. "Gimme your fucking shirt!"

Gilbert hesitated. Willie put the pistol in his face, and so he pulled the shirt off and handed it over. Willie wrapped it around the gun, covering part of his trigger hand in the process. "Get down! Down on your knees, you sonofabitch!"

This time Gilbert did exactly as he was told, kneeling at Steelman's feet. Willie stretched his arm and the gun down upon the top of his head. Steadying it with both hands, he squeezed the trigger.

Click. Nothing.

He pulled it again. It still didn't fire.

He looked at the gun and realized the shirt he was using as a makeshift silencer had jammed the hammer, causing the misfire. He pulled the gun back and tore the shirt from around the pistol. Sierra, seizing this blessed opportunity, got up to run, heading blindly towards the darkness of a small ravine. Doug yelled he was getting away, just as Willie cleared the hammer. He wheeled and aimed the gun at the back of Sierra, who had managed to get only a few feet.

Willie fired. This time the gun crackled and Gilbert slumped as the bullet entered his back. His knees buckled and his legs gave way, and he rolled down headfirst, disappearing into the same ravine he had only seconds earlier sought for safety.

Steelman ran down after him. Doug followed and stood at the edge of the ravine, giddy with delight, watching what was taking place at the bottom of the black wash, his tall skinny frame dancing wildly in the moonlight. Willie hovered over his victim and placed the .22 under Gilbert's left eye. Again he pulled the trigger, and fire snapped from the barrel. The impact at point blank spun Gilbert's head into the dirt. Willie's taste was still not satisfied. Another shot pierced Gilbert's skull at the temple, and only then was there complete silence.

Willie walked up from out of the gully and over towards Joanne and Michael, who were still hiding next to the car. He looked over a Marsh. "Go down there and tell me he's dead." He did as he was told, returning moments later to announce the guy was as dead as someone could be, hoping those words might satisfy the rage.

Willie's anger immediately subsided. His only warning was that the two of them better not say a word, because just by being there, they were just as guilty. They got back in the car, this time Michael behind the wheel, as they headed back down the hill, the lights of Tucson scattered as far as they could see. For that brief moment, those inside the car were silent, but even that did not last long.

"Shit!" Willie cursed, his voice startling the others; all of who thought maybe someone was behind them and had witnessed what had gone on. "Shit!" he repeated. "I always take the belt off people I dust! I forgot the fuckin' belt!"

Doug laughed at him. "Bill, you fucked that one up! You don't deserve no belt!"

Not another word was said until the Charger crossed back under Interstate 10 and they were again safely downtown.

But this rush had drained them. They were desperate for a fix. Marsh said he knew of a dude named Dickie Boy who was always good for a score. The problem was, this guy would more than likely rather kill him than sell him any dope, the reason being some squabble about Marsh not settling his debts. But they decided to try anyway and pulled down a side street near Ray and Red's Bar, where Willie set out to find this guy.

Dickie Boy dealt only in speed, and even though every junkie knew it was 10-20 percent pure at best, Mr. Boy's business was always brisk. Willie tracked him down and handed over sixty dollars; a gram and a half worth. Split four ways, it wouldn't last them more than a day. They ditched into an empty building, each of them with their kit; a lighter, a spoon, cotton, and a needle. Willie tied off a vein. Doug found a spot in his neck closer to his brain.

Willie said they shouldn't hang around the Avenue tonight, so Marsh drove them back towards Speedway and a little crash pad where he knew they would be safe for a while.

Marsh found the house. A Jesus freak named Andy lived there and Michael said he was cool. It was just a two-room place, a converted garage actually, and it sat behind the main house on Mabel Street. Andy was home and welcomed them in, introducing them to Don, who was sprawled out on a mattress that filled the tiny living room.

With the crank now taking a firm hold, Willie and Doug made themselves at home. Of course it didn't take long for Willie's to start in with the stories. He talked fast and long and well into the morning before he realized everyone else had crashed around him.

Up in Phoenix, Dave Arellanes' day was about over as well. Just like every night this week, it was midnight before he got out of the office. Following the same routine and route, he dropped Miller off, then continued on to his West Phoenix home. It had been a helluva day and he was flat out exhausted, operating on autopilot, numb to his surroundings. The two-way radio in car snapped numbered codes, signals and street names in a static monotone, now a noise suddenly unrecognizable to Dave. In fact, there was nothing in his immediate world he could identify, not a street, or a house or a landmark. Places he had passed a thousand times before on his way home from work were now strangely foreign to him. His head spun, his stomach growled, his breathing was again heavy and forced. Dave was conscious enough to realize he was having a heart attack.

He panicked. He knew he needed help and he tried to reach for the radio mike, but he couldn't move. Every muscle froze. He had no idea where he was or even who he was. He saw bodies with no faces, stacks of reports with no endings, every note scribbled this week fanned before him. He stared at the lights in the dash but was helpless to make even the slightest move. He was resigned to the fact that he would die here, and that there would be no one left to find the killers. That's what bothered him the most, that they would now get away with it. Everything went black. Time stopped.

"Hey, buddy, you OK?" the voice asked. It startled Dave. "Hey, what's the matter?" the voice repeated. "You OK?"

Dave could hear it, but didn't know to whom it belonged. He still didn't move. His eyes were open but vacant, and he felt the beam of a flashlight cover his face. He blinked and turned towards the light, squinting at the face in the window.

"You need help? Hey, unlock the door."

Dave stared.

"You an officer? This looks like a county car. Roll down the window and talk to me."

Silence.

"Do we need to get you an ambulance? Hey! Fella. C'mon! Talk to me!"

Then as quickly as it had come on, Dave came to his senses. The face in the window was a recognizable one – a sheriff deputy from work – and Dave took a deep breath and looked around. His car was sitting at an intersection, one he had passed every night on his way home. The engine was still running. He rolled down the window, but still found it impossible to speak.

"I saw you stopped here," the deputy explained. "You never moved. I noticed it was one of our cars. Hey, listen, I better get you some help. You don't look so good."

Dave finally found his voice. "No, uh listen, uh, I'm alright...I'll be OK. Just tired."

"You sure?" the deputy asked.

Dave was not very convincing, but was starting to come around. "No really, I'm OK. Just the long hours. I just live up the ways a bit. Don't worry, I'll be fine."

The officer watched as Dave crawled through the intersection. He was home in a couple of minutes. The patrol car followed close behind and waited until he saw the guy close the door and a light go on inside the house.

27

Friday, November 2, 1973 | 8:45 am.

The images in the bath took on human form and experience told him when to pull them. He fished around with his tongs and held the wet photos up to the red light. He had no idea who these people were, but he knew these were good shots. He clipped the prints on the line to dry, then called Homicide to let them know they were ready.

Frilot fingered Bill and Doug in the photos taken from him yesterday and Cantwell sent them to the lab at ID to pull the suspects out of the group picture. His request arrived too late Thursday afternoon to be processed, so it was done first thing Friday morning. *Top Priority!*, his note stated, along with specific instructions to call upstairs the minute the photos were finished. That being done, the pictures were handed over to Gilchrist and Wissman, and this became their first look at the two suspects they had been tracking all week. They, like every other person who viewed them, agreed there was an uneasy evil about the pair. Gilchrist called Phoenix to tell them about the photos and said they would be on the next flight out of Denver.

In the days before electronic communication, fax, or even next day air, it was a common practice to use the airlines to transport time-crucial material, especially in homicide cases. It wasn't discussed, let alone approved of, nor was the method of delivery ever mentioned in any police report. Few would admit to the custom, but it was, without question, the quickest and surest way to deliver evidence critical to a case in progress.

The material was taken directly to the captain of the plane, who would then personally deliver it to the officer waiting at the gate at the other end. As public policy, the airlines frowned upon the procedure, as did the post office, but until technology made the system obsolete a decade later, hundreds of mug shots and crucial matter was transported in this fashion. The photos of Steelman and Gretzler were sent to Phoenix tucked inside the captain's coat, and within two hours they were at the Frontier Airlines terminal at Sky Harbor, where Lt. Jerry Hill from the sheriff's office was waiting.

There was one more person Wissman and Gilchrist needed to talk to before returning to Arizona themselves. Frilot said yesterday the only guy he knew who could tell them more about Bill and Doug was Art Wallen, so they made it a point to pay him a visit Friday morning.

Wallen said things were going pretty well between him and Frances up until the end of August when her brother showed up. He had arrived unexpectedly, "along with every no-good hippie in Denver," and within a couple of days every single one of them was staying at the house. He didn't recollect exactly when the kid named Doug arrived, but he did remember how close he and Bill became. Art said he didn't take a liking to any of them, but it wasn't much he could do; it wasn't his house so he couldn't really kick anybody out. One day he and Frances had a big argument about it and he gave her an ultimatum. "Either they go, or I go." But Frances told him she just couldn't kick her own brother out, so Art packed his bags.

Wallen made it clear he didn't have much use for Willie Steelman, or any of his friends, for that matter. "For my money," he said, "her brother ain't nothing but a piece of shit. And you can write that down." He made his point by adding that the very same day Willie and Doug left town, the stove, refrigerator and furniture from France's house were gone as well. "You tell me that asshole didn't have something to do with it," he demanded.

Where was Willie now?

"Shit, I don't care. Long as it ain't here." But he did say that Frances told him their family lived in a town out in California called Lodi – like the song – and that's where Willie had been before he showed up in Denver. She said her brother had been in a mental hospital there a few years back.

While there was that chance he might return home, the detectives also had to consider the possibility Steelman might come back to Denver, so they asked Art to try and get as much information as he could from Frances about her brother, but under no circumstances should Steelman find out they were looking for him. Wallen said he would be happy to do whatever he could to make sure that shithole got what was coming to him.

Back in Apache Junction, the manager of Vista Grande called the sheriff's office just before noon Friday and said he had received a notice from the post office indicating there was an important letter waiting there. "Think it might have something to do with the murders," he said.

"Why's that?"

"Cuz they said it's addressed to that Yahfah woman," he answered. "And it's from that friend of hers, Marsha."

When the letter was retrieved and opened, it confirmed Arellanes' suspicion that Marsha knew a lot more than she was letting on. Even after she supposedly told them everything she knew during her interrogation, the letter indicated otherwise. "Have you heard anything from Ken or Mike? They might have got it from Bill and Loki!" Dave read that line several times to Bill Miller. He shook his head. "That pretty much tells us how we'll find those two," he added.

When Lieutenant Jerry Hill left the airport with the photos, he carried with him instructions from Arellanes to go to the trailer park and get as many positive IDs as possible. Along with the snapshots of the two suspects, he also carried pictures of other men who had no connection to the case. Hill managed to find five witnesses, including Miss Jerred, who had helped build the composites on Wednesday, and Bret Quimby, the manager's son who remembered the two guys playing music in the rec hall one night. All five identified Willie and Doug from the photo lineups. Hill called Arellanes to confirm there was no question these were the same two men who had been hanging around the park, at least up until the time the victims were last seen.

The next step was to prove Steelman and Gretzler had been inside the trailer. The lab had spent the last several days trying to pull prints off both the Ford sedan and the Chevy convertible, but without success. They had also requested prints from California and New York DMVs, but those could easily take a week to get, and a week right now was much too long to wait. At Miller's request, Officer Edwards from R & I checked out nine items from the property locker. All had come from the nearly one hundred items removed and tagged during the investigation at the trailer; everything from matchbooks to cough drops, from coke spoons and roach clips to pornographic photos of Yahfah.

Yet Edwards could only get two prints that might possibly be from either suspect. Only one of those came from the Ford, and even it was questionable. The search for positive proof of either man being in the trailer – the kind of proof needed for a warrant – seemed impossible to obtain. By mid-afternoon, Edwards admitted his search was a futile one and notified Miller of the disappointing results.

And now Friday was quickly coming to a close, and with it the first full week of their investigation. Arellanes knew they had gotten more than their fair share of lucky breaks, but he and Miller had worked their fannies off too, and they still weren't any closer to an arrest.

Every single hour was important, and Dave hated to waste even one of them. Now, when the long days spent on the case were just starting to pay off, it was all going to come to a screeching halt. When he was on a case as intense as this one, Dave hated the weekends. While their bodies and minds could certainly use the rest, he knew they would be at the office anyway, worrying about what Steelman and Gretzler might do in the next 48 hours, fretting over how much of a head start they already had, and wondering what terrible news he might find on his desk Monday morning.

So all he could do for the next two days was to stay by the phone and teletype, and hope somebody somewhere had crossed paths with Willie and Doug, and were still alive to tell him about it.

Today, ironically, it was the desert's beauty that helped uncover this ugly secret. Photographer Joe Andrew knew prickly pear cactus were plentiful around this particular area of Tucson, often growing right next to the roadway, and all he hoped to do was to take a picture of one. He drove a few miles out from town, parked the car and grabbed his camera. He walked a short distance from the road, took several shots, then stumbled down into a shallow arroyo. In the middle of a small clearing at the bottom, was where he found the body.

It was lying on its back, arms spread wide like an angel who had fallen from the sky. His shoulder length, straight black hair was blood-matted and glistened in the late morning sun. There was no question the man was dead. The body was still, the air warm and silent, and the cream-sand earth around the head was darkened by blood that had seeped from the small holes in the skull. The man wore soiled Levis and black engineer boots, but the dark skinned torso was unclothed from the waist up, and Joe stayed only long enough to remember those few things.

He sprinted back to his car, drove to the nearest phone booth, and was still panting when he called the police. Doing as he was instructed, he went back to the body and waited. He was still there twenty minutes later when the first officer showed up. The desert gave up its secret a mere 12 hours after Willie had pulled the trigger.

There were already a half-dozen officers at the scene by the time Weaver Barkman got there. A detective for Pima County Sheriff's Department, he was one of only a handful working out of the Crimes Against People Unit whose job it was to investigate everything from assaults and rape, to murder, so Barkman wore his homicide hat this afternoon. On the way, he had already begun his ritual of trying to enter the mind of the killer he would be soon be tracking. Barkman's goal was to arrive at the scene with a criminal mentality, and therefore view the death display 180 degrees out. Years before it was fashionable, Barkman made guerilla police work his style, and long before TV shows glamorized it, Weaver was a considered a maverick cop.

He was just three days shy of his 27th birthday, but he was by no means a rookie. He had been in the department over four years, surviving the turmoil and politics that's part of a cop's job in just about any town. Problem was, the situation at Pima County was far worse than usual in recent years and most cops didn't do well in such an atmosphere. But the lack of strong direction from the top allowed Weaver to pretty much go his own way and do his own thing. It was not uncommon for him to break a few written rules, and a helluva lot of unwritten ones, all in the pursuit of being as effective as he could be at his job. Weaver would be the first to admit he didn't always go by the book, but the way he saw it, the means could usually justify the end if he was successful. There were times, in fact, when Weaver stayed so long in this criminal mindset that sometimes it was tough to tell what side of the fence he was actually on. And those were the times when he confessed even he could have gone either way.

He was big on action, but light on the endless paperwork that came with the job. Which in his case was just as well, because some of the tactics he used would have been grounds for discipline, or even dismissal, so Weaver decided there was no use making a permanent record of the questionable procedures used while working a case.

He might have been young, but Weaver Barkman was no novice, and chances were his training started 10 years earlier, when at 17 he quit school and joined the Army. While kids back home were screwing around, getting in trouble, letting the cops chase them around town, he was jumping out of airplanes over North Vietnam. The experience there taught him something he carried over to being a cop in Tucson. First you get inside the other guy's head, then simply out-think him.

Barely five-six, Barkman just hit the shoulders of most of his co-workers. The complexion of his small, pudgy face looked like maybe his teenage years had been tough on him and he sported a nose that appeared to have taken a fist or two. Nor was he real big on the fashions of 1973; the bell-bottom slacks and the big collars, brown polyester jackets, and all those fat obnoxious ties every guy in the office wore. Weaver just laughed at them and shook his head at how idiotic they all looked, knowing full well it was probably their wives who dressed them. True to style, Weaver usually came in wearing jeans, a wrinkled shirt and a tired sport coat, looking more like the culprit than the cop.

And over the years he would be reprimanded, shifted to other departments, pulled inside to a desk job, delegated to lecturing kids about drugs, even privately scorned and taken down a notch or two by those pushing pencils above him. But when it was all said and done, Weaver would eventually be considered one of Arizona's best criminal problem solvers. He had a lost a few battles over the years, but never his original focus. As far as he was concerned, his mind never left those days in Nam. Regardless of how tough it got, he never left the department and he never left Tucson. Didn't matter where he was, to him it was all the same. There are good guys and there are bad guys, and the only hard part was telling who was who.

Commitment to his career cost him dearly, personally and professionally, and it wasn't always storybook, but maybe that's why James Weaver Barkman was considered such a good cop. And maybe that's also why, when they found a no-name Mexican with a couple of bullets in his face, they sent Weaver to find out who killed him.

A few high clouds spotted the ice blue sky and left their shadows as dark patches of desert earth. Detective Barkman joined the others, scouring the area surrounding the body, stopping to make notes on their well-worn pocket pads. Empty Budweiser cans littered the ground and their best guess was these were from a party that preceded by several days the vicious gathering of last night. Cops stooped down to check out items of even the smallest detail, while ID techs clicked rolls of film from every conceivable angle and viewpoint. Landscapes were sketched using a stick figure for the victim, who, for the time being at least, stayed exactly as they found him. The body, for the most part, was ignored. The guy was dead. Very dead, and would stay that way as far as they knew.

But the crime scene was different. It was constantly changing. Every footprint from every cop who trudged the ground in every direction ruined forever the ability to determine just exactly what happened and when. Sure, they were careful, or at least acted like it, but Weaver was never comfortable watching big clumsy cops scatter potential evidence to the wind. He cringed as they shuffled around, yapping and going on about crap that had nothing to do with the job at hand. Jesus! How a dead man could attract a crowd! And sure enough, within just a few minutes, Weaver watched the mob climb to eleven, including the Mexican kid, who somehow managed to stay out of everyone's way.

Barkman used his feet to brake his way down into the small ravine so he could get a closer look at the reason so many had gathered. He checked the body; his touch telling him it was in full rigor, indicating it had been dead at least 10 to 12 hours.

His partner this afternoon, Detective Mike Tucker, joined him and they went through the evidence found on and near the victim. Tucker scribbled as Barkman reeled off the facts. Mexican or Indian male, approximately 25, 5'10", 180 pounds, wearing Levis, black socks and brown hiking or engineer boots. No shirt. A silver Timex watch with blue face on descendant's left wrist shows the correct time, 1:36, Friday the 2nd. Long, shoulder length black hair, thin mustache with 1/8" stubble. Face, chest, hands and arms covered in blood, and there appears to be a wound under the left eye. Blood under victim's head covers the ground and is still slightly damp. There are several thorns sticking in the arms and hands of the victim, several more in the jeans and in his stomach area. One thorn, well over an inch long, is embedded in the nose and reaches up to the eye. These appear to be from one of the prickly pear cactus from the top of the embankment.

Tucker went back up to the top of the ravine and examined the cactus. He found a sizable pool of blood underneath one of the plants and the thorns from it matched those in the body. He and Barkman continued to cover the rest of the area and it was clear a car was involved. Tire tracks arrive, then leave the dirt clearing, just off the pavement. Disturbed earth near the tracks showed signs of a struggle. Marks in the sand, a foot and a half wide and almost five feet long, are in a direct line from the tire tracks to where the body apparently fell into the ravine. Photos are taken and plaster casts of the tracks ordered.

Over an hour after taking the call, Tucker requested an ambulance, and the County pathologist, Dr. Brucker, arrived to officially pronounce the subject dead. At a few minutes before three, the body was taken back to town for the autopsy, after which the crowd in the desert gradually thinned out. The Public Information officer arrived and gathered just enough details from the detectives to satisfy the few media hustlers milling about. The *Daily Star* managed to get a couple of paragraphs about the killing in the late afternoon edition, but the evening radio and television news reports would have little to say about the body found earlier that afternoon. A single uniformed officer stayed to protect the small piece of desert as Barkman returned to his car and followed the ambulance down the hill.

He headed to the office, allowing Detective Tucker to accompany the body to the Coroner's office. They had no ID on the guy, and a search of the body and the area around it turned up nothing. No wallet, rings, slips of paper, tattoos, absolutely nothing of substance. Even the front pockets of the kid's Levis had been turned inside out; as if the killer had beaten Barkman to the very info he was looking for. He first checked with Missing Persons. Nothing. He called dispatch to see if there might be any connection with his body and cases being worked on elsewhere in the department. Ditto. He phoned over to Tucson P.D., and the Department of Public Safety, all without success. There was the slight possibility that the news reports on TV might solicit a call, a name, or at least a clue as to who the dead man was, but for now, Barkman was stumped. Four hours into the investigation and he had hit a roadblock. Weaver liked activity, some action, a little turmoil, something to get off dead center, but there was absolutely nothing going down on this one, so he stayed at his desk and typed out his first report on the crime. It consisted of just two brief paragraphs and two short sentences, and he finished with, *" having drawn the scene, I departed."* He looked it over, crossed out the word 'drawn' and replaced it with *sketched*. It sounded more police-like. He hoped to hell someone would appreciate the extra effort.

Dr. Brucker, who was only a few minutes ahead of Tucker, was already examining the body when the detective walked in. Brucker was busy talking into the recorder and a camera was clicking as the autopsy began. The wound beneath the left eye became the focus of the initial examination. Dr. Brucker was cleansing the wound, explaining that it appeared to be a contact burn and would not wash off. An officer from Identification assumed the task of gathering fingerprints, hair samples and removing the many thorns embedded in the body. The autopsy found three bullet wounds along with the .22 caliber slugs that created them; one under the eye, one at the left temple, and the third one entering the back just above the shoulder blade. Brucker stated the suspect most likely died from the wound at the temple, but the shot to the back would have killed him too. Once opened, the chest cavity was found completely full of blood and the victim could have just as easily bled to death. His task complete, Brucker pieced the body back together and prepared it for the morgue.

But before they went any further, Barkman wanted to see the victim and the autopsy results for himself. At 8 pm the body was wheeled back into an exam room and Barkman began his own investigation. His frustration erupted into anger. The body was clean. Weaver had discussed this matter with Brucker before, and once again the doctor had completely washed off the body; an ignorant act as far as the detective was concerned. Barkman wanted the body as it was found, with all the dirt and all the filth that accompanied the killing. Maybe it was just another of his mind games he played, and admittedly he was having trouble getting on track with this one, but he thought he had made himself clear on many occasions. He did not deny Brucker's qualification, or how well the doctor did his job, but he wasn't a cop, and he just screwed with a cop's job. *His* job. He was absolutely livid, and he noted his displeasure between the lines on his report, stating that he started his investigation only, after the victim had been "cleaned off".

But for a man with a history of few written words, Barkman now had much to say. Fueled in part by his indignation as much as his frustration, the report covered over two pages and described even the most insignificant details. Clearly he was groping, fumbling blindly for some insignificant item that might trigger a clue. He described in desperation nearly two dozen scars, long since healed and having nothing whatsoever to do with the fatal wounds. Callouses and small hairs were noted, as were fillings in his teeth that were 'essentially silver in color', as he put it. Writing it all down helped. Maybe looking it over later would give him a new slant, but for now he found nothing to lead him any closer to the killer.

In Yuba City on Friday, Laurence Loughran finally admitted something was wrong. His son, Steve, had not been heard from in almost two weeks. He was long ago resigned to the understanding that his boy suffered from wanderlust, and could disappear for days on end – traveling, hitchhiking, whatever it was that young people do these days – but God help him, Steve always called home to let everyone know he was okay. But Mr. Loughran had a helpless feeling this time, so he phoned the police Friday afternoon and gave them a brief physical description of his teenage son. "He has a grandmother in Phoenix, Arizona," he told them. "He always talked of going down there to see her."

Friday was Joanne Parkin's birthday. But it was also the first Friday of the month, and those were always hectic days at the United Market, so Wally decided they could better celebrate over the weekend when they could get together with a few friends for dinner. Joanne agreed, but reminded her husband how awkward she felt when people fussed over her, even if it was her birthday.

Joanne left the store early and upbeat, while Wally stayed behind to finish up. He had already flipped off the lights and was locking the doors when it dawned on him that he had totally forgot to get her a gift. Not wanting to make the trip into Lodi at such a late hour, he walked over to the TIMEX display and removed a woman's watch, peeling the price tag off the box as he headed towards the front door. It would have to do until he could get something a little nicer, he rationalized, and at least he wouldn't be going home empty handed.

28

Saturday, November 3, 1973 | 9:30 am.

Because what he had done would be discovered soon, Willie knew his time in Tucson was over. He felt suffocated, like the walls of the tiny bungalow, and the city itself, were closing in on him. There was talk about Chicago or California, but it meant dragging Marsh and Joanne along too. It drove the shit out of him – even more than their constant whining and sniveling – this idea that he was going to have to keep an eye on them for awhile. Even Doug, who rarely noticed or cared about such matters, admitted they made him nervous. If there hadn't been so many people crammed into the small house, he considered killing them too, if for nothing more than shut them up and to put his mind at ease.

In addition to Andy, who rented the place, there was another guy staying there by the name of Donald Scott, a waifish, blond haired head case who had a fondness for long capes and good weed. He said he was from back east, but claimed to be more comfortable on the road, and had drifted out west again this winter, looking for a righteous high and a free place to crash. But when talk got around about leaving Tucson for California, Scott said he was ready for a new adventure and told Willie to count him in. Although Michael and Joanne were scared of Willie – they had witnessed first hand the rage in him that could erupt without warning – they acted like they were in too, but privately Joanne said she didn't want to go anywhere with this lunatic and wind up like the Mexican kid. Michael told her to chill out, pretend like everything was still cool, promising when the time was right he would find a way out.

Early Saturday morning, while Mike and Joanne were still asleep, Willie, Doug and Don walked up to a gas station on Speedway and used the restroom to shoot up the last of the crank. Willie admitted he had been holding out, but only because he didn't want to share what little was left with the other two. He told Don they were going over to a friend's house to borrow his car, and when they got back they would take off for California so be ready if he still wanted to go.

Awake now, and realizing Willie and the others were gone, Michael bolted up and yanked Joanne by the arm, not even taking time to find their shoes. Slipping barefoot out the front door, they scurried down side streets, constantly looking over his shoulder, dodging in and out of alleys towards the safety of 4th Avenue a dozen blocks away, certain Willie already had his car and was closing in, ready to run them down in broad daylight, right there on the streets of Tucson.

His had been in the shop all week, and he was tired of hitchhiking, so Vince Armstrong talked his wife into letting him use her car this morning, convincing her he was heading over to the university library and then maybe run a few errands afterwards. He hopped in her metallic blue 1969 Firebird, but instead of going to the library, his first stop was a nearby convenience store where he bought a quart of beer. It was a great morning; warm and sunny, and Vince rolled the window down to let it all in.

At the next light, he noticed two guys with their thumbs out, and although it was nearly eleven and already quite warm, they were dressed in jeans and heavy jackets. That first impression alone – that nervous feeling in his gut that something was out of place – should have been enough to tell him to just keep driving, Maybe he was hoping for a little karma payback for all the quick rides he had got this past week, or maybe he was just in a good mood this morning and wanted to share it, but whatever the reason, at the very last minute he pulled over to the curb. But as they approached the car, Vince got his first good look. They were older than most of the college kids he usually saw thumbing rides around town, and they were terribly dirty. His concern suddenly shifted to just what kind of filth they were going to track into his wife's car. They fumbled around with the door, trying to decide who was getting in first and Vince had yet to see their faces.

"It's unlocked," he announced as one reached for the handle, then bent over and glared in. A chill ran through Vince. It looked as if the entire right side of the guy's face was bruised black and blue, and his eye was blood red and ready to explode. The man opened the door, pushed the front seat forward so he could slide into the back, but the opening was small and he wrestled the knapsack ahead of him. "Thanks, man," he mumbled.

As he squeezed in, the skinny blond guy was right on his heels. With what he had seen already, he knew he didn't want them both sitting behind him. Hell!, they might even try and rob him, was his first thought. Somehow he mustered the courage to reach over and push the seat back, blocking the blond guy's path. "Hey, wait a minute," Armstrong said. "Why don't you sit up front? It'll look pretty stupid with both you guys in the back."

To his relief, the guy stopped, looked in the back seat for an okay, then without saying a word, slid in up front and yanked the door closed. It was too late now, but Vince realized he had made a huge mistake. He could only hope they didn't want to go very far. They had not even traveled more than a few blocks, not even long enough to start a nervous conversation, when he felt something hard jammed into his side. He looked down between the bucket seats to see the dull black steel of a handgun.

"We just killed a couple of dudes," the stranger boasted from the back seat. "A couple of fuckin' Metro agents, man, and we gotta get outta here. So we're taking you and your car. I suggest you just keep driving."

Vince felt his stomach wrench up. He looked at the guy sitting next to him and watched him finger a large hunting knife.

"We just want your car," the voice from behind him continued, "so you turn this thing around and get us out of town – out in the desert somewhere – and do exactly as I say."

"You're gonna kill me, aren't you?" Vince stammered.

"We just want the car, so just shut the fuck up and drive," came the reply.

Vince did as he was told, turning down a side street, then onto North Campbell Road, heading towards the northern outskirts of town. The farther they drove the more nervous both men became and Vince got a slap upside his head more than once. "Don't you even think about fucking with me on this!" he was warned.

But by now Vince was so upset and so sick to his stomach, he didn't know how much farther he could drive. He was afraid he was going to throw up, or worse, soil himself, and then the guy in the back would kill him for sure. They reached the intersection of North Campbell and East River Road and waited for the cross traffic to pass. Just ahead was the edge of town, and the desert beyond. There would be no help past this point. This was his last chance, and he took it.

"Jesus, I can't drive anymore, man. I just can't do it!" Words that angered the gunman, so he hit him again, knocking Vince's glasses off. "Shit! Pull over here then! Doug, you drive!"

Vince managed somehow to creep through the intersection, then pulled over into a small parking lot. He fumbled for his glasses, leaving the engine running as he slid into the passenger seat, the gun from the back following his every move. When the blond haired guy got behind the wheel, Vince looked over and apologized. "Sorry. I'm just too nervous."

"That's okay man, no sweat," the blond answered as he pulled the car back onto the street. "We don't want to hurt our driver, now do we?"

Okay, so maybe the gun wasn't loaded and maybe they hadn't even killed anyone yet. Maybe they were just a couple of punks who wanted to steal a car. But whatever it was, Vince wasn't willing to hang around and find out. So just as the car was getting back up to speed and headed once again towards the remote north end of town, Vincent opened the door and dove head first out onto the pavement.

"Jesus Christ!" Willie yelled as Doug automatically spun the car around. It was a toss up as to who was the most surprised.

Armstrong rolled several times across the pavement, then looked up in time to see the car turning around. He sprang to his feet and hurdled a low wall encircling the grounds of a nearby church. He darted behind the tall palm trees of the courtyard, then disappeared between the buildings.

Willie was screaming, directing the action, because Doug didn't really know what to do. Initially he aimed the car right at the guy, then watched him scurry through the low trees of the plaza. Somehow Willie managed to get up to the front seat, spinning his head around to try and see where the guy went. It was hopeless. "Let's just get the fuck outta here! Do you believe that guy! Didja see that? He jumped right outta the goddamn car!"

Doug whipped the car around in a one-eighty, hit the gas and sped back in the direction they just came.

Beat up and out of breath, Vince stumbled across a gardener working in a nearby school and tried to explain what had just happened, but the man did not understand. "Telephone! I need a telephone!" Armstrong repeated. The gardener finally answered in very broken English that there was no phone because the school and church were closed. Armstrong remembered a professor he had who lived nearby and he somehow convinced the gardener to take him there. He crouched down low in the front seat of the pick up, terrified the two guys were still driving around looking for him, or that they found his address on the registration and were heading there this very minute. From his professor's house, he called his wife and begged her to get out of the house, promising to explain it all later.

When the call came in to Tucson Police, and there was something in his story about an officer being down, dispatch performed a quick head count. Although there had been no shooting reported, and all patrol staff were soon accounted for, a detective remembered the John Doe Pima County had in the morgue. He didn't even know why he thought there might be a connection – a long shot, at best – but he decided to go with his gut and call the sheriff's department, just to fill them in on what was going on.

Weaver Barkman had a dead body but damn little else; no name, no motive, no witnesses, and very few clues. Even though he had been up late last night, Barkman was at his desk early Saturday going over the autopsy reports again, hoping to find some seemingly insignificant detail he might have missed. Once again, nothing. Just before noon, he and Mike Tucker meet with Lt. John Lyon, Commander of the Criminal Investigation Division at Pima County, to prepared a nationwide APB on the murder. The two page bulletin contained no new information, so they filled it with useless details such as the victim's "well healed scars a quarter of an inch long", and that the subject had a callous "from pencil use". They pinpointed the time of death at 12:30 am, and the weapon as being a .22, but that was all the solid info they could offer.

A phone call for Barkman interrupted their meeting. Somebody said he might have something for him on the dead Mexican kid.

"This is Detective Zimmerman from PD. I was told you were you were the one to talk to regarding the homicide out near Gates Pass yesterday."

"Yeah. What's up?" Barkman's reply came off short fused.

"Well I'm not sure there's a connection, but we just got a call about a stolen car and possible kidnapping out on the north side. Apparently an ex-employee of our department picked up two men hitchhiking. They pulled a gun on him, but he was able to get away. They've got his car though, so we've notified our units in the area."

"So what's the connection? What makes you think it's got something to do with my guy?"

The caller was taken back. He was certain the sheriff's department would welcome any lead, regardless of how far out in left field it came. "Well, ah. . .the two suspects said they had just shot a Metro agent and were desperate to get out of town."

Although he still wasn't clear just what the connection might be, Barkman gave in and decided to hear him out. "Okay, tell me what you got."

Barkman wrote it all down, including the brief description of both suspects, noting one had "a black eye that is bloodshot". The victim claimed he had been a cop at one time and that he recognized the weapon as a short barreled .38 revolver, although no shots had been fired.

Weaver stopped right there and put his pen down. He wasn't looking for a .38, it was a .22, and if the guy was an ex-cop, then he would sure as hell know the difference. Barkman thanked him for the call and hung up.

Lt. Lyon hovered over Weaver's desk during the brief conversation. Barkman knew he was there, but didn't bother looking up. Lyon was a huge man and he towered over him. His presence could not be ignored for long. "P.D., huh? Anything new?" Lyon finally asked.

There were only a few men Barkman respected and listened to, especially on the Pima County force, and John Lyon was one of them. He was not only his commander, but mentor as well. It was not often that he wouldn't appreciate his involvement. But not now. Not today.

"It's nothing," Weaver shrugged, head still buried in his clutter of paperwork. "They're chasing a couple of dudes who stole a car over around Campbell and River Road. I can't see the connection."

"I've always told you to follow your hunches, Weaver, but I'd say it's worth checking out. What else you got to go on?"

"Christ!, John, I gotta body here that I don't have a name on, but I do know that he was done with a .22. These guys gotta .38. I don't have time to go chasing P.D. around looking for a couple of car thieves!"

He closed up the folder and walked outside for some air. He flipped his shades down and let the warmth of the sun wash over him, wondering when the hell he was going to catch a break.

The blue Firebird turned off North Campbell and onto Fort Lowell Road. They drove slowly, eyes peeled for another chance. Willie told Doug to pull over on Vine Street, which was nothing more than a dead end graveled alley. In front of them were some new apartments under construction, and in the parking lot was a guy washing his car.

Willie pointed to a covered stall and told Doug to pull in so the car couldn't be spotted from the street. He got out, scoured the area, removed his coat and folded it over his arm, concealing the weapon. He walked towards the man, then flashed the weapon to get his attention. The guy looked down at the gun, then looked up and smirked, shaking his head as he did. He checked out the

Firebird and saw another guy sitting inside. He made a little laughing sound as Willie waved the gun, motioning him to start moving. He thought about it for a moment, then grudgingly obeyed. He tossed his rag down, turned and walked slowly towards the stairs. Willie jerked his head towards Doug, the signal for him to follow.

When the police began questioning Vincent Armstrong, this whole wild story started sounding a little different from the one he gave over the phone. His wife arrived shortly after the police did, and he now acted as if he was trying to hide something from her.

One of the first things Vince said was that he had been on the police force for a short time, and indeed, one of the young officers remembered him. Vince pulled him aside and confided that he really wasn't going over to the university, but over to visit a girl he knew, and he didn't want his wife to find out. With that, and other discrepancies that kept popping up, the cops began wondering if he was just using this wild stolen car story to cover his ass about a girlfriend. But he swore every word of it was true, convincing the officers into going back to where he jumped out of the car so he could prove it. They did, and on the pavement they found his busted glasses. They decided to take him downtown to continue this discussion, and the first thing they did when they got to the station was ask him to take a polygraph test to make sure he wasn't lying. He did, and apparently he wasn't. Later that afternoon he helped prepare a composite identification on each of the two men who kidnapped him. All units in the northwest section were advised of a possible stolen car, but no additional backup was sent to look for it. Soon thereafter police were all called out to control traffic at a large fire that had erupted in the same part of the city, so now the wail of fire sirens pierced the air, echoing throughout the afternoon as more and more fire trucks were called in. Armstrong's story had to take a temporary back seat

Michael Sandberg bucked and laughed all the way up the stairs. He never turned around, refusing to even look at the man holding the gun, but mocked him with each step. A nervous response. His way of dealing with the shock of having a weapon drawn on you in your own driveway. He wanted it made absolutely clear that he wasn't afraid of some punk with a gun. Willie coiled at this lack of respect he figured was due him, and his rage-filled face felt ready to explode.

Patricia Sandberg was in the kitchen and heard her husband come in. She peeked her head around the corner, surprised to see they had company.

"These guys are robbing us Pat," he announced sarcastically, still amused at the very idea. "It looks like we're their prisoners."

She had not the slightest clue what he was talking about. He was laughing, so she smiled too. It was just another one of his silly jokes, she thought. He had put these two up to the gag. Goodness, they were probably just two of the workers from the complex. Leave it to Michael. She tried laughing now too, for that was her nervous reaction as well. But it was slow to come, uneasy and snappish when it did. So she directed her attention towards the two men standing behind her husband, as if for an explanation, hoping to hear them break out laughing as well, that this was all just a big joke, all just in fun. But there was no laughter, and her jagged smile quickly disappeared when she noticed the gun placed at the back of her husband's head. "Michael?" she quivered.

"I told you, they're robbing us! Well, actually they said they just wanted the car." His tone was smart-ass and spiteful, as if to prove to her there was nothing to worry about.

To further make his point, he left them all standing in the doorway – including the man with the gun that was now pointed into thin air. He walked over, plunked himself down on the living room sofa, and then folded his arms across his chest to signal it was their move.

Seeing this, Doug whipped the knife from his belt and leveled it at the woman's neck. He had their attention now. Sandberg got the message, jumped from the couch and ran towards her. "Michael!" she screamed.

"We need a car, so we're gonna take yours," Willie said, before a word could be uttered in protest. "But we can't leave right now, so we're gonna stay here for awhile. Least 'til things calm down a little bit, so I suggest you get used to it."

The knife dropped away. Patricia fell into her husband's embrace.

"So then," Willie continued as he closed the door behind him, "if anyone asks, we're just some friends from out of town. If there's no hassle, then we split when it gets dark and everything's cool. We just take the car. But you gotta help us and do everything we say. And no hassles." He waved the gun at them. It was now his turn to laugh. "So, tell you what, let's get to know each other. Whaddaya say?"

It was late 1970 when they first met at a Christmas party in Hawaii – he the handsome Marine Corps captain, she the adventurous, slightly older woman from Southern California – and they both admitted later it was love at first sight. Michael Sandberg was a combat pilot who had just returned from his last tour of Vietnam. He told her he was going back to school when he got out, hoping to be a teacher. Surprisingly it was a goal they both held and it was just one of the many things they shared with each other that first night.

Their romance quickly blossomed, and within six months they had a wedding planned. They called the mainland and gave the families the news, and Patricia's father was especially excited. His daughter was in her early thirties, and while she wasn't a child anymore, she had always been his little girl. Now he had a son, one that he could brag endlessly about to his buddies at work.

Within the year, Michael's hitch in the Marines was over and they both agreed to finish their studies at the University of Arizona in Tucson. They found an apartment close to campus and started the fall term, however, it wasn't long before Michael decided he wanted his own place. They spent weekends driving around looking at small condominiums, finally choosing one in the new Villa Parasio complex on Fort Lowell Road on the north end of town. The down payment wiped out their savings, most of which came from Michael's hazard incentives while on bombing runs over North Vietnam.

The complex was so new, they were the only ones living there for a while. But it wasn't long before a few more people moved in, and although they hadn't meet any of their neighbors yet, they did become friendly with the project manager, James Nelson, who always had the time to say hello and chat for a few minutes while making his rounds each day.

Patricia Sandberg was in a particularly good mood Saturday morning. It was a beautiful fall day and she and Michael decided to take a drive later, so while he went out to wash the dirt and construction dust off their car, she phoned her parents in San Francisco to talk to them about their upcoming visit to Tucson over the Thanksgiving holidays. Maybe next year their family would be even bigger, she teased her father, because she and Michael had talked about starting one of their own soon. News that had pleased him no end. She said her goodbyes, announcing there was much work to do before she and Michael left for the afternoon. She turned the stereo on, continued with her housework, and was standing in the kitchen when the men came in.

After the initial shock had worn off, and she was promised nothing bad was going to happen, she calmed down a little. Michael had returned again to the living room and sprawled out on the sofa, announcing again his defiance. He turned on a football game, acting as if he could care less about the men, or their continuing threats. If Michael wasn't worried, Patricia figured she shouldn't be either, deciding to just do whatever was asked of her and wait until it got dark so the men would leave.

As the minutes crept by, Willie's paranoia grew; he had totally boxed himself in. He swore he heard sirens all afternoon, and he nudged Doug to listen for them. It wouldn't be long now, Willie said, promising he wouldn't go without a fight, and he would sure as hell take some pigs with him when the time came. *Listen!* he demanded. *They were all out there looking for us, and they closing in fast. Sooner or later we're going to have to make a run for it. It's our only chance to stay alive.*

So while Willie was tense and jumpy, pacing around the small apartment, Patricia tried to stay calm and agreeable, although her husband did little to cooperate. He and Willie argued about everything, especially when he found the Sandberg's wedding photo with Michael in his Marine dress uniform. So now Willie began unloading about the war, giving Michael an earful about killing all those innocent people with his bombs. "You're nothing but a fuckin' murderer," he spit. "You ain't no better than me."

Doug offered nothing, except to say he was hungry, so Pat led him into the kitchen to fix him a sandwich. He was polite enough towards her now that they were alone, and after all the screaming and cursing going on in the other room, she seemed to find a little comfort with him there. They made small talk while she made lunch. Just to make sure her peace of mind continued, Patricia excused herself to the bathroom and gulped down a couple of Valium.

Tired of arguing, at least for the moment, Willie announced he was out of smokes and said he was going across the street. He swore to Doug the cops were still out there and he wanted to take a look outside, so he made Patricia escort him across the parking lot to the street, just to make it look like he was a friend visiting. He told Doug to keep the gun on the husband. When Patricia and Willie walked across the parking lot, James Nelson spotted them and waved hello, surprised Mrs. Sandberg did not stop to chat or introduce him to her friend.

When Willie returned he told Doug they would have to wait until dark before they could leave. "The town is dirty with cops," he announced. "They're fucking everywhere."

As the afternoon wore on, they began making plans and Willie decided the best idea was to change their identity. He found some hair coloring in the bathroom cabinet and told Patricia to help Doug dye his hair while he kept an eye on her husband. Doug stood on the balcony in the late afternoon shadows and dried and brushed his hair. Willie shaved his mustache and patched up his black eye with her makeup, then rifled through Michael's closet to find a change of clothes.

Throughout all this activity, Patricia Sandberg was again becoming more nervous and upset. At her husband's request, she was given a another Valium from the bottle Willie found along with the hair coloring. Even before it had a chance to settle her down, Willie told Doug to tie them both up. Doug padded her wrists, then with twine found in the house, he cinched them tight behind her. He put her on the floor of the bathroom and shut the door, warning her that if he heard even the slightest noise, he would come back and slit her throat.

Michael was next, still laughing at the games being played and the lengths these two were going to to make their point. Once again Doug carefully placed cloth between his victim's wrists so the heavy twine would not cut into his flesh as he cinched the knot. He escorted Sandberg into the bedroom and told him to lie face down on the bed. Doug wrapped the twine around Sandberg's ankles and made him bend his knees. He tied another piece around his neck and connected the head with the feet, then removed the slack. If Sandberg even tried to stretch his legs out, the cord around his throat would strangle him. A necktie was taken from the closet to gag him and quiet the laughter once and for all.

What little gray light there was came from the bedroom window. It was not even enough to leave a shadow on the wall as Doug performed his task. He rolled the man over on his side, wrapping part of the bed sheet around him as he did. Doug admired his work, then shut the bedroom door tight behind him.

Willie was waiting for him, sitting at the dining room table looking over a map of Arizona and California, planning their route. He had given it a lot of thought, he told Doug, but the car wasn't big enough for all of them. They would have to leave them both here, and there could be no one left who could identify them later. It wouldn't be safe.

There was no argument. Doug brought Mrs. Sandberg to the living room where Willie made her lay face first into the cushions so they could finish tying her up. Willie went and turned the stereo up, handed Doug the gun, and nodded towards the bedroom. Doug's gut wrenched up. But it was a familiar feeling, and he knew from experience his discomfort would quickly pass. Michael Sandberg had not moved, still resting on his side, his back to the door. Doug took only a single step before he lowered the gun to Michael's head and pulled the trigger. The bullet tore into his skull. It was all that was needed. Blood was already soaking into the bedspread before Doug had a chance to turn and leave the room.

Willie had placed a blanket over her body and a pillow over Patricia's head. The music was loud and the room dark, and if she had heard the gunshot from the other room, she had not flinched to show it. Doug could see her moving only slightly, but breathing heavy. Again, without a word from Willie, he forced the gun deep down into the pillow until he could feel the hardness of her skull. The bullet exploded and her body jerked. Willie yanked the pillow away and grabbed the gun, firing another round into the back of her head. Then another, and as her body twitched spastically. He fired again. But her movements did not cease. Her hands tugged furiously at the bindings, while the rest of her body continued to convulse. So her shot her again, firing his last round through the makeshift pillow silencer and squarely into the back of her head. To his shock she still moved and shook furiously. In a fit of desperation he ran over and grabbed a golf club out of a bag resting in the corner, and with a #3 driver, he proceeded to smash her face into a bloody mush. He didn't stop until she did, finally succumbing to the destruction caused by five .22 slugs and a relentless, brutal bashing to her skull. Her body relaxed and eventually ceased its movement. It was only then when Willie stopped swinging.

He stood triumphantly over her. "Holy Christ!" he panted. "Women are so fucking hard to kill!"

He and Doug grabbed some more clothes and threw them in a suitcase, then went through the place again and found some stuff to hock later. Willie dug through the dead woman's purse and grabbed a couple of credit cards, a checkbook and whatever cash he could find. Cigarette money at best. Willie turned the stereo down while Doug wiped off door handles and drinking glasses, but neither seemed in a real rush to leave. Finally, with whatever they could find to take, and neatly attired in their new look, they walked downstairs and threw everything into the Datsun. The sky was dark now, and they pulled out of the parking lot – the blue Firebird right where they left it, under the parking canopy and out of view from the headlights that rushed by on Fort Lowell Road just a few feet away.

When they eventually found their way back to the little house on Mabel, only Donald Scott remained. He barely recognized them. They had left early that morning in grimy clothes and long, unwashed hair, and here they were, all dressed up and looking quite respectable. They stopped for gas on the way out of town, then got on I-10 and just drove. A huge desert moon hung overhead as they headed north. The original plan was to drive all night, taking the southern route into California, but it was now decided being out late on the open road might not be a good idea. About an hour after leaving Tucson, they hit Casa Grande and turned off at the junction of Interstate 8 heading west to California. They drove another 20 more miles but were dead tired. When they came across a small truck stop motel, Willie told Doug to pull in.

Vic's Table Top Motel, Restaurant & Service Station sat on the outskirts of Stanfield, Arizona, which itself wasn't much more than a spot where I-8 and Highway 84 came together. Wherever Vic was at 9:30 this Saturday night, it wasn't behind the motel desk. That job belonged to Ray Garrison, who with his wife Jean, ran the whole show, including the Arco station next door.

Ray greeted the visitor graciously as he entered the tiny cluttered office. It was a bit unusual for someone to stay three nights, but that's what the man wanted, so he filled out the registration card as such. The guest, a 'Mr. M. Sandberg' paid for the 3 days in advance with an American Express card. He then asked if he could cash a small check, but Ray said sorry, he would have to wait until the next day when there was more money in the till. Ray gave Mr. Sandberg the key to cottage #1, and didn't see him again until the next day.

The three men squeezed into the small motel room, smoked some weed, and eventually, one by one, nodded off.

Back in Tucson, their new home was dark, peaceful, and with the dim light and soft music flowing from the stereo, it had a strange romantic feel about it. Yet tonight, she was on the sofa and he in their bed, the door shut tight between them, like a couple who had argued earlier and separated in anger for the night. Both were bathed in the gentle moonlight that found its way through the back windows of their home. The air inside was still and already somewhat stale. Even the traffic sounds from downstairs were muted, and for the first time that day their home was quiet.

29

Sunday, November 4, 1973 | 12 noon.

The car hadn't moved. Yesterday, when he first noticed it sitting there, he just figured it belonged to one of his workers, but they were off today, and yet the Firebird remained, parked slightly sideways, resting in the shade of the newly built carport canopy.

James Nelson remembered the car very clearly. Walking back to work after lunch yesterday, he watched it crawl past him on Fort Lowell Road as if looking for a specific address or someone's house. The car traveled ahead a few more blocks then pulled off the road and disappeared from Nelson's view. Thinking it may be a prospective customer looking for his condominium project, he was happy to see the Firebird in the parking lot when he arrived several minutes later. But to his dismay there was no one in or around the car when he arrived, so it must be one of the worker's, he told himself, and he made a note to remind whoever owned the car that the work crew parking lot was around back.

It was now Sunday afternoon and the car still hadn't moved, so he walked around the vehicle, wondering again whose it was. He took great pride in his new condo project, and while this one was too nice to have just been ditched, he didn't necessarily want to have a bunch of abandoned cars sitting around. So whose was it? Certainly not one of the new residents, because with less than a half dozens units occupied, he made it his business to know everyone, along with the cars they drove. He wanted this one towed away, but decided to call the cops first, just to be safe.

An hour later, and after hearing Nelson's story, Tucson Police Officer Young radioed in the description and license number. It confirmed his suspicion. It was the car they had been looking for, and he told Nelson it had been stolen yesterday at gunpoint. They notified Vince Armstrong of the discovery and asked him to come down and pick it up, adding there didn't appear to be any damage done, although they were still going over it. Armstrong was relieved, resigned to the fact that if the car was ever found, it would be just some burned out shell left in the desert somewhere. He was still having difficulty explaining this entire mess to his wife, but at least she would have her car back.

The police found nothing out of the ordinary, either on the car or the area surrounding it, although they were still dusting for prints. For all purposes it was just another stolen car with a pretty far-out story wrapped around it. After a quick search of the complex, and with the help of Nelson, they tried to locate just one of the few people who lived there, hoping they could offer something. He pointed out the occupied units and they knocked on the doors and poked around, but with no response. Their last chance was with the young couple who lived upstairs and whose condo overlooked the lot where the Firebird was parked. Nelson said he had seen both of them about the time the car showed up, so they pounded on the door repeatedly, and could hear the radio playing inside, but there was no answer. Officer Young finished up his work and left, while Nelson took another look around and followed him out, pleased to have the car gone, satisfied the Villa Parasio was safe and secure once again.

The afternoon sun was hot and it bore down hard. Willie felt sick and wanted to hit the road – nauseous, with these horrible headaches, magnified now by the glare and the heat – that sick Sunday feeling of being far from nowhere. But it was more than that. He knew they had keep moving. Where to was not important. Once more he explained to Doug that they were going to have to run for any chance at all to stay alive.

After waking up late, they drove the fifteen miles back to Casa Grande for breakfast. Willie slouched over the table and practiced scrawling Michael Sandburg's signature. He peeled a couple of checks out of the book and signed them, scrutinized his work with an experienced eye, then tucked them back inside for safekeeping.

On the way back to the room Doug announced the car would need some work if it was going to get them anywhere. So back at the gas station at TableTop, Willie tracked down Ray, who was not only the motel manager, but the mechanic at the station as well, and asked him to do a tune up, flashing the American Express card as payment. Always eager for an extra buck, Ray promised to get right on it.

While the car was in the garage, and Scott was asleep in the room, Willie and Doug took a walk out in the desert behind the motel. "We're gonna need a plan," Willie said. "You know, if it gets hot, we're gonna need a story we both agree on."

Doug listened, waiting for Willie to continue, knowing his input wasn't necessary, or welcome.

"I was thinking we would just say that you're driving me to my mother's funeral and we just borrowed the car from a friend."

Doug nodded.

"And then we picked up this hitchhiker cuz we felt sorry for him." Willie added to his story as they walked. The kid could be a problem later, he admitted, but for now he liked the idea of an extra person in the car.

Minutes later Scott wandered out and Willie filled him in on most of the plan. Don didn't quite grasp the reason they needed to make up any story, but knew better than to ask a lot of questions. Regardless of what Willie said about borrowing the car, Scott guessed that it was probably stolen, and while he really didn't care one way or another where it came from, he was starting to feel a bit uneasy about who he was hanging out with.

Willie sensed this sudden edginess. "Man, if this gets too hot for you, just say so. You can leave anytime you want."

Whatever the intent, these words brought little comfort. Scott now figured he wasn't riding along with just a couple of car thieves. Something was wrong here, and the offer seemed more of a threat than anything. Scott was nervous, and more than a little freaked out by the company he was now keeping.

Doug had woke up Sunday morning with a fierce migraine as well, and not coffee nor weed could chase it from his brain. The sun's piercing glare, as it bounced off the sandy earth or the windows of passing cars, shot right through him, and he spent much of the day removing his glasses, rubbing his eyes, desperate for relief. Nothing worked, so the suffering grew. A small baggie of some mediocre weed Scott couldn't stay out of was all the dope they had, and even it wasn't enough to ease Doug's misery. He ached for the prick of the needle and the warmth that always followed. He loved how it wrapped its arms around him, how it smothered him, and how it drove away all that was bad, allowing him to live with who he was and what he had done. For years that had been the only true comfort he knew, but today he didn't even have that. That's all he could think about, getting something soon that would help him find that place.

But unlike his partner, Willie was always thinking. Mostly about what they had done, paranoid about keeping a step ahead of anyone who might be after him, cops or otherwise. Soon, he would be the most sought after man in the country, and the magnitude of that was not lost on him. His significance could no longer go unnoticed, and for the first time in his life, Willie Steelman felt like he was really somebody. He was important today, not so much for who he was or what he knew, but solely for what he had done. So this continuing flight, this desperate escape, this constant running, was a large part of the high. If they could just keep going, then they could hold off the inevitable maybe just a little longer. "Gotta keep moving," he had reminded Doug many times. "Just run like hell and buy some time." He said that with time comes opportunity, and maybe some much needed luck as well. However, the thought of eventually being captured did not bother Willie. If anything it only added to his self-importance, and he could picture that day in his head and imagine how it would come down. By now, of course, it wasn't just the cops who were on their ass, Willie told Doug, but the people back in Denver, the Smaldones, who were really the ones to worry about.

"Shit, the fuckin' pigs ain't got nothing on those dudes! We'll be damn lucky if the cops find us first, cuz I've seen what the Smaldones do to people like me who's turned on them, and it ain't fucking pretty."

Of course, if it was the cops, then all the better. "You can bet your ass," he promised Doug, "that I'm gonna take out a few of them when I go, and I won't be taken alive, that's for sure."

It must have occurred to him that afternoon, as they lingered around the motel, that they were not far from the Sandberg's apartment – two hours maybe – and for all their driving, they had not distanced themselves very far from their deeds of last night. There was no way of knowing if the people had been found by now, or how long it would be until they would be missed, so Willie guessed that by tomorrow someone would go looking for them. He decided they only had one more day before things would get really hot. Just one more day to run as far as they could.

But here they were, sitting around, wasting time, so as Sunday droned on, and the afternoon shadows began to retake the TableTop Motel, Willie's paranoia finally overcame him. He talked the motel clerk into cashing a check, then walked back into the room and told the others it was time. He was so determined to leave right this instant, he offered to take the wheel first, and with the little car packed back up again, and Doug trying to get some rest, Willie drove off into the night.

Interstate 8 dips southwest from Casa Grande and it's just this side of 300 miles to San Diego. The freeway cuts through Gila Bend, but bypasses long forgotten spots like Dateland and Mohawk, before crossing the border at the Colorado River, the natural division between Arizona and California. The three hours to Yuma is full of nothing with only the occasional far away glow of lights as a reminder that you are not totally alone.

The Datsun whined and strained as Willie keep his foot in it, hoping to make some time, but not so fast as to attract the attention of the highway patrol lurking on the next onramp. Doug closed his eyes to hold off the throbbing in his temples, and Willie fooled with the radio as he drove. In the back, Donald Scott remained silently stoned, content to gaze out the window into the nothingness of the desert night.

Eventually the lights of Yuma flickered in the distance and it was then when Willie complained out loud that he had done his share of driving. Even a few hours were too much for him. He had never been into it like most guys are – guys like Doug who lived for it. Cars never interested Willie. He had owned a couple of them back in Lodi, but it was no big deal. Drove them, trashed them, then tried to figure out a way to get another one. He would much rather be up front riding shotgun, arm stretched over the back of the seat. Seemed a little more cool, and a helluva lot more important, to be chauffeured around.

His head raged with a pain that ripped down his neck and into the muscles of his back – the kind of headache that made his eyes go black. Enough of this driving shit, he told Doug, he had to stop for a while. It didn't matter that they hadn't crossed the border yet, Willie started looking for a place to stop. Just before Yuma, he spotted a rest stop along the highway and pulled in.

It was 9:30. The rest area was silent, empty and dark. What little light there was now came from the pale overhead lamps and a large moon draped in a thin cloudy veil. Several big semis had lined up for the night at the far end of the parking lot, but other than that, the Datsun had very little company. Willie announced they would stay here for a little while, then Doug could drive.

They climbed out of the car and walked around to stretch their legs and get some air. They were in no hurry to leave, and even once back inside, they merely closed their eyes and tried once more to block out the pain still raging in their heads. It took only a minute or so before Willie noticed another set of headlights crawling through the lot. He turned around to see the silhouette of the light bar on top of the big sedan, and an official state seal on the door as it rolled by. He nudged Doug.

Officer Charles Wright of the Arizona Highway Patrol was stationed out of Yuma, working the interstate halfway to Casa Grande. It was a desolate run of asphalt, and there were times, especially on these quiet Sunday nights, when he wouldn't make even one stop. His presence on the freeway was mostly to keep speeders in check and tag the occasional car left abandoned on the side of the road a hundred miles from nowhere. For the past few years however, the rest areas along his route had become the source for far more problems then ever found out on the freeway. Panhandlers, thieves, and transients who camped out there were beginning to hassle motorists who had stopped. Wright kept his eyes peeled for potential problems, usually an old hippie van or a beat up truck, whose occupants were the ones usually causing the most trouble. Even so, most of Wright's time was spent rescuing motorists rather than bothering them and his detours through the rest stops were very quick and very routine, and almost always very boring.

So it wasn't so much the newer Datsun that caught his attention, as it was who was sitting in it. The headlights from his big Dodge lit up the interior of the little car and revealed three men who appeared to be sleeping. It was automatic to first scan the plates – the expiration date was always the easiest excuse to run a check – but the Datsun had current Arizona tags. Still, even in the dim light of the rest stop, Wright had that cop-gut feeling that these weren't your run-of-the-mill businessmen on the way to the coast. He pulled in close enough to thwart their possible getaway, but not so much that he would be blocked if they made a run for it. He shoved the car into park, radioed his stop and location, did a fast check of his gear, then grabbed the flashlight from the dash and got out, walking slowly, cautiously, towards the vehicle.

When Willie first spotted the patrol car, the adrenaline rush kicked in quickly. He had no idea in hell what was going on back in Tucson; for all he knew they could have found the bodies and reported the car stolen. Just to be safe he pulled the pistol from his waistband and placed it under the seat near his feet, determined to use it if need be. He looked at Doug. "Turn around and look, but stay cool."

But Scott saw what was happening and flipped out. Cops made him nervous and the thought of getting busted again sent him into a panic. He had been smoking dope and the inside of the car reeked with the undeniable sweet smell of pot. It was now much too late to start looking for a place to stash it. Doug rolled the driver side window down and waited. "Evening," he said.

The patrolman shined the flashlight in as he spoke. He spotted two fairly well dressed young men in the front and a sorry looking kid in the back. He did not return the greeting. "Taking a little break huh?"

"Yeah, we've been driving for a while. . .kinda got a little tired."

"Like to see your driver's license, please."

Doug pulled the tattered New York permit from his billfold and handed it over. Willie patted around nervously for the gun under the seat.

"Where you heading?" Wright asked as he looked over the license.

"Going to California. My mother's funeral" Willie interrupted, making sure there was the right measure of pain in his voice. Wright said nothing. His interest was not so much in the two up front, but more towards the hippie kid in the back. As the beam from the flashlight blinded him, Scott stumbled around all of the questions about who he was and why he had no ID, or what he was doing in the car and where he was going? If he was indeed just out on the road, why didn't he have any bags or a backpack? Wright was jumping on him hard now, and while Willie and Doug felt a slight sigh of relief, they realized that if he got busted, it could all come tumbling down. This interrogation lasted several more minutes. Wright ran the driver's license through dispatch. Negative. Somewhat reluctantly he handed it back to its owner. With nothing more to go on, he offered them a safe journey and stepped away. He returned to his patrol car and soon pulled out into the darkness, his gut lecturing him about how he had probably missed something back there.

They stayed at the rest stop for a few more minutes, if only to let the rush fade. Eventually Doug pulled the car back onto the freeway and drove the few miles to Yuma, over the Colorado River and into California. Well into the night they drove, while Willie replayed the scene over and over, all the time bragging about how so goddamn smart they were. But the close call forced him to admit that even if the cops still weren't on to them yet, they would be soon. They needed out. They needed to get so far gone no one would ever find them. Canada, maybe. Mexico would work, but that meant money. Big money, not this nickel and dime shit they had been doing. The answer to their dilemma suddenly came to him.

"You remember me showing you that market back in Lodi?"

Doug nodded that he did.

"I know we could go in and take it. Probably four or five grand in there. Maybe more. Dude that owns the place cashes a lot of payroll checks so I wouldn't be surprised if there wasn't twenty thou in the safe. Know where it is too. Plus, he buys and sells tons of drugs out of the store, and he has fucked my people over one too many times. He's dirty, man, and my people have givin' me the go ahead to go in and take him out. Keep whatever I find, but they want him gone."

Doug kept driving, but he said little about Willie's plan. Admittedly it was much bigger that anything they had come up with so far, and that was their original idea, to rip off drug dealers, so it made him feel better to know they could still get back on track. But this was Willie's deal, and Doug had no idea what he could offer, so there were long periods of silence as Willie thought out loud. The only thing Doug could think of was that if he ever got his hands on that amount of money – the kind of money Willie was talking about – then the very first thing he would do was go out and buy a real nice guitar. Pretty funny, he thought to himself as his partner rambled on, that after all he had been a part of, all he had done, the only thing that would make him happy was a brand new Gibson twelve string.

About twenty miles outside Yuma, at a place called Gray's Well, the freeway cuts through the dunes and dips within a few hundred yards of Mexico. Doug watched the highway signs announce the names of the little border towns on the other side. All spelled freedom. All so close. All so untouchable. The night was black, but during the day the naked eye can see the tall cyclone fences and barbed wire that runs forever through the rolling sand, the barrier keeping him from the peace of mind he so desperately needed. He thought about his guitar, and about how so damn close he was, and how different things would be if somehow he woke up in the morning and found himself on the other side. Damn! He could just hear the sweet sounds coming from that guitar, getting loaded while beautiful, dark haired women brought him bottles of cold beer, big plates of tortillas and beans, and bowls of righteous smoke, waiting on him like he was some kind of king. And if only they would take the time to talk with him, to really get to know him, then they would have to understand he was not the kind of person who could have done the things they had heard about. *That guy isn't me*, he would protest. So don't worry, he would be sure to promise, who you see now is the real me, the real Doug. . .laid back and mellow, peaceful and generous and caring. If he could only have that chance. If he could just somehow wake up tomorrow and be on the other side. It all sounded so good. It was the only good thing he had felt in a long time.

"So who is this guy again?" he asked when the dream ended and reality set back in.

"Shit, I know you heard me talking about him," Willie answered. "Name's Wally. Wally Parkin."

On this chilly Sunday night in November, with his children tucked safely in bed and his wife already fast asleep, Wally made one last pass through his house on Orchard Road. Outside, the steady rain of the past few days had transformed the surrounding fields and vineyards into a sea of mud. He looked out the large picture window and saw the ground glisten in the darkness.

This was a busy time of year. They had spent the weekend with friends, celebrating Joanne's birthday in the low-key way she always requested. His little boy would be ten in a few days. Ten! But unlike his mom, Bobby liked big parties, and so there was certain to be one. Even his birthday was coming soon and he knew everyone would make a big fuss about it, all of which he enjoyed, and expected.

Now the hectic holiday season was approaching. The harvests were coming in and the paychecks would be sizable this year, just rewards for the hard work of the people of Victor. Soon the United Market would be a blur of activity – the cooler bursting with dressed toms and the storeroom stacked to the ceiling with cartons of canned goods and cello sacks of potatoes. There were decorations to put up, displays to arrange, parties to plan, and of course, the annual Christmas pageant at the kid's school. It was the time of year for rec basketball, league doubles on Tuesday nights at the Tokay Bowl, or just a night at home with Joanne, sitting in front of the fireplace, his small hands wrapped tightly around the warmth of a coffee mug. How he loved the vivid colors of fall, the smell of wood smoke in the air, even the drizzle from the gray skies of morning. There was comfort in the sound of the chimes, and even in the cool damp air that followed a customer through the front door of the market, and it pleased him when he could hear the echo of season's greeting offered over the clamor of the checkout counter.

It was, without a doubt, his favorite time of year, and he never lacked for someone to share the season with, because there was not a soul around who didn't proudly boast they knew Wally Parkin.

And tonight that list included Willie Steelman.

30

Monday, November 5, 1973 | 6 am.

Ken Francisco was awake early. He walked outside, and it was strictly his curiosity that drove him to check the license plate of the car that came in late last night. Why it bothered him so much that he couldn't sleep, he didn't know, but it infuriated him when people just flat out lied about it, or claimed they couldn't remember the number, or something equally as pathetic. But there it was; cream colored Datsun. Arizona RWS 563. They were right. Ken felt a little twinge of disappointment that it matched up with what the guy said. He always figured himself a pretty good judge of character, and he had that guy last night pegged as a no good lying sonofabitch.

The car had pulled into the Ocotillo Motel around 11:30 the night before. The Francisco's ran the place and were already in bed when front door buzzer alerted them to late arrivals. Ken got up and grumbled out loud about the hour – wondering if he had remembered to turn the CLOSED sign around – then unlocked the door and let the two men inside, his ever-accommodating wife close behind. The motel was the only one in the desolate town of Ocotillo, although even referring to the place as a motel was being generous to the term. The interstate had bypassed the desert village years earlier, but faded signs still led desperate and weary travelers to its door. A whitewashed, low walled building held the manager's quarters along with two additional rooms for rent. A long covered porch connected them, offering not much more than a few patio chairs and cactus plants, an old Coke machine, and some much welcome shade. Two other well-worn structures contained the other units. They, and a couple dilapidated travel trailers, formed a small circle that made up the Ocotillo Motel. There was no paved parking, no pool, no sidewalks, no grass, but plenty of sand;

fine white powdery sand that shifted and rearranged itself with the constant western wind blowing down through Tecate Pass in the mountains Ocotillo nestled itself against.

So last night, while Joan Francisco reached for a registration slip and offered her standard polite greeting, her husband returned to their living quarters and waited impatiently in his easy chair. His wife could be nice and cheery if she wanted, but by God, he didn't have to.

"On our way to San Diego. . .my mother's funeral," the visitor was quick to explain. "We just got too tired. Thanks for letting us in."

"That's quite all right. Sorry to hear about your mother."

"Take American Express?"

"No we don't. Sorry. Check is okay though."

The man reached into his coat pocket, pulled out a checkbook and began writing as Mrs. Francisco completed the paperwork. Two. One night. Room 4. Nine dollars plus tax.

"Any identification?" she asked.

He fumbled for his wallet, found it and flipped it open. She noted the American Express and Veteran's Card, and jotted both numbers, along with the license plate number of their car, on the back of the slip. The two men stood side by side at the counter. Outside the wind drove cold and they could hear it swirl around the parking area. Suddenly a gust hit the office and threw the door open. The man with the wallet was noticeably startled and apparently had decided the gale and the open door was all his friend's fault.

"Jesus Christ, man! You didn't close the door. You're lettin' all the goddamn cold air in this lady's office!"

The culprit, who had not yet uttered even one word, remained that way as he walked over and closed the door, this time rattling it to make sure it was shut good and tight. But even that didn't seem to appease Mr. Sandberg, who continued to complain and accuse. Mrs. Francisco was more than a little embarrassed by this violent display, but the man continued his scolding.

"Jesus, you're letting this lady's office get all cold!"

"Oh, that's quite all right," she interrupted. "Here's your room key, Mr. Sandberg. . .room number four. . .right next door here. You can park your car over there."

As quickly as he had exploded, he turned and thanked her for her patience as he tucked his papers back inside the billfold. "Can you wake us at nine-thirty?"

"Nine-thirty it is," she replied and wrote it on the slip for the morning attendant. "Good night," she said. The men returned to their car and moved it to the spot they had been directed to park. When she saw them disappear into their room, Mrs. Francisco snapped off the office light.

Minutes later, as she lay in bed, she could hear the wind whisper and cry as it curled up under the eves. But there were other sounds even more chilling than the noise of this November gale. The sound of faint laughter from the men in the room next door. It frightened her. She swore she could hear three distinct voices now, not just the two who had checked in. As she lay there listening, she wondered just what in heaven's name she and Ken were doing taking in these strangers from the highway at all hours of the day and night? An invitation to trouble was what it was! And just what kind of people are out on the road at this hour anyway? People up to no good, that's who. Right there, in the room next to her, not a foot away – crazy, loud, laughing, scary, people. Three of them! Who knows what they have done or where they've been?

But eventually the noise from the room next door faded into an eerie silence, like the calm that precedes a desert thunderstorm, and it was well into the early morning hours of Monday when the familiar hiss of the wind finally comforted Joan to sleep.

The Datsun and its occupants were back on the road by mid morning, heading west once again on Interstate 8 towards San Diego. After sleeping in late, the day seemed to have given them a fresh start. The headaches were gone, only to be replaced by hunger pains growling in Doug's belly. Willie continued off and on with his plan about a market and a guy named Wally. Doug listened and watched the road as they climbed up through the mountain pass, trying to pay attention, but more distracted by the wild boulder formations rising skyward on both sides of the highway. During the rare moment when Willie managed to stop talking long enough for them to hear, Doug's stomach made loud rumbling noises and Willie laughed and gave him shit about it.

Things were not so pleasant for the passenger in the back. Donald Scott was now convinced he was in over his head. He knew for certain the car was stolen, and now he watched Willie pass out bad checks like Halloween candy. Willie's talk was getting more violent too, as he boasted about slitting throats and snapping the necks of people who had crossed him somewhere down the line. This was some weird shit he had found himself in the middle of. Hell, all he was trying to do was get to California and find a place to hang around and mellow out, just looking for a tranquil scene, but instead he found himself in the back seat of the tiny Datsun. Listening to talk like this, and to hear all the wild stuff coming from up front, Scott was wondering if it was time to take Willie up on his offer. But before he could decide, Willie said something to Doug that made the decision for him.

"You know, we really need to ditch this car and get another one. This thing is gonna be real hot real quick."

And it was at that moment when they came upon an elderly couple parked on the side of the road, resting against the passenger side of a late model four door. As the Datsun overtook them and sped by, Willie pointed to the unsuspecting woman. "Now we could throw down on somebody like that pretty fuckin' easy."

That was all it took. Donald thought about his own grandmother and knew he didn't want to be around when these two began busting up old people. He was surprised to find his eyes well up as he remembered his grandparents and how long it had been since he had last seen them. For the first time in a long time Don felt homesick.

Minutes later, when Doug pulled in for gas in town of Pine Valley, Scott found the courage to speak up from the back seat. "Think it's time to go it alone," he said.

He wasn't sure what the response would be, relieved when there wasn't any.

Donald gathered his stuff and the three exchanged goodbyes and good luck, with fumbling handshakes signaling the end of their time together. Willie and Doug watched as Scott walked across the highway, set his pack down, put his thumb out and point it back in the direction from which he had just come.

Doug topped off the tank, and Willie failed in his attempt to pass more bad paper, having to use precious cash instead. As they wheeled back onto the highway, they looked over to where the hippie kid was still standing. The Hippie Kid. That's what they would call him from now on. Willie laughed at him as they drove away, an unlit Marlboro bobbed between his large lips.

Lodi. He was back at it. The first thing they had to do, he said, was to get another gun, because it would be flat out impossible to pull this thing off with just the little .22 they were packing around.

"Man, I wish we still had all the other shit," he lamented, referring to the weapons taken from them back in Tucson, recalling how people sat up and paid attention when they opened the cases to reveal the sawn off rifles. But he was confident he could reach a friend who had a large collection of guns, and he assured Doug they would find the guy as soon as they got to Lodi.

Willie also reminded him this Parkin guy might have to go down. The guy wasn't clean, he said again, and his people might look favorably upon him if he was the one to handle the job. Such talk did not bother Doug. Maybe Bill was telling the truth, maybe not. Didn't matter. If they had to do one more, well, it wouldn't make one bit of difference now. Even Willie's incessant boast of big money didn't impress him because he never had much anyway, despite all the big talk and big ideas that began back in Denver. The thought of a lot of money only meant they could maybe get away and finally buy some decent drugs, and of course, get that guitar.

What would he do with his share? Doug didn't have to think long when Willie asked. It was easy. Get loaded and stay loaded. What else? But right now all Doug really thought about was eating. On the eastern edges of San Diego, in the city of El Cajon, Willie decided they had gone far enough from Tucson to pick up some cash. At a storefront on the main drag, a place called Bud & Ray's Pawn Shop, he hocked the 35mm Petri camera for $40, the entire take from the Sandberg's.

Across the street was an International Houses of Pancakes. Doug hated the place, but Willie insisted he wasn't about to drive all over looking for something more to his liking. Doug gave in, figuring it was better than nothing, his hunger pains now overwhelming his finicky eating habits. Over breakfast around lunchtime Willie kept up the talk about Wally Parkin and Lodi, getting more excited with each word he spoke.

Tucson. Monday morning. The weekend was over and no one had come to claim the body. No new leads. No one reported missing. No closer to an ID than he was on Friday night. Except for one long shot lead to follow up on, Weaver Barkman was stumped.

The long shot was all he had to work on this morning. Barkman noted in his report the victim had been wearing black engineer boots and the soles were clearly stamped with the logo "Sears". They appeared to be fairly new, so Weaver's slim hope rested on the outside chance somebody there might remember the man who had bought them not that long ago. The only Sears store in Tucson was downtown on Broadway and Detective Barkman pulled into the lot shortly after ten. If he was nothing else, he was direct and quick to the point. He found a salesman, gave the reason for his visit and a description of the man in question, then stood back and waited for his answer.

"Lopez."

"What's that again?" Barkman asked.

"The man who bought those boots last week was named Lopez," the clerk repeated. "I should know, I sold them to him."

Weaver perked up. Now he was getting somewhere! Lopez. Yeah, that sounded Mexican enough to him. The salesman added that he also remembered the boots were put on a charge card so there would be permanent record of the transaction back in the office. Not one to stand in line, he contacted store security, flashed his badge and was escorted inside.

Barkman barged in and announced, "I need the name of a man who charged some boots here last week, Your guy out front said he remembered the last name as 'Lopez'".

The woman behind the counter listened to the story, then without a single word, slowly rose to her feet and took a few steps to the Cardex file. Weaver fidgeted, realizing things were moving too smoothly. A bad sign.

"Loper. . .Lopes. . .Lopez. Here they are. Which one do you want?" she asked, flipping through the file.

"I don't know. . .Lopez. . .pick one. I don't have a first name. Find the Lopez who charged something last week and that's the one I want."

The woman lifted her head from the file cabinet and looked right at Barkman. "That might take awhile. Care to wait?"

"How long?" Weaver was not a man comfortable wasting time.

"Well, sir," came the quick reply, "this is Tucson, remember? We have hundreds of people, maybe thousands, named Lopez who have charge accounts here."

Barkman threw up his hands and left in a huff. He hoped it wouldn't come to this, because he didn't have the time or patience, but it appeared he had no choice. The only avenue left to explore was something taken directly off the dead man. His fingerprints.

A set had been sent to the Washington D.C office of the FBI on Friday, but because of the weekend, Barkman was sure nothing had been done about it. Unlike local agencies, even one as large as Pima County, only the Bureau had the technology to computer scan the prints to locate a match. But even with the computer, that process could still take hours. And even that, of course, was dependant upon the victim sporting a criminal record, although Barkman would bet his last dollar his guy did.

But he couldn't wait for the FBI. Waiting was not his style. So Weaver drove straight over to Tucson Police to see what they might have in their files on his mystery man. For the rest of the morning and well into the afternoon, with the help of an officer in the Identification Section, Barkman began the task of going through the records of every person the department had booked in the last couple of years. Hundreds upon hundreds of white 5 x 8 cards, each with a name and a set of prints. It was the ultimate in working backwards, but it was all he had. There was no guarantee his man was even here, but with every name, he figured he had eliminated someone and got a little closer. If the age wasn't close, or the card didn't have a Mexican surname, it was discarded. Weaver found an empty desk and jumped in. He knew this was going to take a while, but at least it was keeping him busy.

Two hours north in Apache Junction, Maricopa detectives were also conducting their own wild search for fingerprints in a haystack, or as it was in this case, a house trailer.

Dave Arrelanes, accompanied now by Detectives Wissman and Gilchrist, who had returned from Denver Friday night, drove back out to Vista Grande to try and recover any prints possibly left behind by the suspects – the one missing piece, along with the murder weapon itself, of course, – that they didn't have. With such prints, Arrelanes believed the D.A. would have no choice but to go ahead with the murder warrants. But to Dave's dismay, the trailer again yielded very little. A palm print, maybe, a couple of other possibilities, but nothing substantial enough to match up with something on file somewhere.

The trip to the mobile home park wasn't a total loss however. While there, Arrelanes met with John Holliman, who claimed to have met a guy named Bill staying in the trailer with Bob and Yahfah. All this Bill did was brag about weapons and dope and music and stuff, John said. Did you see these weapons, Dave asked, and Holliman said all he had seen was some kind of pistol that was being flashed around. When Arrelanes showed him the photos, Holliman quickly passed over the two ringers and pointed to the white guy with the big afro.

"Shit; I'd know that face anywhere," he bragged. "That's the dude there. That's Bill".

So John Holliman could place Steelman in the park with a weapon, and most importantly, with the victims. That in itself was probably enough for his warrant, but Dave decided to keep going while they were still in the area. His next stop was Fremont School, where he hoped to talk again to the Sexton girls.

Tarnyn and Teresea were still standoffish when Arrelanes arrived, as if they owed it to Yahfah and Bob not to give in to the cops, regardless of whose side everyone was now on. Dave viewed their teenage snub as simply a cover to hide just how scared they really were. Bill and Doug were still out there somewhere and they were old enough to understand that they were two of the few people still alive who could recognize them. Might even come back and finish them off too, Dave hinted.

The girls cringed at the very idea, and while they were very scared, they tried not to let it show, and yet couldn't help but feel more than a little important to be a major part of such a big deal. To be called out of class, to talk to the cops about the story everyone in town was talking about, made them very special indeed. Their friendship with not only the victims, but with the killers themselves, making them the most important people of all. It took several minutes, but Arrelanes managed to find a way to get them to both open up, so back and forth, the girls took turns telling what they knew.

Sure, we knew Yahfah. Yeah. . .Bob too.

Yes, we saw two men in the trailer with them.

Yeah. We saw them all on Thursday.

No, Tarnyn. Not Bob, remember?

Oh yeah, Bob wasn't there then.

We don't know. Yahfah said he was hiding.

From who? Well from the cops, I guess.

Yeah, Yahfah said they were gonna bust him. It was later that night when we stopped by. Neither one was there. Just the two guys. They said Bob and Yahfah had gone downtown. But would be back. So we waited. But then we heard our parents and got scared. And we tried to hide.

Freeze! he said.

No, no one hurt us. We just couldn't go in the bedrooms. Then they just let us walk out.

Yeah, the girls echoed when shown the photo. *That one's Bill, and that's his friend, Doug.*

With two more positive IDs added to the list, Arrelanes decided to pay Mr. and Mrs. Weld another visit on the way back to the office. While both were adamant about the suspect's stay at the Tahiti, neither could be quite so sure they were the same two men in the photographs. While it wasn't a major setback, Dave hoped the day would end on a more positive note.

Back at the office he again tried to locate the college kids robbed near Globe. He finally got through to the County Sheriff there, thankful to learn the young couple was brave enough at least to report the incident when they finally made it back to town, despite the threats made to them. Dave arranged a meeting with them for the following day.

It baffled Arrelanes though, the fact that this couple, and apparently others now as well, had come in contact with Steelman and Gretzler, even held at gunpoint and robbed, but were not harmed. Even as close as the Sexton girls came to discovering the bodies, they were spared, as if the killers enjoyed deciding who would live and who would not.

So why Yahfah and Robbins? What had they done? What was it they did, or knew, that made such a horrible difference? Even Marsha Renslow could not offer a good reason. Steelman and Gretzler didn't even know the victims until she introduced them just a few days earlier. So what had they done?

Dave was positive he knew who killed Bob Robbins and Yahfah Hacohen, but he still had no idea why.

It was well after six pm in Tucson. Barkman had not stopped since late that morning, determined to keep looking until he had found his man. Now with the help of I.D. Officer Bob Heims, he reclassified the prints once more, going card by card, one by one, scanning hundred and hundreds of possibilities in the search.

As the day wore on, it was clear they were running out of cards, but when they got to "S", Weaver Barkman's heart jumped up into his throat. He checked it again, then had Heims do so as well. It was agreed. This was the their dead man.

Gilbert Rodriguez Sierra. Mexican male, born June 16, 1954. Everything fit, right down to several FBI numbers, which would certainly substantiate his findings. Barkman called Tucker to tell him the good news, and just to be sure, asked him to contact the Bureau to verify his findings. The phone call was made, but because of the late hour, almost midnight in D.C., the agency said it would be morning before an answer could be given. Tomorrow would be fine by Barkman. It was just a technicality anyway. It had been a damned good day and he knew he was now finally getting somewhere. Usually didn't take three days for him to get a name. Hell, most of the time it's plastered all over the body, or at least spills out of the loud mouths of the know-it-alls who migrate to murder scenes. But this one hadn't been quite that easy, and it had bothered him.

But maybe the hardest part of the Sierra murder was behind him, Barkman told himself, encouragement to keep up the pace. Now he could concentrate on finding the person who pulled the trigger. It was long after nightfall by the time Barkman left the building, and a fall chill filled the air as he headed to his car. A good day indeed, he decided.

In fact, today was Weaver's birthday, and he figured finding Gilbert Sierra was a pretty damn good gift.

By nightfall the Datsun had traveled halfway up the state, and both driver and passenger were wrung out and ready to call it quits. Tomorrow they would breeze into town, see a few people, take care of a little business, then split. Go as far as they could with the money they had and not look back. But by now the deal with Wally Parkin and the United Market had taken on a whole new meaning to Willie. Certainly they needed money, and of course the market always had plenty of that, but it had become less about a payoff and more about a payback. Hell yes, they needed every dime they could get – there was nowhere to run without it – but what excited Willie more were the thoughts swirling in his head about how he would soon have his turn with this town. With every word spoken, with each part carefully planned, the more hateful and vengeful he became. The more he rehashed details with Doug, the more he remembered the town he grew up in. The more he remembered the people who had laughed at him, the more he craved the chance to show them exactly who they had screwed with. He remembered his brother and his ex-wife, cops and judges, in-laws and so called friends, and how small and worthless they had all made him feel. He remembered every face of every man who had ever fired him and the name of every person who had lied to him.

Of course he said none of this to Doug. He just kept talking about the big money. Loads of money. At least five large. More than enough money to keep them gone for along time. Who knows, could be ten. Whatever. It's the kind of money that's going to take care of them. That's guaranteed. Hell, might be twenty! Heard he had that in there once. All they had to do was just get through until tomorrow, then everything would fall into place. That was what Willie told Doug.

He decided they needed a good night's sleep, so they found a little out of the way place in Madera, a dump motel chosen for how little it cost and the seclusion it offered. For as much thought as he gave about shrouding his identity, Willie again checked in under a mindless derivative of Steelman. They stayed up and watched some TV, smoked some weed and eventually drifted off. Willie had come down from his earlier high and reclined on the bed trying to think through all the important details, his mind burdened, knowing it would be again all up to him when it came down.

He might have felt better that night if he had known just how important he had already become. Ten lawmen throughout five cities in three states were hot on his trail. None were able to see the big picture, or knew the magnitude of his crimes, let alone comprehend where this would all lead. In some cases they knew nothing about the others in pursuit, nor imagine what tomorrow might bring. Which was indeed a shame, for Willie Steelman would have loved the attention.

Lodi's first week of November was a wet one. Rain had fallen off and on for seven days straight. In the vineyards, ruts left by summer tractors overflowed and the muddy water rippled across the roadway. Even when the rain stopped, the days were short and gray, the nights cold and damp. And yet despite all of this, they had no choice but to ignore the weather and proceed. Tonight, Richard Earl and his family stood outside in the cold drizzle working by only the dim glow of a lantern.

Between trying to finish the house and taking care of the vineyard, the hard work was wearing Richard down and it was clear to everyone he was exhausted. Field help was in short supply, and without the connections afforded the older more established growers, Richard had difficulty hiring laborers, not that he could pay them if he did. So Wanda, Deb and Rick were put to work in the vineyard, with an open invitation to the rest of the family – even friends of the kids – to come and help cut grapes. They came, not for the 25 cents a bushel Richard offered, but because they cared, willing to do what they could to help the Earl family. Months later, several of the small checks Richard wrote to them for their efforts would remain uncashed.

But the grapes had stayed too long on the vines and his agreement with Gallo Winery called for the harvest to be in two weeks ago. That, plus the race with the weather, was weighing him down. You could see it in his face. A cold wet November was now firmly entrenched in the San Joaquin Valley and the damage it could cause would be serious; to the grapes and the crop money Richard so desperately needed.

So tonight the family donned parkas and lit lanterns and slogged through the vineyard surrounding their home on Orchard Road. The Zinfandels clustered in huge bunches and nearly touched the rain swollen earth. The leaves, having long since turned color, collapsed under the weight of the rainwater and fell, exposing the grapes. Only when these scraggly, twisted vines were bare of their fruit and foliage did Richard feel he could rest.

The weather report was not encouraging. A new and potentially strong storm front was racing down from Alaska and was expected to hit California within 48 hours. With it would come the first snow to the mountains, along with torrential rain and bone chilling temperatures to the valley floor. Richard knew it would be a race to finish the harvest before the crop was totally damaged.

So tonight, the first Monday in November, in the soggy darkness, they worked furiously. Richard and Wanda, Deb and Rick, even Mark and a few friends, laboring by the light of lanterns, kerosene torches, and the dim headlights of a pickup aimed down the rows. In the blackness, as rain tried hard again to fall, the band of workers, bogged down in the muddy soil, toiled to strip the valuable clusters from the vines.

It was well after eleven when he finally yelled out that they were done for the night. They hadn't finished, but it was late and they were soaked, cold and tired. As they left, Richard thanked them for their help and half-joked they were all invited back tomorrow night to continue their work.

There's always tomorrow, he reminded them.

The boarding house off 4th Avenue in Tucson where Willie and Doug stayed.

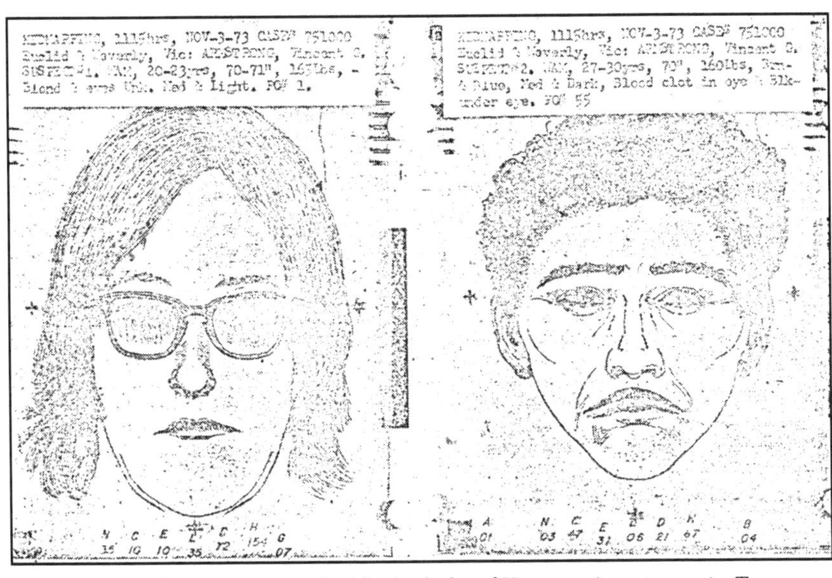

Composite drawing created with the help of Vincent Armstrong in Tucson.

The body of Gilbert Sierra as found in the desert west of downtown Tucson.

The crash pad in Tucson where Willie, Doug, Joanne, and Mike Marsh went after the murder of Gilbert Sierra. It was here where they met Donald Scott.

Michael and Patricia Sandberg on their wedding day.

The Sandberg's condominium in Tucson.

The scene inside the Sandberg condo when Tucson Police entered the home.

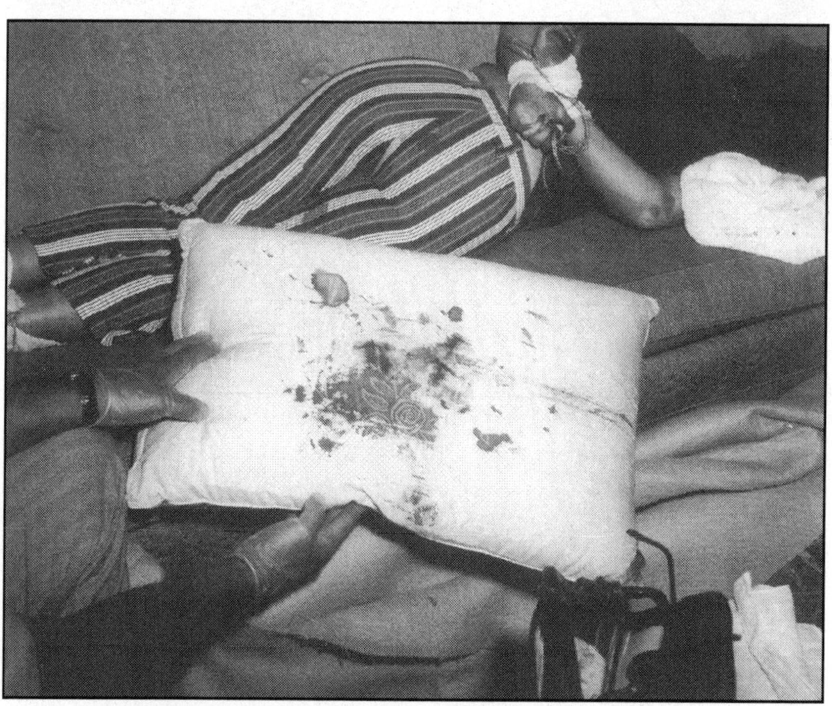

The pillow used as a silencer. Patricia Sandberg's body remains as it was uncovered on the sofa.

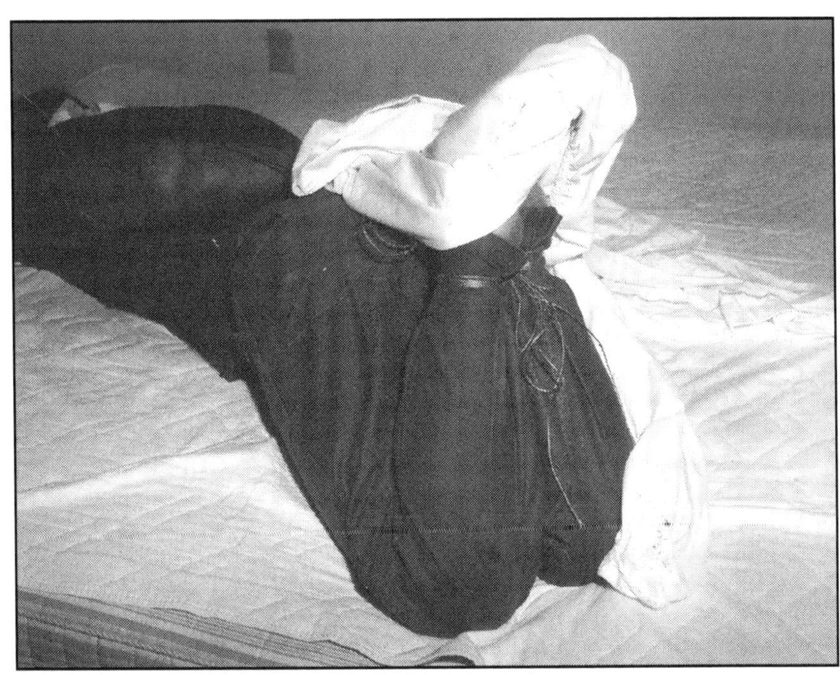

Michael Sandberg's body with intricate knots and padding.

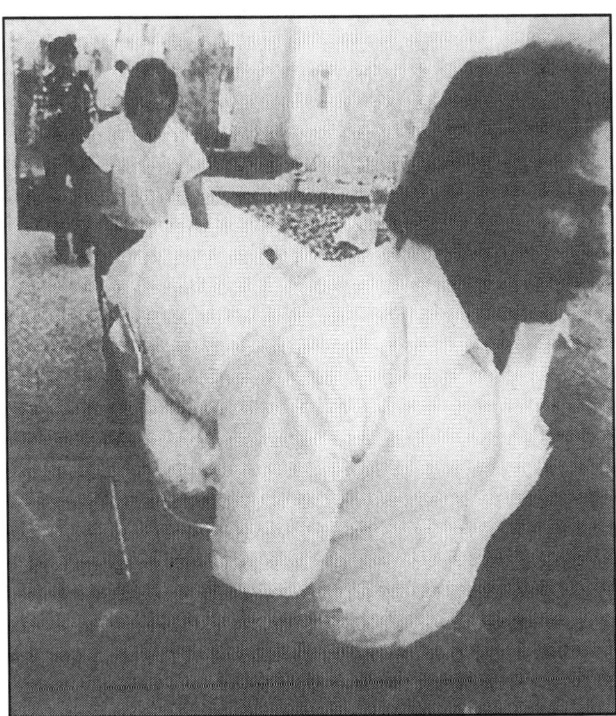

Michael Sandberg's body is removed from his home in Tucson.

Their room at the Table Top Motel where they spent the night after leaving the Sandberg's condo.

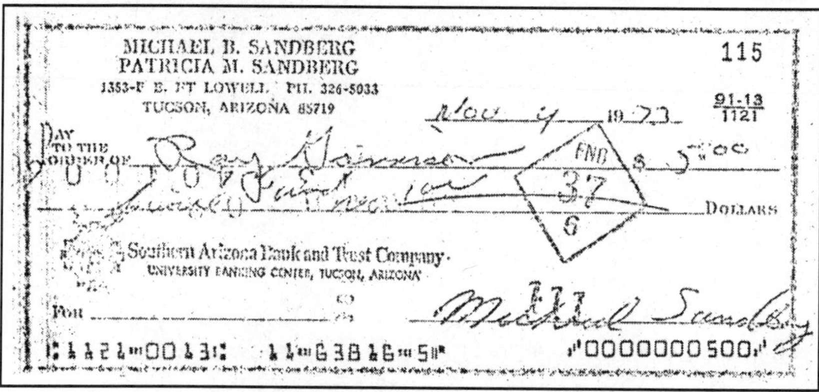

MICHAEL B. SANDBERG
PATRICIA M. SANDBERG
1353-F E. FT LOWELL PH. 326-5033
TUCSON, ARIZONA 85719

115

Nov 4 19 73

91-13
1121

PAY TO THE ORDER OF

$ 5.00

DOLLARS

Southern Arizona Bank and Trust Company
UNIVERSITY BANKING CENTER, TUCSON, ARIZONA

FOR

Michael Sandberg

The check Willie cashed at the Table Top Motel forging Michael Sandberg's signature.

The Ocotillo Motel. The room Willie, Doug and Don Scott stayed is directly in the middle of the photo.

A-24

GUEST REGISTER

ARRIVED	ROOM
DATE 11-4-73	#4
HR. 11:20 PM	

RATE DAY	WEEK	MONTH	NO. IN PARTY
900			2

S	M	T	W	T	F	S

MISCELLANEOUS

DATE	ITEMS	AMOUNT
		9
	TAX	.36
	TOTAL	$9.36

DATE OUT

NAME: [illegible]

STREET ADDRESS: 4412 4TH ST

CITY: [illegible] STATE

CAR LICENSE — NUMBER: RWS 322 — STATE: ARIZ

MAKE AND TYPE OF CAR: FORD

THIS PROPERTY IS PRIVATELY OWNED AND THE MANAGEMENT RESERVES THE RIGHT TO REFUSE SERVICE TO ANYONE, AND WILL NOT BE RESPONSIBLE FOR ACCIDENTS OR INJURY TO GUESTS OR FOR LOSS OF MONEY, JEWELRY OR VALUABLES OF ANY KIND.

REMARKS: Wake at 9:30

AICO-UTILITY Line Form No. 25-018

The registration slip from The Ocotillo Motel. Note his scrawled name and that the address on the form did not match that on the check and although the license number matched the Datsun, Willie said he was driving a Ford.

31

Tuesday, November 6, 1973 | 7:45 am.

The morning began in a dark drizzle, promising another useless day of gray in the San Joaquin Valley. The wet face of a small dog peeked from a dirty army-surplus field jacket that overwhelmed the young woman wearing it. Next to her, a bundled up man with his thumb out stood singing to himself, dancing from one foot to the other to stay warm. Together they waited in the damp morning, feeling the roar of the road scream by just inches away.

South of where they stood, Willie and Doug, an hour or so earlier, had stumbled from Room 11 at a no-name motel. It was still dark out when they got back on 99, and for mile after mile; the only sound in the car was the D.J. banter and morning news coming from the radio. Willie had already laid out what would happen later in Lodi, yet he struggled for something to add. He could think of nothing, so he simply fidgeted with the radio. Doug drove, and the only conversation he could offer was to say he was hungry. Willie ignored him.

Miles later, Willie pointed out two people on the side of the road and told Doug to pull over. He was tired of the present company and was ready for a new audience. The hitchhikers gathered their knapsacks and ducked into the back seat, having to kick trash out of their way to find room. Willie started right in with the bullshit. Doug stayed silent, his head now pounding, his stomach knotting, a nervousness he attributed to hunger. He knew food would help calm him. Again he suggested they stop.

At an off ramp Denny's on the south side of Modesto, Willie had heard enough complaining and announced to his guests it was his treat. They ordered and ate, Doug returned to the living, and while Willie made all the motions of picking up the check, a patron at the counter swore he watched him stiff the waitress as the others walked out to the car.

A dozen miles south of Stockton, Willie offered one last boast. He pulled the .22 from under his seat and held it up. "This," he promised, "is just in case we run into any trouble up the road."

The young couple had seen and heard enough. Guns were not their bag. There had been a lot of wild talk over the last couple of hours, but this was getting too weird. Free ride? Free food? Yeah, but it wasn't worth it. This guy was a freak. They gave each other the look that said it was time to get out. "Have a good trip brother, wherever it is you're going," the young man offered as he pulled his knapsack from the Datsun, relieved to be cut loose.

"Thanks man, but we're not going far," Willie replied, still waving the gun around. "Just headin' up to Lodi on a little business."

Detective Barkman wasn't in the office Tuesday morning when the FBI called. It wouldn't have made any difference anyway. Tucker took the call that merely confirmed what he and his partner already knew; the fingerprints belonged to a man named Gilbert Sierra. But answers to the next questions would be a lot tougher to come by, and Washington wouldn't be any help here either. Just who was this Gilbert kid anyway? The detectives had asked themselves that a dozen times. And more importantly, who killed him? And why?

There were two things Tucker and Barkman were certain of, however. Drugs were involved for one, and two, Sierra was not simply murdered, he was executed. And if that was the reason – if the killing was performed simply to make a statement – then there was every reason to believe their guy was still in the area. The way Barkman saw it, there was no sense going to all the trouble to waste somebody for show if you weren't going to hang around long enough to see if anyone was paying attention.

And that was the part that didn't fit. Sierra wasn't a known commodity to the authorities, at least when it came to drugs. Nor was his face or name recognized or remembered as having anything to do with the local drug trade. At best, Sierra was figured by Barkman to be a little mule that got a bit greedy with some of the packages he was hired to carry. So when he was caught skimming some off the top, his employer terminated their relationship. What Tucker and Barkman needed to do now was find that missing link, the connection between the little guy and the big guy. Maybe then they would find the person who shot Gilbert Sierra in the back, and then point blank twice, right in the face.

At nine am, Tucker received the teletype from Arizona Motor Vehicle listing Gilbert's long time association with the law. The printout consumed an entire page of infractions – most of them moving violations – and Tucker counted a dozen DUI's, all within the last 24 months. His license had been suspended for five years and he had been caught driving without it several times. But nowhere on the page was there any indication he was anything more than a young punk, stupid enough to get busted, not once, but about a hundred million times.

Barkman drove back over to Tucson P.D. to see if they could shed anymore light, but again nothing unusual, and only two names came up in his search; the victim's probation officer and an emergency number, Gilbert's brother, Gregorio. Although the emergency in Gilbert's life had come and gone, Barkman did try to contact Gregorio. That too proved unsuccessful, although he managed to find the person responsible for keeping an eye out for Gilbert Sierra while he was alive.

That seemingly impossible task belonged to Al Mulleneaux, his probation officer, who acted not one bit surprised when he was informed his client would not be checking in anymore. All Barkman wanted was a recent address, but even that Mr. Mulleneaux could not provide. He offered to try and find a next of kin and Barkman accepted, but insisted nothing be said of Sierra's death.

Later in the day, Mulleneaux called Barkman and told him he had reached the grandparents, but they had no idea where Gilbert might be. They were worried about him, claiming he was running with a pretty tough bunch down in Tucson. Mulleneaux asked Barkman when they could notify the family, but was told they would need another day. (Indeed, the next morning, Gilbert's grandparents, who had adopted him, but could never control him, were told of his death.) Barkman spent the rest of Tuesday trying to reach the only other person who might have something to add. But Tucson was a wide open city, and it hid Gregorio Sierra much better than it had hid the body of his brother. Barkman again came up empty.

But word of the murder had spread, and the elder Sierra found Barkman first, telephoning the Sheriff's office to say he had heard the news. His lack of emotion surprised Barkman, especially when he said he could have predicted the outcome. "My brother could be a real sonofabitch," Gregorio conceded. And while there were probably a hundred people who wanted to beat the shit out of him, he could think of nothing Gilbert could have done to make someone want to kill him.

When Sierra got around to asking about his car – explaining Gilbert was the last one who had it – Barkman stopped him mid sentence. *What car?* Gregorio backed up and told him how he had let his brother use his car last week and how he never saw either one again. He described it in great detail. *Had they found it?* He wanted to know. *Where was it?* He asked.

That's just exactly what Barkman now wondered. He jumped at the new lead. Find the Dodge Charger, he decided, and possibly the killer as well.

It was exactly twelve noon, she remembered, because she was just fixing the kid's lunch. The man at her front door showed his badge and Frances invited him in. He didn't have to say anything, she knew who he was looking for. She had heard the rumor. She knew it was only a matter of time before her brother would find bigger trouble, as if he wouldn't be satisfied until he did. And now the cops were at her door, telling her he might be involved in the death of two people. She got this terrible retching in her stomach, the same sick feeling she had a few weeks back when his stare sliced right through her. She hated to admit it, but she wasn't surprised to hear Willie might have killed somebody.

Detective Lawless was still handling the Denver legwork for Arizona and Frances Bender was one of his last contacts. She made him promise her name would not be in the papers or used in any way during their investigation. She didn't want her children to hear what their uncle might have done. And good heavens, she declared! If Willie ever felt she had turned on him, well, she didn't want to even think of what he might do! Lawless understood her fears and agreed to her request.

He was a surprised to find a woman in her forties, clearly much older than their suspect. When he asked about it, she admitted Willie was many years younger than she and more like a son than a brother. She just about raised him herself, she said, and although at one time it was something she was proud of, she appeared embarrassed by that now. When shown the photo, Frances identified him, and in almost the same breath, acknowledged his years of trouble as a teenager and his many run-ins with the law. He was even in a mental hospital for a time, she allowed, although adamant that he wasn't crazy, merely confused. There were two different people living inside him, she explained, hoping such information could help Willie when they caught him.

She told the detective about how much he loved his father, and how he was barely 13 when he died, how her little Bill was never the same after that. She regretted moving away and leaving him alone back then, and how over the years the family wrote to her of his troubles, and she often wondered if there was something she could have done, like maybe it was somehow her fault. Then one day this past summer he showed up on her doorstep and brought all of his problems with him.

It wasn't long after that, Frances added, when another guy showed up at her house – a quiet young man named Doug – and he and Bill soon became inseparable. "They were frightening pair," Frances shivered, "and I guess I knew all along the trouble those two could cause someday." She said nothing about the stolen purse, or the threats made toward her, only that she heard they had left town, and she hadn't seen either one of them in almost a month.

Lawless asked if she knew where they could be now and Frances could only shrug. Their brother, Gary, still lives in Lodi, but he and Willie never did see eye to eye, so she was positive he wouldn't go see him. At the detective's request, she called Gary, just to be sure, but he could only growl that he hadn't seen the no-good since early summer, and that was just fine with him. *So what kind of trouble is he in now?* Gary snarled, but Frances did not say, changed the subject, and said her goodbyes.

She told Lawless her oldest daughter, Terry, was staying with family in Modesto, California, and she and Willie got along well, so that was a possibility. She also heard that Doug was from New York, and they had talked about going back there, but that was about all.

Lawless left the house realizing Willie Steelman could be just about anywhere. When he called Phoenix later to relay his conversation with Frances Bender, the only positive thing he could report is that she identified him in the photo. Her description of Willie's days in Denver paralleled Marsha Renslow's, but she was no help in determining where he may be headed next.

While Jack Gilchrist was on the phone with the detective from Denver, Arellanes and Miller were interviewing the couple robbed near Globe. After going over what happened that day, the young man was asked to look at several photos. Without hesitation he pointed out Steelman, as did his girlfriend, but neither could be positive about the second suspect. The other guy stood back a ways, they remembered, and didn't say anything. Nor did they get a good look at him. The one that scared them the most, the kid explained, was the guy holding the shotgun. "He acted crazy enough to kill us. He took our money, then threw some of it back. He laughed at us and told us to be more careful. He was scary. We could hear them laughing all the way back up the hill."

Arellanes was now certain that the man holding the shotgun – William Steal, or Bill Steel, or Will Steelman – was indeed Willie Luther Steelman, and that he and Douglas Gretzler were responsible for the homicides in the trailer. Never mind the shortage of fingerprints or the lack of a weapon or motive, Dave figured he had enough for a murder warrant, and by late morning he and Miller began preparing the documents for the County Attorney.

Ten days had passed since Dave had first viewed the bodies in the bedrooms, and everyday since he wondered where the killers would show up next, always fearful more victims would surface before Willie and Doug did. But today Dave was confident he now knew exactly where Willie Steelman was heading. Maybe it was his years on the job, or maybe just a hunch, but either way Arellanes was damn sure Willie was on his way home to Lodi.

Detective Nelson had hit a dead end on his case in Northern California. Since hearing from Arizona about the double homicide and recovering the stolen Ford, he had received no further communication. The two departments had traded reports and compared notes, but that was all he had. Their common difficulty was tying the few available fingerprints to their suspects. Nelson's team had recovered several quality prints from the van, but had no way to link them with either suspect. Maricopa apparently had a few prints as well, but the same problem in identifying them. It was Arrelanes who suggested that if they could compare the prints side by side, then it would be much easier to determine who they belonged to. If a print found in the van matched up with one recovered from the trailer, then there was a better than average chance it belonged to one of their suspects and their case would be that much stronger. Nelson agreed. They had to meet face to face and compare notes.

So Tuesday morning, Nelson grabbed an early flight out of San Francisco. Upon arriving at Sky Harbor, a sheriff deputy stood with a handwritten sign spelling out in black marker, "Nelson". And just to be certain, he left his sport coat open to reveal his badge and service revolver.

Arrelanes and Miller were pleased to have a fresh look at their investigation, so after introductions, Arrelanes piled the reams of reports and several dozen photos on his desk, and for the first time Nelson saw the men he too had been looking for. "Convict-Quality," he announced. It was one of his favorite phrases. "Definitely the look of people who have done time."

They compared notes and Arrelanes brought his counterpart up to speed on the Arizona investigation. They retraced the killer's steps over the past few weeks, and Arrelanes said he was certain Steelman was heading back to California.

"But why?" Nelson asked. "He was there once, then he came all the way back here. For what? You said even his own sister didn't think he would go back home. There's nothing there, except a warrant for busting parole."

Arrelanes shrugged. "Dunno really. My gut tells me the guy would feel more comfortable in his own territory. There's no one there who would connect him to any of this. Really, who evens knows about it? So it would give him a few days to regroup and catch his breath. He needs it."

Nelson thought it over. The argument made sense. He remembered all the people he had nabbed right in their own backyard, even weeks after the crime. For all the talk about fleeing the scene, it was amazing to him how so many were dumb enough to go right back home. "Have you talked to them about all of this?" he asked, referring to the authorities in Lodi.

"Not yet. Was hoping to have a warrant ready before I did. Should have it ready to go before the day's out." Still, Arrelanes made a mental note to make the call. He needed to let them know what was going on, warrant or no warrant. But it was fast approaching five o'clock, and he had much to do if he hoped to get papers signed before the day was done. Nelson was taken to his hotel with an appointment to meet with them again first thing Wednesday morning, while Arrelanes and Miller started in with the paperwork.

Once complete, protocol stated they should have traveled to the East Mesa Court, in whose jurisdiction the crime were committed. Arrelanes checked the clock. After six. The hell with formalities, he told Miller, let's get these things signed. They hurried over to the courthouse, hoping Judge Murphy was still in his office. He wasn't. No one was.

Arrelanes debated whether or not to call the judge at home, but honestly, what could he do with the warrants if he had them tonight anyway? It wasn't as if he could go right out and make the arrest. All he could do is send them out and keep his fingers crossed. The judge might not want to be wrestled away from a restful evening at home just so he could listen to a long sales pitch. No weapons? No motive? Only a guess where the suspects might be? *So what's the rush, detective?* Dave could hear the judge lecture. *Can't you see I'm trying to relax here?*

So Arrelanes decided against it. Tomorrow morning he could go into court, get the papers signed and out over the wire, all before most people were having their first cup of coffee. Yeah, tomorrow he could get the warrants, then get on the phone to Lodi and explain everything. Besides, it was late, and there was probably just some nightshift flunky up there in Lodi answering the phones now anyway. Let's go home, he told Miller. Tomorrow will be soon enough.

The weekend business had been brisk at the United Market, and after accepting all the paychecks of the area's farm workers, the first weekend of the month had depleted their cash. Problem was, Wally was supposed to have done their banking yesterday. His mother, who also kept tabs on the market's finances, smiled as she scolded him for putting it off. Eula Parkin was a small woman, but she didn't even have to look up to stare her little Wally right in the eye. "We *needed* thirty two hundred," she said, reminding him of his procrastination. "But of course that was yesterday, and I'm sure we could use more today." She decided on a new amount, then rattled off the denominations the market was in need of.

By eleven-thirty, Wally was at the Wells Fargo Bank in Lodi, and was his custom, he had to first say hello to everyone before getting down to business. His was a familiar face and there was no mistaking that friendly voice. Marilyn Munoz waved him over to her window, but again casual conversation was given priority over his banking transaction. It was always the same; the weather or his latest basketball game or bowling score. Wally snapped a check out of the book and filled it out as they chatted. $3,778. Marilyn flipped it over and hit it with the endorsement stamp, failing to notice that he had forgot to fill in the date. Per his instructions, Munoz pulled out three thousand in banded twenties and laid them in front of him. She then filled the balance of the amount, counting the currency out loud as Wally stuffed the cash into the bag. He was back in Victor before the lunch hour was half over.

The backroom of the United Market was the usual catch-all; storeroom, office, lunchroom, mop closet, and right in the middle of the room, a small floor safe. Most everyone who ever visited the store, or at least knew the Parkins, knew about the safe. Wally didn't feel like there was much of a reason to keep the safe a secret – he knew them all on a first name basis anyway – so when he got back to the market, he dumped the contents of the bank bag into it.

His parents were the first to arrive each morning, well before the store opened, so it was customary for them to leave shortly after the lunch traffic let up. After Wally returned and things quieted down, Ken Parkin stepped out from behind the meat counter, hung up his apron, and waited for his wife to finish her chores. He gazed out the huge front windows. The late autumn sky was tall and somber, and although the rain in the forecast was still hours away, he grabbed his windbreaker, walked into the storeroom and waited by the big sliding door. From his new vantage point he continued to watch the clouds shift and roll. It was nearly 2:30 when he finally heard his wife tell their son goodbye.

The two lanes of Highway 12 runs east-west, and it is on the outskirts of Lodi where it passes directly over State Highway 99. Years ago, 99 was scooped out of the sandy loam so traffic on both roads could speed right along. While Highway 12 becomes one of Lodi's main boulevards in town, travelers on 99 can ignore Lodi all together if they choose. So, because their timing was so unintentionally precise, there was a very good chance that when Wally wheeled his old Chevy pickup down Highway 12 on the way back from the bank, he passed right over a cream colored Datsun heading north on 99.

Willie knew he was a wanted man there, for he was certain there was a warrant out for his parole violation in July. He wanted to stay clear of Lodi, at least until the time came when he too would head out Highway 12 and to the market in Victor. So Willie decided to go directly to Galt, a small town just five miles up the road. He had some of his people there, he told Doug, people who could help later. Plus, Willie knew Galt was on the other side of the Dry Creek Bridge that separated San Joaquin and Sacramento counties. The cops would have a tougher time hassling him there.

Duff Nunley had known Steelman for several years, but hadn't seen him for quite some time. Like Cliff Wardrobe before him, it was easy for Willie to impress people like Duff, and convince him to do things he might not have done otherwise. Although he didn't necessarily always act like it, Willie was years older and Duff could usually count on him for some dope and a few extra bucks. A lot of guys like Duff would put up with the stupid shit Willie got them into just to have stuff like that available.

Among their regular crimes was to swipe beer and cigarettes from the D & A Market near where they both lived. With logic never quite explained, Duff also made a practice of stealing empty soda bottles from the market's storeroom and hauling them all the way into Lodi to cash them in instead of simply stealing from the register the dollar or two they would bring. For that one deed alone, some questioned just how bright Duff Nunley really was. Nor did it seem to matter to him that his parents owned the D & A Market he was stealing from.

Duff was like most of the people Steelman called friend; younger, less experienced, eager to please, willing to do whatever was asked just to fit in. Most of Willie's old acquaintances, the ones from years back, were long gone, tired of him, his excuses, his mooching, not to mention his endless parade of promises and BS. So, after traveling eight hundred miles to get back to Lodi, it could only be a sign of sheer desperation that the first person Steelman went to see was Duff Nunley.

Duff still lived with his parents in the small house right next to the family store, and the Datsun pulled off at Collier Road, crossed over 99, and coasted to a stop at the edge of their driveway. Leonard Nunley had long ago let his son know what he thought of Bill Steelman, and made it clear he was not welcome in or near their home. So when Willie pulled up, he coaxed Doug into going to the door, saying he was certain that if the old man saw him he wouldn't hesitate to call the cops. But it was Mrs. Nunley who answered, and Doug was left waiting on the doorstep, and more than once looked back at Willie as if to ask just how long he was supposed to wait. A few moments later, a disheveled figure appeared, nervously eyeing the blond headed stranger standing in his doorway.

"Bill's out in the car," Doug announced. "He wants to talk to you."

Duff didn't say anything, just looked back over his shoulder to see if the coast was clear. "And just who the fuck are you?" he shot back.

Doug decided to ignore him. He just turned and walked away while Duff bent down and peered out to the small car parked in the street. It *was* Bill! Sure as shit! Duff looked around to see where his folks were, then followed Doug down the walk. Before he could even say hello, Willie told him to get in.

Nunley acted excited to see him, but was taken back by the way Bill looked. He always remembered him as a pretty cool dresser, at least a lot better dressed than the rest of them, anyway. But he was really a mess now; filthy Levis with big silver medallions sewn down the sides and a crappy brown polo shirt and dark leather jacket, both stained and smelling of dirt and dope and smoke and sweat. And his hair was a lot longer than Duff remembered, frizzing out way past his ears in a really bad fro. He had this half-assed moustache, resting just above where his trademark Marlboro dangled. And then there was the swollen eye, still a raging purple with a blood red center. Wherever it was that he had been, Nunley figured things weren't going real well for Bill Steelman.

"Holy Shit, man!" Nunley laughed, his voice ringing loud in the little car as he reached over to clasp hands, "Where the fuck ya been?"

Willie made sure he didn't answer right away. "You know. . .places, man. Just got in from Arizona last night. Mainly been in Arizona. Could use some help though. How 'bout takin' a ride?"

Duff wasn't sure he wanted to go anywhere with Bill looking like he did. He kind of scared him, but he would never let Bill know it. Duff slammed the car door. "Hell yes!" he said. "Let's go!"

Willie got the car back on the highway for the short drive into town and small talk loosened Duff back up. "Shit, man, I was fuckin' paranoid when you showed up at the house. Didn't know who in the hell you were!" Getting no response, he laughed nervously and nodded towards the stranger in the back seat. "Hell, I thought I might hafta hit him, or dust him or sumthin. Fuck! You know, . . .Shit, I didn't know who the fuck he was!"

Willie cracked only the slightest smile, so again Nunley broke the awkward silence and forced a weak wicked laugh, just to let them know he wasn't serious.

Willie again ignored him, like he had done so many times before. "I need to get in touch with Gary," he said. "I figured you could help me with that. Whaddaya think?"

Gary Jr. was his brother's oldest son, and the fact he worshiped Willie, divided father and son even further. Choosing between a strict uptight father and the wild life his uncle lived was not much of a choice at all, so Gary choose Willie every time. Gary still lived at home, not far from the Nunleys, and although growing up in the same small town and having the same rebellious attitude as Duff made them acquaintances, it hardly made them friends. Willie let Duff know he needed to talk with Gary without his old man finding out. He didn't have to explain; Nunley knew nobody's old man ever liked Bill Steelman.

They drove around Galt, checking the school as students filtered into the parking lot and out onto streets for lunch break. Young Gary wasn't to be found, but as they drove by Estralita High, Duff saw a friend of his named Mike Jackson. Estralita was a continuation school comprised of a few portable classrooms dropped in a graveled lot where the buses used to park. Nunley knew he would feel a lot better if he had a familiar face in the car with him, so he pointed out the window and yelled. Jackson turned around, as did the Datsun to pick him up. Willie remembered Mike only because he hung around a lot with Duff, and that he had given the two of them some free gas one night when he worked the station out in Victor.

"Hey," Willie yelled. "Get in."

Jackson took up the offer, and they continued to cruise up around town for awhile, then got on the road heading east out towards the country. Willie pulled a joint from his jacket, lit it, took a toke, then passed it over to Duff, who did the same before sending it into the back seat. Duff had no idea why they were heading away from town, but he was too scared to ask. He took another hit to calm his nerves.

"Got the law after us," Willie proclaimed.

"No shit?" Jackson piped up, acting impressed.

"Yeah, got into a gang war down in Arizona. Lotta people got killed. . .eight. . . eight people got wasted. I took some shot in my stomach." He pointed to his eye. "Shit, that's how I got this. Pistol whipped."

"Jesus!"

"That's where we got the car. Killed a black dude. It was his. Got rid of the body and took the car." He turned and looked over at Nunley. "Anyway, that's why we headed back here. We got another job to do. Gonna go tonight and pick up five grand."

Both Nunley and Jackson knew that most of the time Bill Steelman was nothing but a damn liar. In fact, Duff and Mike argued a lot about Bill's lying. Duff said he lied about half the time, and Mike said no way, it was all the time. But they agreed that with Steelman you could never figure out when the truth stopped and the crap started flying, because he was really good at it. Yeah, Steelman might have been nothing but Mr. Bullshit, but he could get you going sometimes. And besides, he always had a good story, even if it wasn't true, so they would listen to all of his shit, then argue about how much of it to believe.

But Duff decided this trip with Bill was getting too weird. People getting killed and stolen cars? Five grand? There's some big bullshit right there. They were getting further and further from town, and he wanted out, but Willie had other ideas. "Duff, you drive."

Duff spun around to Mike with this '*what do we do now?*' look on his face. But the car stopped and Nunley had little choice but get behind the wheel. As the car got back to speed, Willie reached into the glove box and pulled out a gun.

Jackson's heart jumped into his throat. Willie toyed with the weapon for a moment, turning it and admiring it, allowing the others to do the same, then pointed it out the window and fired out into an open field. Other than the pistol crack, the car was quiet. Jackson finally broke the silence and stammered, "Thought I should let you know, ah, I have a dentist appointment at two."

They continued out New Hope Road several miles west of town. Willie told Duff to pull over, and the car came to a stop near a small bridge crossing a slow, stagnant creek. Willie climbed out, aimed the revolver into the water and fired until he had emptied the chamber. He hunched back into the passenger seat and signaled Nunley to turn around and head back to town.

"What were you shootin' at?" Duff asked.

"Bottle."

"Hit it?"

Steelman laughed. "Shit yes! What do you think?"

On the way back Willie said, "We're gonna need a ride to the airport tonight. You plan on bein' around?"

"Yeah, sure. Where ya goin'?"

"Mexico. There's a murder warrant out for me and we gotta get outta the country pretty quick. Murder one, man."

Nunley gulped.

"Tell ya what," Willie continued. "You give us a ride to Stockton and you and Mike can have this car. I'll just give it to you guys."

"Yeah?" Duffy faked enthusiasm, but wondered what in the hell he would do with a hot car taken off a dead man. If he really was dead, that is. Jesus! Bill was such a goddamn liar. He wasn't going to give anybody no new car.

"But you guys know it's hot, right? So you'd have to strip it. Couldn't leave anything hangin' around. Probably get a few hundred outta it, though."

"Shit, yeah!" Duff agreed, and Willie considered the arrangement a done deal.

Tuesday afternoon dragged along painfully slow. The gray skies parted on occasion to let the sun pass through, and it was during those brief periods when the inside of the small car became hot and stuffy. Back in Galt, Willie splurged for a six-pack of Olympia Beer, and the Datsun did another quick search, in vain, for Gary.

Mike Jackson hoped that he wouldn't have to mention anything again about that appointment, and the sudden silence made him even more nervous. He turned to the blond haired guy sitting next to him in the back seat. They were separated by a suitcase that crowded them even more. "Heard you were from outta town. Where 'bouts?"

"New York. The Bronx."'

"Man! I hear people from New York are crazy!"

Doug took it as a compliment and agreed it takes a different kind of person to live there. Those were the only words spoken between the two the entire afternoon. Mike Jackson was dropped off in the school parking lot; relieved the whole ordeal was over. He knew Steelman wasn't going to call them later for that ride to the airport, or for that matter, give him and Duffy the car. He shut the door behind him, flashed them the peace sign, turned and hurried away. If he never heard about Bill Steelman, or about his friend from New York again, then that would be just fine by him.

Now Bill was asking for another favor, and Duff really hated to do it. He begged Bill to figure something else out, but no luck. He knew Ted would be pissed about it, but Willie would not let up. "Jesus, Duff, you know him better than I do, just take me over there then you can split."

Willie needed to crash. The ride, the glare, the smoke and the beer, he was zonked. What he needed was a place to crash for a couple of hours. Problem was, there was nowhere to go, no one up on the north side who would welcome Steelman into their home. The only one Willie could even think of was a guy named Ted Ryan, and he needed Duff's help on this one. "Come on, Duff, you know him better than I do. Just take me over there and then you can split."

Willie would not let up, so Nunley relented.

About a mile up the road from Galt, near the Twin Bridges Road off ramp, was a semi-circle cluster of cottages facing out onto the frontage road of Highway 99. Three people shared one of the units, but only Ted was there when the Datsun pulled up out front. Ryan had known Steelman for a few years but was never comfortable around him. He walked out to see who it was in the little car, and while he recognized Nunley, it took a little longer to figure out the skinny guy was with the afro was Bill Steelman. Both Willie and Duff were out of the car, and while Ryan was not pleased to see them, he didn't let it show.

"Bill! How's it going? It's been a long time. Where ya been hiding?"

"Overseas man. . .just got back." Duff looked confused.

The two shook hands, and Ryan shot Duff a look. Nunley knew he would get shit later for bringing Steelman over. Ted couldn't help but mention the black eye.

"Oh, that," Willie shrugged. "I got it in a fight in Lodi. That's why I'm here. Wonderin' if we could hang out for a couple hours. Don't want the Lodi pigs hassling me."

Ted said it would be no problem, although he really wanted nothing to do with him. He was just about to go to work, he said, but finally consoled himself with the fact that as long as Duff was here then Bill couldn't swipe too much out of the house.

Doug had gotten tired of sitting in the car and had now joined them. "Hey, Ted, this here's my partner." Willie offered. "Name's Doug. From New York."

Gretzler remained silent, but nodded his head hello and moved inside.

"Really, man," Willie continued, turning his attention back to Ted, "we're just gonna lay low for a few hours cuz we gotta go later and pick up some money from a friend about nine thirty, then we're leavin' the state. We won't be around long."

Ryan nodded and left for work. Willie slept for three hours while Doug sat stone faced in the darkened room staring down the TV. Duff slipped into the kitchen and called his girlfriend, talking until he heard Willie rustle awake in the other room. Willie was upset to see it was now after five, and he told Doug they had to get going because the market closed in less than two hours.

Wally Parkin managed to talk his way out of the store by a quarter to six. Basketball game, he explained, and as he left he reminded Joanne about league later that night, promising her he would be home by eight.

Joanne seemed out of sorts and it bothered Carol to see her that way. After Wally left, Joanne asked Carol three times if the back door was locked and each time she told her that it was. Then Joanne asked her to pull the car around to the front so it would be close by when they closed the store later on. Joanne acted odd, afraid of something or someone. Several times Joanne simply stood by the window and peered out into the darkness, as if just waiting for something bad to happen.

Finally, after Carol had asked her for the umpteenth time what was bothering her, Joanne broke down and said that she had been getting obscene phone calls lately, the last one just a few minutes earlier. She had no idea who the caller was (although Carol had a hunch, she kept quiet about it). For the next hour, both women jumped when the phone rang or a customer entered and the door buzzer sounded, counting down the minutes until they could lock up and go home.

Along with basketball and bowling, and every other thing he did, Wally spent a lot of time helping out young people around town and had developed a real soft spot for those who found themselves in tough times. That's how Carol came to work for him at the United Market, and how just a few weeks back, came to live in his home. Her troubles started several years earlier when she was barely fourteen. Wally watched her come into the market every once in awhile, and usually with the wrong crowd. People started to gossip. Carol was just another one of those bad girls, they said, but Wally thought otherwise and decided she was just making the wrong choices and hoped she would come to her senses soon. Not too far back, her life appeared to take a positive turn when she got on at the Vista Ray Convalescent Hospital. Wally was pleased. He had offered her a job at the United Market, but this sounded even better, and he told her to keep in touch.

There was another new person at the hospital who started just after she did, and they kidded each other about being the rookies. His name was Bill Steelman.

Actually Carol knew Bill long before Vista Ray, having been casual friends with Denise. She was even a little hesitant to work with him at first because she was always so uncomfortable when she was around him. But he seemed kind of different now, even going out of his way to help her when she needed a hand or got behind in her work. It wasn't long before they started acting like the best of friends, getting along so well the other employees figured something must be going on between them after hours too.

What feelings Carol might have had for Bill, she never confided to anyone. She knew about his drug use; heroin, pills and weed, probably coke as well, even while he worked at Vista Ray, but she swore she never saw him do any of that while on duty. Carol believed Bill had really only one true fault. He lied. A lot.

Both had talked about going to Delta College, even planned on sharing a ride down to Stockton to attend, but when Carol left Vista Ray in the fall of 1972, the plans disappeared. After she left, they would run into each other around town every so often, but she didn't act the same towards him. Eventually he left the hospital as well, and she heard he was drifting around Lodi, lost and loaded, and that Denise had finally left him for good. Someone told her Bill had skipped town that past summer and Carol felt like maybe she had let him down.

Wally again offered her a job at the market, and when her parents kicked her out of the house over an older man she was dating, he gave her a place to live as well. Although she had moved in just two weeks earlier, they had already welcomed her as a regular member of the family, a closeness she hadn't felt in a long time. At eighteen, Carol felt like her life was starting to turn around, and she had Wally and Joanne Parkin to thank.

The final hour at work that night was a slow one and the two women managed to get all the clean-up chores done early. Carol had a date later and was rushing to finish up so she could be ready in time. Joanne double-checked the clock, then closed out both check stands, taking the receipts and large bills to the back room where Carol watched her put the money in the floor safe. She made sure to leave the registers open and a little cash showing just in case someone broke in they wouldn't bust up the store looking for money. Joanne flipped off the lights, hung the CLOSED sign on the door, and locked it behind her. Carol looked at her watch and laughed. "Two minutes to seven. We always get out early when Wally's not around!"

Even Joanne had to laugh. They climbed into Carol's Pinto, pulled out of the parking lot, and headed towards the Parkin's house on Orchard Road.

Debbie Earl, on the other hand, was running late. She had tons of homework, but had promised the Parkins she would baby sit tonight. Rushing out the door, loaded with schoolbooks and binders, her purse hanging desperately over one shoulder, she yelled goodbye to her mother and asked her father if he wouldn't mind driving her and Ricky down to the Parkins. Her brother often came to hang out with her when she babysat, just to keep her company.

Her father obliged, and Debbie walked in to the Parkin's home, put her books on the desk in the kitchen, then went into the family room where Carol and Jim were on the sofa, each nursing a drink. Lisa and Bobbie spread out on the green shag carpeting, eyes glued to the television. Debbie greeted everyone, looking for a chair to plop down in. Joanne pulled two TV dinners out of the oven and called the kids, who jumped up and disappeared. Debbie and Carol made small talk as they had done on other occasions, but while they were the same age, the lives they had each led up to this moment had left them little in common. Carol walked into the kitchen, gave Joanne a hug and told her she would be home late. Joanne made her now standard offer to leave the lights on.

Joanne went in the back bedroom to get ready, and after the kids had finished eating, Debbie made sure they were occupied, then looked for a spot to spread her books out. Wally returned, grabbed a quick shower, and by eight o'clock, he and Joanne were headed into town to the Tokay Bowl.

Debbie locked the doors behind them and returned to the books. She had a good solid hour to study before she would have to get the kids ready for bed. Mark promised to come by later to stay with her and give her a ride home, a routine that had become commonplace. Debbie could hear the television laughter cackle from the other room, then the tiny giggles that would soon follow.

The hour passed quickly and Debbie was surprised to hear the crunch of gravel in the driveway and saw headlights beam through the large picture window. Funny, she thought, Mark usually called first to tell her he was on his way. She jumped up to see who was it was, but in the darkness could not recognize the small car, or the man who was now getting out of it. Her stomach tightened. She could tell it wasn't Mark, but she suddenly wished he were here with her right now.

Tuesday was fading fast and there was still only one gun. Night was upon them by the time they left Ted Ryan's house, and Willie told Duff he needed to get to a phone.

For all his boasts to Doug about a guy he knew with 'an extensive gun collection', there was no such person. Willie's only hope in getting a back-up weapon relied on finding his nephew. He remembered his brother had an old camp trailer parked out in his driveway, and hidden in a drawer inside was a small caliber derringer. It was rarely used and would not be missed anytime soon. He also knew he could talk little Gary into getting it for him.

The phone booth out front of Lind's Airport Cafe north of Lodi was illuminated only by a faded Standard Oil sign above it, and its pale white light washed over the booth, the Datsun, and the broken asphalt parking lot. Willie asked Duff for one last favor. Call Gary.

By now Nunley was more than a little eager to cut this evening short. He just wanted to go home. He had been with these guys all day, and there had been gunfire, and talk of gang wars, killings, and questions about whether or not bodies had been found. He was so tired and confused, and these two guys were so fucking crazy. But Duff also knew he was too chicken to run and it was too uncool to beg, so he told Bill he would agree to this one last thing, then he was done. Willie nodded, then stood over him while Duffy flipped through the phone book and found the number. Willie dropped a dime and Duff dialed.

"Ah. . .hello. . .is Gary there?" Duff paused, then narrowed his request. "Ah. . .little Gary."

Steelman grabbed the phone, put it up to his ear, and waited. "Hey, Gary! This is your uncle Bill!. . .Yeah, right, I know, it's been awhile. . .No, doin' okay. Listen I need your help man. . ." His voice trailed off. He made sure he got to the story about a race war down south and how these dudes were gonna kill him if he didn't get some help. He stopped talking and listened to the voice on the other end, then boasted, "Shit yeah, I got one of 'em! Listen, we'll stop by your place in a few minutes. Gonna be driving a little white Datsun so look for us. And don't let your old man know. Okay brother, see ya in a little bit."

Duffy drove and Willie nagged him about keeping off the highway as they snaked their way back to Collier Road. Duff pulled up in front of the Steelman house, and a few seconds later a shadow darted out from the pitch-black yard and Willie opened the door. "You think you could find me a gun?" he asked.

Gary thought it over, then beamed. "You know he keeps that little derringer right there in the camper! Do you think that would be good enough? I don't think he would even miss it."

"Yeah!" Willie exclaimed, like the idea had never occurred to him. "That'd be perfect. Can't let the old man find out though, don't need the hassles. You know that dude hates me."

Gary did indeed. More than once his father jumped his ass, screaming about him turning out just like his no-good uncle. Gary ignored him. What did he know anyway? For the last couple of years Bill Steelman was off limits and even the mention of his name would create a huge yelling match between father and son.

"You take care of it," Willie instructed, "and we'll be back in a half an hour."

With some time to kill, Steelman told Duff to find him another phone, there was one more person he needed to talk to.

Lisa answered. Willie was relieved. Lisa's stomach jumped at the sound of his voice. She had not seen him or talked to him since May and had no idea where he had disappeared. She knew only that her life had been slowly getting better with him out of it.

"You know I can't talk to you, Bill."

"Listen, Lisa. Wait. I'm leaving the state tomorrow. For good. Forever. I gotta see you tonight."

Bill Steelman was not welcome at her home. Her parents had made that very clear, something she reminded him of again at this very moment. But like times before, he wouldn't listen. "Lisa. . .I gotta know. . .I've been wonderin'. . .I gotta know. . .Lisa, I heard you were gonna have a kid. That you're pregnant. Listen, I gotta know. . ."

She didn't answer. But he knew. "Lisa. Tell me. It's mine, isn't it?"

"I've got to go Bill. I can't talk to you." She shivered, remembering the ice-cold glare that came down on her whenever he got angry. But to her surprise, tonight he sounded different. Like he was hurt and sad, not mad at her like she had expected. He was begging her to talk to him, not demanding like he had done every other time before. But she knew him well enough to know how quickly his mood could turn, and he still frightened her because of that. "Bill! I've got to go!" she repeated.

"I'm going to see you tomorrow." He threatened. "I'll see you in Galt." He hung up and tried calling Denise at her parent's house, but there was no answer.

Twice rejected, Willie walked slowly back to the car and stared out the window. "You seen Denise lately, Duff?" he asked.

"No Bill, sure haven't." Now that was a lie. He had heard all about what happened with Bill and Denise and the high school girl he knocked up. But he could see Bill was upset, and this didn't seem the time to make matters worse. But hell yes! He had seen Denise around town a bunch of times these past couple of months – everybody had – and always with that Ivan dude. But he knew better than to tell Bill the truth. Not right now anyway.

"No Bill," he repeated. "I sure haven't."

The Datsun returned to Collier Road. Little Gary walked out of the house on cue and climbed into the back seat. The car pulled away as he slid the gun from his coat pocket.

"Here it is." He handed it to Willie, who held it up and inspected the two shot derringer.

"Yeah, this might do," He passed it to Doug, who also gave it a quick once over. It was an older piece and a far cry from the sawed off .22, or shotgun, they once packed.

Now that Willie had the second weapon, Duff was free to go. He told them to just drop him off Ronnie Bretbrunner's house, which was close by. Nunley was anxious to get out of the car, but before he could, Willie reminded him once more about their plans. "We're gonna need your help real early tomorrow, Duffy, so you be around and we'll get with you then."

"Right, Bill. Tomorrow," Duff nodded as he slammed the car door behind him. He turned and walked up the drive. Tomorrow my ass, he muttered to himself as the Datsun disappeared. I ain't gonna be anywhere to be found come tomorrow morning.

Willie made up a score of stories about where they had been and what they had done, and Gary was stoked. He asked about this race war and how he had managed to get out in one piece. Wasn't easy, Willie answered, because there was just a shit load of them. But we're going back, he said, and that's why I needed your help.

Even Doug got into the act, telling about the black guy he killed for raping his sister. Willie told Doug that he was right on for doing it too, then lit a joint and passed it to Gary; the reward for a job well done.

"Gonna be in school tomorrow?" Willie asked as they pulled up in front of his house. Gary replied, that unfortunately, he would.

"Then maybe I'll see ya before we split town. But do me a favor, okay? When you're at school, find Lisa and tell her that I'll see her before I leave town. Tell her I gotta talk to her."

It was now after seven, and if he worked it right, maybe there would still be someone at the market closing up. Maybe even Wally. If so, this could go down even easier than he had planned.

"Now this ain't gonna be your standard rip," Willie explained again to Doug as he guided the Datsun over the dimly lit back roads towards Victor. "This Parkin dude is dirty and I have been guaranteed all the cash is ours. Probably won't find many drugs 'cuz he's real good about not handling it himself. But I got the word. We take whatever we want."

That was the story he had fed Doug since they left Arizona. Wally Parkin was dealing dope, sure as shit. So much dope that this no good punk – who worked in a little decaf-ass country store, no less – was now living in some big spendy custom place. "No way!" Willie howled. "No fucking way this guy makes that kinda money baggin' groceries!"

And besides, Willie thought, just who in the hell did he think he was? Everybody in town acting like he was some kind of god or something. A big fucking fish in the goddamn little mud hole of Victor, that's who. Willie got himself worked up all over again just talking about it.

Doug nodded. Made sense to him. Besides, this was Bill's turf and his call. That was the pact. Doug certainly didn't need any explanations or excuses, but even up to this point Doug had failed to make the connection. Bill kept saying they had driven by the market when they were in town a few weeks back, but Doug couldn't place it. He still didn't have a clue as to where he was or what this store even looked like. The way Bill talked it was a big store - damn near a supermarket, loaded with cash - but even after they pulled right up in front of the place, Doug still couldn't quite piece it together. This big market he had tried so hard to picture was no more than just a little country store with a very empty parking lot. What's worse, it was closed.

"Well, fuck!" Willie groaned.

"Yeah, so now what?" Doug surprised himself with his critical tone.

Willie continued up the highway for a few hundred yards then did a u-turn. His original plan was for it to all go down at the market, but that idea was shot. Now he looked bad. He had to think fast. Doug's remark had pissed him off, but he brushed it aside like he hadn't noticed.

"No big deal," he answered. "I know where he lives."

Problem was, Willie realized, it was too early to go over there. Have to wait until later, he said, just to make sure they catch Parkin at home. He allowed another car to pass, then turned around and drove back by the market to catch another look.

Doug said, "We'll then, if you really know these people like you say, and they know you, do you really think it's such a good idea to keep driving by?"

Willie took his anger out on the brakes and spun the Datsun back towards Lodi.

It was now seven-thirty. He still had time to try and reach Denise. He hadn't talked to her since the day left town, but he had heard about her new boyfriend. He knew the guy's name. His phone number was etched in his brain so he found a pay phone and dialed it,

"Yeah, this is Bill Steelman. Wondering if Denise...my wife...is over there?"

The woman on the other end answered that she was not, but offered to let her know about the call, if and when she saw her.

"Yeah, well you make sure you tell her I'm looking for her." Willie slammed the phone down.

At the Tunnell home, Denise and Ivan congratulated his mother on her acting skills, and yet Denise knew Willie wouldn't give up that easy. She knew one day Willie would come back looking for her, and while that frightened her terribly at one time, now she felt protected by Ivan. They grabbed a bottle of wine and walked across the road to a vineyard, then hid out and waited. Sure enough, a few minutes later, a small car with out of state plates crawled by. After making several passes in front of the house, it eventually drove away. Denise had seen him. Just a glimpse, an outline, but that was enough. It was him, she was sure of it. And he would be back for her, she was sure of that as well.

It was, as Sharon Lang would lament later, her final act as his big sister. Dinner at McDonald's. Her treat. They ate outside, but even the crisp November air did little to revive him. Sharon could see he just needed to go home to bed.

"Mark, just call Debbie and tell her you're too tired to pick her up," she suggested. "I'm sure she'll understand."

Mark knew she was right. He had been dragging all day at work and now it was all he could do to keep his head up. But Tuesday nights were special, and he hated to spoil it. Every Tuesday night, Debbie babysat the Parkins kids and Mark would always stop by. They would watch some TV until the Parkins got home, then drive into town for a pizza. It didn't seem to matter that Deb had her own car and was babysitting just down the road from her home, Mark always stopped by to get her.

Recently, Mark Lang and Debbie Earl had announced something that surprised almost no one; he had asked her to marry him. An engagement party had been arranged at the Earl home just a few weeks earlier, and while it was small and informal, and on somewhat short notice, it seemed to fit the young couple.

Debbie was, well, Debbie, and Mark was her equal in every way. A good kid. A good student. A good son. A good friend. His only sign of rebellion was last summer when he let his hair grow down over his ears. But even that was short-lived. When he was lucky enough to get hired on at Pacific Gas & Electric, he cut it back. He didn't want to blow a good job. Good enough job he could quit college and go to work full time. Mark was already looking ahead, knowing there was no way he could dare ask Debbie to marry him unless he had a stable job. But this job was the very reason he was often so tired. His day started at 4 am, and after staying up late last night helping out in the vineyard, well, Mark was dragging.

"Debbie will understand," Sharon repeated. Besides, she felt a bit guilty, having insisted he drive all the way up to Sacramento after work to help her with her own wedding plans. Sharon was getting married in less than a week as well, and Mark had waited until the last minute to be fitted for his tux. She told him it had to be done today. No excuses. He obliged and drove to see her.

Now she watched him finish his hamburger. She smiled. Sharon always just thought of him as her little brother, yet here they both were, all grown up and planning weddings together. It was only a month earlier when Mark told her he had asked Debbie to marry him. Again he drove up to Sacramento afterwards and pulled the wedding ring from his coat pocket, as if needing Sharon's approval.

"She said yes!" he announced that night, sounding half-surprised and half-relieved.

Sharon laughed. "Well what did you think she would say? You're a good-looking guy, have a good job, and you just bought her a huge engagement ring!"

"I don't believe it!" he trembled a second time. "She said yes!"

She remembered how happy Mark was that day, but tonight Sharon could only think of how tired and pitiful he looked. It was the mother hen in her. Always protecting. It was going on eight, and it was a long drive back to Lodi. She felt responsible for keeping him up. "Come on," she ordered, standing up and gathering the empty wrappers and cups, "we're going to go back to the apartment and you're going to call Deb. Then you're going straight home and go to bed."

Mark didn't argue and followed her over to her apartment. He dialed the Parkin's number and the conversation was brief. By the time Sharon walked back into the room, Mark was off the phone and standing there with a puzzled look on his face. "That was weird," he said, staring down at the phone.

"What's wrong?" Sharon asked.

"I dunno. That's not like her. I told her how tired I was and how I really just wanted to go home, and she said that she really needed me to be with her tonight."

"And. . .?"

"I'm not sure. It just didn't sound like her. She sounded kind of worried." He stopped and looked at Sharon. "You know, she's right down the street at the Parkin's and she still wants me to drive all the way out there to get her."

He shook his head, then looked around the room and grabbed his things. "Guess I'll go pick her up." He gave his sister a hug and promised to see her over the weekend. He got behind the wheel of his Impala, found his way back to 99, and headed south back to Lodi, and eventually out to the house on Orchard Road.

Only a mere slip of a moon could find its way through the clouds tonight; a soft blur of pale gray light, its crescent hanging slightly out of focus in a deep charcoal sky. The air was cool and still moist from the showers that had fallen off and on throughout the day. Earlier that afternoon, as if to announce the advancing storm, winds from the north began to stir, but failed in their efforts to rustle the wet leaves still pasted to the pavement.

But even the wind was silent now, as if holding its breath, bracing for what was yet to come. An uncomfortable stillness blanketed this blackness, and it was this very silence, this God awful sound of things not heard, that had now fully embraced the house on Orchard Road.

It was the hour of not quite rain.

Debbie held her breath as well, and listened.

The Parkin home was barely two miles from the United Market, sitting well off the road of its address, although still quite visible from the street. The graveled drive to the house was not lit, nor did the mailbox announce who lived there. It was a new house, which was unlike most of the others in the area. The porch lamp was the only light in the darkness, yet sufficient enough to guide the Datsun up the drive and to the front door.

Surprisingly, for all the talk up until now, there was no further discussion of the matter, nor were there any last minute instructions from Willie. He was close enough now to look directly through the large picture window, but could see no movement inside. The interior of the house was brightly lit and he paused for a moment in hopes of catching a glimpse of whoever was inside. Suddenly a young girl walked into view. She stood motionless, like a deer caught in headlights, looking out at him. Then, just as quickly, she was gone. Willie shot a quick look at Doug, then got out of the car.

The Parkin home rambled awkwardly amidst the gravel and the November muck, looking a bit out of place amongst its older and more traditional neighbors. It was a modern structure of redwood and glass, three separate buildings, actually, connected at right angles with a common sea of shake shingles on the gradual pitched roof. To the rear, the attached garage stood, a good distance from the front door, so a rutted path connected the two. A child's bicycle lay nearby on the soggy sparse lawn where several twigs of newly planted trees stuck out of the mud. A graveled drive circled to the entrance of the home where the massive double front door set inside a small entry area, bordered on one side by two floor-to-ceiling picture windows revealing a large open living room. Overhead, a large globe fixture poured yellow light onto the walkway, and onto the stranger who now made his presence known.

Debbie never hesitated, answering the door almost before she heard the bell ring, and if she was scared, she didn't act it. It was the visitor who spoke first.

"Looking for Wally. Is he home?"

The man at the door startled Debbie. He was a frightening stick of a human; thin and drawn, in soiled Levis and a t-shirt. A well-worn black leather jacket rode high up on his waist, appearing much too small for his long frame. His hair was a wild mess, his mustache hung over the edges of his mouth and straggly hairs protruded from his chin. His face had been cut or scraped, and his eye was a sickly mix of purple, red and black. There was no white to it, only blood red.

Debbie looked up at him, his eye, and then stole a quick glance around him, spotting an unfamiliar car and the outline of someone sitting inside it.

"No," she replied, trying to find her voice. "He and Joanne are out bowling."

Debbie offered no more information, but still stood with the door wide open.

Willie could hear the sound of child's laughter from behind her.

"Okay then," he said. "Thanks." He turned and walked back to the Datsun and Debbie closed the door behind him. *Shit! Bowling?* Once again embarrassed by his foul up, he climbed back in the car, knowing full well what was waiting for him. "He's not here," he announced.

"What!?"

"He's out. He's not here. He won't be back 'til later." Willie started the car up and headed back down the driveway.

Push comes to shove, none of this really mattered to Doug. Hell, if it was his call he could just as well hit the road and looked for something easier. But down deep it seemed to him this Wally guy was all they had. It was sure as shit all he had heard about since they left Arizona. Here they had traveled a thousand miles, discussed this whole thing a million different times, even figured out how they were going to spend their take a hundred different ways, and now this Parkin dude isn't even home? That's it? They're done? All this way for nothing? Well, that just wasn't good enough, and Doug lashed out. "Now what the fuck you gonna do now?

The Datsun had reached the end of the drive. Willie fidgeted with the steering wheel. He didn't like being on this end of their conversations. "There's kids in there," he said. "There weren't supposed to be no kids there."

"Yeah? So now what?" Doug demanded. "This was all we had."

Willie hit the brakes and glared over at Doug. "I don't see you comin' up with any big fuckin' ideas! Why don't you think of something for once!"

Doug remained silent for what seemed like the longest time.

"Shit, let's just do it!" Willie ordered.

He turned the car around and headed back up the drive towards the house, and as they approached for the second time they could see the young woman through the large window. She had the phone cradled between her ear and shoulder. Afraid she was calling the cops, Willie jumped out and hurried to the front door, but the girl had disappeared from sight.

But again he knocked on the door and again she was quick to answer.

"Hey listen, we're just some friends of Wally and we owe him a little money. We're just headin' outta town and would like to settle up with him before we go. I'd feel better about it, so would you mind if we just used the phone and leave a message? Just take a minute."

The girl paused for a moment as if to think about the request. Willie could hear the TV in the background and the squeal of little voices. She looked back over her shoulder at the telephone on the table just a few feet away, then again at the man standing in front of her.

"All right," she replied, stepping aside to let him in. He waved at Doug to join him, then entered the house.

Once inside, Willie took a quick look around. The entry opened to the large main living area. To his left was the front room and the picture windows he had just looked in through. On the other side a stone fireplace consumed an entire wall and family photos sat upon its mantle, including several children. The same kids, Willie assumed, that were making all the racket in the next room. There was a dining area, and beyond that some kind of rec room with a pool table in the middle of it. Still further back, a long hallway. The bedrooms, he decided. He could see no other exits. Two doors stood to his right, but it was clear they didn't open to the outside.

Debbie pointed to the phone. Willie picked it up and pretended to dial. Turning his back and feigning privacy, he held a make believe conversation while he listened to the sounds of the house. The television and a child's sporadic giggling was all he heard.

A teenage boy appeared from the doorway of the adjacent room. He surprised Willie. He wasn't a child. Certainly not young enough to be the cause of the laughter. The boy stared at the stranger.

"Deb?" the boy asked, as he moved towards her.

"It's okay Rick. They just need to use the phone."

Ricky Earl was a couple of years younger than Debbie, but even barefoot, as he was tonight, he was much taller than his sister. He had, for many years in fact, decided it was his job to look out for her, and it was clear to him that she was very nervous about the two strangers inside the house. It upset him to see her this way.

Willie could not be sure there weren't even more people somewhere in the house, but he could wait no longer. He cradled the phone, then reached inside his jacket and removed his gun. Wheeling around, he grabbed Debbie by the arm and jammed the pistol against the side of her head.

She gasped and let out a half-scream. Ricky lunged towards them, but Doug was following closely Willie's moves and had the derringer aimed directly at the boy. Ricky froze.

"Now listen!" Willie threatened. "We're only here for Wally, so both of you stay cool and nobody is gonna get hurt. That understood?"

Debbie nodded as the blunt force of the gun pushed her head to one side. Tears were already rolling down her cheeks.

"Anybody else in here?" Willie demanded.

Debbie swallowed. "Just the two children."

Bobby and Lisa had pulled themselves away from the television and their faces now peaked from around the corner to see what the commotion was all about. They huddled side by side, staring wide-eyed at the two men with the guns.

Willie threw his head in their direction. "Is that it?"

Again she nodded.

"Okay then. We're just gonna sit down and wait."

He waved everyone over to the sofa. Debbie reached down and grabbed the children's hands and sat them down next to her. They cuddled close, burying their heads into her sweater.

Willie walked over to the picture window. "So how long Wally gonna be gone?"

Debbie whimpered. "Couple of hours, I guess. I don't know."

Willie turned his head to hide his frustration and anger. *Christ Almighty!* he muttered to himself. *This is all so fucking wrong!*

Richard Earl had just got up from the dinner table when the phone rang. The conversation was brief. Wanda had started clearing away the dishes when he raced past her, disappearing out the back door and into the garage. "If I'm not back in fifteen minutes," he yelled, "call the sheriff!"

Debbie was so frightened by the man who had come to the door, as soon as he had left she called her father to tell him what had happened. She was on the phone with him when Willie returned for the second time. Now just minutes later, Richard's big Pontiac was barreling up the drive, its bright headlights warning of his arrival.

"Who the hell is that," Willie demanded, ducking out of view behind the front door.

"My father."

Richard hustled up to the porch, glancing through the window, hoping to see Rick and Deb safe and sound inside. He noticed the Datsun, but didn't recognize it. He knocked on the door, breathing relief when Debbie opened it. He stepped inside and noticed she had been crying. Her face was red, her eyes wet and swollen. He saw Rick and the two kids sitting on the couch as he reached out to comfort his daughter. And then he saw a blond stranger.

Before he could utter a word, Debbie closed the door and Richard felt someone come up behind him, then the steel pressed against the back of his neck. He was pushed out into the room. Debbie again burst into tears. "OH DADDY!" she sobbed.

"Now you listen man!" the shadow behind him warned. "You listen real close. We ain't here to hurt no one. We came to settle with Wally, so you stay cool... tell these kids here to stay cool...and nothing's gonna happen."

The gunman spun Richard around and looked down on him. "I'll tell ya right now...and if you don't listen...if you try and be a big shot or somethin'...I promise I will kill each and every one of you...and I'll start with her!"

By this time Doug could only wonder what in the hell was going down here. There was a house full of people, including a bunch of kids, and the one guy they wanted wasn't even here. This was getting out of control. The knot in his stomach tightened.

But the father was defiant. "I'll tell you right now this isn't going to work," he shot back. "I just told my wife that if I'm not back in fifteen minutes to call the cops. They're gonna be here any minute."

But Willie wasn't buying. "Well we can fix that," he replied. "We'll just go get her and bring her back here too." He gathered everyone together, then switched guns with Doug, keeping the derringer on the father while giving Doug his last minute instructions. "You cover 'em. If I'm not back in twenty minute, dust 'em. Then get the hell out." The show was strictly for the old man's benefit, just to make sure he wouldn't try anything stupid while they were gone.

Richard drove. Willie kept the gun on him as they entered the Earl home. Startled, Wanda dropped a coffee cup off the counter. Willie reached down and picked it up, cursing himself the instant he did so, knowing that he would have to come back later and clean up. He hurried the couple out to the car and was back at the Parkin's within a few minutes.

When Mark Lang got back to Lodi, and pulled his Impala off of 99 and onto

Cherokee Lane, he found himself behind his two friends, Steve McFadden and Wayne Nitschke. He flashed his lights and pulled them over. From about 8:45 to 9:15 the three of them just talked, until finally Steve asked Mark if he wanted to cruise around with them that night.

But Mark declined. "Can't guys. Deb is babysitting and I promised I would pick her up. In fact she supposed to be done at nine, so I'm late." He would see them both tomorrow, he promised. He got back in his car and pulled out onto Cherokee, turning east on Highway 12 towards Victor.

When Willie returned with the mother and father, his problem was how he was going to keep all these people in line until Parkin showed up. He soon discovered the babysitter was the answer. Anytime he threatened to hurt her, the parents buckled and he got their attention.

But it wasn't long before his task became even more difficult. There were more headlights coming up the drive. It was too soon for Wally, and he wasn't sure he was ready for him anyway.

He looked again to the babysitter for the answer

"It's Mark," she said. "He's my boyfriend. He's coming over to pick me up." Willie grabbed her and pulled her away from the window, shoving the gun into her face as he reminded her once more what to do. Doug kept the others covered and out of sight while Willie hid behind the door, motioning for Debbie to open it. Repeating the procedure, Willie stepped up from behind Mark as he entered and aimed the gun at his head. As Mark reached for Debbie, all the others suddenly came into view, and he could see that he and her were by no means alone. He felt the presence of someone behind him.

Willie pushed the newcomer towards the others, then again reached for Debbie. The gun went back to her head as he barked orders. "Let me tell you all again! We are here for one thing and one thing only. Wally. We have no hassles with any of you people. But if anyone tries to interfere or tries to escape or be some kinda hero, well, we won't think twice. We will kill every single one of you, and I will personally start with her. Now, just in case any of you still want to be the hero, let me warn you that the house is surrounded by my people. They have instructions from me to waste any of you who takes even a single step outside."

And with that he opened the front door and yelled, "Clear!" He then proceeded to converse with people he said had been strategically placed around the house as their back up. Finished with his show, he turned and walked back inside. "All right then," he smiled, "let's just relax and wait."

For the next hour and a half, the seven hostages and the two men who guarded them did just that. They watched TV, played pool, talked, and watched the clock. Mark was allowed to comfort Debbie, and the two cuddled on the sofa, she continuing to weep off and on.

But for however tranquil the scene had become, occasionally Willie took the time to remind them of what would happen if at anytime anyone tried to cross him. But even the father, who Willie felt could try and overtake him at any moment, seemed content to watch over his family and make sure they stayed relaxed and reasonably content. Everything would be fine, he reminded them again, if they all would just sit back and wait for Wally.

Earlier that evening, on their way to Tokay Bowl, Wally made a quick stop at the market to rattle the doors to make sure they were locked, and although they were running late, they still made it to the lanes with enough time to grab their bags from the locker and even roll a few warm-ups before league began.

The United Market Team did well that night and Wally was in his usual good spirits. It had become a weekly ritual to join their teammates, Cindy and John, in the restaurant afterwards for a cup of coffee. At 10:45, with league play finished, Wally told his friends to go on ahead, they were just going to put their bags back in the locker and they would be right in to join them. Wally and Joanne strolled by the front counter and nodded goodnight to the clerk.

Cindy and John waited in the coffee shop. They had another cup and waited some more, but neither Wally or Joanne had returned to join them. It was not uncommon for them to call home and check on the kids, so neither gave their absence too much thought. But just to be sure, they checked the phone booth on the way out, but even it was empty. They had waited almost thirty minutes. Wally must have gotten sidetracked talking with friends, John decided, so he would just have to find out tomorrow what happened. He and Cindy drove home and gave the episode no further thought.

Wally and Joanne made it home as well. This time Willie didn't even bother to hide. But before he even had a chance to yell, "freeze", Wally was screaming at him, demanding to know what in the hell was going on. He knew this punk. Now he wanted to know what in the hell he was doing in his house?

But his cockiness was short-lived. As soon as Joanne followed him through the door and heard the screaming and saw the strangers with their weapons, Wally had no choice but to listen.

This was no joke, Willie said again, and if you're smart, he told Wally, you'll shut up and listen. Joanne ignored the threats and raced over to comfort her children.

It was simply a matter of money. Even to Doug, it had all boiled down to simply taking what cash they could find, and getting the hell out. At Willie's direction, Doug retrieved the wallets from Mark, Richard and Ricky. Any other money they had on them, included even down to their last nickels and dimes, was pulled from their pockets. Debbie and Wanda's purses were rifled for anything of value, their wallets taken as well, and what was left was tossed on the living room floor. At sometime earlier in the evening, and fearing the worst, Debbie had removed the engagement ring Mark had given her just weeks before and hid it in her purse. She replaced it with a large shiny, but worthless, birthstone ring. Willie yanked it from her finger and threw it in the bag.

The entire take was less than $30. In Richard's wallet was a single one-dollar bill, of which Willie pocketed as well. But Willie knew that the money that really mattered was at the United Market, but he didn't dare leave until he knew it was safe to leave. "Tie 'em up," he said.

Doug retrieved a coil of nylon cord from the Datsun and herded everyone into a large bathroom that was separated from the master bedroom by a large walk in closet area. While Willie watched over Wally in the front room, Doug pulled towels off the rack and slit them into long strips. One by one, he pulled their hands behind them, padded their wrists, then cinched the rope up snug. Doug asked each if it was too tight, concerned he might hurt them, especially the slender wrists of the women.

Earlier, at Joanne's pleading, she was allowed to put her children to bed, so now Bobby and Lisa slept side by side in the big bed in their parent's room just a few short steps away. A short hallway connected the master bedroom and its bath. On one side were built-in drawers and cabinets, and on the other was a large open closet area. All the men had been tied first, then Wanda, Debbie, and Joanne. Doug was finishing up when Willie said he was taking Wally down to the market. Doug moved everyone into the closet and cleared a space on the floor. They sat in a semi-circle, backs to the wall, while Doug sat just out of view in the bathroom, and waited for Willie to return.

Upon arriving at the market, Willie knew exactly where to find the safe. Grabbing a paper sack, he handed it to Wally, and with the gun at his head, forced him down on all fours. Even then, Wally was cocky and defiant. Still, he pulled out the contents of the safe and tossed it at Willie's feet. "Take it," he sneered. "Doesn't make any difference to me. Insurance is going to cover it."

Willie had had enough of Wally's shit. He pulled him up off the ground and marched him back out front, guiding him through one of the checkout counters as he did. Although money was clearly visible in the registers, Willie left it untouched, but grabbed a carton of Marlboros instead and threw it in the bag with the cash. Within in minutes they were out of the store and headed back to the house. Willie was proud of how well it all went down.

"Carol is staying with us now," Wally announced as they drove back. "You know that, don't you?" Wally had heard about the two of them, although he had a hard time imagining what she saw in him. He said it just to get a reaction.

For some reason the news about Carol didn't surprise Willie, but he panicked for a second, wondering if maybe she had already walked in on Doug. He felt a twinge in his gut.

Doug was relieved to hear Bill return, especially when shown the money. He tied Wally up then sat him down on the outside edge of the closet with the others. Doug took the rest of the rope and cinched it around their ankles and tied one to another, once and for all eliminating any possibility of escape. Still they twisted and groaned, Wally protesting the loudest until Doug gagged him with a necktie like he had done the others minutes earlier.

With that he and Willie turned and left them in the closet, and for the first time that night the storm in Doug Gretzler's gut started to recede. They had their money. Everyone was tied up and out of their hair. He started to relax. He wanted to leave. He wiped water glasses and pool cues for fingerprints. He listened for noises. He watched for headlights. He awaited the word from Bill about their next move. He followed him around. He wished he was high. He wished he so fucking high that this would all go away. He wished he was someone else. He wished he was somewhere else. He wished they could leave. Just take their shit and go.

But Willie was in no big rush. He roamed the house, digging in drawers and opening cabinets. He combed through boxes and book shelves, never once letting on what it was he was searching for. He didn't even look up when he finally got around to breaking the silence.

"Did I ever tell ya about this chick I knew named Carol?" he asked.

Doug couldn't place the name, but hell, he had a hard time remembering anything anymore. It was all a blur. Besides, Bill was always, ALWAYS, talking shit about something or someone or somewhere. *Carol?* He thought to himself, *What in the hell does she have to do with anything anyway? Let's just go. Carol Fucking Who?* Doug didn't answer the question. It was his way of letting Bill know he was done with all the bullshit.

"Kinda had a thing goin' with her," Willie continued, still scouring the house, oblivious to his partner's silent treatment. "Man, she's a groovy little thing. Worked with her at the hospital. Did some shit together, you know, hung out and stuff."

Doug had enough. "Listen, why don't we split?" He didn't feel like waiting to hear whatever it was Bill was getting at. His gut rumbled again. He couldn't figure out why they were still hanging around. All he could think of was the idea of just one more person walking through that front door and ruining everything. His stomach roared. "Look," he reminded Willie. "We got what we came for. Let's just get outta here"

Willie stopped and turned around, nearly bumping into Doug, who was shadowing him around the room, pleading his case. He snaked his way right into Doug's face and lowered his voice. "You know we can't do that. You know we can't leave these people here. These people are witnesses, man – witnesses to everything we've done. I said all along, no witnesses – I know you remember me saying it. We stay alive by runnin', and leavin' no witnesses."

Doug thought about it for a second. Bill was right, of course. Seemed like the one single thing in this world that Bill really knew anything about was just staying alive, and that meant staying far enough ahead of anyone who might want to bring them down – cops or whoever – people who always seemed to be just few minutes or a few miles behind them. Yeah, he remembered now, he remembered 'no witnesses'. After all, this was Bill's town, Bill's deal, Bill's call, and while his nerves began racing and his stomach again started roaring, he was comfortable in what had to be done. Bill was right, and he knew it.

Doug pointed down at the gun. "Well then, do it," he said. "But then let's get the hell outta here."

Willie didn't flinch or change the tone of his voice as he offered up his excuse. "You know I can't be the one. I know these people, man. They're my neighbors. I can't look them in the eye and do 'em."

Doug was taken back. His gut dropped out, knowing now what Bill was getting at. But he was right. This wasn't a copout. It was almost more righteous for Bill to admit this couldn't be his play. It took a lot to admit that, Doug decided, and he felt a new respect for him with his honesty.

Okay, he didn't want to, and this wasn't his idea, but he would do it, and they would be even and equal from here on. He would do this and then they would leave. Out of this house and out of this whole fucked up deal. For good. Doug groaned. "Alright, then. Let's do this." He checked the double chamber of the tiny derringer as he turned and headed towards the back of the house. "But we're gonna do this quick," he promised as he stormed down the hall, "then we leave"

But before they reached the bedroom Willie grabbed Doug's shoulder and stopped him. "That means all of them," he said.

"Whaddya mean, all of them?"

"Everybody. Kids too. They're old enough to be witnesses, so them too. You know that."

Doug paused. He needed to think this over. Shit! This was different! He could have drawn the line right there. *No kids!*, he could have said. He could have stood his ground. It would have been the right thing to do. He knew that, didn't he? Yeah, Bill would have pitched a fit and complained, and reminded him who was calling the shots here, but he would understand. He would have to, right? Jesus! They were just a couple of little kids! How in the hell were they gonna be a problem? He could have stopped right there and said, *NO! Absolutely not. No kids. No way. Not me.* He could have told Bill, *if you want 'em done then you fucking do it, cuz it sure as shit ain't gonna be me!* He could have said that. He told himself that a million times. Later, of course, later when he had a chance to think. Much later, when his head was clear and Bill wasn't staring him right in the fucking face. He could have handed the gun to him and said it, and Bill would have had to listen to him, because Doug kept reaching for this one thing - this one true thing inside him - buried deep down somewhere, hidden by all the shit he had been through and all the things he had done - this one real thing that would tell him this was wrong. *FUCK IT! Killing kids was wrong!* He would have no part of it. He could have drawn the line right there, and once and for all called his bluff. He could have told Bill, *"No way! NO FUCKING WAY am I'm killing any kids!"*

But he didn't. He didn't do any of that. He didn't say any of those words. At least not right then. Later? Yeah, much later. Later, when it was too late. Later, when he was alone with only his thoughts and regrets to convict him. But now, in this brief moment, this fraction of a second, within this twisted, fucked up excuse for logic he carried around, convinced him Bill was right, so he caved. *Yeah, right on. Makes sense. I can do that.*

Bobby and Lisa Parkin were fast asleep, laid out like two dolls in the middle of the oversized bed. Not more than a half hour earlier their mother had placed them fully clothed, sided by side, on top of the pastel yellow blanket, then pulled the blue quilted bedspread up to their waist, kissing their cheeks as she did, softly urging them to go to sleep. Limp and groggy, their eyes heavy and only half opened, they obeyed, and so there they still lay.

Doug walked to the side of the bed, and with his right hand he placed the gun just inches away from Bobby's small chubby face. Using his large left hand to shield the boy's face from his view, he pulled the derringer up to the forehead, resting it between the two tiny eyes. Without hesitation, he squeezed the trigger.

The sound was not much louder than that of a child's cap gun. One solitary *CRACK!*, and the damage was done. Blood poured out of the wound and onto the yellow blanket. Without waking, without even opening his eyes, Bobby's head slumped over and dark bloody fluids began to trickle out from between his boyish pink lips. Groans and grunts came from the closet.

Before the noise could awake her, Doug placed the gun on Lisa's head and repeated the process. Again blood rushed out, soaking the pale blanket. A crimson spray dotted the headboard and the wall behind the bed. Willie came up from behind and pulled the blanket over the children's head, hiding what had been done. The soft pastel quickly turned scarlet as the blood flowed.

Doug's attention was now drawn toward the closet and the muffled moans and wails coming from just around the corner. Willie handed him the fully loaded six shot as the pair stood over those huddled on the carpeted floor. Doug reminded himself not to look at them, not to make contact, but to act swiftly and decisively.

The bodies were contorted. Their legs, and the bindings around them, were twisted and knotted together into one large mass, like a den of snakes, writhing to escape. Another shot of adrenaline kicked in and raced through Doug's body, piercing his stomach with a wretched pain. He fought it off, reminding himself to think clearly, it would all be over soon.

The babysitter's father was his biggest worry. His body was small but well muscled, and Doug could see the bulging veins in the man's large arms. Even though he was tightly bound, the man still arched his back and tugged at the ropes that wrapped his wrists. The father glared up at both men as if daring them to act. As much as he tried, Doug could not avoid the stare of the father's eyes, a brilliant blue that drilled right through him. He was the one who frightened Doug the most, so it was he who would be first.

With the revolver hidden behind his back, Doug stepped into the middle of the pile, bodies flailing away, their bindings unyielding, they arched and grunted. Then together, in one last effort, as if choreographed and rehearsed a thousand times, the people in the closet contorted in a spastic unison, straightening their knotted bodies like fish snagged and twisting on a line. Doug whipped the pistol from behind him, placed it on the father's temple and fired. Blood gushed from the small hole, momentarily startling the gunman. It began to spurt in thick eruptions as the man's body bucked up against the violent intrusion and the surprise of the attack. His eyes bulged and his face puffed out as he forced air through the necktie gag. His back arched up, his eyes still wide open, his head finally coming to rest momentarily on the outstretched legs of Wally Parkin.

Cries now consumed the closet. Closing his senses off to the bellowing, Doug backtracked, focusing now on the man whose dark blue pullover was now wet with his neighbor's blood. Again, the revolver was lowered against the skull and the bullet rocketed from the chamber and into its target. It had been his plan to hit everyone once, then return to finish his work with each. Without delay, he repeated his actions to each person in the closet. The teenage boy was next. Then his mother. His sister. Doug's last bullet tore into the woman in who's house he was in, its inertia slammed her head back up against the closet wall, then snapped it forward once more, coming to rest against the front of her soft white sweater. White turned crimson as her own blood, and that from the young babysitter lying at her side, drenched her.

Doug was now out of bullets, but not people. He turned to Willie and exchanged weapons.

The boyfriend was the last. Doug had watched him out of the corner of his eye as he had circled the room and knew he would have to switch guns before he would be able to complete his task. The boyfriend had watched calmly as each one went before him. Now their eyes met and Doug was taken back by the expression on the young man's face, for it wasn't so much a look of fear, but one of intense excitement. For a fraction of a second the killer and his victim connected. Finally, he turned his head to one side, away from the man who stood above him. His eyes remained open but his expression had changed from a look of curiosity to one of intense concentration, as if waiting for the end he knew would come shortly.

As the last shot was fired, Doug's stomach knotted up and the pain nearly doubled him over. He was worried he had messed himself.

All of the bodies were silent now. All except the father who continued to struggle and groan. He had somehow found the strength to lift his head up and his blue eyes screamed at his assailants, as if daring them all over again.

It was Willie's turn. Now that the initial dirty work had been done, he pulled Doug out from the pile and went to work. Having reloaded the revolver, he followed his partner's pattern and unleashed another bullet into each person in the closet. He squeezed each one off recklessly, round after round, then reloaded. Wildly, he proceeded again around the closet, an orgasm exploding with each bullet, his fury and rage cresting with each pull. Again he reloaded, carefully pocketing each empty shell. Again he circled the room. And again. Then once more he reloaded the chamber and hurriedly readied himself. Their faces were so bloodied he had no idea where to aim his next round, so he searched for a clean spot on their head and fired. The only sound now was the never-ending pop of the gun and the click of the trigger when it eventually hit an empty chamber.

But the father still shook violently, his taunting eyes still cursing his killers, his grunts letting it be known he was not giving in. Willie focused upon him, and now holding the gun with both hands, sent the fifth and final bullet into the man's skull, finally silencing him as well, his blond hair dirtied with his own blood. His face covered in it as well, but his blue eyes remained open, staring at the two men who looked down upon him, and the others in the closet.

Content that their work was complete, they turned and walked back towards the front of the house. This time there was no loud talk or boastful bravado. They were drained. Spent. Silent.

Willie wandered into the middle of the living room, starring out through the picture window and into the black of night. Doug went straight to the kitchen. He poured a glass of wine and devoured a huge piece of Joanne's birthday cake. He leaned up against the counter and breathed deeply, waiting for the pain in his belly to go away.

Willie resumed his search of the house. He had found a bottle of Seagram's and was sipping from it as he walked around, rummaging again through drawers and cabinets.

"Fuck! Would you look at this!" he shouted at Doug as he held up a blue steel .38 revolver pulled from a drawer. It was the first real firearm he had held since Tucson, and the feel excited him as he fingered it and worked its smooth action. But it also scared him, realizing the weapon was there all the time. Certainly Wally had known about the gun, but not an opportunity to get his hands on it, Willie shuddered to imagine how different things would have turned out if he had.

"Shit!" Willie gushed. "We coulda been shot!"

Doug repeated his argument that to wait around for this Carol girl was dangerous. Willie stared out the living room picture window and changed his mind several times before finally agreeing. He shoved the .38 in his jacket, grabbed the paper sack full of money and the bottle of Seagrams, then flipped off a few lights as they walked out the front door.

They were shocked to see so many cars parked out front. Looked like a damn party going on, Willie thought. Enough cars, he decided, to cause a problem with the first person who came up to the house. They needed to go back down to other house to check it out anyway, so he would take the old man's car and park it back inside the garage. That would get rid of one, anyway. He instructed Doug to follow him.

Once inside the Earl house they were greeted by the barking of the family's cocker spaniel. They had no idea if there was anyone else inside, and so even after they managed to quiet the dog, they moved around cautiously until they could be sure they were alone. Willie remembered the cup he had touched and wiped it off. All the lights were still on, so he took his time looking into each room, opening drawers and cupboards as he wandered. He walked upstairs and Doug followed him into one of the bedrooms.

"Jesus, look at this!" Willie yelled. Lying on a neatly made bed was a 410 shotgun. First the .38, and now this. He reached down and grabbed it, carefully cradling it in his arms. But as excited as Willie was, Doug felt sick at the sight. After what had been done, the thing looked obscene to him. He could not imagine having to use it. Not now. He didn't want it near him.

"Shit, Bill, we don't need to be dragging that thing around." Willie looked disappointed. "And where the hell are you gonna hide it in that little car? We just don't need the heat that it'll bring. I say we leave it and just get outta here."

Willie didn't argue and placed the shotgun back on the bed. They left the rest of house the way they had entered it. They took nothing with them.

Willie pointed the way back to the highway. North on Dustin Road, past the old houses and the bunk shed where he had stayed with the Billingsly boys. Down past the neighbor's garages he had broke into a dozen times. He had walked this road for as long as he could remember, and now he was on it for the last time. They turned left at his old school on Collier and hit 99 heading north. He rolled down the window and let the cold November air slap him in the face. He recalled all the night drives back from Santa Cruz and Frisco – middle of the night, windows down, eight tracks pounding Tower of Power – so perfect. Everybody used to give him shit for letting the cold air in, but that's how he liked it. Stoned and rolling. He put the bottle of Seagrams up to his lips and had another taste.

He reached into his coat pocket and began tossing shell casings out the window, flinging them as far as he could, scattering them from the Liberty Road overpass to the county line. Twenty-seven brass jackets carefully saved from the closet. It wasn't long before Doug complained, just like all the others, so he took another swig and rolled the window up.

On the outskirts of Sacramento, less than forty minutes from Victor, Willie decided that to stay out on road was just asking for trouble. Better to find a place to crash. There would be no late night flight to Mexico. No calling Duff for help out of town. They would be hot within a few hours, and he was sure every cop in the country would be on their ass by morning. He saw the Holiday Inn sign at the 47th Street off ramp and they pulled in. Doug avoided the brightly lit covered parking and instead parked off to the side, out of the night attendant's sight. Willie walked in and registered as W.J. SIEMS from Colorado, paying for the room with a twenty-dollar bill he had folded four ways, just to be a smartass.

Upstairs in room 216 Doug smoked some weed as Willie counted out the take. Nearly four thousand dollars. A long way from the twenty grand Bill had boasted about, Doug thought, and a pathetic amount for the shit they were now in. But he took what was handed over to him, about $800, and shoved it in his coat pocket.

Willie sat on the bed, sipped from the bottle and played with his latest toy; the newly found .38. As he did he kicked around some ideas about what they would do next, but he never said anything to Doug, who rested on the other bed, eyes closed.

It was almost 2 o'clock before Willie finally crashed too.

32

Wednesday, November 7, 1973 | 3:00 am.

Try to explain the unexplainable. Carol could not. Not then. Not ever. And yet her senses told her something was out of place at the house on Orchard Road. As she reached the front door, a wall of dread washed over her. She felt like she didn't belong there, like she shouldn't be there. She froze. She looked back over her shoulder at Jim, but wondered what she would say to him. How could she make him understand? Carol could feel a chill tingle on her skin, even under her heavy jacket. You are being silly, she told herself. But there was something not quite right about the house, and if it hadn't been so late and so cold she would have certainly just stopped right there, right in the mud and the drizzle and the dull headlight glare, and she would not have moved even one inch until she could put her finger on exactly what felt so wrong.

Jim sat in the truck as Carol walked up the graveled path. He always made sure she was safely inside before he left, and it was her routine to wave goodnight before he drove away. But tonight, as she fumbled with the key to unlock the front door, she hesitated for a moment, then looked back at him, as if asking his permission to continue. Jim had never seen that look before. Carol turned, opened the door and went inside, and although there was no wave tonight, Jim hesitated as well, wondering, waiting for what he really didn't know, before he crept down the drive and back onto Orchard Road.

Once inside, she decided it was the lights that bothered her. None of the lights were right, but she wondered why she remembered that. First, the light over the stereo was not on, and Joanne always left it on, like a night light to guide Carol into the house on nights just like this one when she came home long after everyone had gone to bed. Then there was light filtering out of the small bathroom window down the side of the house, and that too seemed odd. She was certain she had turned the light off when she left. No one else would have any reason to be back in that part of the house. And she could see Wally and Joanne's room at the end of the hall, but the door to the master bedroom was closed. Odd as well, because Joanne always left the door open, and regardless of how early or late the hour, Carol would walk to the door and whisper that she had made it home safely, even though Joanne was usually fast asleep by the time she came in.

Carol thought about going into the back bathroom to turn off the light, but that would mean going through their bedroom to get there. And it was late, and maybe the door was closed for a reason. Besides, everybody would be up in a few hours anyway, so Carol went back to her room and climbed into bed, telling herself she could sort it all out in the morning.

Steve McFadden was very much asleep, but at a quarter after six a ringing telephone changed that. It was his dad.

"Hey, sorry to wake you," he apologized, "but is Mark over there?"

"Lang? No, why?

"Well, I just got a call from his mother. She said he didn't come home last night and no one knows where he is."

Steve was still groggy and realized this conversation was going to require him to think a bit. He blinked, coughed, rubbed his eyes and came up with his best guess. "Anyone try Debbie's?"

"There's no answer there. Mrs. Lang is really worried, Steve. Listen, I told her I'd have you go look around a little. You know, check out a few places you think he might be."

"Yeah, sure. Wayne and me will go take a look."

If there ever was a guy more perfect than Mark Lang, Steve figured he had never met him. Probably never would. Mark was the perfect son. Sometimes to the point of making all the other guys look bad. Steve had to laugh. He had finally figured out a way to spend the night with Deb. Maybe he wasn't so damned straight-laced after all.

Lodi was just waking up when Steve and Wayne hit the streets. The ceiling was low and gray, and in the distance the morning sun began to brighten the edge of the eastern sky. Steve made a few loops around the town then headed towards the sunrise. Wayne reminded him that Mark told them last night he was going out to pick up Debbie, so they decided the best place to start was at the Parkin's place out in Victor. Knowing Mark, it would have taken something pretty serious for him not to at least call his folks. And even if his car had broken down, he still would have been close enough he could have walked home. No, this was not like Mark, Steve realized, and now he started to worry a little himself.

So he intentionally took the roundabout way to Orchard Road. But even on the back roads, there was no sign of him or his Impala. At the corner of Dustin Road and Orchard was Debbie's house. They pulled around the corner and into the drive, and were surprised to see Mark's dad walking from around the back of the house. The front porch light was on, but other than that the house appeared empty.

"Nobody home," Mr. Lang announced. He was visibly upset.

Knowing that Debbie babysat just up the street, Wayne told them both to wait here and he would drive up and see if he could find Mark's car. He wasn't really sure which house was the Parkin's, but halfway up the road, out of the corner of his eye, he spotted the white hardtop on Mark's Impala. Just like they figured, Mark had spent the night. He turned around and drove back to the Earl's house to tell the others the good news.

Mr. Lang did not have the patience to wait – he was gone by the time Wayne returned – so Wayne and Steve headed back up the road to let Mark know his parents were looking for him.

Wayne checked his watch. Seven am. And as they walked up to the front door he worried he would be the guy in trouble if he were late for work this morning. *Let's get Mark and go,* he told Steve, *because I've got to hurry*. But there was no answer at the door, so they waited a minute, then walked around the side and knocked again on the patio door.

The sound eventually wrestled Carol awake. She couldn't understand why someone didn't answer it, and she grumbled her way out of bed. But as she walked towards the front door, she could hear voices and see their shadows on the sliding glass door around the side of the house. She realized she was the only one up. Usually by this time of the morning the house was bustling with breakfast and getting kids ready for school. She looked around for a moment and listened. All was quiet. She opened the slider. She recognized the two faces.

"Hi Carol." Steve said. "Hey, is Mark here? Did Mark spend the night here?"

She thought about it for a moment, remembering now it was his car in the driveway when she came home, but Carol just scrunched her shoulders to indicate she didn't know for sure.

"Well," Steve continued, "he's supposed to be at work, and his mom and dad are getting pretty worried."

"Wait a minute," she replied, maybe a little perturbed she got woke up for this. "Let me go ask Joanne if he's still here."

She walked down the hall and stopped. That eerie feeling returned. The bedroom door was still closed. Now she was certain something was wrong. She opened the door slowly. "Joanne?" she whispered. "Wally?" The room was dark and the air still.

"Joanne?" she called out again, now groping her way towards the bed. Then, as her eyes finally adjusted to the room's dim light, she found the reason for her dread.

Back on the other side of the house, Steve and Wayne had stepped inside, waiting for the chance to tell Mark just how much trouble he had caused. It was then when they heard Carol's bloodcurdling scream.

Seemed like everyone in town met at Emma's. Each day before work – seven, seven-thirty – they started filtering into the little hole in the wall coffee shop across from the courthouse in Stockton. Regulars from the offices around the square; an odd mix of beat cops and deputies, judges and prosecutors, lawyers and their clients, all gathered at the tiny spot next to the Fox Theater on Main Street. There was nothing fancy about Emma's, and that included the conversation. It was shop talk mostly, sometimes a little football or hunting, just the sort of place that made men feel at home.

Sam Libicki stopped by most mornings himself, and although younger than the other regulars, he was not opposed to having a cup with his boss or some of the others from the Public Defender's office where he worked. Couldn't hurt keeping yourself seen, Sam decided. You never know what kind of information or leads might come across one of the tables.

It had rained again overnight – off and on, but hard when it came – and the morning was cool. Coffee weather, Libicki called it, and that must have been the reason Emma's seemed busier than normal. Despite the crowd, and the lack of an empty chair, Sam liked the bustle and noise. He found a place and settled in, but hadn't even finished his first cup when it hit him. There was much too much coming and going for Emma's. It was too loud and too hectic, and none of the comfortable background laughter he had become used to. Around him he watched deputies in their crisp khaki storm in, look around for a coworker and whisper in their ear, before both hurried out, leaving full cups of coffee and plates with a half eaten Danish in their wake. Within minutes there wasn't a uniform in the place.

It was all too curious for Sam, who finally managed to grab the last deputy heading for the door. "What's up?' he asked.

The officer looked around, like he wasn't supposed to talk, but lowered his voice. "Not sure," he replied. "Sounds like we may have a multiple 187 up outside of Lodi. Canlis wants everybody on it."

Sam was only slightly taken back, but a murder, or even two, wouldn't create this much commotion. "What do you mean, multiple?"

The deputy was anxious to leave, but stopped long enough for another gulp of coffee and to answer the question. He had seen Libicki around. He figured he could trust him. Figured he would find out soon enough anyway. "We're supposed to keep a lid on it, but it looks like maybe a couple little kids got it. That's all I know."

Sam sat back and watched the scene at Emma's continue to unfold. The deputy was right, word was out, and those left behind began speculating about what was going on up the road in Lodi. He sipped his coffee and listened. It was times like these, whenever he was confronted with the shitty side of the human race, when he contemplated what he did for a living. He enjoyed his job, it wasn't that, but as a public defender he had met every kind of lowlife out there. Hell, he defended them! But he still couldn't come to grips with the kind of creep who could hurt a kid, let alone murder one. He had stood up for a killer a couple of times. He had done a pretty good job, too. But to kill a kid? Jesus, that would be a tough.

So the secret was out, and the voices at Emma's had risen to a point where those who remained all had an opinion, an angle, and their own take on what was going on. Everyone who walked in had something new to add and were welcomed to the group of the guessing. Empty chairs were pulled back and more hot coffee poured. Talk was now there were more people missing. Someone flipped on a radio and the morning news was all over it. The announcer said two entire families were still unaccounted for.

Sam got up and tossed his money on the counter, still shaking his head in disbelief. That's gonna be quite a case someday, he told himself, never thinking for one minute it would be his.

"Oh my God! Oh my, there's blood everywhere!"

Carol tore out of the room and screamed down the hall where a startled Steve McFadden attempted in vain to intercept her. She was ranting hysterically, little of it understandable, all laced with high-pitched shrieks and wails. She broke way from his grip, lunged for the phone and started punching numbers. "Help me!" she screamed into the receiver. "There's so much blood! Blood on the bed! Oh, Dear God Jesus, help me! There's blood everywhere on the bed!"

Steve pleaded with her to tell him what was going on. She ignored him, dialing the first number she saw. On the Parkin's phone was a bright orange label with the emergency number for the Liberty Fire Department. David Blackwell answered, hearing only the sobbing pleas of a very upset female yelling on the other end.

"Hurry!" the voice screamed over and over. "Oh please, please hurry! So much blood! So much blood everywhere! Call the sheriff. . .and an ambulance! Come over to Wally Parkin's house! Hurry! Please hurry!"

Blackwell managed to jot down the address, along with the time. 8300 Orchard Road, Victor. 7:05 am. He reported the call to his Chief, Frank Terra, who in turn called the Woodbridge Fire Department, asking them to notify the sheriff as to a possible homicide at this location.

At 7:12, the San Joaquin Sheriff's Office logged the call and the desk sergeant asked dispatch to check to see who was closest to the scene. Patrol Deputies Levesey and Mello responded that they were about fifteen minutes away.

But Liberty Fire Chief Terra got there first, only to find a terribly distraught young woman running in and out of the house, wailing, screaming for someone to help her. Chasing her around the front yard were two teenage boys, clearly helpless in their efforts to catch her and calm her down. The woman stopped long enough to point down the hallway in the direction of the back bedrooms. Out of breath, she waited only a split second to repeat, "So much blood! There's so much blood!"

Terra hesitated, not sure of who or what he might find, but headed to the back bedroom with a great deal of caution and anticipation. The gray morning light was just now finding its way into the room, and he could barely make out an oversized bed with an ominous dark stain in the middle. It was obvious to him that there was someone beneath the covers, so he carefully peeled them back. There he saw the bodies of not one, but two, very small children.

The discovery caught him off guard. He backed away, sickened, knowing there was no need now trying to help them. A chill hit him. He wondered if he was alone. He backtracked out of the room and did a quick check of the other bedrooms and the living area, then walked out the front door of the house.

Seven twenty-nine. Officers Levesey and Mello arrived, as had several of the neighbors, curious as to what the commotion was. Terra led the deputies to the bedroom as Levesey pulled his service revolver from its holster while Mello grabbed the shotgun from the dash. He pumped it hard as they followed Terra back inside.

But after seeing the bodies, and realizing this particular crime had been committed at least several hours earlier, they caught their breath. Terra said he had made a check of the residence and found nothing else out of order. They took him at his word and walked back out front. Their concern now was preserving the crime scene.

Steve McFadden stopped Mello long enough to let him about all the others who were still unaccounted for. Mello relayed the information to his partner. "The kid's baby sitter is missing," he said.

"*All* the Earl's are missing," Steve interrupted. "We went to their house. The lights are all on, but we couldn't wake anybody up. It doesn't look like they're even home."

Thinking this baby sitter might have an answer, Levesey told Mello to secure the house. Absolutely no one goes in until homicide arrives. He motioned to Terra to come with him.

At 7:40 they arrived at the Earl residence and found all doors locked and no answer to any of their repeated attempts to rouse whoever might inside. They circled around to the back, continuing to yell out as they did. Terra found a kitchen window open and lifted Levesey through it. Inside, they called out again, but still no response. Downstairs, the home was neat and clean, void of any sign of a struggle or intrusion. A pair of shoes at the foot of the stairs and a pair of men's socks on the floor nearby was all they found out of place. Upstairs, a different story. In what appeared to be a boy's room, they discovered a 410 shotgun lying on the bed. They wondered if that might be part of all this, although it had not been fired. They left it where they found it.

They had only been gone ten minutes, but in that time the crowd at the Parkin's house had swelled. By now some members of both families had arrived, all begging for some one to please tell them what was going on. Some demanded to be allowed inside. While Terra and Levesay were gone, Mello had talked with them all. He told Levesay not only was the baby sitter missing, but her boyfriend, her brother, her parents, and the owners of the home they were now standing in, were gone as well.

The scene out front was bursting. The crowd crept ever closer to the front door and several attempted to enter the house, or at the very least, peer through its large picture windows. Sobbing and hysteria overwhelmed all conversation, and while Mello did his best to keep everyone at a distance, it was difficult watching and listening to them. But he knew enough not to let anyone in, no matter who they said they were, although he found it difficult to be so cold and abrupt.

More officers were on the way, but Levesay decided they needed to go over the house once more, this time completely and carefully, just to be sure there was nothing being overlooked. The house was large and rambling, and it would take some time to accurately perform such a task. He told the fire department to guard the front door, then motioned for Mello to follow him in.

They looked in each room, working their way back to the hall that lead to the master bedroom. They forced themselves to view once more the small bodies on the bed. Walking around the side to get a better view, Mello noticed a hallway that lead to a bathroom. There were floor to ceiling cabinets on one side of the short hallway, and what appeared to be an open closet on the other. He could see a shower stall and another door at the far end of the bathroom area. It became clear there was another way in and out of the bedroom – an area they had failed to investigate earlier.

Mello took the first step, wondering out loud how anyone in their right mind could leave two small children alone in such a large house. But one step was all he needed. On his right was the large open closet. He looked down. On the floor he found the seven answers to his question.

Immediately after her call to the fire department, Carol dialed Jim and begged him to come get her. There was trouble at the Parkin's house, was all she told him. She had still said nothing to Steve and Wayne. All that they knew was there was a lot of blood and someone was dead inside.

Jim Mettler arrived within minutes of Carol's call – even before Terra, Mello or Levesay did – and he found her racing in and out of the house, screaming and crying. He had an impossible time trying to catch her and comfort her. "They're dead!" she wailed. "They're in the bedroom, and they're dead!"

"Who?" Jim asked. " Who's dead?"

"Wally and Joanne!" she answered. "They're both dead!"

Carol had grabbed her jacket on the way out and threw it over her nightclothes. She was barefoot and muddy. Jim insisted she go sit inside the truck and let the police take over when they arrived. But she was like a caged animal and she finally convinced Jim to at least let her go into the bathroom in the back of the house and wash the mud from her feet.

Jim agreed and followed her in, and as she washed, she was certain the bathroom was not in its usual order. That same feeling came back to her again. For one desperate moment she recalled that feeling of last night. She saw that there were drawers open and in disarray, like someone had gone through them. And the medicine cabinet was open, its contents scattered all over the counter. There were towels left on the floor of the shower stall, something so out of place, she automatically reached down to pick them up. Jim pulled her away and reminded her again not to touch anything, before carrying her back outside.

The fire department had arrived by this time, as had Eula Parkin. A neighbor had called her about all the ruckus going on over at her son's house. She looked around. Her husband was not there. She needed him now. As was his routine, he had left their house early to go open up the market. For some reason she now worried about him. Was he all right? No one would talk to her. What was going on? she asked.

Carol walked over and gave her a hug, but didn't say anything about what had been found inside. She just couldn't find the words. Besides, someone had certainly told her the bad news by now, Carol decided. Where's Ken? Eula asked. Have you seen him? Carol said that she hadn't, but he was probably still at the market. She looked at Jim, who offered to go over to get him and bring him back, and when they pulled out of the driveway and not a single deputy bothered to stop them.

It was still before eight am, and the store was not open yet, so they went around back and found Mr. Parkin arranging the shelves.

"Ken, there's been some trouble over at Wally's," Jim said, trying to be as casual as he could. "Eula is there. You better get over there too."

Mr. Parkin did not ask for any details, and for that Jim was thankful. They told him to go, that they would lock up the store, so he tossed his apron aside and hurried out. They checked the front doors, then walked into the back storage area to leave when they discovered the door on the floor safe was open. Back at the house, Jim alerted the officer at the front door that it looked like maybe the Parkin's store had been robbed too. Mello phoned in to dispatch, that in addition to Homicide, they would need Robbery Detail called out as well.

Carol found Ken and Eula in the crowd. They seemed unusually calm and it was Eula who broke the news. "I'm afraid it's Lisa and Bobby in the bed, Carol. They're still looking for Wally and Joanne."

Carol, who had finally managed to regain some of her composure, became unraveled once again, wailing and pleading for someone to tell her who could have done such a horrible thing? Jim put his arm around her, walked her over to his pickup and put her back inside. Still, her sobs, moans, and screams could be heard across the yard. Even her parents, who had not been close to Carol as of late, came and tried their best to calm her down. Nothing worked. Finally, San Joaquin Sheriff Detective Biancalana had heard enough. "Listen to me," he barked. "They're gone now and you're going to have to help us here. We need to get some information."

But Carol ignored him. He could get nothing from her and she had now become a major distraction. Against his better judgment, he relented and allowed her to leave with her mother, who had somehow convinced him that what she really needed was a doctor, not some policeman yelling at her. With that, Carol Jenkins left the crime scene without ever having to account for her recent whereabouts.

By now Deputy Mello had separated Steve and Wayne, making each stand on opposite sides of the front door. They were both scared senseless. Steve watched as Carol drove away. That seemed really weird. She was the one who lived here. She was even the one who found them. Shouldn't she have to stick around like them? Then it hit him. His heart sank and his shoulders slumped. He looked over at his friend.

"Wayne!" he moaned "They think *we* killed 'em!"

A million dollars worth of walnuts had gone up in smoke Tuesday night, so at eight o'clock this morning, the fire at the Diamond Plant in Stockton was the only thing Dan was concerned with. The story, and the few photos he could shoot, would go along way towards filling his daily quota. Dan Walters was a reporter for the *Sacramento Union* assigned to their Stockton bureau. His daily requirement was to fill one full page of news from his beat. Twelve stories a day is what it took. Ten, if they were big deals and he could manage to get a few pictures to go along with them.

And the Diamond Walnut disaster was very big. A million bucks was a lot of money, not to mention the people who were going to be out of work as a result. Unemployment always made for good copy, especially with the holidays coming. The fire, along with the Board of Supervisor's meeting scheduled later that morning could make Dan's day. Might even get home early for a change.

At first he was a little embarrassed by taking the job in Stockton, but Dan decided it would have to do until something better came along. The whole idea of stringing for a paper felt awkward to him now, because at the young age of 30, Dan considered himself a seasoned veteran. Having dropped out of high school, he got his first job at a small paper on the northern California coast. He began as a copy boy, but was a fast learner, so was quickly promoted to the coveted police beat. By the time he was 22 he had worked for three different papers and became the youngest managing editor of a daily in the U.S. when he accepted a job in Fresno. But Dan would be the first to admit the newspaper business was a fickle one, and despite a shining young career, he found himself out beating the street for a job just a few short years later. But as luck would have it, an old friend put in a good word for him at the *Union* and Dan was offered the job. But it was only until something bigger and better came along, he assured himself.

Being on the tall side and able to carry a few extra pounds around was actually to his benefit. His stocky frame, along with a full face and high forehead, managed to add a few years to his looks. Dan parted his dark hair low on one side, then slicked it over his head, and when the style everywhere was large, long and loud, Dan dressed more conservatively than his peers, which made him appear older and more experienced about how things got done, which in his business, and with the people he needed to associate with, was a big advantage. The people in Stockton, especially around the courthouse and cop shops, trusted him and seemed comfortable with the articles he wrote. So even though Dan had been on the job only five months, and was many years younger than those he wrote about, he fit in well, discovering quickly what made the town tick and who pulled the strings that got things done.

So as Dan headed out to the fire, he let the dashboard police scanner crackle in the background. It was a habit from his days on the police beat, looking for leads to stories he was constantly chasing. He recognized the voice of Sheriff Canlis, who gave his location as Orchard Road in Victor, but Dan attached no particular significance to it when the Sheriff announced he was 'going out of service'. This was a fairly common practice, especially on sensitive matters, and was simply designed to keep people like Dan Walters from knowing too much of their business. In any event, seconds later the channel was reduced to loud static and Dan didn't give it much more thought.

Finishing up with the fire, Dan returned to his downtown office where he checked the mail and prepared for the supervisors meeting scheduled in a few minutes. He walked the two blocks over to the courthouse, but as he entered the building one of the supervisors stopped him.

"Didn't figure I'd see you here, Dan."

"And why's that?"

"Well, I thought you would be up in Lodi." He sized up Dan's puzzled expression. "Guess you haven't heard. They found some people murdered in a home up there."

A murder every once in awhile didn't surprise Dan, let alone register as a big story. But since he was already in the building, he decided to go down to the Sheriff's Office in the basement and see if he could dig up anything more on it. Although they were hesitant to talk, they eventually confirmed the report. The desk sergeant, who knew Dan well, still had difficulty letting the information out. No one else knows it yet, he told Walters, and we're supposed to keep it under wraps for a while.

"So what are we talking here?" Dan inquired. "How many?"

"Nine," he answered, as if to get it out and over with as fast as he could speak the words. "Worse part of it is two of them are little kids." His head hung down with the very magnitude of it all. "Canlis is up there right now, along with everyone else from the department we could rustle up."

He had Dan's attention.

By now all sheriff personnel were told in the most emphatic of terms to use only the telephone for any communications in regards to this matter. Still, as Walters raced north on Highway 99, he flipped through the all the channels, hoping for any additional info. But very little came across – a Highway Patrol broadcast and a fire department transmittal – so he arrived at the scene with little more than he had left Stockton with. But the department's overall efforts to keep a lid on the story had failed terribly. On the way to Victor, Dan realized that he had gotten a lucky break on the story, a head start maybe, and he prayed he might be the first one to arrive. But he was sadly mistaken. When he finally managed to find a spot to park on the narrow lane, he was shocked at how many people had beaten him there. Cars lined both sides of the road for a long country block. People milled around in small clusters, some still wrapped in their robes and nightclothes, warding off the morning chill, talking and crying, comforting those overwhelmed with grief and uncertainty.

Now Dan felt a little sick himself, seeing how many reporters had beat him to the biggest story to hit the area in a long time. The only good news was that one of those early arrivals was a fellow reporter from the *Union* by the name of Ted Thomas. He was not only a co-worker, but a friend as well, and the man who had gotten Dan his job with the *Union* in the first place. They agreed to divy up the assignments; one would pick up the color of the scene while the other would interview the people in the driveway. While Dan learned that most of those were neighbors and friends, some of the people were relatives of those still officially listed as 'missing'.

By the time Dan arrived, most of the onlookers had heard that Wally and Joanne had not been located yet, nor had any of the Earl family. They were missing, not dead, they assured themselves, but no one knew anything for sure, and Dan soon learned, that with the possible exception of sheriff personnel, he was the only one who knew the magnitude of the horror inside the house, and he kept that information to himself.

The only truth circulating at this time was that the two Parkin kids had been found murdered in the bed where they slept. No other names were mentioned, although everyone whispered and wondered where the parents were. When word filtered through the crowd that the Earl family was missing as well, rumors started to fly. Mark Lang, it was now told, had a violent argument with Debbie, and in his rage killed not only her but Lisa and Bobby as well. These people could not say for sure where Mark was now, but they were certain Debbie's body would be discovered soon. As for the rest of the Earls, or Wally and Joanne for that matter, they could only guess, but Mark was involved someway, that much they knew for sure. Look, his car is right there in the driveway, they proclaimed, and he had been in the house, they were certain about that as well, so that explains it. When one of the onlookers expressed their surprise at such news, being what a nice young man Mark Lang had appeared on the surface and all, another answered her sharply. "It's always the nice ones, the ones you would never expect, who goes and does something crazy like this."

So in the minutes after Dan arrived, Mark Lang had became the first suspect, at least to some of those huddling out in front of the house. A short time later, when news of the killings reached Mark and Debbie's old high school, the two took on cult hero status. A modern day Romeo and Juliet, it was said. Better yet, Bonnie and Clyde. The rumors swirled. Mark and Debbie, in a perverted lover's bond, killed the two kids, and all the parents, and had dumped the bloody bodies somewhere out in the fog shrouded delta. It mattered little, even to those who knew Mark and Debbie well, and those who certainly knew better, just how farfetched such talk was. But for that brief period, at least until the horrible truth surfaced later, the pair had become the most romantic, if not most deadly couple in Lodi High history.

Walters and Thomas continued to circulate the crowd, which by late morning had increased substantially. Many of these new arrivals were law enforcement officers, gathered from agencies all over the valley, many whose sole responsibility was simply crowd control. Every few minutes there would be a loud violent scene outside, an outburst created when a distraught family member couldn't take the not knowing any longer, demanding to be told what was going on, begging to know all that the police certainly knew by now. Who had they found? How many more bodies?

But those guarding the house would not talk. Could not talk. The orders requiring their silence were sent from the top man himself, and were therefore viewed as the enemy by those left dangling in the driveway. So it was, not long after the discovery was made earlier that morning, that a line was drawn in the mud and gravel, a barrier between the cops and the victim's families, as well as all of their friends and neighbors who huddled together in the dull mist chill of this deadly autumn morning.

It was well after nine before Dave Arrelanes could get into court with his case against Willie Steelman and Douglas Gretzler. Yesterday afternoon he had contacted Deputy County Attorney Ralph Fenderson with his request for warrants. The attorney was well aware of the investigation and was half expecting to see Arellanes last night so it didn't take him long to review the complaints. He personally walked the case over to the courthouse where Judge Murphy signed his name to them.

Both suspects were charged with two counts of murder. Bail was set at

$220,000 each.

Murder warrants in hand, Arrelanes returned to his office at 11 am. Robert Nelson was there, waiting to get back at their now mutual investigation. Shortly after Dave returned, an assistant from the communications room barged in, anxious to show him a teletype that had just come over the wire from Stockton, California. Dave read it, then looked up at the others. He read it again to be sure. He had never felt so sick in all his life. His heart sank. Dammit to hell! He knew this was going to happen. He took it personally. Why in the hell didn't he listen to his instincts last night?

SHERIFF-CORONER SAN JOAQUIN COUNTY
ALL POINTS BULLETIN – RUSH RUSH RUSH

Mass murder 9 victims rural area of Lodi near the town of Victor in San Joaquin County. One off the deceased is the storeowner in the town of Victor. Rural fire dept discovered 2 deceased children and after officers arrived at the scene 7 more bodies were discovered in a closet at the residence. Discovered that the contents of the safe at the deceased owner's store was empty with no force used that could indicated a kidnap-hostage type of robbery. Investigation at this time indicates all victims had been shot with small caliber weapon. Post mortem exams pending. No suspects at this time.

Attn – Homicide Details
Attn – CII any similars
Refer replys to Sgt Blythe / Detective Ambrose File #73-27315

Dave felt like they were always just a few steps behind these guys, and now it appeared just a couple hours too late as well. He grabbed the phone and made the call he had planned on making earlier. He called Stockton to tell them all about Willie Steelman and Douglas Gretzler.

It was only mid-morning, but the switchboard at the San Joaquin Sheriff's Office was lit up like a four alarm fire. There were nearly a hundred calls logged before they stopped keeping track. Some were know-it-alls, a few were sadists scrounging for some sick thrill, others simply friends and acquaintances seeking answers and solace. Many, however, were lawmen desperate for a lead. The APB had apparently stirred up every unsolved murder case in the country.

The calls poured in. Flagstaff, Nogales, Williams, Arizona. Sioux Falls, South Dakota. Virginia. Oklahoma City. Lakewood, Colorado. Henderson, Nevada. Santa Clara, San Bernadino, San Diego, Santa Paula and Salinas, California. Calls from private investigators and Missing Persons Bureaus, from big city police departments and one-man sheriff offices. Florida made the list. So did the NYPD. The Texas Rangers called from Lubbock. All had one thing in common. All had a murder in their town and no one to hang it on. All were hoping whoever did this, did theirs. A connection. A lead. That's all they wanted.

Unfortunately for those left to answer the phone at the sheriff's office, the deluge was overwhelming. The cops on the other end went nonstop about cases and victims and dates and possible suspects, pleading to have their call returned.

The harried switchboard staff scribbled as many notes as they could before the other lines started ringing. Still, they made promises they knew the department and its limited staff could not keep.

In addition to the inquires from other agencies, a steady stream of calls came in from concerned citizens offering help; suspicious people they had seen, odd circumstances near the market, unexplained coincidences last evening, and possible suspects capable of doing such an evil deed. Once again, notes were taken down quickly and passed along to field deputies for a follow up when time permitted. There was an outpouring of concern and rage from San Joaquin citizens, and it would only get worse very soon.

Then, of course, there was the media. As the story hit the nationwide crime wire, it found its way into every newspaper, press bureau, radio and television station in the country. Nine people found murdered in a rural farmhouse. Two of them kids. Now this was one helluva story! Everybody wanted in. So calls came in from every major news service and newspaper in the country. By nightfall the list would include *The New York, The Los Angeles*, even *The London Times*. CBS called, as did other networks, all leaving a special number they could be reached day or night. This was big! Absolutely huge! Just think of it, they declared, nine people killed! Stacked in a closet like firewood! Bigger, by God, than Manson himself!

When Arellanes made his call, he let it ring, got put on hold, got a voice, introduced himself and asked specifically for his San Joaquin counterpart.

"That would be Detective Ambrose and he's not in," came the reply. "In fact there's nobody here. They're all out on a big murder we've had."

"I know," Dave answered. "That's the reason I called."

Pause. "Ah, where did you say you were calling from?"

"Maricopa County."

"Ah. . .MariPOSA County?"

Dave was getting frustrated. "Mari-COPA County. . .Arizona. . .Phoenix, Arizona. Please! This is very important."

The next thing Dave heard was a dial tone. He came unglued. But he called back. Somehow he got a higher-up. He got right to the point, afraid he would be cut off. "Listen to me," he demanded. "Our department is holding murder warrants for two men, one who is from Lodi, and we have every reason to believe they were heading to your area. We think they're involved."

There was no response. Maintaining his patience, however difficult, Dave continued to explain the nature of their investigation and the crimes committed in their area, but it seemed like he was making no headway. Dave had the feeling that this guy either didn't believe him, or didn't want to. Arellanes could just picture this guy thinking he was some hick sheriff way out in the desert somewhere.

"Hey, tell you what," the voice came back. "Gimme your name and number and we'll call you back."

Dave did so, reluctantly, along with the other info asked for. He hung up and buried his head in his heads.

But a few minutes later his phone rang. It was San Joaquin County. "Tell this to me again," the voice requested. "Start from the beginning and tell me what you got."

The morning broke wet and depressing. A wave of storms had moved in off the Pacific overnight and had pummeled Northern California. While there was now a temporary break between downpours, the overcast skies were heavy and looked as if they could come right down and touch the earth. Suddenly his world felt much smaller. The wide-open euphoria of last night had vanished.

Willie stood on the 2nd floor walkway that ran the length of the motel and looked out over the pool area and the parking lot just beyond. By now most of the overnight guests were gone and only a few cars remained scattered about. He could just barely see the front of the Datsun sticking out from around the side of the motel. The air was damp and cool, cleansed from the rain and scented from the eucalyptus trees that bordered the motel and sheltered it from Highway 99. The morning commute was on and traffic was heavy. Willie couldn't see the cars speeding by, but he could hear the tires hiss on the wet pavement. The moist air felt good and he sucked it in. It would have been easy for him to feel sick. Natural, maybe, considering what had gone down last night. But he didn't. It happened, so what? Nothing he could do about it now. Except run. They had to run. It was time to hit the road, man. Time to run like all hell. He walked back inside.

"Come on, let's go," Willie ordered

Doug said nothing, just grabbed his coat and took a quick look around the room. Willie tossed some stuff into the suitcase, clicked it closed, and headed for the door. He switched off the television, tossed the room key on the dresser, took one last look around and closed the door. He pointed the way out of the motel lot and back on the highway north. Doug got up to speed and found a comfortable spot amongst the morning traffic racing into Sacramento. Willie screwed around with the radio, and while twisting the dial back and forth, heard something he didn't like. The weather report.

"A new storm has brought more rain into northern California and snow into the Sierras," the announcer reported. *"Overnight eight inches of new snow was on the ground at Truckee and the Highway Patrol tells us chains are required on Interstate Eighty this morning, as well as Highway Fifty into Tahoe. And get ready for more. Another system is expected late today or tonight and more snow is expected."*

Willie grumbled and cursed, taken back by the bad news. Doug didn't need to ask. He knew the weather had changed their plans. Willie had told him they needed to get into Nevada. "My people will back us up," he said, "but we gotta get to Reno." A flight to Mexico was waiting, he promised, but Reno was a couple of hours away, on the other side of the Sierra Nevada. Willie shook his head. "I don't want to get into that shit, man," he said

Doug's first reaction was that Bill was worried about driving in the snow. "That's no big deal," he offered. "Drivin' in snow don't bother me. Man, I've driven in damn whiteouts before."

"Ain't the snow!" Willie shot back. "There's gonna be a shitload of cops up there! Hell, there's always a goddamn army of CHP on the roads when you gotta chain up. No way! We're not goin' up there. Not today."

They had long since reached the south side of Sacramento. Highway 99 had turned into Interstate 80 and the Datsun was still heading towards the mountains. Doug said nothing. He figured Bill knew what he was doing and where they were going. Willie broke the silence with his decision. "We're gonna need to cool it for awhile. Couple of days maybe. Get off at the next exit."

The off ramp sign announced downtown Sacramento/Capital Mall and Doug did as he was told. Signs of last night's storm were everywhere. Leaves and branches covered the front lawns and sidewalks, while puddles of rainwater reflected the morning's platinum skies. The downtown was a maze of one-way streets and it required Doug's close attention. Willie guided him around like he knew right where he was, although Doug wasn't quite so sure. Within a few minutes Doug swore they were going in circles.

"In here!" Willie pointed into a multilevel parking garage and Doug wheeled up to the ticket booth. The attendant watched the car pull in and lectured the driver for coming in the wrong way, then directed them to the ramp that would lead to the third floor. Dark, hidden and remote. That was fine with Willie. They found a spot, grabbed the suitcase, locked the car and walked away.

It was referred to as the Weinstock Garage, after the large department store nearby, and everybody who shopped or worked downtown parked there. Standing on the corner of 8th and J streets, it overlooked the Downtown Mall, where a few years earlier, in an effort to combat the exodus to suburbia, the city closed off traffic on K Street and created an outdoor shopping plaza. For Willie and Doug it was Mecca. For the first time since they had met, money was no object. They had wads of it. Pockets full of it. Billfolds fat with it.

Willie insisted they first needed to change their look, but this time they would do it right. Clean up with some new clothes, a haircut, whatever it took to look more respectable. They started to window shop their way up the Mall, before finally entering a men's clothing store called The College Hi Shop.

Michael Palmer and his assistant manager had been open only a few minutes, and these were their first customers of the day. Palmer was in the storeroom and David Unger was behind the counter, so it was Unger who first noticed how dirty and shabby these two were. It was not uncommon for someone off the street to wander in, but College Hi catered to a more stylish breed of young male, and these two definitely were not of that caliber. Despite that, Unger greeted them with his usual friendly hello, although he knew they were more likely to swipe something than to buy it, so he kept an eye on them as they cruised the store and pulled items off the racks. Unger noticed that while one was very loud, the other was unusually quite. A little spaced out, as he saw it. The more vocal one was quick to show off the stuff he found, and didn't seem one bit concerned if everyone heard him or not. Finally, when both had picked out a shirt and pair of pants, Unger relaxed a little. The men walked up and placed their clothes on the counter, and it was then when Unger could not help but notice the one man's black eye. He tried not to stare.

"Figured it was about time I bought some new stuff," the guy barked. "I've been wearing these pants five years!"

With one look of the man's filthy jeans, Unger didn't know if he was kidding or not, but when the guy laughed, Unger cracked a smile too. Then, when both pulled out their wallets to pay, he was floored by the bankroll they carried.

A few minutes later at a beauty college down the street, both got their hair cut. Doug's long straggly hair, still brown from the dye, was neatly trimmed back to collar-length, while Willie's afro was taken down a notch by a student who gained a healthy tip, but had to endure a nonstop line of chatter to get it.

The Clunie Hotel stood a block away at the corner of 8th and K Street. Built around the turn of the century, it was a well-known downtown landmark, and during its glory years had housed a theater, a prestigious jewelry store, and even an opera house at one time. But now it housed mostly the down and out, and although it advertised itself as a "family hotel", few families would have been brave enough to walk in the front door, let alone spend the night there. So the Clunie was known less these days for its storied past than for the current cast of characters who called it home. If there was trouble downtown, the culprits often gave it as their address. In fact, the city and state used it as a halfway house for ex-cons finding it their first stop after release. A few businesses were still located on the ground floor, while upstairs, long hallways and small rooms were filled with people, who like the hotel itself, had seen better days.

Bill Reger was behind the counter this morning and watched as two men entered through the K Street side. During his years at the Clunie, Bill boasted that he had seen just about everything, and while he didn't necessarily judge people, he studied them a great deal. None of the people staying at the Clunie were special, and that included him, but even with that as his guide, these two seemed out of place. Reger couldn't quite put his finger on it – he told himself it would come to him later – but he watched them both cautiously as they approached his counter.

"Good morning," he offered, checking his watch to make sure he was correct. It was almost eleven. He was safe.

"Need a room for the two of us."

"Alrighty. Can do. How long you plan on staying?"

Willie had to stop to remember what day it was. He wanted to hang around until the weekend, hoping that would be long enough to let things die down a little. "I dunno. I guess about three days," he replied. "One room, three days."

Reger placed a registration slip and pen on the counter and recited the procedure. "Just fill this out please, and that'll be thirty-one fifty." He took another look at the two men. "In advance. You know, hotel rules."

Willie did as he was told, using 'Simen' as his name, then turned it to his partner who signed in as 'Doug Gretzler'. Reger handed them the key to room 319 and pointed the way upstairs. He paid little attention to the names, but he knew he never forget a face, especially one as beat up as guy who had just walked in.

Peter Saiers was the Deputy District Attorney on call when word came in about the murders in Victor, and noting the magnitude of the crime, Saiers was adamant his office be there during the initial investigation. The District Attorney, the Sheriff, and the Stockton Police for that matter, had always enjoyed a close working relationship, and Saiers was firm in his belief it was far better to enter a case from the very beginning, than days later when a pile of police reports had been tossed on a desk somewhere. He knew all of them from the sheriff's department anyway; Canlis, Pappy Wagner, Carl Ambrose, Kenneth Stewart, and the countless others who, by now, were certainly on the scene. So it wasn't that he doubted the integrity of their work, or questioned their professionalism, but with a case as big as this one, nothing could be left to chance. He not only wanted to be there. He *had* to be there.

From the moment he first learned of the murders, Saiers knew this one was something special, because Sheriff Canlis had immediately taken command of the investigation.Experience told him that Canlis did this only on high profile cases; ones with lots of media coverage. He was also well aware of Canlis' wide-open style with the press, and for all Peter knew the good sheriff was leading reporters on a first hand tour of the crime scene at this very minute.

He arrived at the Parkin home at 9:30, then got a quick review of the situation by the familiar faces in the front yard. To a man they forewarned him of what he would see inside. Saiers was worried about only one thing at this point; what Canlis was doing, but after spotting him wandering around inside the house, and seeing the mob of reporters being kept at a sizable distance outside, he relaxed a bit.

But his comfort was short lived. The carnage in the closet was by far the most staggering sight he had ever witnessed. It was not so much the visual condition of the victims, for he had more than once seen a body literally blown apart by the blast of a shotgun, but the overwhelming number of people lying twisted on the floor of that closet caused him to turn away, not once, but several times before he could regain his composure. The bodies, grotesquely intertwined, were bound together with rope and rags. Their mouths remained open, stiff and gaped wide by the neckties that had been neatly knotted behind their head. Neckties that had once been loud and brightly colored, but now were merely blood brown. Each was dressed in a pool of scarlet, their taut skin the color of waxed paper. Flies flitted about the bodies, their annoying buzz filling the tiny room. Nothing had been touched. Nothing moved. Saiers learned that the sheriff had requested two specialists be sent from the Department of Justice in Sacramento, and they were on their way to help coordinate the investigation. For now the focus would be on preserving the scene, and it was agreed that nothing more would be done inside the house until the crime scene specialists arrived.

Story had it, all Mike Canlis had to do was say 'yes', and the job as Director of the FBI was his. That was the story he told anyway, and he told it often. But Sheriff Canlis was so well liked, that if one of his deputies was sent to pick up a suspect in the smallest of towns, in the most remote corner of the country where the law is run by a mom and pop cop shop, the first thing they would ask the newcomer from Stockton was, "Hey, how's ol' Sheriff Canlis doin' these days, anyhow?"

Everyone knew Mike Canlis. Everyone. He was little more than a homegrown boy from the south side of Stockton, but he grew up to serve not only the Sheriff's Department for nearly four decades, but to be one of the most respected law enforcement officers in the nation. That's why his supporters claimed San

Joaquin was so damn lucky to have him. So instead of the FBI, Canlis accepted the post of president of the National Sheriff's Association and stayed in Stockton where he felt the most comfortable. "This is my home," he assured everyone, usually around reelection time. "This is where I belong."

And so on the surface everyone liked Mike Canlis, and that included most of the reporters who shadowed his every move. He was never shy in front of a camera or a recorder, always offering more than enough information necessary to write a good story. Many times the reporters knew more about what was going on than his own deputies did, which often led to a pissing match between the two sides. There was little doubt that early on Canlis understood the ever-important public perception of him and his office, because he was a god in San Joaquin, and his campaigns for reelection were seldom challenged.

So naturally, Canlis was one of the first to hear about Victor. On his way out of the office to the crime scene, he could be heard barking commands to those left in his wake. Canlis stayed in contact with the radio dispatcher as he drove north, but when he was gently reminded about keeping the frequency silent, he broke off communication.

Inspectors Ken Stewart and Carl Ambrose had been the first plainclothes officers to arrive. Deputy Levesey guided them to the walk-in closet, passing by the bed with the tiny bodies on their way. Ambrose knelt down amongst the victims in the closet. It was strictly habit that enabled him to touch each one of them, although his mind knew the answer before his fingers confirmed it. The closet was stuffy and hot, but the bodies were cold and rigid. He walked over to the bed and repeated the procedure on the two children. There was silence in the room as he moved about. Levesey sketched the configuration of the bodies as Ambrose fought for the words to clinically describe the horror of the scene. His first thought, and one that he kept to himself, was that after all these years as a cop, he had just borne witness to a massacre.

Inspector Stewart left for the United Market, having been informed of a possible robbery connection at the Parkin's store, while Sheriff Canlis stayed in the house, staying out of the way, demanding continuous updates on the details of the investigation. He told Ambrose he fully expected each officer assigned to the case to file written reports on every aspect of their work. Those reports were to be filed as often as needed to keep him informed. "I want to know everything," he demanded. "Absolutely everything."

When Jim Streeter and John Cockerham, the specialists from CII in Sacramento, arrived at 10:30, they made it clear they were there to collect ALL evidence. This was not going to be a collaborative effort. From here on out they would give the orders. Their first decision was that San Joaquin would process all prints; being determined gathering evidence for a crime of this magnitude in a home this size could take days, maybe even weeks to complete, time the two from Sacramento did not have to spare. Secondly, Officers Gurrola and Page from Technical Services were directed to take photographs, and Cockerham said they would start with the victims in the closet.

So it was in this order. Wally Parkin, being classified as victim #1, as Gurrola began photographing those on the closet floor and systematically went around the room. By the time he had finished with victim #9, Lisa Parkin, Gurrola had snapped over 70 black and white close-ups. When he was through in the closet and bedroom, he was pulled outside, where he continued shooting roll after roll.

With the crime scene properly preserved on film, Ambrose and Levesey felt a little more comfortable examining the bodies. They began by describing in intricate detail the style of their dress, the position of the bodies and the manner in which they were executed.

But it was at this point when someone came up with a revolutionary idea. Before any additional movements were made, before the bodies were disturbed any further, a decision was made to videotape the entire crime scene. Revolutionary for the simple fact that even the newsmen gathered out front were still using film to record their footage for the nightly broadcast. Videotape was still in its relative infancy and this was the first time anyone of the crime agencies, including CII from Sacramento, could recall using a video camera in an investigation. Peter Saiers was especially enthusiastic, firmly convinced that black and white photos could in no way capture the magnitude and horror of the crime. If and when his office went to trial on this, he wanted everyone to see the unbelievable savagery of the killings.

So as Gurrola manned the bulky camera, he also described the layout of the Parkin home. He walked down the long hallway and entered the master bedroom, then panned down on the bed to the children. Slowly he turned the corner and revealed the massacre in the closet. The bright floods bounced light off the walls, creating a surreal feel to the room. Like a rolling nightmare, the video could not help but magnify the ugliness of the work left by the killer.

The air outside the home had warmed only slightly in the three hours since Walters had arrived. The crowd, on the other hand, had exploded, and it appeared as if every cop and every reporter for a hundred miles milled about under these graveyard skies. It also seemed like the entire town of Victor was on hand, all standing about in the driveway, waiting, whispering. But for all who were outside, Walters' only concern was with the one man who remained inside. Dan wasn't going anywhere until Canlis left. The sheriff was a reporter's dream, and the first lesson Dan learned after coming to Stockton was to always wait for Canlis because the guy will write your story for you. It was just before noon when he spotted him coming out the front door, saddled by Ambrose and Detective Biancalana. When Canlis eyed the throng of newsmen milling about at the end of the driveway, he broke away from his two aides, then brushed aside the victim's friends and family members who had been languishing for hours. They had been totally ignored, their questions having gone unanswered by the silent treatment Canlis himself had ordered. Instead the Sheriff headed straight for the cluster of news people. Deputy Mello, who had been one of those forced into this uncomfortable silence, could only watch. He knew what his boss was about to do, and the very thought of it made him sick to his stomach.

Canlis' demeanor changed as he approached the media. His pace slowed and his shoulders slumped. His face appeared pained and shaken. He held his head low against his chest, staring down at the gravel as he walked the final few yards.

Stopping a few feet short of the group, he waited, then looked up, his signal for them to come gather around. "We have nine bodies in the house," he announced. "All nine victims have been shot in the head at close range – a professional job, in my opinion – the type of job usually done to destroy witnesses."

The reporters groaned, including Walters, whose heartbreak was in not having an exclusive earlier. Now it was all out. Everyone was equal. Everyone knew what he had known for hours. As the others pushed their pens across their pads, Walters watched the sheriff's face, hoping to discover that little something extra he was sure Canlis was hiding.

Mello listened too, wishing Canlis had done the right thing and talked to the families first. He could have eased their burden and lessened their pain, but not now. Now they were going to have to read about it in the newspaper or see it on TV. Something wasn't right when *their* sheriff, their very own goddamn sheriff, the man they elected a hundred times to serve them, ignored them, just so he could see his name in the paper for the umpteenth time. The whole thing made him sick.

"The scene is unreal," Canlis continued. "There is no disturbance in the house, yet here are all those bodies in the closet." He hesitated for a moment, as if searching for just the right words to describe he and only a handful of other had seen. He shook his head several times in disbelief, then stared straight ahead as he spoke.

"It is the work of a madman," he declared.

The *Sacramento Union* had been around since the Gold Rush. True to its creed, the slogan, "The Oldest Paper in the West" was bannered across the front page. While it may have been the oldest, it had been years since it had been the most stable. That honor belonged to its cross-town rival, the McClatchy owned *Sacramento Bee*. With the big money the McClatchy family could pour into the *Bee*, the *Union* was always scrambling to find clever ways to one-up the competition.

The *Union* was the morning paper while the *Bee* ran in the afternoon, so it was clear the *Bee* would dominate the news racks this afternoon with its late breaking story from Victor. In fact, most of their reporters left early, racing to beat the late morning deadline for Wednesday's edition, its editors now clearing front page space, holding it open for as long as they could to give their readers the very first grisly details from the murder scene. While it drove Dan crazy to get bested on a story this big, there was very little he could do about it. Sometimes stories fell his way in the late afternoon, allowing him to turn the tables, but this would not be one of them. So he tried looking beyond just the murders themselves, deciding for his story tomorrow that he would focus on two key questions. Why were these people killed? And more importantly, who killed them?

Walters headed straight to his Stockton office, just minutes behind Canlis, who before he left, had invited reporters to check in with him in a couple of hours, telling them he would have information on the case at that time. But Dan wasted no time and began typing his story for tomorrow's edition, holding his closing line open, hoping for something more when Canlis held his promised news conference later that afternoon. Peter Saiers left the Parkin's house with the others, following the sheriff back to Stockton, not only reeling from the horror he had witnessed, but cringing from Canlis' 'madman' reference as well. "Good heavens!" he thought to himself on the drive back. "We haven't even got the guy who did this to court yet and my own sheriff is giving him an insanity defense!"

But Michael Canlis understood the value of a good quote and close ties to the media. He knew which ones were in his stable and Dan Walters felt he was one of those who had the Sheriff's confidence. Although he had been covering Stockton for only a few months, it seemed as if Canlis had taken a liking to him. More than once he had given Dan the inside track on a pending case, while Walters, understanding fully the nature of a two way street, was quick to compliment Canlis and his staff whenever possible.

Before the afternoon was over, part of the story that Dan would send to press praised the sheriff about an investigation that would have crumpled lesser men.

> *Stockton – Sheriff Mike Canlis is the man in the middle of a nightmarish mass murder. But Canlis, whose law enforcement career stretches back nearly 35 years is taking it all in stride. He exudes confidence and crisp attention to detail as he commands the investigation of nine execution-style murders in a rural Lodi home the search for the killers, and the invasion of his domain by dozens of newsmen from throughout the west.*
>
> *His department is a model of spit and polish efficiency whose deputies appear in modish double knits and departmental blazers more often than hard hats.*
>
> *When Canlis issues orders in the San Joaquin Sheriff's office, they are obeyed with military-like speed.*

When Walters headed back to the Sheriff's office a few hours later, he found Canlis waiting for him.

Dave Arellanes had spent the last few hours trying his best to convince anyone in Stockton who would listen to him that he had a plan for catching the killers. "We're holding murder warrants for both suspects," he explained. "Steelman has family and acquaintances in the Lodi area. It was his home. We know he has been there in the past couple of weeks and we had a hunch he would be heading back there again."

Dave found himself rushing his words, racing the clock. He was certain the suspects could not have gotten far. "In my office is Sergeant Nelson from Sonoma County. He's been here working on a connecting case. Steelman and Gretzler have been in his area during the same time frame – it's a rape-kidnap apparently. In any event, Nelson is flying back home in a couple of hours. I'll send copies of the warrants and everything else we have with him. You have someone meet him at the plane in San Francisco and he'll have everything you need. I'll make sure to include a recent photo of Steelman. You run it on the news and in the paper, and I guarantee someone will recognize him."

Dave spit out orders like he was talking to a deputy in his own department. He did indeed have a plan to catch these guys and he was caught up in all the excitement going on hundreds of miles away. The voice on the other end of the line interrupted him. "San Francisco? Do you know how far the airport in San Francisco is from Stockton?!"

Dave stopped dead in his tracks. He couldn't believe it. He drops two weeks of hard work in this asshole's lap and the guy is worried about racking up mileage.

"Sergeant Nelson will be at the airport late this afternoon!" Arellanes barked. "He will have what you need."

The conversation was over.

Later, when Canlis got back to the office, he was told about the call from Arizona. He asked if there had been any action taken on the information supplied, and the answer was no. When Deputy Jim Allen came on shift at 12:30, he was ushered in to meet with the boss. Canlis told him there was a lead he wanted him to follow up on, but was no need to meet anyone in San Francisco. Instead, he told Allen to contact a Sergeant Colstad at the Sheriff's office in Sonoma County who would brief him on a kidnap and rape case they were working on against two guys named Steelman and Gretzler. Canlis gave no reason for the connection. Doing as he was told, Allen made the call to Colstad, who promised he would have Nelson get back to him the minute he came in. (When Nelson's plane landed in San Francisco later that day, there was no one from Stockton waiting, so he carried the packet from Arellanes with him to his office in Santa Rosa. It was almost five o'clock when he finally returned the call to Allen, who agreed to drive to Santa Rosa and meet with him the following morning at 8 am.)

The call from Phoenix had given Canlis a good idea. If the Arizona lead was correct, and he had no reason to think otherwise, then he could create his own story, his way. He told his deputy to go over to the County Probation Office and see if he could dig up anything on this Steelman guy. "And get a photo if they have one," he added.

So he did just that, inquiring about a Willie Luther Steelman. It was a toss up as to who was more surprised; Allen, or the probation officer he was talking to. The file on the man he was asking about sat right on the top of the stack. Apparently the San Joaquin County legal system was interested in this guy too – Judge Papas had signed a warrant for his arrest for violation of probation only yesterday. After being granted probation in July, their records showed Steelman made only one meeting and then disappeared.

It had taken well over three months for them to miss him, but finally, last Thursday, November 1st, county probation officer Jeff Kenyon went to the Machell's home in search of his client. It was the last address Steelman had given. When Willie's father-in-law admitted he hadn't seen him since August, and heard he had even left the state, Kenyon figured the worst. His last employer, the Vista Ray Hospital, had no contact with him for at least four months. After checking with the Lodi Police, he also found that a $1,000 traffic warrant had been issued as well.

Willie had been right, he was a wanted man, and on Tuesday Jeff Kenyon made it official. He got a warrant for the arrest of Willie Luther Steelman, and Jim Allen raced back to the office, carrying with him a booking photo of Willie Steelman taken from the file.

When Sheriff Canlis met with reporters, as promised, late Wednesday afternoon, he briefed them on the progress made by his men. In his news conference he announced, for the first time, the names of the suspects. "Gentlemen," Canlis announced. "Earlier this afternoon I called my friend Clarence Kelly at the FBI. I told him of our tragedy here and asked him if he had any similar cases that might help us with our investigation. Kelly informed us of two recent killings in the Phoenix, Arizona area that may be related. We are told one of the suspects is from the Lodi area."

Canlis passed out copies of the photo to the reporters. "This is one of the men we are looking for. His name is Willie Steelman." He never mentioned the phone call from Maricopa County. Not one word was uttered about their lengthy investigation or the murder warrants they had issued earlier that morning in Arizona.

All afternoon, Arellanes had communicated with San Joaquin, answering a barrage of questions as fast as he could. The teletype clattered away at a feverous pitch and the phone rang constantly. Dave was confident his hard work was about to pay off, and despite the self-criticism earlier, he was now proud to be the critical part of the ongoing investigation. The arrest was imminent, he was positive of that, and he and his team would be the reason. But the name Dave Arellanes was not mentioned. As far as Canlis and his staff were concerned, this whole thing was all the Sheriff's grand idea.

Walters, photo in hand, hurried back to his office and put the finishing touches on the story. His teletype operator then began the tedious process of sending it northward over the wire. While the words arrived in Sacramento almost instantly, the photo of the murder suspect would take longer. Willie had to ride the bus. It had long been standard practice to send photos, sketches or artwork by late afternoon Greyhound, still the most practical, not to mention the least expensive way, to get it north. At first the photo did not seem overly significant. It was a plus, certainly, because the *Union* would be the first newspaper to publish a picture of one of the murder suspects. They would beat the *Bee*, and that was the best part. Surprisingly, even Walters gave no particular importance to the photo of the bushy headed man with the surprised look on his face, thinking of it merely as fill. He didn't even suggest to his editors, as was his custom, how they might best use it, he just told them it was coming. At the top of his story, now being fed over the wire, he typed his advisory for them to send someone down to the bus station to pick up the photo. It read: *11-7-73 Stockton Murder with pics on bus*.

At the *Union* office in Sacramento, copywriters and editors awaited the words from their man down south. When the photo arrived later, they made a quick decision on where to place it. It proved to be the most important move anyone could have made.

Willie and Doug's universe had become the few blocks surrounding the Clunie Hotel. They hung around the room just long enough to change their clothes and clean up, both anxious to get back on the street to throw around some of their new found riches. Willie had been telling Doug about this great place to eat just around the corner from the hotel. Doug thought that was a little odd because he never seemed to care much about food. It was like he was showing off when he went on and on about 'these fuckin' great steaks'.

They found the restaurant and ordered. It was clear they were hot now, as radios and televisions blurted news about the murders, and about the huge manhunt underway to find who was responsible. Doug could hear people in the restaurant talking about it, and he caught himself trying to listen in, eves-dropping on their conversation like some kind of snoopy bystander. Occasionally something was said and Doug took the news like everyone else, surprised to hear about things he didn't even know about. Is that true? He asked himself. Did all that really happen? Did I do that? None of which seemed possible. It was all just too weird, he thought – the whole thing – like someone else was to blame. The consequences had not sunk in yet. The TV made it sound like every cop in the world was looking for them. How could that be? Here they were, sitting right out in the middle of a damn restaurant, surrounded by a bunch of people, and they couldn't find him? He wanted to scream out, "Here we are!" He had this sudden urge to tell everyone who he was. "If you guys are so smart, just walk over and get this whole damn thing over with!"

It was all too strange. Funny and sad at the same time. He knew right then, sitting in that restaurant, that his life was over. It didn't bother him. Bill had a plan. He wasn't scared. Not one bit. Still, he fought off twinges of remorse, slashing seconds of hating himself for what he had done – all he had done – especially what he had done to Ken and Mike, and for some stupid sick reason that that still ate at him. Even more than what had happened last night. Christ! He was still pissed at himself about Ken and Mike. But it was over, so be it. Nothing he could do about it now. All he really had to worry about now was how they were going to fix his steak.

While they waited for their food, Willie started talking about what they were going to do next. Next, as in like running for their very lives, and next, as in what clubs they were going to go to that night.

The restaurant had a big lunchtime crowd, and they had been sitting for quite some time, before they realized that they were surrounded by cops. There were a few uniforms that Doug could see, but mostly plainclothes cops. There was no doubt, they were in a sea of pigs, as Willie laughed later. But however many there were, he smiled and said it was just his luck to pick a place that was hosting some kind of police luncheon. While their first reaction was to get up quietly and get the hell out of there, Willie found his composure and cockiness, and convinced Doug that if these dumbfucks had any clue who was sitting at the table next to them, they would have opened fire a long time ago. No, the cops were there for the same reason they were. The were hungry.

So they decided to wait it out. Hang loose, finish their meal, then casually get up and leave. Stay cool, Willie said. They were safe as long as these guys next to them were content on feeding their faces, telling stupid jokes, and ignoring everyone else. Willie actually enjoyed the company. There was a certain twisted justice in being one of the most wanted men in America, and be having a nice leisurely meal right in the middle of a fucking police convention. He looked at Doug and laughed. They're so stupid, he said, we ain't got shit to worry about. So they relaxed and had a good time with it, although Doug had to remind Willie about the .38 shoved in his waistband. Every time he reached across the table, his coat would open up and reveal the handgun. But even that was funny, they decided.

Back out on the street, and strutting a bit from their amazing good fortune, Willie walked Doug around the corner to the Happy House Massage Parlor. Doug had confided earlier that he had never had a massage, so this was Willie's treat.

Since everything she did was by the clock, Melinda checked it automatically as the two men entered the room. It was 1:30 when she greeted the pair. "Hi. How you guys doin'?"

"We're doin' alright," Willie announced. "How 'bout you?"

"Great! Massage, guys?"

"Yeah. I think we will."

The two men reeked of Hi Karate aftershave, and both were cleanly dressed. Melinda always checked out the new customers first for tip potential. These guys weren't rich businessmen, that's for sure. Maybe worth five apiece, tops. Just like a thousand other 'judys' off the street. "Well, it's nineteen-fifty each," she said.

Melinda motioned to her partner to help her out as Willie reached for his roll of money. He handed her two twenties. "Hey ah, ah..."

"Melinda. It's Melinda"

"Do you like counting money, Melinda?"

"Ah, I guess. Sure."

"Well Melinda, I'm Willie, and this here is Doug." He showed her the huge wad of bills he had pulled from his coat pocket. He handed it to her. "Why doncha help me out and count this."

The large roll of cash floored her, quickly calculating what she would have to do to get some of it. Again, at Willie's urging, she began peeling off bills, counting twenty dollars at a time. She got to more than nine hundred, then quit. "That's a lot of money," she gushed, handing it back. Willie just smiled.

While Doug was in the other room with some girl named Kay, Melinda took extra good care of her client. Willie did most of the talking, adding he always had lots of cash because of the work he was in. He was the manager of a rock group named "Mountain", he said, and that his friend Doug was the drummer. "Personally signed a few people myself," he bragged. "You know James Taylor? I signed him."

Melinda feigned interest. "Wow. Trippy."

Willie said they were on the road a lot and were heading back to a gig in Arizona. Where he really wanted to go was to Mexico. "Love it where it's warm," he confided. "Don't like the rain at all."

When Melinda was finished, which was almost two hours later, Willie got dressed, handed her a $20 tip, and asked her if he could see her again. He told her several times about a call he had to make to someone around eighty thirty that night, although she didn't quite understand what that had to do with her. All she could think about was the money he had wadded up in his pocket. She gave him her address. Stop by if you're in the area, she said.

It was early afternoon. More than six hours had passed since Carol opened that door to the master bedroom, and now she was nowhere to be found. However, with the many people who had remained, their worst fears were coming true. It had not been officially confirmed, but they knew. They knew who was inside the house. And they knew it was bad. Although the Sheriff's Department still refused to release the names of the victims, they knew. Family members viewed this silence as arrogance, and more than one shouting match could be overheard as the hours, the frustration and the crushing sense of loss wore on.

Sharon Lang had arrived earlier that morning after another brother heard on the radio about what was going on in Victor. He did not know how to tell Sharon about Mark, but he knew she would want to be there. Sharon quizzed him constantly as to what was so important, so he finally told her, as carefully as he could, that Mark might be in trouble. Now she was left standing with all the others, for hours on end, in the muddy yard. Weary and overcome with the grief of the obvious, she finally confronted a deputy, demanding, pleading, begging for him to tell her if one of those inside was Mark Lang. She was nearly hysterical, drowning helplessly in her fear and sorrow, crying for someone, anyone, to please tell her what was going on. Tired of her relentless ranting, his own nerves severed by what he had seen inside and the emotions that consumed the yard, the officer snapped. He turned around and shoved his face directly into hers. "Get your crying ass off the driveway!" he screamed. "This is no place for a woman."

Wanda Earl's brother, Carl Cummings, was there too, arriving shortly after the first emergency crew did. He too was defeated from the wait, and yet determined to stick this out to the very end. When one of the plainclothes officers approached him and asked if he would be able to identify members of the Earl family, his worst fears were confirmed. Even then he would have to endure several more hours, standing, pacing the perimeter of the police line, waiting for the end he was certain would come.

Officer Hellyer, a Highway Patrol officer and a friend of the Parkin family, had heard the reports over the radio that morning and arrived at their home immediately. He was one of many who counted Wally and Joanne as close friends, and it was just last Saturday night when he had gone out to dinner with them to help celebrate Joanne's 33rd birthday. Although he was privy to more information than the others standing outside, he kept it to himself. When he was asked if he could help identify the Parkins, he agreed, consoling himself in the realization that this would be his final act as their friend.

At 2:15, the Lodi Funeral Home, who also been kept waiting for several hours, were advised to begin preparations to remove the bodies. They had worked crime scenes many times before, but never one with this many victims. The only requirement made by the sheriff's department was, due to the nature of the investigation, each body would need to be removed and taken to Stockton separately. They had brought several vehicles to perform this task, although this was far from a normal undertaking. At first they had no idea how they would transport nine victims to Stockton for the scheduled autopsies, so they had arrived earlier with every hearse they could find, plus a few borrowed station wagons for good measure. They even brought along a truck with a camper shell, just to be safe. Eventually Hellyer was brought in to first identify the two children. Then, only minutes later, Carl Cummings struggled as he looked at his sister and her family, telling officers he was certain they were the bodies of Richard, Wanda, Debbie and Ricky Earl. Hellyer again stepped forward and identified his friends, Wally and Joanne, after which Michael Lang was called in to identify his brother.

As the bodies were moved for the first time, Gurrola continued to photograph the activities. One by one the victims were placed on stretchers and wheeled down the hallway to the front door. The neckties gags were left in place and their wrists remained bound behind them. Only the rope that wrapped their ankles had been removed in order to separate the victims. A blanket bearing the mortuary's name was draped over each as they made the journey out to daylight and the awaiting hearse.

A reporter for the Stockton Record, Bill Cook, had stood watch out front all day, determined to witness this final act. But it was soon clear he was not prepared for the unbearable agony it created.

By way of his mobile radio, Cook broadcast this grueling episode back to the office, where his associate at the paper, court reporter Hugh Wright, listened as a very distraught newsman tried to find the words to describe what was taking place at the Parkin home. Stunned by what he was hearing, Wright knew he would never forget Cook's torturous account of that slate gray afternoon.

"Here comes a gurney," the voice relayed. "Three men are wheeling it out the front door. They are loading it into the hearse."

"And here comes another one..." Silence.

"Oh my...another!"

The voice cracked, "Oh good Lord! Another..."

Cook continued, his voice choking more with each announcement. He knew beforehand how many were inside. He knew the number was nine. He just wasn't ready for the extent of despair that came along with witnessing it firsthand.

"Oh, Dear God!" he sighed, his voice barely audible. "Oh Dear Jesus...they just keep coming!"

The removal of the nine murder victims took over an hour to complete.

And Bob Cook stayed until the very end.

Willie and Doug walked the downtown streets with little concern of being recognized. Willie couldn't be sure the cops even knew who to be looking for. How could they? There wasn't anyone left in that house to finger him, that much he was sure of. No way they had a name, let alone, a place to start looking. Or maybe they did. He didn't know. Maybe Duff talked. Yeah, it was Duff. Never could never trust that little bastard. Or maybe he left something at the house.

Maybe someone saw him around town. He didn't know. He was paranoid. Speed was the usual culprit, but now even that was gone. There was some grass and a few pills left, but nothing good. He needed something good. It wasn't that he was worried about scoring – not with the money he had, shit he could get some really good stuff – but he was in unfamiliar territory and had no idea who to call. Who could he trust, anyway. No one, that's who. So he waited, left to coast through the afternoon until the right deal came along. He alternated between extreme suspicion of everyone, and a fuck-it attitude about everything.

At Joe's Style Shop, a men's store hidden in the middle of J Street, a block away, Willie went in to buy the new leather jacket he had long promised himself. When the owner, Joe Faraci, a small Italian man with a loud, jet-black hairpiece, fitted his latest customer, he was certain he patted down a handgun tucked inside the man's shirt. As long as the guy didn't try and use it on him, Faraci wasn't worried. He had plenty of regulars who were packing. In this neighborhood you would be fool if you didn't, was how he saw it. Hell, he had so many guns shoved in his face over the years, he even thought about carrying one himself. Would have too, if it didn't make his tailored sport coats bulge. Bad for business, he decided, for the owner of a clothing store to look so ill fitted.

So Willie handed over $132.50 and tossed his old jacket to Doug. Joe was a little surprised to see the money and not the gun. He had grown to distrust anyone he didn't know on a first name basis. His initial reaction to a new face was that they were there just to case the place, then they would come back later to rob him. So he was a little edgy about these two. The one guy, the one who bought the jacket, couldn't stop talking for a minute, but his friend never said a word. Not even a thank you when the other guy tossed him the old jacket. Quite a pair, he thought.

Oh, they'll be back, Joe decided. Later tonight about closing time they'll show up to get their money back. He had already decided to put his little .22 under the counter, just in case. As the two turned to leave, the man with the brand new jacket turned around one last time. "Any of these cars out front belong to you?" he asked.

The shiny blue Lincoln Continental parked at the curb was Joe's pride and joy, and he wasn't about to give it up. "No," Faraci replied. "I walk to work. It's good for you."

The stranger turned and disappeared out the door.

Shit, Joe thought, their going to come back tonight and get my money, AND my car. The pricks!

At a music store around the corner, Doug bought a new Gibson twelve-string guitar, and a harmonica to go with it, making sure he got a receipt in case it didn't feel right later. It had been a chilly day, and it was getting dark, so they headed back to their room. But first Willie decided they better take care of the car. They had left it in an hourly space and all they needed now was for the attendant to have it towed away. They walked back over to the garage and made arrangements to leave it overnight. Doug was impressed Bill was still so on top of things. He would have never thought about the car.

When they got back to the hotel lobby, Willie spotted a newspaper rack. He slid a dime into the slot and pulled out a copy of the afternoon *Bee*.

NINE ARE SHOT TO DEATH IN LODI, BURGLARY LINK IS CITED. Underneath the bold headline was a photo of the Parkin home surrounded by cops and cars.

In the elevator, on the way up to their third floor room, Willie got real quiet for the first time that day. Their run was about over. He could feel it. The shit was about to hit the fan. He had to think. He glanced through the paper, tossed it on the dresser and slumped down on the edge of the bed, making sure that Doug could not see the defeat he felt closing in around him.

By the time Willie and Doug got back to the room, Walter Cronkite was breaking the news to the nation of what they had done. Another mass murder, he announced in his trademark sober style, this one discovered earlier today in a modern farmhouse in central California. Superimposed on the screen next to him was a crude map showing the general location of the rural town of Victor. Cronkite gave only the basics of the crime before turning it over to the CBS affiliate in Sacramento for the latest update. Indeed, the networks knew very little of this story, and therefore clamored for details, pleading with their local stations to send whatever film they could gather. The stations in Sacramento and Stockton covered the murders on their evening news, but surprisingly not even one mentioned the name, let alone the photo of the lead suspect Sheriff Canlis had released earlier at his press conference.

However, radio stations throughout the San Joaquin valley, from Sacramento to Bakersfield, continued to cover the story in depth, including the most recent information that an extensive manhunt was now underway to locate a man now known as Willie Steelman. Because of that, up and down the state, doors were bolted, windows latched tight, and in many homes, the nightstand pistols were double-checked just to be safe. The people in California were justifiably frightened; a madmen was on the loose, and no one had any idea where he might strike next. A woman interviewed on the radio spoke for many when she said, "This whole thing is crazy. There's no rhyme or reason to any of this. I don't really know what to do. I don't know how to protect myself from crazy people."

Back in Lodi, Willie's onetime friend and roommate, Kathy Stone, double locked her front door after catching the news that it was Willie they were looking for. Around 7 pm, her new husband answered the phone and the voice on the other end asked to speak to Kathy. Not knowing about anyone named Steelman, let alone the relationship his wife had with him years earlier, he could not understand why she flipped out when he said the caller identified himself only as 'Bill'.

Kathy covered her mouth and gasped. Shaking her head, she made it clear she was not coming to the phone. She remembered that look in his eye. How did he find her? Bill was scary like that. He had a knack of sneaking up on people and just plain scaring the holy shit of them. How did he get her number? What did he want with her? Her bewildered husband could only watch as she threw clothes into a suitcase and rattled off endless excuses why she could not stay in Lodi until the killer was captured and behind bars.

"I'll be staying with family," she told him, but never saying where, or with who that would be. She left, and even her husband had no idca where to find her.

She remembered how Bill used to tell her about never having a family he could count on, and how she was she was his family now, and that families had to stick together. Well she didn't want to be his family. She didn't want to be anywhere near Bill Steelman tonight.

And then there were those who were not scared, but outraged. In the close-knit communities of Lodi and Victor, vengeance was now considered an option, if not a right. Of course there was no one in custody, and little reason to believe the killer would be captured anytime soon, so their self-imposed justice would have to wait. Many were resigned to the fact that they were probably long gone by now. Ruthless and cold yes, but not stupid enough to stick around a place that would shoot them on sight if given half a chance. Talk about what the town would do to them, if and when they were caught, flowed freely over dinner tables and telephone lines. As it had been for decades, at the very center of such conversations was the fact that California still had no death penalty. Like many other states, it had been struck down by the United States Supreme Court, who then required the states to rewrite the law to conform to their changing guidelines. After much wrangling in the State Senate, a new capital punishment law was approved last August, but it would not go into effect until January 1st, 54 days from now. To the citizens of Lodi, the families and friends of the Parkin, the Earls and young Mark Lang, there would be no true justice. No real punishment. Not the kind of punishment they deserved. Certainly not with the legal system California had.

By order of Sheriff Canlis, deputies guarded the homes of all the victim's families as they returned home from the murder scene, and as they gathered to comfort themselves. Deputy Michael Clark was placed at the senior Parkin residence and paid little attention as a fellow deputy entered the house. Clark looked at the face of his colleague. It looked like he had been crying, but at the same time, seemed flush with anger. It had certainly been a difficult day on everyone in the department, but this guy seemed overly worked up, if not downright angry. Nothing made sense to Clark until he learned that the man was Douglas Pasco, a Deputy Marshall with the Lodi Municipal Court, and more importantly, a cousin of Wally Parkin. Pasco emerged from the house several minutes later and stopped to talk about the murders with him. He got even more agitated as he spoke. "I'm just waiting for them to bring them sonsabitches into my court and I'll take situation myself!"

Clark could understand, even sympathize, but nevertheless he felt compelled to report the incident to his supervisor later that night. But Pasco had suddenly disappeared. He called in sick the next morning, offering nothing as to his whereabouts, or about if and when he might return. Although the department made every attempt to talk to him about his comments, they were unsuccessful, and members of the Parkin family admitted he was very sincere about his threats.

It was a wake up call for Canlis and his staff. If it had not been a consideration before, it was now clear security would be a huge problem if Steelman and his partner were captured anywhere near San Joaquin County. Well into Wednesday evening, he and members of his staff discussed what steps would need to be taken to protect the suspects in that event. There had never been a case of this size. They searched for written procedures that might already be on file, but found nothing.

So they began drafting their own memos, preparing for the moment, hopefully soon, when they had the killers in custody. This action seemed most appropriate. Especially when the very first threats had come from within their own ranks.

After being cooped up in their hotel room for over an hour, Willie announced he wanted to hit some clubs and listen to some music. They tried a few places Willie suggested but the nightlife on a Wednesday night in Sacramento left much to be desired. After a couple of drinks in a few very quiet bars, Willie gave up. He told the cabbie to take them to an address on 29th Street, but even that turned out a bust. Melinda Kashula was not home.

Once more back in the room, Doug toyed with his new guitar while Willie played around with the .38 revolver. By ten o'clock Doug had crashed out and was sleeping like a baby. Willie stayed up, still thinking about tomorrow.

As night came, there was very little new information released to the media, so the newsmen waited, their vans circled around the courthouse in Stockton. They huddled and sipped hot coffee as the cold November air lapped around them. The local television stations, as well as those in Oakland and San Francisco, made plans to lead their late evening news with the complete coverage of the killings, so they had held back their story until the very last minute, hoping that something new about the manhunt would come from the Sheriff's Office.

But there was nothing, so they ran footage taken earlier of the house, the United Market, and tearful comments from a devastated community. There was little said about either suspect, although it was mentioned authorities were seeking a former resident of Lodi by the name of Willie Steelman. On the surface at least, Dave Arellanes' suggestion to have Steelman's name and picture plastered across the news had been totally and purposely ignored.

Like the news people covering the story, Deputy Mello's day was far from over either. After being at the Parkin home for over eight hours, he was told to follow the bodies back to Stockton and help with the autopsy. His reports were generated mainly from the photographs, however other information still needed to be gathered on each of the victims, including next of kin, which in this case was difficult. Mello struggled to find out who could be listed, noting to his supervisors that two entire families had been wiped out. He described how each body was found, the position it was in when discovered, and the type of clothing each was wearing. Studying the photos carefully, he first described the head wounds, nothing they had been caused by an "unknown caliber weapon". Nine times he filled out such a form. Mello would not leave the morgue until early Thursday morning.

The autopsies had begun at 5:30 p.m., after a brief delay when it was discovered that Mike Lang had incorrectly identified Richard Earl as being his brother, Mark. In the emotion and confusion inside the house on Orchard Road, the funeral home had two bodies tagged with the same name. If it had not been gut wrenching enough for him the first time, Lang was brought back in to view his brother's body. With the mistake corrected, the remains of Mark Lang were the first to be examined.

Each autopsy began by describing the decedent's physical features, including age, height and weight. In this case, the examiner made note of the bindings that remained on the body, and the visible head injuries. Other than the obvious gunshot wounds, no other lacerations were noted. Nor were there any signs of struggle, such as bruises or contusions normally associated with a fight, or physical resistance by the victim. From there, with Jim Streeter assisting, individual wounds were traced, marking the entry and exit of each by placing a pencil into the opening to indicate the bullet's trajectory. With each demonstration, the camera clicked to record the finding, because the next procedure would obliterate it forever. The top of the skull was removed, the brain examined, weighed and photographed. When they were uncovered, slugs were removed, bagged and marked for identification.

From there, the body cavity was opened and the organs examined. With just one exception, everything appeared normal. During the autopsy of Debbie Earl, an exit wound was discovered near the collarbone, yet there was no matching hole found in her sweater. After the body was opened, a large amount of blood was found in the chest, and the doctor, noting the unusual, continued to search for the source. At first he surmised that Debbie might have been shot before the others, and therefore internal bleeding had most likely caused her death.

But he eventually found the culprit. A bullet that had gone undetected, had entered the base of her skull, ricocheted off a bone and pierced her lung, after which it exited just below the collarbone, creating the mysterious wound. If it had been the only bullet (Debbie's skull indicated she was shot four times) it alone was enough to have been fatal, the doctor noted. One after one, the bodies were rolled in and dissected. Each autopsy took anywhere from ninety minutes to slightly over two hours. The doctor, Streeter, and their assistants would take a quick five minute break between bodies, step outside for a cup of coffee and a smoke, then go back in and start all over again. After the first four, which was now well after midnight, the doctor began to lose his voice. The nonstop dictation into the recorder and a continuous monotone of medical chatter had taken its toll. He began sucking on Life Savers, hoping they would allow him to get through the next five.

As difficult as it was, especially with the two small children, he continued to view each as patients. With each exam, his first remarks into the tape recorder were to recognize them by name, as if politely introducing them to his small circle of friends. Wednesday became Thursday, and the autopsies continued.

He didn't know why he was staring at television late that night – it was something he seldom did – but as he watched the lead story on the late night news, a chill came over him. Mike Jackson looked over at his girlfriend and blurted out. "Jesus Christ! I think I know who did this!" He called the Sheriff's office and asked for the only guy he knew down there, the cop who had hassled him a hundred times, an asshole by the name of Barbieri.

Detective John Barbieri had helped Duff Nunley on a minor beef a year or so back, and it was only his good word that kept Nunley out of the joint. So Nunley, along with his friend Jackson, returned the favor by snitching to Barbieri about some of the petty stuff going on around Galt. They had become his informants.

By Barbieri's book, Nunley and Jackson were nothing more than a couple of punks, but in some twisted sort of way, he took a liking to the two guys. They had gotten pinched doing some of the most stupid shit stunts he had ever heard of, but they weren't really bad kids, or even dangerous, just dumb. For some reason he couldn't explain, Barbieri kind of felt sorry for them, and soon found himself going out of his way to look out for these two whenever the occasion arose.

Barbieri was forever pissing him off, but Jackson still trusted him. The news on TV didn't say who the police were looking for, and Jackson certainly didn't know Steelman as well as Duff did, but he was positive Steelman and the other guy in the car had something to do with it. He didn't even bother to call Duff, he went straight to Barbieri.

It was ten minutes to midnight when the office finally tracked down the detective who was still going full tilt on the investigation. Not only did the caller say that he knew who had killed all those people, dispatch told Barbieri, but he had been with them yesterday afternoon and said that he might even know where they were right now. "They said they were going to pick up four or five grand," Jackson told Barbieri after the detective had called him back. "Then they were heading down to Mexico."

Barbieri had spent most of the day out at the house on Orchard Road, and like all the others who had witnessed the aftermath of the crime committed there, the picture of that bedroom and closet would haunt him forever. But the crime scene itself was not his department – he left that for Ambrose and the others – his job was to track down the few clues found at the house. By 5 pm it was official. The San Joaquin County Sheriff wanted to talk to Willie Steelman and Douglas Gretzler.

So Barbeiri spent the balance of Wednesday trying to find anyone who had ever known Willie. He also exhausted their files hoping to get something on this Gretzler character, but came up empty. He did find the names of a few of Steelman's old associates, and he got some help from other deputies to follow up on them to see if anyone had seen Willie lately. None could offer much help. The magnitude of the killings, especially the two kids, shocked all of Lodi, and even those who Willie might have been considered a friend at one time, would have quickly turned him in, if they only knew where he might be.

So Barbieri had came up short. Then he got the message Mike Jackson wanted to talk to him. Jackson confirmed what the Arizona authorities said; Steelman had been in the area.

Barbieri called him back. He knew immediately Jackson was being on the level with him. He had no reason to lie, and actually sounded frightened by what he knew; fearful, it seemed, of what Steelman might do if he found out who snitched on him. Barbieri told Jackson to stay put, he would be right over.

It was a twenty-minute drive to Galt. It took another couple of hours for Jackson to tell Barbieri about he and Duff spent yesterday afternoon hanging around with Steelman and a guy from New York named Doug. He described the car they were in, the gun Willie had, the knife on Doug's belt, even the two suspects themselves. He told Barbieri that Steelman bragged several times about getting 'four or five grand' that night from someone in Lodi, then going to Mexico.

While the two talked, Nunley called and Barbieri got the same story out of him. Duff sounded afraid too and blurted out that he 'was going to stay up all night, just in case'. Barbieri pulled out a picture of Steelman and showed it to Jackson. He didn't hesitate. That was the guy. He was sure of it. Barbieri stopped by his house, got a shower and a shave, then returned to the office, pulling in around four Thursday morning. He knew now that the call from Arizona had been right on. He went right for the typewriter in the communications room and updated their earlier alert.

> *APB NATIONWIDE 1110873 0415 PST SPECIAL ATTN MARICOPA COUNTY. S/O ATTN: ALL HOMICIDE DETAILS*
> *Supplemental info to APB LTS 002 & 003 Nationwide Suspects:*
> *1. Willie Luther Steelman, WMA-28, DOB 3-20-45 6 ft., 140, Brown 4 inch Afro, Brown eyes.*
> *2. Douglas E. Gretzler, WMA DOB 5-21-51, 6 ft., 140, Blnd hair, Blue eyes.*
> *Suspects observed this county in area of Galt, Calif. on 11-6-73 at 1220 hours and 11-7-73 at 1200 hours. Suspect vehicle: A 1970-1973 Datsun 2 door sedan, cream color. Black interior and black tires with Arizona Plates Refer reply Detective Barbieri File 73-27315*

With the updated APB, including the important vehicle info now in the hands of every cop in the country, Barbieri could only sit back and wait for someone somewhere to cross their path. He found his coffee cup and decided to hang around the teletype, hoping for a quick reply. If it didn't come soon, he knew he would be in for another long day.

It was about this time, before morning light dawned a new day, when drivers for *The Sacramento Union* wheeled their delivery trucks out of the downtown printing plant and headed to the neighborhood drops. There they would meet the carriers who would pick up the morning edition of the paper.

Less than a mile from the *Union* office, the carrier responsible for the downtown route entered the Clunie Hotel. The lobby was dark and quite. Even the desk clerk, who was usually head down on the desk at this hour, wasn't in his usual spot. The carrier looked through the full glass doors that led into the Clunie coffee shop. The restaurant was just coming to life in the early morning.

He took his key and opened the *Union* rack, tossing a bundle of papers inside. He pulled one off the top and placed it in the display window of the machine, reading the headline yet another time.

LODI SLAUGHTER!

But for some reason this time he could not help but stare. His eyes remained fixed. Not only at the large bold type of the staggering headline, but at the unsettling picture of the man the police said they were now looking for.

2 Suspects Sought

Lodi Slaughter

Willie Luther Steelman

Robbery Motive In Nine Murders

By DAN WALTERS
Staff Writer

The Sacramento Union

Oldest Daily In the West

Thursday, November 8, 1973

10¢

STREET EDITION

Robert Parkin

Lisa Parkin

Ricky Earl

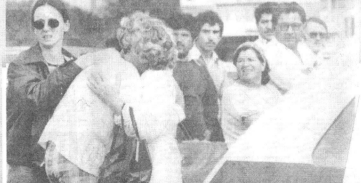

The Thursday morning edition of the Sacramento Union as it showed in the newspaper rack at the Clune Hotel. After hotel clerk Bill Reger spotted Willie and Doug coming downstairs, then noticed the picture of Willie Steelman on the front page, his suspicions were confirmed and he called the police.

Photo courtesy Special Collections Department, UC Davis

Richard, Debbie, Wanda and Ricky Earl 1972

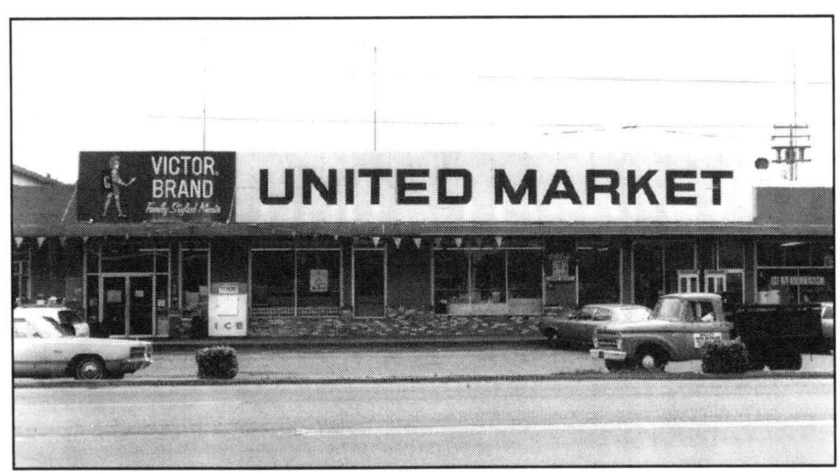

The United Market in Victor owned by Wally and Joanne Parkin.

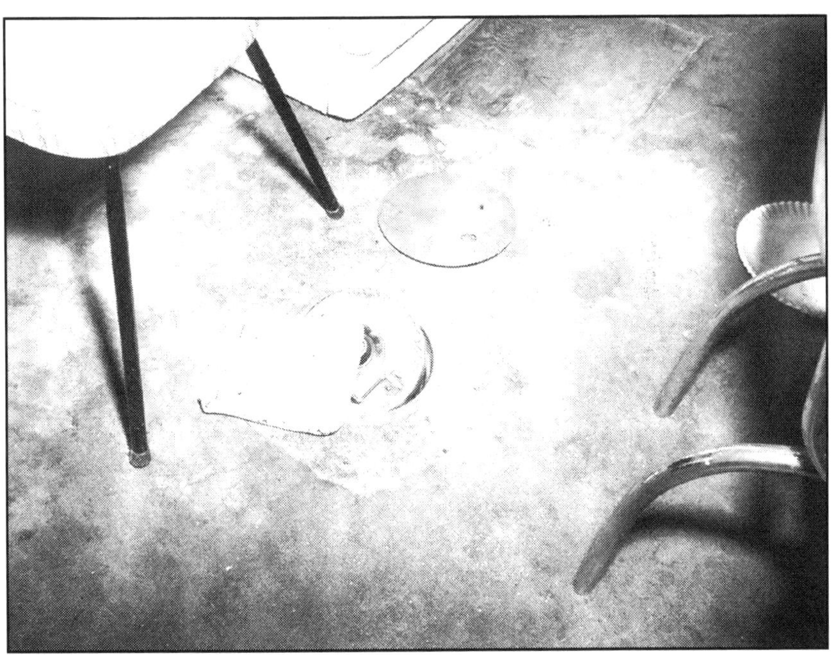
The floor safe in the back storeroom of the market as it was discovered by San Joaquin Sheriff Detectives.

Photos courtesy Special Collections Department, UC Davis

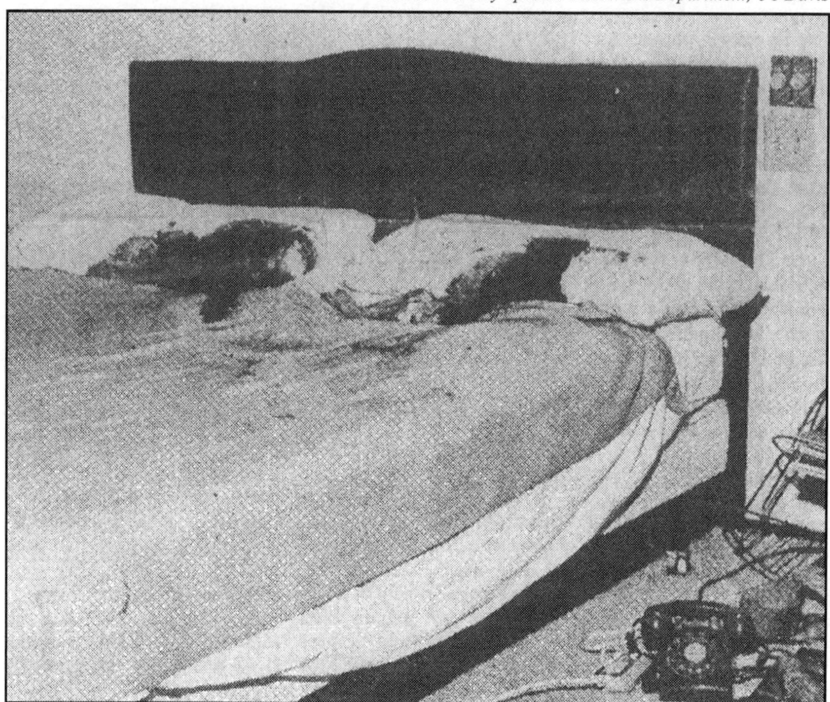

The children's bed.

Lisa Parkin

Bobby Parkin

The Parkin's home in Victor. Mark Lang's Chevrolet Impala is in the foreground.

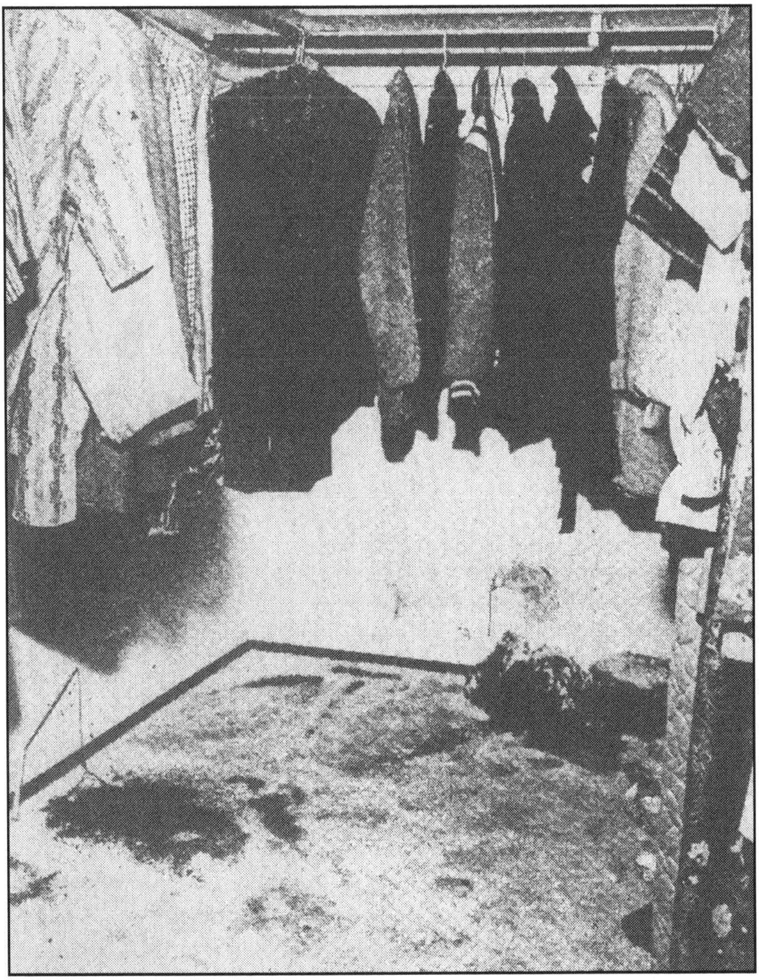

Photo courtesy Special Collections Department, UC Davis

The closet where the bodies were found.

Sheriff Michael Canlis meets with reporters after touring the Parkin home in Victor. "The work of a madman," was how he described the murder scene inside.

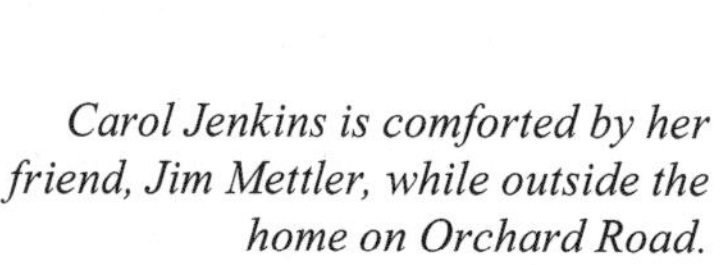

Carol Jenkins is comforted by her friend, Jim Mettler, while outside the home on Orchard Road.

Photos courtesy Special Collections Department, UC Davis

Photo courtesy Special Collections Department, UC Davis

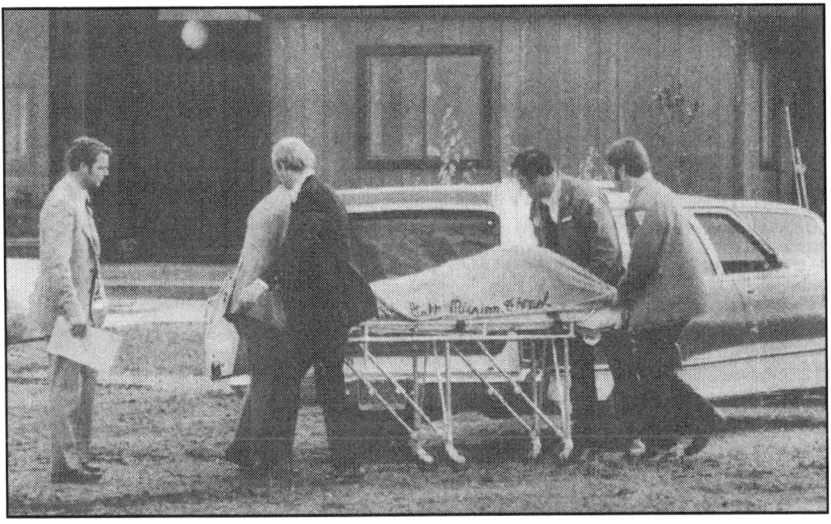

Bodies being removed from the home.

Photo courtesy Special Collections Department, UC Davis

Mourners gather at graveside rites for the Earl Family.

33

Thursday, November 8, 1973 | 6:00 am.

At exactly three minutes before six the last victim was wheeled into the examination room. It was Bobby Parkin.

So the procedure was repeated for the ninth time, and by a 7:45 Thursday morning, his tiny body was pieced back together and placed in storage along with his sister, his mother and his father, all awaiting the official approval that would release them to the funeral home later that afternoon. Bobby was just one day shy of his 10th birthday.

A total of twenty-seven bullet wounds had been discovered during the examinations, although not all of the slugs had been recovered in the bodies. Even the children had multiple wounds; Bobby with three, and it was obvious with each that the weapon had been placed at least very close to the head, if not directly upon it.

Doctor Lawrence completed his task, exhausted, sickened. He considered the magnitude of what destruction he had just documented, remembering what Sheriff Canlis had said yesterday. He had to agree. Only a madman could have done this.

Of all the people interviewed the previous afternoon, most made the paper Thursday morning, and residents of Lodi poured over the *News-Sentinel*. With the exception of a small article about President Nixon asking every American to turn the thermostat down to help out with the looming energy shortage, details about the murdered families consumed the entire front page.

"Everybody liked Wally," offered his aunt, a tissue dabbing her nose. "He was always smiling, always happy. We can't believe this has happened to them."

"You couldn't find nicer people," a former co-worker said of Richard Earl and his family.

Lodi and Victor were numb. These were the type of things that happened somewhere else. And even though California had been the scene of many terrible murders in recent years, mass murder was still a foreign subject in the rural areas such as this. But now, if this could happen here in Victor, then by God, it could happen anywhere.

But even more so, the citizens seemed embarrassed, ashamed these crimes had apparently been committed by one of their own. A man who had grown up here. Lived his entire life here. An outsider? Yes, to some degree, but still part of this community. A community that knew each other, and until now had trusted and looked out for each other. It was difficult to admit even the best of families sometimes have a bad seed, that even their town could create someone so horrible. Some even hoped that Sheriff Canlis was wrong, that Willie Steelman was not responsible, for he had not only killed nine of them, he had shamed all of them. How about the other guy? What's his name? Yeah, the one from New York. Maybe he did it. New York people are crazy. That city is sick and twisted. Those people live like animals. He probably did it. Some hoped as much, because today the people of Victor and Lodi grieved, their heads and spirits bowed low, as much in hurt and heartache, as in humiliation.

The United Market remained closed Thursday morning, a handwritten note taped to the door apologizing for the inconvenience, and a sheriff deputy standing guard nearby, shooing away the curious. Down the road, the staff of the elementary school in Victor scrambled to find ways to talk to Bobby and Lisa's classmates about what happened. Some of the children said they were scared the bad men were going to come back to the school and hurt them too. School pictures of the Parkin children made the front page of the paper Thursday morning, as did a photo of the coroner removing Bobbie's body from the home. The Lodi *News–Sentinel* did manage to offer its readers some hope with a banner "ACTIVE LEADS IN MASS MURDER", explaining two men wanted in a double slaying in Mesa, Arizona were now being sought in this murder. Within the story, next to the photo of Bobby Parkin, was a picture of one of those suspects, Willie Steelman.

The killings were the single topic of conversation. Over busy phone lines, over coffee at the Hollywood Cafe, behind the counter at Woolworth, across office desks and in line at the post office, it was all anyone could talk about. The media swarmed, snapping photos, scribbling notes, talking constantly on the cloesest pay phone they could find.

"Lordy, Lordy," Mrs. Cummings sighed to a reporter. "It is unbelievable. I just don't know what kind of people would do this."

The frail woman of 69 years sat in the living room of her mobile home in Victor, her grief stricken husband silent on the nearby sofa, his head in his hands. "And I do hope someone takes care of Patches," she rambled, wringing her hands as she spoke, "cuz you know, after her little black one got run over by the pickup, Debbie wouldn't even let poor Patches out of the house."

She stopped for a moment and stared out the window, chasing ghosts in the dreary morning fog. "Jez think about it," she lamented. "Nine bodies in one pile. It's jez awful!"

Especially when one them was her very own daughter, Wanda Jean.

Willie had now decided they would have to get out of town sooner than originally planned. With the headlines, and all the TV and radio coverage, he knew it was only a matter of time before the cops started closing in. Running was again their only option. The visit to Melinda's apartment last night was not a social call. Willie was hoping he could talk her in to leaving town with them. There would be no returning to the Datsun. Its owners had probably been found by now, so Melinda was their only chance. He knew he had a good shot at convincing her to leave with them, in her car, of course, although he had no idea where to.

So he and Doug got up shortly after seven Thursday morning, got dressed, and walked downstairs, intent on having breakfast at the hotel coffee shop. There Willie would have some time to think this through. He nodded good morning to desk clerk, and on the way into the restaurant, he glanced down at the rack of newspapers. There was his picture, right on the front page, staring back at him.

He stopped in his tracks and grabbed Doug by the arm, motioning down at the paper, but not saying a word. They turned around and hurried out the door, not even taking the chance to get their belongings upstairs. The clerk, Bill Reger, his restlessness still itching from yesterday, watched the two walk outside and disappear around the corner. It was now ten minutes after eight.

Peter Saiers was a senior in high school when his parents packed up the family and moved to Tucson. But he was so homesick, even a year later, that on the last day of school, he got in his car and drove straight back home to Pennsylvania. He stayed there in college for a couple years, then traveled north and entered the seminary at St Mary's in Boston. After studying philosophy, and still not knowing what he wanted to do, he dropped out and headed back to Arizona. He laid brick while he tried to sort his life out.

But the draft board stepped in and made the decision for him. But even after a two-year hitch in the Army, he was still up in the air about where he was heading. There was not much a man could do with a Degree in Philosophy. But one day it hit him that law could be an interesting field, and after writing to several schools, he was accepted at the University of Arizona, right back in Tucson.

But while he was at U of A, his parents moved again, this time to Stockton, California, so Peter spent summers there, working in construction, helping to pay his tuition. After graduating a few years later, he decided to take the California bar exams instead. He passed in the spring of 1970.

But it was in Arizona where he met his future wife, and while neither had given any thought about living in California, that all changed when Saiers was offered a job in the San Joaquin County District Attorney's Office, yes, back in Stockton. He was just 27 years old. And now, just three short years later, Saiers was right in the middle of the biggest, most brutal murder case in the County's history, and it was looking very much like this one was all his.

Saiers checked out a county car Thursday morning and drove to Victor, stopping by the United Market to follow up on the robbery portion of the investigation. The identification team was wrapping up their work, and they reported it was now clear that whoever robbed the store did so with the help of the owner. There were no signs of forced entry, either to the store itself, or to the floor safe in the back. Saiers made a note that Walter Parkin must have been brought here at gunpoint, and therefore he would add a charge of kidnapping to nine counts of murder.

But over at the Parkin home, the investigation was still going full throttle. When Saiers arrived he was surprised to find several members of the press still camped out front, along with several neighbors buttoned up against the morning chill. He wondered if any of them had ever gone home. Inside the house was a disaster. It looked like the bottom of a fireplace. Fingerprinting had not begun until late Wednesday afternoon, hours after the bodies had been removed, and the work was still in progress. The Parkin home was huge and their work sizable. Every square inch would need to be gone over, so there was black print powder everywhere. As far up the walls as a man could reach, on every appliance, every counter, every piece of furniture, any surface that could possibly hold a print, there was black dust. Fingerprint powder is about as close to soot as something could get, and it covered the Parkin home from top to bottom. Every fingerprint of every person who had ever visited the house found its way to one of the print cards being assembled that morning. The victim's prints, taken prior to the autopsies, were given to investigators, so at least they could rule those out during their search.

Sheriff investigators had developed a list of people who within just the past couple of hours had called claiming to have seen the suspects recently. Some simply had information they felt was crucial to the case and the name Carol Jenkins came up more than once. Most reported she once worked with Steelman at the Vista Ray, while some went so far as to suggest she and Willie were more than just friends. In any event, John Barbieri decided it was time to have a long talk with Miss Jenkins.

As he had arranged yesterday, Deputy Allen was already on his way to Santa Rosa to meet with Sergeant Nelson. Nelson handed over the packet of material brought back from Arizona and gave Allen a rough timetable of the suspect's activities of the last month. The information included the names of the murder victims in the trailer, along with the two missing men, Ken Unrein and Michael Adshade. Nelson also gave him a copy of his report on the kidnap/rape of the young couple in Sonoma County. Allen thanked him for his time and returned to Stockton.

Saiers was back at his desk by nine. Waiting there when he arrived was an important message from the Sheriff's office. Sacramento Police had just called to inform them the suspects had been spotted and their department was closing in.

Bill Reger shared his desk duties at the Clunie with Larry Beebe. Reger had the morning shift, Larry the afternoon, and both resided in the hotel. They had stayed up late last night, glued to the television, waiting for anything new about the killings. Bill had still not made the connection, but when the two men came downstairs this morning and said hello, that strange feeling from yesterday came over him once again. When one of them looked down at the newspaper, Reger did as well. It suddenly all clicked. He called and told Larry to hurry and get downstairs.

It was Beebe who had been on duty when both men returned to the hotel last night, and Reger asked him if he didn't think the guy in the newspaper wasn't the very same guy staying at the hotel? Larry said damned if it didn't, adding the TV said the cops were looking for two men, one named Steelman, the other, Gretzler. Bill pulled out the registration slips from yesterday and checked the names. One of the men had signed in as 'Simen'. The other wrote down 'Doug Gretzler'. Reger shot a look at Beebe, then reached for the phone.

Willie and Doug flagged down the first cab they spotted, giving the driver Melinda's address. They were relieved when this time she answered the door. She, on the other hand, was surprised to see them. It was barely eight thirty and much too early for company, especially two men she didn't know. But she invited them in, and apologized for not being home last night. Willie shrugged it off and told her that they were out hitting some clubs and just wondered if she wanted to go along. Willie soon got around to the real reason for their visit. "Me and Doug are going to take off for Florida," he announced. "How about going with us?"

Melinda was taken back by the offer, but acted interested at first. She listened to Willie's line, then apologized that there was no way she could go. Willie seemed disappointed but didn't push her. He acted if there was no hurry. He said he was still was going to find a way down to Florida one day. "I'm tired of the rain," he complained. "I gotta get back to some sunshine."

So he changed the subject and asked her if she could find them a place to stay around here, someplace close, and Melinda offered to check out a few places she knew around the university in nearby Davis. Willie said he would really appreciate it if she could help them out.

It was a little after nine when Willie pulled Doug aside and told him to go back downtown and get the rest of their stuff out of the room. "They already know me, man. Hell, they even got my picture! But they don't know who you are."

All of which sounded logical to Doug, who then told Melinda he was going back to the room to get his guitar. He walked around the corner to 29th and P Streets and called another cab.

Willie and Melinda sat around the apartment, smoked some cigarettes and listened to the stereo. Willie bragged about all the places he had been and all the rock stars he knew. He had a comment about every song, and it seemed to Melinda that he somehow had a hand in each and every one.

The taxi came, and during the ten-minute cab ride back downtown, Doug was in a cheerful and slightly stoned mood. He chatted to the cabbie the entire way, most of it about nothing at all. "Yeah, just goin' down to get my guitar, then I'll have ya bring me right back." He took a swig from his soda and continued to babble on. He looked at the can he was holding and became almost reflective. "You know, I much prefer Coca Cola to all the other cola drinks. How 'bout you?"

Lieutenant Taylor from the Sacramento Police was the first to arrive at the Clunie. Reger held a copy of the newspaper, all the time pointing to the picture on the front page as he again went through the events of the morning. He showed Taylor the registration slip to prove what he was saying was true. Reger told him both guys were long gone by now, but Taylor and two other officers checked all the floors just in case. He radioed back to headquarters, advising them he would need help. He sent officers Brown and Wilson back up to Room 319 and told them to wait there. They yanked the shotguns from their squad cars and hurried back upstairs. It was now 8:40 am.

The Police Department first notified the Bureau of Investigation, then the Sacramento Sheriff's Office, then and the California Highway Patrol. By 9:00 am, a command post had been set up in a parking lot on the corner of J and L, the two streets bordering the K Street Mall, only a couple blocks from the Clunie. Taylor ordered the entire outdoor mall area checked for the suspects, as well as the streets and businesses surrounding the hotel. Officer were stationed on every floor, including two on the roof, three behind the front desk, and one on a stool at the coffee shop counter.

From the command center, Sacramento Police began their positioning around the Clunie. Within minutes, rifles could be seen from nearby windows, all aimed at the hotel. Undercover cops with long hair and droopy mustaches saturated the mall streets, keeping an eye on the crowd and an ear on their walkie-talkie. They scoured the park around the State Capital, just two blocks from the hotel, knowing full well how easy it would be for someone to hide in the heavy foliage, or disappear amongst the hundreds of tourists and office workers who walked the grounds. By nine-thirty, nearly 75 police and sheriff officers were positioned downtown. The Highway Patrol covered all major roads and bridges in and out of Sacramento, including Interstates 5 and 80, Highway 99. The Greyhound Bus Station came under surveillance and flight departures were screened at the airport. Officers notified the terminal of the critical nature of the situation, and were told there was a possibility some flights could be put on hold.

But with the police came newsmen and their vans, all plastered with logos and call letters, all screeching to a halt on the side streets surrounding the Clunie and command post. Like the officers they followed, cameramen could be seen lugging their heavy gear into position, battling for the best spots. Emptying from the outdoor mall, beat reporters with notepads, tape recorders and small cameras raced up K Street. The media monitored the police band and were as fast as the cops at getting ready, and in a few cases even beat them to the most critical and strategic locations.

It had been less than an hour since Lt. Taylor first spoke with Bill Reger, and by now the entire city of Sacramento was on alert.

The Yellow Cab carrying Doug Gretzler wiggled through morning traffic and pulled up to the K Street entrance of the Clunie. The cabbie, Charles Dukes, was told to wait at the curb and keep the meter running. There was already a buck on the meter, and as the guy disappeared into the hotel, he wondered if he would see him, or his dollar, ever again.

Police Lieutenant Harold O'Kane pulled into a spot near the 8th Street entrance to the hotel, at almost the same time the cab arrived right around the corner, not 30 feet away. As O'Kane climbed out of the car, his radio crackled, "Possible suspect entering the hotel! Repeat! Possible suspect now inside!"

Sergeant Chatoain, who was on a car stakeout near the corner of K and 8th, watched as a man fitting a suspect's description got out of a cab and scurried inside the Clunie. He had broadcast the urgent message before beginning his pursuit. O'Kane had already spotted the sergeant's sedan and ran over to intercept Chatoain who was hurrying towards the hotel. "He's inside, Harold!" Chatoain reported breathlessly. "I saw him get on the elevator!"

Bill Reger agreed. "That's the man. That's him! That's the guy named Gretzler!"

By now other officers had stormed the lobby and looked to O'Kane and Chatoain for instructions. They all knew about some of their men positioned upstairs in the hall and suspect's room, so their first concern was to block every exit to the hotel. Once upstairs, it would be almost impossible for anyone to get back down without being seen. Reger said that the only way out were the fire escapes on each floor, so their sharpshooters outside were instructed to focus their attention there. O'Kane knew they would need to evacuate the building quickly if they didn't get their guy in the first few minutes. Every report had both suspects armed and considered extremely dangerous. He wasn't going to chance it. He had no intention of any more people being killed.

The elevator returned to lobby, the operator, surprised to be bombarded by so many men and so many questions, said he had taken the guy to the third floor, but had no idea which way he went after that.

Police Detectives Pane and Blanas had been at the scene for almost an hour. After Gretzler was spotted going inside, the detectives and two officers from the Sheriff's Department were sent to seal off the second floor so there would be no way back down.

Indeed, Doug got off on the third floor and headed to his room. As he reached down to put the key in the door, he noticed the hair he had stuck to the crack of the door was gone. Someone had been in the room. The doors to the rooms at the Clunie were not solid wood. Thick louvered slats covered the lower half allowing ventilation into the stuffy rooms. As he waited, Doug heard the phone ring twice, then the voice of a man answer in a whisper. He knew he had been spotted. The phone call was warning whoever was inside his room of his arrival.

Doug hurried back down the hall, and not seeing any cops, took the stairs to the fourth floor hoping for a place to hide, or better yet, another way out. He climbed out a window and onto a fire escape, but while standing out on the ledge, he looked down in the alley only to see a man standing next to a blue-gray sedan looking back up at him. As he scampered back inside he saw cops loaded down with rifles standing on the nearby rooftops. He rattled every door on the fourth floor, desperate for at least a place to crawl into. Down the hall he stumbled across a storage room. A cleaning woman was standing inside folding towels.

"Can you tell me if there is another way out through here?" he asked.

She looked back at him like he was some kind of crazy. "You mean goin' through dis lil' room? No way. You gotta go all da way down da stairs to git outta here." She had no idea what was going on around her.

"Well, thanks anyway."

The only way out was down, and once more Doug headed for the stairs, making sure to avoid the third floor, knowing the cops were already there.

From the staircase at the second floor landing he could look down in the lobby and see it was packed with cops. He hit the brakes, turned around and headed back down the hall when he heard a hammer cock.

"There he is!" came the yell.

Detectives Pane and Blanas had been on the second floor for only a few minutes. Guns drawn, they covered the hallway and rattled the doors, clearing the floor as they walked. Larry Beebe had joined them and pointed out another stairway on the west side of the hotel when a shadow emerged from the stairwell at the far end of the hall and began walking towards them.

Beebe recognized him. "Here he comes!"

When Doug Gretzler heard the voice, his first reaction was to hide, but he had run out of room. So he decided that if he couldn't hide, at least he could get rid of the derringer. On each hallway were small portals, cubicles of sorts, leading to the rooms. Each cubicle had three doors, each one to a numbered room. Over each door was a narrow ledge, no more than seven feet up, and only a few inches wide. Making sure he was out of the view of the cops approaching fast, Gretzler yanked the derringer from his coat pocket, reached up and placed it on the ledge. He took a deep breath, stepped back out into the hallway, put his hands in the air, and waited. He heard someone yell, "We got him!" He could also hear the stampede coming up the stairs behind him.

Lieutenant O'Kane was still discussing the evacuation with Chatoain when he heard the shouts from upstairs. He raced up one flight and saw Pane, Blanas and the two sheriff detectives pulling wads of money from the handcuffed suspect.

"Man I'm glad this is over," their guy gushed. "I've seen enough killing, and man, I don't wanna see anymore."

"Where's your partner?"

"He's at a place over on 29th...1514 A 29th Street," he blurted, surprisingly anxious and overly willing to tell them where Willie could be found.

It was 10:04 am.

The wait was getting to Willie. Doug had been gone too long, almost an hour, and he was getting restless. No way he could go out on the streets, or back to the hotel to look for him, and he knew of no one he could call to help him out of this. He felt trapped. Smothered. The only thing he could do was hang around and hope that Doug got back soon. When he did, Willie would try again to talk Mindi into going with them.

Mindi. Her friends called her that, she said, so Willie did too. She said she was nineteen, but seemed older to him. She told him about how she had just moved to Sacramento from Berkeley, but she grew up in Pennsylvania, and that's where her parents still lived. Willie said he lived in Berkeley awhile back, and that he always wanted to go to Pennsylvania just to see what it was like.

Mindi was slender, attractive, athletic, with dark blonde hair straight to her shoulders. And she had some great legs. "Fucking far out legs!" was how Willie described them to Doug after their massage yesterday afternoon, and he swore she wore those tight shorts just so she could show them off. Shoes were worn only when she had to, content to parade around the apartment barefoot, as she did this morning. She boasted to having been on the Olympic Swim Team a year or so back, and that explained her great figure. She looked damn good. He wanted to stay. Maybe he was worried about nothing. Maybe Doug would be back soon and things would be cool. He knew he needed more time with her. He needed to make her understand exactly what had happened. He had his whole story to tell her, his whole life, and how things, no matter how hard he had tried, just never went his way. He wondered if she would care. He wondered if he could somehow get her to understand. He wanted desperately to at least try.

There was a pounding on the door and it shook Willie back to his senses, realizing how this whole mess had gone to hell in a hurry. Turned out it was just some guy from the utility company and his only threat was that the power was going to be turned off if someone didn't come up with the payment. Mindi was in tears as she tried to explain a roommate, not her, owed the money and she didn't have it anyway, but none of that mattered to the meter man. So Willie stepped in, flipped him a twenty and told him to get out. Mindi thanked him a dozen times over.

But his euphoria was short lived, his paranoia again took over, and Willie started looking out the front window on a regular basis. Mindi noticed how nervous he was and it made her a little uptight too. Willie still didn't say much, just gazed out the window, claiming to be looking for Doug. She asked him again if something was wrong, but he shook his head and told her no, everything was cool.

So Mindi went into the bathroom, and when she came out Willie was standing in the middle of the room with a gun in his hand.

"The police are out there," he said, waving the gun towards the window. "They're after me, Mindi. I guess you should know that."

Mindi covered her mouth, like she was catching her breath. She was much too frightened to scream.

Back at the Clunie, Dukes couldn't help but notice the commotion going on. People were rushing in and out of the hotel – cops with big rifles and men with big cameras – all running around and yelling at each other. He had waited almost ten minutes for his fare to come back. Nothing. Didn't take a genius, he grumbled to himself, to see that he had been stiffed. So he decided to go on inside, curious to find out what was happening. It was Reger who filled him in, and it was pretty clear that they were all looking for the same guy. Pissed him off too. Dukes knew for a damn fact that he wouldn't get his money now.

As soon as their guy started yapping away, O'Kane interrupted him and gave him his rights. The suspect stopped himself long enough to explain that he knew all about his rights, then jumped right back in and kept talking. So after O'Kane covered all the legalities, he asked him if he wanted to talk about what happened in Lodi? Suddenly the guy balked, saying he didn't feel right talking about it in the middle of the hallway.

"I'm feelin' really strange. I just wanna get out of here as soon as we can."

O'Kane didn't press the question. He would leave that for the others. He tugged at the guy's arm to move him downstairs. Doug balked, then decided to buy himself some more goodwill and started talking once more. "I think I should tell you though, the other guy is armed and says he won't be taken alive. Says he'll take as many cops as he can with him when he goes down."

So O'Kane listened, then radioed for a car to be brought around to the far side of the hotel. When word came back they were ready, O'Kane hustled the suspect downstairs, through the mob in the lobby, and out to the waiting car.

Dukes watched as four big cops slammed his fare through the crowd and out the front door, shoving him into the backseat of a car, before speeding away. Reger pointed out to the cops that this was the cabbie who had brought this Gretzler guy back to the hotel. Dukes was told to stay put until they could talk to him. He obeyed, but it was over an hour later before they let him go back out to his cab. The meter had been running, but Dukes was right. He never saw his passenger, or his dollar, ever again.

At 10:15, Lieutenant Waters got word that the suspect, Douglas E. Gretzler, was in custody. Ten minutes later, they had him on ice in the second floor interrogation room at the Police Department. Five minutes after that the calls started pouring in from people wanting to help assist in the manhunt, many of whom were at home, watching the drama unfold on TV. Television and radio stations had interrupted regular programming to report live on the biggest crime story in the city's history. One of those callers was the attendant at the Weinstocks Garage. He said had seen both these men just last night and they had asked if they could leave their car overnight.

"It's a white Datsun. Arizona license number RWS 563," he claimed. "It's still here, if you guys are interested."

When Waters was assured the situation downtown had been successfully resolved, he reformed the squad, keeping a small unit in and near the Clunie in the event Steelman returned, while sending the rest over to the apartment on 29th Street. Waters had Ambrose and McColl driven there so they could observe the operation firsthand. Ken Wagner stayed behind, relaying updates over an open phone line to Sheriff's office back in Stockton. Saiers, knowing at least one suspect was in custody, began drawing up the search warrants he hoped to use later.

The north-south streets of downtown Sacramento are numbered, while a letter designates those running east west. The Clunie Hotel was at the corner of 8th and K, while Melinda's apartment was about a mile and a half away, on 29th between O and P. The area she lived in was mainly residential, with small homes, duplexes and large older houses that had been long ago converted into apartments. On the corner near Melinda's was a Texaco station where Doug called the cab, and a half dozen blocks the other way, the historic Sutter's Fort. Across the street from the apartment was Farmer's Market, a seasonal produce stand, and next to it, a large parking lot. Above that was Business 80, the elevated freeway where traffic roared day and night.

Melinda's place was an old two story clapboard style building divided into three units, two down and one up, all facing east onto 29th Street and the freeway beyond. The enclosed stairway to her apartment was located on the north end of the building. Her upstairs kitchen window faced out to the rear, and onto the extra parking, community trash cans, and into the alley that ran around the back of the building.

The first to arrive was a detective in an unmarked car. He drove by a few times then parked in the lot across the street, soon joined by several others. Around back, more cars pulled in and blocked off the alley. Again, the media was directly on their heals. TV crews raced in, set up shop at the Farmer's Market and in the parking lot next to it, still with no concept of the term, undercover. The surveillance van arrived, as did the swat team units in the camper.

At 10:50 Deputy Police Chief Jack Kearns arrived and took control. He ordered all side streets blocked off and the neighborhood around the apartment evacuated. Tear gas and arrest teams were formed and surrounded the building. Guns and canisters were loaded, awaiting Kearns' orders. Sharpshooters found protection in the trees up and down 29th Street, as well as behind the cars scattered in the parking lot. The Highway Patrol had already begun to shutdown 80 and traffic trickled to a stop. In its place, rifle units could be seen peering over the railing, their weapons trained on the apartment.

After he calmed her down, he told her again. "The cops are after me Mindi."

"What?"

"The cops are after me. They've come for me."

"Why? What for? I don't understand."

Willie stumbled around about how it was really his brother they wanted, and that his brother lived down in Modesto, but that the cops must have got mixed up, and now they were here, and he had a parole violation from New York, and the cops must think he's him, and now with the violation and all...

"Wait a minute," she interrupted. "Who had the parole problem?"

"Well," Willie flustered. "That one was mine."

By now more than 70 officers from 5 different agencies had assembled on the area. Still, they seemed greatly outnumbered by the news people and spectators lining the parking lot and side streets. As the tension continued to mount, a kid on a bicycle busted through the barriers in 29th Street and zigzagged around the command post; pedaling full bore, dodging all the cops chasing after him. While many of the officers were wise enough to be wearing bulletproof vests, the gawkers and the media made no attempt to stay protected, although most were with an easy gunshot distance from the window of the second story apartment.

This morning's edition, its rubber band still wrapped around it, was on top of a pile of papers, most of which were unread, and stacked on the kitchen table. When Mindi went into the bathroom, Willie opened the paper and looked it over. There was his picture, and ones of the dead kids. When he heard Mindi came out, he pulled a wad of money from his jacket, wrapped the rubber band around it and shoved it up under sink, hiding it behind the drainpipes. That's when he told her that they were looking for him, not his brother. She screamed and started running around the room, stopping only long enough to ask him if he was telling her the truth, or if anyone was going to get hurt.

"Don't lie to me!" she screamed. She started to cry. "All this for a parole violation?" she sobbed. "I don't understand."

Back at the window, Steelman noticed all the cops arriving. He saw the automatic weapons and the sharpshooters in the camper. He watched as they scrambled around trying to get set up. He could not believe how stupid they were. If he just had something bigger than this pathetic little pop gun, he could set up here and pick them all off, one by one, like shooting fish in a barrel. Mindi walked over to the window and he yanked her out of the way, telling her go over and sit on the couch, which she did. Willie opened the window and started yelling. She heard the bullhorn from out front telling him to surrender and come out. Willie turned to her and confessed hopelessly. "They've got me. What am I gonna do?"

At 11:28 a.m. Chief Kearns heard the voice from the apartment. He was relieved. Until now they weren't even sure they had the right house. His confidence bolstered, he grabbed the bullhorn and once again ordered Steelman to give himself up.

For the next few minutes, Willie sweated it out near the front window. He put the gun up to his temple and told Mindi that maybe this was what he should do. She screamed at him to stop. Put the gun down, she begged, sobbing. No, he replied, this really was the best way out; at least she wouldn't get hurt. That's what worried him the most, he confessed, her getting hurt over all of this. "Never mind me," he said. "I'm thinking about you." She cried and pleaded for him to stop talking so stupid. There had to be another way out of this.

"Willie Steelman!" The voice boomed again from the loudspeaker out front. "This is going to be your last chance to give yourself up peacefully.

Willie yelled back through the open window. "I'm not coming out. How do I know I ain't gonna be shot?"

Kearns assured him he wouldn't be harmed, but Willie could see a hundred rifles out front – even a machine gun, he swore, all pointed at him. "What's your word?" he yelled back. "How do I know that for a fact?"

Kearns and Steelman continued to argue back and forth, neither convincing the other to budge. Then Willie said, "Well, then you get the news people around, you get all the media around when I walk out so I don't get shot," he shouted. "Then you announce it on the radio that I ain't gonna get shot at if I walk outta here!"

Kearns looked at the men beside him. What in the hell is he talking about, he asked? Announce it on the radio? The two conferred for a moment and Kearns nodded, then pointed the bullhorn back up towards the window. "Okay then, what station?"

Without hesitation Willie yelled back. "K-ZAP!"

It was 11:32 a.m. and Robert Williams was in the second hour of his 10 to 2 shift when he got a strange request on the station's 'Listener Line'. A television station, KCRA, was calling to tell him that the police wanted him to broadcast a special message about some guy they had cornered and who was supposed to surrender, but only if the station would announce it on the air. The excited voice on the phone rambled, out of breath.

"Wait a minute!" Williams interrupted. "What are you talking about?"

Just then the entire KZAP staffed rushed the control room. "It's for real!" They all screamed in unison. "We gotta do it! The cops want us to do it!"

Sacramento Police was now on the other line; not knowing KCRA had beaten them to the punch. Williams picked up the phone and listened to their story. He couldn't really say if he knew what the hell was going on, or what his role in this deal was supposed to be, but he told the caller to hang on. He let the record run out while he gathered his thoughts.

Willie moved away from the window and told Mindi to turn the stereo on to K-ZAP and get him a piece of paper. But when she handed it to him, he shook his head and waved her off.

"I'm too nervous," he said. "You write what I tell you. You write this all down."

And amidst the radio and the bullhorn, and the noise from the street and her own heart pounding in her chest, Mindi scribbled down the few words he gave her.

> *THE LAST WILL AND TESTAMENT OF WILLIE LUTHER STEELMAN.*
> *I hereby leave all of my personal property and real estate to Melinda Kashula.*
> *Nov 8, 1973*

Willie signed it. She was sure there were tears in his eyes and she could hear his voice choke. "I got nobody else," he said. "I got no friends, Mindi, and you're a really nice person." He told her to put the note where someone would be sure to find it.

Habit forced him to check the clock. It was 11:35 a.m. Robert Williams opened the microphone and started in. "You are listening and there are some people who would like you to follow these instructions and no hassles are going to come down on your head."

Willie was indeed listening. The voice on the radio was laid back and comforting.

"The girl you are with should come out first," the announcer continued, "and then you should come out with your hands up and nothing is going to come down on your head right then."

Williams stopped, then went right into another song. No one had told him what to say, or how to say it, and he wondered what effect his words were having. He had no idea in hell what was going on across town. All he was told was that the guy who had killed all those people down in Lodi was cornered. Williams couldn't help but feel a bit honored that the guy, regardless of what he had done, had asked for him. Too bad it wasn't ratings week, he thought.

But Willie hadn't give up yet. He told Mindi to leave the house. Just walk downstairs. He said he would let everyone know she was coming out and not to shoot. "I'm not gonna get you hurt in all this," he promised.

But she refused. Thinking again what he had said about killing himself, she said, "If I go out there, I'm taking the gun with me."

Outside, Kearns was getting restless. He gave himself two minutes after the radio announcement before he made his move. Steelman would surrender, or he was going to force him out. While Willie and Melinda argued about who was going to save who, Kearns gave the order.

The two of them were standing in the middle of the apartment when a shot went off and exploded through the kitchen window behind them. A tear gas canister had been fired from the alley, but instead of landing in the apartment, it just kept going, right out the front window and into the street. A direct shot straight through the building. It came to rest on 29th street, gas trickling from the broken casing.

Willie heard a shot and breaking glass and he figured they were opening fire. The canister came within inches of his head. He went over to the window and yelled. "Jesus! Wait a minute...hold your fire, there's a girl in here!"

As Willie and Kearns argued back and forth about who was going to do what next, Williams came back on and broadcast his second message. "Willie Steelman, the girl first. Please. And then you come out with nothing in your hands."

Whether it had been Melinda's tearful plea, the realization he didn't have the nerve to turn the gun on himself, or knowing he didn't stand a chance in hell in getting out of the apartment in one piece, Willie gave in. He walked back to the window and shouted at them to hold their fire. They were coming out.

The instructions on the radio were specific; the girl first, then him, so Melinda started down the stairs with Willie close behind. Halfway down she turned around and held her hand out for the gun. Willie handed it to her and told her when she got to the door, just open it a little, then toss the gun out the lawn. She nodded, and continued down.

Willie reached out and stopped her. "Mindi, one other thing. About my brother. It's not him, it's me they're really after."

She looked up at him like she already knew that.

"But I didn't kill anyone. I never killed anybody. You believe me, don't you?"

She nodded and whispered she did. The police arrest team was positioned all around the building. One was hiding next to the entrance, inches from where the screen door hinged. Some were near a small drive on the other side, others in flak jackets stood on the far edges of the sidewalk. Across the street several dozen rifles had the front door in their sights. They could not see their suspect come down the enclosed stair way so there was no guarantee he wasn't going to come out firing, or that he might use the girl as his shield. They were prepared for the worst.

There would be no more victims, Kearns had decided, unless of course Steelman gave them no choice. Cop adrenalin ran high. Kearns wasn't so sure one of his own men wouldn't want to deliver some kind of swift justice right then and there. He prayed Steelman wouldn't do something stupid to give any one of them an excuse.

The front door opened. Behind the screen they could see the girl. Voices barked in unison for her to throw the gun out, although they did not know for sure if she even had it. Melinda opened the screen and tossed the gun out on the lawn a few feet out in front of her.

"Now step out and to the side!" they ordered.

She did as she was told. Two officers raced into the picture and hustled over her to the side of the building, out of rifle sight. She turned and struggled to see what was going to happen, still afraid of what was going to happen to Willie.

Steelman now came into view. His hands were raised behind his head. Again, every voice yelled for him to come out and lay face down on the lawn.

Now he too obeyed, a cigarette dangling dangerously between his lips.

He walked out and the lawn was covered in uniforms and reporters. Two cops dove down on top of him. Handcuffs opened, they straddled him and pulled his arms back, snapping them tight behind him, while Willie twisted his head to glare up at them. Newsmen pounced in as well, their cameras and tape recorders rolling. They got right in Willie's face while the cops were attempting to pull them out of the pile.

All this within just a matter of seconds, and all within just a few feet of the gun that Melinda had tossed out on the lawn. Sergeant Chatoain saw weapon, scooped it up and stood back away from the ruckus. A reporter came right over top of him. He noticed the suspect's black eye, so as Steelman was sprawled out on the grass, he stuck a microphone in his face. "Did they do this?" he yelled. "Did the police do this to you?"

Even as the cops were dragging him away, the reporter never let up. "Tell us, did they hit you? Did the police give you this black eye?"

The cops lifted Steelman to his feet and patted him down. "Guess I'm going back to Stockton" he snarled.

They threw him into a car and sped away, leaving everyone else standing on 29th Street with their adrenalin racing and their mouths wide open.

After Chatoain picked up the gun off the lawn, he made his ID mark on it, then handed it to Ambrose. The other items taken off Steelman in the front yard were passed along as well, including a wallet with $330 in cash and nine live rounds of .22 hollow point ammunition. He handed it over to Saiers.

At 11:25 a.m., still minutes before Willie walked out of the apartment, Sacramento Police began their interrogation of Doug Gretzler. He had been searched, stripped, photographed, then left to sit and wait. On him they found the key to room 319 at the Clunie, some matchbooks, $4.91 in change, and a receipt for a comb. He was overly polite as Lt. O'Kane again advised him of his rights and asked if he could turn on the tape recorder. Gretzler assured him he knew his rights and was willing to talk, again making it clear he had seen enough killing and wanted to tell them everything they needed to know. The guy he was traveling with, the guy in the apartment, was very dangerous, Gretzler warned. He had killed before and would certainly kill as many policemen as he possibly could before they caught him.

When asked his partner's last name Doug had to think for a minute. "You know, I'm not really sure. I think his real name is William Stillman. . .with an i."

O'Kane told him that they had his partner surrounded. He asked about whether the girl inside was involved and Gretzler replied no, explaining about them going to the massage parlor yesterday and meeting Melinda.

"She got any kids in that house?" O'Kane asked.

"No."

"Phone?"

"I don't think so, I had to call the cab from a pay phone at the gas station."

Having no idea at this point if this Melinda girl was an accomplice or a hostage, O'Kane figured he needed to know more about her. He pulled Ken Wagner into the room and invited him to have a go with their suspect. Again, Gretzler was cordial, waived his rights and talked freely. Wagner had no idea at that time, but much of the story Gretzler told was a lie, but he was dumping the whole thing on Willie.

The Happy House Massage Parlor was just a couple blocks away and Hal O'Kane was there in minutes. Louise Knowlton and Sarah Endicott were both in and he showed them the morning paper. They recognized the photo as the man from yesterday afternoon, and were frightened to learn Mindi was now held captive by him inside the apartment. But to O'Kane's repeated questioning, they both replied there were no kids, no phone, and no way Mindi could be involved with this guy. She had just met yesterday. She didn't even know them. They agreed to lock up and accompany the Lieutenant back to the station to continue the interview, but by the time O'Kane reported his information to the command center, Steelman was already in custody.

In the car on the way to the station, Steelman was in his usual talkative mood. He leaned forward and started jabbering. "Hey man, you guys didn't give me a chance! I asked for a man from K-ZAP to come to the house so the girl would not get hurt! And then you guys shot that tear gas shit through the window and damn near hit her! Shit, I thought it was a damn mortar or something 'til I saw it out front. Man, it went all the way through the house and out the front and hit a police car!"

At the station, Steelman went through the same procedure as did his partner; stripped, searched, photographed. He was quick to complain about being sick; said he was coughing up blood and that he had been hit by the tear gas canister. A nurse was brought in to see him. She reported back that the black eye was an old wound and whatever scratches and cuts he had on him were minor. She said he was fine, and could wait until they got him back to Stockton to have him fully examined. The police photographer saw what appeared to be blood on his collar and pants leg, and showed it to his supervisor. He was instructed to get several good color close-ups of the stains. When Steelman saw what was going on he was quick to answer it was his blood, and it was O positive.

Steelman started back in. "Are you going to take me back to Stockton?"

"I don't know, I'm not working the case."

"Hey, the girl won't be involved in this, will she? I don't want her name in the paper or anything."

"I'll check."

"She held up good, didn't she? She didn't know what was happening until I told you guys were outside. She started crying when the tear gas went through. I saw my name and picture in the morning paper and decided to go to her place 'til the heat was off."

The officer kept a close ear, but he was worried. There had been no rights given, no recorder running, nothing to capture the confession he knew was coming.

"Hey, lemme ask you something," came the voice inside the room. "How did you guys get Doug?"

"I don't know."

"Is he hurt?"

"I wasn't there."

There was a pause from the room. "So how in the hell did you guys know I was at the girl's place?" Steelman asked.

Doug Gretzler claimed he 'wanted to get it cleared up as soon as possible', so he continued his cooperation. During the interview with Wagner, he admitted being at the Parkin house, but made sure to distance himself from the crimes. "I was in the front room, watching for this chick named Carol – just like Bill told me to – and then he comes out from the back of the house and said, 'Let's go.'

"Did you hear anything?" Wagner asked. "Any gunshots?"

"No, not really. The TV was on and, you know, that noise, and the fact that it was a big house and I was a long ways away. . .no"

"So you didn't know the people had been shot?"

"Not until Bill told me later."

At the end of the interview, Gretzler was asked to sign a waiver to allow them to search the room at the Clunie Hotel. He did, and also told them where they could find the car.

"Will you also allow us to search the Datsun?"

"I have no control over that," Gretzler admitted, "being that it's a stolen vehicle and all."

Finished with Gretzler, Sacramento took him to the county jail where San Joaquin authorities were to pick him up. As promised, the police let the media know when the suspects would be moved. Flash bulbs exploded as two plainclothes officers escorted Gretzler out of the building. It was 12:55 pm.

Over at K-ZAP, reporters from all the media gathered around Robert Williams, and after telling him of the successful capture, asked him how he felt to have been part of catching a suspected mass murderer. "Well, you know" Williams said, still in his laidback, FM style" My approach was just. . .mellow. I didn't want to yell at the guy like another policeman might. I just figured that if he's listening to K-ZAP, he might be more susceptible to a suggestion than a command."

Williams also gave a pitch for the station. "You know, we're more noted for our human involvement. . .we 're just more of a human radio station. . .more able to relate to people."

At 1 p.m. Lt. Ed Burt and Sergeant Guerrero from Burglary were sent over to the garage to find the Datsun. They had power to seize the car, but until the owner could be contacted, they were uncertain as to if they had the right to search it. They agreed that for now just to impound the car to maintain control and protect the evidence possibly still inside. They ran the license number, but there were no hits, no warrants, nothing to suggest the owners even knew it was missing.

But the tow truck was too tall to get inside the multilevel garage, so they had no choice but to enter the vehicle so they could at least put it in neutral and roll it out. The driver's door was opened and out fell a bottle of Seagram's. That's just perfect, Guerrero moaned, another damn report to fill out. They pushed the Datsun down to the first floor, and followed the tow truck to the crime lab where it was secured behind a cyclone fence in the basement. An officer was assigned to standby the vehicle until the investigators arrived. Guerrero's first reaction when he looked inside car was how filthy it was. He knew whoever owned it was going to be really upset when they got it back.

Steelman was still talking. Most figured he was stoned. He rambled on about what 'they were going to do to him', how he was going to be snuffed out by 'the same people who were following him' in Lodi and even down in Arizona. When someone mentioned gathering evidence, he laughed. "Find the car and you'll find everything you need."

They didn't say a word.

At 2 p.m. having been given her consent, officers entered Melinda's apartment. Four members of the Police department were there, including Chatoain. Two were from the State Investigation and Identification Bureau and three from the Fire Department, including the Chief himself, along with Ambrose and McColl from San Joaquin. The tiny apartment was very crowded.

On the coffee table in living room they found the will. On top of it, a pen from the H.J. Nicoletti Funeral Home. In the kitchen they located the *Union* newspaper from that morning. On the bedroom nightstand was the cover jacket to Truman Capote's book, IN COLD BLOOD.

Both suspects had been told they were going to be booked on a murder warrant from Arizona, although nothing was asked about those crimes, nor was anything offered. They were also advised that they would stay in Sacramento only long enough to finish the paperwork and then would then be turned over to San Joaquin County. Willie and Doug were kept separated and the decision made earlier they would be transported back to Stockton at different times, for security purposes.

Because of that, John Barbieri raced up to Sacramento to assist in the transfer. His first order of business after arriving around 2:30 was to interview Melinda Kashula. He tried convincing her how serious the situation was and that he needed to know everything that went on from the very first moment she met these two. She did, and gave the same story she had given Sacramento. Although it was his nature to suspicious of everyone, Barbieri decided that she had simply got mixed up in something out of her control. He told Sacramento that as far as he was concerned they could cut her loose. Too bad though, he was overheard telling one of the other cops, she sure is a cute little thing.

His next stop was county jail where he signed to take possession of Douglas Gretzler. The prisoner was wearing borrowed jail clothing and was handcuffed and shackled. He was also barefoot, his shoes having been taken as evidence. None of which mattered to Barbieri, who manhandled him to the car, accompanied by two guards. Barbieri drove back to Stockton angry, and Gretzler remained quiet during the trip. That was okay with Barbieri, who wasn't about to waste the energy giving this piece of shit even the time of day.

Sacramento was done with Steelman as well, although his departure was held up for another half hour. During that time, as he and the guards waited for the word they could leave, Steelman gave his first recorded interview. It was a long, rambling, back and forth bullshit session with investigators, who gave the impression they were just killing time, rapping with the one of the guys. All the time the recorder ran. Willie bragged about how good a shot he was and how his dad used to take him out hunting, making sure his kills were clean. "Oh, shit yeah man, if you shot an animal and wounded it and let it get away then you deserved to have your butt whipped. He would tell ya, if you're gonna shoot it, then you kill it, or don't shoot it."

"So how do you feel when you kill someone?"

"Nothing. Nothing at all. Not even a feeling of elation or happiness. I got off fine, you know, I'm a sadist but I didn't even feel that. Nothing."

"Were you high?"

"Yeah, on all the time and maybe that had something to do with it. Maybe it kills the only piece of morality in you. It could have been my own mother there and I don't think I would have felt anything. . .kids. . .anybody, I've stopped feeling anything. There's something dead inside me."

"What are you in, some kind of cult or something? What makes someone do this kind of thing?"

"I don't think nobody makes you go out and do something like that by talking to you, not unless there's something wrong with your head in the beginning. I just remembered that about an hour after it happened I had to get a couple shots of whiskey in me. I'm just thankful that I didn't mean to take somebody's life. Now, maybe that's wrong."

"Ever think about killing yourself?"

"Sure."

"Why?"

"Why not?"

"Then you don't care if you die, do you?"

"I've been dead. The first time I pulled that trigger I was dead. I'm not that big a fool. The first time I put that needle in my arm I died, because there's no remorse after that."

Having been told by Gretzler about staying there the night of the killings, Sacramento Police showed up at the Holiday Inn South. They were told that the night manager, the one on duty Tuesday night, would not be in until later, but the woman who cleaned the rooms, Ocie Hard, was there, and she took the officers up to Room 216. She said she didn't think it had been occupied since that night, and claimed she didn't notice anything out of the ordinary when she cleaned the room late Wednesday morning. There were no bloodstains on the bed or on any clothing left behind, she said, if that's what they were looking for. There was a wine bottle or something like that under the sink, she remembered, but she had thrown it in the trash. She couldn't say for sure that it was even theirs. When the police followed her out to the dumpster, they were disappointed to find the garbage had been picked up earlier that morning. But Mrs. Hard picked up a piece of paper on the ground and announced excitedly. "Look! You know, I can't be sure, but I'm almost positive I took this out of the room!" The officer looked over the orange colored piece of scratch paper. Written in pencil was the note:

> *AirWest Orange County Airport 540-4550*
> *flight #725*
> *2:00 arrives 3:30*

Lt. Waters overheard the conversation going on with Steelman and broke it up. He had instructions not to talk to the prisoner until Lodi authorities arrived.

Willie bolted. "Why are the Lodi officers gonna talk to me? It's not even in their jurisdiction. It's San Joaquin's. It happened out of Lodi's area!"

At half past three, thirty minutes after Doug left, Willie followed, but unlike his partner, Willie remained real talkative. Sergeant McColl was the driver, and the listener.

"So, who's gonna try me first?" Willie asked. "Arizona or California?"

"I think we will," McColl answered. "We have you."

"No, no, I don't think so cuz Arizona had their charges first."

"Well, I don't know if that matters."

"Hey, do you know if the other guy made it to Stockton okay?"

"Yeah, why wouldn't he?"

"Well, neither of us will never live to be tried," Willie promised. "The same people who sent us to get Wally will kill us too."

There was several miles of silence, until Willie asked, "You know I didn't kill those kids."

"Well someone did!"

"Then it musta been the people who followed me in the pickup when Wally went to the store."

McColl acted like he didn't know what in the hell he was talking about, so

Willie made sure to explain. "When Wally went to the store he drove his Pontiac and I followed in the Datsun, but these people followed us to the store and then back to the house."

"And just who are 'these people'?" McColl asked.

"Well, everyone knows Wally was involved in drugs, and the same people who were killed in Arizona were after me and Wally's partners."

The San Joaquin Sheriff's Department is located downtown in the basement of the county building. A driveway leads from street level down to a sally port that enters directly into the holding cells, offering maximum security when taking prisoners into custody – needing only a few feet from the squad car to the lockup. On the street above, a walkway led around the building and into the main entrance of the courthouse. By late afternoon crowds had already gathered in hopes of catching a glimpse of the killers. They were a cold, angry and vocal mob. The evening fog had already begun to settle in and visibility was reduced to less than a city block, even though it was not yet dark. On the nearby streets, sheriff officers kept a watchful eye on any suspicious characters. Several death threats had already been received and there would be many more to come. In the crowd could be heard loud talk of what they would do to these two guys if given half a chance.

"Child killers!" one man screamed. "If we had any sense at all we would hang both of them right here!"

A half block away were the offices of the San Joaquin Public Defender. Like many others, Sam Libicki had kept a close ear on the radio listening to the latest news from Sacramento. He was relieved the suspects had been found so quickly, and even more surprised they were already talking about what they had done. There was always the outside chance that a crime of this magnitude would attract some big names in the legal business, but more than likely, Libicki realized, it was his office who would be called in.

As word came in the prisoners were on their way, Libicki's boss Robert Chargin, came into his office and closed the door. "I'm thinking about assigning this case to you,"

Libicki was flattered and excited, but confused why he was Chargin's first choice. Although he had been in the office for a few years and worked several felony cases, including homicide, he thought the logical choice was Joel Karesh, who had much more experience than he.

"Why aren't you giving this to Joel?"

Chargrin thought for a minute as if he was trying to find a delicate way to put it. "Well, for one thing, Joel's got kids."

Libicki was confused by the answer, not having any idea what Joel's kids had to do with it.

Chargin said he had given it a lot of thought. But because kids had been killed, he explained, it might be hard for a father to block that out and give his all to the case. That, plus the lynch mob mentality that was festering throughout the county was going to make things very tense for the defender. Chargin suggested there was even the possibility that Karesh's children could be threatened in some way, and it was a chance he wasn't willing to take. "I'm told the arraignment has been scheduled for eleven tomorrow morning. I want you there."

Municipal Court Judge Woodward was advised the arraignment would be in his courtroom. He looked outside and saw the crowd. He called downstairs to the Sheriff's office and requested an extra twelve armed deputies in his courtroom the next morning for the hearing.

The Sheriff's Office had several holding cells, and the courthouse only had enough cells for those prisoners with a court date upstairs. The actual County Jail was a few miles down the road at French Camp. There had been a county jail there ever since there had been county. It was a old multi-story brick building; dark, massive and just a little haunted looking. It sat well off the road, surrounded by open land, fenced with razor topped cyclone. After a brief stay at the holding cell downtown, it was certain Steelman and Gretzler would be taken there, so when the jail commander, Chief Bailey, was given that news, he conferred with Sheriff Canlis, then wrote a very detailed, very specific, and very confidential memo to his staff about how the prisoners would be handled.

> *These men are to be kept separated at all times, and under no circumstances will an officer allow the inmate to be moved without full security procedures. When possible more than one officer should make the movement as it will be in leg irons and handcuffs. Newer clothing will be assigned to these men and no photographs will be taken if not in neat appearing clothing. Inmate Douglas Gretzler will be assigned to Cell Block #23 – Cell #26. It has been cleared out and no other inmate will be confined to that cell block. Inmate William (sic) Steelman will be place in Cell Block #15 – Cell #16 and will never be moved with another inmate. This man has previous suicidal tendencies and a strict routine check will be made on this man and his cell. We have been alerted to his tendencies and we must use every caution to protect his life.*

Back at the courthouse, the sedan carrying the first of the prisoners arrived. It rolled down the ramp and into the back dock amidst curses and threats hurled from the crowd on the walkway above. Barbieri left Gretzler and deputies in the car and walked inside for instructions on how Canlis wished to proceed. They were all anxious to get their first look at the men responsible for the massacre and there was an uneasy, tense feel around the department.

"It was kind of like Christmas and Halloween all rolled into one, and I think everyone was a little nervous," a deputy told his wife later that night. "It was like a gift, you know, we had 'em. I mean we had 'em sure as shit, but we didn't know who we had. Jesus, I saw those pictures later, the pictures of all those people in the closet of that house, and just couldn't help but wonder who could of done something like that."

Canlis had authorized several photographers to be present when the prisoners were brought in, but they were held back away from the vehicle during the delay. Barbeiri didn't like the idea of any news people at all being around, and he gave them a dirty look as he passed by. He was surly and anxious as he approached his boss about their next move. He had been up all night and not in the best of moods. He just kept thinking about all those people – and those kids – and him having to chauffer around the prick who did it. And now fuckin' photographers. It all just set him off.

To make maters worse, the first thing Canlis asked him was how the prisoner was doing?

It put Barbieri over the top. *Dammit, Canlis!,* he fumed, always worried about what people are thinking of him. Barbieri snubbed him, so Canlis walked out to see for himself. In the back seat of the car was a very skinny, very young, very bored, straggly looking little punk.

"Where's his shoes?" Canlis demanded of Barbieri.

"In Sacramento. They took 'em and never bothered to give him jail issue is what I was told." Barbieri couldn't believe Canlis was so worried about this asshole's lack of proper footwear.

The Sheriff reached into his wallet, pulled out a $100 bill and handed it to his detective with a firm warning. "I'm not going to let a prisoner of mine be photographed coming into my jail without any shoes! You go find him some, and then you let me know. We will bring him in at that time."

Canlis turned and walked back inside while Barbieri seethed. He grabbed the first deputy he could find and shoved the money in his hand. "You go across the street to the Florshiem place and buy the most expensive goddamn pair of tennis shoes you can find. And I don't care if you spend the entire hundred fucking bucks! Just go do it!"

Minutes later, Doug Gretzler was escorted in, and photographed, wearing his brand new black and white tennies courtesy of the good sheriff, Michael Canlis.

Sacramento had finally got word back from Arizona DMV as to the registered owner of the Datsun: Michael B. or P.M. Sandberg 1353 East Ft. Lowell Rd. #49-b Tucson, Arizona There was no phone number listed and reaching the vehicle's owner was not considered a top priority. The information was passed along to San Joaquin so they could follow up on it when time allowed.

Sacramento did get around to notifying Maricopa County that their department had captured both suspects with the murder warrants issued yesterday morning, and both were talking freely. They had been turned over to San Joaquin County and were being transported back to Stockton to await charges on the Lodi killings. Arellanes told Bill Miller of the arrests, then made plans for both of them to fly to Stockton immediately. He then called San Joaquin to let them know they were on their way. Their hard work had paid off.

With release forms signed by Gretzler, and to some extent the information offered by both men, Pete Saiers had what he needed to proceed with search warrants. From the moment he arrived in Sacramento, his primary focus was to gather evidence and to keep it clean and legal. He wasn't involved in the capture, nor did he conduct any interviews. In fact, he had to be careful his involvement did not destroy the very case he was there to build. So while the others were at the apartment, interviewing the suspects or locating the stolen vehicle, Saiers sat in an office at the Bureau of Investigation preparing information necessary for obtaining search warrants. The release by Gretzler removed a large stumbling block, but it did not give anyone the legal right to start looking through the room at the Clunie, or the Datsun. That decision could only be made by the courts. Assisting Saiers was Sacramento Deputy D.A. Ken Hake. While Ken Wagner obtained releases and other information in his session with Gretzler, Saiers wrote the documents in long hand on a yellow legal pad – 14 pages of information the court would need to review before it would sign any warrants.

Spelled out were the crimes themselves and why the attorney believed the two men in custody were responsible for these acts. Teletype copies of the Arizona murder warrants were included, as were lists of other items they were seeking, including additional weapons, clothing and money. It was Saiers' responsibility to indicate exactly where these items might be located. But as he compiled the list and prepared the document, he was worried about only one thing. He hoped the judge could read his scrawl. Saiers was the first to admit he had terrible penmanship.

But there was no time to type all this information and still attempt to find a judge to hear it. It was now after 4 o'clock and court personnel would be going home soon. Confident he had prepared the requests as best he could under the circumstances, he and Hake scurried over to the Municipal Courthouse. It would be necessary for Hake to present the documents, being that they were in his jurisdiction.

The only problem was, it was late Thursday afternoon and there were no judges left in the building. Saiers impressed upon the clerk the urgency of their request, who remembered that Judge Grossfeld might still be around. Although he taught a law class on Thursday and was usually gone by now, the clerk reported, he was their only hope.

"If he's in would you please tell him this is very important," Saiers pleaded. "It concerns the murders in Lodi."

Minutes later the clerk returned and said the judge had agreed to stay and hear their request.

At the proceedings, along with the documents presented, Sergeant Wagner explained about the information he had obtained from one of the defendants. There hadn't been time to transcribe his interrogation with Doug Gretzler so the judge allowed his verbal recorded statement. Yet despite the severity of the accusations and of the crimes in question, the presentation to Grossfeld was no easy task. The judge pointed out problems in allowing the search. First, only one of the defendants had agreed and signed the release, even though both had property inside the room and vehicle. Secondly, the suspects were arrested on out of state warrants and Grossfeld was concerned that without Arizona authorities present he might not be hearing the whole story. He said that there was no specific information given in the teletyped warrants explaining exactly what would be found when the suspects were eventually captured.

It was not as cut and dry as Saiers had hoped. The judge interrupted him several times to express his concerns. But after listening to arguments for well over two hours, he finally agreed to the request. He told Saiers he was shelving his planned lesson, and would use the legalities of this impromptu hearing instead. A class he was now late for, he added, and hurried out.

Arrangements had been made with the Department of Justice for a criminalist, a latent print analyst and a photographer to be present during the search, and later to process whatever evidence they uncovered. They were on standby at the Clunie when Saiers, Ambrose and Wagner arrived with the warrants.

The room at the Clunie had been kept under constant guard with officers sporting sawed off shotguns. Upon entering the room, Wagner made a quick inspection, then instructed the photographer what shots to take and specific close-ups of items that would be dusted for prints. When the camerawork was finished, another inspection was performed and a more detailed search began. Saiers noticed the open suitcase and the Sandberg's checkbook, and on a nearby table, car keys. There were receipts from pawn shops, motels and gas stations. In addition to the checkbook, there was identification cards for a Michael Sandberg and a Michael Marsh. There were coins and ammunition scattered about the dresser, as was yesterday's *Sacramento Bee* with headlines about the mass murders. Under one of the beds they found a guitar case. Inside it, wrapped in a sock, was a Smith and Wesson .38.

While the work at the Clunie was underway, the same San Joaquin team hand delivered search warrants to the storage area where the Datsun had been moved. The process was repeated.

Evidence linking Steelman and Gretzler to the house on Orchard Lane literally fell out of the car. Bloody boots and Levis, along with a knife and a receipt from a Woolco department store in Colorado for a .22 rifle. On the floor of the back seat was a small brown grocery sack, and inside it, a field day. Four empty wallets and a federal money band with a serial number and a date of issue. There were over twenty pieces of ID, from driver licenses and social security cards to credit cards and hunting and fishing licenses. Each and every one belonged to one of the victims. In the bottom of the bag was a handful of pennies and a woman's pearl ring. The fingerprint analyst remarked, "I don't know who they belong to, but we've got a lot of 'em here."

Saiers was ecstatic. "We nailed 'em!" he proclaimed to all. "We really nailed 'em!"

In Phoenix, Arellanes and Miller were having trouble getting out of town. There were no direct flights to Stockton, and it was late and impossible to make any connections. Arellanes was anxious to start. He wanted to be there now, when these two guys really started talking. There was one flight with a final destination to Stockton, but just minutes before it was scheduled to depart Sky Harbor Airport, it was canceled. Stockton was socked in with heavy fog, so the closest they could get to Stockton was San Francisco. There was a red eye leaving just after midnight and Dave and Bill made sure they were on it.

In San Francisco they hustled a rental car and headed to Stockton, but when they hit the legendary Valley fog, they ran into a whiteout, and it was six in the morning before they finally got to town.

But Dave couldn't wait. He told the first man he spotted at the Sheriff's Office that they had come all the way from Arizona just to talk to Steelman and Gretzler, and to wake them up if they had to.

Willie had been talking with anyone willing to listen. His conversation earlier with Sergeant Clifton in Sacramento was lengthy, detailed, occasionally honest and often very incriminating. Willie knew Clifton was a cop. It didn't matter. Problem was, it was just that, talk. There had been no rights given and no way any of what he said could ever be held against him. In the car back to Stockton it was the same story. It wasn't until an hour later, when Wagner tried giving Willie his Miranda rights, that Willie balked for the first time. He told Wagner that he decided that he would wait until he had an attorney.

So everything the cops had, at least legally, they got from Doug Gretzler. Later that evening, the D.A.'s office sent over Deputy District Attorney Richard Eichenberger, and Investigator Donnie Brooksher, to sit in on the ongoing interviews of both suspects. Again Gretzler was cooperative. He gave a full statement, beginning with the day he left home, right up until the moment they caught him in the hotel. And once again, he blamed Bill for everything.

Steelman said he was still a little strung out and hurting, but other than that, refused to talk. "I'd be a fool to sit here and talk to you without an attorney present to help me, because I don't have any idea what I'm doing. Besides, I'm not thinking too straight right now."

He asked again to see a doctor, 'to get something for the pain' and they told him one was on the way.

It is at all not uncommon to have a murder suspect examined by a psychiatrist, even before an attorney is appointed. It's critical for prosecutors to discover early, as soon after the crime as possible, what frame of mind the suspect was in at the time of the occurrence, or if drugs or alcohol were involved. Willie had been saying all along that he was strung out during the entire episode and claimed to in the early stages of heroin withdrawal, hence the pain. He told Sacramento police he had downed a couple of Percodans and was smoking some grass at Mindi's apartment, and was 'doing my second number when I walked out of there'.

So the District Attorney's office called on two psychiatrists, Dr. Rogerson and Dr. Austin, to interview the suspects soon after they arrived in Stockton. Doug once again pointed the blame on his partner, and confessed that 'he felt a little sick when I heard the shots go off in the other room'. But he didn't protest because 'I didn't want to be the 10th person dusted'. When he told them about his problems with his father and marriage, even his association with the crimes he was being held for, he just shrugged his shoulders and said, 'some people just have bad luck'. The doctors agreed he was fully capable of understanding what he had done. Rogerson stated that as to Gretzler's extent of involvement in the killings, 'when he was with Steelman he probably just mimicked his behavior'.

Steelman, who would later claim he thought he was talking with a medical doctor, opened up and proceeded to tell Dr. Rogerson everything. "I wasn't planning on shooting or killing anyone but Wally, but since they were all there and they were witnesses, they had to be silenced." Wally was a sleazy individual, Willie claimed, and killing him was like 'cutting open a watermelon'.

Dr. Austin maintained he told Steelman up front that any comments he made could be against him. He said that Steelman acted surprised at first and responded by saying that he had asked for an attorney and didn't want to say anything more. But seconds later, Willie started talking again. He was polite and cooperative, but this time careful only to talk in general terms about his life and the crimes he was charged with. Austin and Rogerson conferred briefly following their sessions with the suspects, and then informed the D.A. investigators that, without question, both men fully understood what was going on around them.

It was late Thursday night before Steelman was returned to his cell. He spent the next several hours complaining of his pain and demanding he be given something to help him sleep. When Ambrose showed up, Willie made him an offer. "Hey, I wanna get this over with as soon as I can. If you can get me one (an attorney) down here, and let me get on with it, hell, we can clear this right now. Cuz I can guarantee you by tomorrow I'm going to be a lot sicker than I am today."

Willie had been complaining about being sick since he got there. It was withdrawals, he told the jailer, and he begged to be given something for the pain. While he had an audience present, Willie started playing the role they seemed to expect; strung out, delusional – a madman, just like Canlis said.

Doug Barr was a young deputy in the department in charge of the holding cells. He had grown up in Lodi and had known Bill Steelman, or at least had heard of him over the past couple of years. They were about the same age, and while Steelman went one way in life, Barr went the other. He was as surprised as anyone to hear that it was Bill they were looking for in the Lodi killings. It was hard for him to believe that the same stupid dope-head he knew out on the streets was the same guy they were holding for the murder of nine people. So in between the complaining and the constant demands, Barr wandered over to Steelman's cell and asked him point blank. "Bill, for chrissakes, what happened? How did you get yourself into all this?"

Willie didn't move, like he was maybe thinking the same thing, but he eventually looked over and smirked. He rose to his feet and took the few steps to the edge of his cell. He glanced around, like he was making sure they were alone, then got right in the deputy's face.

"Hey," he whispered, "you stay close, and keep me in cigarettes, Doug, and we'll make ourselves a million dollars. Cuz right now I'm fucking bigger than Manson himself."

34

Friday, November 9, 1973 | 6 am.

Late last night, San Joaquin moved their two suspects to the French Camp facility. Willie said he had been up all night. Said he couldn't sleep. Said the heroin withdrawals were killing him. Said he needed a doctor. "A real one this time!" he screamed. He was given Thorazine as much to ease his alleged pain, as to shut him up. An hour later they told him two detectives from Phoenix, Arizona were there and wanted to talk with him. He repeated his stance. He wasn't talking about nothing to nobody until he got his lawyer. He fell back on his bunk and waited for his court date later in the morning.

After arriving in Stockton before dawn, and learning it was going to be awhile before they could speak with Steelman and Gretzler, Arellanes and Miller checked into a nearby motel, got cleaned up, then called back to the sheriff's office. Ken Wagner told them that one of the suspects was still holding out, but the other – the one named Gretzler – was talking and they had just brought him back to the basement of the courthouse downtown. Meet him there in a few minutes, Wagner allowed, and they could *sit* in on the interrogation. Wagner wasn't real interested in sharing. Just sit in, he reminded them again. No questions.

When Saiers returned to the office Friday morning, he met with Investigator Brooksher about the items they had recovered in Sacramento. He mentioned specifically a checkbook and identification cards with the names Michael Sandberg and Michael Marsh, both of Tucson. It appeared the Datsun belonged to Sandberg, and he suggested someone call Tucson to let them know what was happening. At 9 am Brooksher gave his counterpart at Pima County Sheriff's Office the information about the car and thc ID recovered in Sacramento. All they had to go on was the name 'Captain Sandberg'. However, he did say that one of the suspects mentioned being in Tucson sometime around the last of October or first week of November, and a guy in a white Datsun picked them up while hitchhiking. He said they tied him up and left him the desert, then took his car.

The information was given to Tucker and Barkman, and although confused about how any of this pertained to them, Tucker returned the call to Stockton. He admitted to Brooksher they were indeed working the only homicide in the county, their body was found in the desert, and the victim was named Sierra, not Sandberg, a young Mexican male with a long rap sheet of drug and alcohol arrests, and certainly not an officer in the Air Force. Plus, he had been driving his brother's 1972 Dodge Charger, not a Datsun. Despite the inconsistencies, Tucker said he would follow up on it and get back to him if he found any connection.

Meanwhile, Barkman called nearby Davis Monthan Air Base and asked if a Captain Sandberg was stationed there, and if so, was he missing? The name didn't ring a bell, but they too promised to look into it. Per Brooksher's request, Barkman also passed the message about Captain Sandberg to Tucson Police, who in turn advised Sergeant Larry Bunting of the call. Bunting wasted no time in getting back to Brooksher, anxious for more details, but was disappointed in the answer. The San Joaquin investigator could only say, once again, they had captured two men who had in their possession the afore-mentioned items, and because the physical evidence was still being processed in Sacramento, all he could offer was a few vague notes and a license number off a late model Datsun two door sedan. "Everything is a little confusing around here," Brooksher apologized, "but maybe you should check on these people." If nothing more, he said, than to let them know their car had been found.

As suggested, Bunting phoned DMV and got the Sandberg's address. The car had not been reported stolen and all the other leads came back negative. Regardless, he still sent two men out to the Sandberg's address on Fort Lowell Road to tell them about their car.

Less than ten minutes later, the two Tucson police officers called from the apartment complex on Fort Lowell Road. They said things didn't look good at the Sandberg place.

The interview with Doug Gretzler began a few minutes after ten in a basement office of the Courthouse. In addition to the suspect and a shorthand reporter, Peter Saiers, Ken Wagner and Carl Ambrose were present, along with Miller and Arrelanes. They had been kept waiting almost a half hour while Brooksher finished with his phone calls. After introductions, Brooksher told Gretzler they had asked him down to clear up some questions about their interview last night. They knew he was lying, but they also knew that within the hour Gretzler would be arraigned and would have an attorney, so this was probably their last opportunity to have him all to themselves.

Brooksher and Wagner first asked about his clothing and the boots he was wearing the night in Lodi. They wanted to hear again what he knew about the girl known as Carol, and why all the Earls were in the house at the same time. Gretzler offered nothing new.

"Then I want to ask you one more time in regards to the actual shooting of these people," continued Wagner. "I want you to just go over this particular part of the incident again. . .and lay it to us straight because there is a lot of things that don't correspond with what you are telling us here in regards to the shooting, I mean in reference to physical evidence and other statements. Do you understand that?"

"Yes I do," Gretzler answered firmly, and then repeated how he had been in the front of the house at the time. But unlike yesterday, he now admitted to hearing 'low pops from back there'.

"Ever see the bodies?" Saiers wanted to know.

"Not after the shooting."

"What about the kids?"

"Just that he said he did them too."

"How do you account for any blood being on your clothing?" Wagner demanded.

". . .or boots?" added Saiers.

"I don't know," Gretzler shrugged.

About twenty minutes into the interview, and seeing their questioning wasn't getting them anywhere, and with an okay nod from Wagner, Saiers introduced Arrelanes and Miller, who informed Gretzler that they were interested in a double homicide east of Phoenix near Apache Junction.

"Is that up towards. . .this is a trailer court up towards the Superstition Mountains?" Gretzler asked.

"That's right," Arrelanes replied. "Are you familiar with this area?"

He was. Even admitting he had stayed there with some people he met named Bob and Yahfah. He proceeded to tell Arrelanes the long story about how he had come with Bill from Denver in his MGB, and how they were supposed to go do some jobs and then go see this guy who's name he couldn't recall. Then he told them about the Preacher deal, but somehow Bill got shot and he lost the MGB at the Tahiti Motel and there was a Volkswagen van that they drove out somewhere but had to ditch it and hitchhike and got picked up by a dude and two girls who dropped them off maybe ten minutes later and Bill got them another car and told him it was going be okay. He said they went back to Phoenix again where they went to see Bob and Yahfah. Then one day Bill sent him out for some cigarettes or chocolate milk or something, to a Circle K somewhere close by, and when he got back Bill had all their stuff in Bob's car because the Ford had a flat tire, so they left and ditched the car, then got a cab, then got a bus down to Tucson.

Arrelanes' head was swimming. He stopped him in his tracks. "Let's get back to Bob and Yahfah. Do you know a Marsha?"

"Yes."

"She has given us the whole story, Doug. Were you aware that Bob and Yahfah are dead?"

"Yeah, I gathered."

"How did you gather that?"

"Well, when it was mentioned to me I was wanted in connection with a murder in Phoenix, in a trailer court, I figured, hell, the only trailer court I've been to was Bob and Yahfah's, and it must be in connection with something there."

"So in other words what you're telling us is that you weren't present when they were killed?"

"No, I didn't know in truth they had actually been killed."

Just listening to Gretzler's long-winded explanations, it was easy to see how Donnie Brooksher had the story so backwards, and yet, fortunately for him, it had worked to his advantage. In his conversation with Gretzler the previous night, Brooksher somehow mixed up the part about the guy with the Datsun, (the guy Gretzler said they had gagged and left in the desert near Tucson) and Captain Sandberg, (the name found in the room at the Clunie Hotel). In attempting to sort out the jumble of info coming from Gretzler, had mistakenly combined both stories. Something wasn't adding up, yet he felt a connection. He excused himself from the room and again called Pima County. He asked for Weaver Barkman and told him again of 'a man who they left in the desert named Sandberg'. "Don't you have something about a kid being left in the desert?" he asked. So Barkman repeated the story of the murder of Gilbert Sierra, and Brooksher knew in his gut there was something, or someone, that linked the two killings?

Brooksher returned and took his best shot. "How about the seventy-two Dodge Charger, white over orange, young Mexican kid by the name of Sierra, five-seven, a hundred and seventy, long hair? Can you tell me something about this?"

He knew immediately he had caught Gretzler off guard. He had caught everyone off guard.

"Uh. . .seventy-two Charger?" Gretzler stammered.

"Dodge Charger. His body was discovered about six miles west of Tucson. He was blown away. . .shot three times with a twenty-two. Name is Gilbert Rodriquez Sierra. Third of November."

Gretzler sat stone-faced.

As did Arellanes and Miller, who were hearing about Steelman and Gretzler's activities in Tucson for the very first time.

Gretzler stumbled around for words. "Third of November? Well, that was already. . .that was Phoenix too. I remember a Charger. . .we had for a little while,. . .not too long."

"Who squeezed the trigger?" Brooksher shot back.

On that matter Doug did not hesitate.

"Bill did."

In Tucson, Detectives Condiss and Phillips arrived at the Villa Parasio Condominiums and did a quick check of the area. They found the unit marked 49-b and walked upstairs. On the balcony they noticed a newspaper dated Sunday, November 4th, along with a pair of flip-flop sandals and two hairbrushes. Huge black flies slammed against the inside of the front door slider. The detectives could hear music inside, but after repeated pounding and yelling, they gave up and walked back downstairs.

Mr. Watts was working the sales office and the officers advised him of the reason for their visit. Watts said had been concerned about the Sandbergs too. They're a pleasant young couple, he said, and up until recently he would see them every few days or so, because while the project is being built, all the mail comes to his office and all the new residents pick it up there. He had been saving the Sandberg's for almost a week but neither of them had come by to get it. Thought that was strange. Hadn't seen their car around either. He just figured they had left town without telling him. He had a passkey to all the units, he offered, and could let them in to look around if it was really important.

It was, they replied, so back upstairs they went and Watts unlocked the door, then stepped aside and waited for Condiss to open it. The sweet sickly smell overpowered them and flooded on onto the balcony. Condiss took a few steps inside and looked around. He knew what they would find, so he walked back to the door and shut it tight behind him, telling Phillips to stay put, he was going down to call Bunting.

With the report in from the Sandberg's residence, Bunting called the Coroner's Pathologist, crime scene technicians and a photographer. He also tracked down Homicide Detective Larry Hust who would take control of the investigation upon his arrival. Soon, several marked units were crowding the parking lot as well, awaiting their instructions. Bunting got there a few minutes later and walked inside, doing his utmost to fight off the odor. In the living room he noticed a blanket covering something on the sofa. He gently lifted one corner and confirmed his suspicion. In the bedroom he found another body, this one a man, lying face down on the bed. His arms and legs were bound together with twine, which was then looped up and around his neck. His wrists and neck had been padded prior to being tied and a white bed sheet partially wrapped the body. Both of the victims were in a severe state of decomposition. The apartment showed signs of criminal activity; closet doors were opened and items scattered about for example, but there were no signs of any struggle by the victims. Bunting waited for the photographer to record the scene before he went any further.

The interrogation of Douglas Gretzler continued for another thirty minutes. It covered Phoenix, then Tucson and then back again. Despite his best efforts, Arrelanes could never get him back to Bob and Yahfah's trailer. Doug was adamant about Bill being the one who killed the Mexican kid, as well as the one who pulled the gun on the guy in the blue Firebird, and yet he never said a word about anyone named Sandberg. The closest they came to it was near the end when Brooksher and Saiers brought it up.

"How about the other kidnappings back there in the Tucson area?" Brooksher inquired.

"Which?"

"Well, the guy Sandberg for one."

"That was...that was...that was..." Doug stammered.

Saiers was more direct. "What did you do with the people who owned the white Datsun?"

"I don't know...I never, you know...all I knew was that when we went in we had the Firebird and we saw the guy washing his car and Bill told me we could throw down on him and he told me to stay by the Datsun and he and the guy went upstairs and he stayed up there until around six or seven and it was dark by then and he came back down said, 'I got the Datsun. Let's go'."

"Did you hear any shots?"

"No I didn't."

It was not even a half hour later when Tucson Police called about finding the two bodies in the apartment. The news did not surprise Brooksher as much as infuriate him. They had just finished with Gretzler, and got some info about the Sierra kid, but never bothered to nail down exactly what had happened to the Sandbergs. By now Gretzler was on his way to his arraignment and would be assigned a lawyer. Brooksher knew he might never have the opportunity again.

Bunting told Brooksher the initial indications were the couple had been shot. Fingerprinting had begun, but the autopsies wouldn't be performed for at least another couple of hours. Any solid comparison between the killing of the Sandbergs and the people in Lodi would have to wait. Bunting said that what he could really use right now were fingerprint samples on the suspects, and Brooksher promised to see what he could do. The two agreed that one common thread seemed to run through both crimes. All of the victims had been bound and gagged in a similar fashion, right down to the padding of their wrists. Bunting hadn't paid too much attention to that particular detail, but later, after the bodies had been removed, he sent an officer down to the Coroner's Office to photographs the elaborate bindings, along with instructions to remove them, but keep them intact for evidence.

Also, during the final few minutes of their interrogation of Gretzler, after the Sierra murder had been brought up, Gretzler told them where the cops in Tucson could find the white Charger. Brooksher relayed the info to Bunting, who in turn called Barkman. "Gretzler said it's parked near an apartment by a Jack in the Box on Speedway," he reported.

An hour later sheriff deputies found the car exactly where they were told it would be.

Bold headlines in Friday morning's *Lodi News Sentinel*:

> ***TWO ACCUSED OF VICTOR MURDERS***
>
> *Steelman pulled trigger, Gretzler reportedly said (Friday, November 9, 1973) Douglas Gretzler, suspect in the Victor mass murder case has fingered Willie Luther Steelman as the triggerman, a source close to the investigation told the* News-Sentinel *last night. Gretzler, according to the source, freely admitted the Victor slayings and said Steelman was the one who did the shooting.*
>
> *Meanwhile, the pair will be arraigned in Stockton Municipal Court this morning in the courtroom of Judge Wm. Woodward.*

At ten minutes to eleven, in a convoy of sheriff patrol units and a motorcycle escort surrounding it, Willie Steelman was brought to the Stockton courthouse.

The basement delivery area had been cleared and the nearby streets scoured for anyone who looked suspicious. Two blocks away, a man carrying an air rifle was pushed up against a patrol car and searched. The death threats had continued through the night. Sheriff deputies were tipped off late Thursday about a plan conceived where several men were going to be arrested in separate incidents only to regroup once in jail and kill the two men with their bare hands.

But overnight security at French Camp was so tight only a few people even knew what cells the suspects were in. They remained separated at all times, including this morning when Gretzler was brought to the courthouse hours before his partner.

Five minutes before the scheduled hearing, county marshals swept through Woodward's court and cleared it. Many of those who were simply waiting for an appearance suddenly found themselves not just out in the hall, but all the way out on the street. Outside the courtroom a pack of newspaper, radio and television reporters jockeyed for position, of which only thirty managed to get inside, while those remaining were forced to wait in the hall. No cameras were allowed and Woodward permitted only one sketch artist in the room. The rest of the seats were open to the public. First come, first served. The line for that had started forming hours earlier. At the door entering the courtroom the delay was a long one as marshals checked bags and briefcases and ran an electronic wand over every person allowed inside. Inside, plainclothes officers mingled amongst the spectators, while armed patrol officers guarded each door and paced the hallway, all of which was responsible for a 40-minute delay in the proceedings.

But the delay also had allowed the interview with Doug Gretzler upstairs to last longer than planned, and when it was time, Arrelanes and Miller accompanied Gretzler to the elevator and continued to talk to him as they rode upstairs. "You know, Doug," Arellanes remarked, "they told us you had been real truthful with everyone here in Stockton and that's all we're looking for; just to cooperate with us. We just want to know about Bob and Yahfah and how they were murdered, that's all."

Doug could not hold out any longer. He broke down. In the elevator he told Arrelanes he admitted knowing all along that Bob and Yahfah were dead. Bill garroted Bob with a wire and they took him to the bedroom where he helped Bill put him under the mattress.

"How about Yahfah? When was she killed?"

The next day, Doug confessed. Bob had got it at night while Yahfah was at work, so she never knew.

"How was Yahfah killed?"

"She was kneeling over a candle or incense or something and Bill came up and put a towel on the end of the twenty-two and shot her in the back of her head." This happened in the living room, he said, so he helped Bill carry her to the master bedroom. "Yahfah was still moving, so Bill shot her again in the head."

The elevator stopped and they started to move Gretzler out into the waiting area next to the courtroom when word came in to take the prisoner back downstairs, they weren't ready yet.

"How about Ken and Mike? Where are they at?"

"We dumped them somewhere out in the country?"
"Are they dead?"
"Yeah."
"How were they killed? Did you shot them too?"
"No. One was stabbed, the other garroted."

The District Attorney's Office had stayed late through the night preparing the information to be used in the arraignment. Because he had not even left Sacramento until the wee hours of the morning, Peter Saiers conferred only briefly with Richard Eichenberger, Chief Trial Deputy for the county. It was Eichenberger who would present the prosecution's case. The San Joaquin D.A was Joe Baker. And with a case of this magnitude, it would seem only logical that Baker would be front row center. After winning election, and running on the skirts of a well-organized political machine, Baker was reelected to office several times, usually unopposed. Baker was up again in 1974, and while it may have been early, it was obvious this was going to be huge case with an excellent chance of conviction – two things most men in his position would give anything for. But Baker seldom tried cases anymore, and in fact, when they were quizzed about it, few people in the office could remember the last case he prosecuted. Come to think of it, they added, he was hardly ever *in* the office anymore.

Judge Woodward's first call Friday morning, hours before the scheduled arraignment, was to George Dedekam. He had picked Dedekam's name from a lawyer's reference list supplied to the judges. Dedekam was one of the lawyers on the county "Serious Felony Panel" and Woodward felt comfortable he had not only the experience, but also the low-key style necessary to represent either one of the defendants effectively.

Dedekam had arrived at the courthouse just minutes before the arraignment and all he knew about the case was what he had read in the papers or saw on TV. And although Sam Libicki knew yesterday he would be in court this morning, he wasn't any better prepared. The Public Defender's Office had received nothing on the case or the suspects, and like Dedekam, could only rely on the media for what limited information they had. Still, Libicki arrived at Woodward's courtroom as excited as everyone else to get his first look at the two defendants.

At exactly 11:38, the judge entered and the room fell silent. A middle aged man with a surprisingly large face and a high forehead, Woodward was considered by those who stood before him to be a firm disciplinarian of the law who ruled over his courtroom with a no nonsense approach. But understandably, even he was a bit aprehensive this morning, and his eyes scanned the room as he approached his bench. He knew what he was about to face this morning. He had heard in great detail the depravity of their crimes, and the hideous scene they had left behind at the house in Victor. It seemed as if there was nothing sacred anymore, not even his courtroom, and there was no telling what might take place, especially with the tension clouding this community over these killings. He had seen the crowds that gathered last night. He heard the hatred in their voices, their open threats of retribution, their call of swift justice. He remembered that even the judge at the Manson trial just 2 years earlier had resorted to packing a gun, and some said remnants of The Family were still out there, waiting to even the score. And now talk buzzed the building that one of the defendants this morning had been mentioning Manson by name, boasting that 'his own people would never let him get to trial'. Many noticed how uncomfortable Woodward looked, and agreed he had every right to.

Gretzler was the first to be brought in, shackled, handcuffed, and ringed by deputies. The jail jumpsuits were intentionally different colors, each signaling the level of security that would surround the prisoner. His was red, and baggy, and hung about his skinny frame like a draped parachute. His hair was dirty, stringy, falling over his pale white face, a face forever looking down, as if not even he could bare to see what was going on around him.

"Douglas Edward Gretzler.You are charged with a violation of Section one eighty-seven of the Penal Code. Murder."

Woodward paused for a moment, then fanned through a stack of papers in front of him.

"Count One. The victim being Walter Parkin."

"Count Two. The victim being Richard A. Earl."

"Count Three. The victim being Ricky Earl."

"Count Four. The victim being Wanda Jean Earl."

"Count Five. The victim being Debbie Earl."

"Count Six. The victim being Joanne Parkin."

"Count Seven. The victim being Mark Allen Lang."

Woodward had paused between each name, but now the wait became even more pronounced, as if trying to find the strength to continue, or reluctance to be the one who read the names of the final two victims. He took a deep breath, then raised his voice, making sure to emphasize the number to show his disdain for the fate of these last two, the children.

"Count Eight. The victim being Robert Allen Parkin."

"Count Nine. The victim being Lisa Parkin."

Gretzler's eyes never left the floor. Woodward was not finished. The prosecution had added one more charge.

"Count Ten. You are charged with a violation of Section 209 of the Penal Code. Kidnapping for the purpose of robbery." Woodward advised the defendant he had the right to choose his own attorney. However, if he didn't have one, or couldn't afford one, the court was going to appoint George Dedekam as his representative. Dedekam stood up as his name was mentioned. Gretzler looked up long enough to nod his head and mumble.

Woodward took that as a yes. "You will be remanded to the custody of the Sheriff," he ordered. "And there will be no bail."

The hearing complete, Gretzler was escorted through the side doors and back into the elevator to the basement. Making sure the defendant's paths never crossed, there was a few minutes delay before Willie Steelman was ushered in and the procedure repeated almost word for word. But unlike Doug, Willie was animated and cocky. He spent a lot of time looking around the room as if he was expecting to see someone he knew. His head was up and he glared right back at Woodward as the judge read the long list of charges.

But if the tension wasn't thick enough, Frank Dean, a member of the D.A.'s Investigation Unit, was in the courtroom, and he fidgeted in his seat to get more comfortable. As he did, his service revolver fell out from his waistband. In an already hushed room, the pistol hit the floor and went spinning across it. Bailiffs jumped, as did Woodward's nerves, as they watched the firearm slide out onto the courtroom floor. Willie saw it too and cracked a smile as he watched an embarrassed Dean fetch his revolver.

Woodward brought the hearing to a close by appointing Sam Libicki as Steelman's counsel, and with that, Willie was hustled out of the room. Libicki ran up to his new client as he was being taken away and pleaded with him. "Don't talk to anybody! I'll try and be out to see you tomorrow."

If it was anything, the Lang family was quiet and close knit. For the past 48 hours, the Langs had gathered in their Lodi home to reminisce, and grieve, about Mark's life. And for every single one of those hours, under explicit instructions from Sheriff Canlis, a uniformed deputy stood watch outside the home. The Lang's took no comfort in his presence. They wished he would just go away. It only reminded them of their loss. They also decided their family would remain private, and they agreed that from that moment on they would never discuss Mark, or his death, with anyone outside their family. As sensational as the murders had become, they did not wish to see their son and brother be a victim twice. As family members and close friends came and went from the home, reporters swarmed, asking for a comment, searching to know how the family felt, or how they were holding up. Each time their requests were refused. They would not talk about Mark's death, or even damn his killers, in public.

Each member took it very hard. Mr. and Mrs. Lang were elderly, and yet Mark was especially close to his father, despite the years. Mark's brothers did their best to shield their father from the details of the tragedy. Mike Lang even told the officers at the crime scene on Wednesday that he wanted to be the one to identify the body and to break the news to his father. The request was granted. Mark's older sister, Sharon, who had been the last to be with him Tuesday night, scolded herself for not being able to do something, anything, to have helped save her baby brother. Nor could she believe the news when it was reported who police were looking for. Up until the eighth grade, she and Denise Machell had been the best of friends. Those days had long since passed, and by that time she heard Denise had married an older man by the name of Bill Steelman.

So to save themselves additional pain, the Langs decided as a family that they would move through this episode as quickly as possible. At 2 o'clock Friday afternoon they buried Mark. Three hundred people, mostly friends he had met in his young life showed up to pay their respects. Per the family's request, reporters and cameras were not allowed anywhere near the services. As the frigid San Joaquin fog began to lift, haunting harmonica strains of one of Mark's favorite songs could be heard; "And When I Die" by Blood Sweat & Tears.

"I can swear there ain't no heaven,
and I pray there ain't no hell.
But I'll never know by living,
It's only by dying I can tell."

Two of the pallbearers were Steve McFadden and Wayne Nitsche. The pastor read from the New Testament and recited the story about how Jesus consoled another family who were grieving over the loss of a brother. Those believing in Christ, he quoted from the Bible, will live again. He reminded everyone, despite the lyrics of the song, that Mark loved Christ. He knew him intimately, he promised, and believed in him deeply.

And from that day forward the Langs made good on their word not to discuss Mark with anyone outside their family. The only comfort they could gather was knowing he and Debbie were now together forever, just as the two had planned only a few weeks earlier.

After his arraignment, Gretzler was brought back down to the basement. The earlier interview was resumed so Detective Ambrose could clear up the matter up of the double murder in the trailer park, the killing of the Mexican kid, and now two new names, Ken and Mike, victims who had suddenly surfaced out of nowhere. Five bodies in the past twenty minutes, and that did not include the nine they had from Victor. Ambrose could not help but wonder just how many more they would find.

Now that he had an attorney, Ambrose wanted Gretzler to notify Dedekam of the ongoing interrogation. Because of security, Ambrose could only reach the attorney by phone. Ambrose prodded Gretzler. "You're going to advise him that you are going to make further statements to us. Do you understand that?" He handed Gretzler the phone.

"I understand. I'm willing to make a statement, with or without him," he replied.

Surprisingly, Dedekam protested only slightly to Ambrose. "I told him not to, but I didn't have much of a chance (to talk to Gretzler) in court."

But he made it clear he wanted his client to remain tight lipped, at least for the time being, and he told Gretzler just that. "No more statements, then. Okay? I don't have many reports, so it will be sometime this week before I come out and see you."

Doug sounded disappointed and Dedekam changed the subject. "Now, do you have any parents to be notified?"

"I already talked to them," he said. "I want to find my wife.

There were two important pieces of evidence missing in the San Joaquin investigation. Money and guns. Doug admitted they had split up the money at the motel that first night and said he thought Bill 'had about fifteen hundred on him' when they were walking around Sacramento. Melinda Kashula told Barbieri that when they came to the massage parlor, Bill invited her to count his money and said she 'got to $900 and then quit'. Yet when Steelman was captured, he had a mere $330 on him. So where was the rest of the money?

Detective Ambrose called Sacramento and asked if there was a possibility it could still be inside the girl's apartment?

At 2 p.m. the police tracked down Melinda, who answered that she saw him in the kitchen with a lot of money, but did not see what he did with it. She assumed the cops got it when they captured him. Sacramento police met her an hour later at the apartment and the first place Melinda looked was under the sink.

"Oh, here it is!" she exclaimed as she pulled a huge roll of bills from their hiding place, not knowing she had just tampered with evidence. The officer cringed as he congratulated her, but asked that she put it back exactly where she found it. The photographer then took a several pictures for the evidence file. They then pulled it back out from its hiding place and counted out $1064.

The second problem were guns. Friday afternoon the Department of Justice called to say they had examined the lead slugs removed from the bodies and determined they came from two different weapons. Ambrose looked back on the notes received from Sacramento and learned that Gretzler was indeed carrying .22 caliber bullets on him when he was captured. The detective figured maybe Gretzler knew he was about to be caught and had time to dispose of the weapon. If that was the case, it still had to be somewhere in the hotel.

Ambrose called Sacramento once more, this time about the possibility of a second weapon being hidden in the Clunie. He told them they were on their way up to begin a new search. Meanwhile, Sacramento said they would send someone over to start looking for the missing weapon. They found nothing in the areas they knew Gretzler had access to, and a few places he didn't, such as the roof. They even searched adjoining rooftops speculating that he may have tossed it out an open window. Each time they came up empty. Ambrose said they would return the next day to resume the search, hoping Gretzler would start talking again.

STOCKTON RECORD

TWO MORE BODIES FOUND IN ARIZONA

> *(November 9, 1973) Tucson, Arizona authorities have found two bodies in a residence there as a result of questioning Willie Luther Steelman and Douglas Edward Gretzler following their capture in Sacramento Thursday. Officials fear there may be more bodies uncovered in Arizona and elsewhere. In addition, authorities believe they are responsible for the disappearance of two men, Mike Adshade and Ken Unrein, both 22 and both of Phoenix, on October 17.*

The afternoon *Stockton Record* was going to print just as word leaked out about the phone calls back and forth from Tucson. They stopped the presses and cleared front-page space for the pending story. They also followed the lead of the Lodi *News-Sentinel* from that morning that had splashed a huge bold headline across top of Friday's paper.

STEELMAN NAMED TRIGGERMAN BY PAL

After returning from Sacramento, Brooksher told Peter Saiers the rumor circulating at the Sheriff's Office was that Canlis had promised reporters he would let them tour the Parkin home later in the day. Saiers was beside himself! The fingerprint team had not even left yet, physical evidence was still being gathered, and now his very own Sheriff was going to take any newsman who signed up on a field trip through a working crime scene. Yesterday's *Stockton Record* was bad enough. On the front page of the paper were splashed gruesome pictures of the bloody closet and bed where the youngest victims had been found. It was the type of publicity that destroys an otherwise solid case. All a defense attorney had to do is point the picture to a judge to show pretrial prejudice. Either that, or you have major problems seating a jury, or possibly sufficient grounds for reversal on error in the appeals process. The very least was that there was little room to argue when the defense motioned for a change of venue.

The newspaper photos came as a huge surprise, because the media had never been allowed inside the Parkin house. And while it appeared to Saiers that the photos looked suspiciously like scenes from the videotape, no one was willing to point the finger directly at who they thought the culprit might be, although more than one person suggested the problem with news leaks started and ended at the top.

Saiers could not reach Canlis, and fearing he was already on his way to Victor, he raced to intercept him. Much to his relief, Canlis was nowhere to be found. Saiers explained his problem to the technicians on duty who agreed to do whatever they could to dissuade the Sheriff if he did indeed show up with members of the media. Whatever Saiers said to them must have found its way back to Canlis, because there were no newsmen allowed in that day, or for many, many days to come.

When Pete Saiers graduated from the University of Arizona, one of his many classmates was a fellow named Jim Howard. After graduation, Howard stayed in Tucson and hooked on with Pima County District Attorney's office, and the two had managed to stay in touch over the years, so Saiers called Howard Friday afternoon to fill him in on the California developments. Saiers was especially enthusiastic about how everything was falling in place. One of the suspects was talking, he said, but unfortunately he was also describing other murders they had apparently committed as well. Howard replied that he had just been to one of them, the Sandberg home, and it was the most revolting sight he had ever laid eyes on. Saiers understood completely.

Larry Hust wasn't even in Tucson when he got the call from Bunting about the double homicide. He was returning from Phoenix, heading south on I-10 when he got word over the radio that Bunting wanted him. Hust was sharp enough to decipher the vague message and knew Bunting was trying to keep the media from overhearing their conversation and swarming the crime scene, with limited success.

Hust was not too far behind the officers who first opened the front door, although by the time he arrived, Bunting had already reviewed the scene and started the investigation. The officers who made the discovery got the passkey and checked inside every other condo unit in the development, but found nothing. They interviewed several other residents, but because the condominium development was so new, the Sandbergs didn't even have a neighbor below or next to them.

Tucson Police had finally connected the homicide to the Armstrong kidnap attempt. His blue Firebird had been found in the same parking lot the previous Sunday, an officer noted on his report, and it was also shown that officers attempted to knock on some of the doors in their investigation that day. One resident mentioned seeing the Firebird, but not the white Datsun. She told officers that some people said they saw a negro and a white man, both in their twenties, wandering the complex last Saturday, but she couldn't recall who she had heard that from.

They were having slightly better success inside the apartment. When they eventually lifted the blanket from the sofa, they found, in addition to a body, a pillow, which appeared to have been used as a silencer to muffle the gunshots. In the kitchen, analysts found quality prints on a mayonnaise jar and assorted glasses and dishes. In the bathroom it appeared as if someone had used hair dye, and the containers were taken in as evidence. On the coffee table in front of the sofa was a ball of twine and a woman's purse that showed signs of having been rummaged through. Next to it, an Arizona road map.

Soon after Hust arrived, so did Randy Stevens and Jim Howard from the D.A.'s office. The sights and smells were too much for Howard and he left quickly, but Stevens stayed. He remained there for most of the afternoon, gathering as much information as he could store in his head. He made sure he looked several times at the victims in an effort to remind himself later the disgust he felt. He chose to take this personally. He walked in and out of each of the rooms of the small apartment. In the back bedroom he saw a photograph he forever etched in his mind. The picture was of an attractive young woman in a white gown and a handsome Marine in his dress whites. They were smiling and the woman held a delicate bouquet of flowers. It was a wedding photo, and Stevens had to study it for several minutes before realizing that it was the same two people who's bloated and spoiled bodies they had just uncovered.

Bunting knew he had no choice but to go up to Stockton to interrogate the two being held there, and while he certainly did not want to, he knew he should ask Mike Tucker to accompany him. Tucson Police and the Pima County Sheriff's Office never had what would be considered a tight working relationship. They cooperated when necessary, and some even had friends on the other side, but there had existed a tension between the two for many years. Tucson thought the sheriff department was a little backwards, and Pima County considered the city cops nothing more than snobs, so they always seemed to trip over each other near the city limit sign, especially as the town grew. But despite which side of the street they worked, almost every one of them agreed that Mike Tucker could be a real sonafabitch to work with.

Barkman had him as partner, and was quick to bit his lip when asked about him. Hust, on the other hand, just out and out didn't like him, said so every chance he got, and the two would square off more than once before the Steelman and Gretzler story ran it's course. But for Bunting it was just that he really didn't feel like traveling all the way to California with the guy, let alone staying a few days in the same motel room together.

Tucker could be a little cocky, a little arrogant, a little pushy. Or he could be a lot of those, depending on who you asked. But he had a homicide case to wrap up just like the others, and every reason to be in Stockton with the rest of them, so Tucker called the airport and got flight times for he and Bunting. They would leave Tucson around 3:30 p.m., and after a layover in L.A., be in Stockton before nine that night. Tucker picked up $500 in traveling money from the county and even got a letter from his boss, Sheriff Cox, introducing him and giving him full authority to, *'proceed to Stockton and take custody of __________, a fugitive from justice and return said fugitive to the County of Pima, Arizona'*. Cox decided to leave the line blank because he didn't know if Tucker was going to come back with one, or both of the suspects. Tucker, on the other hand, decided he was not coming back empty handed. Screw Tucson. Screw Stockton. He had a job to do.

But Bunting and Tucker ran into the same adversary Miller and Arellanes did. San Joaquin fog. Just minutes before they were to takeoff, word came back the flight had been cancelled. So they took the same route as the others. They drove up to Phoenix, flew into San Francisco then rented a car. They got to Stockton at 12:45 Saturday morning and found the French Camp jail. Introducing themselves, they said they wished to talk with Willie Steelman and Douglas Gretzler regarding an ongoing homicide investigation in their jurisdiction. The jailer said he was certain they couldn't talk with Steelman because he was insisting on no interviews, but he would check with Gretzler. He promised nothing, considering the late hour.

A few minutes later the jailer returned and announced that Gretzler said he would be happy to talk.

When Doug was brought into the interrogation room, the officers introduced themselves and the reason for their trip. They wanted him to know he was going to be charged with three murders in Arizona, and did he want to give his version of it. He replied he had been advised by his attorney not to give any more taped statements, but if they wanted to just ask him some questions he would be happy to answer them the best he knew how. Bunting told him that anything he said, taped or not, could be used against him, and asked him again if he understood his rights.

Bunting's tone grated on Gretzler. Here he was trying to cooperate and act nice and all, and all he hears is that anything he says is going to be used against him. Like he was stupid, or something. He snapped back. "I've know what my constitutional rights are and I know all about my Miranda rights and all that since I first got myself arrested!"

"Then you know you don't have to talk to us?"

"I know all that."

But with their first question, Doug calmed down and started in. He didn't stop until an hour later. The conversation was not recorded. Tucker and Bunting decided not to force the issue. The last thing they wanted to do was to piss the guy off and wind up with nothing out of the deal, especially after coming all this way. They hoped there would be other opportunities to tape his statements. Gretzler was relaxed and cooperative, smoking the cigarettes offered him as he casually explained how they got picked up by the kid in the Charger, and how Bill shot him.

He remembered Michael Marsh's name but not that of his girlfriend. She had a friend or a sister named Sue and that was all he could tell them. He mentioned getting the Firebird, then ditching it because they were so hot. He said Bill spotted the guy washing his car and threw down on him and took him upstairs. A few hours later he came down and they left in the white Datsun.

"Did you ever go inside the residence?" Bunting quizzed.

"No I did not."

"Are those the only three homicides you were involved with in the Tucson area?" asked Tucker.

Gretzler thought for a minute and said yes, in Tucson, that was it.

How about elsewhere in Arizona?

Gretzler said before going to Tucson there were two people in a trailer near Phoenix and then he and Bill brought two guys from Phoenix to California and Steelman killed these people and dumped them in Santa Rosa, California. They then went back to Phoenix, and then to Tucson.

At the end of the conversation, Doug asked them if they were going to talk with Steelman. "Don't tell him anything about talking to me. Don't tell him I gave you anything. I'm afraid of him and if he finds out I talked to you he'll kill me."

How would he do that, they asked, both of you are in jail?

"I don't know, but he would find a way."

But Tucker and Bunting did get an opportunity to talk with Steelman. Several minutes after Gretzler was taken away, now well into the early morning hours, the guards showed up with Willie.

"I'm not interested in speaking with you guys," he said. "And my attorney said not to anyway."

"Well, that's your right," Bunting acknowledged. "But we want you to know that you're going to be arrested and charged with the Sandberg murders back in Arizona."

Steelman nodded he understood.

"Might be something for you to think about," Bunting added, "because Arizona has the death penalty, and if you have your version of the story, well, we would be interested in hearing it."

Bunting let it sink in, then added. "And you know it might be important because you definitely will be charged, I can guarantee you that."

Steelman tossed aside the suggestion and said that he would think about it. For right now, however, he said only that he had nothing more to say to anyone.

35

Saturday, November 10, 1973.

Around mid morning, a woman walked into the Pinal County Sheriff Substation near Apache Junction to retrieve a wallet they had been holding for her. It had been brought into their office almost two weeks earlier, and after finding an address inside, deputies notified them by mail of their recent discovery. A week later they received a letter from a woman residing in nearby Glendale explaining the wallet actually belonged to her grandson and that she would be in as soon as possible to claim it.

When she arrived to collect the billfold, she said that it was not unusual for her grandson to take off at any moment on one of his grand escapades. She acknowledged he had been gone for three weeks now, but did not seem overly concerned, that while his empty wallet had been found, he had not called to declare it missing. She patted the billfold and announced. "Steve will show up soon and I know he'll be glad to have this back."

Steve Loughran's grandmother was partially correct. He would indeed show up before the day was over.

He was told there were more authorities coming in to talk with him. So now there would be more stories to tell, more lies to spin. It was all getting to be too much, and Doug Gretzler wondered just how long he could hold on. Friday night a detention guard at the jail told him what the newspapers were saying. They said Douglas Gretzler was talking and he was pointing all the blame at his partner, Steelman. Up to now, Doug had not seen any of the papers, but what the jailer told him only confirmed what he already suspected; the talks he had with the cops were somehow getting out.

He had no idea if Bill was talking or not, but he knew if Bill ever found out he was copping him out, then he was a dead man. With all his connections, all his family, all the Mafia people and shit, well then, Doug knew he didn't stand a chance in hell of staying alive. In or out of jail, Bill would get him.

Arellanes and Miller stopped by the jail at nine-thirty Saturday morning to try one more time to get the truth about Bob and Yahfah. Dave got right to the point.

"Douglas. We'll call you Doug, okay? What we are interested in is in the murder of Bob and Yahfah in the trailer park. Could you tell us how this murder came down?"

Gretzler replied that it all started with Ken and Mike, because Bill said stealing the van meant Bob would know what happened. So after Ken and Mike, they drove all the way back to Phoenix and took care of Bob because Bill felt it was important to get rid of him just to be sure there weren't any witnesses to the Ken and Mike deal. But afterwards they couldn't get Bob's body out of the house because Yahfah wouldn't leave to go to work, so Bill did her too. Doug spoke in great detail, but made it clear Bill was the one who did them both. His job was simply to stand guard.

"You understand we have missing person's reports on Ken and Mike?" Miller asked.

"Yeah," Doug acknowledged. "I'll give you an explanation as to the best way I know to find the bodies."

"Okay."

"Alright, they were garroted and stabbed to death near San Jose, California... out in the country, way out in the country, and uh, you'll probably have to use a helicopter to find them." His directions consisted of "just up a road...we drove in a van...there's a bridge...cement bridge...a small indentation in the ground... dragged them across a little river...there's a marsh...some tall reeds..."

Miller was confused and stopped him. "I think yesterday you said it was Santa Rosa."

"Oh yeah...Santa Rosa...Well it was one of them." He chuckled under his breath at his confusion. "There's so many 'Sans' towns around," he complained.

Miller and Arrelanes knew right then Gretzler couldn't lead them anywhere – hell, he didn't even know what part of the state he was in – so before they left, Miller pleaded with him one more time, that if he really knew where they could find the bodies, he had to come clean. "These families deserve the right to bury these people. Let's find them now and get it taken care of."

"Well, that's all the bodies," said Doug, not replying directly to Miller's request.

"All you know about?"

"Yeah, cuz I was with Bill all the time. He never let me out of his sight and I really didn't care to get out of his sight. And for awhile there, I was too frightened to."

Gretzler was sent back to his cell and Arrelanes decided to give Steelman another shot at telling them where to find Ken and Mike. Still, as a precaution, Dave called Sergeant Nelson in Santa Rosa to tell him there was a slight possibility the bodies could be in his area. By late morning, officials there had mobilized the Sonoma County Volunteer Posse, who started searching the banks of the Russian River on horseback near where the van had been found. It was a miserable day on the coast; rainy and windy, and with only their plastic rain gear to protect them, they fanned out to cover the trails and back roads to where the river meets the ocean.

Arrelanes had figured out by now that Steelman was the lead guy, and he was from around this area, so his intention was to get Steelman talking long enough to find out where they had dumped Adshade and Unrein. In the very brief conversation they had with Steelman in the early hours of Saturday morning, Arrelanes had encouraged him, even if he did nothing else, to at least come across with the location. It was the only good thing that could out of all this, Dave told him.

Willie said if they would promise not to talk about the Lodi thing, then he would go back and sleep on it. He made a point to complain again about his heroin withdrawals and how much pain he was in, and if they could help him get something for it, then maybe he could get some sleep. He needed sleep if he was going to help them.

So now, hours later, they were back to try it again. Willie said nothing about the drugs he had requested earlier. He began only by saying that if they would give their word not to 'get into the California thing', meaning Lodi, then he would try and help them find Ken and Mike. It was agreed.

Willie started off by talking about the Preacher incident, then eventually working his way back to Ken and Mike and how they took them to California.

"You said you dumped them off. Did you kill 'em'?"

"Yeah – strangled one and I hit one over the head – I don't know, I think it was his head. I pushed him and Doug strangled him and cut his throat."

"Near what town?"

"Modesto. You turn off 99 and it's maybe 70 miles out in the country. I'm not really sure."

"Does Santa Rosa ring a bell to you?" Miller inquired.

"Yeah I've been there. They're nowhere near Santa Rosa." Willie spent the next several minutes trying to describe the area where it happened. About halfway through the forty-five minute interview, while Willie was explaining how they took Bob's car to the bus station, he stopped dead. He rubbed his thumb across his temple and closed his eyes. "It seems to me they dumped one of those bodies on the first day. . .out past Bob and Yahfah's." Willie seemed genuinely puzzled with this new revelation, like it had just occurred to him what had happened.

"Past their house?" Arellanes asked, anxious to get him back on track.

"Yeah. It seems to me they said they were taking them out to the Superstition Mountains and maybe, you know, drop them off?" He sounded as if he was maybe even questioning himself, as if he wasn't really sure that it even happened at all. "Man, my head's really messed up," he announced.

"Hey, just take your time. . .take it easy."

"I don't know, things kept coming down every time we turned around. . .and somebody else got shot."

"Who was that?" Dave asked again, taking the time to walk Steelman back through the towns and the killings, and having him count each one they happened. Willie still looked confused, so Dave went easy on him, trying to work it all out in sequence.

"It seems to me I'm forgetting about somebody somewhere. I'm trying to figure it out. I shot three people in this whole mess and trying to think of the one I'm forgetting."

"Was it in Phoenix?"

"Yeah, out in the desert."

"Was it the Preacher deal?"

"No, that wasn't included in it. It was somebody else. How can you forget about shooting somebody?" Willie was upset. "Damn it! I put somebody in a sleeping bag, and shot 'em."

"Why did you shoot them? " Arrelanes asked. "Was it a man or a woman?"

"Man."

"Do you know where he came from, or how it happened?"

Willie paused before he answered. "Before we got to Phoenix, we picked him up, and he ended up being a tough guy. A big muthafucker."

"Was he hitchhiking?"

"Yeah! He was. That's right!" It was all coming back to him now. "I don't think I ever knew his name. He's a big tough dude."

"And you put him in a sleeping bag?"

"Bob's sleeping bag."

"Bob's?" Arellanes questioned. Now he was getting confused.

"Yeah. Bob knew we were going to do him."

"Okay, this guy in the sleeping bag. Did you kill him right on the spot?"

"Right out there on the spot." Willie was back to boasting, now that it was all coming back. "I made him get into the sleeping bag. . ."

". . .and you shot him?"

"Yeah, right in the head." He smiled when he spoke. Like a huge weight had been lifted from him for simply remembering.

Arrelanes had not even considered there being another body somewhere. He was just hoping he could find Ken and Mike. Now this. He wondered how long this could go on.

"Is there anybody else that's been shot and dumped someplace?" he asked, not quite sure he wanted to know the answer.

Willie smiled and leaned back. "Nope. I think that's all."

In Tucson, Weaver Barkman had located his witness in the Gilbert Sierra killing.

Larry Hust had given Barkman an arrest report for a Michael Marsh dated October 30, 1973, and while Marsh had been arrested for driving under the influence of a dangerous drug and carrying a concealed weapon, they merely charged him and let him go. But on the arrest sheet there were listed the names of two women who were with him when he was stopped. One of them was named Sue Harlan, the other Joanne Lily McPeek.

The name rang a bell to Barkman, only because at 4 a.m. that very same morning, he was jarred awake by a phone call from Stockton. Tucker told him that Gretzler had mentioned that the only person who may know about this Michael Marsh guy, or his girlfriend, was some woman named Sue.

Up until now, Barkman assumed Marsh was an accomplice to the Sierra murder. The woman known as Sue had given an address on the report, so Barkman went over Saturday morning to check it out. When he arrived he at the shabby little house, he peered through the window and saw young woman sleeping on the floor. When he finally got her to answer the door, he told her the reason for his visit. She acted nervous and scared and stammered on, denying she knew anything about any shooting. She fidgeted as she spoke, grinding her fingers together as she made excuses.

But Barkman caught one look at the needle marks on her arm, and he knew he had found Joanne. So he came down hard and stayed in her face until she finally caved. He took her downtown and she told him everything about the night a guy named Bill killed the Mexican kid. She also promised Barkman she would try and convince her boyfriend to come out of hiding and talk to him about it too.

Continuing to interrogate Steelman, Arellanes asked him again about finding the body in the sleeping bag. Willie sketched out a crude map and handed it to him.

"Does this guy in the sleeping bag have any papers on him, or identification or anything?" Arellanes asked as he looked over the map.

"He did have. A billfold, but we threw it away."

Arellanes decided it was time to wrap this up and try and find the victims. "Okay, eleven murders in the Phoenix and Tucson areas. Bill, we sure do appreciate it and we thank you and we appreciate the fact that you have cooperated with us."

"How long will it be before you people start extradition so I can get out there?"

"Well, we don't know."

"You know they don't have the death penalty in California."

"Don't have one in Arizona either," Arellanes replied, incorrectly, as it would be pointed out to him later.

"They don't?"

"Not that I know of."

"That's funny," Willie remarked, "cuz they told me you did."

Arellanes asked a deputy to call Stanislaus County to tell them of the possibility of the two homicide victims being in their jurisdiction. Dave said to let them know he and his partner were on their way. But before they left, Dave called back to Phoenix and told Calles that they may have come up with yet another victim. He asked Calles to check all the missing persons reports in the Phoenix area, and all of Arizona if he could. He said one of the suspects remembered killing a young man and putting him in a sleeping bag somewhere near the Superstitions. And if his location were accurate, the body wouldn't be in Maricopa County, so they would need to advise Pinal about the possible 187. Arellanes added the suspect said they probably couldn't find it without a helicopter, so they should have the Department of Public Safety get a chopper ready, just in case.

Arellanes and Miller drove down to Modesto, arriving just before 1 p.m. They told Stanislaus Sheriff's Department one of the suspects was apparently familiar with the area and had recalled a Yosemite sign and an old covered one lane bridge. He said they left the bodies just off a paved road about two miles from the bridge. Their best guess was the area he was talking about was around a small town called Knights Ferry.

They searched there for three hours. The land was cold, wet and immense, and Arellanes realized he would need much better directions if they were going to have any chance to recover any bodies. They called it quits just as nightfall set in. Arellanes said they would give it another go tomorrow, trying to sound encouraged about how close they were, but down deep wondering if this Steelman guy was capable of remembering anything.

While their search was still underway, word leaked out about the possibility of more bodies being hidden somewhere in the remote countryside near Modesto. Once again, newspapers around the nation picked up the story and flooded the San Joaquin Sheriff's main switchboard. The now standard reply was the investigation was ongoing and there would be no word about the results until the Arizona lawmen advised them of the status of the search.

True to form though, the news media still knew more about what was going on than the Sheriff's Office. In fact, it was a reporter from the *Stockton Record* who called in minutes earlier to let the department know the search near Modesto had been suspended until tomorrow.

The *Arizona Republic* in Phoenix was also reporting on the mass murder in the California farmhouse and the capture of the two suspected killers. The story said two Maricopa County detectives were in Stockton questioning the men about a couple found murdered in an Apache Junction trailer, and the disappearance of two Phoenix men named Ken Unrein and Michael Adshade who had been missing for almost a month. There was a definite connection to the events in Arizona and the Lodi killings, the detectives were quoted, and they were doing everything they could to get to the bottom of it all.

Mike Adshade's father came by the San Joaquin Sheriff's office at twelve-thirty Saturday afternoon to let them know he and his other son had come to Stockton to await word on the fate of Michael. He sounded tired and defeated. They would be staying at the Travelodge downtown, he said, and would appreciate a call if there was any news, good or bad.

Soon afterwards, the Sheriff's office took a call from a woman who asked if what she had heard was true? When he asked what that news might be, she replied that a San Joaquin Correctional officer told her there was a contract out on both suspects because they had killed the kids. According to the anonymous caller, the job was going to come from inside the jail. Based on that tip, Canlis notified all jail personnel to again be very careful when moving or transporting the prisoners. He also advised them again that some of those people being taken into custody might have larger motives for being arrested.

Directly following his interview with Arellanes and Miller early Saturday morning, Doug Gretzler decided to find out once and for all who was telling the newspapers that he was being a snitch. The guard told him that if he wanted to see anybody, he would have to put his request in writing. He asked for pencil and paper and wrote;

> *11-10-73 @ 10:40*
> *I, Doug Gretzler wish to see Detective Wagner as soon as possible.*

At one-thirty Saturday afternoon, Gretzler got his meeting. It would be the longest interview held to this point – nearly four hours – and what would begin as a simple request for a newspaper would lead to him finally admitting everything.

On their return from Modesto, Arellanes confided to his partner that this whole trip to California was like finding yourself at a party you weren't invited to. He was right. They were not welcome in Stockton. He could sense that from the moment they arrived, although Dave did not know why. Didn't he give them the lead on Steelman in the first place? Weren't they the ones who figured out who was responsible for all of this? Didn't he tell Stockton, pointblank, how to catch these guys? Weren't the arrests made on their warrants?

He knew about Steelman and Gretzler long before anything happened in Lodi. He called them and tried to tell them that, but they wouldn't listen. That still ticked him off. They were all in this together, weren't they? They all had work to do and murders to solve. Wasn't that their code? So why the cold shoulder? Why the grunts and snide remarks whenever he said something, or tried to make a point or offer a suggestion. Why the roadblock? Why did they ignore him and what he had to say? All he was doing was what he was hired to do in the first place. Find the killers. Solve the crime.

But Stockton didn't want to hear it. This wasn't about Arizona, or some people in a trailer, or the possibility of two more hidden in a pasture somewhere. It wasn't even about an apartment in Tucson, or Tempe, or where ever the hell it was they found those people.

Hell, this was about Lodi. Plain and simple. This was about nine people killed in their backyard. This was about the cold-blooded execution of two entire families, about two little kids killed where they slept. It wasn't about some drug punks getting their due; being stupid enough to hang around with the likes of these two. Whoever Arizona was looking for probably got what they deserved anyway.

No. This was about nine very innocent people, nine very young, very good and very decent people, who were minding their own business, in their very own home, being murdered for absolutely no good goddamn reason in the world. This was not about Arizona. This was about Stockton and Lodi and Victor. This was about the safety of their own people. About their own credibility. Their backyard. Their murders. Their crimes to solve. Their suspects. Fact of the matter was, San Joaquin authorities didn't like Arellanes or Miller, or whoever else was on the way, traipsing through their office, asking their prisoners questions about things that had not one damn thing to do with their case. Outsiders made them nervous, anyway. They didn't have to cooperate. Really, they didn't have to share anything with anybody. And they were sure as hell weren't going to be interrupted, or one-upped, by them or anybody else.

So Dave was right. He and Miller were not welcome in Stockton. And when the time came for them to leave, Dave was certain they would be going back alone, because there was no way in the world Stockton was giving up Steelman and Gretzler.

Carl Ambrose gave Gretzler his rights and made him sign off once again just to be sure. He had a gut feeling this was a keeper, and he did not want to screw it up.

"All right, Douglas," Wagner began, "there's been an awful lot of things happen since we talked to you last."

"Yes."

"And I understand you want to talk to me in regards to the newspapers. Go ahead and tell me."

"All right. I wanted to ask you if you knew, or could find out, how the newspaper found out that I was talking to you people and giving you information."

Wagner fumbled along about the problems of transcribing tapes and not knowing who was typing them, or how the tapes from Sacramento leaked out or who was really responsible. His tone oozed concern. "I honestly don't know, Doug. I just read the paper last night myself. You know, there were other officers present. I do know that our radio is monitored by newspapers and that part of the statement referring to where Mr. Steelman was at was monitored over the air."

Gretzler nodded, like he understood the confusion.

"In other words," Wagner continued, "you were telling the officers, and the officers were radioing in telling them where to go, and that is why all the press was out at the scene when Mr. Steelman was arrested."

He went on to assure Gretzler, that while he and Ambrose weren't responsible, they would do everything in their power to try and find out where the leaks where coming from and get them stopped. And just so Gretzler could keep track of what was going on, Wagner promised to get him a subscription to the newspaper. "We'll have it delivered right here to your cell," Wagner offered. "Just like home delivery."

Doug thanked them for understanding. He felt better.

"Now Douglas," Wagner said, casually changing the subject, "this lab man who works on bullets and stuff like that, well, he tells us the people were definitely shot with two different weapons. . .two different twenty-two weapons. So therefore, we have a weapon missing – a twenty-two weapon missing. We recovered one from Mr. Steelman, and then there's one more."

"Uh-huh."

"So we theorized that you were armed with a twenty-two weapon when you entered the hotel, and you hid it somewhere in the hotel before you turned yourself in to the officers. Is that correct?"

"Let me make a few corrections," Doug snapped back, not ready to let them assume anything. "First of all, I don't know about another gun. Second of all, I don't rightfully feel I turned myself in."

His backlash took Wagner and Ambrose by surprise. Until now, Gretzler had been as cooperative as could be. They thought they had him. Sure, he had been lying through his teeth, but he was very mellow about it. Suddenly he was angry and defensive, so Wagner got him off the gun question and let him talk about anything he wished.

He talked about his wife and baby and family, and about how Bill Steelman was lying to them if he said he was suffering from withdrawals, "He's not going through withdrawals because he didn't shoot up anymore than me, and he wasn't no habitual user, no more than me." He talked about Denver and the robberies in Phoenix, and while he talked for over an hour, he made sure to avoid any mention of another gun.

"Are you giving it to me straight?" Wagner asked. "You didn't have a gun of your own?"

"Right, I did not."

"You remember we talked yesterday in the elevator and I told you eventually everything comes out. . .?"

"Yeah."

". . .it just takes a little longer, you know."

"Yeah."

"Doug, you know you are in as deep as you can get in."

"Yeah."

"All right, you understand that. Can you give me a reasonable explanation why we're finding these two different weapons?"

Doug stayed firm. "I do not know."

So again Wagner let the gun go. "Douglas, is there anything in your previous statements that you want to change in regards to the incident that occurred?"

"Huh?"

"Well, the reason I'm asking is that also through our criminologist, and what I've seen too, is that there is far more blood on your clothing than there is on Willie Steelman's, and I would like you to give me an explanation for this."

Doug was unmoved.

"What we are asking you to do is answer some unanswered questions for us. Why are we having ballistics coming from two different weapons? Why have you got more blood on your clothing that Steelman has on his? See, these are unanswered."

Doug nodded. Wagner didn't let up. "We've got two guns. We can't account for one. We got blood on your shoes, blood on your pants. How? Tell me how are we going to explain this?"

He sat for a moment to think about his answer. "I don't know. He might have been wearing my pants."

Wagner was dumbfounded. "Well he can't be wearing BOTH pair of pants!" He had run out of patience, and cassettes. He sat back, shut the recorder off, then called for more tapes. Ambrose left to go get rid of some coffee. Wagner just looked at Gretzler and shook his head. He didn't say another word.

Ed Calles couldn't wait any longer. Darkness would be upon them soon and there still was no word from California. He went ahead and called Pinal County, breaking the news about the possibility of a murder victim hidden somewhere in the foothills of the Superstitions. Calles admitted he had no idea if this was a wild goose chase or not. The helicopter arrived and Calles gave the pilot the only directions he had. The body is apparently hidden in a sleeping bag in this general area. That was the best he could offer.

At 4:40 p.m., the copter radioed back that they had spotted the sleeping bag. Using the helicopter as a guide, the officers on the ground drove up Mining Camp Road, past the old café, and another quarter mile on a dirt road. With the chopper hovering above, they soon found the mark. In a dry wash about a hundred yards off the nearest fence line, and partially hidden beneath a small Palo Verde tree, they found the sleeping bag.

It was nearly dark, so they searched the area with as much care as possible. Pictures were taken and the body was prepared for removal. It was badly decomposed. It was all they could do to keep it in one piece while getting it into the plastic bag.

There they were, high above the desert floor, the lights of the valley twinkling beneath them. The fire of an evening sunset burned on the horizon, and with it came just enough light to help guide them through their work. It was the most morbid of sights in the most beautiful of places.

Calles called back to Stockton and told Arellanes they had found the kid in the sleeping bag.

At 4:10 p.m., after nearly two and a half hours, Doug Gretzler could take no more. These final moments, the stares, the silent treatment from Wagner, all had combined to wear him down. He took a deep breath and told Wagner that he had changed his mind. He would make a statement. "About Lodi. About Arizona. About everything," were his words. Once and for all he wanted to be done with it.

Wagner switched the recorder back on and spoke into it. "There was a brief pause," he reported. "And during this pause, Mr. Gretzler had made some statements that he would like to get them cleared up and give us a true account of what actually happened at the Victor incident, and in Arizona. He has also made statements that he does not want counsel and that he does not want to advise him at this time. Is that true?"

"That's true."

"And you will relate the same information to the Arizona authorities?"

"Yes."

And so Doug began. "I was really nervous. I was watching out the window. Then Wally came back with Bill and I tied Wally up, and I tied Wally's wife, and Bill got jumpy and wanted to get the hell outta there."

"So you guys had already decided to. . ."

"They were witnesses to the whole thing and they would have a complete description, you know. . ."

"Yeah, go ahead."

". . .and Bill, he wanted to talk to me, which he did, and then he said he couldn't do it, cause he knew 'em."

"And so you had them in the closet..."

"And Bill said...'You'll have to go in and dust 'em..."

"And?"

"And, so I did."

Wagner relaxed, but Doug kept talking. He gave the shooting order, and how the father just wouldn't die. He said he shot them with the six-shot .22, and when he ran out of bullets, Willie handed him the derringer. But after he went around once, Willie jumped in and started shooting. And he kept shooting. But the father still wouldn't die. "It took a lot of shots to make all his body processes and functions stop."

"Okay," Wagner interrupted "The last question..."

"It took five shots," Doug continued. He went back over it again – just so they knew it all. He told them about the wallets and the money, and exactly where he hid the derringer.

"You won't have any trouble finding it," he promised. He also admitted being the one who shot Bob in the trailer, and that he helped kill Ken and Mike. "They were garroted. That's the dirtiest way I know to kill somebody. That's probably the reason why I could take so many deaths as that because after the first, I was steeled too. I never seen anything like that before."

"How did you do it?" Wagner asked.

"Cord around the neck – the small piece of chain that was taken off me when I was arrested – that's my belt. That's the one I used."

"So you used that?"

"Yeah, he was tied, and you come up behind the dude and then you clip it around his neck, then put your knee in the back, high up between the shoulder blades and pull back. That's how Bill told me to do it..."

"Yeah?"

"...but I couldn't kill mine, I couldn't actually kill mine completely dead because it made me sick and he was kicking and shuddering and blood came out of his eyes...and it was like his head was exploding. And I'm sure he was half dead, brain damage or something, so I let up and Bill came back over and helped me finish it."

"What did Bill do?"

"He used his belt. Then we took the bodies and we dragged them towards the marsh and Bill proceeded to strip them of their clothing and he stabbed them with that large knife I was telling you about."

"How many times did Bill stab them?"

"Couple times in the back, you know, one on either side, and then through the throat. They were stark naked, and we dragged them into the reeds and took the clothes back with us when we left. Then we dumped them off of another bridge we were passing over."

Wagner reminded Gretzler of what he had said at the beginning of the tape and how he had waived his rights to an attorney. "Do you have anything that you want to add at this time?"

He seemed anxious to keep talking, but replied. "Not unless you have further questions."

And with that, Wagner shut the recorder off and thanked Gretzler for coming clean. He called Sacramento and told them were they could find the other weapon. They called him back thirty minutes later and told him that the gun was right where he said it would be.

Ambrose and Wagner reported to Sheriff Canlis about what had happened with Gretzler. Canlis said he was pleased how things were developing. He told them to try and get some rest. He said they both looked beat. They walked out of his office and were handed another note from the County Jail:

> *11-10-73*
> *I, Willie Steelman want to speak with Sergeant Wagner.*

So at 10:30 Saturday night, Wagner and Ambrose returned to French Camp and interviewed Steelman, who said he had decided to tell them the whole story, start to finish. They shrugged and told him that they knew all of it now anyway, but would listen to his side, but only if he had something new to add.

Admittedly they were both a bit surprised by what they heard, because for the very first time, both stories matched up.

By the time they left the jail early Sunday morning, Ken Wagner and Carl Ambrose were riding a pretty good high. They had just wrapped this one up real tight. With a nice big bow on it.

36

Sunday, November 11, 1973.

Headline in this morning's *Stockton Record*:

> ***15th BODY FOUND; HUNT 3 MORE.***
> ***2 Sought in Stanislaus***
> *A 15th body was found Saturday in the Arizona desert and three more were hunted – two in the river bottomlands of Stanislaus County – in the unfolding saga of mass murder which came to light this past week. The latest victim, an unidentified man, was spotted in the desert east of Phoenix by a helicopter. A search resumed today in the Knights Ferry area for two bodies sought yesterday by Stanislaus and Phoenix officers.*

On Saturday, television stations were reporting the total dead could eventually reach 22, and again, law enforcement agencies from around the country were asking the San Joaquin Sheriff's Department for help in unsolved murder cases in their jurisdictions. But by Sunday morning, Stockton authorities knew enough about the suspect's whereabouts over the past thirty days to discredit most calls. Still, there were a few with enough similarities to warrant a closer look, and those were turned over to Inspector Ken Stewart who had been coordinating the investigation for Canlis. The follow-up work generated by those investigations found its way to the workhorse team of Wagner and Ambrose.

One inquiry in particular seemed especially close to home. Detectives in Santa Clara County were investigating the bludgeoning death of a young man found in a creek near the town of Cupertino. Now certain Steelman and Gretzler had been in nearby Mountain View, San Joaquin authorities agreed, reluctantly, to allow those detectives to speak with their suspects. On Sunday morning they questioned both vigorously, but it was soon obvious neither had any idea what the officers were talking about.

In Arizona, Pinal County deputies returned to the Sleeping Bag Murder scene to sift for any evidence they might have missed last night, or anything that might help identify the victim. Remembering the woman who came to their office for the billfold yesterday morning, they called her and asked that she try learn more about her grandson's whereabouts. Within minutes she called back, and in a defeated voice, informed them that Steve's father in California had filed a missing person's report on him over a week ago. She sounded resigned to the real possibility the body found in the desert was that of her Stevie.

An autopsy was scheduled for Monday, the officers told her, but because the victim had been there so long, visual identification would be very difficult. They needed his dental charts, and she said she would see what she could do. In the meantime she agreed to return the wallet for their investigation.

Meanwhile, back in San Joaquin, Detective Larry Hersey and Sergeant Chuck Curtis from Stanislaus County drove up to Stockton to meet Arellanes and Miller and discuss their next move. They brought with them a highly detailed map of the area where Steelman said the bodies could be found. Arellanes set up another interview with Steelman, but before he got around to talking about Unrein and Adshade, he asked again about any other bodies that might be hidden in Arizona, especially near the Superstition Mountains.

"Okay, Willie," Arellanes started in, "these officers are going to talk to you about where you killed Ken and Mike, but before we do that we need to go into Phoenix and locate another body. Our officers found the guy in the sleeping bag. Now we would like to try and find the second one you say is in that area."

"Should be farther up the mountain."

"Were you present when he was dumped?"

"No."

"Who told you he was. . ."

"Larry. Yeah, Larry told me they put him out there and there were places out there they would never be found."

"Do you think they could be found or seen by air?"

"They didn't say nothing about that, only that they dumped a body out there and no one would find it. . .nobody would ever stumble on it."

Arellanes phoned Phoenix with the sketchy information. There was talk of resuming the search in the Superstitions, but without a better location, Calles agreed that Willie's mysterious accomplice was correct; no one would ever 'stumble over a body' in those mountains. So Dave dropped it, deciding that finding Ken and Mike was more important.

Curtis and Hersey spent the next thirty minutes going over the map with Steelman. They knew the area as well as anyone and were able to steer Willie around by mentioning bridges, trees and landmarks, such as the windmill he remembered seeing close by. They finally felt confident enough to believe they could find the location, but just in case, they asked Willie if he would mind going out and showing it to them if all else failed.

"I would probably have to get a Superior Court order, but you wouldn't mind taking a ride in the country, would you?" Curtis invited. "You probably would be glad to get out of here for awhile and get a little fresh air, right?"

"Long as there's no publicity about me going out."

Curtis assured him there wouldn't be, but Willie worried about leaving the security of his jail cell, so Curtis, Hersey, Arellanes and Miller left Stockton at 9:20 a.m., without Steelman, and drove to the same general area east of Modesto where they had searched yesterday. They crossed the bridge over Littlejohn Creek and parked, huddling in the car for a moment to check the map one last time. In the distance, through the mist and fog they could see the oak tree and the windmill Willie told them about.

Another storm had pounded the valley Saturday night and the ground was soft and muddy. The rain continued to pelt them as they headed towards the only indentation they could see. They were no more than a few hundred yards from where they were yesterday, but as they closed in on the shallow spot in the earth, the rancid smell told Arellanes all he needed to know. He followed the odor to a tall stand of brush and reeds, motioning to the others to circle around the marsh and focus their search on the small gully below. There, in the middle of the matted cattails, were the bodies of two nude men, one on top of the other, face down in the shallow water. At 11 a.m. Curtis walked to the car and radioed in that they had found the remains of Ken Unrein and Mike Adshade. They asked that someone pay a visit to Mr. Adshade at the Travelodge to break the grim news.

"When Michael was a little boy," the father remembered, an overwhelming sadness burdening his words, "he wasn't even 10, I don't think, just a little guy, and he was outside playing, and he broke his arm. Two places, as I recall. I thought you might want to use that to identify him."

Ironically, Ken and Mike had been the first killed, and the last to be found.

Sunday afternoon in Tucson a reporter asked Pima County attorney Randy Stevens about the killings. Stevens had carried that vision of the scene at the Sandberg home with him, and he responded with a firm resolve. "We would like to prosecute them first, and we will begin immediately the process that will enable us to do that."

The attorney reminded the reporter that Arizona has the death penalty and California did not. That said, the most the pair could receive in California was life in prison, and could be eligible for parole in seven short years. "Yeah, we want them," he said, adding state statutes required Arizona to bring the defendants to court within 150 days for the filling of charges. That would be impossible, he added, if a trial was held in California first, leaving the impression the Sandberg's killers would never be held accountable for their crimes in Arizona. Steven's comments were printed over the next several days in newspapers throughout Arizona and California, and became the initial spark in a firestorm of dispute over who would be the one with first crack at Willie Steelman and Doug Gretzler.

Coincidently, *The Stockton Record* ran a story on page two of Sunday's paper reminding its readers what small punishments were being handed out to

California killers. The Lodi Slaughter, as some now referred to it, happened just 56 days before their new death penalty law was to take effect.

In 1972 the California Supreme Court had struck down the state's capital punishment law, and soon after, the U.S. Supreme Court ruled the method used in most other states to determine how capital punishment would be applied was unconstitutional. That decision sent everyone back to the drawing board to try to find a way to meet the new Supreme Court guidelines.

Arizona's death penalty law was on the books, but it had never been tested, as Stevens had pointed out. After the high court's most recent ruling was made, most death sentences were commuted automatically to life, with the possibility of parole. To further infuriate already irate citizens, the new sentencing laws did not differentiate between the number of victims. A killer of one hundred would be given the same life sentence as a murder of one. And in California in 1973, life meant seven years. Period.

So that meant that people like Charlie Manson and Sirhan Sirhan would never be executed and could possibly even walk the streets again. A spokesman for the Parole Board attempted to calm the fear and frustration being generated, allowing that although the law required parole hearings to be held for even the most evil of men, there was almost no chance they would ever be released back into society. Still, the majority of California citizens were outraged, and in September, passed a new death penalty law, enthusiastically signed by Governor Reagan, guaranteeing mass murderers like Willie Steelman and Doug Gretzler would face the gas chamber if convicted.

Problem was the new law went into effect 56 days too late. So the talk began Sunday of what to do with them. Some realized what the Arizona attorney was saying might not be a bad way to handle the situation. The good people of Lodi, and all of California, for that matter, were set on revenge, and a few years in prison was hardly their idea of vengeance. Let Arizona have them, some said. Let them kill them. At least it will get done.

So the battle over Steelman and Gretzler would begin this Sunday, fueled by a man who had seen first hand the vile remnants of their deeds. A man who promised himself he would do everything in his power to make them pay with their very lives.

Also in Tucson on Sunday, Joanne McPeek made good her promise to bring her boyfriend in to see Detective Barkman. She was in big trouble already, being on three years probation on federal charges of heroin smuggling, so Barkman warned her up front not to screw around with him on this. As far as he was concerned, anyone could have pulled the trigger on Sierra, and he would not hesitate one second to get all their names on a murder rap. He had given her until noon Sunday to bring Michael Marsh into his office, and although they were over an hour late, they arrived and Marsh retold Joanne's story, placing the gun in Bill Steelman's hand the night of the killing. Barkman could see Marsh seemed upset; maybe even a little scared about what he had been a part of. The first chance they had, Marsh admitted, he and Joanne split, afraid Bill would track him down and kill them just as easy as he killed the Mexican.

When Barkman asked, Marsh agreed he would do anything he could, including testifying at a trial, if there ever was one.

For his help, Barkman found a judge who agreed to give Marsh a few extra days to pay the fine he had skipped out on (the reason there was an arrest warrant on him in the first place), after which Barkman had a buddy at the department sign off the warrant. For his help, Michael Marsh was free to go, courtesy of Weaver Barkman.

Back in California, Larry Bunting and Michael Tucker had spent the weekend gathering evidence linking Steelman and Gretzler to the Sandberg and Sierra murders. Although they weren't present, they had heard about the marathon session Saturday night when Doug Gretzler finally admitted everything, including tying up and killing the Sandbergs, as well as watching while Bill offed the Mexican kid.

The confessions would help make their work back home a bit easier, but confessions weren't evidence, and often a suspect's admission of guilt was thrown out, or never used by the prosecution because of the problems confessions could cause. It was near impossible to get a first-degree murder conviction just because the guy admitted he pulled the trigger. And junkie witnesses like Marsh and McPeek in the Sierra case were even more trouble for all the obvious reasons.

What Bunting and Tucker needed was evidence – good, solid undisputable evidence to attach the killers to the crime – so they drove to Sacramento to look at the items being held at C.I.&I; items that included gas and motel receipts, the checkbook, and a pill bottle bearing Patricia's prescription. C.I.&I. promised that as soon as they were finished, and if San Joaquin gave them the go ahead, they would send it all down to Tucson.

During their first interview session earlier back in Stockton, Bunting and Tucker had obtained handwriting samples from both suspects. Willie knew what they were driving at and smart-assed them. "I'll make it a lot easier on you," he said. "I'll sign like I did before." He laughed and wrote out the name, 'M. Sandberg'.

Remembering the Clairol bottles found in the Sandberg bathroom, Bunting asked for a hair sample from Gretzler. Both the signatures and hair would be sent to the FBI for comparison. Matching the .22 with the slugs found in the three victims would be an important link as well, so they tracked down James Booker who was handling the comparison work for San Joaquin. He suggested they send the slugs found in their victims to his lab and he would analyze them as well.

Bunting had brought a Xerox copy of the Sandberg's house key with hopes he could match it to the keys found on the suspects. For some reason, Ambrose was still holding on to them and had never sent them to the lab. Bunting got the key ring from him and held them up together. They were a perfect match.

Peter Saiers promised to send transcripts of all the interviews and psychiatric reports as soon as they were available, as well as fingerprint cards.

So Detective Tucker and Sergeant Bunting flew back to Tucson Sunday, and although they returned without Steelman and Gretzler, they were convinced they had enough on them to obtain a First Degree Murder conviction for the deaths of the Sandbergs and Gilbert Sierra.

San Joaquin deputies were out early Sunday morning looking for bullet casings. Not one spent shell was found in the house, and Doug said he saw Bill pocket them and toss them out the car window sometime after they left they house. Not knowing the exact route taken from Orchard Road to Highway 99, Doug was asked several times which way he drove. He remembered turning right at the Earl place and going all the way out to the end of the road, then turning left to get on the highway. Asked if Willie had tossed them out before that, Gretzler shrugged, saying he wasn't sure. He held on to that question for a moment, then said it must have been on the highway, because he remembered how cold the wind was when Willie rolled the window down.

Sunday morning, six deputies searched the shoulder of the northbound lanes of 99 from Liberty Road – where they believed the car entered the highway – to Twin Cities Road, a distance of almost five miles. With squad car lights flashing to protect them in the fog, they walked the entire length of roadway. By mid afternoon they gave up and reported their lack of success to Canlis. He told them to try it again tomorrow, this time in a different stretch of highway.

John Barbieri had better luck. With the help of Nunley and Jackson, he returned to the bridge outside of Galt where the two boys said Willie shot at bottles in the water. On the ground near the bridge railing he found several .22 casings, some of them shiny and seemingly fresh.

About the time Barbieri returned to the office, George Dedekam called to report, somewhat nonchalantly, that he had received several threatening phone calls over the weekend. Dedekam had managed to speak only a few words to his client since he was assigned the case on Friday.

"This kooky woman called and told me an assassination plot was being planned if I don't get off the case". He sounded neither worried nor frightened, just that he felt someone should know. He laughed as he added, "You know, if anything really happens". He agreed not to tell anyone else about the call, at least for a few days, just to see if the woman called back. In the meantime, the department said they would continue to monitor and tape record all calls coming into their office. Dedekam refused their offer of a phone tap.

Later that night, a Lodi Police dispatcher called Stockton to report the details of a phone call she had just received asking if there was a "Wetzler" checked into the jail there. "No, not here," she had told the caller. "But are you referring to Doug Gretzler?" Yes, that was the person they meant. What is the bail amount? The dispatcher replied that she believed it was $100,000. The caller offered to pay it. Informed immediately by a co-worker that there was no bail set for either suspect, the dispatcher corrected her mistake, whereas the gravely male voice yelled, 'I'll take him out by force then!' and hung up. Forty-five minutes later the same man called the Sheriff's office with the same threat.

Dave Arellanes and Bill Miller were making their own plans to leave town, buttoning up a few loose ends Sunday after their return from the search in Stanislaus. When they arrived back at the courthouse, a reporter from the *Stockton Record* was waiting, insisting Arellanes speak with him before he left. Feeling he had his work here pretty well wrapped up, Dave agreed to the interview and told how he and his partner had investigated the case from the very beginning. The story would hit the front page on Monday.

STOCKTON RECORD

How 2 Arizona Lawmen Linked Pair to Murders

Maricopa County, Arizona is big and sprawling. Its sheriff's office is small. There are only four men available to investigate homicides. But this investigative team is credited with connecting the names of Willie Steelman and Doug Gretzler to the murder of nine persons in Victor, as well as at least eight others in Arizona and Northern California.

Dave Arellanes, a tall, copper-skinned veteran of the Maricopa sheriff's office made it sound easy when the Record interviewed him on Sunday. Arellanes said how he and his partner were investigating the murder of two people found inside a trailer near Phoenix prior to all of this. He mentioned the long hours, the team effort, and the lack of sleep. Hard work paid off and they finally they had some names. Last Wednesday, when they heard the news about the murder of nine people in a farmhouse near Lodi, he was sure it was the same people he was looking for. That's when he called Stockton and told them about Willie Steelman and Doug Gretzler.

"When we heard they were in custody, Miller and I grabbed our bags and our notes and started out here."

Arellanes and Miller reportedly got Gretzler and Steelman talking about other murders in (Arizona and California) Asked how they got Steelman and Gretzler to talk, Arellanes shrugged his broad shoulders, "Oh, we just told them what we knew, and they told us what they knew."

Before they left for the airport, he and Miller paid a final visit to the jail, simply to clear up a few loose ends.

"Okay Willie, we just want to know what happened."

"About Ken and Mike?"

"Yeah, the whole thing."

Willie lit a cigarette. "Well after we drove around for awhile, and I was hot and shit and no one to help, we figured we would leave them and split with the van. So we drove around the area for at least an hour trying to find a place to leave the two men."

"Had you planned at that time you were going to kill them?"

"No, not definite."

"No decision?"

"Right. I was supposed to have my niece – she was supposed to be there – get a hold of another vehicle and follow us. Then we would drive the van, oh about sixty or seventy miles south and leave them. But I don't know what happened to my niece. She never showed up. So we walked them down there and talked and tied them up and shit, then untied them and smoked a joint, trying to figure out what to do."

"Did they know what was happening?"

"No. Well the tall one, Mike, he was nervous and paranoid and shit and he kept saying 'what are you going to do? You gonna kill us?' and I truthfully didn't know. Anyway we tied them up and left and I told them we were going to leave and for them not to try and leave, cuz we might be watching. And Douglas and I left.

"So what happened when you left?"

Willie took a long drag. "Well, we were walking back to the car and I tell Doug, you know, this isn't right. I'm hot and people are going to be all over me and, you know, these guys are witnesses to the whole thing'. So I tell Doug we got to go back, and I tell him I would take Ken and he take Mike."

"So what happened to Ken?"

"Well I stand him up and start walking him in front of me over closer to the reeds, just me and him, and I come up behind him and. . .uh, at that point I break his neck."

"How did you do that, do you recall?"

"Uh, it was a karate hold, a keeto hold. I can't explain it, want me to show it?"

"No, that's all right."

"So, Douglas was coming out of the indentation and as I walked in he said he was through, but when I went to help him move the body, he wasn't dead, well, he may have been dead, but still had reactions and all, and my heart was beating so fast I couldn't get a pulse. I couldn't tell if it was mine or his."

"Was he cut?"

"Yeah, there was blood. Douglas tried to garrote him and it looked like he may have broken the larynx, cuz, uh, there was blood coming from his nose and mouth. So I tell Douglas I wasn't sure he had done a thorough job on him, his body was still quivering. Occasionally he would make a breathing sound and it was best to, uh, finish it because I don't want the guy laying down there for two days. It wasn't that easy to kill a guy without breaking his neck, so he tries to strangle the guy some more and wasn't doing a very good job."

"With what?"

"A belt. And he was getting blood all over himself, so he asked me where to cut his throat and I showed him, but instead of cutting it he tried to stab him two or three times – which did very little or no good at all – and then he stabbed him in both lungs, which was a mistake, because then the air went into those wounds and it was making even more noise. So I showed him how to break a man's neck, and uh, I don't think he even did that properly. Then he took a rock and smashed him across the face with it, and I think that is what finished him off."

"At that point do you strip him of his clothes?"

"Yeah, same time as the other. We just threw them in the van and we left."

Minutes later Doug told the same basic story, except he said they weren't stripped at first. After the killings, they started to leave, but Bill remembered he had left his coat down there, so they went back. But it was almost dark and they had to use a flashlight to find the jacket and a missing silver concho that had been ripped off Bill's Levis during the attack. It was then when Bill said they should take everything off them so nobody could identify the bodies. So they removed the clothes and carried them back to the van, only to throw them out a short distance down the road.

After Arellanes and Miller left for the airport and their flight home, Sam Libicki finally got around to visiting his client. It was nearly 7 p.m. Sunday night when he arrived at the jail, only to find Steelman once again talking to Wagner. Willie, who thought he could trade more info for a quick favor, requested the session. He wanted to see his old girlfriend, Lisa. He told Libicki to wait outside until he was finished.

Lisa, of course, was one of the many reasons Denise had told Willie that their marriage was over. She was a 17-year-old student at Galt High School when she first met him, although it was several months later before she learned he was married. Willie explained he was separated and the divorce was only weeks away. He also told her long, sad stories about how his wife mistreated him, and about how all he really ever wanted was for someone to care about him.

Lisa bought into it, and was soon spending a great deal of time with him. It was not uncommon for her to ditch class, and then have Willie waiting out front to pick her up in his old beat up Ford Falcon. They would drive out to Comanche Dam, stopping by the United Market on the way for beer, bread and lunchmeat. Lisa waited patiently as Willie gabbed with the people at the check stand, always acting like they were old friends.

Soon he began giving her small gifts; like a necklace, and one time even an expensive antique hunting knife, but by early May of 1973 her parents began pressuring her to stop seeing him. She tried hard to obey them, and for the first few weeks went out of her way to avoid him, but he would not let up. Finally, she came out and told him she couldn't see him anymore. Willie exploded at the news, more violent than she had ever seen him before. He doubled up his fist and smashed it against his car, then climbed in and sped away. That was the last time she ever saw him, although he tried calling her several times during the weeks to follow. Finally the calls stopped and Lisa thought he was gone. But then out of the blue he called her Tuesday night. Again she said she couldn't talk with him.

All of this was driving Willie nuts, him being stuck here in jail, not being able to talk to her. He had to find out if what he had heard about her being pregnant was really true. So he told Wagner about her and how it was important for him to talk to her. He couldn't get a hold of her himself, he admitted, so maybe a cop could help. Especially, he reminded Wagner, after all he had done for him.

Wagner shook his head at Steelman's gall, but he promised to see what he could do. He jotted down the girl's name, even her phone number that Willie had memorized. Wagner decided he wouldn't mind talking to this Lisa himself.

"By the way," Willie added as Wagner got up to leave, "there's a big rip coming down in Tucson tomorrow. Western Union office. Heard that ten grand was just sitting in the safe. Maybe you guys should check into it."

Wagner feigned interest, but told Willie that he would get right on it.

When Sam Libicki finally got to sit down with his client, he was not a happy man. He had no idea in the world that Willie had been talking all weekend. From what he had heard and read in the papers, Libicki was under the impression that Gretzler was the one doing all the yapping and Willie was obeying orders to keep quiet. When he found out otherwise, he exploded.

"What in the hell were you thinking of?" he demanded.

Willie said that he thought if he talked, especially to the Arizona people, it might go easier down there.

"Why would that be?" Libicki asked.

"Well, you know, they got the death penalty in Arizona and they said, you know, what I had to say might make a difference."

Libicki was flabbergasted. "Willie, I don't know what they told you, but those guys don't have the authority to make any deals with you!"

Willie just sat, head down, like a scolded child.

"Willie, I'll tell you. You have just been fucked over big time!"

"Yeah, well, shit! It don't make any difference anymore," Willie shot back. "I've talked to so many people, I can't even remember who I told what to."

But Libicki wasn't finished. "And another thing Willie. Those two 'doctors' you talked to the other night. . .they're shrinks! And everything you told them went right back to the police!"

Willie could only sit and listen. It didn't matter anymore. It was all over. He was sick and he was tired, and he knew that no amount of lies could change anything. He actually felt relieved to have it all out in the open.

Libicki eventually cooled down, and they stopped talking about killings and guns and drugs and running and all the other things they should have, and they just talked. They talked about life, and about people, and family, and politics, and how Willie could solve all the problems of the world if someone would just listen.

Libicki was impressed; a realitization that struck him as so odd, so twisted, and somehow so hypocritical. He should not become this absorbed. He knew full well what Steelman had done, how vicious his deeds, how callous his manner had been in not only committing them, but later admitting to them, and just how little remorse he had shown either time.

And yet Libicki could not help but be overwhelmed by Willie's intelligence and his ability to express himself with so much emotion and conviction. He could feel Willie's charisma wrap around him, and within just minutes of meeting him, could see how Doug Gretzler could believe every word he had to say, and do everything he asked, regardless of what it might be.

After three hours, Libicki announced, rather reluctantly, that he had to leave. As he waited for the guard, he was struck by this powerful sense of duty. There had to be something there to grasp onto, something could use to defend this man.

It was a challenge he could not wait to get started on. As he left the French Camp jail late Sunday night, ideas of how he would defend Willie swirled through his head. The bottom line, he concluded, was that Willie was like no other client he had ever represented. He was articulate, seemingly intelligent, and at times, very personable. Somewhere in there was the strength for his defense.

As he drove home Libicki told himself, that if you could just forget about the fact that he had orchestrated the brutal murders of seventeen people, then Jesus!, Willie Steelman could be a real likable guy.

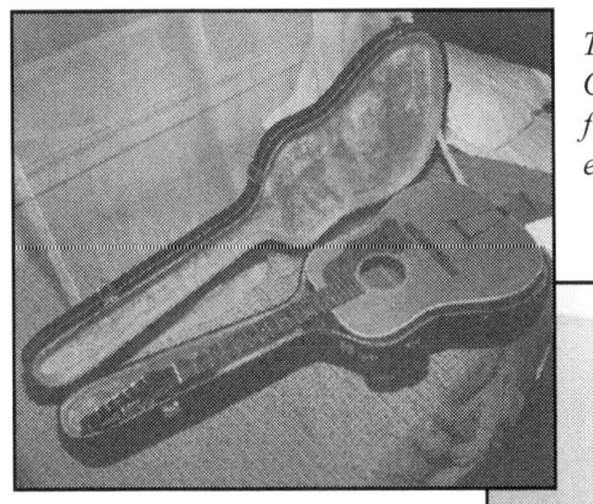

The Gibson 12 string purchased by Doug Gretzler with his share of the money taken from the United Market. The guitar was eventually returned to the Parkin family.

Willie and Doug's room at the Hotel Clunie in Sacramento.

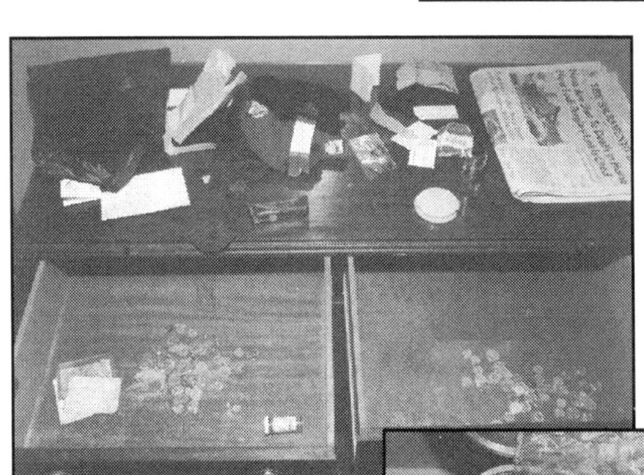

Evidence found by authorities upon entering the room at the Hotel Clunie. The newspaper headlines reads. . ."Nine are Shot to Death. . ."

GUEST LEDGER No. T3991

HOTEL CLUNIE
SACRAMENTO CALIFORNIA

№ 4938

ROOM No. 319

3 nt
adv 31.00 GRETZLER

DATE 11/9

NAME Doug Gretzler
Willie Simen
SIMEN

ROOMS

NO. OF PERSONS 2

STREET ADDRESS 1919 Wadsworth Ave ARRIVAL 11:00A

CITY AND STATE Bronx, New York RATE 10.50

CLERK

AUTO LICENSE NO.

NOTICE TO GUEST: A SAFE IS PROVIDED FOR THE DEPOSIT OF VALUABLES.
THE HOTEL CANNOT BE RESPONSIBLE FOR VALUABLES NOT DEPOSITED.

GUESTS NOT PERMITTED AFTER 10:00 P.M.

The registration slip at the Hotel Clunie. While Willie makes up another fake name, Doug has no problem giving his real one, as well as his hometown.

A Sacramento Police Officer removes the Derringer hidden by Gretzler moments before his capture at the Hotel Clunie.

All photos courtesy Special Collections Department, UC Davis

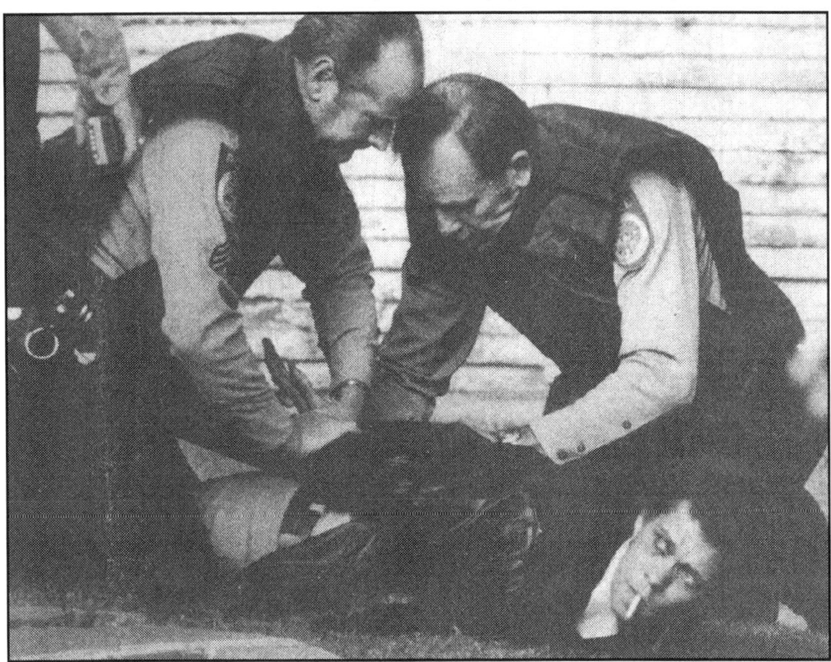

Police handcuff Willie Steelman moments after his surrender in Sacramento. He had once promised Doug if he was ever captured he "will take some pigs with me."

Melinda Kashula's apartment where Willie and Doug went to hide out the morning of their capture.

Melinda Kashula waits outside her apartment during the capture of Willie Steelman.

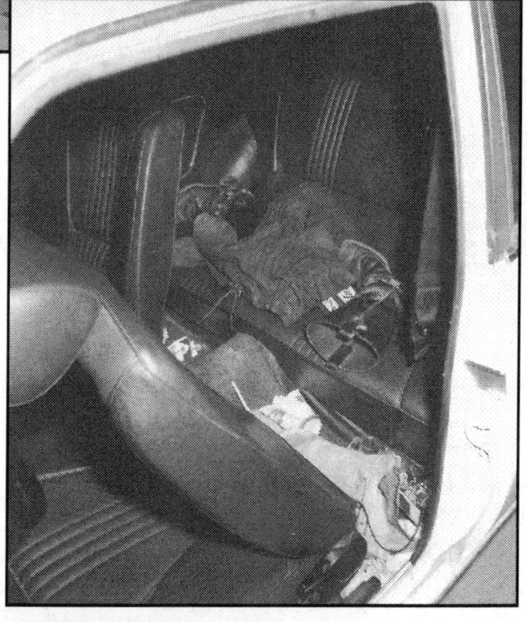

The Sandberg's Datsun with evidence found inside.

Willie bought a new leather jacket from this store with a portion of his take from the market. He was wearing it when he was captured.

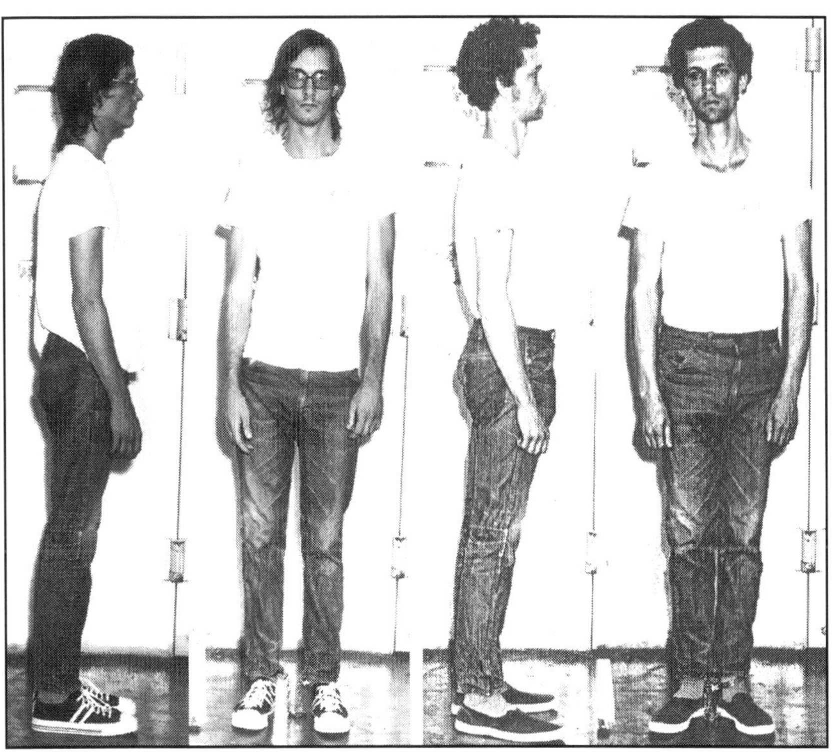

Booking photos of Gretzler and Steelman after their transfer to San Joaquin Sheriff's Department from Sacramento on November 8, 1973. Notice Gretzler's new tennis shoes.

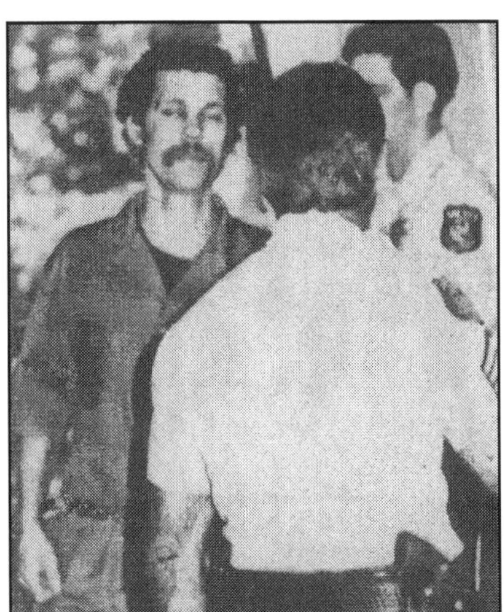

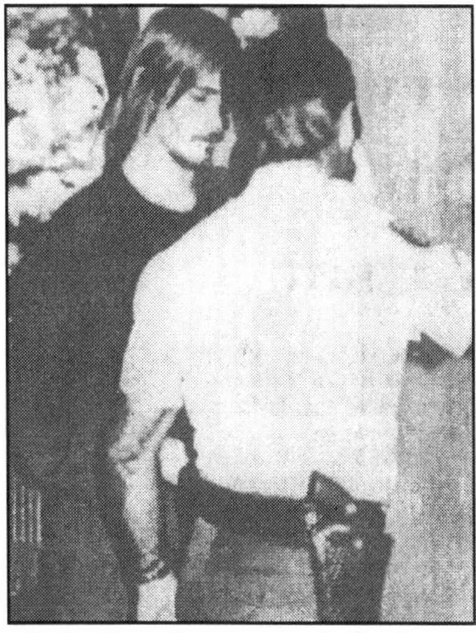

Willie Steelman and Douglas Gretzler leave Judge Papas' courtroom in Stockton July 8, 1974 after being sentenced to life in prison for the nine murders in Victor.

Photos courtesy Special Collections Department, UC Davis

Book 2

THE TRIALS.

1

Monday, November 12, 1973 | 10:00 am.

Years before, when he opened his first gas station and customers were few and times were lean, Richard spent many hours hunched over the counter in his small office watching cars zip by, waiting, hoping for someone to pull in. If not for the few dollars they might spend, at least for the few minutes of conversation he might have. Some days were just that lonely.

But Richard's first regular came not by car, but on foot. The newcomer lived just up the road, but even then it was a painful struggle for him to make his daily trek to the corner station. He was a young man, about Richard's age, but with a body crippled with cerebral palsy. And yet he somehow managed to hobble the short distance on brittle legs; his movements uncontrollable; his head jerked and his arms could flail about in a spastic rage at any given moment. His speech was no less painful to endure, as he labored to utter even the simplest of words. Although few understood him, eventually Richard reached the point where he could, and the two sat and talked for hours at a time, somehow comfortable with each other even during the many moments of silence.

But it was the man's laughter, so deep, so real, so loud and infectious, that Richard came to appreciate most. He looked forward to the daily visits, which soon came like clockwork. On the rare occasion when his friend was late, Richard wandered out to edge of the road to await his arrival. The man lived only several hundred yards away, but because of his condition, it could take him a half hour to complete the journey. When he did arrive, Richard was quick to pull a bottle of Coke out of the machine and help him hold it to his lips while the young man caught his breath.

But one day he did not show up at all. It was an unusually busy day at the station and Richard had not noticed his absence until late afternoon. The days turned into weeks, and there was still no sight of his friend. One evening after work, Richard walked up the road and questioned the neighbors as to the young man's whereabouts, only to learn he had become ill and had passed away unexpectedly; the funeral being held just days before.

There was an awakening in Richard that day, and it dawned on him what few friends he really had. Here he was, already twenty-five, and he could count on one hand the people he knew. He had spent every moment working, raising a family, his ambitious goals solely for them, and almost no time trying to meet people or developing any real friendships. And what was so equally concerning was that he realized there was very little he could do about it. It was his nature to be reserved; cautious about the way he approached others, cool to show his feelings. His one friend, the handicapped man from the gas station, had somehow found a way, through his disability maybe, to break Richard's shell.

One day soon after that, Richard's brother stopped by the station and Richard told him about what had happened. For the first time ever he opened up and confided to his brother his disappointment. "You know, I've spent all these years working hard, worrying about Wanda and the kids, trying to do the best for them, and they're still the most important people in the world to me, but..."

Richard stopped for a moment and sighed, the air leaving his body in a long slow gush; as if life itself was rushing from him, uncertain about confessing his weakness to one of the few people he had ever looked up to.

"...but it seems like I don't have any friends, and that really bothers me. I don't want to spend my whole life that way."

Monday morning woke to another thick covering of fog, locking Lodi into graveyard gray gloom. Somehow the town had managed to survive the weekend, but the hardest part was yet to come. Lodi still had to bury their dead.

The Parkin family gathered early, coming together at The First United Methodist Church downtown, a large brick building where 13 years earlier, in a bright cheery celebration, Wally and Joanne had confessed their love forever. Now this morning, friends, business associates, customers from the market, even a few total strangers, had arrived several hours before the scheduled ten-thirty start. Most stood outside, huddled in the mist, cigarettes lit to ward off this dreary chill, their voices as low as the spirits of their small town. Eventually they followed each other inside, their places on the sidewalk soon taken by the arriving crowd of reporters. Eight hundred people now packed a church that had seldom held a congregation half that size, most of whom now jammed the isles, staircases and hallways, the balance content to stand outside in the cold, hoping to hear even a small portion of what was being said by the two reverends chosen to address the mourners and the merely curious. Four identical gunmetal gray caskets rested beneath the stained glass windows high above the church alter.

"They have touched our lives in so many ways," Reverend Herbert Hirshfield eulogized, "that none of us can escape the belief that lives of great people have been snuffed out."

The Reverend Paul Donovan from the Congregational Church quoted the Apostle Paul often in an attempt to answer the grief, frustration and incomprehension felt by the onlookers. "We have run the gamut of human emotion. We live in a society that suffers from an inner sickness, and so I ask each one of you to dedicate yourselves to now build the kind of society in which these tragic events will disappear, so that these fine people shall not have died in vain."

After the service, Norm Parkin escorted his parents to a waiting limousine which would follow the four hearses, each bearing a single casket, to the cemetery. Because of crowd and size of the procession, there was confusion and difficulty getting underway. During the delay, while overcome by the finality of the moment, Mrs. Parkin cracked her window open slightly for a bit of fresh air. Within seconds, a television reporter shoved a microphone and a camera at her and asked if she had anything to say to her son's killers.

She recoiled, and somehow managed to close the window, but not before the reporter had repeated his question several times. She was heartsick. There was nothing with to compare her grief, no images to help her explain it, no words to describe how she felt, even if she wished to. And she didn't. Over the last several days, she had great difficulty even talking with her husband about their loss, and he too decided it was easier to keep the pain to himself. Mrs. Parkin knew that if the words ever came to her, she would certainly keep them, and her feelings, private, and under no circumstances share them with a stranger, let alone the rest of world. How could they ever understand how she felt?

And the TV reporters? She had lost all respect for them. Such savages! She swore she would never watch their news programs again. How cold and callous they were! "Please, just go away," she sobbed, as they stuck microphones in her face. "Please, just leave us alone." But they would not.

As the crowds filtered out of Cherokee Memorial Park after the Parkin service, the Earl family began arriving. Four copper colored coffins had been delivered earlier that morning and were arranged in a semi circle. Brilliant sprays of color stood behind the caskets, all in front of a pearl white satin backdrop. Per instructions from Richard's parents, the coffins remained open, although the remains resting inside were not immediately recognizable. Even the artistic hand of the mortician could not overcome the damage done by not only the shooter, but the doctor as well. The only sign life had resided here once, were the grape-stained fingers on Wanda's small porcelain hands, testimony of her late night toils a week earlier

The funeral motorcade had been lengthy, beginning across town at the home of Richard's sister, Della, and now proceeding slowly through Lodi; past police officers and their orange cones, through streets closed to all other traffic, past grocery store reader boards bemoaning the tragedy, and past other cars with headlights blinking in condolence. As the train of vehicles turned the final corner before entering the cemetery, the sun burst through the fog, and in the brilliance of an early autumn afternoon, those within the procession could see the crowd had completely overwhelmed the intersection.

There were hundreds of townspeople standing almost stage struck, gawking, hoping for one last glance of this grief stricken family. Among the bystanders, reporters and television crews huddled over their cameras and tripods, while others jogged to keep up with the long line of cars, scrambling for a final shot, dodging traffic across the intersection until this sad caisson had passed.

The Reverend John Hughes from the First Southern Baptist Church wasted no time in getting to the point of his message. There had been talk among family members, despite how private they had intended to keep it, about the possibility of administering justice themselves. There had been several late night sessions around the kitchen table at Aunt Della's as to how, or even if, a weapon could be smuggled into the courtroom. Revenge was believed to be their duty, their right, and while spoken in grief, there was a certain seriousness attached to the idea. Both sides of Richard and Wanda's families had discussed the plan in earnest, and Richard's brother, being the oldest of all siblings, fully expected this was his duty to perform, although the intense security at Friday's arraignment gave him little hope that such an attempt at retribution could succeed.

"Express your opposition to the evil that has been so terribly displayed!" Reverend Hughes implored the family, and, as if asking for their guarantee that any additional violence would not be repeated, he held his Bible high in the air for all to see as he quoted from it. "Vengeance is mine, sayeth the Lord. I will repay!"

The number of people at the service was so great, the guest book had to be replaced three times, until finally a yellow notepad was offered so everyone could at least leave their name. Besides family, there were people from school who knew Ricky, or friends of Debbie from Rainbow Girls, women who had been close to Wanda, as well as friends and neighbors who had known the entire family. And yes, there were many who knew only Richard. Some from work, some from his business, some just friends. In fact, there were a lot of friends.

By late afternoon all were laid to rest. Eight new graves, two entire families not a hundred yards apart. Debbie was buried only a few feet away from Mark's grave, the ground still bearing witness to his service on Friday.

As the Earl's service was coming to a close, Sheriff Canlis held a news conference in Stockton and announced "We are now documenting our evidence and re-interviewing a lot of people." And while he wouldn't confirm Steelman and Gretzler had confessed to the murders, he indicated much of the evidence linking them to the crimes had already been uncovered. He also stated the investigation was solely in the hands of his department and not the Arizona lawmen who had flooded his office over the weekend. All of whom now, much to his staff's relief, had finally returned home.

"I think they've found all the bodies they can account for," he stated, and that Steelman and Gretzler could now be linked to 17 murders in all. "But at this stage, with these guys talking, anyone with an unsolved murder in the past two month wants to talk with them."

Canlis also reported the additional key piece of evidence his department was seeking were casings from the .22 used in the killings. As he spoke, his men searched the fields and vineyards from Orchard Road west to Highway 99 and north to the county line. Deputies lined both sides of the roadway, hunched over looking for anything that shimmered, and for the rest of Monday afternoon, until the fog returned and daylight disappeared, they searched for as long and as far as they could. They found nothing.

It was also at this time when Carl Ambrose drove to the Steelman home in Acampo to find out about the derringer recovered over the weekend at the Clunie. Willie had admitted where he got it, so these last several days had been a nightmare for the Steelman family too. Because Willie's mother was out of state, spending the winter in Arizona with her new husband (her third), and therefore not subject to the wrath of her neighbors; all of the town's hatred fell totally and completely on the senior Steelman, his wife Patricia, and their teenage son, Gary. Since first mentioned in the papers, the name Steelman was uttered with nothing but contempt. It did not matter Mr. Steelman hadn't seen his brother since early spring, or would have turned him in if he had, they shared the same last name, and that was all most people cared to know. And yet until now, Steelman had been a respected citizen of his small community. He had a good job, did his best to be a good neighbor, and made it a point to keep out of other people's business. His most difficult task was trying to keep his son from taking the same path as his no-good brother.

Little Gary, as the family referred to him, struggled simply to be accepted. He was not the best student at Galt High, nor did he hang around in the best of company. He was only seventeen, but already his life revolved around getting high, goofing off and giving up. With every step it seemed all he cared to do was to follow in his Uncle Willie's footsteps. He knew he was in a load of trouble, as scared as he had ever been, knowing the truth would soon be discovered and his role in the murders revealed. He also knew he was just as responsible as anyone for all those people being killed. His old man had no idea the gun was missing, so Gary lied, denying having anything to do with it, swearing up and down the last time he ever saw his uncle was over the summer when Aunt Frances came to visit. Even now, as Ambrose quizzed him again, Gary was still willing to lie about the gun, creating excuses and alibis to try and save his skin, not knowing his uncle had already fingered him in the deal.

When Ambrose told him that, Gary broke down and cried, admitting what he had done. His uncle said some badass black guys were chasing him and all he was looking for was something to protect himself with. He was just trying to help, he promised. He had no idea what was going to happen. Soon Ambrose was confident he played no active role in the crimes, but requested they both come down to Stockton to make a formal statement, although there was still some question as to whether charges would be filed against them for their involvement.

The anger and disgust over what had happened overwhelmed the senior Steelman. He had spent his entire adult life distancing himself from his low-life brother, and now, with the help of his very own son, his gun had become a murder weapon. *His* gun had helped kill nine perfectly innocent people. *His* gun linked him with these murders. *His* gun. *His* son. When the newspapers reported where the weapon had come from, Gary Steelman and his son were as hated as two men could be, and Lodi would never let them forget what they had done.

When Ambrose was finished with the Steelmans, there was a note for him to call Jim Brooker at his home in Sacramento. Brooker told him his department had linked the revolver taken from Steelman to a slug removed from the body of Walter Parkin. He also said several of the other slugs were from a different weapon: definitely a .22, most likely some kind of derringer, yet it appeared the weapon was used only four times during the shooting. He also reported ballistic tests on the bullets left by Pima County were complete, and although he couldn't discuss the results until he had contacted them first, Brooker promised they would be pleased at their findings.

Pete Saiers' boss at San Joaquin was the long standing District Attorney, Joseph Baker. Next June, Baker would run for re-election, and because he was so entrenched in his position, there was some question whether he would even be opposed in the upcoming primary. Baker was fifty-ish, bald, with a preference for dark suits, white shirts and bright, cheerful ties. That single piece of clothing seemed such a contradiction, because most who knew him agreed Baker had no such personality.

"He was a half-drunk, sleazy excuse for a human being." These words were spoken years later from a man who never would have considered himself Baker's enemy at the time. But there were other similar comments; enough to paint a picture of a man who such enemies feared, co-workers tolerated, and for some reason, voters loved.

And that made him a man to be reckoned within Stockton. During his reign in office, there were rumors about his unyielding control of the unions, and how he had exerted this influence to swing city and county spending projects to his favorite cronies. Years later, because of those continued accusations, a newspaper reporter ran a series of articles that connected him to what was then being referred to as Stockton's 'Lebanese Mafia'.

That reporter, who would later win a libel suit brought on by Baker over the allegations, was Dan Walters.

Whether his staff and peers respected him, however, was something else again. Even his own employees managed to work around him, and if he wasn't in the office after a long lunch, or failed to show his face for days at a time, it was not considered a huge loss. Seldom did he even try a case these days, or help work on others, but he could always be counted on to press the flesh at an important news conference or public event that could further his political career. So after the murders, Baker was quick to jump into the fray. The D.A.'s office was in the spotlight these past few days, and while Pete Saiers and the others were running the show and doing the work, Baker managed to position himself center stage.

But today Baker found himself in the uncomfortable position of having to explain the actions and motivations of his department. Assuming San Joaquin was successful in winning their case against Steelman and Gretzler – and most were confident it was a done deal – it was now clear the most severe punishment California could impose was life in prison, handed out in seven year increments.

But Arizona could kill them. The Death Penalty. The Gas Chamber. All of which sounded a lot better to the people of San Joaquin County than what they could do. What's more, Arizona acted like they wanted them first, which was beginning to make perfect sense. Send them to Arizona. Try them. Convict them. Kill them. Save the money. Spare the hassle. Sounded good. Even this morning, word was spreading that Willie was anxious to go and had already signed a waiver of extradition.

But Baker remained adamant Steelman and Gretzler weren't going anywhere, although he was having a tough time defending his stance. "While we got them here, the witnesses are here, and we've got all the evidence, we should go ahead."

It was, at best, a half-hearted proclamation, as if Baker himself wondered, knowing the vengeance-inspired will of the people, if this could backfire in a coming campaign. He promised the trials could begin as early as January, although privately admitting they would most likely be moved out of San Joaquin County due to overwhelming publicity. And in an effort to further assure maximum punishment for the defendants, he announced his office was in the process of adding kidnapping with intent of robbery to the list; surprisingly a charge far more serious than that of murder. If convicted of this new charge, life without parole would be the punishment, and he declared Willie Steelman or Doug Gretzler would never walk their streets again.

But his own Board of Supervisors was not totally convinced in the logic of holding on to the pair. Still smarting over the California legislature delaying implementation of the Death Penalty Amendment passed a year ago by voters, (the law was written to exclude crimes committed before January 1, 1974, thereby excluding Steelman and Gretzler), some elected figures agreed with their constituents and thought turning the killers over to Arizona was not such a bad idea. The Board decided to hold a meeting to discuss the subject.

While feelings were mixed, the people's frustration over what now passed as justice was clear. Supervisor Carmen Perino summed up that feeling when he suggested that after the trials were over, County government should reexamine its legal procedures, referring specifically to Willie Steelman's lengthy record of being in and out of their local justice system. "You begin to wonder," Perino questioned, "what has happened to our system."

It was slap at the system Joe Baker represented, and the accusation did not go unnoticed.

It was not yet official, but Arizona was indeed making their intentions known, and they were using the press to explain how justice would be better served with a quick extradition. Maricopa and Pima County, along with the City of Tucson, all had expressed the desire to try Steelman and Gretzler first. Dave Hatfield, a reporter for The *Arizona Daily Star* in Tucson, quoted Pima County Deputy Attorney W. Randolph Stevens as saying he was worried that if the trials were not held soon, there might not be any trial at all. The Rule of Criminal Procedure in Arizona required a trial be held within 150 days of the filing of charges, and if they went on trial in California first, Stevens said, the Arizona charges probably would have to be dropped.

Whether Stevens was serious, or was just trying to instill a bit of fear into

California authorities, the threat appeared to work. For the next several days the big topic of conversation in both states was what should be done, and who should be allowed to do it first. But even Tucson was not immune to the controversy. In today's *Daily Citizen*, a lawyer by the name of William Risner wrote a letter questioning the rationale of extraditing both killers to Arizona for what would certainly be a costly trial. Considering that California was willing to go to all the trouble and expense not only to try them, but to house them for what was most likely to be life in prison, Risner wondered out loud what the County Attorney's Office was really attempting to do, and if their efforts were more political than an honest concern for justice.

Later this same night, soon after he had finished overseeing the statements given by Gary Steelman and his son, Pete Saiers was leaving the Sheriff's office when he noticed Doug Gretzler sitting in one of the interrogation rooms. He had never spoken to the suspect, nor should he now, knowing what his role would be during the upcoming legal proceedings. But there was something inside him that could not let this moment pass, so he stepped inside the room and looked down at the scraggly prisoner slumped over in his chair. His red security jumpsuit fell in layers around him, his long dirty hair poured over his face, manacles and leg irons clanging as he squirmed to find comfort. He did not look up until he heard someone speaking to him.

It surprised Saiers that he felt no anger towards this man, nor was he in the mood to be confrontational, yet he could not help but wonder what was going on in this man's head while all of this swirled around him. There had to be some remorse, Saiers thought, some measure of guilt, a tiny speck of shame or sorrow. He decided he would be satisfied with merely an admission of that.

"Does any of what you did bother you?" he asked.

Gretzler looked up and shook the hair hanging across his forehead. His eyes were so dark and sunk so far back in his head that Saiers could not tell if they were even open at all. For a moment, Gretzler did not say anything, he just stared. Finally, he held his hands up, twisted the chains around so he could move, then held his two index fingers less than an inch apart.

"It bothers me about this much," he snarled, "that none of this shit bothers me at all."

2

Wednesday, November 14, 1973 | 6:00 am.

Denise Steelman was awake early. She had been having trouble sleeping, and horrible nightmares, so she decided that this morning she was going to go down to Stockton and get it over with. It had been exactly one week since she had last left the safety of her parent's house, and she was tired of being held prisoner there.

Like her brother-in-law and his family, Denise was now cursed with the Steelman name. For the past week, she, and now her mother and father as well, were subjected to continuous torment. There were constant crank calls, or worse, only deep breathing on the other end. An endless stream of cars drove slowly by the Machell residence at all hours of the day and night yelling obscenities and terrible threats, while others did nothing more than stare and point at the house where the monster once lived. Occasionally a car would stop and someone would jump out, snap a photo, and tear off again. Even some of the same people she once considered friends wondered out loud just how much she knew about the killings.

And then there were the cops. Starting with the Sheriff's Department, and every other law enforcement agency anyone could imagine, all pressing her for information on her husband, asking questions about things she didn't know or ever would, insinuating she must have been in on the whole thing from the very beginning. And the news media never let up, hour after hour, calling and hounding, pleading and promising, demanding Denise had an obligation to tell what she knew about her husband, the mass murderer.

Of course, she knew nothing. But that wasn't good enough. The phone rang and the doorbell buzzed constantly and Denise stayed inside, a prisoner in her parent's home.

So Wednesday was the day, she decided. By noon she had gathered her things, made sure the coast was clear, got in her car and drove to Stockton. Fearful she would be recognized, never considering that no one there could possibly know who she was, she took the elevator to the third floor, walked up to the empty counter and handed over the papers.

Denise was filing for divorce.

She stated there were no children and no property, and that her husband had left suddenly on August 20th of that year. That was the main reason for dissolution, she explained, abandonment. Denise paid the extra few dollars to have a third party serve her husband with the papers, and considering the circumstances, it was not necessary for her to explain where they might find him.

On Wednesday afternoon, Detectives Ambrose and Bowling drove to Sacramento to continue gathering evidence. Their first stop was at the police department where they retrieved a photo of Doug Gretzler that had been pulled from a line-up and identified by the cabbie who had dropped him off at the Clunie. Other stops included The Happy Hour Massage parlor, but of the four witnesses Ambrose hoped to interview, only one was left. Kashula and the two other girls who were working the night Willie and Doug dropped in had all quit and left town. Melinda left a note saying she was scared and was going back to Pennsylvania to stay with her father. When the two detectives drove across town to her apartment, they found it empty.

Ambrose was slightly more successful at Joe's Style Shop where Willie had bought the leather jacket. Joe Faraci was happy to see the cops, and more than anxious to fill them in on not only that incident, but every run in he had ever had with all the lowlifes ever to come into his place. He drug out all the stories, and Ambrose had his hands full just trying to keep Faraci on the subject at hand. But the bottom line was, yes, he did remember the two men and handed the detectives a yellow receipt showing the transaction. He identified Steelman from his picture in the newspaper and when Ambrose showed him the line-up photo of Gretzler, he IDed him as Steelman's partner that day. "Didn't say much though," he remembered. "He just stood over there by the counter and watched. I don't think he said one word the whole time. Not even thanks when the other guy gave him his old jacket."

Faraci did offer one more item. When he was helping the customer try on the new jacket, he smoothed down the edges like he always does, just to show the customer how well it fit. "He had a piece on him, I can tell you that. Never saw it. Never had to. I could feel it stick out of his waistband." Faraci added that when the two left, the one known as Steelman turned to him and asked if the car out front was his. "I told him it wasn't. Good thing too. He probably would a killed me for it if it had been."

Before leaving town, Ambrose and Bowling stopped by the Department of Justice to pick up a current rap sheet on the suspects. There was a lengthy history for Steelman, but nothing on Gretzler. Had to be some kind of glitch in the system, they assured the detectives, promising to call just as soon as the information came through.

Some members of the Earl family were not so sure others weren't involved, nor were they comfortable with Carol Jenkin's version of why she hadn't come home earlier that evening. They were certain Debbie had told her father that she was going to be home by nine pm because Richard had told his brother-in-law precisely that when asked if he and Wanda would like to get together to play cards after dinner.

That brief phone conversation was just minutes before Richard received the message from his daughter, after which he flew out of the house in a huge hurry. Even Mark's friends, Steve and Wayne, recalled Mark saying he was late and had to pick Debbie up from babysitting at nine o'clock. So it was inconceivable to the family that there just wasn't more to this whole thing than people were letting on. Carol's story simply did not fit.

But the Sheriff's Department could not find anyone anywhere to dispute it. They had spent nearly five hours over the weekend interviewing Carol, and later her fiancé, Jim Mettler, and there was no reason at all not to believe the two were telling the truth. The only lead they had was a cryptic phone message the Stockton Police Vice Squad received the afternoon the murders had been discovered. The caller was identified only by the jail number given to him on a burglary charge months earlier. The following information was taken directly from the daily report.

> *"(73N113) called me tonight. . .stated when he was pulling burglaries in Lodi, Bill Steelman was his partner. . .stated Steelman is flakey dude and likes to rape girls and is capable of anything. . .stated that Bill would carry a gun on the burglaries and said he would smoke anyone that came in one them. . .stated Bill is very capable of the 187PC (murders). . .he indicated that the girl that lived with the Parkin Family is a tramp and that Steelman and the whole group have been having relations with her. (73N113) thinks she would have set up the deal, not knowing it would be a 187PC."*

The officer on duty promised the caller he would hand the info over to the Sheriff's Department and get back with him the next day. Supposedly the department followed up on the lead, but there was no written report found about this matter anywhere in the vast file of information on the case. Nor is there an interrogation recorded where the question was ever asked of Willie concerning Carol Jenkins being somehow involved.

Steelman and Gretzler were back in court Friday morning, a continuation of last week's arraignment. A four-car caravan brought them from the jail at French Camp to Judge Woodward's second floor courtroom. Like last week, security was tight, and more than a dozen marshals and deputies escorted the suspects in.

Gretzler was brought in first, and this time stood erect and attentive as Judge Woodward repeated the charges, now adding the tenth count, that of kidnapping. The accused answered clearly that he understood, unlike Willie who during his turn, could only mumble and nod his head when questioned by Woodward. Each session lasted less than three minutes.

Woodward finished quickly and continued the matter until December 4th when, he announced, a preliminary examination would begin for the two defendants.

It was doubtful, however, that such a session would ever take place. The District Attorney was already making plans to take the evidence to the Grand Jury, and if they returned the expected indictments, the case would go directly to the Superior Court and ultimately to another Judge.

Later that day, Tucson papers reported the Pima County Grand Jury had returned secret indictments of three murder charges against both suspects in the Sandberg and Sierra killings. They were going ahead with plans to prosecute the cases as soon as the accused were returned to their jurisdiction, whenever that might be.

That weekend, Tucson Detective Larry Hust and Pima County Attorney David Dingeldine left for California with the same thought in mind. Dingeldine was getting antsy, worried about the possible extradition, wondering if there was something he could do to get the ball rolling, so he had Jim Howard call his buddy Pete Saiers to set it up. They decided to drive the suspected route Steelman and Gretzler took almost two weeks earlier. Hust had known Dingeldine for years, since the days he spent at law school and the nights he spent working at the El Rancho Market in Tucson, just trying to get himself through college. Hust had known them all, even Randy Stevens, who had started his career trying traffic tickets. Hust got along with just about all of them, but he worked especially well with Dave. Piecing together what little information they could from recent interviews, they followed the killer's path through Stanfield, Yuma, El Centro and up through California, gathering whatever evidence they could find along the way, arriving in Stockton Sunday morning.

The next day was spent introducing themselves to their counterparts in San Joaquin, but they were not well received. No one wanted to give up anything they had on Steelman and Gretzler, which pissed Hust off no end, because that was not the way most jurisdictions treated each other.

"You know what the problem is, Dave?" Hust whispered late that afternoon while cooling their heals in Wagner's office, "They think we're gonna try and sneak these two guys outta here."

A thought that had already crossed their minds. But after the reception they had received, they realized Stockton wouldn't trust them alone with the prisoners for even one minute, so that idea had gone south in a hurry. Up to now they had got nothing from their trip to Stockton. Tired and discouraged, they returned to the motel, packed their suitcases and got ready to head back home the next morning.

But for some reason Hust was willing to give it one last shot. He called the Sheriff's office and asked for Ambrose. "Can you make arrangements for me to at least go down there and try and talk to Steelman and Gretzler?"

Ambrose and the others had just about had it with each and everyone of these guys from Arizona traipsing into their office, asking for this, demanding that, big shots, wasting everyone's time. He wished to hell they would just leave, and stop screwing everything up, and go back to the goddamn desert so they could finish their work.

Ambrose tried to make that clear in his short response. "They won't talk to you. I can tell you that right now."

"Can I at least go try?" Hust pleaded. He could hear the frustration in Ambrose voice and waited a long time for his answer.

"All right," Ambrose relented. "But don't you go trying to check those sonofabitches out of my jail!"

Finally having something to get excited about, Hust grabbed his jacket and asked Dingeldine if he wanted to go with him.

"No," Dave smiled, suddenly feeling a little more confident about things again. "No, I think I'll stay right here. I plan on prosecuting these two one day, and I don't think talking to them would be such a good idea."

When Hust got to the jail just after the dinner meal, he found everyone waiting for him, including Willie Steelman, who was sitting in the interview room, shackled, chained, handcuffed, snarling, fidgeting. It had been over a week since he had talked to anyone and he appeared ready to go.

So was Hust. He had been interrogating people for over eight years and it was the part of the job he loved most. Loved getting on their side, making them feel good, feel important, feel powerful. He loved the game, all the time getting inside their head and messing around with it. That's all it was, a head game. Most of the perps he interviewed, especially killers, were very smart, and really stupid, all at the same time.

"Hey wait a minute," Hust interrupted, stopping the guard as he was leaving the room. "Think you can take the handcuffs off this guy? He ain't going anywhere."

The guard looked at Willie, like this wasn't a real good idea, but pulled the cuffs off just the same. Hust looked over at Willie and smiled. "Now, I could use a cup of coffee. How 'bout you?"

"Yeah, sure."

"Cigarette?"

"Yeah."

"Just wanted to talk, you know, things are kinda confusing and all. Just wanted to get this all sorted out. You understand, doncha Willie?"

"Yeah, sure."

"Mind if I tape this?"

"No."

"Gotta read you your rights. Ready?"

"Yeah, go ahead."

Hust rattled them off. Willie said he understood. "Still wanna talk?" he asked.

"Yeah. Where do you want me to start?"

"Right from day one, Willie. Right from the very beginning."

And Willie started in. He told Hust that by now he had blown everything anyway. Made no difference anymore. He had talked to 30 to 40 people and he couldn't begin to remember what he had said to who. Libicki had told him he was so deep in shit now about talking so much that nothing much mattered anymore, so Libicki said he didn't care. Hell, talk to them all, Libicki said, say anything you want, it's all out now, you're screwed big time.

So everything was brought up and Hust was kept busy changing the tapes, feeding Willie cigarettes and having the guards hustle in fresh coffee.

After Steelman came Gretzler, and the scene repeated.

Hust made each of them feel comfortable and special. Maybe it was the week in captivity, or the clear head that came with a few days without drugs, but Doug's story finally matched Willie's, and it was told in great detail. He even copped to killing the two kids, and that was something no one was able to get til now.

Although he had opened up like never before, Willie remained cold and calculating throughout the entire session. But Doug acted like he had finally found a friend, someone he could trust. When it was all over he seemed sad to see Hust leave.

3

Thursday, November 22, 1973.

So there was this one day, this one single day when the world did not revolve around Willie Steelman or Douglas Gretzler, or the horrific murders they had been accused of. There were no articles about them in the paper, no stories on TV, no press conferences or heated discussions on how society could best punish them. For this one day we forgot about Willie and Doug, and turned instead to another murder exactly ten years earlier.

Frances had not spoken with her brother since that afternoon on her front porch in Denver when simply his glare frightened her beyond belief. She said her goodbyes that day, not imagining they would be forever. And now this. Somehow she knew this would happen. She knew in her heart that one day he would lose it all and let the pain of his troubled years destroy those in his path. But seventeen? Good Lord, Frances cried out each night. Why so many? Why the children? Why all of this?

So for Frances this day was heartbreaking for many reasons, but mostly because when she looked back on this very same day a decade earlier, the only picture she could recall was her brother sobbing.

He had come to Denver to visit her in early fall of 1963. It was an effort, his mother decided, to somehow try and get him to leave his problems behind in Lodi. Frances went out of her way to make him feel at home, knowing how much trouble he had been in, hoping somehow she could help him, to at least assure him she still cared, and he was still part of her family.

He was eighteen now, and France was startled when she picked him up at the bus station. He was not the little boy she remembered. He was thin and mean looking, with the angry skin of a teenager. Even his tone of voice sounded hateful, and at first glance Frances tensed up, realizing he was now her problem to deal with. Her kids did not seem frightened, and they were all quick to pounce on him in a playful tussle. So despite his appearance and age, Bill fit right in with the family, and weeks later, on this particular Friday morning in Denver, and while Frances was painting one of the rooms of the house, Bill was still doing what he liked to do; wrestle around on the floor with the children.

She had run out of paint, so Frances left for the hardware store. "Watch the kids. I'll be back in a minute," she yelled, although Bill had a difficult time hearing her over the giggling children and the noise blaring from the Motorola. He just looked up, nodded, and went back to tickling the youngest.

Frances was gone less than an hour, but in that short time, the world had turned upside down. As she headed up the walk, the front door burst open and Bill tore out, waving his arms hysterically, running in circles in the front yard, screaming at the top of lungs. "They've killed him! They've killed him! Jesus, my God, they've killed him!"

He turned around and ran back inside, Frances right on his heals, thinking one of children was hurt. Relieved to see them startled but okay, she turned to her brother to find out what in heaven's name was going on. Bill lunged towards the television, and without thinking, picked up the littlest and hugged him tight. Sitting on the edge of the sofa, eyes never leaving the black and white screen, he unconsciously rocked back and forth, consoling the child, and himself.

"They've killed him!" were the only words he spoke, repeating them now in a mindless drone. Frances moved next to him, concerned more about her brother than what was on the TV. He continued to rock, tears now rolling down his cheeks.

"Bill?" Frances got right in his face and shook him hard to get his attention. "Killed who?" she pleaded. "Who killed who?"

Finally she turned to the television and saw the news from Dallas. For a mere moment in time, for a split second, before the overwhelming tragedy struck home, Frances gasped a sigh of relief. It was only the President. Because for a tiny moment, she thought Bill was talking about their dead father again, and having another one of his many nightmares.

"Jesus Christ," he wailed repeatedly, "they've killed him!"

Frances was long convinced her brother had not been the same since their father died. It was the only reason she could offer for his current state of mind; as if he blamed himself. There had not been a day go by during these past five years that she didn't think about her little Bill; worried about how he was doing, heartsick she wasn't there to help. He was always the first topic of conversation on those calls back home, and most of the time her mother confessed he was only getting worse and harder to handle. admitting she was beside herself about what stupid thing he might do next. "You know, he's gonna hurt somebody one day,"

It was she who suggested Bill go to Denver to stay with Frances. Maybe she could help him. Maybe being with her and the kids would help get him back on track somehow. It was her only hope.

And Frances wanted to help more than anything; guilt ridden that she had left him at a time when he needed her the most. Sometimes they would talk to her about their dad, and he pleaded with her to tell him about their times together; about camping trips and going fishing, about all the things they did when he was too young to remember. He wanted to know everything about him. He wanted Frances to fill in the missing pieces of his life, however brief those times might have been. So she told him stories, stretched them out, even made a few up, just to assure him that times were good back then, very good, and that their father loved them both very much.

Now he sat on her sofa, weeping at the death of a young president, and for that brief moment Frances felt relieved, thankful that was all her brother was crying about. She would be ashamed to admit those feelings later, knowing how shallow and uncaring they must have sounded. But all she could remember about that day was how worried she was for her brother, how tight the thread of his sanity had been tautened. She was certain he was about to snap; he was just that close, so close to the edge that she gathered him in her arms, like she had done many times years before, and try and comfort him.

"Bill, it's all going to be okay," she whispered. "Don't cry now. Everything is going to be just fine."

So today, as the blood cold November winds whipped through Denver, just as they had on that Black Friday ten years earlier, Frances sat in the front room of her home and recalled that day long ago. She thought of her brother and wondered what he was doing, and how he was holding up. And she thought how terribly sad this all was, and how ironic it was that her little brother, her little Bill, who now was responsible for so much pain to so many others.

In the California judicial system there are two ways to bring a murder case to trial. One is to go through the Municipal Court first and have a hearing there – a mini trial of sorts – and if sufficient evidence presented, the judge can move it up to Superior Court where the case will be heard. The other to by submitting evidence directly to the Grand Jury and having them determine if there is enough evidence to proceed. If there is, the indictments they deliver can move the case up automatically to Superior Court, and that's exactly where the D.A. was taking this one.

On Wednesday morning, November 28th, Baker and his staff assembled the Grand Jury to hear their case against Steelman and Gretzler. In a grueling nine-hour session, they brought almost forty witnesses to present testimony and evidence. It was a steady stream, from law enforcement officers to members of the victim's families. Ambrose, Barbieri and Wagner revealed the evidence their office had recovered. Wanda's brother Carl was there, as was Mr. and Mrs. Parkin and their son, Norm. Doctor Lawrence explained the autopsy findings, James Brooker, the bullets from the guns that killed them, while Gary Steelman and his son were asked to explain how their weapon got into Steelman's hands. The videotape from the killing scene was introduced, although deemed too gruesome to present before the panel. The guns and slugs recovered were labeled, as was the wad of money found under Melinda Kashula's kitchen sink.

Richard's wallet, Debbie's ring, Wanda's purse, Mark Lang's glasses, all were shown to the jury. During the hearing, Baker interviewed just two witnesses, then left the room. Peter Saiers handled the rest; autopsies, ballistics, fingerprints, all the physical evidence. When it came time to take the matter to Judge Papas, Baker returned to again take charge of the procedure.

The jury only took five minutes to decide they had heard enough to indict both suspects with murder, robbery and kidnapping. Minutes later, Joe Baker presented those indictments to Superior Court Judge Papas.

Judge Chris Papas had been around long enough that everyone in the District Attorney's Office had argued a case in his courtroom at least once, and therefore knew fully what to expect. But that didn't necessarily mean they enjoyed their time spent before him. He could be a gruff sonofabitch; a label he was quick to give himself, especially if you wasted his time. Pity the lawyer who went before him uncertain or unprepared.

"Don't you go trying to pull the wool over this old Greek's eyes!" he roared on many an occasion when he felt some wise guy attorney was trying to sneak something past him. "You just leave that crap back at your office! You know better than that!"

So while he had scolded many a young counselor in his days, he had also made it clear he respected the strength that came with experience. Come before him well prepared, attentive to the standards he felt the law demanded, and Judge Papas would give you all the time you needed.

Pete Saiers liked him. Liked his loud laugh and booming voice, his curly, close-cropped salt and pepper hair, and his big flat nose. He liked the way Papas set the stage in his courtroom, the guidelines he expected all to adhere to, the leeway he allowed when the situation called for it, and how he would go to bat for the underdog if necessary. And yet the Judge held no court with the pompous, and Saiers had witnessed Papas give his own boss Joe Baker a good ass-chewing more than once. Saiers decided years earlier Chris Papas was the kind of guy who would make a great neighbor.

So after reviewing the documents presented to him, Judge Papas announced to all, including members of the media, that the prisoners would be arraigned on these charges in his courtroom Friday at ten am.

But he also had a surprise. After the reporters had left to file their story, he told the others to show up at eight o'clock and to bring Steelman and Gretzler with them. The concern for the safety of the prisoners had reached a point where no one was willing to take any chances. On Wednesday, Steelman and Gretzler had been secretly moved from the county jail at French Camp just outside of town, to the Deuel Vocational Institute, a high security prison near Tracy, thirty minutes south. The taunts and threats from fellow prisoners at county made keeping them there impossible, and the increased cries of retribution from outraged local citizens made any public appearance by the pair a huge risk. So when the two were rousted out of bed Friday morning and ushered into the courtroom for their semi-secret arraignment two hours earlier than announced, except for two people from the media, the courtroom was empty.

However, nearly one hundred armed officers still patrolled the surrounding blocks, the entire county building that sat upon it, as well as Papas' third floor courtroom. It was, without question, the tightest security to date. Willie and Doug, clad in their new khaki uniforms from DVI, wore the same heavy manacles and leg irons they had since their capture. They stood together in front of Judge Papas as he quoted from the documents before him.

"You are charged with one count of a one eighty seven from the California Penal Code, that in the death of Wanda Jean Cummings," at which time he looked at the defendants, paused a moment for dramatic effect, then continued, "a human being."

And he did that nine consecutive times, once for each victim, each time closing with those same chilling words. When he was finished with the murder charges, he moved on to those of robbery and finally to kidnapping. Each time he asked if the defendants understood. Each time they answered yes. Initially Gretzler's response was loud, firm and seemingly without emotion, but as the charges grew, and the mind numbing severity of his predicament mounted, it appeared even too much for him, and eventually he bowed his head as he listened.

The arraignment took nearly thirty minutes. When the proceedings were complete, it was clear it had also taken its toll on Judge Papas. His emotions seemed shaken, and his voice cracked several times during the readings, most noticeably when he came to the children's names.

He set Tuesday, December 18th for the continuation of the hearing, and told the defendants he expected their plea at that time.

4

Wednesday, December 6, 1973.

In the letter to the editor Tucson lawyer William Risner penned several weeks earlier, he stated what he considered the obvious, arguing the County Attorney's Office intention of extraditing Steelman and Gretzler to Arizona.

"The alternative to the possible death penalty," Risner wrote, "would be incarceration for life in California for the numerous murders allegedly committed there."

But the portion of the letter that created the firestorm was yet to come.

"So could you be so kind as to give me a cost estimate for all the expenses incurred by the taxpayers in Pima County should your office continue with your plans?"

It took only two days for Deputy Attorney Randy Stevens's response to reach the editorial pages.

"Simply take the cost of extradition," he advised Risner in his stinging reply, "plus the cost of prosecution and the cost of legal defense, and add to that the cost of appeals, and multiply that by one million."

And even that, Stevens continued, would be less than the value of the lives of the murder victims.

"Or, maybe the parents could be able to give you an idea of what they would give to have them alive today,"

There was one parent who would have given anything. Roderick Mays came to Stockton today to let that be known to all who would listen.

Mr. Mays lived in San Francisco with his wife, and was an advertising executive there within only a few years from retirement. But business had him in Los Angeles the day the bodies of Michael and Patricia Sandberg were discovered. For the few days prior, Mays had seen the events in Lodi and Sacramento unfolding on Los Angeles television, never imagining for a moment he would soon be pulled deep into the tragedy. All that changed when his wife called him with the news.

Roderick Mays had been beside himself for weeks. After the services for Patricia were held, his life seemed so useless and unimportant. He could not fathom what had happened; disheartened to realize on that Saturday in October, only minutes after he had hung up the phone with her, these two worthless bastards barged into her home and murdered her. He had no idea in the world how he would go on without her. His hurt was so deep he couldn't even bear to carry a picture of Patricia anymore. His pain so intense, even the mention of her name caused him to buckle with hopelessness so overwhelming, he sometimes felt his life should not go on either.

While Mrs. Mays tried to find some way to resume a semi-normal life, her husband's torment would not allow him to do the same. While she tried staying busy with simple projects to keep her mind off what had happened, he could not do anything other than try and think of things he might have done to protect his daughter from scum like this. At night, when she tried to rest, he paced the floor, planning, pleading to God for justice, praying for relief from this nightmare. Patricia had been his everything, and now she was gone. But these two pieces of shit were still alive. His heart hurt, his soul ached, he could not let go of her, certain he could not live again, could not breathe again, until these two were just as dead.

"I'm here to communicate my feelings, and to convince the residents of this county that I want the killers of my daughter executed," he announced.

Mays had come to Stockton with his newly hired Lodi attorney and made the rounds of every newspaper that would see him, every radio and television station that would listen. He knew nothing of the letter in Tucson, or the debate brewing there as well. He knew only that Arizona had the death penalty and California did not, and he wanted the killers returned there for trial and to face the ultimate penalty for their crimes.

Joe Baker, however, had no intention of letting them go until he was finished with them.

When he learned this, Mays was dumbfounded. It was a concept as foreign to him as the very murders themselves! How could any man, especially a father, not want justice to prevail? Real justice – not this California slap on the wrist malarkey – justice applied swiftly to those who had caused so much damage and left behind so much pain. So Mays decided, before he had even met Joseph H. Baker, he didn't like him. For he was certain that Baker was the only man standing in the way of what was right, and what was just.

For the next several days Mr. Mays toured the county, talking to anyone who would listen, trying to drum up support for extradition, noting "there is so much a stronger chance in California that a plea of insanity or some other pleas could be applied." He was hitting the local citizenry right in their weak spot, because there wasn't any doubt that Californians considered their state too soft on crime. But it was more of a direct slap at Baker, and one that did not go unnoticed, because the DA was now forced to explain his decision to a crowd being worked to a frenzy by a man who had lost so much. How dare Joe Baker tell the father of a murdered daughter what is, and what is not, justice?

Roderick Mays was making Joe Baker's life difficult and that was something Baker was not accustomed to. While Mays asked citizens to write letters to Baker showing their support for immediate extradition, Baker tried to convince them he really was on their side, that his actions were in their best interest, and that his was the right decision for everyone, including Roderick Mays. Willie Steelman and Douglas Gretzler must be tried here first, he argued, and they had to answer for what evil deeds they had wrought upon their community.

Eventually Baker and Mays came face-to-face Thursday afternoon. The meeting was amicable but neither was successful in changing the other's mind.

"Mr. Mays had nothing new to offer that we haven't already considered," a stubborn Baker announced afterwards, adding that anyone who assumed Steelman and Gretzler would be automatically convicted and executed in Arizona were just plan wrong. "There are no such guarantees."

Dan Walters, who had been busy covering the courtroom proceedings, drove out to Victor to report on how the people there were holding up. His article appeared December 6th, exactly a month after the murders.

"The shock has worn off a month after nine persons were executed here," he began, "but the memories will remain for decades. The initial outburst of anger and outrage have given way to a grim determination that the Parkin and Earl families will not be forgotten, and a widespread disgust with the judicial system."

"I blame the judges more than them," Walters quoted Norm Parkin who had worked with Steelman for a brief time at a winery just down the road from the United Market, and was reluctant to give the killer any credit for anything. "Willie was just a pothead who couldn't hold a job." Parkin insinuated that if he was smart enough to see that trait, then why couldn't the judges?

The article said the Parkin family was intent on keeping the house on Orchard Road and finishing it the way Wally and Joanne had planned. The market had reopened and was busy with holiday shoppers. "They stayed away for awhile," Norm admitted, "but only because most didn't know what to say."

A memorial fund set up in the names of the Parkin family a few days after the murders was up and running, and the chairman, a long time friend of the family announced it was up to $7,000. There was no decision made yet on just how the memorial would be created, but most thought a small park in town would be a nice way to remember some of Victor's most popular citizens. The head of the memorial fund agreed with Norm Parkin and others who directed their anger and frustration at the judicial system more than at the slayings, noting Steelman had been released on probation from a local judge just this past summer, even after the county probation department recommended against it. But his real concern was for Victor and how everyone would get by from here on out.

"A lot of the shock has worn off, but it will never be the same."

The following week, with the extradition debate in full swing, Joe Baker came out with his strongest attack to date. Suddenly concerned he might be standing alone, defending an unpopular position; he placed a call to Governor Reagan's office to see if he could count on their support in his efforts. Reagan had long talked of being tough on crime, and had campaigned hard for the reestablishment of the death penalty a year earlier, but Baker wasn't quite sure where the Governor stood on the situation in Stockton. He had heard the rumor that Arizona Governor Williams had already discussed the case privately with Reagan, and had attempted to get his agreement on the extradition. But as of today, there was no word on what way Reagan was leaning. Baker was worried. He didn't want to be hung out to dry. Not with the primary a little more than six months away.

So before going even further out on a limb, Baker called Sacramento on Monday and asked for a commitment from the Governor. Reagan's advisor, James Garbolino, told him he could count on their support. The governor decided there would be no extradition to Arizona until California justice was served. Willie Steelman and Douglas Gretzler would be tried here first. Baker had Reagan's word on it.

The announcement was made public Tuesday afternoon, and coincidently, at exactly the same time Roderick Mays had been invited to address the San Joaquin County Board of Supervisors. He had stayed in Lodi and Stockton all week, talking with everyone from elected officials to people on the street.

He claimed the letter writing campaign he had requested was gaining favorable response to his idea. He walked into the Supervisor's meeting armed with a stack of letters. The news from Sacramento had not diminished his determination in the slightest.

"The will of the people is what really counts," was the message he repeated over and over.

At the end of the three-hour meeting it was clear he had failed to sway any members, even if their decision carried any weight, which it did not. It was also revealed that out of the eighty letters of support he carried into the meeting, only twenty were from the San Joaquin area.

The argument between the two men carried on for several more days. Mays announced plans for a countywide petition to make it easier for everyone to voice their support, while Baker issued a news release stating the three basic reasons for keeping the trials here. Mays claimed the letters were still pouring in, and Baker admitting somewhat sarcastically that he indeed had received two letters himself, but one person had called to tell him they had already changed their mind and they were now supporting him.

Mays finally attacked Baker's reasons for his position, saying the D.A.'s actions were merely political. Baker responded by telling the press that he understood the pain Roderick Mays was going through, but he could not use that to change what was the right thing to do. "We are not emotionally motivated," he said, referring to Mr. Mays' relentless efforts. "We are being professional in our judgments."

By now the two attorneys for the accused stepped into the act and said, that regardless of what had been rumored earlier, neither one of their clients wanted to go anywhere. Waiving extradition was not in their plans. "We'll fight any attempt," Libicki announced, "Now, or anytime in the future."

By Friday the commotion had calmed down somewhat. Roderick Mays had poured his heart and soul into what he knew was right, and still it was not enough. Dejected, he mentioned he was the only member of any of the victim's families to press for what he termed "the maximum punishment". He could not understand their hesitation, their silence, or their lack of commitment for justice, even if some viewed it only as revenge. He had done the right thing. He was sure of that. He made once last request for letters to be sent to his attorney in Lodi, and then he went home to San Francisco to wait. If nothing more, his activity of the past week was therapeutic. At least he was doing something, he decided. That was more than he could say for the others.

And he knew he was not finished. He vowed not to quit until Willie Steelman and Douglas Gretzler were dead and gone. Just like his dear sweet Patricia.

On Tuesday morning, December 18th, Steelman and Gretzler returned to court accompanied by their attorneys and a small army of officers.

But unlike before, this hearing had been widely publicized, and the turnout was substantial. Lines began forming long before the courthouse opened and each person allowed inside were herded through metal detectors and individually searched. Once more the entire building was surrounded and armed guards covered every entry. When the spectators were seated, bailiffs sealed all courtroom doors before motioning deputies to escort the prisoners inside. A concealed passageway and elevator brought Willie and Doug from the DVI into the basement then up to the third floor courtroom. With the exception of the guards who shadowed their every step, there hadn't been anyone within a hundred feet of either one since they had arrived downtown. But now the courtroom was packed and that made every officer nervous. It was during this court appearance, newspapers had reported, that Willie Steelman and Douglas Gretzler were supposed to answer to the murder charges.

They stood along side their attorneys as Judge Papas entered. Doug bowed his head slightly, silent, his stringy hair covering his face. But Willie, with his bushy afro and a new Fu-Manchu, was animated and talkative, turning to look at those who had come to get a peek at him. At one point, while Libicki addressed the bench, Willie smiled and waved to a young woman sitting in the back of the courtroom.

Dedekam and Libicki made the usual motions.

The public defender requested juvenile records of his client, and Dedekam asked the court for permission to hire a psychiatrist and a private investigator.

Joe Baker introduced himself, but asked for nothing.

Papas quizzed Dedekam for a cost on his request, then continued the hearing until after the first of the year.

The entire session lasted nine minutes.

And those who had come to see a guilty plea, or justice moving swiftly, left disappointed.

Life at Deuel was not all that unpleasant. Willie and Doug were housed on the same run of the more popular L Wing, a newer section of the prison known for its nicer living conditions and wider variety of drugs. Their cells, while not adjoining, were within shouting distance of each other and both learned quickly how to use the ventilation system as a method of communicating with the others. They were not allowed access to fellow prisoners, but the cellblocks were designed around a fenced courtyard and each prisoner had his small piece of ground, enclosed by cyclone and razor wire. There, for a few minutes each day, they could mingle in lieu of the scheduled exercise period.

Willie spent the time handing out his usual line while Doug just tried to blend in and get along. He listened and learned from Willie and the others on how things worked on the inside. He found it odd and uncomfortable that he was actually respected, and a little feared, for what he and Willie had done. He was a novelty item. A freak show. He heard his name being whispered, and his story told and retold through their wing, their hideous glory now magnified and exaggerated with each new accounting. He thought it all quite odd. He never considered himself dangerous, let alone being a serial killer. He admitted not knowing one thing about being a prisoner; didn't have a clue as to how things worked or who called the shots. He looked to Willie for all the answers and realized how much he still depended on him just to get through each day. So, as he had done most of his life, he tried not to think at all. This was all so new, so murky, so surreal. During the day he took all the drugs he could get just to stay comatose. At night he popped pills called "red-eyes" so he could sleep. Life in prison was not unlike that on the outside; drugs made being who he was, and what he had done, a little easier to tolerate.

There were nights as he lay on his bunk, when he could hear guards sneak in and beat the hell out of two black guys housed in cells on either side of him. Word was they had attacked another guard in another wing – bad enough to send him to the hospital – and this was their payback. He listened to the crack of a wooden club on flesh and the dull thud made as a body slammed against concrete. He had learned enough to keep quiet about what he heard.

December at Deuel was bitter cold. A damp fog covered the grounds until mid afternoon, depositing moisture even inside his cell. It was not uncommon for the small wire-screened windows in each cell to be broken, letting in even more cold and wet air. If he was lucky, he sometimes found a piece of cardboard to cover the barred windows. If it was still there when guards made their routine inspections, the coverings were ripped down and he would have to begin his search all over again. The blankets for their bunks were thin and did little to ward off the cold, even in the daytime. While jackets or coats were not allowed, he managed to get an extra blanket and fashion it into a poncho to wear when the guards were away, just to try and stay warm.

He found time to write Judy on occasion, although she ignored him. He wrote to his mother, and she sent him a box of cookies for the holidays. He read every book he could get his hands on, slept whenever his mind would allow it, and stumbled to fit in.

Christmas was now a week away. It had been exactly one year since Doug Gretzler left to discover the world.

This is what he had found.

5

Thursday, January 3, 1974.

George Dedekam did not understand Doug Gretzler anymore than anyone else ever did.

He tried. When he had a spare moment, he drove down to DVI to talk with him, each time hoping his client would cut the silent treatment and give him something he could work with; a hint of remorse, a faint cry for help, just one 'I'm sorry', something to get the juices flowing. Anything at all he might work with.

But there was nothing. Doug was not only quiet, but unemotional as well, never once giving the indication he was sorry for what happened, never once begging for mercy or pleading with his lawyer to find a way to get him out of the this huge mess he had created. Dedekam couldn't understand it. The clock was ticking. What would he tell a jury about Doug Gretzler?

Initially, Dedekam thought he had it figured out. It was all Willie. His first look at the guy told him that. Doug was nothing more than a simple-minded follower who went along for the ride; the frightened one, the weak one, the one who could never muster up the courage to find a way out. Just look at the two of them, Dedekam thought. Anyone could see whose idea it was to kill all those people. It was Steelman. It just had to be.

But after his first long talk with Gretzler soon after his capture, Dedekam realized he was wrong. Gretzler didn't say much to him then either. Every word had to be yanked out like a bad tooth. He just sat there, dragging long and hard on the cigarettes offered, muttering only that he wasn't really sure how he felt about what he had done, or even why he did it, for that matter. *What's the big fucking deal? The guy Parkin was dirty,* Doug reminded his attorney. *Didn't you listen when Bill said that? So anyway, they're all dead and there's nothing I can do to change any of that now, so why is everybody hassling me? Let me say this again. It was all Bill. The whole thing. I mean I did it, I helped, but it was Bill who called the shots and made the plans and decided where we were going and when. That's the story. Anyway, Bill said these guys were following us and all we could do is keep moving and stay ahead of them because if they caught us they would kill us too. It was just a matter of time, so we couldn't leave anyone behind who could tell these people where to find us. No witnesses, Bill said, and I said yeah, that makes sense to me. I mean this was Bill's call, his territory, his deal. Who was I to say otherwise?*

But at the same time Doug didn't want to talk too much about his family or what he had left behind. It wasn't their fault he did what he did. His mom was all right, but the rest of them, they didn't care about him, didn't come see him or write him, or call to see if he was okay. *They won't talk to me,* he told Dedekam, *so why would they bother talking to you?*

It had been almost two months and Dedekam realized the only things he knew about his client was what he read in the papers. He warned Gretzler there was only so much he could do to represent him unless he gave him something more to go on. "If you even just acted liked you were sorry," Dedekam pleaded, "then at least that would be a start."

But there was nothing. He couldn't break into Gretzler's world, so he asked Judge Papas for a psychiatrist, hoping he would be more successful. Dedekam never once thought Doug Gretzler was insane, nor did he for one minute ever plan on using that as an excuse for what he did, but he had to find out more about this guy, or else his work might just as well stop right here, because this guy Gretzler was as guilty as they come.

Dedekam and Libicki talked several times on how to best defend these two; trading ideas on how to handle a sure loser. At twenty-six, Libicki was half Dedekam's age with twice the enthusiasm. He still enjoyed the struggle for the underdog. Unlike the stylish, yet conservative Dedekam, Libicki just looked the part of public defender – his suits crumpled, his long curly hair battling gravity with each visit to the courtroom, his briefcase bulging with tattered papers and notebooks. Sam Libicki acted as if he looked forward to the fight, couldn't wait for the court dates, loved each and every sick and twisted conversation he had with Willie, appreciated what a terrific uphill road he had to climb each day. He was a whirlwind of energy, always excited about what he was faced with.

Dedekam could only smile. He had been there once – hell, he had been just like him – but now days he was a bit tired of it all. He cleared his throat a lot, buying time, waiting for the inspiration that never came. There wasn't a damn thing in Douglas Gretzler that interested him other than seeing his constitutional rights honored. Nothing much more he cared about than that. Sometimes that bothered him; not to have the fight that Libicki had. He would do his absolute best, of that there was no question, because that is what he always did, but he wasn't excited like Libicki was. Wasn't anything here that got him revved up like the young guy. To Dedekam, Gretzler was a punk. Yeah, a sorry sack of shit punk with the back bone of a worm, but a punk just the same, and it was his job to speak up for the punks who came his way. He just wished he had the energy young Sam had, but he wondered whether he would waste it on somebody like Gretzler if he did.

George Dedekam was in his mid twenties when he came out to Stockton from his hometown in Ohio. Like the young man he now represented, all he could think about was heading west to California, and after the war that's exactly what he did. He went to school at the College of the Pacific, earned a law degree, and like so many others, got his first job at the San Joaquin County D.A.'s office.

It was there where Pete Saiers met him, and they stayed friends when Dedekam left to form a partnership with two other attorneys. Their office was a few blocks from the courthouse on East Channel Street, and on payday Saiers and Dedekam would meet after work for a few beers at a little bar across the street, just to catch up on cases and spread a few rumors. 'Shorty' was the nickname Dedekam answered to, given to him years ago by his fellow deputy attorneys at the county, and Saiers thought it was perfect.

"He was just beginning to slow down, the illness maybe, but let me tell you, the George I remembered was a funny, feisty, sonofagun," Saiers lamented later. "Man, I'll tell you, he used to crack us all up with his stories and remarks about things that were going around us. Sometimes his wife Charlene would join us and those two were such a kick! He called her 'Dirty Mouth Charley' and I never in my life heard two people have more fun than George and her."

But at the same time George Dedekam had earned the respect of his peers. After starting his own firm, he was appointed by the Lawyers Referral Service to sit on the Serious Felony Panel, where only a few were deemed so worthy. It was from that panel that George Dedekam had been selected to defend Doug Gretzler. And as confident as Pete Saiers was that Gretzler was guilty, he knew his friend George Dedekam would give all he could to defend him.

"Anything new?" Dedekam asked each time he stopped by Saiers' office to pick up the latest transcripts of witness interrogations, ballistic findings and crime scene reports, all required to be shared by the prosecution.

"It's all in here," Saiers joked in a singsong newsboy manner. "Read all about it!"

Dedekam looked over the documents in silence; so quiet that Saiers finally had to ask. "What's up, Shorty? What's new with you?" It was only then when he could see weary look on the face of his friend.

Dedekam let out a sigh and confessed with a shrug. "Not a thing, Peter. Not a single goddamn thing."

It was the New Year. The people were anxious for justice. They wanted Steelman and Gretzler in court now. But they weren't the only ones interested in getting this thing off the dime. There was already huge pressure building in the San Joaquin legal circles to get this case to trial. Baker was promising everyone April 1st at the latest, confiding to associates most likely first of May, hoping silently it didn't go past that. So knowing how all eyes were on him to proceed, and how he would be looked upon if he became part of any shenanigan to purposely delay the trial, the decision Dedekam made with Sam Libicki was a difficult one. It was Libicki who pointed out the obvious. Neither one had much choice. They had to buy time. Time was always a defense attorney's best ally. So they came to court today and asked that all charges against their clients be dropped.

A familiar tactic, indeed, but it left a sour taste in the mouths of many who were demanding justice be swift. That included some of people Dedekam knew and worked with, and yet both Libicki and Dedekam argued strongly at this morning's hearing that the evidence presented to the Grand Jury was insufficient, and made their joint motion to quash the indictment. They wanted Papas to give them two hours to make their case. Papas could do little more but continue the hearing to January 18th.

At that hearing, Libicki lead the charge, and while the original motion claimed the evidence against their clients in all charges was insufficient, they only argued the kidnapping count. Even with nine counts of murder preceding it, the kidnapping charge was by far the most serious. If convicted of kidnapping Walter Parkin, both Steelman and Gretzler would be given life without parole, a sentence that did not come with a murder conviction. Searching for anything he could come up with to serve his client, Dedekam agreed to go along with Libicki.

The public defender argued the evidence relating to the charge was presented to the Grand Jury in a speculative manner. In other words, there was no physical evidence given to prove Willie or Doug used force to take Parkin to the United Market. Libicki argued Mr. Parkin may have just offered to take Willie Steelman to the store just to satisfy his request for money, and there were no witnesses or physical proof to say otherwise.

But Saiers countered that the store and the safe were not broken into, and that could only indicate that Wally Parkin was there.

"But there is no *proof* that Parkin was actually taken from his house to the store," Dedekam answered during one of his few responses. "At best this may have been larceny or grand theft, possibly burglary, but not kidnapping. The evidence is totally circumstantial. We don't really know who opened that safe."

Saiers came back and offered that the Grand Jury could have inferred the events that took place, while Libicki claimed they all could speculate what happened that night, but it was proof the prosecution needed. Proof they didn't have. Judge Papas tended to side with Saiers when he told both attorneys, "The prosecution doesn't need proof beyond a reasonable doubt to sustain charges for trial." But at the end of the hour-long hearing, the longest to date, Papas said he would take the matter into consideration and rule next week.

Having an idea what that decision might be, Libicki told reporters after the session that he and Dedekam had already agreed to appeal the decision to the state if the reply came back against them.

Which it did. On January 25th, Papas ruled in an indictment all the prosecution had to do was to create "a strong suspicion" and they had done that. "There is sufficient reason to believe that the offenses have been committed," Papas stated, while noting the burden of proof would be a lot higher when they have to prove those same charges to a jury. He rescheduled the entering of pleas for February 8th.

As promised, Libicki and Dedekam appealed the ruling to the state on January

30th. The District Court of Appeals could be asked to suspend all other charges in the matter until the hearing was held, a delay that could last two months. But as if to appease the public, Dedekam told reporters he believed the state would speed the normally slow process along because of the circumstances of the case. At the same time the D.A.'s office said the appeal would not hinder their case in the slightest. Until they heard otherwise they expected everything to move along as planned and they equally expected both suspects to enter a plea at the next hearing.

The appeal by Libicki and Dedekam would be the last time both attorneys would work so close together. From here on out they would handle their particular case the way they saw fit, and it soon became quite clear each man saw the need for a different direction.

At least until the time she met Willie Steelman, Dr. Patricia White had been a respected member of Stockton's psychiatric community.

She was petite, mid forties, and very stylish. Being a woman did not endear her to the male dominated law enforcement community in which she had to ply her trade. Nor did it help that she often embraced the weaknesses prevalent in the people she diagnosed. She immersed herself in her clients, and usually became their most vigorous supporter, regardless of the crimes they were accused of.

But Pete Saiers saw it differently. He said there wasn't a criminal Dr. White ever talked to that she didn't think was insane. She made sure of that. Willie was perfect for her.

Sam Libicki knew of Dr. White for several years. As a public defender, it was sometimes necessary to have a client examined, and certainly with the more serious, higher profile cases such as this one. Dr. White was on the local psychiatric panel judges used to select from when it was clear the mental state of a defendant was in question, so her name was not an unfamiliar one in Stockton. Libicki had contacted Dr. White immediately after his first visit with Willie in November, and asked for her help. After hearing the news reports of this horrible crime, White was more than anxious to talk with the person who was apparently taking responsibility.

Dr. White first spoke with Willie on November 15th, one week after the murders. He was reserved at first, remembering how he got burned talking with the other 'doctors' the night he was captured. But he eventually loosened up with White, especially when it became clear that he fascinated her. At Libicki's request, she saw him again on December 8th, this time while at Deuel. Now comfortable with her, and excited to know she was authorized to prescribe drugs, Willie opened up and began describing the nightmares he claimed to have had off and on over the past couple of years. He talked of how he slept very little and the nightmares would come even in the middle of the day. He said he was now hearing voices again, something that had happened at other times in his life, and those voices now laughed at him. He claimed only to be able to hear them on his left side and there were three or four people heard constantly throughout the day, but he could never understand what they are saying because the voices were garbled, as if coming through a radio. Willie confided in her about the rage that builds inside him and how he lashed out at whatever was within his reach. It is during these times, he said, when he wants to kill someone, or maybe even turn the hostility upon himself. Willie told her he was again thinking more and more about suicide.

By now Dr. White was extremely concerned about Willie and she expressed that fear to Libicki. "If Mr. Steelman does not receive immediate and intensive psychiatric care in a hospital environment, he is only going to get worse and his suicidal urges will increase until he is successful."

On January 26th, the day after Judge Papas denied the motion to dismiss all charges against Steelman and Gretzler, Libicki began planning his next move. He asked Dr. White to again visit Willie at DVI. By now White was adamant Willie Steelman was insane, and she told Libicki that, so he asked her help in preparing such a report for the court. When she again examined Willie on the 26th, everything he had been telling her was intensified. The nightmares more frightening, the voices louder and angrier, his rage more violent, his homicidal and suicidal thoughts more frequent. Willie had been on some form of medication since his arrest, but now the quantity and variety had been increasing steadily. His act was now being rewarded, and he understood Dr. White's importance and involvement in that matter. He made sure not to let up.

Libicki's talks with his client were not nearly as interesting or revealing. Sometimes Willie would be cordial and open about what was going on, other times close lipped and standoffish. Libicki was still impressed with his intellect and ability to communicate his feelings, but never could seem to get real grip on how his client viewed the charges against him. One day Willie acted like he worried about what was looming before him, other times he was just angry and combative, willing to take on any bastard who stood in his way.

There were days when Libicki himself felt the wrath of Willie Steelman, heard the threats and curses he spewed, felt the very rage that Dr. White had talked about spread over him. He listened as Willie accused him of conspiring with the D.A. to crucify him. "You think I don't know you? Shit, you're no better than they are! You get your money from the same fucking machine, the machine that oppresses all of us who know your game!"

And yet many times Willie was polite and talkative, but at no time did Willie ever want to say he was guilty, refusing to admit he had done anything wrong. He also let Libicki know he wasn't interested in helping a twenty six year old county defender, someone even younger than he, send him to jail for the rest of his life.

It seemed the only person Willie really trusted was Dr. White, so it was she Libicki turned to convey Willie Steelman's mental state to the courts. After her last visit to DVI, she returned and again told him of her concern. Libicki called Judge Papas and asked for an immediate hearing on the matter. New information has come to light, he said, on the sanity of Willie Steelman. Papas agreed to listen, and Libicki was off and rolling.

On Friday, February 1st, Papas held a special session to hear Libicki's motion to grant psychiatric evaluations on his client. Only Willie Steelman was present, and while George Dedekam was in the audience observing, Gretzler had remained behind at DVI. Libicki began by insisting the court order an immediate examination to decide if Steelman was even able to stand trial. Libicki submitted a personal affidavit to Papas claiming in the visits with his client, Willie appeared to be having "difficulty distinguishing between fantasy and reality" and that he was "undergoing oral hallucinations", meaning that Willie was hearing things.

"He is not remembering facts material to the case," he told Judge Papas, and for that reason, Libicki explained, Steelman could not understand what was going on, or help in his defense.

Libicki made his motion "under the penalty of perjury", he offered, and his contentions were made by his personal examinations of the defendant while incarcerated at DVI. He added that he based his findings on the section of the California Penal Code that states *when at any time while an action is pending if doubt arises as to the defendant's sanity, then the court must order a trial to determine his mental state, and at that time all criminal proceedings must be suspended until that question is fully answered.* Libicki added that while he had a "psychiatrist out looking at Steelman", this motion was based solely on his observations. Not once did Libicki mention Dr. White by name, or her involvement, but everyone in the courtroom knew exactly whom Libicki was referring to.

Joe Baker, who happened to be in court that day, replied that his office had talked with DVI guards and that Willie Steelman had been a cooperative prisoner, and at no time did he act insane.

At the end of the hearing Papas once more ruled against Libicki, stating Steelman had been examined twice already by psychiatrists and counsel's personal observations were still not enough for the court to require further examinations. The judge did offer to postpone the hearing for one week to give counsel time to have a psychiatrist talk with Steelman and decide if a full scale examination is warranted, but the offer was declined. Libicki knew that if the psychiatrists' findings were presented in court, they would be subject to cross-examination by the prosecution. Privately, he was not that comfortable with Dr. White's findings or how she would come across in court. Dedekam had watched in silence, sitting amongst the handful of newsmen covering the proceedings. Afterwards he told them that he had no intention of raising a similar issue about Doug Gretzler's mental condition. "I was out to see him yesterday and he's fine." Dedekam announced casually.

Outside of the courtroom, Libicki told reporters he would again take Papas' ruling to the State District Court of Appeals and expressed his concern with how this case was being handled by the courts and the prosecution. "It's being given special treatment," he complained, noting that in other cases less serious than this one, mental exams had been ordered based only on counsel's word. Libicki concluded by admitting he really didn't know why he was being singled out, or why they were making it so difficult on him. "For all I know there may be political ramifications involved."

This was the second time Libicki announced he was going over Judge Papas' head, and when Dan Walters later relayed Libicki's accusations to the judge, Papas coiled in anger. "Goddamn attorneys!" he barked.

Dr. White again visited Willie on February 7th. This time she brought some books for him to read.

Libicki had asked the officers at Deuel if reading material for his client was allowed, and the answer was only if the content was "not adverse" and they went through proper channels. So after her visit, White handed the guard two books she wanted given to Willie.

The two books, *The Joyous Cosmology – Adventures in the Chemistry of Consciousness* and *The Book on the Taboo Against Knowing Who You Are* were both authored by a man named Alan Watts. The guards examined the books, but there was little in them they could comprehend. "It was pretty far out stuff," one guard noted in the daily logbook, but there wasn't anything that they could find that was against the rules. A guard delivered the books to Steelman that afternoon.

The next day both Steelman and Gretzler returned to Judge Papas' courtroom, once again amidst the overwhelming security each of their previous appearances had received. They remained cuffed and manacled as their attorneys conferred privately with Papas in his chambers. The one o'clock scheduled start was delayed nearly twenty minutes for the secret meeting.

Eventually Judge Papas took the bench and began reading the charges against both defendants. Steelman and Gretzler, now flanked by their attorneys, each answered "Not Guilty" to each charge as it was read. At one point, when the charge of robbery against Richard Earl was being read, Steelman turned around and winked at a young woman sitting in the rear of the courtroom. Guards closest to Willie turned him around to face the judge. He was still smiling when he answered that he wasn't guilty of that one either. All eyes were now focused on the young black woman, later identified as a college student, who said she was fascinated by Willie Steelman and was doing a term paper for her police science class. Although embarrassed by the attention, she admitted they had written to each other and Steelman had asked her to be at each hearing, "to keep me going."

After the reading, Libicki again asked for a moment with the Judge. Joined by Dedekam, Saiers and his assistant Al Norris, Libicki informed the court that he was so busy with other issues involved in this case that he wasn't sure he could go to trial anytime in the near future.

In an impressive show of restraint, Papas allowed him more time, making sure there was no objection from the prosecution. Papas set the trial date for May 6th, nearly three months away. "I have your assurances then gentlemen," he said, "that you will do everything possible to have this case ready to go on that date."

Dedekam said he would be ready. Libicki said he wasn't sure, "But I will do my best, Your Honor," he promised.

That promise went out the window when Libicki announced moments later to reporters in the hallway that he and Dedekam had discussed a change of venue motion, and that such a document was being prepared. In addition, he still was planning on appealing the ruling against the appointment of a psychiatrist for his client. Confident such a ruling would be overturned by the state, Libicki said all criminal matters against Steelman would then be put on hold, although

Dedekam and Gretzler would proceed. Libicki speculated that his case would most certainly be moved out of the county at that time.

Now armed with a little breathing room, Libicki arranged for Dr. White to visit Willie Steelman again. On February 18th, White returned to DVI to see how he was doing, and if he had a chance to read any of the books she had brought to him. This time Willie was even more animated and descriptive, explaining in vivid detail about a green snake that slithers around him in his dreams, attacking him, biting him, and how any attempt he makes to stop the snake is in vain. What little sleep he has is interrupted by this terror and his days are filled with a fantasy of changing body sensations, always on his left side. He complained that now he often couldn't feel anything at all, and he had burned himself with a cigarette, but didn't feel any pain.

He told White, "they're all out to get me"; the officers, his guards, even his attorney, and he didn't think he could fight them off much longer.

By now Willie's prescription drug consumption was higher than it had ever been. He was currently taking Stelazine twice a day, plus huge quantities of Thorazine four times daily, along with Artane and Sodium Amatol at night to help him sleep. Dr. White was convinced the tranquilizers were completely necessary and were the only reason Willie Steelman was keeping it all together. Of course, when it came to drugs, who was Willie to argue with a doctor?

Two days after this visit, more concerned than ever, Dr. White relayed her findings in a written report at the request of Sam Libicki. It was an extensive, three-page document listing every little detail of her six examinations with the patient. Before she even got started though, she stated, Willie Steelman was, without question, presently insane and mentally incompetent to stand trial.

Sam Libicki decided to give it another shot. This time he would take his chances and use Dr. White, even if it meant putting her on the stand. On February 21st, he filed a motion to grant a full psychiatric examination of his client by Dr. White, claiming she, not him, had witnessed Mr. Steelman's difficulty in distinguishing between fantasy and reality. Dr. White claimed Steelman was suicidal and could not assist in his defense. Libicki was in a position to give Papas more than just his word; he now had the expert Papas talked about, even if it was Patricia White.

While Libicki filed his motion and waited for the judge to respond, Willie Steelman remained on hold at DVI, wondering how his recent display with White had been received. On those days when he had no visitors (and those days were many because Libicki and White were the only people who came by) he was content to stay in his cell and bullshit with whoever would listen. Some days that included Doug, whose cell was within shouting distance. In any event, Willie was not unlike any other prisoner locked up in the L Wing, also known as The Adjustment Center.

In fact, the DVI daily logs for the last few days of February show Willie Steelman as very cordial guest.

> *February 25th: "During the last month and a half that inmate Willie Steelman has been under my supervision, in my opinion his behavior*

> *and mental attitude has been normal."*
>
> *February 28th: "Inmate Steelman gets along well with staff, asks for no special considerations, is willing to talk with a pleasant attitude, and in fact, has been a model inmate".*

When Pete Saiers got word about these books Steelman had received from Dr. White, he sent for his own copies, just to see what Willie was up to. He could only laugh at what he read. All the nightmares, all the hallucinations, all the nonsense about burning bushes and green snakes that Willie was spouting off about was vividly described in the books. Willie was merely repeating what he had read, damn near word for word. What Saiers found even more incredible was that Dr. White was buying the whole thing, not even bothering to have him change it around a little.

"It was like Willie had gone to the trouble of cramming for this big test and was dumb enough to write all the answers on his forehead," Saiers joked.

6

Friday, March 1, 1974 | 9:00 am.

The deadline was exactly one week away, but as of yet, no one had filed to run against Joseph Baker for San Joaquin District Attorney.

Libicki's recent contention that the D.A.'s office was using the Steelman/ Gretzler case to further a political agenda may have appeared to be nothing more than a hot shot attorney shooting his mouth off, but to those covering the trial; a list that included Dan Walters, the comment hit home. They knew Joe Baker would offer no deals, cut any slack, or give even one inch, unless it could somehow sweeten his position in the San Joaquin political circles.

Regardless of his age or experience, Sam Libicki knew one thing; the final determination in the case against Willie Steelman did not rest on whether doctors thought him insane, or whether evidence was circumstantial, or even whether Judge Papas liked him or not. None of that mattered, because Libicki knew his client would ultimately be convicted of the murder charges. What he wanted was to receive a token for his efforts; proof he had done his best for his client. Neither he nor Willie wanted to plead guilty to all the charges. In fact, Libicki decided weeks ago he would just slow plea this whole thing out to avoid having to do just that. He would file appeals, make motions, request delays, clutter the record, whatever it took to drag this trial out until he got what he wanted. And what he wanted was to be tossed a bone.

That bone was having the kidnapping charges dropped. Both he and Dedekam decided it was probably the most they were going to get out of Papas and the prosecution, and both understood only Joe Baker had that kind of power. If he was running unopposed, then his reputation could afford such an offer. If not, they knew damn good and well the D.A. would not allow the voting public to see him negotiate with killers, especially before an election.

The absence of a candidate to run against Baker was viewed as a sign of the D.A.'s strength and support from the community, and Libicki felt if the ballot remained that way, then they could have a settlement in a week or so. If not, well then Libicki was ready with Plan B.

Papas scheduled the hearing on Libicki's psychiatric motion for nine am Friday. Armed with Dr. White's recent report; the very information the judge had insinuated was missing from the public defender's earlier motion, Libicki got right to the core of his request. Although Gretzler and Dedekam were in the courtroom, they were only observers. Dedekam made it clear to Papas this was Libicki's deal.

The argument was good enough to convince Papas to appoint three psychiatrists; Doctors Robert Austin, Kent Rogerson and Gary Cavanaugh, to examine Steelman. There was no objection from Saiers.

But instead of embracing his victory, Libicki continued his battle, arguing the selection, saying Austin and Rogerson technically work for the D.A.'s office and had already examined his client, "It's a conflict of interest. All they're doing is changing hats," he complained.

But Papas disagreed, "Then they're all the more qualified to see if there have been any major changes in Mr. Steelman's mental state."

If that is true, Libicki countered, then why couldn't Dr. White be appointed to the panel as well? She had examined Steelman six times over a three-month period. Surely she was now more of an expert on him than anyone else.

Papas' normally soft voice erupted. The judge had a short fuse when it came to attorneys telling him what to do in his courtroom, especially a smart-ass public defender still wet behind the ears from law school.

"NO!" came his reply, and he reminded counsel he wasn't all that thrilled with Dr. White's report in the first place. "First she says that Steelman is presently insane and incapable to stand trial. Then she says he is able to understand the nature and purpose of the judicial proceedings against him. What one is it?"

Libicki knew he was walking on thin ice, but he wasn't finished. Having been denied a say in who was going to examine his client, he asked to be present during the examinations to protect his client's Fifth Amendment right, maintaining that since the two doctors were in the employ of the county, and on the same payroll as the District Attorney, he wanted to be able to advise Steelman when he should remain silent.

Papas rejected that as well. When Libicki asked that the court at least allow White's report into the testimony, Papas again interrupted. "Let's just take these things one step at a time, shall we?"

He ordered the three doctors to exam Willie Steelman and report their findings to him by March 22nd. He would give his answer at that time.

Before the week was over, a former deputy attorney with the D.A.'s office by the name of Al Tassano announced he would oppose his old boss Joe Baker in the June primary. Baker was livid at being forced into campaigning once more for his own job. And Dedekam and Libicki realized their task would not be over anytime soon.

Dr. Robert Austin was informed of his selection and arranged an interview with Willie Steelman for later in the week. He met with Steelman as planned, and then prepared his written report for Judge Papas as requested. But just days before either Rogerson or Cavanaugh could do the same, they were notified by Libicki that he had instructed his client not to talk with them, and their services were therefore no longer needed.

On Thursday, March 21st, the day before the scheduled hearing, Papas realized he had not received all three reports, and when he found out what Libicki had done, he came to court the next day ready for battle. Before he even uttered a word, courtroom observers realized there was trouble brewing. Papas stared directly at Sam Libicki as he opened the session. "There will be no hearing on any reports today," Papas announced, his voice rising as he spoke, "because the ink was not dry on my order and you went out and instructed your client not to talk with anyone!"

Libicki tried again to explain his ongoing concern over the selection of Doctors Austin and Rogerson, and that he was in no way questioning the credentials of either one, but only trying to make his position clear. Once again he suggested maybe there were other doctors both he, the court, and the prosecution could agree on. Libicki, anxious to cool Papas' wrath, added that he was not trying to circumvent the court's decision and had only sent letters to both doctors to again show his deep concern about protecting his client's constitutional rights.

But Papas pounded his fist on his bench, cutting him off in mid-sentence. "I will not have you dictating to this court who it should or should not appoint! That is the discretion of the court! That's what the public has me up here to do! I will not have a gun behind my back, and I feel you are doing a great disservice to this court and to Mr. Steelman!" He was livid, but as if realizing he was losing control, he stopped, took several short breaths, moistened his lips with his tongue, swallowed, then returned to his glare at Libicki. The entire courtroom was now focused on the young attorney. The sudden silence was overpowering. Finally, if out of nothing more than nervousness, Deputy D.A. Al Norris, filling in for Saiers, attempted to play intermediary and offered the court the names of two new doctors for consideration. Libicki, announcing that he was not familiar with either one, suddenly began a direct conversation with the prosecution.

"What are we getting into here?" Papas roared, again seeing the proceedings crumble into a free for all. "Whomever the court appoints, one of you is going to be suspicious!"

Norris countered that he was just trying to help. His office didn't care who was appointed because his case against Steelman was cut and dried, regardless of what any doctor said, and here he was trying to be cooperative. He backed down. "We are perfectly willing to leave it all in the court's hands," he conceded.

But as Norris spoke, Papas interrupted him, holding his hand up like a stop sign. He again turned his attention to Libicki. "You have plenty of funds in your budget to hire as many private psychiatrists as you like, you can bring a dozen in here if you desire, but you will not tell this court who is, and who is not, acceptable!"

Papas recessed the hearing for fifteen minutes. As quickly as he had exploded, he calmed down. As he left the bench, he turned around and advised Libicki to use the time to check on the doctors Norris had suggested. The fifteen minutes became a half hour, and when the three men returned to the courtroom, the air was quiet again. Judge Papas announced the hearing on the matter was continued until Monday to allow both sides to confer with the psychiatrists recommended.

That afternoon, even while the courtroom clash was in full swing, prison guards at Deuel made a surprising discovery. It appeared to them as if Willie Steelman and Doug Gretzler had been planning an escape. While both defendants were in the Stockton courtroom, guards entered Gretzler's cell for a routine inspection. Inside they found what looked to be cut marks on the window bars, and hidden under the bed, a blanket that had been cut up and fashioned into some kind of jacket or poncho. A more aggressive search uncovered two razor blades hidden in a stick deodorant container.

Guards checked Steelman's cell and found identical cuts on the bars, and blankets altered in a similar fashion. The cuts on the bars were fresh, but not very deep – no more than a sixteenth of an inch – so there appeared no immediate chance of escape. All had been covered with some form of paste to hide them from routine inspections, most likely made from a powder cleanser.

When the prisoners returned from court that afternoon, they were placed in other cells and confronted with the evidence. The discovery was noted on the log sheets and information about the possible escape was relayed to their attorneys, as well as the D.A. and Judge Papas, late that afternoon. Both Steelman and Gretzler tried to explain the ponchos, but neither could explain the cut marks on the bars. Gretzler claimed he hid the blades only for safekeeping, but their words fell on deaf ears. Their personal items had already been moved to another unit of the prison, a section known by other inmates as "The Hole".

On Monday all parties agreed to keep Dr. Gary Cavanaugh and add Dr. Erwin Lyons and Dr. James Richmond to the group who would examine Willie Steelman. But while Libicki should have again been pleased with the outcome of his latest efforts, he instead used the court hearing to lodge another protest. Before Papas could close the proceedings, Libicki asked if there had been any thought given to, "the other matter which as been brought to the attention of the court?"

And with a visible sigh, he ordered guards to, for the first time, to remove the handcuffs from the defendants and escort them, their attorneys and the assistant D.A. into his chambers. The conference lasted twenty minutes. When finished, Steelman and Gretzler were ushered straight out of the courtroom and into the elevator. Both of them had been recuffed. Papas never returned. The hearing was over.

Outside in the corridor, Libicki told reporters both defendants had been complaining about their treatment at DVI, and that's what the meeting with Judge Papas was about. "They've been kept isolated from one another and are being treated as convicted felons, deprived of the many things they could have if at county jail."

The situation had been building up over the past couple of months, Libicki told reporters, and it peaked on Friday when both men were "thrown in a hole." He still said nothing of the escape attempt, but Dan Walters sensed Libicki was acting nervous and fidgety, which was very unlike him. After the press conference was over, Walters managed to get a quick meeting with Judge Papas who told him what was going on out at Deuel, including the supposed escape.

This was the first of what would be many meetings he would have with Papas in closed chambers. From these meetings Walters would soon learn what was really going on behind the scenes. It was evident to Dan Walters that Judge Papas was becoming increasingly tired of not only Libicki's tactics, but what he too sensed as a game of politics coming from Baker's office. The only stipulation the judge made at these private meetings was that he could not be quoted directly. So from here on, when Walters used the phrase, "it is known", in his articles, he was referring to information gathered in those meetings.

Increasingly frustrated, Papas would continue to talk with Walters throughout the trial, and of course, there was no one who knew more about what was going on than he.

Libicki's motion regarding Steelman's ability to stand trial was to be heard on Thursday afternoon, April 11th, but was postponed. It wasn't Libicki who was stalling, but the U.S. Postal Service seemed the guilty party, because while both Lyons and Cavanaugh had submitted their reports to the court, Richmond's was missing. He said he mailed it, but it still had not arrived, so Papas had no choice but to continue the matter for another week.

Still, there was some unfinished business they could attend to. Libicki had been complaining that certain documents he had requested from DVI had not been sent, and he had filed a motion of discovery in that regard weeks earlier. Saiers claimed Libicki had all the reports available and the motion was simply another delay tactic. Papas agreed, reminding Libicki there was some information deemed classified by the Department of Corrections and not open for review.

The pending joint motion for a change of venue was also brought up, and the handfull of reporters in the courtroom snapped to attention when the subject was mentioned. But Papas ended the public portion of the hearing and invited both sides into chambers to discuss the venue matter in private. When an associate asked him what happened in court that afternoon, Walters replied the most interesting topic he could possibly report on was Willie Steelman's new afro.

On the afternoon of Thursday, April 18th, with all three reports now in, the hearing on Willie Steelman's sanity finally got underway. According to one doctor, Willie told him the victims deserved to die because they had humiliated and mistreated him for years. Dr. Lyons reported Steelman told him, "he had finished one off who was in a bad way," after first being shot by Doug Gretzler, and "they deserved it because they oppressed people economically and spiritually." Lyons stated Steelman claimed to have known some of the victims for some time and they, "had the habit of treating him in an arrogant manner. . . injuring his self-esteem and allegedly humiliating him over the years."

Dr. Cavanaugh quoted Steelman as saying "I've never trusted anybody. I've always felt like I was an outsider. I don't feel very much for people. I don't let them get too close."

Cavanaugh went on to report the patient has a similar hostile attitude for society and that he would never conform. "They're going to have to kill me," Steelman told him.

Dr. Richmond agreed with Cavanaugh's assessment and said Willie Steelman expressed no fear of death, and in fact, looked forward to being released from his body because after that nobody could do him further harm. The doctor said Willie's use of drugs apparently had a calming effect on him, but eventually the rage built to a point where he felt the need to commit assault. It was then, Steelman told him, after he first killed someone that he experienced a brief, yet highly relieving sense of inner calm that continued with each killing. When Richmond asked him if he could bring back to life the people in Lodi he was charged with killing, Willie answered he would not. It wasn't that he still hated them, but because "life on this earth is so painful, I would not want the responsibility of subjecting them further to such pain."

Regardless of whatever else Willie told them, each doctor made it clear they felt Steelman had some psychiatric problems, but they all agreed on one thing; Willie Steelman was sane and capable of cooperating with his defense at trial. "If he does not actually do this," Dr. Lyons concluded in his report, "it is because he does not choose to do so."

None of the above information came out in the public courtroom, but was reported the next morning in The *Union*. Dan Walters had managed to obtain copies of each of the psychiatrist's reports, information only Libicki, Saiers, and of course Papas, was entitled to.

On April 24th, Judge Papas ruled Willie Steelman sane and able to stand trial, but not before Libicki asked the court to appoint additional psychiatrists because Steelman might be affected by "diminished capacity" and while considered sane, not fully able to understand what was going on around him.

Papas denied the request. "We've got enough doctor's reports already," he announced.

With that ruling, Libicki's three-month odyssey came to a close. For those three months, George Dedekam had remained very quiet, although it was Dedekam who started the whole sanity issue back on December 18th when he asked Papas for permission to hire psychiatrists to examine Gretzler. Although the Judge agreed, Dedekam never followed up, and the last time a psychiatrist spoke with Gretzler was the day of his capture when the County called in Austin and Rogerson.

So it seemed a bit odd that Dedekam waited until this morning to finally speak up. Even Saiers was surprised by what could only be viewed as a stall. This was not like Dedekam, but at today's hearing, just as Papas had finished with Libicki,

Dedekam started in. First off, the change of venue motion he had requested earlier was granted with no argument whatsoever from the prosecution. Dedekam then motioned for a separation of trials, of which Libicki joined, adding it appeared the District Attorney was preparing to use one defendant's statement against the other.

Saiers said they had no such intention, and agreed to the separation if that's what it would take to get things moving. "We do not intend to use any of defendant's statement as evidence," indicating their confidence of a conviction even without the many incriminating statements given to the police by both suspects.

Dedekam then made an oral motion to suppress evidence. He wanted Gretzler's statement to police on how he hid the .22 derringer at the Clunie Hotel removed from the transcripts, explaining his client was not fully represented by counsel when he talked to police, and therefore the information was obtained illegally. Papas told him to put his motion in writing and he would consider it. He asked again for the money to hire three psychiatrists to decide if his client was presently sane, and at the time of the alleged crimes, as well. Papas agreed and told Dedekam just to try and have it all done before the start of the trial, which was still on for May 6th.

During all of this discussion, Willie remained seated with his head buried in a newspaper. Libicki had given him the April 20th edition of the Lodi *News-Sentinel* that had a story quoting the doctor's reports of his recent examinations. The article said Willie admitting feeling guilty about the crimes, but he wasn't cooperating with his attorney because he thought Libicki was collaborating with the prosecution and Judge Papas.

The article was a two-part piece that ripped into Libicki's ethics, style and courtroom tactics. He was no more pleased with it's content than he was with his client.

"You see Willie," Libicki lectured him when he tossed him the paper, "this is what happens when you open your big mouth."

It was Monday, May 6th, an anniversary, of sorts. Six months to the day that Willie and Doug barged into the house on Orchard Road and coldly executed nine people. They had already admitted what they had done, and overwhelming evidence proved their guilt, yet the trial would not begin this morning. In Sunday's *Sacramento Union*, Dan Walters penned an article explaining just what was happening behind the courtroom doors in Stockton, and who was responsible for the delays.

"It has been six months since two entire families were killed in the bedroom of a rural home near Victor. It has been a period of intense legal maneuvering over the fate of the two young drifters accused of the murders, seasoned by election year politics. The most bizarre aspect is that there is no doubt in anyone's mind that Steelman and Gretzler actually committed the murders. The evidence is massive and the factual basis for the case against them is conceded by all parties, including the attorneys who pleaded the pair, 'Not Guilty'. Nonetheless, the case remains in the court because of a three way standoff among the District Attorney's Office, the defense attorneys, and Judge Papas."

"Judge Papas, it is known, has made several attempts to get all parties to agree on a compromise settlement involving guilty pleas to some of the 15 charges against Steelman and Gretzler. District Attorney Joseph Baker has insisted he would accept guilty pleas only to all 15 charges, while the defense attorneys have told Papas the kidnapping charge must be dropped as a pre-condition to plea negotiations. Publicly, Libicki will say that removal of the kidnapping charge would remove a major stumbling block to a non-trial settlement."

"Baker, sources say, is not willing to drop any of the charges because of the possibility that he could be accused of softening on the sensational case during a campaign period, and yet denies he is wedded to the kidnapping count. Baker says the only offer made thus far was a plea of guilty to only seven counts of murder, 'and I won't take it!' The defendants, he said, were unwilling to plead guilty to the two murder charges involving the Parkin children."

Walters ended by acknowledging the obvious. There would be no trial on Monday and little possibility of a settlement of any kind before Election Day, now just one month away. Later, Walters conceded his article was prompted by Judge Papas' growing frustration with all parties involved. This was not about justice; Papas confided to Walters in their now frequent meetings, this was all about politics, stubbornness, and saving face.

It was Papas who encouraged Saiers not to use the defendant's statements as evidence against them, hoping it would spur some movement from the other side. The kidnapping charges were based solely on such statements, Papas explained to Walters, and it would take an complete idiot not to see that if there were no statements, then there was no way to convict anyone of such a charge.

"So then what's Libicki do when Saiers makes the announcement?" Papas asked. "He goes off and makes some other meaningless motion! He just doesn't get it!"

Papas believed he had them all close to an agreement back in April, but now he too realized nothing was going to happen until after the election.

"Goddamn attorneys!" Papas cursed in each private meeting with Walters. "I hate this case!"

7

Monday, May 20, 1974.

Two weeks earlier, on May 6th, Judge Papas had scheduled June 11th as the date for the trial to start. Coincidently, that was just one week after the primary election. He also acknowledged the trial could not be held in Stockton, so he instructed the State Judicial council to select a location. But of all the places in California available to hold the upcoming murder trial of Steelman and Gretzler, the selection of Santa Rosa came as quite a surprise.

Just the other side of two plus hours northwest of Stockton, it was an odd choice, if for nothing more than the county in which it was located, Sonoma, still had rape and kidnapping charges pending there. While they had not yet held a formal arraignment for them, sending Steelman and Gretzler there to stand trial seemed a huge risk for San Joaquin to take. The prisoners would be housed in Sonoma jails, guarded by Sonoma deputies, and processed by Sonoma officials. San Joaquin was taking its chances the much-awaited trial could be yanked right out its hands if Sonoma County decided to move ahead with their very serious charges of kidnapping.

But privately, Sonoma County had agreed not to interfere, and admitted to their counterparts in Stockton their case was shaky at best. With a lack of hard evidence, and only Fulkerson's and Hallock's testimony go on, they had not even prepared for a trial after learning what Steelman and Gretzler had done in Lodi. Pretrial publicity about the couple's kidnapping was virtually nonexistent in Sonoma (only one small newspaper article could be found by the Judicial Council) but Steelman and Gretzler's murderous activities in San Joaquin were very well known, and Santa Rosa seemed much too close for an impartial jury to be assembled.

But on the plus side, Santa Rosa had a new state-of-the-art jail facility tied directly to the courtrooms, so security would be as good as could be expected. The journey from Stockton to Santa Rosa was an easy one, with most of the distance over rural two lane roads easily secured with a standard sheriff motorcade. And most importantly, Santa Rosa could meet the time table required. Being a fairly small town, as California cities go, their crime rate wasn't as high as it was in places like San Jose, so their court calendar was pretty much wide open.

So Santa Rosa was selected, and while everyone prepared for a trial slated to begin in three weeks, Judge Papas still hoped he could settle this whole thing without one.

In the meantime, the argument over conditions at Deuel continued as Bruce Avrit questioned both sides. DVI officials maintained their institution was perfectly within state standards, while Steelman and Gretzler, along with their attorneys, claimed otherwise. In addition to the original complaint, the prisoners upped the ante, protesting the lack of music, or even a radio. With a new attentive audience in Mr. Avrit, Willie decided he now wanted a harmonica to play. When Doug heard what his partner was asking for, he went one better and demanded a guitar, going so far as to suggest, "they can just get the twelve string I had in the room".

Arvit's final report to Judge Papas stated conditions were not acceptable, and regardless of what DVI claimed about standards or security, the area where the prisoners were being housed was not even close to being satisfactory, even for the likes of Steelman and Gretzler. Before Monday's hearing, Papas confronted Deuel officials with his findings and gave the prison a chance to quietly move the prisoners back to general population before he announced his decision publicly. DVI refused.

So Papas opened the hearing by reporting what his investigation had discovered. He again asked the DVI official present at the hearing to reconsider his request.

DVI Lt. George Legris balked. "Where they are now is the safest place in the institution," although adding he would be willing to discuss the judge's recommendation with his superiors, just to make sure.

Papas gave him 24 hours. However, if they weren't moved by then he would have the prisoners transferred directly to Santa Rosa. He said neither of them should have contact with other prisoners, 'for their own protection', but that he was not going to allow them to be kept in inadequate conditions just to do so.

Libicki pressed the court for a ruling right now, but Papas told him to sit down.

"My concern is for their protection," he said, while reminding counsel his client's personal safety should be his primary concern as well.

The only other discussion was regarding Libicki's previous request for funds to travel to Arizona to check out several matters there. Papas reminded him the Public Defender's office had plenty of cash to do whatever they want. "But don't look at this court for money," he scolded. "I'm not going to send anyone to Arizona on a fishing expedition."

Tuesday, May 21st was Doug Gretzler's 23rd birthday, and the only one who even mentioned it was Dan Walters, who began his article in the *Sacramento Union* with a simple such acknowledgement.

Judge Papas spent the morning on the phone with Sheriff Canlis, doing his best to convince him to take Steelman and Gretzler back to French Camp, but to no avail. For all his media parading months earlier, Canlis was now quite pleased to be rid of these two. Their short stay in his facility was a constant, nerve-wracking few weeks full of conflicting schedules, countless interruptions and stacks of time cards bloated with budget-busting overtime. The threats against them from other prisoners and the public alike had been relentless, the security required unending. No sir, Canlis informed the judge, he was happy they were gone. Let someone else worry about them, because they were not welcome back in his jail. He hinted that he hoped the good judge would not press the issue. Canlis wielded that kind of clout.

So Papas was faced with a tough choice. Leave them at Deuel and gamble that Libicki would take his writ to State Appeals (where Papas conceded the public defender would more than likely win his case, thus delaying the trial even more), or try and find a place close by to move the prisoners. Problem was, there was no other place.

As tight as county jail was, it was no match for these two. If the escape attempt at DVI was legit (and Papas had his doubts), then certainly their county facility wouldn't hold them. There were just two many loose ends there, nor was it ever designed as a maximum-security operation. Papas' true concern, however, was for the threats against the pair. He was convinced, beyond any doubt, that if another prisoner, or anyone from the outside for that matter, could get to either Steelman or Gretzler, they would kill them. Given half a chance, he conceded, most of the prison guards would probably do it themselves.

The only place that made sense was to send them to Santa Rosa and let them sit for a couple weeks until the trial started.

So at a hastily called court hearing late Tuesday morning, he made his intentions known, and because of obvious security reasons, did not elaborate as to when the transfer would take place. He said he had urged DVI to reconsider, but they were defiant in their refusal.

Of course, Sam Libicki protested the move, claiming the distance would prove much too far to allow him to confer freely with his client, especially at such a critical time. The judge sharply reminded him it was his idea to get his client out of DVI in the first place and he couldn't have it both ways, despite what he might have heard while working for the Public Defender's Office.

"I did everything I could to hold up the transfer until the last possible minute but you insisted they be moved." Papas answered. "Besides, you've had seven months to talk with your client!"

At dawn, two days later, Willie Steelman was removed from his cell and driven back to town for a brain scan Libicki had earlier requested as part of his psychiatric studies. Originally scheduled to be preformed at Dameron Hospital in Stockton, it was shifted to the medical facility at French Camp at the very last minute. While the appointment was only for Steelman, Doug Gretzler was also rousted from his bunk and told to gather his few personal belongings for an impromptu inspection. Both prisoners were taken from DVI in separate vehicles, and while Willie made the stop at the jail hospital, Doug continued on to Santa Rosa, where his partner eventually joined him. Canlis announced the transfer to the press late Thursday afternoon; long after the move had been successfully completed.

Sonoma County Jail was much newer, and by far a nicer facility than they had been used to at either San Joaquin or Deuel. Both were placed as far away from the other inmates as possible, eventually landing on the upper floors of the A Wing. While Willie and Doug were housed close to each other, an attempt was made to keep them from communicating with other prisoners, but as usual, Willie's mouth proved too much for everyone. Before the day was over he had raised enough of a ruckus to require they be moved again. According to jail deputies, Willie was quick to brag about his extensive connections to "people on the outside" who were just waiting to bust both of them out at any moment. His real downfall came, however, when he insinuated that his Hell's Angel friends, (ones very tight with the Manson Family, as he made sure to point out), were just waiting for his signal. Willie was unaware that some of the men suspected in the murder of the young Marine found along the Russian River – a crime later connected to Manson stragglers – were his new neighbors in jail. When Willie started bragging about 'his family', and all the people he knew, more than one fellow prisoner told him the shut the hell up. Which, of course, Willie did.

It was now Tuesday, May 28th, just one week before the primary election. The battle between Joe Baker and his only challenger, Al Toscano, had turned the debate into an almost single-issue campaign. The real problem, as Toscano was sure to point out at every stop around the county, was the spiraling crime rate, and more specifically, what the D.A.'s office was doing to confront it.

Toscano did not mince words. He said that for well over six months Joe Baker had two of the most hated and vile criminals in the county's history in custody, and still had not been able to bring them to trial. These men had admitted their guilt, the evidence against them was unshakable, and while local citizens demanded justice, it appeared to many the D.A. was merely arguing about a string of senseless, insignificant details.

Toscano had worked the prosecution's side for Baker long enough to know how the game was played, so he forced Baker into trying to explain the unexplainable. Trials of serious crimes take time, Baker reminded voters whenever the subject came up, even though it was an extremely solid case. Justice can't be rushed, he conceded, regardless of how anxious everyone is to see it carried out. Be patient, Baker soothed, his office was confident conviction and punishment would come soon enough.

It may have been simply Toscano's way of ruffling the feathers of his old boss, for whom he had much contempt, but most insiders saw it as something else.

It appeared the only way he could possibly unseat the long-standing D.A. was to force him to make a fatal mistake with the most despised criminals anyone could remember. People wanted action now, and Toscano's only hope at this late date was to try and pressure Baker into negotiating a plea bargain with the killers, and then let the voters scream bloody murder at the polls.

Baker, on the other hand, knew all along that would be the worse thing he could do. So he held tough, counting down the days, repeating he would never plea-bargain with a pair of murders as disgusting as these two. Never. He pointed out how, through their lawyers, they had tried to bargain away the punishment for killing the little Parkin children, along with the nerve to claim Wally Parkin was never kidnapped or forced to open the safe at his market. Plea bargaining was sometimes a necessary part of moving the criminal justice system along quickly, Baker admitted, but not with these two. Not as long as he was in office. Not with Steelman and Gretzler. Not now. Not ever. If it took ten years to bring them to trial, then he was willing to wait.

Privately, however, Joe Baker knew exactly how long it was going to take. If everything went his way, it would be, coincidently, only another week.

Despite the scene he created in the courtroom, or the constant commotion he made in the media, behind the scenes Sam Libicki was coming down hard on his client. Because unlike Doug Gretzler, Willie Steelman was painfully aware of the turmoil swirling around them. He might be acting like none of this bothered him, but Libicki knew otherwise.

For the past several weeks, Libicki had made it perfectly clear to Steelman there was little left to bargain with. Baker and Saiers held all the cards, and he reminded Willie that shooting his mouth off to authorities during those first few days had proven to be his downfall. Libicki's attempt at diversions and roadblocks, trying to wear everyone down and buy some time, was coming to an end. If they went to trial today, he told Willie, he could guarantee they would lose everything. His problem was convincing Steelman to agree to let him negotiate some kind of plea bargain with Baker or Saiers right now.

"I'm working on the kidnapping charge," Libicki explained to Willie while at DVI. "You plead out to the rest and I think we can get it dropped, and you know that's the big one. That's all we have, man."

But Willie couldn't. There were times when Libicki thought he might have him leaning, only to have Willie change his mind the very next day.

It had taken him six months, but Sam Libicki was finally seeing the real Willie. He had simply assumed a guy who could do the unbelievable things Willie did, and then freely admit his involvement, would not have any problem saying, "Yeah, I did it."

But that was the last thing Willie Steelman could do. Libicki was just now beginning to realize his client was a lot of things – calculating, manipulative, egocentric, sociopathic, irritating, incredibly stupid, remarkably intelligent, well read, poorly adjusted, a dreamer, a junkie, a loser. But the one thing he was not, was a man. He had no spirit, no nerve, no backbone, no guts to come out and say what everyone knew. That he was guilty. That he had murdered all those people. His brain couldn't comprehend the consequences. His lips couldn't form the sentence. Whenever Libicki brought the matter up, Willie couldn't even look him in the eye while he stammered to change the subject.

So back and forth Willie went. At times angrily denying he had done anything wrong, screaming he was simply protecting himself against a corrupt system that only sought to execute him. Moments later, head hanging, whimpering, eyes moist, voice breaking, he begged Libicki to help him, but not even once could bring himself to admit his obvious guilt.

Now he was hours away in Santa Rosa, and it was even more difficult to talk with him. The clock was ticking, and for the first time since he had met Willie Steelman, Libicki began wondering what in the hell he was going to say to a jury.

On Thursday morning, May 30th, Steelman and Gretzler were taken from their cells, fully expecting a trip back to Stockton. Instead they were led downstairs and into a Sonoma County Municipal Courtroom where, to everyone's surprise, they were arraigned on the long-standing rape, assault and kidnapping charges involving Jim Fulkerson and Eileen Hallock.

Sonoma authorities gave no reason for going back on their promise to San Joaquin, other than to say both men were in their custody and the time seemed right.

A shocked George Dedekam told the press that he, "thought it was a pretty stupid thing", for the Sonoma D.A. to do, while Libicki expressed his concern about jeopardizing the upcoming trial. Both men promised to look into any pretrial publicity Thursday's court session might have created, saying they could only hope the trial would not have to be moved again.

8

Tuesday, June 4, 1974 | 8:00 pm.

The dominos began falling as soon as the polls closed.

There had been little doubt about the outcome of today's primary election. Publicly, Joe Baker talked the good talk about what a worthy opponent he had in Al Toscano. Privately, he was annoyed with having to go through all the crap of another campaign. Down deep Baker knew he had the D.A. job in San Joaquin for as long as he wanted. Tonight, when the ballots were counted, he overwhelmed Toscano by a 2 to 1 margin. Michael Canlis, who had held his office since 1960, fared even better. He buried his challenger by taking nearly 80% of the vote for sheriff.

At his acceptance speech to a small gathering of friends and reporters late Tuesday afternoon, the District Attorney thanked everyone for their help, congratulated Sheriff Canlis in his landslide victory, and summed up the reason for their overwhelming success on election day. "I think our prosecution record spoke for itself," he boasted, adding he felt the lopsided vote simply recognized the success his department had in prosecuting some big cases during the past several years, and that included the current one.

And although his opponent had made plea-bargaining a major issue in the campaign, Baker admitted that he didn't particularly care for the practice either. "It is a necessary evil," he told the *Stockton Record*, adding without it some cases might not be tried at all. But with the system, he boasted, "we get substantial justice."

Baker finished the evening with a victory dinner, joined by both family members and his many supporters; political and otherwise. Judge Papas was not in attendance, but was pleased with the outcome of the election just the same.

It was not that he was a big fan of the District Attorney, but with the campaign now over, he felt they could finally come together and settle this Steelman and Gretzler problem once and for all. So Tuesday night he stayed home and relaxed, watching the election results on TV, half-expecting the phone to ring at any moment.

George Dedekam was not having anywhere near the trouble with his client that Libicki was having with his. For several months now, Doug Gretzler had made it clear, or as clear as his frame of mind would allow, that he would go along with whatever plan his lawyer suggested. Guilty. Not guilty. What did it matter anyway? All he knew was that he was behind bars, and would most likely remain that way for many years to come. And yet surprisingly, with all that faced him; the killings in Lodi and the multiple murder trial certainly waiting for him in Arizona, Gretzler actually believed that if he went along with his lawyer's recommendations, and cooperated with the court, then he might even be a free man one day, especially if Dedekam could get the kidnapping charge dropped. All Gretzler had learned while in jail was that a murder conviction in California was 7 years, period. After that, it was mandatory parole hearings from there on out.

Nor did Dedekam discourage such hope, offering every indication he believed he could separate the actions of his client from those of Willie Steelman. He felt that if the case did go to trial, a jury could not help but look at the two men differently. And while admittedly a long shot, a jury could quite possibly offer different sentences as well. Who knows? Maybe by being agreeable and cooperative, Gretzler could work out something a little better than his partner. George Dedekam told Doug Gretzler exactly that.

He also told his client what was pending here in California would have no bearing on anything that might happen in Arizona. Two separate situations, he said. "But let's just concentrate on what's facing us right now. There's nothing I can do to help you with Arizona, so don't worry about that until we take care of this."

Doug went along with what Dedekam suggested, content with not having to devote any energy to thinking, forgetting most of what was said from one meeting to the next.

There was still another truth. George Dedekam was a weary man. Much too tired to raise a fuss or make too many promises. Drained of any new ideas and void of his usual enthusiasm, Dedekam felt that once the election ran its course, then everyone would sit down and agree on how to best handle this situation. He just wanted this all behind him. Doug Gretzler would get his day in court. Justice would be served. The legal system would prevail. After that he could rest. He just needed to rest.

Joe Baker didn't break any traffic laws getting to the office Wednesday morning. He came in at his usual time, showing his face about the time everyone else was making lunch plans. He conferred briefly with Saiers, and promised to meet with him again later in the afternoon. There are no official records to verify exactly the sequence of events that happened next, although it is clear Baker and Papas talked sometime around noon, and let it be known his office was now ready to reopen discussions in the Steelman/Gretzler matter.

Papas relayed the message to both attorneys, asking them to set aside the rest of the day, not having any idea what Baker's timetable might be. He also took a moment to quiz them on whether or not they were still ready to negotiate a middle ground with the prosecution. Dedekam assured the judge there would be no problem on his end, while Libicki could make no such promises.

Baker and Saiers met to discuss the kidnapping charge but Saiers remained adamant he would have no difficulty getting a jury to understand and accept the fact that Willie Steelman took Wally Parkin at gunpoint from his house to the market. He cited two very simple reasons. First, the door to the market was opened with a key, and secondly the safe was opened with the combination. Granted, it could be argued that Willie took the key from Parkin, or memorized the combination sequence to the safe, but that was highly unlikely knowing how sloppy other details were handled that evening. The absence of his fingerprints in the market actually worked against Willie, Saiers argued. Steelman let Wally open the front door and the safe, plus having Parkin along guaranteed a smooth operation. No, the market was way too clean and orderly for anything Willie Steelman could have done by himself. Saiers didn't like the idea of dropping any charges, and he made a strong case for their office to stay the course.

But Baker needed something to give up. Something substantial. Something he could trade for a guilty plea. Something the defense had been asking for all along. Pete Saiers knew immediately he was going to lose his argument. So Baker called Papas to suggest all parties meet the following morning, and that the defendants be present as well.

Doug Gretzler's cell at Sonoma County was now far enough removed from Willie's that for the past several days the two seldom talked, but Steelman was still boisterous and vocal when word came down Wednesday evening his attorney wanted to speak with him.

"Time to make up your mind, Willie," Libicki demanded, for what he hoped would be the last time. "Looks like the D.A. is ready to talk now."

But Willie still wasn't ready to say the words, so he changed the subject. Libicki reminded him a big trial would only work against them by once again stirring up everyone's anger and hatred. He told Willie what the D.A. was offering was the best they were going to get, and that he had heard Gretzler was ready to okay the deal. Willie felt the rage return and his stomach sour. Deal? The *only* deal he remembered was the deal he and Doug had made in Denver. He could feel his head pound. He was the one who called the shots! He made the deals! Willie's fists clinched up and his eyes throbbed as he counted up all things he had done for his so-called partner. This wasn't Doug's decision to make! He would have starved to death a long time ago if it hadn't been for him. The anger slammed into Willie as he realized it was all over. He didn't want it to end this way. Not after all this. Not without a fight.

But he had to ask. "So Douglas finally fuckin' gave in, huh?"

Libicki nodded. Maybe this would be enough to make Willie see the light. He had fought hard for him, going further than most, considering the odds. He really did want the best for his client, and hell, he wasn't ready to give in either, but in his gut Libicki knew this was it. He looked at Willie as if to say, '*You're done. It's finished. Game's over. This is as good as you're gonna get, man. Listen to me. For God's sake, would you please listen to me just once?'*

So he told him what he knew. "Yeah Willie, he's ready."

And Willie knew he was once again on his own.

The distance between the jail facility in Sonoma County and its counterpart in Stockton was 134 miles exactly. With the exception of a freeway-like stretch of Highway 101 near Santa Rosa, those miles were covered almost entirely on remote two lane roads across rolling hills and delta farm land, through small levee towns and past scenic inland harbors. Recent travel had shown San Joaquin authorities the one-way trip took almost two and a half hours.

So it was well before dawn Thursday morning, June 6th, when two San Joaquin County cars headed west out of Stockton with orders to pick up Willie Steelman and Douglas Gretzler and bring them back in time for a hastily scheduled court appearance later that morning. A call was placed to Sonoma County to have their prisoners up and dressed by 7 am. The early hour visit did not come unexpectedly to Willie. The rattling of keys against cell bars only managed to reawake the festering anger towards his one-time accomplice.

Doug, on the other hand, was surprised by the guard's predawn visit. He had not spoken to his attorney for several days so he was not aware of yesterday's activity in Stockton. However, each was brought down at slightly different times and taken into the 2nd floor Clothing Room. It was here where inmates changed out of prison uniforms and into street clothes, either for transfer out of the system, or as was usually the case, an appearance next door at the courthouse. The inmates shared a rather large, drab room, while guards viewed the proceedings through wire reinforced glass from a small office where switches, levers and intercoms, controlled movement through several iron doors; the only way in and out of the room. Security was taken very seriously at this point, for it was decided that if prisoners ever planned an escape, it would be attempted from this room. In Willie and Doug's case, a short elevator ride would take them down to the rear sally port entrance to the facility where the San Joaquin caravan would be waiting.

Doug appeared tired, confused maybe, by this last minute change of events. He tried to find a logical reason for the trip back to Stockton. A guard mumbled something about a change of venue, but even that didn't make any sense. He couldn't help but notice the angry look sealed upon Bill's face – he had seen it before – and knew that if anyone had a clue as to what was going on it would be him. Already Willie's silence was uncomfortable and Doug felt the need to break it, having no idea he was the reason for Bill's pissy mood.

"Why we goin' back? Do you know?" he asked.

That was all that was needed for Willie to explode. His eyes jumped from his skull as he leered at Doug, his voice low and threatening. "Yeah, I know. You made a fuckin' deal with 'em, that's why!"

Gretzler acted shocked at the accusation, stammering that he hadn't made any deal. He hardly ever saw his lawyer and he reminded Willie of that. No, there was some mistake, he repeated. Willie had it wrong and Doug told him so.

"BULLSHIT, MAN!" Willie had stopped dressing to devote full attention to his rage, trembling as he spoke. "I talked to my lawyer yesterday and he told me all about it. Don't lie to me, man!"

"I didn't! There's no deal! What are you talking about?"

"You know what the fuck I'm talking about!" And with that Willie took several steps towards Doug, clinched his right fist and smashed Doug across the face. The blow didn't hit him square on, but connected enough to knock Doug's glasses to the floor and cut him slightly on the cheek. Before Willie could land another, two guards were on him, one putting on a chokehold, the other cuffing him hard behind his back. As they pulled Willie away to lock him in an adjoining room, they could hear Doug pleading in exasperation for his partner to understand. "C'mon, let's just cop, man," his voice reduced to no more than a whimper. "They're gonna kill us anyway. Let's just cop and take our chances."

One month earlier, Joe Baker disclosed to the *Stockton Record* that both of the accused had recently offered to plead guilty to not only the kidnapping charge, but to seven of the nine murder charges well. According to Baker, the two counts the defense wanted dropped were those for the deaths of Bobby and Lisa Parkin, because neither wanted to be known as a child killer while in prison.

"Of course I couldn't accept," he assured the reporter. "I have seen pictures of those two young ones. I couldn't let anyone get away with the horrible things that were done to them. These two will answer, I promise you." Baker claimed this was the only time he had ever been approached by either defense attorney in regards to a negotiated settlement. During this brief interview in early May, he said nothing about any plea bargain involving kidnapping charges.

Sam Libicki shook his head when reminded of that claim. He said he never once asked the D.A.'s office to reduce any murder charges. In fact it was he who went to Saiers many times offering a guilty plea to all the murder charges in exchange for a dismissal of the one count of kidnapping. An offer that was always declined without discussion. Even this morning, when the same reporter quizzed the District Attorney about the surprise court session, Baker sounded as innocent as anybody. "All I know is that the judge has asked all parties to meet with him this morning. I have no idea what will be discussed."

Steelman and Gretzler were escorted into court several minutes apart, and remained separated while waiting for Judge Papas to arrive. With the skirmish in Santa Rosa and the delay in getting the pair back to Stockton, it was now late morning. The defendants sat at their respective tables, chairs turned away from the other. Willie was loud, overly animated, and could be heard laughing with the guards who surrounded him. Doug sat hunched over, head bowed, stringy hair covering his face, seemingly afraid to dare even look up to see what was going on around him. Again, the guards comprised the largest group. Dan Walters was there, having been tipped off by Papas himself.

No sooner had the session got underway, when Libicki stood and made a formal motion asking the prosecution to set aside the change of venue, allowing San Joaquin to, once again, become the location where this case would be resolved. The motion was agreed to, and both sides were called into Papa's chamber. Steelman, Gretzler, their guards and everyone else in the courtroom were left to sit and wonder what was going on behind closed doors.

Inside, it was apparent there was going to be a problem with Willie Steelman. Almost apologetic, Libicki announced his client was not ready to plead guilty to anything, despite what might have been insinuated over the last few days. He then asked that the charges of kidnapping and robbery be set aside. Baker was livid. But Libicki knew that the prosecution wanted this wrapped up today. Although he had earlier implied he could deliver a guilty plea from his client if just the kidnapping charge would go away, he also understood that, at least in Baker's mind, given one murder count or nine, Steelman was going to get the maximum the law could allow, and the time was going to run concurrent. He reminded the prosecution of that. "What difference does this all make?" Libicki asked. "You can only sentence him once."

On the other hand, while Dedekam had already made it clear his client was ready to plead, he was not going give in to all counts either, so he watched with interest while Libicki made his move. Dedekam promised early on he wasn't going to create a problem for the District Attorney, but he wasn't going to roll over either. If his client was going to make things easier for them, then he expected a helluva lot better deal than Steelman was asking for.

So while Libicki and the prosecution argued back and forth, a loose agreement was struck with Dedekam. Doug Gretzler would plead guilty to nine counts of murder, and in return, the prosecution would drop the kidnapping and the robbery charges. It was the same deal Libicki was asking for except Willie wasn't ready to plead guilty.

A half-hour into the meeting, Libicki changed his offer to a "nolo contendere" plea if the said charges were dropped. Willie could apparently utter the words "no contest", but that was all he was capable of doing. Actually, the prosecution gave the offer brief consideration knowing that 'no contest' was, in this case at least, the same thing as guilty. The three men left Papas' office and returned to the courtroom for a moment to discuss the offer. Huddling in a far corner, they agreed the offer would not play well with the public, regardless of how Judge Papas viewed the plea or how he would eventually pass sentence on it. Saiers especially didn't like the sound of it and he led the argument to hold out. "We've got 'em," he reminded the others. "Why do want to give anything away?" They walked back into Papas' chambers with their answer. No deal.

Libicki still had one more card. Although he had never used this before, nor could he find anyone in the Public Defender's office who had, he had heard of a plea arrangement where the defendant would submit his case to the judge solely on the basis of the evidence contained in Grand Jury testimony. In essence, the defense would let Judge Papas decide Willie Steelman's guilt or innocence based on the information presented to the Grand Jury. Steelman would waive his right to a jury trial and all the provisions that accompanied it, thus allowing the judge to determine his fate totally on what information had been gathered against him. With the offer, Willie Steelman was waiving all of his constitutional rights, and considering the overwhelming amount of evidence against him in those documents, was cutting his own throat right there in Papas' courtroom. Libicki had explained the idea earlier to Willie, claiming it to be a last ditch stand at best, and Willie gave him the go ahead to use it if necessary. Anything but having to say the word, "Guilty".

Both Papas and the prosecution were somewhat taken back by the offer. It was such a farce, such a total waste of everyone's time, knowing what the Grand Jury transcripts contained. Papas reminded Libicki he would have no rebuttal, no cross-examination, could present no witnesses, nor could the defendant even testify in his own behalf. There was absolutely nothing to gain by going this route.

But Baker took it. He agreed to drop the kidnapping count, but insisted the robbery charges were not negotiable. Libicki accepted.

It was now mid afternoon, and with everyone back in court, the events just discussed were repeated for the record. Libicki went through the judicial jargon to present his offer, after which Judge Papas addressed the defendant, pausing several times to carefully pick his words, each time asking Steelman if he understood. Each time Willie answered clearly that he did indeed.

Papas explained the rights being forfeited by the defense through this offer, stopping at one point to announce this whole thing was 'tantamount to a plea of guilty'.

"Do you understand what I'm saying?" Papas asked, and for the first time, Willie replied that he really didn't. He didn't like being associated with the word. Libicki noticed his client's sudden concern and stepped in to smooth things over.

"Excuse me, Your Honor. As I advised the defendant, even with submission on the transcripts, the court would still be bound by the same rules of evidence. . ."

Judge Papas realized he was already passing sentence and interrupted to agree. "There is certainly no question about that. . ."

". . .just as if the matter were before a jury trial or court trial," Libicki also reminded the judge.

"That's right," Papas again agreed, while explaining he still would have only one side of the story to base his findings on. Turning to the defendant he again tried to clarify what he was agreeing to. "You, in a sense, are waiving your right to testify in your own behalf. Is that what you want to do?"

For the first time Willie actually looked like he was paying attention. "I'm not sure I understand that."

Judge Papas fell all over himself trying to paint the big picture. In as fatherly a tone as he could muster, he leaned forward and looked at Willie. "Thank you for telling me. I will be happy to explain it to you again." At which time he started all over, carefully repeating each right that was being relinquished, each time asking if the defendant understood, and each time Willie answering indeed he now did. "Although I am somewhat reluctant about this proceeding, obviously you gentlemen have a right to it." Papas added.

There were days during these past six months when Doug was sour and moody, days when he was demanding and unreasonable, others when he was cordial and responsive. Today he was merely alone and defeated. Willie's blow had taken care of that. His defeat was seen in his slouch, heard in his hesitant voice, felt in the quiet tension that built as Judge Papas asked the defendant to stand.

Dedekam stood beside Gretzler and addressed the court, motioning to withdraw his client's previous plea to all counts. "We are ready to enter a new and different plea."

At which point Judge Papas began, as he had done almost a half year earlier, to slowly read from the Grand Jury Indictment, the names of each victim and the crime committed against them. Each presented in a loud voice, each hanging in the air until replaced by the next, one by one, until all nine had been offered, all 'separate but related felonies', as Judge Papas was clear to point out.

But with each name there seemed to come a renewed strength in Doug Gretzler, as if this was the last time he would ever have to hear them. As if this raising of the dead would, once and for all, rid their ghosts from him. With each name came his answer. "Guilty." With each name his voice became a little louder, a little more absolute and defined, his thin frame more erect, the shake of his hair from his eyes more defiant.

"Guilty". Nine times he repeated the word.

Papas reminded him of each right he was giving up with his guilty pleas. He asked the defendant if he had any doubt about we he was doing. "If there is," he warned, "then now's the time to say it."

Gretzler looked right at him. "No, I'm guilty."

Peter Saiers motioned the court, that with the new pleas, the prosecution was willing to dismiss all other counts against the defendant. Accepted. Papas then ordered mandatory probation reports on each. He announced oral arguments in the case against Willie Luther Steelman would be continued until Wednesday of next week. It was then when Judge Papas asked both Dedekam and Saiers to approach the bench, thereby setting off a controversy that would last for as long as Doug Gretzler could remain alive.

Papas merely wanted to discuss a sentencing date with both attorneys, but Dedekam seemed anxious to clear up questions regarding the pending extradition to Arizona. He first asked, due to the altercation earlier, that his client be kept separated from Willie Steelman from this point on. Secondly, after sentencing was complete, he wanted Gretzler out of San Joaquin County as soon as possible due to the community's anger and hostility towards him. Dedekam seemed to be asking Papas to provide his client protection while Arizona waited to bring him back to their state.

The conversation at the bench soon led to a larger discussion, again inside the judge's chambers. There was no way Papas could make such guarantees and he advised Dedekam of that. Extradition is handled through the State Department of Corrections, he reminded counsel, and all prisoners are shuttled into the system through the facility at Vacaville. Papas would have no control over how each man would be handled after they left his jurisdiction. He offered to have Steelman sent back to Sonoma County for the next several weeks while his case was still pending, and to keep Gretzler here while probation reports were being prepared, but that was all he could do. He could not keep them separated after that. He set July 8th as the date for sentencing.

Before the meeting broke up, Papas told Gretzler his guilty pleas would not affect any charges currently pending against him anywhere else. Papas sensed Gretzler was suddenly concerned the crimes he was going to be charged with in Arizona were being connected to those he had just pled guilty to. Now he would be forced into pleading guilty there too. Papas claimed he was only attempting to calm Gretzler's fear when he assured him that nothing he admitted to today would have any effect him down the road.

But in Arizona, one of the prerequisites the prosecution can have in obtaining the Death Penalty was the presence of a prior felony conviction, such as a murder conviction. And any first year law student could clearly see Douglas Gretzler had just plead guilty to nine of them.

For the next several days Papas spent his extra hours and evenings doing his homework, reviewing the lengthy Grand Jury transcripts as he had promised. On Friday, June 14th he requested a copy of the videotape taken inside the Parkin house and asked that both Saiers and Libicki be present in his chambers when he viewed it. Willie had signed a waiver indicating he wished not to be present at the showing and his request was granted. Papas spent much of the time grimacing and shifting in his chair, trying hard not to show his revulsion and contempt for what he was seeing.

Throughout the course of reviewing the Grand Jury documents, and now seeing firsthand the video, he had to keep reminding himself to maintain an open mind. He knew that from the very beginning Gretzler had admitted responsibility for the initial shots, and he wondered if there might be testimony from someone or interrogation transcripts that might indicate Steelman's lesser activity at the crime scene. He could find nothing. What's more, with every report he read the more he understood how it was Steelman who had instigated and choreographed the entire episode.

The Sonoma County District Attorney's Office dismissed the charges against Steelman and Gretzler. That left Stanislaus County as the only jurisdiction in California with the possibility of future prosecution against the pair. With that in mind, and discussions of extradition heating up once again, Stanislaus District Attorney Don Stahl announced his office was considering an agreement recently presented by Pima County that would allow Steelman and Gretzler to be prosecuted there first, then be returned to Modesto to stand trial for the murders of Mike Adshade and Ken Unrein.

On Wednesday, June 19th, Judge Papas made official his findings. Willie Steelman stood up, dressed in blue coveralls, manacles clanging, flanked by Libicki and several guards, he turned and twisted to see who was in the courtroom behind him, smiling and goofing around, trying what seemed his best to ignore what Papas was about to say.

Papas said he had read the entire transcripts several times before making his decision, and while he admitted the case against the defendant was circumstantial, it was impossible to dispute. The transcripts and evidence, he said, "unerringly points to the guilt of the defendant beyond a reasonable doubt." He pronounced Steelman guilty of nine counts of murder plus five counts of robbery, and set July 8th as sentencing for both men.

Wanda Earl's younger brother, Carl Cummings, had been at every hearing during the past seven months. He took sister's death extremely hard, and during those first few days after the murders, when both sides of the family talked of vengeance, Carl was the most vocal and the most anxious. Even after seeing the security amassed for each court hearing, he remained willing to try anything to find a way to strike back at her killers. Often his voice could be heard in the crowded courtroom, cursing and threatening the two men.

After the verdict was announced, guards moved in to take Steelman from the crowded room, Carl jumped up from his third row seat behind the defense table and lunged toward him. "Hey punk! How tough you feel now?" he shouted. "How tough you feel now?"

Startled by this outburst, the deputies shielded Steelman from the possible attack, while those sitting next to Cummings grabbed him as he started climbing over the railing. "C'mon Carl. It won't do you any good," they comforted. "C'mon on back, Carl"

His taunts soon turned to sobs. He slumped over and buried his face in his hands; his crying now uncontrollable, as Willie disappeared through the closest doorway.

9

Monday, July 8, 1974.

"Our system has decided that the worst person in our society is still entitled to one person, his lawyer, to be on his side. I'm Willie Steelman's one guy, and I didn't get much of a hand to play."

– Sam Libicki

A strong summer storm began brewing over the San Joaquin Valley Sunday afternoon. It was the end of a long 4th of July weekend, and the rain started coming just as campers and boaters were returning home from the rivers and reservoirs in nearby Calaveras foothills. The temperatures dropped rapidly and the rain fell hard.

Throughout the night it came, so this morning, windshield wipers flapped on the sheriff sedans bringing the prisoners to the Stockton courthouse. Judge Papas had arrived early and was ready to begin, as was Saiers, while Libicki grabbed an umbrella and left his office two blocks away, walking the short distance to the courthouse. Papas took his place at the head of a courtroom filled to capacity, then, without a word, flipped through the pile of paperwork stacked upon his bench. Finally, after an uneasy silence, he spoke. He described Willie Steelman as 'the architect and engineer', and Doug Gretzler as 'a willing follower'. He pronounced them both guilty to all charges resulting from 'this tragic odyssey', while adding the robbery counts to Steelman's list. He sentenced both to life in prison, adding he would strongly recommend neither man be released for the rest of their natural lives. There was no emotion shown from neither Papas, the spectators, or on the faces of the guilty.

The sentence was not a surprise to anyone, although Libicki rose and took exception the judge's final recommendation. Papas barely looked his way when he replied the said objection was so noted.

He ordered the pair returned to the custody of the sheriff's department who would be responsible for delivering them to California Medical Facility at Vacaville, where all inmates were prepared for their entry into the state penal system, or in this case, out of the state altogether. Experienced observers to this morning's sentencing were quick to note their stay at Vacaville would be a brief one, and highly unlikely either would ever see the inside of another California prison. Following the hearing, Peter Saiers told a reporter from the Lodi *News Sentinel* he expected no roadblocks in their extradition to Arizona, indicating the pair could be gone within two to three weeks.

But California law allowed sixty days for appeal, and so the last word Libicki had for his client was, because he was going to Vacaville and out of his jurisdiction, he could not be his lawyer for that process. Willie snapped back that he wasn't sure he even wanted to bother with any appeals.

"Well, you've got sixty days, man," Libicki warned him. "Make up your mind, but don't wait too long. They're tough on that. They don't give you any second chances."

Doug Gretzler remembered only one thing about Vacaville. He remembered that on the day of his arrival, he walked by another prisoner's cell and was encouraged to find inside a small television, a typewriter, and an unusually large amount of books. But most surprising, on one wall there were shelves holding what seemed to be hundreds of amber prescription bottles. "It looked like a damn drugstore in there," he would remember later.

The prisoner was not there, but the guard noticed Gretzler's interest and pointed out, almost proudly it seemed to Doug, the man whose cell this belonged to was none other than Charles Manson.

"Now, I'll betcha you heard of him," the officer smirked.

The discussions between Arizona and California's respective governors, Williams and Reagan, continued throughout the next two weeks. On July 23rd, Reagan signed the extradition papers releasing Steelman and Gretzler to Pima County, who had made every effort to keep their activities low key, hoping to catch Maricopa County off-guard. It looked as if their plan was working. Maricopa had not bothered to contact anyone in California – San Joaquin County, the prison system, or the Governor's office, for that matter. They acted as if, when the time came, California would simply call and tell them to come pick up their prisoners, they were that smug in their self-importance.

After the sentencing, George Dedekam took a few days off, trying to forget about the past seven months. He felt worn out and rundown. Guessing that maybe he was coming down with one of those summer colds, he made an appointment to see his doctor the following week. On August 2nd he presented his bill to San Joaquin totaling $4,917.73. Judge Papas approved the request the same day, and

Dedekam felt he could finally relax and focus on other things in his life.

On the other hand, Sam Libicki still thought a lot about Willie and wondered how he was doing. He got his one week vacation out of the way and went back to work, burying himself in some other cases, still trying his best to earn his thousand bucks a month, and before he knew it, the Labor Day Weekend had arrived. On Saturday, August 31st, Libicki realized he had not heard anything from Steelman, and was worried maybe he had fallen through the cracks in Vacaville. With the holiday, he knew it would be days before he could find out anything, and neither he or Willie had any days to waste. So his first call Tuesday morning, September 3rd, was to his counterpart at the Solano County Public Defender's office to see if there had been any contact with a prisoner housed at Vacaville by the name of Willie Steelman.

Marvin Brookner took the call, and yes, he was familiar with the name, but replied he knew of no action pending with his office, nor was he aware of the approaching deadline the prisoner faced. Libicki asked if he would be willing to represent his former client on appeal and Brookner agreed. Libicki urged him to reach Steelman as soon as possible because this Friday would be the last day to file. When Brookner asked on what grounds an appeal could be made, especially at this late date, Libicki told him, "Just get a hold of Steelman. I'll come up with something."

Brookner did as Libicki asked, but because of strict guidelines regarding prisoner visitation at the maximum security facility, as well as Brookner's heavy workload, it was the following Monday, September 9th, before he could get in to see Steelman. At first Willie did not appear anxious to see another lawyer, let alone discuss anymore legal stuff, but the more Brookner talked about the seriousness of what he faced in Arizona, the more interested Willie became. Brookner told him his office was going to file the appeal, with or without his help, and Willie, somewhat reluctantly, agreed to go along.

Over the next several days, Brookner and Libicki came up with an appeal based on the concept that state law did not allow the extradition of persons already convicted and serving time in California. It wasn't that the penal code specifically denied such actions, but only that Libicki could not find anything on the books that discussed it. Knowing full well that the time for appeal had come and gone, Brookner raced to get a court date.

Early on the morning of Monday, September 16th, in the nearby city of Fairfield, Solano County Superior Court Judge Raymond Sherwin heard the petitions that attempted to block the transfer of both prisoners to Arizona. He also wasted no time in denying the appeal. Afterwards, while waiting to be transported back to his cell, and at the suggestion from Brookner, Willie created what he hoped would be a legal document outlining his wishes, a letter chock full of misspellings and incorrect information.

> *9-16-74 To the superior court I, Willie Luther Steelman am wrighting to let the court know am appealing the dispositions of my cass, the last day of my prosecution was on 7-8-64 and I was convicted in you court for 9 ct 187 pc and 5 ct 211 pc all C C. All corresponce should be sent*

to Mr sam Libicki of the P.O. office in Stockton, Calif.
Thank you
Willie Luther Steelman

Over the word *Thank* he drew a tiny heart, but without any reason to rush the process, Willie held onto the note. The court did not receive it until ten days later. By that time he was long gone.

Shortly after Monday morning's hearing in Fairfield, Dave Dingledine got a call from California advising him the prisoners would be available Tuesday morning for Pima County to pick up. He gave Larry Hust the news. "Get some guys together," he said. "Whatever you need, you got it."

Larry said he would get back to him within the hour, then relayed the news to Sergeant Bunting, who suggested he contact the Sheriff's Office to see if they wanted to send anyone along. "It would be a good gesture," Bunting told him.

But more than that, it was an absolute necessity they be included, a matter Michael Tucker was quick to make when Hust got him on the phone. As had been mentioned, Tucker was not the most popular cop in Tucson, and Larry Hust was certainly not his biggest fan, but as Tucker correctly pointed out, all warrants for extradition were sent directly to the county sheriff, including these. Michael Tucker told Hust, in no uncertain terms, he was going to California with him. "I got the warrants, and I'm the sergeant here, so I'm in charge."

"You're full of shit, Tucker," Hust shot back. "This is my fucking case!"

Despite the rough start, each picked one other man from their respective departments to make the trip and all agreed to meet at the airport the following morning. Hust called Dingledine and told him he needed four tickets to San Francisco, and six tickets back, plus a thousand dollars for expenses. True to his word, Dingledine had the package waiting when Hust arrived at the County Attorney's office later that day. But Dave made Hust promise this operation would be made in utmost secrecy. "I don't want the whole town knowing what's happening, especially the papers."

Hust had only a vague idea where Steelman and Gretzler were being housed. Looking over a map of the San Francisco Bay Area the night before, he found Vacaville, and the prison described as a 'medical facility', shown nearby. His best guess was that it was maybe an hour or so from the airport. While laying out plans for the trip, Hust figured if they got into San Francisco before noon, they would still have plenty of time to drive to the prison, take custody, then return to the airport in plenty of time to catch their early evening plane back home.

The four slipped out of Tucson early the next morning, but Dingledine was not just worried about the media finding out what was going on, but that someone in either California or Arizona could be tipped off to their clandestine activities. It was clear Maricopa expected the prisoners to be handed over to them when the time came, and equally clear they would be ready to block any movement that indicated otherwise. In addition, the agreement between Stanislaus and Pima counties had never been finalized, and Dingledine feared they, or any other jurisdiction in either state, could have second thoughts about letting go of such notable prisoners. Then there was always some do-good attorney out there who might find a judge willing to put a stop to any extradition. No sir, Dingledine wouldn't rest until every one of them, Steelman and Gretzler included, were back in Tucson

The party landed in San Francisco shortly before noon and proceeded to the rental car counter. It was there when they discovered their first big problem. There were no cars. At least none the size they needed. There were plenty of small compacts; Pintos and Vegas, even a few mid size models, but nothing that could comfortably hold six large men and their baggage. Already the delays began to set in, so Hust found the manager of the Avis counter and explained his problem.

"So what is it you need?" the man asked.

"I need something big," Hust answered, his arms stretched wide "Something like a big station wagon. Like a nine passenger wagon." Hust had run all the scenarios in his head. He even imagined having to outrun the other guys, so he added, "And something with a lot of power. I need a big v-eight."

The Avis guy listened and nodded, making mental notes of each request. Problem was, he said, most customers these days were asking for smaller economy cars that got good mileage, especially now with the gas shortage on. "But can you wait here for a little while?" he asked. "Let me see what I can do. I promise to be back as soon as I can."

Hust grumped, cussed and complained, but within the hour, the Avis manager returned and waved them out to the curb. Parked with the engine running was a brand new, nine-passenger Buick wagon with a big, rumbling V-8 motor.

"Were in the hell did you get this?" Hust grinned.

"Went down to the Buick dealer and bought it. It's what you wanted, right?"

Hust laughed out loud. All he could think of was that stupid TV commercial about them trying harder. *Damn right they do!*, he told himself.

As the men threw their overnight bags into the back of the wagon, the manager told Hust that he had figured out what they were up to. He knew they were cops. He read the papers. He had heard the stories. He knew about all the people these guys had killed in Lodi, and down in Arizona too. "I got family out there," he said. "Just want to help out whatever way I could."

The delay had set them back hours. Hust drove. Seventy. Eighty, when he could get away with it, which wasn't often. Most of the time it was fifty, if he was lucky. It took them almost an hour to even get across the Bay Bridge, so it was late afternoon before they got to the prison. Paperwork and more delays. Hust did his best to hurry everyone along, but with limited success. Finally he saw the guards bringing Steelman, then Gretzler, down the long hallway, making sure they were kept at a distance from each other. "Strict security," came the explanation. "We don't take any chances here."

Jesus! Hust thought, we're just going to toss these sonofbitches together in the back seat of the car, so what's the big deal?

There was now the problem of making it back to the airport to catch their plane home. It was the last flight of the evening and he did not want to even think of having to keep these two guys all night somewhere. And if traffic was bad coming up here in the middle of the afternoon, what the hell would it be like now? Rush hour was on. He had to get them out of the state, and California couldn't touch them if they were in Nevada, so maybe they could catch a plane out of Reno in the morning if need be. He asked how far it was to the state line? Three hours, came the reply.

Screw it, Hust decided. He got back on I-80 and blasted back towards The City, weaving in and out of traffic, dodging cars, gunning the gas more than he hit the brakes. Even Willie had cause to ask what in the hell the big hurry was, but Hust wouldn't relax until he had them all back on the plane. He got everyone to the airport in time, but their plane was late, so they waited in a room near the gate and Hust sent out for sandwiches. They got the last six seats. Very back of the plane, like he requested. Now they were on board and he let up a bit, ready to go a couple rounds with either guy if need be.

They placed Steelman on one end, Gretzler on the other. Tucker sat in the middle seat next to Willie, Hust on the other side of the plane next to Doug. Both lawmen were unarmed. The other two men were on the aisle holding everyone's weapons so either prisoner would have to go over Tucker or Hust to get a gun. FAA regulations required all prisoners to travel without handcuffs or shackles while on any commercial flight and Hust wasn't about to take any chances.

"I have an objection," Willie announced as the other passengers began taking their seats.

Hust leaned over. "What's the problem, Willie?"

"I don't wanna fly."

Hust thought for a minute. "Well, your problem is, Willie, that if you had waived extradition you wouldn't have to fly. You could go back any way you wanted. But seeing that you didn't waive it, you got no choice now."

"Well I want my disagreement known, you know, for the record."

Hust shook his head and motioned for a stewardess.

She listened, smiled, nodded, excused herself, then returned with a crew member from the cockpit

"Problem here?" he asked.

"Problem is," Hust answered, "he don't want to fly. I told him he didn't have any say in the matter. Now you tell him."

"I'll let the pilot know."

Thirty seconds later the plane pulled away from the gate, and before Willie could utter another protest, they were gunning down the runway and in the air. Hust gave his final warning. "Listen you guys, we're on a plane with a lot of people. None of 'em know who we all are or what we're doin', so I don't want any shit out of either of you. Understand?"

Satisfied he had made his point, and with the plane now safely on its way back to Arizona, Hust burrowed down in the seat to get comfortable. A few moments later, long after his warning had been made, Willie finally decided a reply was in order.

"Don't worry man, you're not gonna get a chance to put a bullet in my head." Hust cracked up. Steelman had such a flair for the dramatic.

"Well, then," Gretzler piped up, "could I at least have a pen? I want to write a letter."

Hust looked over at Doug. At first he thought he was joking, but the expression on Gretzler's face indicated otherwise.

"Oh yeah, sure," Hust answered. "Let me get you a pen so you can fucking stab someone with it!"

Doug acted surprised Hust would even think such a thing.

Hust looked at him and shook his head. What a piece of work, he thought.

10

Wednesday, September 18, 1974 | 10 am.

The Pima County Governmental Center consumes the entire block at Church and Congress Streets in downtown Tucson. Anchored by the substantial Superior Court Building, the cluster sits squarely on top of ancient Indians ruins, not more than a hundred yards from where the town itself began nearly two centuries earlier. The sandy earth contains so many artifacts, that when the city digs up a street for repairs, they're often forced to seal off the area so historians can recover the broken pottery and primitive tools that almost bubble to the surface.

As Pima County had grown, so had the bureaucracy required to run it. By the fall of 1974 they had simply run out of space at the complex and many of the departments had moved to offices nearby. The Sheriff's Department had already relocated to new headquarters south of town, and the Public Defender's office was planning to take over the entire third floor of the Pioneer Title Building across Church Street. What was left of the downtown retail trade – and there wasn't much due to the ongoing exodus to the suburbs – catered almost exclusively to the legal, banking and real estate clientele working nearby. Most of the old-name downtown department stores were gone now, and in their place, coffee counters, bars and sandwich shops squeezed into the spaces left by once-thriving jewelry stores and men's clothing shops.

Late yesterday afternoon, after Hust called to inform him their operation was now going according to plan, Dingeldine leaked details about the extradition to the media. Even though more than ten months had passed since the Sandberg murders, the story of their killers being returned to Tucson made the television news that night as well as the front page of both papers.

From the moment he first walked into the Sandberg home, Randy Stevens lobbied hard for the opportunity to prosecute Willie Steelman and Douglas Gretzler, if and when they were ever returned to Tucson. Whenever a reporter needed an official reaction to the situation in California, it was Stevens they sought for comment. For ten long months he had held on to the rage and disgust he felt over what had happened to the Sandbergs; the startling contrast of their wedding picture to the image he kept in his head of how he remembered their bodies. He promised never to forget that scene, and in his attempt to keep his contempt alive, in the top drawer of his desk he placed a photo of the bodies found in the closet in California.

So it was also during those ten months, that whenever Stevens felt his indignation slipping away, or his attention drifting to another case, he opened his desk drawer and looked down, simply to remind himself how badly he wanted these two guys, and how he wanted so desperately to be the one who would make them pay for what they had done. But while he had worked hard towards that goal, he knew full well that decision was not his to make.

That decision belonged to Dave Dingeldine. As Chief Deputy under Deputy Attorney Dennis DeConcini, it was he one who handed out the prosecution workload, and over the past several days it was becoming more and more obvious to Stevens that Dave was going to take this one himself.

It had been nearly five years since he had prosecuted a case of any magnitude, and as of late, Dave had been heard grumbling about how antsy he felt and how tired he was of sitting behind a desk all day. Having just turned 40, Dave saw himself growing old in his office. "I'm still too young not to be out there," he had complained to co-workers. And now he could feel the excitement of a huge trial building inside him, knowing that Steelman and Gretzler were on their way back to Tucson.

When Hust called from California, Dingledine told only a handful in the office, including Stevens. It was then when Randy knew he would only be working the sidelines. He tried not to let his disappointment show – there was a chain of command and Stevens understood his rung on the ladder – but he couldn't help but feel a tremendous letdown. Still, he continued to open that top desk drawer every day, if only to remind himself the importance of his role, however small it might be.

The prisoners were ushered into Superior Court early Wednesday morning, dazed and bleary-eyed after their late night flight. Under heavy security, they were transported separately to the courthouse. Willie took his sweet time moving, yanking his arms back whenever a guard grabbed him to hurry things along. "Keep your fucking hands off me," he was heard to say more than once. Doug was slightly more cooperative, but when he saw Willie's actions, he too became combative and troublesome.

The extradition had come so swiftly, and so secretly, few people had the opportunity to prepare. Yesterday, as they readied themselves for Steelman and Gretzler's arrival, the County Attorney advised both the Superior Court Clerk and Public Defender of what was happening and asked the arraignment be held immediately. Superior Court Judge Joe Jacobson offered to clear his calendar and oversee the arraignment, while the Sheriff's Department scrambled for additional deputies to handle security. Because the prisoners had arrived so late, and the court session was scheduled so early, there had been little opportunity for any crowd to gather.

Jacobson appointed Public Defender John Neis to represent Steelman and a local attorney named Lars Pederson to defend Gretzler. Neither had been given the opportunity to talk to their clients about the charges they were facing, so both Neis and Pederson first requested a delay so they could do just that. Neis suggested at least a two to three week postponement, but Jacobson gave them a week, then rescheduled the arraignment for the following Wednesday. Each attorney presented several procedural motions; standard stuff, like removing shackles and handcuffs while in court, a certain change of venue, and barring the media from any future hearings. Jacobson said he would rule on them next week. But when Neis requested a bail hearing, Jacobson wasted no time responding.

"That one we can address today," he replied. "Because of the gravity of the charges against Mr. Steelman and Mr. Gretzler, I will not allow them to go free. There will be no bail set."

So as the session ended, neither Steelman nor Gretzler had answered to three counts of murder pending before them; they had not even opened their mouths, and were secreted back to Pima County Jail, to sit and wait.

Like many others before and after him, Lars Pederson began his law career in civil service, starting out with the County Attorney as a prosecutor. Lars was the quiet type, which seemed out of place for his chosen profession, but he was friendly enough to gain the admiration and friendship of those he worked with. His father, also an attorney from New York, was the first to educate his son about the proper respect for the legal system. So while Lars' came in contact with the most unsavory characters, he still expected them to show some shred of human dignity.

The real turning point in his life came seven years earlier. After watching the Fourth of July firework display at the University, he and his family were involved in a terrible head-on collision just outside of Tucson. Lars was severely injured, as was a young daughter, but tragically, his wife and infant son were killed. Although most expected it to be months before he returned to work, Lars showed up at the office one morning a week later with missing teeth and his jaw wired shut, and proceeded to dig back in. Within a few years, he left the county and joined a private law firm. Following the accident, and after he began to rebuild his life, those who knew him claimed his resolve was much stronger, his tolerance lower, his thoughts more vocal, and what he expected from others much greater.

So maybe it was because of all of this, that he knew when he first set eyes on him, he knew he could not work anywhere near Willie Steelman.

It seemed everyone in Tucson knew what Willie had been part of, and that included the legal community who followed the story with a keen and professional interest. Judge Jacobson picked Pederson for the same reason any judge would have; he felt Lars had the background to handle a case of this size and would do the absolute best job he could. But it was not a case that could be won, nor would it be profitable. Still, Jacobson was confident neither Pederson's name nor career would suffer defending one of these men, even though Dingledine admitted his office had every intention of making Steelman and Gretzler one of the first tests of the newly redesigned Arizona death penalty.

Once again, Willie had the Public Defender as representation, with all the resources afforded them, while Pederson understood exactly what he was faced with in defending Gretzler. There would be limited funds, long hours, public ridicule, and the certainty he was going to lose. However, what bothered him the most was not what little he would have to work with, but with who. Knowing the trials could be held together became Pederson's biggest headache, because he also knew the moment he saw Willie Steelman that he didn't like him, and didn't care to be around him even one minute more than absolutely necessary.

And yet initially, Lars proceeded diligently with his assignment. Like everyone else, the murders not only in their city, but in California as well, were hard to ignore because of the overwhelming attention the story had gathered in Tucson. But after reading the official reports and absorbing the staggering evidence presented to the Grand Jury, Lars understood for the first time just how horrible these crimes were.

He met with Gretzler for the first time Thursday morning. As usual, the jail reeked of urine and disinfectant, the men housed there loud, vulgar and obnoxious. And right in the middle of them was Willie Steelman, his voice rising above all the others. Pederson did his best to ignore him – Willie was not his client, nor necessarily his concern for that matter, – but he had caught Gretzler in a nasty, pissy mood that morning as well, and no matter how hard he tried, he could not converse with him, let alone get a straight answer. It was if as long as Steelman could be heard, Doug Gretzler was not to be reasoned with. Not interested in wasting anymore time, Pederson snapped his briefcase shut and called for the jailer.

On his way out he saw Steelman being brought in to meet with the Neis, and Pederson watched several deputies wrestle him into the room. As they did, Willie cursed and threatened each one, and as a final defiant act, he spit into one of the guard's face.

Even after knowing the crimes Steelman was responsible for, it still shocked Lars to witness such a disgusting display. As far as he was concerned, Willie could have slit the jailer's throat and he would not have been more outraged. To Lars Pederson, Willie Steelman did not belong to the human race and was most certainly not anyone he wished to spend time with, let alone help defend.

Lars returned to his office, called Judge Jacobson, and in the clearest of language, resigned. "Tell them what you wish," he said, "but I won't be a part of this. I know of nothing more abhorrent!"

It is not customary to withdraw as court-appointed counsel, especially not with the simple reason Pederson had given, but it took Jacobson by such surprise that he failed to advise him that he couldn't do what he just did. Even after the conversation ended, Jacobson knew he had no choice in the matter. Like so many others in town, he knew Lars Pederson. He knew him well. He knew what he had gone through and what he stood for, and he knew there was no sense discussing the matter further.

The official reason for Pederson's departure, it would be explained later in the week, was the law firm he now worked with had been retained by one of the witnesses in the case and Pederson and Jacobson reluctantly agreed there could be a conflict of interest.

After word spread around town about Pederson's departure, the legal community once again began to lay low. No one wanted this job. It would be, simply put, a losing proposition, time consuming, thankless, and constricting. The attorney soon selected as Pederson's replacement would represent Doug Gretzler with ridiculously low pay, few if any funds for investigative and psychological work, plus a stacked deck against him, including a client who had already confessed to the crimes. And don't even think about other clients. This case might easily drag on for a year or more.

So for the next few days, as Jacobson tossed around whom might best handle the job, lawyers disappeared on last minute vacations or were suddenly called out of town on an emergency. Secretaries were told to take messages. Answering services were given a list of excuses. At home, the attorney told his family he was not in. Almost overnight, the Tucson legal community had gone underground.

Of all those capable of defending Doug Gretzler, the name David Hoffman had to be included. And yet, of all of the names on Jacobson's short list, he was the one with the best excuse not to be selected.

Hoffman came to Tucson in the 60's to attend U of A law school, and after graduation went to the local office of the United States Attorney General. It soon became clear to him that the stuffy, low-key approach practiced at the federal level was not his style. Within a couple of years Hoffman left to start his own firm, specializing in criminal defense. By 1974, and although not yet thirty, David Hoffman's physical presence was close to matching the overwhelming self-confidence he had attained. Large, loud, boisterous and cocky, he was never at a loss for words, making a point to tell you exactly what he thought, even if you didn't care to know. If he didn't have an opinion, he made one up just to keep the conversation interesting. No other lawyer had his style. Very few had his balls. And within just months of setting up shop, every other lawyer in town knew the name David Hoffman. And much to their angst, every judge did as well.

On the weekend before Wednesday's arraignment, David Hoffman hobbled around the house, half way expecting the phone to ring, still not knowing how he would weasel out if Jacobson called. Hoffman had injured his knee and was convalescing at home, waiting for surgery scheduled later in the week. Monday afternoon, as he hurried out the door to a doctor appointment, the phone rang, and without thinking, Hoffman answered it.

It was Judge Jacobson. Hoffman cringed.

The judge promised the moon. He buttered him up and let him know that no one in town could do the job as good as he. He offered him whatever he needed to defend Doug Gretzler, and he wasn't going to take no for an answer.

Hoffman did say no, explaining he was out of commission with a busted up knee and surgery was scheduled in only a few days. He could be out for a couple of weeks, he said, and there was no way he could take the case. But Jacobson held firm and granted Hoffman all the time he needed to get back on his feet, indicating he wouldn't even require him to be at the upcoming arraignment. "Listen, David, it looks like I'm going to be the trial judge on this and I promise you will have everything you need. Everything."

Hoffman knew better. Something inside him said this was a bad deal all around. He also knew from experience that county pay for defending indigents was, at the very best, shitty. But something else inside him said, that of anyone in town, he was the man who could best defend the killer who had no defense. A case like this was a challenge he could not pass up. Few ever got a shot at a capital punishment case, but here it was, right in his lap, and they were begging for his services. Like it would do many times later, his robust ego overruled any common sense. He made Jacobson promise him again he wouldn't starve, then agreed to take the case.

At the hearing on Wednesday, September 25th, the Public Defender's office announced they had also switched gears and introduced Robert Norgren as new counsel for Willie Steelman. Lars Pederson was there just long enough to bail out. As expected, David Hoffman was not in attendance.

Reading of the defendant's rights were waived, and pleas of Not Guilty to the three counts of First Degree Murder, as well as the kidnapping and other related charges were offered.

At Norgren's urging, Jacobson threw a blanket of secrecy on the case, imposing a stiff gag order prohibiting any county employee from the Attorney's Office or Public Defender, courts and Sheriff, even from the Tucson Police, from discussing any aspect of the case with the media. And without any further discussion of the matter he set November 7th at the trial date.

When the announcement came regarding Pederson's withdrawal, it was clear the reason was not about some conflict of interest, but about Willie's vulgarity, Norgren denied the accusation, but Jacobson would have none of it and told the counselor to sit down, the matter was closed

Now Willie felt his good name being tarnished so he stood up next to Norgren to argue. "May I say something?" he asked.

"No sir, you may not!" Jacobson snapped. "You are represented by counsel and are not privileged to say anything."

Doug, who had nothing to do with the incident, could only watch with interest. But with his lawyer now out of the picture, he figured he wasn't represented by anybody, so he stood up to defend his partner. "Well then, can I say something?" he asked.

Jacobson turned his glare to Gretzler and repeated his orders. "No sir, neither can you."

With the spitting matter out of the way, along with Lars Pederson, Jacobson announced his new selection for defense attorney. "Now, Mr. Gretzler; Mr. Pederson has asked to withdraw due to possible conflict of interest charges and that request has been granted by this court. I am appointing a David Hoffman to act as counsel in your defense. Have you any objections?"

Doug looked puzzled. "To what?"

A look of exasperation covered Jacobson's face. "To Lars Pederson resigning and the appointment of David Hoffman as counsel?"

He thought for a moment, fully expecting by the very nature of the question, this was an area the judge felt should be given a great deal of contemplation. He scrunched up his face and pursed his lips as he weighed his options. He looked up and answered as honestly as he could. "Don't know. I've never met him."

It would be several days before Doug Gretzler would have that opportunity, but in David Hoffman he would soon have a trusted friend, a confidant, and to a certain degree, a savior. This would be the man who, for two decades to come, would disturb the Arizona legal system as much as Doug Gretzler disturbed its citizens. During that time they would develop a relationship far beyond that normally found between a lawyer and his client. Doug Gretzler had no way of knowing it then, but a few days later, when he was first introduced to David Hoffman, he had met the man single-handedly responsible for keeping him alive.

Forget that Steelman and Gretzler were brought back to Arizona under the cover of darkness, Pima County's secret was short lived, and this morning, up the road in Phoenix, authorities there were feeling a little foolish, and very angry. Privately, Maricopa County realized it had been out foxed. They had just assumed the pair were as good as theirs, if for no other reason than the California arrests had been made on their warrants for crimes committed in their jurisdiction a week before they ever set foot in Tucson.

Sheriff Paul Blubaum and County Attorney Moise Berger decided to serve Pima County with a writ demanding they release Steelman and Gretzler into their custody so they could be brought to Phoenix to face their open murder charges. Their reasoning, as explained to the media late Wednesday afternoon, was that in accordance with a recent Arizona law, once warrants are delivered – as they had been over 10 months earlier in Stockton – the law required the defendants be tried within 90 days if they were currently in custody. A court decision months earlier said that the 90 days would begin when the suspects were back within the state, so the meter was now running. So armed with the paperwork, Heider, Berger, Blubaum and Dave Arrelanes, drove to Tucson early Thursday, September 26th, with every intention of bringing the two defendants back with them. But Pima jail officials refused to turn them over, and the news spread about what was going down.

David Hoffman was in the hospital and in no condition to oppose the move, but Robert Norgren quickly prepared a temporary restraining order, had it signed, and then raced over to the jail to halt the transfer. But before the document was even served, Sheriff Blubaum, now knowing he was going home empty handed, returned to Phoenix, and the others followed shortly thereafter. Willie and Doug would remain in Pima Jail, at least for the time being.

Late that afternoon, Superior Court Judge Lawrence Galligan, who issued the stop order, scheduled a hearing for the following Monday. Maricopa County Deputy Attorney Chuck Heider explained his department's actions to the press who had gathered at the courthouse. He claimed they were only trying to follow the new law and by no means were they attempting to upstage anyone. He argued neither city would want these two men to get away with these heinous crimes because of an avoidable technicality. Pima County would do the same thing, he assured reporters, if the roles were reversed.

Asked for his appraisal of the events, Randy Stevens admitted that Maricopa County had a strong case, and the wording of the recent ruling appeared to be on their side. "But if Heider wins, it would mean we would have these people (Steelman and Gretzler) traveling up and down I-Ten while both sets of attorneys prepared their cases at the same time."

Stevens added that was a security risk no one should be willing to take.

On Saturday, September 28th, the *Tucson Daily Citizen* ran a banner story on the front page. TUCSONIANS ASK: WHAT MAKES A KILLER?

The article introduced the new staff psychologist for the Tucson Police Department, Charles Galbo, who wrote about the accused killers who were now in Arizona custody. Galbo was the department's first psychologist, and one of only five or six in the country, and had interviewed the pair the day before Jacobson issued his gag order. Like most murderers he had interviewed over the years, Galbo said the defendants were very cooperative and almost eager to talk about their lives, along with the crimes they had been accused of.

Galbo said Steelman and Gretzler were "animated and lucid" during the interviews, "but show no signs of caring about themselves or others. They are often very likable, very amiable, but they only let people get so close. They just can't love. It is hard to say if they are sensitive, but the big thing about them is that they really don't have a conscience – they really don't care."

David Hoffman read the article while still recuperating from his recent surgery, and knowing of the gag order, grinned and tucked the newspaper into his briefcase.

In a surprise move on Monday, September 30th, Judge Jacobson was removed from the case and Judge Richard Roylston heard the matter of the transfer of the prisoners. Richard and his twin brother, Robert, both served as judges with the Superior Court in Pima County, and it was joked that when one did not want to hear a case, the other would step in. Attorneys who appeared before them admitted that the only way to tell them apart was that Robert's arthritis bothered him more than his brother's identical ailment.

David Hoffman hobbled into court on crutches, his first session as Gretzler's defense lawyer. Maricopa County had altered its stance slightly, claiming now that they only wanted Steelman and Gretzler long enough to arraign them on charges, and that Pima Sheriff William Cox would be more than welcome to control the movement of the prisoners if he wished. He also offered to return them to Tucson immediately after the hearing.

Roylston's answer came quickly. The prisoners would remain in Pima's custody throughout the course of the impending trial, adding that his interpretation of the new rule meant that the 90 days now would not start until after such trial, and time spent until then would not be counted against them.

But before Roylston ended the hearing, David Hoffman rose to address other matters; beginning by asking the County provide special lenses for the eyeglasses Gretzler had broken. "I believe he is legally blind," Hoffman announced with what would become his flair for the dramatic. "In order to save whatever vision he does have, we ask that Mr. Douglas Gretzler be provided access to an optometrist, and hopefully at the county's expense, because I am not a rich man."

Roylston said he sympathized with the situation, but replied that he did not have the power to authorize any special requests. He suggested a check with the jail officials and the county hospital to see what could be done. Hoffman said later he got tired of the bureaucratic runaround and bought the glasses himself.

Nor was Hoffman any more successful with his two other requests that morning. He pulled the newspaper out and waved it at the bench. Roylston was familiar with the story and allowed counsel due time to address it. True to form, Hoffman didn't beat around the bush. He asked for a dismissal of all charges based on the defiance of a city official in regards to the gag order, and the comment the doctor made about his client "not having a conscience."

The judge denied the motion, but agreed that it was a serious breech of Jacobson's order and promised that he would look into the matter. Hoffman demanded the writer be summoned into court to explain his actions but the judge quickly brought the matter to a close without any further comment.

Hoffman then asked if the court would allow having his client brought to his office for the all interviews. "I don't think there is any possibility of escape," Hoffman offered. "My concern is that I don't think Pima Jail provides adequate safety. My client is extremely nervous and I've heard constant rumors of the cells and interview areas being bugged."

Roylston smiled, realizing David Hoffman was just getting warmed up. "You may file the motion. . .Go ahead. . .But for your sake I hope it doesn't come back in my courtroom, because Mr. Hoffman, I guarantee you on that one you would lose."

11

Tuesday, October 1, 1974.

Regardless of what he once promised David Hoffman, Judge Jacobson was now out of the picture. During those first few days, some of those on the inside were quick to question his ability to handle a case of this magnitude, characterizing him as "merely a politician sitting on the bench". Others went so far as to say that Jacobson maintained "the lethal combination of arrogance and stupidity". Of all the comments made, the kindest remarks offered by some of the attorneys who had faced him were that he was extremely difficult to work with.

But for whatever the reasons, Jacobson was gone. He would never again hear another motion or make any ruling pertaining to the eventual murder trials of Willie Steelman or Douglas Gretzler.

Which was terrible news for David Hoffman, because all of Jacobson's lavish promises went out the window with him. Hoffman was left holding an empty bag and his work hadn't even started yet.

With the trial scheduled to start in just thirty days, the first week of October was surprisingly quiet. Neither Norgren or Hoffman made any noise about a change of venue, severance of the cases or trials, nor did they request any psychiatric studies on their clients. At the very least, most expected them to have filed a Rule 11 motion by now to determine the defendants' competence and their mental ability to stand trial. There was little doubt such a request would be granted, therefore postponing the November 7th date for an indefinite period of time. But nothing had been said to this point, although Norgren hinted he was in the process of preparing such a motion. Hoffman, on the other hand, took his case in a different direction. On October 9th, he pressed for a Show Cause hearing before Judge Galligan, attempting to bring to light violations of his client's rights he claimed were taking place everyday at the Pima County Jail. Norgren joined in on Hoffman's complaint, and for the first time Steelman and Gretzler were allowed to take the stand.

Under guided questioning from his attorney, Gretzler said he was being taken from his cell almost daily and forced into a small room where plainclothes cops demanded he answer their questions or suffer the consequences. When he told them he had nothing to say and tried to leave, they put a foot in front of the door and told him he wasn't going anywhere. Gretzler told them he didn't want any hassles and managed to get out of the room, but admitted he was frightened by the repeated harassment.

Norgren put Willie on the stand, and true to form, he was much more animated. "I told 'em I didn't wanna talk – that I wanted to see my attorney. But they told me to sit my goddamn ass down if I didn't wanna lose a tooth."

"So what happened then?" Norgren pressed.

"Well, I sat down, but it really upset me, 'cause, you know, I'm a very nervous person."

Assistant Deputy Attorney Callahan, who was filling in for Dave Dingeldine at the hearing, smiled as he rose to cross-examine. "Mr. Steelman, I'm going to ask you some questions. Is this going induce an extreme paranoia in you – the fact that I'm going to ask some questions?"

Willie was still playing serious and hadn't recognized the sarcasm. He crinkled his brow and looked away. "Man, I hope not," he winced.

Minutes later, urged on by Norgren, Willie told the court the words he had heard every single day from jail officials, the same words thrown at him when he arrived in Tucson weeks earlier.

"What do they keep telling you, Willie?" Norgren asked.

"They say, 'now we got you, and you know we're going to kill you'."

"Does that kind of talk upset you?"

"Yeah, it makes me very nervous."

Willie had no sooner taken his seat than Hoffman stood with his new demands. He requested Galligan immediately block all interviews of his client by Pima officials and other outside jurisdictions who, he snarled, "have been traipsing in and out of the jail and violating my client's rights."

Galligan denied the request, visibly annoyed by counsel's bluster. He reminded Hoffman that no judge had the authority to issue such an order. "Law enforcement agencies have the right to investigate matters pertaining to their jurisdiction, just as the defendants have the right not to speak with them."

But according to jail insiders, the relentless interrogation of Steelman and Gretzler continued virtually nonstop for weeks afterwards.

During the second week of October, Robert Norgren flew to Stockton. There he spoke with Sam Libicki at length, gathering as much information as he could about how his fellow Public Defender had approached the case. He visited Dr. Austin and Dr. Cavanaugh to discuss their findings, although he came away with little he could use.

It was when he met Dr. Patricia White that he first felt he might be on to something. White was convinced Willie Steelman was insane and relayed to Norgren the scope of her findings, passionately explaining the details of her ongoing treatment of the defendant. She further bolstered Norgren's spirits when she mentioned how a colleague, a Dr. Peale, agreed with her analysis. She showed a deep concern for the mental well being of her former patient, and now that he was in Arizona, she was afraid he would be misdiagnosed for the benefit of the death penalty. Before Norgren left, Dr. White offered to travel to the upcoming trial and speak on Willie Steelman's behalf.

Suddenly recharged, Norgren drove to Lodi to search for any of Willie's family who might be willing to help. But he found only Gary Steelman, who refused to meet with him. He also tried contacting Denise on several occasions, but she too ignored his requests, hiding out in her parent's home while he was in town.

Returning to Tucson, he briefed Hoffman about and trip and let him know about a potentially serious problem he had discovered while in Stockton. George Dedekam was dying of cancer, and doctors had given him only a month to live. David Hoffman had never spoken with Dedekam, not even bothering as much as a phone call of introduction, nor did even this troublesome news rush him into action. He continued reviewing the material presented to him by the County Attorney's office and preparing motions for the courts. Hoffman's lack of interest in Dedekam surprised even Robert Norgren, but he moved forward, and now armed with Dr. White's enthusiasm, and a better understanding of Steelman's emotional background, Norgren motioned for a Rule 11 hearing.

Granted immediately, it blocked the scheduled trial date, which was now slightly more than two weeks away. It also gave the defense more time to develop strategy on how best to defend a man already convicted of nine counts of murder.

On October 21st, David Hoffman chose another route. He motioned the court to dismiss all Grand Jury indictments against his client. According to his motion, again heard before Judge Galligan, Hoffman claimed that because Randy Stevens had been one of the first at the crime scene, and because he had also presided over the Grand Jury hearings later that same week, the evidence, or at least the emotional manner in which it most likely had been presented, was tainted and therefore inadmissible. He demanded he be allowed to question Stevens on the stand, and subpoena him to court, if necessary.

Galligan was swayed enough with Hoffman's argument to allow the motion and continued the hearing, with Mr. Stevens present, for the following week. Stevens, who had made no bones about his dislike for Hoffman, was livid when he heard the news. Dingeldine was himself running out of patience with his opponent and objected to the court over 'these frivolous motions'. Before the court session was over that day, Hoffman added to the fray by requesting the court provide him with a law student to help him review the case. Claiming the Public Defender and County Attorney had seemingly unlimited funds for their side, he charged that he was being given nothing. "There's over 1500 pages of documents to review here, and Mr. Gretzler is being denied equal representation."

While he was on the subject, Hoffman also asked for an alternate means of payment. Now that Jacobson was gone, so were the mighty dollar promises once made. "Put this on a contract basis and I'll agree to a reasonable fee. I don't intend to make frivolous motions, but I do intend to defend this man with everything I have and everything the law gives me."

Galligan denied both requests.

A week later, at the October 28th hearing before yet another judge, The Honorable Robert Buchanan, Dingeldine began by informing the court about Hoffman's delays, especially in regards to the Rule 11 motion yet to be made. While no one could remember a prosecutor motioning for a competency hearing for a man he was trying to convict, Dingeldine decided to speed things up and take the matter into his own hands. He motioned the court to request a Rule 11 hearing for Gretzler, but surprisingly Buchanan refused to hear it. Exasperated, Dingeldine slumped down in his chair, shaking his head in frustration and disbelief.

Randy Stevens was called to the stand. He loathed Hoffman's style, his bluff and swagger, his bullshit tactics, not to mention all the crap he had pulled in court during the first month alone. Stevens' tone was curt and adversarial, his responses short, precise, condescending and often sarcastic. Hoffman began by insinuating that Stevens directed the investigation at the Sandberg residence and took his anger with him to the Grand Jury hearings. "Sir, you have strong feelings about this case, don't you?" Hoffman asked.

Dingeldine objected, reminding the court Mr. Stevens had been present at 50 to 60 crime scenes during his five years with the County Attorney and had many times presented over a Grand Jury. This was all just standard procedure, he protested, yet Hoffman was attempting to make something sinister about it.

"This is ridiculous!" he roared. "This type of accusation has never been heard in a court before!"

Yet despite his protests, the questioning continued nonstop for over an hour, until finally Stevens was instructed to step down. Buchanan said he would make his ruling known in a week. He was going on vacation and nothing was going to interfere with it.

In the days following his return from California, when they met in the interview room at the Pima jail, Norgren was pestered by Willie to tell him more about his trip. "Did you see Denise?" he asked repeatedly. "Did you get over to her house? You know she's probably staying at her parent's place".

No, Norgren admitted, he wasn't able to see her. She wouldn't talk to him, adding that Mrs. Machell informed him Denise would not have anything to say to anyone. Which was not good news, Norgren told Willie, because they really needed her help. Only Denise could know the real Willie Steelman; the Willie before all of this madness; the one who got so hopelessly involved with drugs that he was unable to separate right from wrong. Forget that she was now Willie's ex-wife; she was the only family he had left.

Willie offered to help. "Mrs. Machell likes me," he boasted. "I know I can get her to talk Denise into it. You let me talk to her."

So before the hearing was adjourned Monday afternoon, Judge Buchanan granted Willie Steelman one phone call to Lodi.

Not to be out done, David Hoffman stepped up and asked for money to travel to Stockton, although the judge set aside his request until a latter date.

On Wednesday, November 6th, the eve of the scheduled trial and exactly a year to the day since the Lodi massacre, Superior Court Judge Robert Roylston granted Norgren's request for a delay. It would be the first of many such postponements. Although sought by Norgren to allow for Steelman's pending competency tests, the delay was actually for the trial belonging to Douglas Gretzler. Neither Norgren nor Hoffman was on record as ever asking for a severance of the trials, but due to some legal quirk, the November 7th date had been officially assigned to Gretzler six weeks earlier.

Dingeldine and the County Attorney's Office opposed any talk of severance. Their official response was that they were concerned of possible complications of using one defendant's statements against the other. To prosecute one by using the other's admissions of wrongdoing could create a problem in getting a first-degree murder conviction, something necessary in obtaining the Death Penalty. In addition, if for any reason some of the evidence was thrown out (like any of the numerous confessions for example) a first-degree conviction could be much more difficult to achieve. Dingeldine said he had no intention of discussing a separation of the trials until he was sure he knew all he had to work with.

But if the truth be known, the real reason came down to money. Two convictions with one trial, in one court, with one jury and one judge meant keeping this whole thing under budget. To do so would look good for the C.A.'s office, especially for the next election. There had already been rumblings, spurred on by the Risner/Stevens tussle, as to why Pima had bothered to bring the pair back for a costly trial in the first place, so it was extremely important that DeConcini's office keep these cases as streamlined and cost effective as possible.

As Roylston listened to arguments from both sides in regards to Norgren's motion, Dingeldine carefully avoided any possible discussion about splitting the trials, and simply pointed out that the 60 day rule would be up on November 24th, saying he hoped they could set the new trial date before then.

But Hoffman was blubberous about the work before him and let the court know that date was much too soon. "I now have well over 2,000 pages of disclosures," he groaned, "and without the help necessary to review them."

While he was getting very proficient at complaining, he failed once again to sway Roylston, who set November 22nd as the new date.

In California, the Sunday *Sacramento Union* featured a full-page article about the people of Victor and how the town was holding up on the first anniversary of the killings. Once again penned by Dan Walters, it portrayed a town still reeling, often times confused about what was happening and why justice had appeared to elude them, even one full year later.

"I don't think there's a night goes by that I don't think about it," Norm Parkin was quoted about his brother's death. His parents had moved into the house on

Orchard Road over the past summer, and other than replacing the carpet in the closet, had not changed one thing inside the home. Photos of the slain family decorated the mantle and Walters made sure to use them in the story.

"It'll be hard enough just getting through the day without any services," Mrs. Parkin lamented, although her husband still refused to speak to anyone about his son's murder.

During the year, Carol Jenkins had become Carol Mettler and she was anxious to show her feelings about how difficult the past twelve months had been. "I wanted them tried on everything here," she announced bitterly, referring to the dropped kidnapping charges. With the lack of a real trial in California, there had never been any true closure, she complained. No way for the family and neighbors to deal with their pain, and now that the killers were gone, they could only get bits of information from the sporadic newspaper reports carried in the local papers. Still, the emptiness lingered in Victor and they collectively prayed that somehow Arizona justice would do what California could not.

"I hope they get the death penalty," Carol said, certain she was speaking for everyone.

But she, or any of the others for that matter, had no way of knowing how slow those wheels were turning, or how long the wait would eventually be.

It was obvious at first sight. Mary Anne Richey was a striking woman. Not so much in a beautiful way, or what most men might consider a looker, but still, extremely handsome. Yet she balanced a rugged femininity with an imposing manner, one demanding of attention. When she entered a room, her long salt and pepper hair pulled back, and her black robe covering a conservative business suit, she turned many a head. Tall and strongly built, she took manly strides, and with her large hands she made bold movements across her desk. When she spoke, the words were loud and decisive, and she had a way of cutting to the bone, clearing away all the clutter carried in the speech of many of the men who humbled themselves before her.

Richey had been around men and their big talk most of her life, so she knew what to expect from them. During World War II she was a pilot in the military, and it was her job to ferry huge bombers from the United States to England for service in the European theater. During those years she worked side by side with men who always had an angle and a line, so she could only laugh when they now came to her with their feeble excuses and sad stories.

It was Judge Mary Anne Richey who was the next to hear the ongoing saga of Willie Steelman and Douglas Gretzler, and on November 12th, David Hoffman stood in her courtroom asking for money for an investigator to help him with his defense. With it he renewed his request for travel expenses to California, even though he had yet to request one single psychiatric exam for his client. In his now customary style, Hoffman ignored what would certainly be an obvious objection, then pushed his weight and words around the room until Richey could stand it no longer, and stopped him dead sentence.

"You still have not filed a Rule Eleven, Mr. Hoffman?" she questioned, knowing the answer.

"Well, not at this time, Your Honor. This is to assist me in determining the need for Rule Eleven," Hoffman stammered.

Richey smirked and called him on it. "I have never heard that you appoint experts to determine if you should appoint experts," she replied coyly, shuffling through the paperwork in front of her. "It seems very foolish to me that I'm the fourth judge to hear motions on this case."

"I have a problem here, Your Honor. . ."

"Mr. Hoffman, my heart doesn't bleed for you that much," Richey interrupted as she looked directly in the large reddened face of counsel. She was leaning forward now, resting her upper torso on her elbows, glaring down on the attorney. "I think you know exactly what is going on and I have the feeling that games are being played. I think we need to get down to business and get this case tried."

"I'm not playing games," Hoffman protested, although failing to end the scolding.

"Let me anticipate what you are going to do," the judge imagined out loud. "You are going to wait until the last minute and then file your Rule Eleven. Am I correct?"

"I'm not playing games," he repeated.

Yet despite her stern lecture, Richey saw the need for David Hoffman's request, although she was already weary of his tiresome methods. Hoffman explained that Robert Norgren had recently returned from California and had informed him that George Dedekam was not expected to live much longer.

"Have you spoke to him?" she inquired.

"No."

"Not even over the phone?"

"No."

"Couldn't you just give him a call?" Richey asked.

"I haven't had time."

Judge Richey rolled her eyes. "But you have time to travel there?"

"I'm not a wealthy man," Hoffman pouted, attempting to get the conversation back to the money angle.

Richey pondered the matter for a moment, then announced that she wasn't in a position to dole out money without a good reason; reasons that so far David Hoffman had failed to offer. She had no intention in giving him a blank check.

"Mr. Hoffman, I think before I give you any money to investigate the sanity question, I must inform you that you are obligated to use whatever sources you have here. If you have any reason to believe the need for a Rule Eleven, then you don't have a reason to go out and interview all these people."

But in the end, Judge Richey gave him one week to bring her more details regarding his travel request, while warning him that he was not fooling her for one moment. "You are putting the cart before the horse here, Mr. Hoffman, and that can be dangerous in my courtroom."

The following Monday morning, November 18th, Willie Steelman was taken from the Pima Jail and escorted by three sheriff deputies to the University of

Arizona Medical Center where he was examined by Dr. Marshall Jones. It was the first of several sessions scheduled for his Rule 11 determination, lasting little more than an hour. At its conclusion, after the patient was taken from his office, Jones sat down and composed a very brief letter to the court to discuss his findings. "Mr. Steelman knows the nature and quality of his acts. He most certainly knows right from wrong. There is no reason whatsoever for him not to assist his counsel or know the contents of the proceedings."

Later that afternoon, Judge Richey continued the hearing from the previous week. David Dingeldine began by motioning the court to consider a consolidation of the murder and kidnapping charges and Richey promised to review his request. There was also mention made of selecting a permanent trial judge to hear these preliminary motions as well and Richey agreed it would save valuable time down the road. Dingeldine made it clear he would have no objection in having Her Honor be that judge, but David Hoffman found a way to change the subject. He wanted nothing to do with her.

After listening again to Hoffman's travel request, Judge Richey offered him a plane ticket to Stockton, a rental car and $30 a day expenses, not to exceed 4 days. Noting the new trial date was still on for Friday, and knowing Hoffman still hadn't made a Rule 11 request, Richey saw the writing on the wall and told both counsels they would meet again on Thursday to discuss lingering matters.

David Hoffman returned to his office and checked his calendar. Thanksgiving was a week away and the Christmas holidays would follow quickly. Now that he had the money, he wondered how long he could hold off going to California. Certainly he could postpone it until the first of the year without too much trouble, that is, if George Dedekam's health cooperated. Going beyond that would certainly insure the wrath of Judge Richey, something he did not wish to do. But before Hoffman left the office Monday, his travel plans were turned moot by a late phone call from Stockton. George Dedekam had died.

On Wednesday, Willie returned to the University for another examination, this time with Doctor Hoogerbeets. In his subsequent report to the court, Hoogerbeets disclosed that Steelman suffered from chronic paranoid psychosis and was 'a very dangerous person, even in jail or a prison situation'. "It is very easy for him to justify his actions," the doctor wrote, "and he is prone to commit acts without any emotion."

Yet Hoogerbeets agreed with Dr. Jones' finding that the patient was able to understand the charges against him and to assist his counsel. He also agreed there was no doubt Willie Steelman knew right from wrong, but he left some hope for Robert Norgren. In his report he claimed there was the possibility the patient might be suffering from some type of organic brain damage and he suggested a complete neurological examination be done, including an E.E.G.

After seeing a copy of the report, Norgren felt a glimmer of hope, for he knew there was no way the State of Arizona could bring itself to kill a man who was found to be mentally ill. It also gave him the ammunition to attack one of the biggest obstacles in Steelman's defense; the California murder convictions. A previous felony conviction, such as the nine given to Willie in California, was one of the preclusions to receiving the death penalty in Arizona. If they could set aside those convictions by proving Steelman was mentally incapacitated at the time, then the Arizona would have a much harder time in seeking death. So armed with Hoogerbeets report of possible organic brain damage, Norgren helped Willie file an appeal to California's 3rd District Court of Appeals, claiming diminished mental capacity as the reason the previous convictions should be overturned.

The problem was the deadline for filing was September 8th, over two months earlier. In his letter Willie stated he was unable to meet that deadline because of poor legal assistance in California and his rapid extradition to Arizona. Norgren rushed the document to Sacramento, and despite the fact it was two months late, California law required them to accept and review it. They had until December 9th to issue their response.

But it didn't take that long. When the action was brought up at the Appeals Court in Sacramento, the justices looked at each other, reviewed the law regarding the time limit for appeal, took a vote, and within less than five minutes tossed aside Willie Steelman's request.

Back in Tucson, again on the day before the trial was to begin, and just as Judge Richey had predicted, Hoffman finally asked the court to proceed with a Rule 11 hearing for his client.

Yet there had been little evidence shown up to now a hearing was even necessary, and David Dingeldine was quick to remind the court of that in his argument. Gretzler had been as close to a model prisoner as could be expected. He had made every court appearance, arriving clean and alert and at least giving the indication he was trying to follow along. While Willie read the paper, stared at the ceiling, threatened the guards or made faces at the visitors in the courtroom, Doug acted like he was paying attention, and at times it even appeared he was taking notes. There was nothing in his manner to suggest he was unbalanced or didn't understand what was going on around him, and Dingledine made sure that was clear to the court.

But Judge Richey granted the Rule 11 motion, and with it stayed all future proceedings against Douglas Gretzler, including the trial slated to get under way the following day. Judge Richey scheduled the Rule 11 hearings on both defendants to be held in her courtroom in three weeks.

In what would later prove to be an interesting selection, Hoffman choose a Dr. Gurland to examine his client, while the prosecution again relied on the well known Dr. Alan Beigel as its representative in the hearing. The repercussions of those choices would not be felt for some time, but the selections would prove significant over the long term.

The next day, Friday, November 22nd, Dr. Biegel met with Willie. Biegel had been selected by the County Attorney's office to handle both cases. He spent less than a half hour with his patient. That same afternoon he sent a letter to the court stating that Steelman had "a distorted sense of reality and was paranoid". There was very little mention of anything else. Nothing was said about the effects of long-term drug use or the possibility of organic brain damage. Along with the report he sent the county an invoice charging them $50 for his services.

Other than an hour session with Dr. Gurland the first week of December, there had been no other action taken on the competency tests ordered by the court for Douglas Gretzler. David Hoffman gave the matter little, if any, attention, deciding it was up to the courts to hurry things along if they so desired. He was busy with others cases, as well as the fast-approaching holidays. He had set a goal to do nothing more regarding Doug Gretzler until at least after the first of the year.

So at this morning's hearing there was no resolution as to his client's mental state, but there was plenty of complaining from Hoffman about his heavy workload and the difficulties in scheduling things around the holidays. Judge Richey brushed aside his rambling and turned her attention to Norgren, who unlike his counterpart, seemed anxious to proceed. He first requested a continuation of the hearing based on Dr. Hoogerbeets report of possible brain damage in Willie Steelman, then asked Richey to provide him with access to further tests, including sleep monitoring and an E.E.G. The judge agreed.

Concerned once again they were running out of time in their second 60 day time limit, Dingeldine pointed out the potential problem to the court. Richey said the delays were defense related and would not affect the time limit, but she set no new trial date, nor did she fix a time when all parties would again return to the courtroom. All pending legal action was suspended indefinitely, which pleased David Hoffman no end.

The holidays approached rapidly, and the warm sunny days of an Arizona December seemed odd and out of place to Doug Gretzler, who could only associate Christmas with snow, and the biting cold winters in New York City. David Hoffman, and occasionally his associate Michael Brown, would stop by the jail from time to time to talk to Doug. They brought him candy and snacks, and the basic toiletries allowed prisoners, but other than that, visitors were rare, and his days were lingering and lonely. Although there were times when he could still hear him ranting and raving, cursing his guards and bragging to the other inmates, Doug had long ago been separated from Willie. Even the cops had stopped barging in.

The one exception was Larry Hust, whose work brought him to the jail on a regular basis. Whenever he had the chance, he would take a minute to check in on him, usually just long enough to say hello. For all the obvious reasons, Hust couldn't give a rat's ass about Steelman, but he didn't mind talking with Gretzler, who seemed naive, even childlike at times, about what was going on around him. Over the past few months, Hust had stopped in a half dozen times or so, and with the holidays here, Hust thought the least he could do was wish the poor bastard a Merry Christmas.

For a cop with a steel plated soul like Larry Hust, it seemed a little out of place to see him get all giddy around the holidays, but for as long as anyone could remember Larry took the Christmas season seriously. While the rest of the world was out shopping the day after Thanksgiving, he was in his yard setting up the Christmas lights and displays. It took him three, sometimes even four days, but his small tract house in east Tucson wound up looking like Santa's Village on acid. There were sleighs and snowmen and candy cane houses and motorized skiers. There were miles of ribbons and at least 30,000 blinking colored lights. A picture of the house always made the papers and people came from all over town to see it. Traffic in the cul-de-sac got so bad some years the neighbors just stayed home on the nights right before Christmas, not even attempting to leave their driveway.

Larry was a self-confessed fool about Christmas, and figured everyone deserved some holiday cheering up, even a sadsack as worthless as Doug Gretzler, so he stopped by the jail and wished him a Merry Christmas. They spent a few minutes yapping about nothing much in particular – nothing about the trials or about legal stuff, most certainly – they just talked about families and big dinners and what it used to be like before all this happened. Afterwards Hust couldn't help but feel a twinge of sorrow for Gretzler. He hoped it was just the spirit of the season making him all sappy, and that he wasn't losing his edge.

On Christmas Day at the jail, prisoners got the usual extra helping of turkey and gravy on their tray along with an amazingly skinny piece of pumpkin pie. Willie got a letter from Frances and her kids, along with a care package with some cheese, salami and a few crackers. Doug got a card from his sister, who said they were all thinking of him, although he knew that was just her way of trying to make him feel better.

A few days after Christmas, when David Hoffman found out who had stopped by the jail recently, he came unglued. He told Gretzler not to talk to anyone from now on.

"Not even my friend, Hust?" Doug asked.

"Especially not him, you asshole!" Hoffman roared, scolding his client like a little schoolboy. "What in the hell are you thinking? The guy is a fucking cop!"

So as 1974 came to a close, Doug Gretzler had to try and figure out how he was going to break the news to Larry that he couldn't talk to him anymore.

12

Monday, January 6, 1975.

The New Year began with very little new activity in the case against Willie Steelman and Douglas Gretzler. Willie had an E.E.G. performed on January 3rd, but Hoogerbeets informed Norgren the lab technician had botched the job and it would have to be redone. Scheduling another date would be difficult because Judge Richey would need to authorize funds to perform such a test. The delay angered an already tense Robert Norgren.

David Hoffman spent the first two weeks of 1975 busy with other cases. His practice was beginning to flourish, and the constant need for money prohibited him from saying no to anyone. Never much for research or busy work – the courtroom was where he functioned best – Hoffman spent surprisingly little time on Gretzler unless there was a court date approaching. Even then, he would wait until the final few hours before he got down to business, and like a school kid the night before a big exam, he would cram as much work in as possible.

He flew to California on January 14 and spent four days in and around the courthouse speaking with anyone he could find. He had done little preparation before leaving Tucson and arrived in Stockton without even one firm appointment. He was not well received. The legal and law enforcement community had no problem with him representing Doug Gretzler, but they could not handle the manner in which he went about his business. They were not accustomed to someone, a visitor especially, coming across so obnoxious, demanding and self-absorbed. Politely, albeit somewhat reluctantly, most still found time to speak with him, but he appeared unprepared, not even knowing the simplest of details or names associated the San Joaquin cases. And yet he expected everyone to stop what they were doing to meet with him, complaining that he "was only in town for a couple of days to do a couple of months worth of work".

And by now everyone knew he had ignored George Dedekam, which was surprising to all, because with the exception of a few doctors like Rogerson and Austin, Dedekam was the only person in Stockton who ever really spent any time with Doug Gretzler. George Dedekam was the only person David Hoffman ever really needed to talk to, but never bothered.

Hoffman did meet with Pete Saiers and complimented him at just how tight the San Joaquin D.A.'s case had been prepared, although it seemed his sole intent was to punch holes in their investigative work. Saiers laughed and he told his guest, that despite what he might have heard, they weren't just a bunch of rookies up here in Stockton, and politely let it go at that.

So Hoffman was content to leave town with a dozen brief interviews and a short list of names he planned to call later, but other than that, there appeared very little substance to his few days in California.

Back in Tucson, on the afternoon of January 28th, Judge Richey held the Rule 11 hearing that had been postponed from December. Norgren explained the problems of the last E.E.G. and asked for another opportunity, while Hoffman only complained that other cases were interfering with this one and that he was having trouble scheduling the psychiatric experts. With nothing else to discuss, Richey sighed and set February 11th as the new date for the hearing. When Norgren asked again about severance, Judge Richey was sharp in her response. "Let's worry about the matter at hand (Rule 11) first. As of right now the trials are together!"

Norgren had not yet heard back from Dr White. A few days before the scheduled hearing date he called to let her know he was still counting on her written opinion. Her reply didn't arrive until the day after the hearing, but its contents boosted his spirits considerably when he read, that as far as she was concerned, Willie Steelman was presently insane and mentally unable to stand trial. One week later, on February 7th, Judge Jack Marks held the final Rule 11 hearing with Hoogerbeets, Jones, Biegel and a technician from the University Medical Center testifying, while Norgren presented his letter from Dr. White. The entire session took less than an hour, after which the judge dismissed Dr. White's remarks and announced Willie Steelman competent to stand trial. Surprisingly, Norgren offered no protest to the decision and agreed with Dingeldine to let a newcomer, Judge William Druke, hear the case. The trial was to begin March 4th, 1975.

Willie had been in Arizona almost five months. During that time his mental condition and ability to stand trial had been the only decision made. Not one other item of business had been discussed, not a witness heard, nor a single piece of evidence introduced. Jacobson's gag order of September had succeeded in keeping reporters away as well. The string of drab court hearings offered little in the way of news excitement, and the inability to interview those people on the inside of the case proved effective in keeping media buzz to a minimum. By February, the newspapers could barely muster an occasional paragraph about the proceedings, and even those were buried deep into the second or third section. The Tucson TV stations didn't even bother mentioning what was taking place downtown.

Judge William Druke was a quiet mannered man in his early thirties, surprisingly young for someone in his position, and at times he appeared to struggle with that dilemma. Even his appearance seemed to contradict his lofty position. With long dark hair crisply styled just over his ears and a full thick mustache, Druke looked more like a young executive than a prestigious member of the Superior Court. He sported a soft, friendly disposition and an ever-present smile, giving the impression that the last thing he would ever wish to do is to hurt someone's feelings.

While he had already served on the bench for several years, he remained a student of the law. It was an area he took great pride in, yet at times it became difficult for him to juggle what he believed in, and what was written as law. There were days in his court when he struggled so much with the legal process, and what he felt down deep was the right thing to do, it appeared he had lost track of his responsibility to guide the proceedings before him. It wasn't that he was reluctant to decide on a matter; it was that he always tried to come at the situation from every side just to make sure he was not missing anything. He wanted every decision to be absolutely right. Unfortunately this gave some the impression that he was intimidated, which was not the case at all. Viewed from the prosecution's side, Druke often appeared pro-defense, because, like a good defense lawyer, he was never one to rush the process. Plus he was yet another University of Arizona law graduates – a few years before both Pete Saiers and David Hoffman – a year or so behind Randy Stevens. But unlike the others, it became clear from the very beginning he wanted nothing to do with practicing law. His only interest was on the judicial side.

Of the half dozen Superior Court judges who had presided over six months worth of hearings, Druke was somewhat new to the fray. When it was decided by both sides that he would be their first choice to hear the trial, he was both flattered and uncomfortable. This would be his first capital case, and although he had no problem presiding over it, (he was rather excited about the opportunity) privately, he had many personal and professional questions with the death penalty. So he tried to create the perfect scenario in his mind, one based solely on the most current legal opinion, where he could impose a sentence of death on anyone, regardless of the atrocities they were responsible for, and remain firm and certain in his decision.

So Druke studied hard. He had just three days to educate himself on the matters that had come before him. The next hearing was scheduled in his courtroom on February 10th, and the first major discussion would be regarding the possible severance of the trials. With a trial date and judge selected, it looked like Norgren was ready to go, but as usual, the problem was with David Hoffman. It finally became clear to Dingeldine and the C.A.'s office they could hold out no longer. If they wanted to get to trial, then they would have to agree to split them. Either that, or suffer along while David Hoffman dragged his feet and all of the legal system along with it.

So at the hearing this morning Dingeldine agreed to try each defendant separately unless, and he was adamant about this point, David Hoffman moved to have Gretzler's confessions suppressed. If Hoffman promised to keep the California confessions intact, then Dingeldine would take his shot at trying Steelman and Gretzler independently of each other.

Hoffman agreed. As did Norgren before the hearing was over, along with agreeing to consolidate the Sandberg and Armstrong cases. Things looked as if they were finally moving ahead. The following day was set aside for final arguments in Doug Gretzler's Rule 11 motion, and Hoffman called Dr. Gurland.

It is a common pun among defense lawyers that, when necessary, you could always buy "a reasonable doubt for a reasonable amount". So there was no shortage of experts in the psychiatric field who could be called on to muscle up a mental question mark for the defense. For whatever the reasons, whether justified or not, in Tucson, Dr. Gurland was one of several who carried that label. So it was bit surprising, that even after Hoffman had hand picked Gurland as his man to examine Gretzler, the doctor came back with the decision he did. As far as he was concerned Doug Gretzler was perfectly able to go to trial. Gurland found very little in Gretzler's mental makeup to claim otherwise. Granted, Gurland had spent barely an hour with him in December, and not much more than that since, but after all the delays about even filing the Rule 11, it was odd that Hoffman seemed to have stumbled so badly in handling his client's mental defense.

David Hoffman produced no other witnesses, made not even the slightest mention of Gretzler's long term drug abuse, the father he despised, or the bizarre history of the tightly wound New York family which he grew up in. There was no mention of his brother's suicide or the broken marriage Doug ran away from. With not much more to offer, Druke had little choice but to find the defendant competent to hear the case against him, and ordered a new trial date.

But Dingeldine advised the court they were once again running out of days in the 60-day rule, and he suggested they proceed with Gretzler's trial even before that of Steelman's.

But Hoffman interrupted once more, demanding Druke hear an oral motion to suppress the California confessions of Doug Gretzler.

Dingeldine flew into a rage, accusing Hoffman again of playing the time-limit games and going back on his word. He was absolutely livid, waving his arms around the room, pointing an accusing finger at the defense table, his blood boiling.

Hoffman shrugged him off, moaning to Druke that he was just doing the best he could under the circumstances. Druke was one of the few who hadn't heard the "one man against the world" speech, but he was now getting an earful. "It is just me, Your Honor. I do not have the same amount of outside help that Mr. Dingeldine has availed himself to. I don't see how we can even think about going to trial on this. How can it be done? First, we have two separate cases here, plus I can't remember the last time we even set a trial date."

Druke thought for a moment and answered. "Let me solve that one for you Mr. Hoffman. We will go to court on this matter one week from today, February 18th."

But February 18th came and went. Hoffman had somehow managed to have that date tossed aside as well, and the month ended almost where it had began, and there was nothing to suggest the State of Arizona was going to get either defendant to trial anytime soon.

With their game plan stalled, on March 3rd, Dave Dingeldine gave in and offered a compromise to try and get things moving again. He offered a stipulation that if he could get a First Degree Conviction on both Steelman and Gretzler for the Sandberg killings, his office would not prosecute them for the murder of Gilbert Sierra. "If we're successful," he said, "then we'll just stop there."

"What do you consider a success?" Hoffman snapped. "Executing both of them?"

"A First Degree conviction," Dingeldine pounced back, ignoring the sarcasm. "Regardless of the penalty."

Despite Hoffman's comments, the offer was accepted, and the Sierra case was out of the way, at least for the time being.

The following morning, Druke opened the Suppression Hearing in the matter of The State of Arizona vs. Willie Luther Steelman. Suppression hearings serve a single purpose; to determine what evidence would and would not be allowed in an upcoming trial. In this case, however, the physical evidence was not necessarily in dispute. The primary focus of these hearings would center on the vast number of statements made by both defendants while in California, and their subsequent admissibility in an Arizona court of law.

Carl Ambrose, Donnie Brookshier and Ken Wagner were summoned from California – each given $30 a day and ten cents a mile for their trouble – while Larry Hust and Larry Bunting were called from Pima County, while Dave Arrelanes represented Maricopa County. Over the next week, each testified as to the manner in which the Stockton interrogations were held, and the question posed to each was, regardless of how many times the defendants were given their rights, were any of the interrogations obtained illegally? Norgren claimed his client had repeatedly made it clear he did not want to talk with anyone. But the detectives involved vehemently disagreed, arguing that even after he was given his Miranda rights for the umpteenth time, Steelman would not stop talking.

Even after Miranda, statements could be thrown out if there was even the slightest appearance they were obtained in unscrupulous manner. For example, Norgren claimed Willie never realized what he told Rogerson and Austin on the night of his capture could be held against him, although it clearly had been. What's more, he said, because of the nonstop string of interviews (held literally around the clock, he pointed out to Druke) and his client's physical condition at the time due to drug withdrawal, went into creating an atmosphere where there was no way Steelman could be held accountable for what he said.

"Listen to him," Norgren demanded, after one of the dozens of taped interogations was played before the court. "He tells them how sick he is and they just keep asking questions. Mr. Steelman honestly thought that when he talked about what happened in Arizona, that there was no way the California authorities were going to hear about it. But the truth was these people were trading tapes as fast as they could get them out of the machines."

When the week was over, it was up to Druke to decide what interviews, if any, would be allowed. It was a mind boggling mess, with hundreds of pages of transcripts and dozens and dozens of tapes to review, and even though Willie had confessed, not just once but several times, to killing the Sandbergs, that in itself still might not be enough. And although he had been given his Miranda rights several times over, and signed countless waiver cards, there was still a reasonably good chance none of those confessions would ever be used against him.

A few days later, David Hoffman moved to suppress all California interrogations made with his client as well, despite the fact a similar hearing for Gretzler had not even been scheduled yet. Still, just for good measure, Hoffman added a change of venue request and a motion challenging the constitutionality of the death penalty.

Visibly overwhelmed, Druke replied he would take each under advisement and rule later. He took the time to remind Hoffman of the new trial date of March 18th agreed to almost two weeks earlier.

"I'm not sure who will eventually hear this case, Mr. Hoffman," Druke conceded, knowing full well the 18th wasn't going to happen, "but it appears you will make sure they will have their hands full."

On March 21st, Willie's 30th birthday, they celebrated with yet another court hearing that saw Hoffman and Norgren again joining forces, this time in a change of venue request. On their way into the courtroom, a television cameraman filmed Steelman being escorted in by a deputy armed with a shotgun. Willie liked it, and on que sneered for the camera. But once inside, Norgren protested strongly to Druke about the harm this type of publicity could do to his client. If nothing more, it gave additional credence to their change of venue motion. Norgren was not quite finished, but Hoffman jumped in with both feet, pulling a small stack of newspaper clippings from his briefcase, then tossing them down on his table for effect. "Prejudicial material!" he roared, then threatened to subpoena every last member of the media, along with transcripts of their coverage, for the past six months.

Druke said he understood their concern, but there was nothing he could do about news coverage or the security of the prisoners. That was up to the Sheriff's Department.

"But there's a man standing out in the hall with a loaded shotgun!" Hoffman bellowed. "I ask that this procedure be stopped! I don't know about you, but it makes me extremely nervous, and I can't devote the attention necessary for the defense of my client! I don't like the idea that this guy with a loaded shotgun jumps up every time I walk down the hall. This whole thing is prejudicial to my client!"

Norgren joined in the motion. "Let me just add that it would be extremely prejudicial if the gun went off."

Druke agreed that it was indeed nerve-wracking, but there was little he could do. Dingeldine leaned over to his associate Rich Rollman and in a loud whisper for all to hear, said." After knowing what these two murdering bastards have done, I'd be a lot more nervous if those guards outside *weren't* armed to the teeth."

The final week of March was a full one. In addition to the suppression hearing decision he had to make in Steelman's case, Druke was now faced with scheduling similar hearings for Gretzler, along with change of venue requests, plus possibly the most complicated motion of all, the joint challenge to the death penalty. The judge was confident that if there was a way to drag this out, David Hoffman was the man for the job. So, because of a possible conflict of interest, Druke assigned the death penalty challenge to Judge Birdsall, who would hear all future arguments regarding it. Birdsall's first order of business was to deny Hoffman's motion to put Druke on the stand.

And if that wasn't enough, Robert Norgren offered one more thing for Druke to consider. The standard of insanity had long been the McNaughton Rule, but Norgren argued the definition was too narrow; that it was possible a defendant could be technically sane, but not responsible for his actions. At the end of his brief presentation, Norgren said Willie Steelman was not really insane, he was just a lunatic.

The term had not been used in court since the mid seventeen hundreds, and even then it was in England. Soon after that, the McNaughton definition was established and subsequently used as the yardstick in the western world. But Norgren said that because of Steelman's brain damage, his troubled childhood and years of constant drug use, and despite the fact he knew what he was doing was wrong, he could not control his actions. He was a lunatic, Norgren announced. Plain and simple. Druke sighed and said he would think about it, and then added the request to his forever-growing list.

On March 28th, Dr. Patricia White traveled to Tucson in hopes of seeing Willie. She was so concerned about his well being that she paid for the trip herself, although Norgren had to receive special permission by the court for her visit. Willie was happy to see her, thinking that maybe she had brought her prescription pad along with her. He wasn't that lucky. While in Tucson, White would be prohibited from recommending or prescribing any of the medication Willie was so looking forward to.

13

Tuesday, April 8, 1975.

Like Arizona in the spring, the days were really starting to heat up for Willie and Doug. Although there were no new dates scheduled, the trials were officially separated and each defense attorney was now free to pursue their case in the direction they saw fit. Although after six months of working side by side, it appeared some of David Hoffman's tactics were rubbing off on Robert Norgren.

Initially content to keep the pace moving along, a change had come over the Public Defender as of late. He was arguing more, filing more motions, and using a more combative approach to his defense strategy, all designed to create more commotion in the courtroom. His recent illogical lunacy concept was a good example. And now, his newest idea was to have the court arrange for a massive public opinion poll of the citizens of Tucson to determine if they had knowledge of, or was biased against, what his client was accused of. It was an idea Druke was quick to brush aside, mostly due to its cost. There indeed seemed a new fire in Robert Norgren, and most agreed there was only David Hoffman to thank.

On April 8th, Druke called for oral arguments in conjunction with Norgren's Motion to Suppress. At the hearing, Norgren claimed all interviews in Stockton were obtained in a coercive, and therefore illegal, manner. "We stipulate that statements made on November 10th, and all those after that, were illegal," he argued. "Here we have a defendant under physical and psychological duress. A defendant without sleep, testifying that he wasn't able to hold any food down and suffering from heroin withdrawal, and a situation where he is being interviewed by various police departments over a two day span. The same place, the same people, the same influences are working on him. There is no break between them."

"Isn't seven days quite a break?" Druke asked, referring to the one week prior to Hust's final interview session the following weekend.

"No!" Norgren countered loudly. "Not when you consider Detective Hust prepared himself by reading all the previous statements. Hey, the cat was out of the bag by now! What did Mr. Steelman have to lose?"

Dingeldine countered that Steelman clearly knew his rights. He knew them from the moment he was arrested, and now he was hiding behind them. "Mr. Steelman was no fool," Dingledine shot back. "He had been here before. . .he even recognized Carl Ambrose from previous arrests. . .and Mr. Ambrose offered him his rights, he took advantage of them. Mr. Steelman even told Ambrose that, 'as soon as you look in the car you'll have all the evidence you need anyway.' He knows what is going on in this game. Don't let him fool you!"

The very next day, April 9th, the Voluntariness Hearing for Doug Gretzler got underway. Like the Steelman suppression hearings, these were to determine if the statements obtained were done so in a legal manner and offered willingly by the defendant. But unlike Steelman, these hearings lasted much longer. David Hoffman managed to stretch the hearings out for nearly two weeks. His focus was not that his client hadn't confessed to the crimes – the transcripts prove he had – but that immediately upon his capture, Doug Gretzler became cooperative and openly remorseful.

So it was fitting Hoffman's first witness in the suppression hearing would be Sacramento Detective Hal O'Kane; the man who had arrested Gretzler at the Clunie Hotel. O'Kane was angry about being called as a witness for the defense – he didn't like David Hoffman anymore than he liked Douglas Gretzler – but despite his vigorous protests, O'Kane showed up in Tucson when ordered.

"What was the first thing Mr. Gretzler said to you?" Hoffman asked the reluctant witness.

"He said that he had seen enough killing and he didn't want to see anymore."

"Did Mr. Gretzler resist or struggle in any way?"

"No, he did not."

"And did he then tell you where you could find Willie Steelman?"

"Yes, he did."

"And did you find and arrest Willie Steelman at that location based on the information supplied by Mr. Gretzler?"

"Yes, we did."

That was all Hoffman wanted to hear.

For the next two weeks, regardless of who was on the stand, whether it was Arrelanes, Bunting, Brookshier, or Larry Hust, the attention remained the same. Hoffman portrayed Doug Gretzler as cooperative, even helpful, to the police investigation. It was also during this time, from April 9th through April 28th, when Druke, already busy with these hearings, was juggling the dozens of previous motions still pending in both cases. Norgren had pestered Druke to no end, anxious to know about the court's decision on his lunacy request.

But he was not pleased with Druke's answer. "McNaughton is the test and nothing other than that will be used," he ruled.

Norgren countered he would take his challenge to the Arizona Supreme Court, and being a faithful student of the law, Druke replied he would await their findings with a great deal of interest. Norgren immediately filed another motion to dismiss the charges against his client due to the lack of a speedy trial. Druke denied that as well, while admitting to colleagues the Public Defender was getting more and more like David Hoffman everyday.

It was also during the hearings when Druke brought in a sample jury from the county to see if the news coverage had tarnished the potential jury pool. The Change of Venue motions were based on the concept that neither defendant could receive a fair trial in Pima County due to such biased and overwhelming coverage from the media. Surprisingly, of the twelve sample jurors called, only one had never heard of Steelman or Gretzler, let alone the crimes they were accused of. The one person who seemed to know everything was a self-confessed news junkie who read both daily papers religiously and watched as many newscasts as possible. Most of the others seemed almost ambivalent to the story. They had either remembered the crime, but didn't recognize the names, or visa-versa. If either of the defense teams were expecting to come away with a mandate for moving the trials, they had to be disappointed. It was as about the most lackluster representation of a jury pool one could imagine being assembled.

When a local TV news director heard about the results of the inquiry, his face dropped in dejection. "Guess we aren't doing such a great job after all then, are we?" he bemoaned.

On Monday, May 5th, Judge Druke ruled on Steelman's confession tapes, and his decision came as quite a surprise, because he threw half of them out.

Druke held that all interrogations from the time Steelman was captured until the session on Saturday night, November 10th, when his handwritten note summoned Wagner and Ambrose to his jail, were potentially tainted. In his ruling, Druke stated, that while it was clear the officers repeatedly gave the defendant his rights, Steelman's physical and mental makeup was questionable. But after Steelman instigated the Saturday night session with the note, Druke decided all bets were off and the defendant was responsible for whatever he said from there on out. The statements tossed included all of those taken by Dave Arrelanes and Tucson Detective Larry Bunting.

The decision didn't bother Dave Dingeldine in the slightest. He had insisted from the start he could convict both men without a single confession tape, his case was that strong. Besides, the state was still left with the damaging Wagner/Ambrose transcripts, not to mention the Hust tapes of the following weekend.

Norgren, on the other hand, fumed at Druke's ruling. For it to have been a victory for the defense, all transcripts would have to be excluded. Even with Druke's decision, one that on the surface clearly benefited the defendant, there was still plenty rope left for the prosecution to hang Willie Steelman with.

On May 27th, still attempting to give the defense as much support as possible, Druke granted the Change of Venue request, although moving the trial out of town was going to be easier said than done. First off, there were only a few days before the current court date of June 2nd, and still none of the groundwork was in place. Secondly, summer was fast approaching, and with it vacations for judges and court personnel. After checking several of court calendars for other counties, Druke knew no one had the time for a trial of this magnitude, estimated by some to last up to three months. And even if they could find a courthouse, they still had to worry about the massive security problem and getting the out-of-state witnesses to Arizona.

By now Norgren had had enough of Druke, and motioned the court to find a new judge to hear his case. The request was made with a poisoned pen, for now Norgren was accusing Druke of bias towards him and his client. Visibly angered over the recent suppression ruling on the tapes, he argued there was no way his client could receive a fair trial with Judge Druke on the bench. To further make his point, he included in his motion a handwritten letter from Willie echoing the same complaint, although it was clear who had really drafted the letter. But through his attorney, Willie had made no bones about his dislike for Druke – openly mocking his preppy looks and the smug smile that lingered on the Judge's face through the countless hearings. Nor did he like the idea the man presiding over this case wasn't much older than he was.

The motion did not surprise Druke, and in fact, during the past several months he wondered whether he would be able to sit on both trials anyway. For the record, he claimed his main concern was always in preserving judicial quality and was quick to shrug off any comment about the overwhelming fatigue that would result in one judge hearing both cases. As he saw it, agreeing to split the trials, then presiding over both, could open the court up for countless defense appeals later. However, the motion required Druke to postpone the trial date one week, to June 9th, but before Judge Birdsall (who Druke had assigned to hear the matter) could even schedule a hearing on it, Norgren complained he was having difficulty getting witnesses in from California. Druke rescheduled it another week out to June 16th.

Actually, Norgren's problems in California centered on just one witness; Denise Machell. She had refused to speak with either side during the past year. She was now pregnant, and her doctor wouldn't let her go anywhere. Regardless, Norgren sent a Summons to Appear and a $205 travel check to her on June 2nd, but Denise sent it back with a letter from her physician. Now only willing to speak to her through her parents, Norgren pleaded with them to make it clear to her that she was Willie's only chance at avoiding the gas chamber. If she couldn't help him show the jury the other Willie – the Willie she feel in love with several years earlier – then Norgren announced in very blunt terms that Arizona would most likely carry out its promise to kill him.

On Friday June 6th, the hearing on Druke's removal was held. Dave Dingeldine told Birdsall he didn't care one way or the other, and as long as the judge's decision, regardless of what it was, didn't delay the trial, then the State would not oppose the motion. Judge Birdsall found no prejudice or bias on Druke's part, but granted the request just the same. He instructed both sides to get together over the weekend and agree on a new judge. He gave them until 3 p.m. the following Monday to come up with Druke's replacement.

During the past month, while most of the attention focused on getting Willie Steelman to trial, David Hoffman was equally busy gumming up the legal works for his client. Since he took the case nine months earlier, Hoffman created stacks of paperwork and consumed untold hours of court time making demands. He had requested everything; from travel money to California to interview witnesses, to funds to go to New York to talk to the Gretzler family. He wanted the court to pay to have all the transcripts copied so he could have a second set. He wanted money to pay his secretary for typing. He wanted to be repaid for Gretzler's glasses, along with more money for more medical tests and more studies. His client needed special dental work, he claimed, and he wanted money for that. Hoffman needed his phone bills paid, his Xeroxing costs reimbursed. He wanted the state to pay for an assistant and another psychiatrist. Hoffman even requested funds to find Joanne McPeek so he could interview her himself, claiming that she was the key to his defense.

With each request came written motions and additional court times, arguments and decisions, and often more delays. Most of the requests were turned down simply because they often exceeded the court's jurisdiction. His latest demand was for money to hire an investigator, and once again he motioned Judge Druke to rule on his request immediately. After Hoffman had spent the past several weeks complaining of his dire need, Druke agreed to hear the matter Friday afternoon.

Exasperated, Dingledine once again said the state didn't care one way or the other, as long as the request caused no additional delays. But Hoffman had another court date and was not even present in the courtroom when the hearing got underway. Sitting at the defense table all by himself, Douglas Gretzler was asked to stand up to hear the matter.

"Mr. Gretzler," Druke explained in a fatherly fashion, "since Mr. Hoffman is not here, let me tell you that in a Capital Case the statutes make a provision for you to have an investigator." Druke chose his words carefully and explained to the defendant what he was entitled to. Gretzler listened closely and nodded his head repeatedly, indicating he was following along and understood what was being offered.

"The only thought expressed by Mr. Dingeldine," Druke continued, "which is of course is shared to some extent by the court, is how extensive the investigator might be utilized?"

Doug thought for a moment, then admitted he was in over his head. "Can you run that by me again?" he asked.

Druke did. Then offered him $250 so his lawyer could hire an investigator.

Down the hall, Dingeldine and Norgren were having a tough time agreeing on a new trial judge. The prosecution's first choice was Judge Ruskin Lines of Safford, but Norgren wanted Judge Barry DeRose of Globe. Going down the list, they agreed on very few, with the exception of a judge out of remote Apache County by the name of Dick Greer, and so after a little wrangling, both sides agreed to give him a call.

On that same afternoon, Druke granted Hoffman's Change of Venue motion and it was now apparent that neither case would be heard in Tucson.

With the trials officially severed, and the decision made that Druke would preside over only the Gretzler trial, it was going to be much more difficult to coordinate the two events. There may be two defense counsels and two judges, but there was only one Dave Dingeldine, and he was bound and determined to prosecute both defendants. When Judge Druke set Gretzler's trial date for mid July, Dingledine apologized to the court admiting he couldn't be sure if he was available or not, so Druke left the date open one more time.

Today, for the first time in nine months, there was nothing standing in the way of the trials. All they needed was a courtroom to hold them in, and in Willie's case, a judge to hear it.

14

Wednesday, June 11, 1975 | 11 am.

On Monday, when Judge Birdsall called Apache County looking for Judge Greer, the courthouse secretary in St. Johns could only apologize. The Judge was not in the office, nor was he scheduled to return for several days. Birdsall could only groan and envision yet another delay looming on the horizon. "Do you have any idea where can I find him?" he pleaded.

"He's in Tucson, I believe, doing some overflow work for the Superior Court there."

Birdsall checked the court calendar, and sure enough, the Honorable Richard Greer was holding court just a few doors down the hall When Birdsall caught up with him and asked if he would consider hearing the case, Greer thought it over for all of about ten seconds. "On two conditions, Ben," he replied. "One, we have it up in St. Johns, and two, we wait 'til after the Fourth of July. I promised myself I was gonna take some time off, and by golly, I'm gonna do it!"

Birdsall accepted, and gave his word both sides would as well. They would, of course, keep the location hush-hush for as long as possible to avoid any pretrial publicity, but Birdsall agreed St. Johns would be perfect. "How long you in town, Dick?" he asked after the details had been ironed out.

"Rest of the week, I guess. Why?"

"Wondered if you might care to hear some of the ongoing motions? I could try and put something together before you leave."

Dick Greer rubbed in hands together like a man anxious to get on with it, then flashed Birdsall a big grin. "Why not! Heard this thing has been draggin' on for quite awhile. Might as well jump right in and get my feet wet!"

In an adjoining courtroom, Dingeldine rose to speak. "Now, as for the change of venue, if the judge for Gretzler is Your Honor, then I ask that we select a place and that this case be set for trial within the next week or so."

Hoffman started laughing.

Dingeldine fumed. "I hear a little snickering from Mr. Hoffman, but let me remind the court that we want to get to trial and get this thing going!"

"Are you through?" Hoffman barked, clearing his throat as he lifted himself off his chair. "I did snicker, Your Honor. I'm guilty of that, but we have many motions still under advisement. Important motions, including the motion to suppress and the voluntariness of the statements by my client, not to mention the motion to appoint a psychiatrist and payments to obtain other expert witnesses. And I've yet to see anything on the $250 promised for an investigator. As to the trial date next week? That's absurd! Mr. Dingeldine knows its absurd! I don't mind the court setting a date – I think it should be set – but we are this juncture because of the prosecution motions, not the defense."

Dingeldine was dumbfounded. These months and months of delays were now his fault. He somehow kept his mouth shut, and it was all he could do to simply sit down and shake his head.

Druke somehow managed to wrestle the proceedings away from David Hoffman and got things back on track. First, he had both sides agree to him being the trial judge. Then he got the defense to agree specifically to drop the Motion to Suppress so the trials could be severed and Steelman's case be heard as scheduled. In return, the money for the investigator would be released immediately.

The trial site for the Change of Venue was now back in Hoffman's lap, and he took little time in crossing courthouses of the list. "Maricopa is out. Pima is out. Pinal is out. . ."

"Wait a minute," Druke interrupted, "why is Pinal out?"

"The potential of charges being filed on my client in the Loughran matter there." The tone of Hoffman's voice made it clear he considered Druke's question an ignorant one.

"So, if I decide to go to Pinal, you would object on those grounds?" Druke inquired.

"That's correct."

"Globe wouldn't be a good idea then," Druke offered, ignoring the rebuke. "I can foresee maybe Kingman, Flagstaff, or Prescott. Maybe Yuma. How about Yuma? I've talked to them down there and they. . ."

"Not Yuma," Hoffman protested. "It's awfully hot in Yuma."

If ever there was a Judge who appeared out of his element in Tucson, it was Dick Greer.

Not that it was necessarily all bad, because for all the legal mumbo jumbo and courtroom shenanigans that had gone on for the last nine months, Judge Greer came on like a breath of fresh air. He didn't take kindly to all this pussyfooting around, and he was quick to say so. As he saw it, they all had a job to do; he, the attorneys, everybody. And certainly the citizens of this good state wanted nothing less than a fair trial, at a fair cost, done as quickly as possible. Good Golly! That always seemed downright reasonable to him, and how a judge could lose control of any proceedings, like some before him had, was always a mystery to the man from Apache County.

Judge Greer understood one thing very well, however, and that was the magnitude of the prosecution's case. So while both sides would have their day in his courtroom, Greer made sure the defendant would have a few extra bones thrown their way. He would force, beyond any shadow of a doubt, the prosecution prove their allegations. That was the way he did it up north in St. Johns and that's the way he would do it in Tucson. Made no never mind where he was, justice was justice and fair was fair.

So on Friday morning, June 13th, after introducing himself to both David Dingeldine and Robert Norgren, Greer firmly laid out the ground rules. The trial in the matter of The State of Arizona vs. Willie Luther Steelman would be held in the Apache County Courthouse in St. Johns. The proceedings would begin promptly at 9 a.m. Monday, July 7th. All pending pretrial motions would be heard at that time, while the rest of the day would be set aside to clear up any of those lingering details. Tuesday and Wednesday were for jury selection, and the prosecution should have their first witness ready to go no later than Thursday morning, the 10th. Greer said he figured the whole trial at three weeks, tops. If either side thought about dragging its feet and wasting everyone's time, well, then they could do it in the slow paced splendor of St. Johns, Arizona, population 3,000, where no restaurant would dare call itself fancy, and what passed as nightlife started and ended when the sun went down.

"Any questions?" he smiled.

Good. Judge Greer clasped his hands and said how much he was looking forward to hearing the case. He thanked both sides and excused himself. He took the next few hours to review what had transpired to this point, especially the many pretrial motions and delays. He acquainted himself with the actual murders as well as the charges brought on by them. He poured over the seemingly endless minute entries of the past nine months and the motion after motion presented in countless Pima County courtrooms. It all seemed such a huge waste of time, he thought, this should have been tried and over with a long time ago.

Still, he called his court clerk in St. Johns and told her what was up. Make the necessary arrangements, Greer instructed, and get everyone ready for company. Call Sheriff Lee and let him know about his new guest staying in his jail. Make sure to get a hold of Edgar over at the Trail Rider Motel and tell him to set aside a few rooms. And while you're at it, clear my calendar for the next two weeks, because I'm going on vacation.

Oh yes. One last thing, the judge added, get a jury pool together. I want you to call at least sixty people. Get as many minorities as you can. Find a few black folks, if that's possible. Call in as many younger folks in we can get. I want as wide a variety of people as we can put together, he said. Because this Steelman fella, Greer told her, was going to need all the help he could get.

On June 19th, Robert Norgren flew to Stockton to videotape Denise Machell. Her recorded testimony would be all he could use at the upcoming trial. It was clear Ms. Machell was a reluctant witness, so Dingeldine decided not to bother with the trip and simply asked Peter Saiers to represent Pima County at the session. He didn't even have any specific questions for Saiers to ask, just that he sit there and listen.

Saiers called him when it was over and reported it was pretty much cut and dried. He promised there would be no surprises for the prosecution when the taped was played. "There were no tears," he informed counsel, "she appeared real anxious to get this over with and out of there as quickly as possible."

There had always been a security concern for the both defendants while being housed at the Pima Jail. The problem was discussed frequently, but nothing was ever resolved. The big hitch was, that while all the legal maneuverings were taking place, both prisoners needed to be kept close by just so they could show up in court on what was now a regular basis.

Willie's trial was already scheduled. There would be no reason for him to return to court in Tucson, but they didn't really want to move him until they sent him to St. Johns in a couple of weeks. The risk of doing so outweighed the benefits, so it was decided to let him sit and wait while they upped the security around him.

There were still a few lingering motions for Judge Druke to decide, but for all practical purposes, Gretzler was a done deal as well. Although his trial was still a ways off, and despite his mild demeanor, he was still a security risk while at Pima, so at the request of the State, and despite the boisterous objection from David Hoffman, Druke transferred Doug Gretzler to the Santa Cruz County Jail facility near the Mexican border and about an hour south of Tucson. It was regarded as a more secure place for a prisoner of his repute, and there would be no way he and his partner could cook up any grand plans of freedom if they were separated.

With due caution however, and just to be safe from the long arm of Maricopa County, Druke ordered Gretzler not be released to anyone other than Pima County officials. No one had forgotten the episode of the previous September. They had come this far. Courtrooms had been selected. Judges were picked. Trials were set. Pima was not about to let it all slip away.

Not after all this.

15

Sunday, July 6, 1975.

The mid-afternoon winds of summer enter St. Johns from the south and hug the rolling terrain of Arizona's eastern high country, picking up specks of earth and bits of grass as it builds momentum, only to drop them as it swirls through town. The strong gusts pull behind them tall gray clouds that will soon blanket the town. As the long days of July burn away, the clouds signal the start of the monsoon season, and each day, like clockwork, they bring heavy rain from the Gulf.

But it had been a long dry July 4th weekend, and like most Sundays in St. Johns, a quiet one as well. Independence Day festivities had been held Friday night and sparkler wires and strings of crepe paper still littered the town square, while charcoal spots could be seen on the random patches of concrete; places where Blackcats and Worms burned during the celebration.

Sundays were strictly for church and family. During the lazy afternoons following morning service, big dinners were planned, cooked, and consumed, all of which proceeded contented catnaps, which lasted until the townspeople returned for evening worship. Even the stores in town were locked up tight on Sunday. All except for the Circle K, and because of that, it was the center of all activity in St. Johns.

So besides the Apache County Sheriff and his Chief Deputy, there was no one else waiting at the small airport for the arrival. Not even the reporter for the *White Mountain Independent* bothered to show. And although the stringers for the Tucson and Phoenix dailies living in nearby Show Low could sell their words for a few cents each, none considered the event worth the trouble. Cost more in gas just to get there, they figured, so they too stayed home and struggled with the continuing urge to doze off in the numbing quiet of another sluggish Sunday afternoon in St. Johns.

So Willie crept in unnoticed, just as he had done in so many other towns before. This time he was flown in, crowded into a small Cessna accompanied by two deputies and the pilot, Jack Bowman. Willie remained cuffed and shackled, but that did not prevent him from talking, which he did a lot of during the flight from Tucson. He tumbled out of the plane and squinted into the afternoon glare, unable to move his hands up to shield his eyes.

Sheriff C. Arthur Lee and his Deputy Bob Gilchrist watched the plane touch down, then taxi back towards the airport office. Lee had grown up on the land surrounding St. Johns, but just as many young people do, he left for the lure of a better job in a bigger town. However, the Lee name was a popular one back home, so when a friend told him he could be the next Apache County Sheriff if he wanted, Lee returned and politicked for the position. He had been Sheriff for only a couple of years by the time Willie arrived.

Lee was a descendant of one of the founders of the large local Mormon contingent, yet he was less than perfect in practicing his faith. It was not surprising to spot him coming out of the Circle K sporting a six-pack, nor did he ever go out of his way to hide his nicotine habit. He decided early on there was no reason to try and fool anybody about his shortcomings, and that included Mrs. Lee, who, like most women in town, had enough LDS enthusiasm for the both of them.

Lee had returned earlier in the week from an FBI training academy in Virginia and was just starting to get settled back into the routine. It had been a long, difficult course – nearly three months – and the locals were proud to be able to send him. So the first he was asked to do when he got back was to smile for the camera and hold up his diploma for all to see, his picture was on the front page of Friday's *White Mountain Independent*. "I feel the course was very helpful in making me a better law enforcement officer," he was quoted, "and I plan on using what I learned to improve the department in the future."

"What do you want me to call you?" Lee asked as he sized up the new arrival.

"You can call me Willie."

"Fine. Then Willie it is."

The trip from the airport to the county jail was no more than five minutes, and on the way, Lee laid out the ground rules. He had nothing against Steelman. Legally speaking, he was nothing more than another guest in his town.

"Okay, now Willie, this is how things work around here. You see, I'm responsible for the safety of the town and of my staff. Now there's three roads into St. Johns, and three roads out. Not too many places you could go where we couldn't find you. Understand?"

Willie indicated he did. Lee glanced back in the rearview to be sure.

"Now, we're not gonna mistreat you – I can promise you that – but you try and escape, or act up in any manner that threatens my town, well then. . .we'll kill you."

Willie didn't even blink. "That's fine by me," he shot back.

It had long been rumored that the jail cell at the Apache County Courthouse had originally come from the old territorial prison down in Yuma. The story was told the notorious Clanton Boys had even stayed there, as had Butch Cassidy, years before he met a kid named Sundance. But regardless of who had been behind its bars, none found it especially inviting. For a hundred years prisoners simply referred to it as The Black Hole.

But this cell was now on the far end of the courthouse and therefore anyone housed there would have to be escorted through the offices and hallways of the busy county office building in order to get to the courtroom upstairs. It was agreed that was probably stretching their security a bit, despite Lee's assurances there was little an escapee could do, or places he could go, even if he did manage to break free. Still, Lee needed an alternate plan.

On the other side of the courthouse, at the base of the stairs, was a small, somewhat newer jail containing four separate cells. It was here where juvenile offenders, or on an even rarer occasion, a female prisoner was held. At the far end of the cellblock was an open shower and just enough room for guards to conduct the required twice-daily searches. From the cell it was only a few steps to the stairs leading up to Judge Greer's courtroom on the second floor. This is where Willie would be housed while in St. Johns.

Dave Dingledine, his assistant Rich Rollman, and an investigator from the County Attorney's office, Rex Angeli, pulled into town on Saturday in Angeli's huge motorhome, loaded down with boxes of files and evidence. For the past several years, Angeli had been Dingledine's right hand man, although Rex often joked that he was little more than "Ding's Flunky". While he never lost the slow comfortable drawl he had dragged along with him from his native Texas, he did manage to lose his first job with the Tucson Police Department when a disability forced him to an unwanted desk position. Fed up with sitting, one afternoon he walked down the street and caught on with the County Attorney, where it didn't take him long to realize a Chief Investigator's job was a lot easier than chasing bad guys, and a helluva lot safer too.

Always in motion, Angeli was forever in search of a golf partner, a poker game, or the lure of a good fishing hole, so it was he who first suggested they bring his RV, just in case any of the aforementioned opportunities presented themselves. Plus, with the staggering amount of paperwork, office supplies and court documents necessary to prosecute this case, Dave figured they were going to need a U-Haul anyway to get it all to St. Johns. So the motorhome it was, giving Rex all the more ammunition to talk Dave into getting away sometime during to trial for a little fishing and exploring. They pulled out of Tucson early Saturday morning, heading towards the eastern edge of Arizona in what Angeli affectionately referred to as "The Rolling File Cabinet".

Larry Hust drove up Sunday, and with the exception of Greer who lived in town, and Robert Norgren, who made plans to stay a relative's cabin in Pinetop, everyone else moved into the Trail Rider. With Dave's personal secretary now in town, his office, and the rooms set aside for the Hust, Angeli, Rich Rollman, and the state witnesses, the group took up most of the lower floor of the motel. The

Trail Rider was one of only two motels in town large enough to accommodate the group and their extended stay. This was an unexpected financial bonanza for the owner, Edgar Udall, for July in St. Johns was typically very quiet.

The motel was a standard two-story affair built around a small parking lot. Out front, a tidy coffee shop served motel guests or the rare traveler passing through town on Highway 61. There were only eight stools at the counter and barely enough room for the four booths snuggled up against the windowed wall overlooking the parking lot. The morning sun poured through the glass so intensely that by seven am the waitress had to drop the venetians to prevent blinding the customers.

The motel office was little more than a chest high counter in the lobby. Several feet away, bi-fold doors opened to a seldom-used meeting room. Around the corner, an unmarked door led to a tiny bar. The mostly Mormon contingent in town did not frequent the lounge, or at least not openly, so it was indeed a hideaway, despite a small, lighted sign outside advertising 'cocktails'. Tucked away below the motel office and restaurant was a large basement. It too was seldom used, except each Wednesday night when it became the home of the only poker game town.

Late Sunday night, Robert Norgren drove into town to see how his client was holding up. Steelman was having his dinner; a sandwich from the Trail Rider restaurant, and wasn't in much a mood to talk, especially to his attorney, so Norgren left after staying only a few minutes. It was nearly an hour back to Pinetop, and he used the time to contemplate the pending trial.

There was no reason at this point to feel he could actually win anything here, so averting a death sentence was all he could hope for, because he had no illusions of his client being found not guilty. He didn't know where to begin, actually. The problem was, he decided, that he really didn't understand Willie. He most certainly didn't trust him. Couldn't really say he believed him either. Willie never let him in to his world, so Norgren never managed to get close enough to find even one single redeeming feature worth saving, even though that was the very thing his job required of him.

He was a human being, Norgren acknowledged, which seemed the sum of his argument. He believed no government should kill its citizens, regardless of what crimes they had committed. And you most certainly don't kill the mentally ill, and there was no question in Norgren's mind Willie Steelman was a sick man.

He was also frightening, and Norgren did not hide his fear of him. Yes, Willie had lived a terrible life and admittedly much of it was self-inflicted, but that was not the point. Norgren believed Willie Steelman should not be killed because of what or who he had become, and he was convinced Willie was not mentally responsible for what he had done.

So Norgren did not know where to turn, and he struggled with what he would tell the jury about his client. The longest of odds told him he might be able to convince them into sparing Willie's life. So this became his primary goal; merely to keep the State of Arizona from killing him.

But that meant keeping him alive. And the point could be argued, what the hell for?

On Monday morning, July 7th, the trial of Willie Steelman began. Judge Greer flipped through the papers in front of him, then turned his attention to Robert Norgren. "The only other matter, I understand," he said, "is pertaining to your defense of lunacy. Correct?"

"Yes, Your Honor," Norgren replied. He didn't really expect Greer to embrace the concept – no one else had – and while nowhere in the history of Arizona could there be found a case where lunacy had ever been used as a defense, he continued just the same. "We have filed extensive briefs that we presented in the court's file on the issue of lunacy. This issue was presented to Judge Druke. We have a psychiatrist, Doctor Hoogerbeets, who testified at the evidentiary hearing. Doctor Hoogerbeets stated that he fit within the definition. . .that Steelman was a lunatic."

Greer nodded as Norgren spoke, but the squint in his eye showed he was having a difficult time buying into the idea. But Norgren, and Hoogerbeets if you pressed him, were convinced a true distinction could be made between the two. Conversely, Dingledine and his associates at the County Attorney's office were adamant in their belief insanity and lunacy were interchangeable.

Norgren was prepared to prove otherwise. After the Arizona Supreme Court ruled not to allow lunacy as a defense, Norgren appealed, arguing the State had now violated Steelman's constitutional rights under the Fifth and Fourteenth Amendments. He filed a motion in Federal Court hoping to have them review the constitutionality of Arizona's decision.

But his motion was denied there as well. They suggested Norgren continue with a regular trial, and if his client was convicted, then he could use the standard avenues of appeal.

"Certainly, upon trial before the judge now assigned to try the case," they concurred, *"the plaintiff can offer the lunacy defense; and the judge may find it available and submit it to a jury. If the new trial judge rules against the plaintiff on the issue, the plaintiff has the right to appeal to the Supreme Court of Arizona."*

So Robert Norgren proceeded only on the slim notion, that while he could not find a law to base his motion upon, there was also no law on the books to say it could not be used. The decision whether or not to allow lunacy now rested fully with Judge Greer.

"So, what is lunacy?" Greer asked. "What's the definition?"

Norgren scrambled for his notes, taken back by Greer's quick query. "Ah. . . it is a condition of the mind. . .I'll get the exact definition from Black's Law Dictionary. . .and read it. . .Your Honor. . .if I can have a minute. . ."

While he waited, Greer repeated what so many others before him had admitted. "This is the first time I ever heard the defense of lunacy being raised."

Norgren began reading directly from the book, but stopped himself. "Your Honor, the definition between lunacy and McNaughton insanity is that a person could be in a state where they could control their acts, but could be mildly insane, and yet know what they were doing. Whereas a lunatic, although he may be aware of what he was doing, would be unable to control his acts."

Norgren realized his analogy was a poor one, and Rich Rollman rose to offer his challenge. "I would like to respond briefly to that, Your Honor. I have a little problem with this because there is a separation of one hundred and twenty five years here. The Owen Case that Mr. Norgren has referred to earlier is not a criminal case at all. It's about an eighty four year old woman – an extremely ill woman – and her capacity to enter into a contract. Never once has Mr. Norgren cited a case as to lunacy itself."

Rollman was assisting Dingledine for exactly this occasion. As a recent law graduate, he was much more familiar with case law than was Dingledine, who during the trial would look to Rollman whenever there was legal research required. "Now, there may be a defense though," he continued sarcastically. "One of the definitions of a lunatic is an insane person who is affected by the moon. But, he is not always insane. Only when the moon is in a certain position. . ."

Greer took note of his horseplay and interrupted. "Are you suggesting to me counselor. . ."

Rollman apologized. "Just let me point out, the definition of lunacy, and of insanity, is changing throughout the times." He then quoted from several legal textbooks, some dating back into the mid 1700's, showing how madmen were locked up at one time, later sent to asylums, and even later treated in hospitals.

He summed up his argument, as if exasperated by the entire idea. "We ought to treat the test of lunacy as being nothing different than the test of insanity. Call it what you want. This was brought up to Judge Druke, then through a special action to the Court of Appeals, and it was denied. The Supreme Court of the State of Arizona refused to take jurisdiction. Then it went over into Federal Court. Mr. Norgren has had an adequate hearing on this point, and everyone has rejected his argument."

But Norgren disagreed. "Mr. Rollman has not cited a single case to state where the test for lunacy should be the test for McNaughton insanity! He has made the inference, Your Honor, that lunacy is the same as insanity. I can call ten psychiatrists and they will all testify that Mr. Steelman was, and is, insane! There is no question about that. There were three psychiatrists appointed by the court; Dr. Peale, Dr. Marshall Jones, and Dr. Hoogerbeets, who will say Steelman is insane. Now, if insanity is synonymous with lunacy, then Steelman is also a lunatic."

This had gone on too long, so Greer put an end to it. "All right, I'll read your memorandum carefully. Now, I think there were some items recently filed by the state."

Later that afternoon, Greer rejected the lunacy defense as proposed by Robert Norgren, again citing the McNaughton Rule of 1840, a ruling that simply stated that it must be proved that a person did not know right from wrong, or realize the consequences of his action. Willie Steelman might be a lot of things, but he was not a lunatic.

Norgren had filed fifteen additional motions before Judge Druke prior to the case being assigned to Greer, and many of them pertained to the constitutionality of the death penalty. Those discussed in the hearings Monday morning included suppression of statements made by Steelman in California. Norgren reminded

Greer that Druke had already tossed half of them, and because the record showed the second batch of statements were tainted by the first, they all should be suppressed. But Greer disagreed and allowed the remaining statements to be admitted.

Norgren also sought to have many additional crime photos removed. There were 200 pictures of the Sandberg apartment, and Dingledine voluntarily agreed to remove all but fifty. Greer went along with Norgren and agreed to review the remaining photos, suggesting that between the three of them they should by able to come to some agreement on which ones the jury would be allowed to see.

"Now, do you think, Mr. Norgren, that this court can be assured there will be no attempt made to escape during this trial?"

He had good reason to be concerned. Just this morning, two men from the Navajo reservation came to Greer and told him of a plan they had heard about to get the prisoner out of jail. The men were brothers, and coincidently both had received jury summons. They said they had been approached by someone at a motel east of Chambers, about an hour north of St. Johns, who invited them to join in a plan to 'get Steelman'.

Greer told Lee to look into it, which of course he did, but he found no one willing to talk. Lee ultimately decided it probably wasn't so much an attempt to get Steelman out of jail, as it was some crackpot trying to get a little attention. Nothing more was ever heard about the alleged scheme. On the other hand, if Judge Greer was concerned of possible jury tampering, he never let on. One of the two men who came to him with the story would be selected to sit on the jury. He would not only hear the case, but eventually pass judgment on Willie Steelman as well.

Greer also had strong feelings about defendants being chained up in his courtroom, especially in front of a jury. Regardless of what he was accused of, Greer wanted to give the appearance of an innocent man on trial. He asked Norgren once more to assure him his client wasn't going anywhere.

"Your Honor," Norgren replied, "Mr. Steelman had been in custody since 1973 and I know of no escape attempts during that time." Apparently the records of Duell Vocational Institute in California had not been made accessible to him.

"All right," Greer announced, "I've thought a good deal on this. I will not require manacles unless there is some indication made by the defendant that he is intending to escape. I will ask the Sheriff's Office to bring the defendant in handcuffed from jail in the morning at nine and have the handcuffs removed and him seated at the counsel table before the jury arrives. However, should he create a disturbance in any way during this trial, I will conduct this trial in the defendant's absence."

Ultimately, the reason they all were in St. Johns in the first place was in the hopes of outrunning the publicity that had surrounded the case in Tucson. Norgren still had his doubts and expressed his concern to Greer. "There has been extensive publicity, and with the size of this town – I understand which is about two thousand people – there could be saturation by the TV stations from Tucson that are received here. Therefore we ask to individually voir dire the jury."

Greer seemed anxious to educate the newcomer to his hometown. "I'll be candid with you, Mr. Norgren. I know that you know nothing about St. Johns, but you will find the community north of us – for which perhaps half of our jury will be drawn – doesn't even know where Tucson is."

Greer wanted Norgren to understand he would have no problem getting an unbiased jury. The vast area of Apache County north of town was almost entirely Navajo reservation and influenced substantially more by New Mexico than Arizona. People there were likely to receive their newspapers and television from Gallup, and were seldom served by the Arizona media.

"It is about that remote from Arizona," Greer added.

He was right. Of the fifty-four people scheduled to appear for jury selection the following morning, only thirteen had ever heard the name Willie Steelman.

16

Tuesday, July 8, 1975 | 10 am.

Apache County borders not only New Mexico, but Utah and Colorado as well. On its extreme northeast edge is Four Corners; the only place in the U.S. where four states join together. It is also home to the massive Navajo Nation, an area so large it totally surrounds the very sizable Hopi Indian reservation. Although only forty to fifty miles wide in some places, the county is over two hundred miles long, and therefore, one of Arizona's largest. But it is also one of the least populated. And because it contains no city of any size, and a large portion of its inhabitants are Indian, Greer was right; it is about as far away from Arizona as you can get and not leave the state.

Greer knew this, of course, so he was confident they would have little trouble finding an unbiased jury. In fact, he was so sure there had been no pretrial publicity in St. Johns, he warned both sides they would probably need to tell potential jurors a little about the case just to explain why they were being dragged into court in the middle of summer.

He also knew what a tremendous hardship he was about to create for most of them. These were just plain folk. Many of them downright poor. Not so much uneducated, but simply uninterested. And maybe a bit uncertain as to why something that happened almost two years earlier had anything to do with them. Their main concern each day was simply the struggle of making a living, holding on to their meager job, running their small business, and watching over their families.

The first concern for Greer was distance. For many, the trip to St. Johns would be a troubling daily ordeal. Jury summons were mailed to residents in remote hamlets such as Ganado, Fort Defiance and Window Rock; some spots over a hundred miles from the courthouse. And while he knew he could assemble an impartial jury, he also knew it would consist of the very people least financially able to serve on it.

However, by nine am Tuesday morning, all fifty-four jurors had arrived as instructed, gathering at the old courthouse, waiting patiently for their name to be called.

"Ladies and gentlemen," Greer began. "All of you have been handed a questionnaire and have filled it out, I assume. We are now going to have you come into the jury room where we will ask each of you a few additional questions."

In that room, located at the rear of the courtroom, Greer, both counsels and their assistants, along with Steelman and his guards, all waited for names to be announced. Then, one by one, each prospective juror entered the room with a grand welcome from Judge Greer. "Come on down!" came the invitation. "Come on down and sit in the hot seat!"

And they did. Perhaps a bit apprehensive at first, but it wasn't long before he had made them feel a little more comfortable, and a lot more important. But there were still many who balked.

"I got a sore throat."

Greer looked concerned. "How long you had it?"

"Since yesterday."

"Feel better today?"

"No. Think its strept throat."

"Think you'll feel better tomorrow?"

"No. Don't think I can serve."

If Greer thought the elderly gentleman was trying to pull a fast one, he wasn't letting on. "Well, Mr. Burnside, it doesn't sound too good. I'm going to have you go back out there with the others and wait for us. I'm not sure I can let you go just yet. You let me see what I can do."

And so the process went. For nearly two hours Judge Greer and the others listened. A young man named Hubert Morris came in and sat down in front of the judge.

"How old are you, Hubert?"

"Nineteen."

"What did you hear about this case, Hubert?"

"Well, just what was on TV."

Greer asked how he felt about what he had heard and Morris replied he had already tried the case. "In my class the teacher usually brings in a newspaper article and we discuss it. You know, debate it."

"This was in the Mormon Church?" Greer quizzed.

"Yes."

"And you said you formed an opinion from that class and you lean towards guilty because the defendant fleeing from Arizona."

Morris sounded apologetic. "Yes sir. Well, we reasoned it – it was ten boys on my committee – and we checked to see how we were thinking about it and we kind of like took a little vote."

"You took a vote?"

"The whole body did."

"In your voting, do you have a feeling that the defendant is probably guilty?"

"I would say probably. I don't know. I'm confused."

Greer smiled. "Well Hubert, I don't know what will happen. I think you would make a good juror. I hope you can join us. It's going to be a fascinating case if you get to hear it."

Hubert Morris would not be selected.

However, in the first two hours Greer narrowed the list of fifty-four down to thirty-six, but he excused no one and added a warning about discussing the morning's activities. There were only a couple of lunch counters in St. Johns and he knew the subject was certain to come up. He told them to return by one thirty.

"Ladies and gentlemen of the jury," he began as they reassembled in the early afternoon, "we have now approached the phase of the trial where the court is going to ask you a series of questions to determine if you can sit as a fair and impartial juror. Now I hope you understand that these questions are not intended to embarrass you or pry into your personal affairs."

Greer knew these were a proud group of people and he had no intention of humiliating them by what their past might reveal. He realized most of the excuses would be monetary ones. And yet there were a few, and Greer knew in advance which ones, who carried around secrets about themselves and their families; secrets they would not divulge to just any stranger. Greer had briefed both Norgren and Dingledine about his idea prior to the start of the afternoon session. His plan was to invite any of the potential jurors into the privacy of his chambers where they could explain their reasons for not wanting to be a part of the trial.

"The court will now call the names of thirty six prospective jurors," Greer began. "Ladies and gentlemen, when your name is called, please come forward and be seated up here as the bailiff will instruct you. We'll fill up the jury box, then start seating yourselves along the front rows right in front of me."

Once the names were called, and the balance excused, Greer once again turned and addressed those who remained. "Now, any of you have anything to tell me? Any special problem you have sitting on this jury? Any relative who has been charged with a crime? Any of you been charged, or any member of your family, or friends, or relatives been charged or convicted of a crime? We'd like to know."

Greer paused, and then took a moment to scan the group. "Please," he offered, "please feel free to come in and talk to me."

With that, he rose from his bench and walked into his office chambers behind him. Neither Dingledine or Norgren had been invited in, and Greer make special note of that. "There are no counsel present," he stated for the record. "We are in chambers and out of the presence of the jury.

It took a few minutes, but Gladys Miller was the first to enter and got right to the point. "You know Judge, this would be a real hardship on my employees. I'm the cashier at the Chieftan Cafe and today you brought me, my relief cashier, plus my head cook! There was no one left in there!"

Greer leaned back in his chair and laughed. "Your boss called me three times yesterday to try and get me not to take all three of you! I'll see what I can do," he promised. "You know the county has spent about ten thousand dollars getting this case ready to go, and we've got to have a trial. And we have to have a jury. But let me see what I can do."

More than a dozen others walked into Judge Greer's chambers that afternoon, if nothing more than to just talk. Some had a good excuse. Others just needed to get something off their chest.

"I came to tell you that my husband is unemployed, and had been for a month now."

The woman who belonged to the tiny voice was cautious, hesitant; uncertain what she was getting herself into. "He can't work, and the only way we have of supportin' our family is me. And I don't have any transportation." She shook her head to set the record straight, "Well, we got an old Chevy, but I don't think it'll make it here ev'ryday."

"You know, I could have a deputy bring you," Greer offered, but even that didn't seem to make any difference. "Or, if you came in your own vehicle, we'll pay you mileage."

The woman perked up. "Oh? How much is that?"

"Twenty cents a mile, one way." Greer replied. "Now from Chambers that's twelve dollars for mileage and twelve dollars a day for being a juror. "That twenty four dollars a day!"

The woman's face brightened. "Well, I'm better off here than I am for the sixteen dollars a day over there!"

"And," Greer pointed out, "you get all the water you want to drink!" They laughed, but down deep Greer knew how difficult it would be for her to serve, she being one of the other employees at the Chieftan. Plus the distance from her home to the courthouse was one hundred miles round trip, and she had no place in St. Johns to stay. "Listen, I'll try and let you off if I can. I promise. And I want to thank you for coming down today."

When Greer was finished he called both Norgren and Dingledine in to discuss what had gone on without them.

"Let me tell you what I've learned," he began. "If I had brought you two in I don't think the jurors would have been fair and open with me. Now Mr. Benallie told me he had a nephew charged with voluntary manslaughter. Mrs. Bloomfield told me about her nephew down in Florence on a second-degree murder charge. Mrs. Sells says her uncle was charged with murdering a policeman. Mr. Lincoln, well, he says he was an alcoholic at one time. Got two brothers who were assaulted, which is typical of an Indian who drinks. But Mr. Lincoln is a fine man and would make a good juror.

"Well, that's it," Greer announced, sitting back in his chair, visibly proud of his work. "That's the extent of what I know."

Norgren was the first to compliment him. "I've never seen that done before."

"Oh I've used it several times," the judge said, brushing aside the flattery. "Usually pick up a whole lot of surprises. Most just want some counseling though. Someone to talk to."

By six o'clock Greer had his jury. He announced the sixteen names, taking extra time to personally thank all of those who were not chosen. Finally, he remembered the older gentleman still waiting in the hall, the one who had been ailing earlier that morning. "By the way, Mr. Burnside, I'm concerned about your throat. I want you to see a doctor."

Wednesday morning, July 9th, Robert Norgren stayed self-sequestered in the cabin at Pinetop, putting the finishing touches on his opening statement, while Dave Dingledine stayed at the motel awaiting the arrival of his first witness. When Jack Bowman's Cessna landed with Vince Armstrong aboard, Larry Hust was waiting. He, along with several others at Tucson P.D., had tried to warn the County Attorney's Office about their key witness's discrepancies surrounding his version of what happened that Saturday in November. Armstrong had changed his story more than once that day, and the police were suspicious from that point on. Hust encouraged Dingledine to spend as much time as he could with Armstrong to get his story straight before putting him on the stand.

Jack Bowman was a very busy man Wednesday. In addition to Armstrong, he also piloted Donald Scott and James Nelson into St. Johns for their testimony tomorrow morning as well. All three would be asked to identify Willie Steelman and recall their role in the activities of November 3rd. A Dessurealt hearing to determine the validity of their identification was scheduled before the jury was seated, and if Judge Greer decided their recollection of the events of that day met the court's criteria, they would then be allowed to tell their story in front of the jury. Bouncing nonstop between the three witnesses, Dingledine and Rich Rollman stayed quite busy on Wednesday. The Trail Rider was filling up fast and owner Edgar Udall scrambled around making sure everyone was being taken care of.

It was Judge Greer himself who introduced Rex Angeli to the late night poker games in the Trail Rider basement. Every Wednesday night, for about as long as any of them could remember, some of the locals got together, and after awhile the poker faces got a bit stale – even among these long time friends – so naturally they were always anxious to welcome a newcomer, especially one who came at the recommendation of Dick Greer. Enter Rex Angeli.

Three bucks would get you a place at the table and a cold sandwich from the kitchen upstairs. The games always started out low key and friendly, but before long the pot would rise, and usually tempers along with it. Word was more than one man lost a week's wages on one of those Wednesday nights.

So while Dingledine and the others plotted their strategy upstairs, Rex spent his evening playing cards. He decided early on to simply pace himself, feeling it would not be neighborly to act overly aggressive. But even with this self-restraint, he walked out that first night a few dollars ahead, a sure fire guarantee he would be invited back next week. Still. everyone at the table agreed he was a damn sight better poker player than Dick Greer, and a lot more willing to part with his money than the good judge.

Greer once turned the tables on a reporter who had come to town to write a story about him. The judge asked if he had been out to the St. Johns' cemetery yet, and while he was only interested in a brief sketch of the judge's background, the writer had done his homework and replied that indeed he had.

Greer was noticeably pleased. "That's my upbringing buried up there," he boasted. "The entire Greer family is in that plot."

A hundred years earlier, when the Greer family came to the untamed Arizona Territory, they became some of the first Mormons to settle the area just north of present day St. Johns. Richard Greer, whom the judge would be named for two generations later, was a boy, barely six years of age when he arrived with his parents and brothers. The settlement, at least until the Mormons came on the scene, was almost entirely Mexican sheepherders, and yet, despite their differences, the two sides managed to get along without too much trouble during those first few years. It was, however, as history records, a very uneasy peace.

The small river north of the settlement was called "El Vadito", or Little Crossing, and even later still, The Little Colorado. After years of being flooded out, the growing Mormon contingent decided to move to higher ground, and closer into the area held by the Mexicans, who by now were feeling mighty crowded in such wide open spaces. For years, June 24th was the day the Mexican community celebrated as San Juan's Day, in honor of their patron saint. On that day in 1882, as the Mexican's held their festivities, Richard's older brother, Nat, and several others from their clan, rode into town to see what all the ruckus was about. Whether they had mischief on their minds can only be speculated.

It was well known, however, that the Greer family had not been popular with the Mexican population ever since the day the Greers tracked down and 'marked' a Mexican who they claimed stole one of their horses. So when Richard and family showed its face that day, they were ambushed and chased to an adobe outside of town where they remained pinned down by gunfire.

Colorful reports tell of the ensuing gunfight. 'A thousand shots had been fired,' the pulp westerns exclaimed, before the area marshal finally convinced the Greer Boys to surrender, promising to sort this whole mess out before someone got killed. They agreed, and were being led to safety when a shot fired from the Mexican stronghold killed one of the volunteer peacemakers accompanying the marshal. Once again the Greers were in danger and the Mexicans threatened to lynch all of them. Another gunfight erupted, and this time several men were killed. Again, somehow the marshal managed to whisk the remaining Greers to safety, taking them all the way to Prescott, where they eventually stood trial for several minor offenses, and received a light punishment for their actions.

Few history books give the names of the men killed that day. But the Greer family remembered, because it was a member of their family who lost his life in that brief battle. His name was Jim Vaughn, and technically he was not a blood relative at all.

"It's a little embarrassing to repeat it now," Judge Greer apologized, "but back then they called him 'Nigger Jim'. He was a black man, but I guess my family figured he was as much a brother as any of the rest of them because they buried him right there in the family plot at St. Johns."

Years later, Judge Greer's father, also named Richard, was born in St. Johns, as was his son several decades following. Senior Greer was first a lawyer, and then went on to serve in the Arizona State Senate. It was fully expected his son would follow in his footsteps of civil service. But as a youngster, Richard worked on the family's cattle ranch. "We had a little place outside of St Johns," he shrugged. "Wasn't nearly as big as the neighbor's, only 'bout twelve thousand acres or so."

The Greers, along with the Udalls, were two of the most prominent families in the county, and Dick became good friends with Udall brothers, Morris and Stewart. Even after graduating high school together, they remained close while attending the University of Arizona's law school in Tucson. In 1955, just barely thirty-two years old, Richard Greer became an Apache County judge. Stewart Udall had already been elected to Congress the year before, and six years later, President Kennedy appointed him Secretary of the Interior. His younger brother Mo would take his place in Congress, and would run for the Presidency himself years later.

"There's a deep soul in St. Johns," Judge Greer reasoned, as he told the reporter about life growing up there. "And there's a strong Mormon belief in achieving your highest goal. I guess that's why such a small place like this has so many good people. Simple people, sure, but hard-working, honest people just the same. You know, we all went to the littlest bitty high school, and none of us were born with silver spoons in our mouths, but I bet ninety percent of all the graduates there went on to college."

So Judge Greer knew in his heart that if Willie Steelman were to ever have a fair hearing for his crimes, it would be in his hometown. He had gone to considerable lengths to gather a wide cross section of potential jurors, going so far as to instruct the court clerk to summons every black person in the county, if she could find one. Like many others, Judge Greer incorrectly assumed the defendant was a Negro. "It was that hairdo," he later admitted when the writer corrected him as to the defendant's race. "I'd never seen one quite like that on a white man."

Still, he knew intimately the people chosen to serve, and was confident in their fairness and honesty. Wednesday night, as he too prepared for the first day of trial, Judge Greer was certain of one thing. If the State of Arizona could not prove to each and every person on the jury, beyond a shadow of any doubt, that Willie Steelman was guilty, then they would acquit him and he would walk away a free man.

It would be, like the people of St. Johns themselves, just that simple.

17

Thursday, July 10, 1975.

Willie Steelman was awakened by six, fed by seven, and ready for court by eight. On days such as yesterday, the rare day when he was not scheduled upstairs, he might be allowed an extra thirty minutes sleep, but that was all the slack his hosts cut him.

There were no other prisoners in his four unit cellblock, and besides Norgren and Gilchrist, visitors were nonexistent. What remained of his small family, which included a distant aunt who still lived near Phoenix, never made the trip to St. Johns. Of course, brother Gary ignored him, as did his mother. Frances wrote to him regularly and told him how badly she wanted to come visit, but she never did. Still, as standard procedure, Norgren asked Willie to compile a list of close relatives who might possibly come for the trial. Only the above names were on it. Sheriff Lee ran a check on each, but no one showed. So it soon came to the point where Willie actually looked forward to those early mornings when Deputy Gilchrist would roust him from his bunk.

Chief Deputy Bob Gilchrist was Lee's right hand man, and the strange twist that two Gilchrists had worked the case of Willie Steelman proved just how small the state of Arizona really was. Bob knew he had a second cousin wearing a badge down in the valley somewhere, but had no idea Jack Gilchrist had played such a key role in the investigation until years later when they bumped into each other at funeral for a fellow officer. As Chief Deputy for the Apache County Sheriff Department, Gilchrist was in charge of getting Willie ready and upstairs in time for court. From past experience, he knew what a stickler Judge Greer was for being prompt, and he would take no chances on a reprimand.

Oddly enough, Gilchrist actually came to enjoy the time he and his prisoner spent together, although he didn't come right out and say so for fear of being thought a bit twisted. In private though, he admitted if he could ever forget what Steelman had done, he would have no problem liking him. "The guy is a joker!" he told Lee more than once. "And believe it or not, we actually have some pretty good talks from time to time."

However, Gilchrist made sure Willie knew what would happen if he crossed the line. Willie, on the other hand, stayed just crafty enough to keep the deputy guessing. That aside, they didn't spare the jokes on each other.

"Now, Bob," Willie drawled, eyeing Gilchrist's holster as the deputy prepared him for court Thursday morning, "just what kind of weapon you carryin' there?"

"Well, Willie, that's a .357 magnum."

"No shit! Don't look like it," Willie shot back. "Here, why don't you just let me see it for myself."

"Mr. Dingledine," Judge Greer announced, "you may proceed with your opening statement."

Dave had prepared long and hard for this moment; constantly fine tuning and refining his remarks, although he was never truly satisfied. His opening was designed to lay out the events of that day, and if he knew just one thing about prosecuting a case, it was to make absolutely sure the jury understood every minute detail. He named the witnesses they would soon hear and the testimony they would give, stopping at one point to remind them, "What I state is not evidence. All the evidence that will be heard will come from that witness stand right there. Now if I say anything misleading, I do not mean to do so. I like to refer to an opening statement as kind of a portrait. A picture frame. I will give you the picture frame, and the picture will be filled in from the witnesses on the stand."

He checked off each. Vince Armstrong. A blue Firebird. A gun. A gardener. Villa Parasio. James Nelson. Donald Scott. Stolen checks and a camera. Larry Hust and Larry Bunting. Fingerprints and the FBI. Bullets and Jim Brooker. Bodies, and Dr. Brucker.

"Ladies and gentlemen," Dingledine stormed, his voice rising in disgust, "deliberate, premeditated, cold-blooded, cruel, brutal, execution type murders were committed on Pat and Michael Sandberg! And at the conclusion of this case, the State is going to ask you for a guilty verdict of First Degree Murder on Michael Sandberg, and a guilty verdict of First Degree Murder on Pat Sandberg!"

It was now Robert Norgren's turn, and he started slowly and cautiously. "I would like to tell you at the outset that a Grand Jury indictment is *not* evidence. It is merely a piece of paper. . .a means of getting somebody to trial. Mr. Dingledine, being the prosecutor, has the duty here to prove, beyond a reasonable doubt, all of the allegations and all of the charges he has made. The defendant comes into this court with the presumption of innocence. It is the duty of the prosecution to prove his guilt."

"I think there is going to be two issues in this case," he continued. "Number one. Did Willie Luther Steelman in fact shoot and kill the Sandbergs? The second issue is, what was the mental capacity or mental condition of Willie Luther Steelman during the crime for which he has been charged?"

He waited for a moment, and then answered both of his own questions. "Now, as to the first issue, who shot and killed the Sandbergs? I think you are going to find Mr. Dingledine cannot prove beyond a reasonable doubt that Willie Luther Steelman tied up the Sandbergs. . .or that he in fact fired the shot that killed the Sandbergs. I think the evidence will show that the bullets that killed the Sandbergs were fired by Douglas Gretzler."

This second point was designed to divert attention from Steelman's guilt, and to get the jury thinking about something less that a First Degree Murder conviction. Norgren knew of two things he could prove. One, Willie Steelman consumed large quantities of drugs for years right up until the Sandbergs were killed, and secondly, his mental disorder, the one that allowed him to be part of such a repulsive act, was brought on by the brain damage associated with the years of drug abuse.

"There are going to be psychiatrists and psychologists testify here, and you will have to listen to that evidence and understand it. At the end of the case the judge will instruct you on what the law is regarding when a person can be excused for a crime because of the mental condition for insanity caused by organic brain damage."

He then mentioned his client's stay in a mental hospital in California, and a long list of the drugs he took to try and mask a very real problem. Because of that, Norgren asked the jury to find Willie Steelman not guilty.

As expected, Vince Armstrong was called first. He took the stand, told of the kidnapping, and stated Willie Steelman was one of his attackers. Next was James Nelson, who said he had first spotted the defendant with Mr. Sandberg, remembering how he was bothered by the blue Firebird still being parked in his lot. He also identified Willie Steelman as one of the men he saw that afternoon.

Under cross-examination, Norgren asked Nelson why he had waited so long to tell the police what he knew. Nelson explained that after the Sandbergs were found, and heard about two men being arrested in California for their murders, he was so upset that he left the next day for the mountains. He said he needed to get away from all the terrible news stories coming out of Lodi, claiming he needed to get his head together and didn't want 'muddy the water'. "When I heard about those kids being killed, I went into shock. I didn't know what to believe."

Several other witnesses were called Thursday afternoon, including Donald Scott. By his appearance alone, Scott was the last person one would expect as a witness for the prosecution. During his opening statement, Dingledine all but apologized to the jury for even bringing him to St. Johns. They had located Scott in Colorado shortly after the murders and brought him to Tucson for the Grand Jury hearings. During the following eighteen months, Dingledine kept in close contact, preparing him for an eventual trial, and in an effort to keep him interested, he granted Scott immunity for anything he might say about drug use during his time spent with Steelman and Gretzler. He also promised to ignore any drug arrests and convictions he might incur during the months prior to a trial. That, along with the travel expenses and per diem allowance, made an irresistible offer that Scott could not pass up.

Dingledine was able to keep tabs on Scott during the long wait, but he was not able to change his stripes. When he escorted Scott into Dingledine's motel room yesterday, Larry Hust was grinning from ear to ear. Donald Scott, Dingledine's star witness – all five feet, five inches of him – arrived in St. Johns wearing filthy jeans, ripped moccasins, long, scraggly hair. . .and a cape.

After the chuckling quieted down, Dave got busy and schooled Scott about the testimony he would give, reviewing every last detail about what went on with Steelman and Gretzler, making sure Scott's story remained consistent. Dave got him some different clothes, a brush for his hair, and somehow managed to create a somewhat more credible witness. Dave even talked him out of the cape. He could wear it around the motel, Dave told him, but not in the courtroom. All of this because Dingledine saw in Scott an honest, almost childlike innocence when it came to his emotions about what had gone on during the time with Steelman and Gretzler. He could tell that Scott was bothered by what they did, and hoped to let those feelings show when he took the stand.

Thursday afternoon Scott told the jury about the crash pad where he first met Bill and Doug. The next day Scott said they both left to get a car so they could all leave Tucson together. They came back, he said, but they looked different. "They had the car and said they were going to California, so I went with them."

They stayed in a place called Casa Grande the first night and Bill came up with this story about going to his mother's funeral. Scott said he didn't really understand why, but it was not a big deal to him. They took off for California and were questioned by the Highway Patrol later that night. "The next day they started talking about getting another car. They saw these old people stopped along the road and acted like they were going to pull over. I just knew they would kill them to get their car."

With that, Scott burst into tears, saying the old couple reminded him of his grandparents, and the thought of them being killed upset him. With the witness still crying, Greer called for a brief recess.

A few minutes later, after he had regained his composure and retook the stand, Scott said his fear of what might happen to those old people was the reason he decided to leave Bill and Doug. "Steelman told me anytime I wanted out to let him know, so I did."

That night, back at the Trail Rider, and his testimony complete, Scott came into Dingledine's room to say goodbye. Sitting in a chair was a familiar face. "I've seen you before, haven't I?" Scott asked.

"This is Officer Wright," Dingledine offered.

Wright broke into a grin. "You're the guy I spoke to on the highway that night! Jesus, you look a lot different now."

Don Scott took it as a compliment, and said it was kind of nice to be on the same side as the cops for a change.

On Friday, as the first week of the trial came to a close, word traveled slowly around town about the going-ons up at the courthouse. Wednesday there was barely a dozen people there, and most of those came only to see what an honest-to-God killer looked like. No one appeared to care a stitch about the mundane legalities taking place in front of them.

But by Friday the group of spectators had grown considerably, and they chatted amongst themselves in their best library voices as they waited for Judge Greer to bang the gavel down. The daily account of the trial spread around St. Johns strictly by word of mouth. The townsfolk didn't put much stock in the Tucson television station, even though it was the only signal they could get. Not everyone watched TV, or owned one, for that matter, but even the radio station from nearby Showlow read only the newswire reports, and initially did not send anyone to cover the trial. Although both the Phoenix and Tucson newspapers were delivered to St. Johns each morning, neither had much more to offer. The only true local paper, The *White Mountain Independent*, published its St Johns' edition each Friday, and of course by then the news was old and merely a recap of what had transpired during the week. This morning's paper ran a story at the bottom of the front page about the Steelman jury being selected and Norgren's attempt at using the lunacy defense, as well as the story about Sheriff Lee returning from the FBI training school. In between Lee and Steelman was the report from nearby Springerville announcing the excitement over the new well the city was digging out at the east end of town.

Of course Judge Greer made it clear to members of the jury they weren't supposed to read the papers anyway, or watch the TV news, or discuss what was going on at the trial, even with fellow jurors. Still, a few stories couldn't help but leak out. But as one might expect, they got a lot more interesting as they made the rounds about town.

The biggest story remained true to the Old West. Several area treasure hunters were excited to hear Steelman and his partner had taken the money from one of their victims and had hidden it, so talk circulated this morning about how they had got all this drug loot and stashed it out in the desert. Rumor was the money was supposed to pay off the people who were ready to bust the killers out of jail at any moment. Of course no one could say for sure just exactly where this money was, or why it was hidden, but it did make for an exciting adventure.

Another tale being told was about a recent visitor to Willie's cell. Apparently a long lost relative, reportedly a Methodist minister from nearly Showlow and a distant cousin of some sort had paid Willie a visit. Supposedly Deputy Gilchrist had even checked out his story, and after verifying his name and that of his church in the phone book, allowed him in. But now, according to the talk around town, instead of praying for his soul and asking Willie to beg God for forgiveness, the minister was bringing him cigarettes and Playboy magazines.

It was a delightful story for the tidy little Mormon community. Before the day was out, the Playboy magazines had become real life Playboy Bunnies, and the story reached a point where the minister was now supplying Steelman with marijuana cigarettes, and the Bunnies were coming to town any day now to tell Judge Greer about how Willie had devised a plan for them to bust him out of jail.

All of which could explain why there was a full house in the courtroom on Friday.

Larry Hust, who had been little more than a spectator himself this week, was called as the prosecution's first witness this morning. Dingledine removed a soiled blanket and pillow from a brown grocery sack and asked him if he could identify the items. Hust pretended to examine them, then stated they were the same articles he had removed from the sofa where Patricia Sandberg's body had been found.

When Dingledine inquired about the holes in the pillow, Hust replied that they were bullet holes and pointed to the blackened gunpowder burns around each of them. The pillow was found near the victim's head, he reported, and the blanket covered both the pillow and the body. Hust was also asked to identify four other items; a woman's purse, a ball of twine, a newspaper and a few misshapen slugs. The first two were found on the coffee table in front of the sofa, he announced, the newspaper was on the front porch, and the slugs were removed from Mrs. Sandberg by the coroner.

"Are the size of the slugs consistent with the holes in the pillow?" Dingledine asked. Hust answered that they were. The items were entered into evidence without any objection.

Shortly before noon, Mrs. Francisco was called to the stand. She told the court two men asking for a room at their motel awakened her and her husband. It was very late, she recalled, about eleven-twenty on the night of Sunday, November 4th, 1973. The taller of the two men registered and asked if he could use a credit card to pay for the room. She informed him they didn't take credit cards but would accept a check with proper identification. The man produced an American Express card but apologized for not having a driver's license, explaining his mother had died suddenly and his friend was driving him to San Diego for the funeral. The check and the credit card both bore the name of Michael Sandberg – she remembered that because he also showed a Veteran's Card issued to a Captain Sandberg – and all three matched, relieving somewhat her suspicion of the pair. From the witness stand she pointed to the defendant as the man who claimed to be Michael Sandberg.

After lunch, Dingledine brought Dr. Brucker to examine the slugs introduced earlier. His responses were short and his vocabulary technical. He was quick to recognize the blunt pieces of lead as the same ones he had removed from Mrs. Sandberg during his autopsy. The doctor became the last of seven witnesses called by the prosecution on Friday. Dingledine had literally run out of witnesses and he approached the bench to Greer of his dilemma, complaining that getting all these people to St. Johns and coordinating their schedules was no easy task.

The judge took the news in stride. He sent the jury home, but not before warning them again about his rules.

Hust and Angeli looked forward to the weekend, hoping to take the motorhome out for some much anticipated fishing. They had pestered Dave all week to go with them, but at the last minute he backed out, explaining that he felt a little guilty about enjoying himself while in the middle of a double murder trial. It didn't seem right, he thought, to go out and have fun after what had happened to the Sandbergs – the reason they were all up here in the first place.

But before anyone could leave the building, Greer changed everyone's plans.

There was a golf tournament tomorrow at the local country club, he said, and he would be pleased to have them all as his special guests.

Dingledine again felt awkward, worried how it might look, and wondering out loud if Norgren had been invited as well. Greer settled the matter before anyone could say no. "See you boys there at seven," he announced with a grin. "And Dave, don't worry, I'll make sure you and Bob aren't on the same team." Hust and Angeli decided the fishing could wait another day.

The afternoon was warm. Probably not like the hundred plus degrees down in Phoenix or Tucson, but eighty-eight at least. The air was thick, heavy, and uncomfortable. The monstrous gray clouds, so familiar during the summer monsoon season now blanketed the southwest sky and there was little doubt the valleys below them were being pounded. By the time Dingledine and the others had left the courthouse and reached the Trail Rider, they could hear the rolling swell of thunder bellowing in the distance. Soon the streets of St. Johns were quiet, dark, unsettling, and empty, especially for a Friday afternoon. As the men relaxed in their motel room, splitting a six-pack, they could hear the giant raindrops begin to hit the asphalt just outside the door.

In his cell, Willie stretched out on his bunk, listening to the sounds of the approaching storm. Norgren had clearly avoided him this afternoon, and would for the remainder of the weekend. And with no Gilchrist to start his day, Willie would be left alone to idle the hours away until Monday.

He was already bored, not so much with his cell, but with the lack of company he was used to keeping. In all the other places he had been, there was always someone, somewhere, to rap with. There was always a radio blasting or the static of the community TV, the clanging bars, prisoner tirades, and the threats guards are always quick to make. And Willie liked it that way. The noise brought him comfort, the daytime commotion made the nights easier to endure.

He thought about his sister and why she didn't write him anymore. He thought about Lodi, and home, and Denise, and it hit him hard how much he missed her, how badly he had screwed up a damn good thing. A wave of loneliness rolled over him and he ached for someone, anyone, to talk to.

If he listened closely, he could hear the sounds of the people who worked in the office next to him. He strained to hear their conversations and laughter, the faint ring of a telephone and the chatter of an electric typewriter. But as their day ended, the room fell silent.

He remained motionless on his bunk, hidden away in the late afternoon darkness of a summer storm. He could feel the rain surround him, and hear its sad whisper on the roof above him. There was no comfort here. No comfort at all.

18

Monday, July 14, 1975.

Deputy Gilchrist noticed nothing out of the ordinary Monday morning as he readied his prisoner for a court appearance. Willie offered his usual greeting of nonstop nonsense, followed by Gilchrist's now customary laugh and stories of his fishing trip over the weekend. They talked a lot about fishing – it seemed their common denominator – and Gilchrist was surprised how much Willie knew and cared about it. Willie said that when he was real young his dad took him out to the nearby sloughs for catfish and bass. It was real nice, Willie said, because most of the time it was just the two of them. He remembered one time when the whole family went up to the mountains, a place called Silver Lake, and his dad showed him how to go after trout. Willie admitted to Gilchrist that trout fishing was a helluva lot different, and a damn sight harder, than just drowning a piece of clam for some stupid-ass catfish. "Jesus. I was just a little kid then," he reminisced, "but shit, I still remember how much fun we had."

Gilchrist noticed Willie always got real serious when they talked about fishing. He never joked about it like he did everything else. Like fishing was sacred or something.

He got Steelman upstairs on time, turned him over to Lee and everything seemed normal, but as soon as Norgren walked in, Willie started acting weird and tripping out. It was just that quick, Gilchrist noticed, like somebody had flipped a switch. Norgren leaned over and started talking to Willie, getting right in his face, making sure the deputies couldn't hear what he was saying, then stood up and motioned to the bailiff.

"Let the records show we are in chambers and out of the presence of the jury,"

Greer said to the court reporter a few minutes later, then turned to Norgren. "Counsel?"

Norgren answered. "I just talked to the defendant, Your Honor, and he said he desired to have handcuffs placed on him, that he doesn't feel he can control himself."

"I'm reluctant to do so," Greer answered. He turned to Dingledine. "Do you have any objections?"

Dave shrugged his shoulders and said that he wished the defense counsel was a bit more specific about what actions Steelman was threatening.

"Perhaps we should bring the defendant in here," Greer suggested, "so the court can make that determination." He called for Deputy Gilchrist.

Willie was hyped up and trembling, his eyes bugged out and darted around the room, eventually settling on the judge, who was the first to speak.

"Your attorney has conveyed to the court a request coming from you to the effect you would like to be handcuffed."

Willie wasted no time in answering. "I think it would be best if I could be set in the room back here with the handcuffs on this morning. I'm hallucinating now pretty bad. I was bothered all last night, and hallucinating this morning. I'm afraid something might happen in court."

Gilchrist couldn't believe it. What a damn acting job! It was all he could do to hold back the laughter. Five minutes ago this guy is swapping old fishing stories, and now he's putting on a full-fledged psycho-show for the judge. But no one asked him, so Gilchrist kept his mouth shut, turning away so Greer couldn't see him snickering.

"I'd like to have the cuffs on," Willie repeated, "so I couldn't hurt nobody when I go like that. . .you know, it's just not good. Keep them on at least until I can get some medication or something."

So that's it, Gilchrist thought. All of this so he can get a little fix. Still, he said nothing.

"What medication do you need?" Greer asked.

Willie perked up. "I usually take Quaalude, usually before I start hallucinating. If I could get an injection of, of. . .I can't remember the name of it. . .the MD would have it. . .but it makes me settle down. I still hallucinate a little bit, but I don't get violent."

"Are you taking any tranquilizers now?"

"Three or four hundred milligrams yesterday and it wouldn't help," Willie answered. He held up his hand for Greer to see. "I broke my hand. I think I broke it. The tranquilizers don't help. Matter of fact they make it worse."

Greer examined Steelman's hand. "This is all a result from taking LSD?"

"I think it is. Never had a doctor say. I start hallucinating, then things start melting. I start seeing visions of people talking to me. . ."

Greer stopped him. "I'm most reluctant to have you handcuffed in front of the jury." He looked at Norgren, as if for approval. "I understand this has been done before, where a defendant has been seated outside the courtroom."

"Yes, that's possible," Norgren replied, an answer that did not appear to please Willie, who decided it was time to speak up again.

"At least if we could get an MD to give me a shot or something. That would be all right."

Greer ignored him and asked Dingledine and Norgren if either one had an objection to the defendant sitting in the back room with handcuffs on. But Willie realized his grand plan was slipping away and spoke up quickly.

"I'd feel a lot safer, I really would, so I couldn't hurt somebody. I wouldn't want to hurt anybody anymore. . .but you know. . .if I could just get a shot – it's a drug store prescription – it's a well used drug, not restricted or anything. I'm just awful afraid something bad will happen."

Greer gave in. "So what's this drug?"

"Quaalude," Willie shot back. "You could go to a drug store for it. Or a shot of demurral. Or I could take morphine or another type of heroin or opium type drug." Willie was rolling now, reeling off names like a kid at the candy counter. All of it so close now he could just about taste them.

"Morphine is out," Greer shot back. "They won't give that to you."

Willie knew he was real close. He could see the old man leaning. He could already feel the needle. He kept it up. "I don't wanna hold up the court proceedings either, because I know it's costin' too much money."

Greer decided enough was enough. He excused himself and went into the next room and called Willie's physician in Tucson. Doctor Hoogerbeets couldn't help but laugh when the judge explained what was going on.

"Don't worry," the doctor said. "He goes through this every three weeks or so when he gets tired of the prescription drugs and wants something off the street." He assured Greer there wasn't any cause to worry about the defendant's mental condition, and even suggested a couple of drugs he could give Steelman to calm him down and satisfy his request.

When Greer returned and advised everyone of his call, Norgren promptly demanded a Rule 11 hearing to again determine his client's competency. Dingledine protested. The two verbally climbed all over each other to be heard. Greer took a deep breath, called for a break, then went back into the courtroom, where the jury had been kept waiting for nearly two hours.

"Ladies and gentlemen, thank you for being so prompt this morning. This is one of those days I've told you about. Some problems have developed – mostly my fault, mind you – and we won't be ready to got until about one thirty. Do what you want 'til then, but remember my admonitions."

Greer returned and announced his decision. Gilchrist would escort the defendant to the medical clinic in Springerville where he would be examined and the prescription filled, if it was so decided. Greer let it be known he did not relish the idea of sending the prisoner that distance – Springerville was thirty miles away – but both Lee and Gilchrist assured him they would have no problem. There was a certain understanding between them, Lee said.

Willie stayed wide-eyed and twitching, right up until Greer gave them the go ahead. The second Gilchrist grabbed the top of his head and ducked him into the back seat, Willie brightened. Gilchrist turned the sedan onto the highway south, checked his rearview mirror, broke into a wide grin and shook his head. Willie could see him smiling. "Hey, Bob," he laughed, "is this the road to that fishin' spot of yours?"

Gilchrist let him know that he hadn't fooled anyone with the act back there, especially him, but Willie simply shrugged him off. Gilchrist decided Willie was just bored and looking for a change of scenery.

The high country was in its summer glory, wide open, gorgeous, and surprisingly still very green. The clouds from last night's storm were long gone and blue skies filled the horizon. Gilchrist kept up the conversation in the rear view mirror. There were times when Willie was talkative and animated, countered with spells when he seemed sullen and close mouthed. It was Willie who first mentioned the Sandbergs, ranting about how Michael Sandberg thought he was joking and how he laughed at him. He got loud, and agitated. The piece of shit thought it was all real funny, Willie snarled, until Douglas put a knife to his wife's throat and threatened to slit it wide open.

A shiver ran through Gilchrist. He had finally witnessed Steelman's fury; the rage the Sandbergs must have felt too. Willie kept it up, claiming he had no choice but to kill them both. And with that he shut up and looked out the window. The view seemed to calm him. There was a tense silence for several miles until it seemed the anger had drained him.

"They weren't criminals or nothin' like that," he said, still staring out the side window. "Just a couple of righteous citizens who got bumped."

Steelman sat on the examining table at the clinic, shackled and cuffed, checking out the room, waiting for the doctor. "Got a Playboy bunny coming to testify", he announced.

Gilchrist cracked up. "Yeah, I heard about that."

Willie laughed too, pleased to see Gilchrist smile. "Yeah, Miss April, I think. Damn! I can't wait! Heard she's got some real big tits."

But true to form, the instant the doctor entered the room, Willie started back in. "Oh, I still see 'em under my bed, trying to grab me," he wailed. "All the people I killed. . .all of 'em talkin' to me in my dreams. I can't get no sleep no more. . .they're all coming after me!"

Willie got the part. He got his prescription. Gilchrist didn't say a word. They got back to St. Johns by one thirty.

"We thought about taking them with us, but Doug figured it would be better to just shoot them."

When the proceedings resumed, Sergeant Kenneth Wagner was called by the prosecution and read aloud a portion of the interrogation he conducted during that weekend in November. The words were those of Willie Steelman. At Dingledine's urging, Wagner continued. "So I turned up the stereo and Doug tied them up in the bathroom while I kept watch."

Both Wagner and Carl Ambrose had arrived in St. Johns over the weekend. While Dingledine had hoped to spend Sunday reviewing their testimony, Hust and Angeli tempted them with talk of some great fishing holes. Hust and Angeli won. Wagner and Ambrose went fishing Sunday, but had their game face on Monday afternoon.

"Then Doug goes into the bedroom and shot the man. I had the woman roll over on the couch so she couldn't see what was coming and laid a pillow over her. Doug shot her three or four times. He did a lousy job, so I shot her again to make damn sure she wasn't suffering."

Charles Richardson, a top FBI fingerprint analyst testified that fingerprints found in the Sandberg apartment matched those of Willie Steelman, while James Brooker, the California firearms specialist, reported slugs removed from the bodies matched the .22 revolver taken from Steelman when he was arrested.

Robert Norgren, who had already asked the court for a mistrial following Wagner's stint on the stand, now moved to dismiss all charges against his client after Brooker alluded to other killings Steelman was responsible for. Again Greer denied the request. Dingledine said he wasn't finished with the witness, but Greer said that he had had enough. "Invite him back tomorrow," he offered. "I think we're done for today."

Gilchrist took Willie down to his cell, then phoned over to the Trail Rider Restaurant to let them know they could send over the prisoner's dinner whenever they were ready.

He walked next door to his office, gathered his things and started home. The blue sky of early afternoon was now gone and giant raindrops bounced hard off his windshield. He thought about Willie and all the crazy stuff he had pulled today. He couldn't help but smile. He knew what was going to happen to Willie when this was all over, and that made him kind of sad. He wondered if he was going soft.

Each morning before court, Dingledine, Rich Rollman, Hust and Angeli would walk over to the motel restaurant for breakfast, usually accompanied by one of the day's witnesses. Over coffee they would discuss their strategy. Other days, on those occasions when they were running late, Dave would send Angeli around the corner for donuts and they would work in their room right up until the very last second. Then, after tossing all their documents and evidence into the motorhome, they climbed the few blocks up the hill to the courthouse.

It was under the threat of Greer's wrath, they all be in place and ready to go on time. But more than once they were seen hustling boxes up the stairs at the very last minute, scrambling to beat the deadline. Yet, it never once mattered how early they arrived, for the good judge was always there waiting for them.

Greer was a stickler for promptness. A few days prior, the wife of a courtroom staff member had given birth to the couple's first child. Greer announced to the courtroom the new father was "understandably delayed", but made it equally clear it would take a similar act of God for him to accept such tardiness from anyone else.

"Please be prompt ladies and gentlemen," Greer seemed forever repeating. "We need each and every one of you to try this lawsuit."

And he used the term 'lawsuit' often. It was never a murder trial, but a lawsuit, or a hearing. At times he became even more businesslike and referred to their work as 'litigation'. Greer insisted nothing be said or done to agitate or inflame the jury. He avoided all sensationalism. He did not care to make the subject matter of these proceedings any worse than it already was.

For example, of the nearly two hundred and fifty crime scene photographs, the state asked to submit fifty. However, after reviewing the photos and discussing their content with the prosecution, Greer encouraged Dingledine to whittle his list down even further. "No need for the jury to see most of these," he said, pointing out their gruesome, repetitive nature. "One or two per victim would be sufficient."

Although Greer's suggestion carried no legal weight, Dingledine got the message. While insisting the grisly death scene, captured so violently in these black and white photos, was his best tool in convincing the jury of the need for a death penalty conviction, he bowed to Greer's wishes and agreed to submit only about a dozen of them into evidence. The jury still winced when the photos were passed around, but Judge Greer had done his best to keep their repulsion to a manageable level.

When Dingledine and the others met for breakfast Tuesday morning, they were hopeful, barring any unforeseen problems, they could wrap up their case before the day was done. They arrived in court well before the appointed time and were in their seats and ready to go by 9:30 am.

Dingledine began by recalling Detective Wagner to the stand. Again reading from the transcripts, Wagner quoted Steelman as saying he had worked for a small drug family in California until just before leaving Lodi in the summer of 1973. He said about three times a year his job was to move heroin from San Francisco to the Stockton area. The money he earned, along with whatever drugs he could boost, went to support his growing drug habit. When he arrived in Denver later that summer, he got involved with a much larger group called the Smaldone Family. He started out as their errand boy, then quickly moved into the role of hit man. One of his first assignments was to off a guy he knew only "as a dude named Randy".

According to Willie's statement, Randy had compiled a list of all the important people in the Smaldone organization – a list that could go a long way in helping him take over the family's operations – therefore the Smaldones instructed Willie to him take out. But Willie did not complete his task, and in fact he admitted to Wagner that he botched the job so badly he decided his life was in danger. It was then when he fled to Phoenix with Doug Gretzler.

Larry Hust was called back to the stand and asked about the interview he had with Steelman on November 19th, a conversation held a week after Willie admitted to Ambrose and Wagner that he and Doug had killed the Sandbergs. On this tape Steelman boasted about the "Preacher Murders", and about how he shot one man and how his accomplice, a guy named Larry, stabbed Preacher's associate with an ice pick. Norgren winced. Willie never gave a motive for the killings, or said who had ordered them, even though Hust was heard asking him that question several times.

Under cross-examination, Norgren asked Hust if it was ever proved that these killings even took place? Was there ever a body found? A weapon? A motive? Hust admitted he knew of no evidence relating to such a crime and agreed there was never a body recovered, nor was the exact location the apartment where it supposedly took place ever positively determined.

With that, the State rested.

Ken Wagner and Carl Ambrose stayed around St. Johns an extra day and went fishing with Hust and Angeli, while Dave decided against it and remained at the motel to catch up on work. However, he was the one who caught the biggest surprise.

When Greer began the trail and addressed the newly seated jury, he read to them a list of witnesses that may be presented during the trial, including names of all the principals in the case; police officers, eyewitnesses, guards, victims, even several doctors and psychiatrists. But nowhere on the list of over forty names was that of the man Dave now discovered was going to testify that Willie Steelman was insane.

His name was Dr. James Peale, and as Dave sat in his motel room Tuesday afternoon, he learned the doctor was already in town.

Joining Peale was another psychiatrist from Stockton; a Dr. Irvin Roy, and both had examined Steelman in May of 1974 at the request of Sam Libicki to try and determine the possibility of using diminished capacity as a defense. Peale and Roy had since been in contact with Robert Norgren over the past six months, and Norgren's boss at Pima County, Ken Peasley, even flew to Stockton to ask Peale personally if there was any chance he could categorize Steelman as McNaughton insane. Peale told him he believed he could, but would need additional examinations with the defendant in order to do so. Without the examinations, or even a session with Peale, Norgren felt there was little chance either doctor would make the trip to St. Johns. However, late Tuesday afternoon he received a message the two were on their way.

They arrived at Norgren's cabin Wednesday morning and went directly to the jail. Peale spent nearly two hours talking with Steelman, after which Roy duplicated the series of tests he had first performed a year earlier. While the doctors were with Willie, Dingledine received a call from the jail tipping him off about what was happening there.

The news that Peale and Roy were in town was not his biggest concern. It was the timing of their visit that upset Dingledine the most. He had just completed the State's case and had made no mention of the mental condition of the defendant. He stayed strictly with the basics; weapons, fingerprints, eyewitnesses, even Steelman's own confession. After listening to Greer tell Norgren to forget about using lunacy as a defense, and after being assured repeatedly that Steelman was considered McNaughton sane, Dave assumed he would not need to travel the insanity path. Just to be safe, however, he had included the doctors Rogerson, Lyons, and Austin as possible witnesses, but had decided not to use them and they were never present during the trial.

So here it was, the day before defense arguments were to begin, and Dingledine was on the phone to Stockton, pleading with the doctors to find a way to get to St. Johns immediately. He knew they could not be used directly, but only as rebuttal witnesses to any damaging statements Peale or Roy might offer. That was better than nothing, which was all he had now.

While Dingledine made the calls, Rollman began preparing himself for the technical side of his certain cross-examination. He buried himself in research regarding mental illness, schizophrenia, organic brain disorders, as well as the numerous tests a doctor might give to qualify his ultimate findings. Rollman had no idea of the specifics that could be brought up, but fortunately Dave have brought with him copies of the reports the doctors had filed while Steelman was incarcerated in California. Rollman had exactly one afternoon to become an expert.

As usual, Wednesday night was poker night at the Trail Rider and Angeli made sure he got back from the fishing trip in time to take his place at the table. He felt lucky tonight. The stakes were getting higher as the night wore on and he was winning more than his share of hands. When one of the other player's money finally ran out, he upped the pot with an unusual wager. It was gorgeous piece of jewelry, a lavish Navajo squash blossom necklace crafted of silver and turquoise. "It's worth nine hundred dollars if it's worth a dime," the gambler boasted.

When Rex walked back into Dingledine's room that night with the necklace draped around his neck everyone broke up laughing. He wore it around town several times after that but the guys gave him such a load a crap about it, he eventually took it off and stuck it in his suitcase. When he got back home to Tucson, he gave it to his wife. She loved it, but Rex didn't think it was necessary to tell her where, or how he got it.

19

Thursday, July 17, 1975 | 9:00 am.

St. Johns woke to cloudy skies, mirrored in the chrome puddles left by last night's storm. The air was damp, warm, suffocating, and eighty degrees by the time the prosecution team steered the motorhome up the hill to the courthouse. They felt the sun's warmth radiate from above the clouds, and could see blue patches of sky to the south where it had forced its way through, painting the high desert in a subtle wash of a hand-colored postcard. But St. Johns itself remained in gray, and as the morning session got underway, giant raindrops began to fall.

In Judge Greer's chamber, Dingledine began. "Your Honor, yesterday afternoon was the first time the State learned that any psychiatrist was going to testify as to the McNaughton insanity, and that is exactly one day before this man is going on the stand and testify!" Dingledine danced with anger. "We have been working very, very hard on this case and it is my understanding now that Mr. Norgren, at least according to yesterday, has abandoned his original defense and now it will strictly be McNaughton insanity, along with drug intoxication."

Because of that, Dingledine continued, he had no choice but to fly in his own psychiatrists from California as witnesses. He wanted a continuance, and yet realized such a move would cause more harm than good at this point. Instead, he requested Norgren at least be sanctioned for his shenanigans, then for the court to inform the jury what was going on.

"Dr. Peale said just yesterday that he knew Steelman was insane back in nineteen seventy four," Dingledine reminded Greer. "But now, Mr. Norgren says he didn't know that, and didn't even know that was going to be his opinion."

Norgren jumped in to defend his position. "Wait a minute! I filed – and the records in this case will show – that a month and a half to two months ago we put down Dr. Peale's name and we stated that Dr. Peale might testify that Steelman was insane at the time. Mr. Dingledine knew about that a month and a half or two ago but he didn't, at any time, try and talk to Dr. Peale."

Greer knew somebody was bending the truth, but he did not care to spend extra hours reviewing the record to try and see who did what when. They were making good time in the case and he wanted no unnecessary delays. On a strictly legal basis, the prosecution had reasonable cause to ask for a continuance, especially if key witnesses could not make it to trial on time. Greer knew that St. Johns' remote location might cause exactly this kind of problem, and if the prosecution could show a sufficient effort being made to get his people here on time, well, a continuance was a certainty. Norgren, on the other hand, might have been a bit devious in this last minute announcement, and by never actually pinning down Dr. Peale as to when, or if, he planned on attending the trial, then it was Norgren who had placed an unnecessary burden upon the court.

And it was he who interrupted Greer's train of thought. "I would like to state for the record that I don't like the insinuation that Mr. Dingledine has made! It's not true, and I will have Ken Peasley come in – and I'll have Dr. Peale come in – so we can set the record straight!"

"That won't be necessary. I'll deny the objection and permit you to proceed." He turned to Dingledine and attempted to smooth his ruffled feathers as well. "And I'll take under advisement what we will tell the jury. I think we can work this out. I am concerned about the delays occasioned by the doctors. . ."

"They're working very hard to clear their schedule," Dave whined. "Very hard, Your Honor."

Greer motioned for the bailiff to call the jury back in and pointed at Robert Norgren to begin.

Denise's divorce from Willie had been finalized in February. She had not seen him since he left Lodi almost two years ago, and vowed she never would.

But he was never completely out of her life. From the moment he was captured, and his wicked story began to unfold, Willie's legacy continued to haunt her. As her ex-brother-in-law had learned, Denise found the Steelman name was hated in Lodi, so she returned to her maiden name and moved back in with her parents, hoping to hide, or even outrun, the insults, innuendo, crank calls and threats. She had little success. Finally, when Willie was taken to Arizona, Denise relaxed, hoping the worst was over. It was, to her painful dismay, just the beginning. Prosecutors, public defenders, doctors, jailers, reporters; they all wanted a piece of her and the information they were certain only she could supply. They called incessantly, wrote her constantly, starting with Dave Dingledine the day Willie was hauled off to Tucson. When David Hoffman came to town, he didn't even bother to ask, he just showed up on her doorstep demanding she speak with him. He left empty handed. She refused him. She refused everyone.

But by the early summer of 1975 the heat was back on. The Pima County Public Defender's office told her bluntly she would be summoned to the upcoming trial. Not only would she have to see Willie again, she would be forced to sit just a few feet from him as she answered intimate questions about their life together.

It was not that she hated him, more that she still could not understand what happened to him. She loved him once, she reminded herself of that often the first year after the murders, but she could still remember the rage he could explode into and the hatred in his eye during those times. She did not care to admit it, but maybe there had been this killer inside him all along and that she was just too blind to see it. A thousand times the thought raced through her head that maybe there was something she could of done. Maybe she could have stopped him, gotten him help, changed what happened, saved all those people. Maybe. There were so many maybes.

She recalled one day in particular, shortly before he left town, the day she confronted him about Lisa and told him it was over, and their marriage was done. Willie answered back by hitting her, grabbing her by the hair and throwing her into the car where he slapped her again. She remembered the devil in his eyes that day. The very thought made her shiver; knowing all those people in the closet saw that very same look, felt that same cold stare just before he...

She didn't want to think about him anymore. She didn't want to see him or think about him ever again. She wanted him gone for good. Out of her life forever.

But they wouldn't let her forget. They kept calling and pestering her, so she eventually caved in and agreed to speak with Robert Norgren on one condition; that he promise her this would be the last time. But now Denise was also expecting her first child with her soon-to-be new husband, Ivan. With the birth just a month away, and her doctor insisting that she not leave town, Dingledine relented, and agreed to allow her to be videotaped for the approaching trial.

The taped testimony of Denise Marie Machell was entered as Defendant's Exhibit Number 97 and played before a quieted courtroom Thursday morning. Willie never took his eyes off the television screen.

She first recalled the incident outside the music store, and later when he fought with their landlord over moving into an apartment. Those were the times, not the only times, mind you, when he would be so violent, and then not be able to remember anything about it later.

"You mentioned a third incident," Norgren asked. "When did this happen?"

"June of nineteen seventy three," Denise replied. "I had found out about his girlfriend and I told him 'if we're going to be married, then we're going to be married. None of this running around'. I told him I was going to leave. Well, he got all upset and we started an argument. And at the times when he was like this he acted like he was crazy, and his eyes were just like a blank stare, and he didn't know what he was doing."

"Did you talk to him later about this incident?"

"Yeah, a few days later."

"Did he have a recollection?"

"Well, he knew we had an argument, but he didn't realize how bad he got..."

". . .and that he had actually struck you during that argument," Norgren interrupted.

"Yeah. I brought it up, but he didn't remember."

Norgren asked about Willie's fall outside the department store in the spring of 1972. Denise nodded and replied that afterwards he constantly complained of headaches – headaches that continued up until the day he left Lodi.

"He didn't tell you where he was going?"

"No, just that he would be gone for a few days, but that he would be back. I haven't seen him since."

"Did he ever make any remarks to you as to what he thought about killing?"

"Oh yeah. I couldn't understand why he didn't like to go deer hunting like all the other guys did. But he said he just didn't believe in killing."

Saiers tested her memory about a few subjects but for the most part remained an observer. The video lasted fifteen minutes, then the screen went black. When the tape was over, the sound of Denise's voice was replaced by the pounding of the rain outside, and the rolling moans of thunder in the distance.

After a brief recess, Norgren called Willie Steelman.

Greer allowed him to testify from his seat at the defense table and Norgren turned the podium to face him as the courtroom grew dark from the approaching storm. Norgren asked Willie about his life as a young adult, moving quickly to his health, and more specifically the headaches following the fall Denise had described.

"They were big," Willie answered. "Real heavy. The ringing in my ears seemed to start inside and bang around through my head. It felt like it was exploding."

"Any other type of feeling you have besides the headaches?"

"I'm not sure I understand what you mean."

Norgren spelled it out again, slowly. "Is there any other type of feeling that you had?"

Willie finally got it. "Oh yeah. Frustration mostly. I spent a lot of time trying to change things within the system the last couple of years. Seems like it was all a waste. I was just frustrated."

"What do you mean, change things?" Norgren's question lit a spark in Willie.

"Well, I worked with AIM; The American Indian Movement. I worked with the black ghetto people in Stockton. I gave up a job making eight dollars an hour so I could be a nurse in a hospital for two bucks an hour. I thought to control the controlling class of people through the system, but it seemed like such a waste of time. Every time I tried to passively resist them they would come up and beat you in the fucking head. They would come after you."

"Did they come after you?"

"Sure! I watched my brothers die in the streets trying to change things and do away with the system. Unarmed people, like a thirteen-year-old black kid, Larry Taylor. . .they shot him down because he was carrying a stick. Shot in the back. It's pretty frustrating when you're not doing anything wrong to these people and all they want to do is kill you because of something you stand for. I've seen too many blacks forced to use drugs, or sell drugs to feed their children. I've seen pigs kick their teeth in and beat them in the head. They chase me constantly. They're always on my back. It got to a point where I had to do things I didn't want to do."

Willie was on a roll and Norgren hated to interrupt him. "Like what Willie? Like what things?"

"Like sometimes hurt people. I don't like to hurt people, but sometimes I had to because they were trying to destroy me and everything I believed in, everything I worked for."

"Why destroy you?"

Willie was getting worked up. "The police, this pig state, the ruling class of America, they use every technique to destroy you!" He swept his arm across the room. "You people in this courtroom that run this government are the shipmasters, the sons of the devil! But I started using acid and came to the awareness that they wanted me dead, wanted me stopped. Not me personally, but for what I know and what I could say. But I wasn't done with my work!"

"What was your work?"

"No black man in America ever asked to be brought to this country, no Indian ever asked to have his lands taken away from him and stuck on some piece of desert and told to shut up. . .'open your mouth and I'll kill you!' No Jew ever asked to be put in an oven. The United States let them put over six million of them in there. They could have stopped them, but it wasn't economical. No Mexican-American ever asked to work in a vineyard for seventy five cents an hour..."

"But what does this have to do with the Sandbergs?"

Willie paused on cue. He glared at Norgren, sneering at his stupid questions.

"Well, he's a Marine! His chest full of medals. He's a killer! A murderer!"

"Did you kill him?" Norgren asked.

"Certainly!" Willie snapped. "I was doing nothing but defending myself. I committed no crime – they can say anything they want – I committed no crime. I defended my rights as a human being, as an individual. I just got to the point where I will no longer stand still for it! When they kill me, I win double, because they will see what kind of garbage train it is!"

"Do you fear death, Mr. Steelman?"

"No! I look forward to it, because when they put me in that gas chamber that man right there loses!" He pointed at Dingledine. "He's the perfect shovel for the organization! He's nothing but a tool. When they put me in the gas chamber I win and he loses because he's proving I'm right and he's wrong. . .every word that comes out of his mouth! They can beat me, stomp me. They've done it before and they can't make me change my mind or make me fear them."

Dingledine smirked at the remark, making sure to keep his amusement from the jury's view. But now, for the first time, he saw what others before him had been witness to. He watched the fury rise up in Willie Steelman, and although he was certain that it had all been scripted and rehearsed, he had no doubt Willie had come to believe the words he spoke. Steelman wanted the jury to believe he was crazy, and he was doing a damn good job. He felt his hands tighten around the arm of the chair as Steelman spoke. He had been sucked in. He knew it. But Dave released his grip and vowed not to be a part of this charade. He scribbled on his legal pad and pushed it towards Rollman. 'Bullshit', it read.

Norgren shuffled his papers. The rain slammed berserk against the building, screaming so hard into the windows above them that all heads turned upwards, certain they would see glass shatter and come crashing to the courtroom floor at any moment. Occasionally as Willie spoke, the lights would dim, followed by the low wail of thunder bellowing in the distant heavens.

"Are you fearful of somebody?" Norgren asked, looking down, returning to his notes.

"The people in my cell," Willie said, his voice barely a whisper now.

Norgren didn't flinch. "Who are they?"

"I don't like to name names. Some of the people that have been in my cell are usually dead people."

"What are they doing there?"

Steelman sparked. "They're out to get me, trying to discredit what I say. If they can make me change, make me give up my ideals, then everything I've fought for is a waste. Fifteen hundred thousand of them will say he was wrong and the ruling class was right. I can't allow that!"

"Was Captain Sandberg after you?"

Willie laughed and shook his head at such a pitiful question. The rain screamed against the courthouse as lightning crashed.

"YES, HE WAS AFTER ME! He's been after me for four hundred years! He was after me that day, and he thought it was funny because he's a Marine...he's America's hero...but he wanted to kill me so bad, just to shut my mouth!"

Willie's voice rose to do battle with the storm. "He was a tool for the class! Every child that died in Viet Nam on Christmas, he killed them! Whether he dropped the bomb or not, he killed them! Murdered them! Every Indian that died, he murdered them! Every black man that died in the streets, he murdered them! But he didn't like hearing that...didn't like hearing that at all!"

Suddenly, an unexpected quiet smothered the courtroom, and Willie's timing could not have been more perfect. He lowered his voice, his eyes bulging as he spoke, the blue blood veins in his neck ready to explode. "He couldn't get away from the guilt feeling inside him. He knew he was the Devil's Child!"

At the very moment Willie spit out those final words, a crack of lightning tore through the skies over St. Johns. Sensing a divine message from above, the people in the courtroom twisted in their chairs, cowering unashamed as the heavens snapped and hissed. The room fell dark. The groan of the ensuing thunder rumbled deep in the earth below until it could hold back this wrath no longer. The storm's vengeance rose up through the floorboards, splitting this nervous silence, sending those in the room for whatever cover and protection they could find.

Seconds later the lights in the courtroom flickered back on and Willie spoke once more. This time his eyes were teary, his head bowed, his shoulders slumped, his voice weak, drained, pitiful.

"I loved Denise," he droned. "I really loved her."

During the lunch recess Dingledine tossed out everything he had planned for his cross of Willie Steelman. Everything. Willie was a showman, a master of the theater, a manipulator, a liar. Dingledine had had a front row seat to Willie's most recent performance. It was good, but he wasn't buying it. He would have no hand in making Willie look crazy.

For the countless times Dave had been in the same room with Willie over the past year, throughout all the countless hearings held, he never once underestimated Steelman's abilities. He had no quarrel with those who claimed Willie was an intelligent man, and he knew Steelman was capable of anything he set his mind to. Today, Willie wanted the jury to believe he was a madman, and with the help of God Almighty above, he had put on the performance of a lifetime. But Dave would have no part of it. He knew Willie was just waiting for him; looking forward to the time when he could renew his act, rekindle his rage, reinforce his role of madman.

Dave told Rollman at lunchtime that he was on to Willie. "We're going to frustrate the hell outta him. You just watch."

Back in court, Willie was waiting, itching to get started, ready, anxious. He stared up at Dingledine and sneered as Judge Greer gave the nod for them to begin.

The rain outside had quieted. Dingledine was all smiles as he strode to the podium to face the defendant.

Q: "You are Willie Steelman?"

A: "Yeah."

Q: "Now is that Willie...or Bill?"

A: "Willie."

Q: "How old are you Willie?"

A: "Thirty."

Q: "Where were you born?"

A: "Stockton."

Q: "Dad's name?"

A: "Lester."

Q: "Mother's name?"

A: "Ethel." Willie was edgy, waiting for the big question.

Dingldine looked over his notes.

Q: "You were married only once, right?"

A: "Twice."

Q: "Twice? What was the first one's name?"

A: "Don't remember."

Q: "Don't remember? Wasn't Denise?"

A: "No."

Q: "Right...Denise was your second."

Dingledine and Steelman sparred back and forth for several minutes, and Willie ready to get it on, but Dave was content to mess with his head. He never asked anything about any crime, just dozens of questions about nothing at all. With each Willie would snarl and snap back a yes or no.

Q: "Remember going to Tucson?"

"Remember a little motel around Casa Grande"

"Have any brothers or sisters?"

"Your brother married, Willie?"

"Have any hobbies, Willie?"

"Did you like your job as a nurse, Willie?"

"You feeling all right now, Willie?"

Steelman glared back at him and laughed. "Yeah. I'm fuckin' loaded."

Dingledine smiled and looked to the bench. "I have no further question, Your Honor." He turned his back on Steelman as he stepped away.

"Sonofabitch wasn't going to show me up," he whispered under his breath.

Dr. Irvin Roy was a pleasant faced, middle-aged man with a substantial background in clinical psychology. His extensive resume included a doctorate from New York University, followed by years of research conducted at some of the finest schools and hospitals on the east coast. After moving to California, Roy began work at Stockton State Hospital where he studied and administered to hundreds of patients, most of whom had been diagnosed with some form of schizophrenia. His most recent work was with the California Adult Authority, evaluating parolees who the state felt might pose future problems; criminals whose obvious mental condition and inability to adjust to life outside the prison kept them constantly circling through the courts and legal system.

People exactly like Willie Steelman.

"Dr. Roy," Norgren began after calling him to the stand, "tell us first what tests you administered, and what the purpose of each test is."

"Yes. Well, I presented a portion of the Wexler Adult Intelligence scale, the Roshault Ink Blot test, the Graham Kendall memory test, several thematic and perception tests, the Minnesota Multi-Physic inventory – which is scored by computer and is designed..."

Norgren glanced towards the jury to see if they were following along, then interrupted. "Neurological doctors," he continued. "Do they request these tests sometimes?"

"Oh yes. Not all tests with every individual, though."

"But there have been occasions where they indicated an E.E.G. test shows nothing, and they then have given you the assignment of making these tests to determine if there is brain damage?"

"Yes. Very common. The electroencephalogram is really a gross measure. It has an error percentage of fifteen percent. That is, fifteen percent of normal people will have an abnormal E.E.G., and likewise, fifteen percent of people with known brain pathology – tumors, epilepsy, or gross brain lesions – will have a normal E.E.G..."

Again, Norgren stopped him. Knowing Steelman's E.E.G. had come back normal, he wanted Roy to state that his client could very well be insane, and yet an x-ray, or all the tests in the world for that matter, may never show it. "Are there any perfect tests to determine...?"

"No." Roy answered, finishing Norgren's thought. "No perfect tests of any kind."

Norgren asked Roy to review for the jury the series of tests administered to the defendant yesterday.

"I started out not looking for anything. I had no idea of what I could expect. It very quickly became apparent to me that Mr. Steelman was of above-average intelligence, and whatever problems he had were not problems due to lack of intellectual ability. However, I did note he did very poorly in certain tests and that gave me the hypothesis there may be a deficiency in the area of perceptual motoring functioning."

"And that is. . .?" Norgren asked, hoping to have this spelled out in layman's terms.

"Minimal brain dysfunction, or organic brain damage," Roy replied.

When asked to describe in greater detail the results of the tests given, and why he had arrived at this diagnosis, again Roy reviewed his procedures and the reasons why he came to his conclusion.

When he was finished, Norgren asked him, "So all this indicates what, doctor?"

"That the results of these tests indicates minimal brain damage. People of this category are typically impulsive, irritable and distractible. They usually have very poor control over their impulses."

Norgren could not have been more pleased. The doctor had described Willie Steelman perfectly. Now he was anxious to move into the area of Roy's examination he was certain would give the jury the most compelling reasons why they had to consider the defendant's mental imbalance; the ink blot test.

Roy again reviewed the procedures taken, the nature of each test, how they are administered, and what findings can be taken from them. "There are ten cards. I would hold one up and he would respond in a certain way." Roy held the cards up so the jury could see them, although he noted that they would be viewing them from a distance much greater than a patient would.

"Now this is the first card. The first response normally would be a butterfly or bird. Mr. Steelman reported that it reminded him of a skeleton, and went on to describe how it was disjointed – the eyes were in the ribcage and it was upside down. This again is a clue to his thinking, which is not very ordinary or logical."

Norgren nodded and looked towards the jury, hoping they would be in agreement as well.

"Now the second one is typically seen as animals; sheep or dogs or mares rubbing their noses together, or sometimes even as two clowns with painted faces. But Mr. Steelman's first response was that he wouldn't even take the card. I insisted he hold it, and he said it looked like blood, smeared blood, and the blood was running out of this hole. Very unusual, the disorganization he draws. Very unusual."

Roy continued to go through each of the ten cards, describing the reaction normal people usually gave to the inkblots, and then what Steelman said he saw. No matter what the usual response might have been, Steelman always saw blood or insects, big human eyes coming off the page to get him, boots with faces on them. He even described a cat that had been skinned out, yet was still alive. He saw an unborn fetus with blood flowing from the umbilical cord and a man's face, 'with deadly eyes'.

"One card," the doctor noted, "he refused to even touch, saying 'there's blood all over it. It's ugly and I don't want to look at it'."

"Doctor, can someone fake these tests?"

Roy answered that a normal person trying to fake the tests could be easily spotted, implying he didn't feel that this was the case. He concluded by saying there was the possibility the actions of the accused could be traced to organic brain damage.

But on cross, Dingledine gave Rich Rollman the task of making Dr. Roy look like a buffoon.

Q: "Doctor, did you administer a factual performance test?"

A: "No, I did not."

Q: "Did you administer a speech and sound perception test?"

A: "No, I did not."

Q: "Did you do a finger oscillating test?"

A: "No."

Q: "A trail making test?"

A: "No!" Roy snapped. "I administered those specific tests I told you!"

Q: "You administered those tests and none others?"

Norgren jumped in, objecting to the state trying to make a mockery of the doctor's work. He was overruled, allowing Rollman to continue.

Q: "Did you do a disfacious scanning test?"

A: "No."

Q: "A sensory perception test?"

A: "I said not."

Q: "Well, doctor, what are those tests designed to indicate?"

A: "We went through quite a category. Many of those tests are also very specific. . ."

Q: "Are they not also designed to detect organic brain damage?"

A: "Yes."

Rollman expressed shock at the doctor's admission. "And you didn't administer them?"

Roy rolled his eyes but did not reply. Rollman had done his homework. He proceeded to rattle off test names, methods of research and scores expected. He bombarded Roy with technical questions about specific test applications and forced the doctor to concede he had only scratched the surface in his study of Willie Steelman.

"Doctor, what do you consider the most extensive test on the Wexler intelligence scale for organic brain damage? The arithmetic test?"

"I don't think there is one test more significant than another in the Wexler. . .all the tests would be important."

"But you did not give him the arithmetic!"

Rollman forced Roy to admit the high probability of error in the findings of the limited tests given, and even more importantly, with only two examinations of Steelman, he could obtain only a general outline of the patient's mental condition on those dates and not when the crimes occurred. Lastly, Rollman made Roy admit the results of any test could vary according to the setting they were in, like a prison cell, for instance.

"Doctor, don't you expect that a man preoccupied with his involvement in a murder trial might have a different response to those tests than a man not so involved?"

Roy gave in. "I think that would be a good assumption."

On re-direct, Norgren pointed out, that despite the prosecution's insinuations, the results of Steelman's tests showed abnormalities, and the most recent test given just yesterday showed a higher degree than the test given in May of last year.

"So, the person is getting worse?" Norgren asked.

"Yes."

"Now, doctor, you were aware of the fact that yesterday Mr. Steelman was taking Valium?"

"We didn't get into that."

"But, if in fact he was taking Valium, would that affect the scores?"

Indeed it would, Roy replied, however not in the way most would expect. A mentally affected person would actually do better on the tests under the influence of valium, stating that Steelman was most likely even more disturbed than the tests led him to believe.

"These other tests mentioned by the prosecution," Norgren asked. "Could they be administered?"

Roy sighed. "One could test Mr. Steelman for the next two years and keep quite busy."

Throughout the afternoon session, a spectator sat in the courtroom scribbling in a notebook with a fever pitch. The man watched with a great deal of interest the videotape of the ex-wife, the look on defendant's face as he too watched, and later seemed immersed in the testimony he gave. The spectator would watch, appear to think for a moment, gather his thoughts, and then proceed to write them down on a legal pad.

He was a stout, rotund, black man – the color of his skin itself an unusual sight in St. Johns. He looked uncomfortable in the compact courtroom, his large frame packed in between the smaller, older onlookers. His face was full, with Dizzy Gillespie cheeks and wisps of kinky gray hair at the temples. His fashionably dark suit was a noticeable contrast to the khaki uniforms of Lee's staff and the casual dress of the locals. The man never spoke to those sitting next to him, nor did he act surprised at anything he heard coming from the witness stand.

His name was Dr. James Peale, and he was convinced beyond a shadow of a doubt that Willie Steelman was insane. It was late Thursday afternoon when Robert Norgren called him as a witness for the defense.

Peale's resume appeared endless, and when asked by Norgren to talk about it, it took Peale several minutes to simply cover the highlights.

He was a Doctor of Medicine from Howard University. Interned at Harlem Hospital. Residency in Connecticut. Psychiatrist training at Yale and the U.S. Naval Hospital. Diplomat of the National Board of Medical Examiners. Certified by the American Board of Psychiatry. Member of the Royal College of Psychiatry in Great Britain, as well as several other notable institutions.

He was responsible for the creation of psychiatrist training programs at more than a half dozen universities in California as well as a guest lecturer and faculty member at each. He held the title of Chief of Psychiatric Services at the California Mental Facility at Vacaville and later held similar positions at correction facilities throughout the state, establishing programs for the mentally ill and criminally insane. He was an examiner for the District Attorney and Public Defender in San Joaquin County. Established his own private practice, founded a mental health center in a San Francisco ghetto, and in his spare time, consulted with the Air Force Surgeon General at the Travis Air Base in the north Bay Area.

"Oh yes," Peale added. "I have been a reserve officer in the Army and Air Force for seven years and my retired rank is that of Major." He paused for a moment. "I believe that is about it."

It was not mentioned here, but word was Peale had also served on the Manhattan Project, but had never been proud of his work and refused to discuss it.

Norgren asked him to describe the history he had received from their client, his patient. Peale recited the story that had been told to him by Steelman, and although it was horribly inaccurate and a terrific piece of fiction, Peale seemingly took it at face value, making particular note the drug use Willie claimed to have had, especially the two hundred acid trips he boasted about.

"As his experience with acid developed, he found emerging from himself an angry part of him. He was now two people; a person who was angry with the need to destroy people, and a person that wanted to help them. After his fall in nineteen seventy two, he underwent a very straining personality change; uncontrollable, aggressive, fearful of hurting someone, including his wife. He had been confused and not able to separate the enemy and the war, from his friends."

"Doctor, were you surprised at the testimony from Sergeant Wagner and Detective Hust?" Norgren inquired.

"Yes, I was."

"And were you present when Willie Steelman testified, and when the video tape from his ex-wife was played?"

"Yes."

"Based upon the history of Willie Luther Steelman, and the other information supplied, were you able to diagnose his condition?"

"It is my opinion Mr. Steelman has two problems...schizophrenia and organic brain damage associated with trauma." Peale explained the reasons behind his findings. Quite surprisingly they were based partly on Steelman's references to the Mafia and the Preacher killing. According to him, the discrepancies found in both stories showed delusion. His false ideas about how to change the world, and his belief that he was somehow a soldier in the war proved his thinking was disorganized, as was his perception of reality.

"It indicates to me several things," Peale offered, "but one thing is that he is severely mentally ill."

The remarkable part of Peale's testimony, at least to those who just minutes earlier had listened to his impressive background, was that he was using Willie's grand work of fiction as the basis for his opinion. When confronted with this accusation, Peale had an interesting reply. He admitted, that while the patient was most likely not telling him the whole truth, it was those same wild stories that reinforced his belief that Steelman was mentally ill.

"The statements made (to Wagner and Hust) are full of inconsistencies and are highly questionable as to validity. He is aware of the fact he had memory deficits and cannot remember, so he fills in the holes. We have a term for this called confabulation."

"Greer was lost. "What?"

"Con-fabu-la-tion," Peale explained. "Fills in the holes."

"Doctor," Norgren asked. "Did you ask him what happened at the Sandberg place?"

"Mr. Steelman could not remember everything that happened. It is spotty. He can remember being there, the Sandbergs being tied, and remembers padding Mrs. Sandberg's wrist to avoid hurting her. He doesn't remember the entire time there."

Dingledine watched and listened, then could only shake his head in amazement. Norgren saw him, and then made sure he brought the witness to the main point.

"So what does this indicate to you?" he asked.

"A real deficit in thinking. . .and I think that the person is grossly unable to know what he is doing."

"Now with respect to the history obtained, the testimony in court, with connection to your experience and training as a psychiatrist. . .and all that you reviewed. . .do you have an opinion whether or not, on November third, nineteen seventy three, Willie Luther Steelman knew the nature and quality of his acts, or knew right from wrong?"

"Peale never hesitated. "I don't think Mr. Steelman is faking anything – either sanity or insanity. He is a man who is doing the best he can just to hang on, and I really mean that, literally. All people who are mentally ill have the fear of falling apart, really losing it. They live continuously with it and there isn't much room left for faking. When he had the hallucinations of people in his cell, he knows they aren't there. . .but they are there!"

"Your opinion is then?"

"It is my opinion he was not able to know the nature and quality of his acts, or know right from wrong.

Dingledine slumped in his chair. He didn't care how many degrees this guy had, it was his opinion that the good doctor from California was completely and totally full of shit.

20

Friday, July 18, 1975.

Deputy Gilchrist arrived earlier than usual for his morning routine and apparently caught Willie off guard. He jumped up from his bunk and fumbled towards the washbasin. There, in full sight, was a bar of soap cut into the shape of a handgun. It was not a very good replica, but startled Gilchrist just the same. Willie looked at him, picked the soap up and started washing his hands, smiling.

"I swear, I can't tell if he's serious about the stuff he's pulling," Gilchrist confided to some buddies later that day. "I can't figure him out. Hell, just a few minutes after this soap deal, he asked me if I wanted to practice some martial arts moves. Said he knew some Ti Kwon Do and wanted to try a few moves on me. I couldn't help but laugh at the guy!"

Gilchrist wasn't the only one cautious of Willie Steelman. More than once Robert Norgren asked the deputy to bring his client upstairs into a small conference room so he could speak with him.

"Want him unshackled?" Gilchrist asked.

"No!"

"Want me to leave then?"

"Hell, no!" Norgren snapped. "You stay right here!"

"Doctor, Willie Steelman said in his confession that he shot a fourth bullet into Pat Sandberg's head just to make sure. Doesn't that show that he was aware somebody had been shot?"

"Not to me it doesn't"

Dave Dingledine had begun his cross-examination of Dr. Peale. This opening question attacked Peale's theory that Steelman was not aware of what went on while he was in the Sandberg home. Peale said he believed the defendant's mental state was so diminished at the time that he could not possibly have formed any malicious intent, not did he know right from wrong, so therefore was McNaughton Insane. Logic so warped, Dingledine decided he could only shake his head in disbelief when the doctor answered his first question.

"Doctor. Mr. Steelman said he turned on the stereo to drown out any noise they might make. Does this indicate to you he knew what he was doing?"

"No, it does not."

"Does the fact that both Steelman and Gretzler used a pillow to muffle the shots to both Michael and Pat Sandberg indicate that they didn't want anyone to hear the shots?"

"No, not necessarily."

Dingledine could not believe what he was hearing. "Let me get this straight. Mr. Steelman puts a bullet in the gun, points the gun at the Sandbergs and pulls the trigger. Did he know it would go through the chamber and into their head?"

"I don't think he did."

Dingledine smirked. "So, he really wasn't much of a soldier then, was he?"

Peale remained calm, oblivious to the prosecutor's sarcasm. "Many people envision themselves as a soldier and don't kill or use weapons."

"Didn't you testify yesterday that he was a soldier. . .part of the war and killing?"

"Uh huh."

"Then what was he going to kill with?"

"That was his problem, "Peale replied. "He saw himself as a soldier, but really couldn't do what soldiers do. He cannot kill. He cannot understand what killing is."

Dave had heard enough. He waved the witness off the stand, muttering under his breath to Rich Rollman, "Willie Steelman knows more about the truth than that asshole ever will!"

Greer called it enough for one day.

Gilchrist joked with Willie as he took him back downstairs. "Any big plans for the weekend, Willie?"

"Nope," Willie shot back. "Think I'll just hang around here and take it easy."

On the way home, Gilchrist thought a lot about all the things those doctors had said over the last couple days. He had heard it all before, and years ago had come up with something he called 'Gilchrist's Law'. It stated the more credentials a doctor carried around with him, the more idiotic he would sound when he opened his mouth. Besides, Bob had decided awhile back that he knew more about people, and what made them tick, than any psychiatrist did.

He did agree with Peale on one thing. Willie Steelman *was* crazy. Not just because Peale was a shrink and said so, but because anyone who acted so strangely and killed so coldly just had to be nuts.

Of course that didn't mean they shouldn't gas him, because if anyone deserved it, Willie Steelman did. And if they needed anyone to pull the switch, then he would be more than obliged to volunteer.

And right then Gilchrist decided that he must be a little crazy too, because Jesus Almighty, he kind of liked the guy. "DAMMIT!" he thought. I *am* getting soft!

If Dave Dingledine had his way, he would be giving his closing arguments this morning instead of listening to more psychiatric mumbo-jumbo from some self-proclaimed experts. It mattered not one iota that these so called mind-gurus were now on his side. Doctors Austin, Rogerson, and Cavanaugh had arrived in St. Johns over the weekend and Dingledine had spent most of Sunday in his motel room planning their rebuttal to Peale's pathetic excuse for an opinion. As usual, while they were studying, Larry and Rex went fishing.

Another thunderstorm had pounded the town Friday afternoon, but no evidence remained of this most recent downpour Saturday and Sunday. It was a spectacular summer weekend in the Arizona high country; nearly ninety and dry, and Dave, not unlike the man he was working to convict, had a bad case of cabin fever. Two long weeks in a small room, in a small town, with a small circle of faces, was wearing him down. He longed for dinner at a nice restaurant in Tucson, and not out of a brown bag from a nearby diner. He missed his family, and although he never believed he would admit it, he missed the traffic of the city and the hustle of his downtown office, the incessant ring of the telephone, and the stack of messages from people about problems other than Willie Steelman. For over a year and a half he had done little else but focus on Steelman and Gretzler. So from the moment he had first heard their names, until today, he had thought of little else. Everything he had done, written about or talked about was aimed at the successful outcome of this trial, and anything short of a First Degree Murder conviction would be considered a failure.

And yet Dingledine realized this was far from over. Even after St. Johns, he would still have to do it all over again with David Hoffman and Doug Gretzler.

So it was, while everyone else was outside enjoying this gorgeous weekend, he was stuck inside, turning pages with three guys who didn't want to be in St. Johns anymore than he did. Dave tried to concentrate, telling himself it would not be much longer. He had already promised his family when his work was done here he would take a week off and they would all go to Disneyland.

So amid the piles of paperwork, the motel room clutter, the endless babble of people he didn't even know, David Dingledine found himself daydreaming a bit, thinking that a few days fighting crowds in the Magic Kingdom sounded pretty damn good right about now.

Monday morning, July 21st, Robert Norgren began by objecting to the scheduled appearances of Austin, Rogerson and Cavanaugh. In his verbal motion, he asked the court not to allow the doctors to take the stand, basing his demand on two areas.

First, the examinations that both Austin and Rogerson performed late in the evening of November 9, 1973 were made under the ruse of being of a medical nature, and therefore should not be allowed.

Greer shook his head, reminding him the matter had already been discussed, and allowed, in pretrial hearings.

Norgren then complained those same exams were based on the California complaints and had nothing whatsoever to do with this trial. Again Greer corrected him, saying that regardless of the crime, the doctor's duties were to try and understand more clearly the defendant's state of mind at the time. The doctors would be allowed to give their testimony to the jury.

Austin was called first and Dingledine steered him to the report he had filed with San Joaquin authorities after seeing the defendant. The doctor, reading directly from that report, stated Willie Steelman had 'an anti-social personality'.

"A person like that is constantly in conflict with society and has little or no guilt feelings," he explained, adding that the defendant's lack of loyalty to any social system, along with his inability to learn from past mistakes and self-centered life, is just one part of what allows him to be capable of murder.

"Then what is the other part?" Dingledine inquired.

"The severe degree in which he is able to dehumanize people, including himself. Studies have shown that people who do commit murder all appear to have this common trait."

When asked about the possibility the defendant suffered the mental illness Dr. Peale had suggested, Austin shook his head. "Anti-social behavior is not considered a mental illness," he said.

"What about paranoid schizophrenia?"

Once more Austin shook off the comparison. "No. That is a serious mental disorder which hampers a person's ability to organize his thoughts and carry on a conversation."

Dingledine, driving home to the jury this message that the doctor did not believe the defendant suffered from either mental condition, rattled off all of the tasks Willie Steelman performed while he was inside the Sandberg's home. With each Austin shook his head. No. As far as he was concerned, Steelman was not mentally ill on the day in question, or the day he first interviewed him, or even today, for that matter.

After lunch, Dr. Rogerson was called to offer his opinion. Dingldine's plan was to use the doctor to downplay the defense position that drugs played a major role in Steelman's state of mind. Peale had indicated the defendant's prolonged drug use was a big factor in his mental incapacity.

Once again, Rogerson's typewritten report of November 9th, stated Willie Steelman barely even mentioned his drug use, so Rogerson stated he felt his homicidal nature "was not the result of delusional, hallucinatory state of mind from recent onset, but represents a pattern of personality that has been present for a number of years".

According to Rogerson, no one could really say for certain what role drugs played in the commission of these crimes because no one was there to examine him when he was taking them. In addition, his mental state would greatly depend on how much he took, how often, the quality of the drugs, and the tolerances he managed to build. The doctor said he agreed with his colleague. Willie Steelman suffered from an anti-social personality disorder. He was a severe, habitual criminal. He was dangerous to himself and others.

Dr. Cavanaugh was called late Monday afternoon. His testimony was brief and uneventful.

Dingledine asked him. "Doctor, in your opinion, do you believe Willie Luther Steelman was sane at the time?"

"Yes, I do."

The next morning, after Dingledine and Norgren haggled for over an hour about the additional witnesses the prosecution had scheduled for the day, Greer finally shooed them both out of his office, saying, "They've come this far, I'm going to let the jury hear what they have to say."

Dingledine, taking no chances, had summoned from Tucson, a psychiatrist, Dr. Marshall Jones, and a psychologist, Dr. Hayward Fox. He told Rollman, "We'll bring in as many people as it takes to dispute all the crap Peale dished out."

As each took their turn on the stand, Dingledine hammered away at the basics, making it sound as if Peale was the only man on the face of the earth who could have the audacity, for even one minute, to say that Steelman was insane. Both Jones and Fox had visited with Steelman during his stay at the Pima County jail, and while the sessions were admittedly brief, neither hesitated when asked if the defendant knew right from wrong, or the consequences of their acts on at the time of the murder. Both said he most certainly did. In particular, Dr. Fox rebutted what Dr. Roy said about the psychological tests he performed proving that Steelman suffered from mild to severe brain damage. Fox said such tests were very inconclusive and proved nothing, except the need for more tests.

With that, Dingledine again told the court that the State rested.

Norgren stayed in the courtroom for a few minutes organizing his briefcase. Willie had complained yesterday about the store-bought smokes they kept bringing him and said he wanted to roll some of his own. If it wasn't too much trouble, maybe he could get him a can of tobacco. Norgren discovered the can he had purchased as he placed papers back into his case. On the way out, he went downstairs to give it to him, along with an apology for taking so long. Willie gushed, and thanked for remembering.

The way Willie acted only made Norgren feel worse. He had all but lost the case, and probably the guy's life as well, and still Willie couldn't thank him enough for a measly little three-dollar can of tobacco.

Norgren drove back to the cabin and spent most of the night working on his final arguments to the jury. He realized it would be little more than a beg for mercy, for he knew in his gut what the verdict would be.

"I have every confidence in you people," he scribbled on his legal pad, "and I know you are going to do the right thing." It was long after midnight when he finished. He knew that if he were to salvage anything from this trial, these words he had written would certainly be his last chance.

It was by mere coincidence that Willie spent most of the night working on what he figured would be his final opportunity as well. He knew the very moment he set foot in St. Johns that he would not leave this place quietly. He decided that up to now he had been pretty damn cordial and cooperative.

He twisted the lid off the can and quietly worked away at this last chance to show them who they were dealing with.

21

Wednesday, July 23, 1975.

Somewhere along the line, Willie got a new cowboy outfit. For the past several days he came to court decked out in new blue Levis and a plaid western-style shirt, brightly adorned with white pearlescent buttons. He wore pointed-toe boots made from rattlesnake hide. And with his new threads came the usual droopy mustache and the ever-bulging afro Willie had become noted for. It was an odd combination, and certainly a look not lost on the courthouse regulars, all of who were getting a good laugh at his expense.

Bob Gilchrist teased him every chance he got. "Willie, I swear to God, those are the ugliest damn boots I think I ever saw."

Dave Dingledine, on the other hand, was seething over the latest defense tactic. Robert Norgren announced Monday that Dr. White had arrived in St. Johns to testify, which forced Dingledine to try and counter the move. This morning, Judge Greer listened to arguments from both sides regarding Dr. Patricia White's appearance. Prior to the meeting, Dingledine and Rollman had even confronted Dr. White in the hallway and demanded to know if she had planned on declaring Steelman insane. White was noncommittal, saying she could not render such an opinion at this point. Dingledine smelled a con job, and told her as much. He worried if White was allowed to take the stand and mirror Peale's earlier testimony, then the last five psychiatric experts he had called, along with the opinions they gave, would have been all for naught. Dave had no one else to call, and the last thing he wanted was for Norgren to have the final word on the subject of the defendant's sanity.

"So just exactly what is she going to testify to?" Greer asked.

"Exactly what Mr. Dingledine said she was going to…that she saw Steelman on a number of occasions and…"

Greer didn't care to hear the all the psycho mumbo-jumbo again, and interrupted. "Okay. I think I'll let it in. It may be in error, but I would rather…"

Dingledine fumed. "May the record show my strong objection! My *strongest* objection!"

Dr. White took the stand and recalled her various meetings with the defendant while he was in custody in California. Norgren asked her, that after these examinations had been completed, if she was able to diagnose Mr. Steelman's condition?

"I made the diagnosis of pseudo-psychopathic schizophrenia," adding that she treated him with tranquilizers, sedatives, and psychotherapy treatments every few weeks until he was removed from San Joaquin's jurisdiction.

"Now, would you say this particular disease is different, or even the opposite, from an anti-social personality or sociopath?"

"It's totally different," White replied.

It was Dingledine's turn. "Dr. White, are you prepared to offer an opinion to the jury as to whether Willie Luther Steelman, on November third, nineteen seventy three, knew the nature and quality of his acts, or right from wrong, when he participated in the killings of Michael and Patricia Sandberg?"

"Yes."

Dave lunged towards her, his voice booming. "Didn't you tell me less than a half hour ago that you could not?"

"I cannot say, with any degree of certainty, exactly what was going on in Mr. Steelman's mind at that moment, but if his mental functioning at that moment is the same as at this time, then I would consider him legally insane."

Dingledine looked at Judge Greer and roared. "If the court is going to allow for this type of testimony, then I must ask for an exclusion of the evidence, and also ask it hold Mr. Norgren in contempt for not advising us what Dr. White was going to do! A half hour ago she says she could not render an opinion, and now she comes in here and says she can!"

Norgren had heard enough. "I told Mr. Dingledine what Dr. White said this morning! I said the doctor could not, with a reasonable degree of medical certainty, say as to whether or not he knew right from wrong! This is the first time I've heard this testimony, and I'm tired of every time Mr. Dingledine doesn't like what he hears he asks to hold somebody in contempt!"

Dingledine ignored him. "The same was true for Dr. Peale!" he complained to Greer. "He never had a McNaughton opinion until he got over here!"

"Hey!" Norgren shot back, "If I could read the mind of every psychiatrist, I would gladly tell Mr. Dingledine what they were going to testify to!"

As far as Greer was concerned, the matter was closed, as was the presentation of witnesses and evidence. He called for a brief recess, the told both sides to have their closing remarks ready when they returned.

Thirty minutes later, Dave Dingledine wasted no time getting to the heart of the matter.

"Ladies and gentlemen, I'm telling you that Willie Steelman is a killer! He committed cold blooded, First Degree murder!"

He walked the jury back over that Saturday, from the kidnapping of Vincent Armstrong to pulling the trigger on Patricia Sandberg. He reintroduced each piece of evidence, from the prints found in the apartment, to the check forged at the Ocotillo Motel. He disputed vigorously the defense of insanity, pointing to the decisions Willie Steelman made that day, and how a person under such an extreme influence of drugs, as the defense had claimed, could not have handled the situation he and his partner found themselves in with the Sandbergs He focused on facts alone, and repeated the details until he was certain they had been etched into the mind of every last juror. He omitted nothing. He did not want any of his words to confuse them, so he chose them carefully, pausing often to find just the right one. When he was finished he asked the jury to find Willie Luther Steelman guilty of murder in the First Degree.

Norgren had remembered something Judge Greer said early on; that the people of Apache County wanted desperately to believe Willie Steelman was crazy because they did not want to admit a man in his right mind would have done such horrible things. Because of who they were and the community in which they lived, Greer said each one had a desperate need to believe in the basic goodness of all people. All the defense would need to do, Greer had insinuated, was to convince just one member of the jury that his client was not a vicious monster. If he could do that one single thing, he might avoid a First Degree verdict.

Norgren first thanked the jury. "Judge Greer told us he could give us a fair trial and that you were good people. We agree with that. Regardless of the verdict, we know we received a fair trial here in St. Johns."

He then appealed to the kindness of their hearts. He spoke to each jury member directly, making eye contact as he appealed to their good nature, asking for their understanding, compassion and forgiveness.

Problem was Willie didn't play along. He slouched and sneered and rolled his eyes, appearing bored, snickering from time to time at the picture Norgren painted of him.

"Now, I told you from the outset, in my opening statement, that Mr. Dingledine cannot prove beyond a reasonable doubt that Willie Steelman was guilty of First Degree Murder. In fact, Mr. Dingledine has not offered a single element of any kind of proof. Remember, we don't have to prove anything. When the issue of insanity is raised, as it has been in this case, it is up to Mr. Dingledine to prove to you, beyond a reasonable doubt, that Willie Luther Steelman was sane at the time of the incident. We don't have to prove anything, and that is very important to remember."

He moved to another area he hoped could help sway the jury. "Reasonable doubt. Think about what that says. You and I can't afford to make mistakes, so when you hear the evidence, and there is any doubt in your mind – any doubt at all that he did not know right from wrong at the time of the incident – then you have to acquit him! It is your duty to acquit him! The statutes require it! If you don't, then it would be an extreme tragedy that you might have to live with for the rest of your life."

He kept up the guilt. "You know, I have lived with this case for many months and I've worked very hard on it. I'm tired. Now I'm going to turn the burden over to you and you are going to have to carry that burden with you when you go back to the jury room. You are going to have to make a decision with regard to Willie Steelman's life."

"Reasonable doubt!" Norgren reminded them. "When Dr. Marshall Jones testified that Willie Steelman was sane on November third, nineteen seventy three, I asked him, 'Are you sure beyond a reasonable doubt?', even he said 'No'. Now here is a psychiatrist with years and years of experience and even he is not convinced beyond a reasonable doubt of Willie Steelman's sanity. So, where does that put you?"

He paused. "Mr. Dingledine has proved nothing. And based on their failure of proof, I'm going to ask you to return a verdict of either not guilty, or to reduced charges based on drug intoxication. I have every confidence in you people. I know you are going to do the right thing."

Dingledine rose to offer his rebuttal. "Ladies and gentlemen, Mr. Norgren did a wonderful job for Willie Steelman, but he doesn't have any facts to work with. None at all. There was a lot of evidence that was brought in that I probably didn't have to bring – the confessions have been enough – but I brought in men to match the bullets, two fingerprint men from the F.B.I. to show they were Steelman's in the Sandberg house. I brought you fingerprints from California and showed you they were from the Datsun. Why did I do this? Because Mr. Norgren is exactly right. I have to prove this case beyond a reasonable doubt."

Dingledine pointed to the defendant. "This man here is sane! He knows that a gun kills! He knew the nature and the quality of his acts! If not, why didn't he just go up and say, 'Michael, I want your car', and leave it at that? Everything would have been fine. He knew what he did with Armstrong was wrong. He knew everything he did that day was wrong!"

"And drug use? I'm not saying that over the years Willie Steelman hasn't been on drugs, but we're talking about November third, nineteen seventy three, and his accountability to the law. I can stand here another twenty minutes and show you why there is no evidence, no evidence at all, that Willie Luther Steelman didn't know right from wrong, or what he was doing. I know this has been a long case. . .a long, dirty case. . .so let me say this now, I would like to commend you people in this community. You've heard the evidence, and now I urge you to come back with a verdict of First Degree Murder. Michael and Patricia Sandberg can't say anything, but I can. Thank you."

Judge Greer dismissed the jury for a short recess. When they returned, he gave them the lengthy and complicated instructions on how they would have to unravel everything they had seen and heard over the last couple of weeks, and at 2:30 p.m. the jury retired to deliberate.

Because it was already mid afternoon, many of the participants felt the jury would probably not return that day with any decision. Although confident in the outcome, Dingledine and the others returned to their motel room, knowing it would most likely be morning before they heard anything.

Deputy Gilchrist took Willie back downstairs to his cell, then strolled over to the office, where he was soon joined by Lee and some of the more prominent names in the community. As was usually the case, the good Mormon men of St. Johns used Gilchrist's office to sneak a cigarette on occasion. Gilchrist, who was neither Mormon or a smoker, waved his arms and coughed, issuing his now standard rebuke, "You Mormons and your damn cigarettes are gonna kill me one day."

Back in his cell, Willie worked quickly. He also knew what the outcome was going to be, and his only hope now was that the jury would stay out long enough for him to finish what he had started.

Upstairs in the jury room, seven women and five men did not hesitate in their task. Foreman Ralph Maness asked each of them to speak their mind. It took less than an hour for them to come to a decision. With all the time they had spent together, there was no urgency to finish, as if just mere minutes together might dull what they had already agreed to. So they stayed and talked, about everything other than Willie Steelman, and the things he had done.

Down the hill at the Trail Rider, the men kicked around where they should all go eat, for what most likely would be their last dinner in St. Johns. It was now after five, and the remote chance of being called back to the courthouse had faded. Hust suggested that they grab some steaks, and maybe a six pack, and celebrate with a little barbeque right out in the motel parking lot. But Dave nixed the idea. It was too early to celebrate anything, he said.

Rex checked his watch, and not willing to miss out on that evening's poker game, said that whatever they were going to do, they could count him out. He would be in the basement if they needed him.

Fifteen minutes later, Larry Hust raced downstairs to retrieve him. The jury was back.

Word had traveled quickly through St. Johns that the trial was over and the jury had gone to deliberate, so many of the townspeople came to the courthouse curious to see what was going to happen next. Greer's courtroom was bustling, full of spectators, family members of the jurors, even a few extra reporters, all mingling about. For the first time since the trial had begun, it was standing room only. The bailiff walked into Greer's chambers and reported the jury was ready. It was five fifteen. The call went over to the Sheriff's Office for Gilchrist to bring Willie back. The phone rang at the Trail Rider as well. Dingledine and Rollman gave each other thumbs up. Less than three hours. A good sign. They headed back up to the courthouse, all of the day's ninety-five degrees still hanging in the air.

Robert Norgren had never left the building. They found him talking with the Apache County Public Defender who had assisted him during the trial. It was said Norgren winced a little at the news, before heading slowly back into the courtroom.

Willie was sitting on his bunk when Gilchrist entered. He locked the main cellblock door behind him. Willie rose, put his hands through the bars and waited for the cuffs. Gilchrist opened the cell door, patted Willie down and did a quick, routine scan of the cell. He saw a red can of tobacco sitting on the ledge above the toilet – he had seen it before – so it was what he didn't see that made him reach for it.

The lid was missing.

Willie didn't flinch.

"Whadda we got here, Willie?"

Silence.

Gilchrist asked again. "What happened to the top off this thing?"

No response.

"Who gave you this?"

"Norgren."

"So where's the rest of it? What did you do with the lid?"

Steelman was done talking. On the floor in the corner of the cell Gilchrist could see scruff marks on the concrete, like where metal had been scrapped across it. He knew now what he was looking for. Again he asked Willie to tell him what was going on. Willie stayed tight lipped. Gilchrist dug through his clothes. Nothing. He was just about ready for a full body search when the light bulb went off. He reached up and buried his hands into Willie's bushy afro. From deep within it he pulled out a crude homemade knife – three inches long, sharpened to a razor edge. He held it in Willie's face.

"Well now!" he grinned.

"Hey, that wasn't for you, man," Willie stammered. "It was for the pilot on the way back."

"Hell, Willie," a relieved Gilchrist laughed, the rush of the moment fading. "I didn't know you knew how to fly a plane?"

Willie cracked a smile. "I'd hafta damn well learn, wouldn't I?"

Gilchrist called upstairs and said there would be a slight delay, telling the bailiff of his discovery. When word got around to Norgren, it was said he turned ghost white, and they were afraid he was going to pass out right there at his table.

Greer got the news and decided there was no sense dilly-dallying any longer. He told Gilchrist that Steelman would remain cuffed and shackled while the verdicts were read. He had gotten this far without a problem and he darned sure wasn't going to let the defendant raise a ruckus now.

Steelman entered the room wearing his usual smirk. He knew that they knew. That was enough. He would have his story to tell later. Gilchrist sat him down next to Norgren, who made no attempt to conceal his fear as he slid his chair away. Two reporters came up as close as Lee and Gilchrist would allow and asked Willie what he was thinking.

"They're gonna find me guilty," he shot back. "I expect the death penalty. Anything less is a waste of time, and I sure as hell ain't gonna spend the rest of my life behind bars." Willie turned his back on them before they could fire off another question. He was done talking.

Ralph Maness stood up. "State of Arizona, Plaintiff versus Willie Luther Steelman, Defendant…"

He read the verdicts, slowly, carefully. All six of them. All six. All guilty.

Dingledine had a clean sweep.

Several jurists were now weeping. Willie was blank. Greer remanded him into the custody of Pima County and set August 22nd for a pre-sentence hearing.

He looked at the jury. "Ladies and gentlemen, I'd like to thank you for your service. It is, I suppose, sometimes the most difficult responsibility, but as citizens that's what we have to bear, and I thank you for filling it very well." He heard the sniffling, then continued his thought. "And if it makes you feel any better, I agree with your verdict."

Gilchrist and Lee started to hustle Willie out of the room. The same two reporters asked, "Mr. Steelman, are you surprised?"

"I'm not surprised. I know I'm gonna die, but I don't hold against the jury. I had no doubt what the result would be."

"Do you think you got a fair trial in St. Johns?"

Willie thought for a moment. Even Gilchrist stopped. He wanted to hear the answer to this one himself. Willie looked at the deputy, then back to the reporters. "The judge has been square. The jury has been square. But there was no way I can get a fair trial in the United States."

Larry Hust stopped by the Circle K on the way back to the room and picked up a couple of six packs. Over a beer, Dingledine thanked each one of them for their hard work.

The decision had been made earlier to take Steelman directly to Tucson following the verdict. Bowman's Cessna was waiting when the sheriff's sedan moved out onto the tarmac. Lee and Gilchrist pulled Willie from the backseat. "Well, Willie," Gilchrist asked, "what do you think they're going do to you?"

"Shit, no question. They're gonna hafta kill me."

Gilchrist didn't miss a beat. He pointed to Willie's feet. "Then can I have them ugly boots of yours?"

Willie cracked up. "Hell, yes! They ain't gonna let me into Florence with these things. They're loaded with steel shanks."

Willie reached out to shake their hands. "You guys been real fair to me and I appreciate it. Couldn't have asked for anything more."

They loaded Willie into the plane. It taxied a couple hundred feet, the engine gunned, and it took off into the southern sky.

"You know," Gilchrist said, not even bothering to look over at his boss, "I gotta feeling it'll be a little more quiet around here from now on."

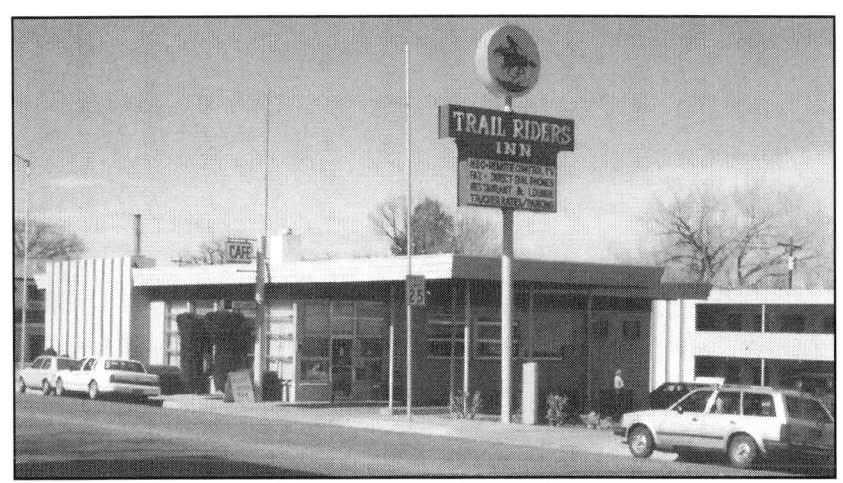

The Trail Riders Inn, St. Johns, Arizona.
Home to the prosecution team while in St. Johns.

Apache County Courthouse, St. Johns, Arizona

Judge
Richard Greer

Judge Greer's Courtroom, St. Johns, Arizona

The Federal Building in Prescott, Arizona where Douglas Gretzler's trial was held.

The courtroom at the Federal Building in Prescott, Arizona where Judge William Druke presided over the murder trial of Douglas Gretzler.

22

Wednesday, August 27, 1975.

Willie had spent four weeks at the Pima County Jail, waiting to hear the words. He was neither nervous, or anxious, or angry. In fact, for the first time, he was considered a model prisoner. It had been a month of little or no outside contact, with the possible exception of Norgren, who stopped by on the rarest of occasions to talk about what was going on.

In Arizona, the Aggravation/Mitigation hearings allow both sides the opportunity to give their final arguments in the sentencing phase of the trial. The prosecution is required to prove the presence of certain aggravating circumstances that occurred during the commission of the crime in order to obtain a death penalty conviction. Those circumstances include such factors as prior convictions involving violence, pecuniary gain, multiple homicides, or the one Dingledine was pressing for; a murder especially cruel, depraved, or heinous. On the other hand, it was the responsibility of the defense to offer mitigating circumstances to show why their client should be spared death. Factors such as the defendant's age, a traumatic childhood, even a low IQ score could be offered to help balance the scale.

But unlike some states where the jury hears this discussion, Arizona requires the original trial judge hear the arguments and determine the punishment. Steelman's hearing, originally scheduled for Friday, August 22nd, had been postponed because Dingledine had not returned from vacation yet. Rich Rollman had filled in for him during several preliminary hearings, but Greer insisted the Chief Prosecutor be present at this one, so he postponed the hearing until the following Tuesday.

However there was very little to discuss and yesterday's session was rather uneventful. Norgren had a difficult time locating even one person willing to speak on Willie's behalf, so he simply rehashed the words spoken in St. Johns; once again pleading for the court to consider his client's mental illness before making a decision.

"It is inhumane to punish a sick man," he argued. "Brutality breeds brutality. It is an absolute myth that capital punishment is a deterrent. How can it be to a mentally ill man? A society is not wholly civilized that punishes the mentally ill."

Dingledine answered by reminding the court how the Sandbergs had been tied up, and the long, agonizing length of time they were held captive, followed finally by the sickening manner by which they had been killed. "That's what was inhumane about this whole sick episode," he countered. "He shot Michael while his wife was within hearing distance in another room...then shot her! The Sandbergs had done nothing to provoke him, and I submit that these are the aggravating circumstances to justify the death penalty."

While both sides made their case, Willie sat, bored and uninterested, rolling his eyes whenever Norgren mentioned his mental condition.

Willie rose and stood erect, looking directly at the judge, hands clasped at his waist. "I don't plan to ask for any mercy," he announced. "I don't expect any and I don't want any. I see no reason for the courts to act any differently than they have for these hundreds of years, so let's just get this over with so I can go."

He started to sit back down, but then, as almost an after thought, he looked at Norgren and sneered. "Oh yeah, just one more thing. I don't agree with my attorney. It was nice to have received a fair trial in the sovereign country of the United States, and in Arizona."

Greer thanked both sides for their 'excellent and highly competent efforts'. "But I'm not here to philosophize on the merits of the death penalty," he continued. "Obviously it did not deter Mr. Steelman in these deeds and it will not deter hundreds of others. The court finds there are no mitigating circumstances to preclude the penalty of death and that the defendant's comprehension of the situation was not severely impaired."

He paused for a moment then looked down at Steelman. "Willie, you know me and I know you, so it is with that, that I'm sentencing you to two consecutive death penalties. In the event on is overturned on appeal, the other will stand."

He added another eighty to ninety-five years for the other convictions, including the Armstrong kidnapping and the burglary and robbery of the Sandbergs, then addressed Willie once more. "Mr. Steelman, I believe you committed these cruel and hideous murders fully aware that you were robbing these victims of the sweet blessings of life, and I believe, that in your present state of mind, that you would do it again."

"Judge Greer," Willie replied, with as close to an apology as he would ever offer, "I don't blame you. I don't want to hurt nobody no more."

Shortly after one o'clock that same afternoon, Willie arrived at the Arizona State Prison in Florence, a small, ancient, desert town that scatters its dusty streets around the northern edge of the sprawling prison complex. He was met by Warden Harold Cardwell, who, in the company of several reporters who had tagged along from Tucson, warned his new arrival, "I expect you to act like a man."

Willie Luther Steelman took his place as the 13th inmate on Arizona's Death Row. Before night fell the paperwork was already in motion to review Greer's decision, an automatic appeal required in all death penalty cases. Ironically, for all of David Dingledine's efforts, and despite Judge Greer's swift dispense of justice, Willie would not live long enough to see the inside of Arizona's gas chamber.

23

Tuesday, October 14, 1975.

Headline of the afternoon edition of the *Prescott Courier*:

"DOUGLAS GRETZLER MURDER TRIAL MOVED HERE"

"A New York City man went on trial in Prescott today for the murders of a Tucson couple in November of 1973. One hundred jurors have been called for duty in the federal courthouse, and panel selection is expected to take two days. Pima County Superior Court Judge William Druke says the trial should take about one month."

Prescott rests in the foothills of northwestern Arizona, more than 200 miles from Tucson, but even further away from the image most have of the Southwest. Here grow tall pines instead of saguaro. Adobe and stucco, so commonplace in the desert below, is replaced by clapboard sided homes.

The Prescott town square is bordered on one side by a somber gray courthouse, its granite walls cut decades earlier from a nearby quarry. In the center of the square stands a statue, not of a well-known Spanish explorer or proud leader of the native Yavapai, but that of Buckey O'Neill, a much-loved mayor of an earlier Prescott. O'Neill's fame did not come from his community service, but years later as one of the infamous Rough Riders in the War with Spain, where he lost his life in a battle charge along side Teddy Roosevelt himself.

So Prescott residents admit, even boast, they are indeed different than the rest of the state. "Our rivers actually have running water in them," is their sarcastic way of distancing themselves from the lowlanders. They do fail to mention, however, that for several years Prescott was everything Arizona, even carrying the title of Territorial Capital, before townsfolk grew weary of the bureaucracy and haggling, and gladly relinquished the honor to Phoenix. The territorial courthouse still stands just a few blocks down from the town square. Before that, justice was handed out at Fort Misery, a two-room log house that served as both a courtroom and a church. Even Fort Misery remains today, walking distance from the county courthouse.

Thirty miles off Interstate 17 and west up Highway 69, Prescott is also the birthplace of Brenda Harris, who in October 1973, at the tender age of 20, suddenly found herself in the middle a grisly murder trial. It was no more than a year earlier, fresh out of Prescott High, Brenda was hired by Yavapai County largely for her admirable shorthand skills. Expecting to toil away forever in the Finance Department, young Ms. Harris was surprised to learn she had been instructed to report to the Federal Building across the street early this particular Tuesday morning. There she introduced herself to Judge Druke, who informed her she would be his new court clerk for a trial scheduled to begin in a few minutes.

The Federal Courthouse in Prescott was once a striking example of judicial decor. After being built in the 1930's by the WPA, years of use and government neglect had left the building extremely worn. It suffered from peeling paint, faded woodwork, and broken fixtures, leaving the building either too hot, too cold, too drafty, or much too stuffy. It was used sparingly now – the Federal judge seated in Prescott oversaw only a handful of cases these days – so usually the doors remained locked.

The upstairs courtroom, however, was still a magnificent sight, with a large gallery at the rear and a massive elevated alcove to the front where the judge's bench rose above the room. To the right was the jury box with ornate railing framing in sixteen heavy wooden chairs. Behind the jury, and along the wall of the courtroom's southern exposure, tall narrow windows welcomed needed sunlight into the darkened room. Facing the bench were the prosecution and defense tables, with a podium positioned between them from which their oration was to be delivered. Next to the judge was the witness chair, and directly in front of and below the bench – literally in the middle of the courtroom – was the clerk table. As Judge Druke had promised, the proceeding was soon underway, and out in front of everyone and everything, sat Brenda Harris, feverously attacking her steno pad.

Like many of her generation, Brenda believed there was good in just about everyone. Love One Another had been the 60's cornerstone, and so she felt killing was wrong – any kind of killing – and while she wasn't adamant about it, she felt the death penalty was probably wrong as well. She knew almost nothing about the case she was now a part of, although for some reason she recalled watching the news one night several years back when the story came out of Tucson. She could still remember seeing the victims being removed from their apartment, shivering as the reporter described the condition of the bodies, trying to imagine what they looked like underneath those blankets. She remembered wondering what kind of person could have done such a horrible thing.

The answer to that question now sat just few feet away from her. And yet, after seeing him up close, and how quiet and shy he was, Brenda could now not help but wonder if there hadn't been some awful mistake.

As she had been instructed, when the bailiff nodded, Brenda pressed the buzzer, signaling the judge they were ready. She glanced around, amazed to find policemen outnumbering everyone else. There was one at each door, several directly behind the defendant, and two more in the spectator gallery. There had been lots of talk about security, not just for the man on trial, but for everyone in the courtroom, so naturally she was scared. What if someone had a gun? There was talk some of the victim's family members were in the courtroom. She worried one of them might try something crazy.

The morning was filled with boring ground rules and arguments between the judge and both sides about how the jury would be picked. Brenda couldn't help but notice right away how loud and dramatic Mr. Hoffman was, even when it was not his turn to speak. The initial rush of the morning was gone, and now the words she transcribed seemed technical, repetitive, boring. Except for Mr. Hoffman, who acted like a carnival barker. She thought he would be a good lawyer on TV.

The boredom was short-lived, however. When everyone returned to the courtroom after lunch, Willie Steelman was waiting for them.

Days before the trial began, David Hoffman had every intention of calling Steelman as a witness for the defense, a threat that concerned Dingledine. If Steelman came off as the bad guy of the two, and could be paraded around in front of the jury, Dingledine knew he could be in trouble. Compared to the wild-eyed Willie Steelman, Doug Gretzler looked every bit the innocent choirboy.

Likewise, Hoffman knew his client's chance would be greatly improved if the jury could get a good look at Steelman. But he also realized if Willie took the stand and turned on his former partner, it could become a huge liability. After all, it was Gretzler who admitted firing the first shots, the ones that most likely killed the Sandbergs. He believed it was worth a gamble.

So when Dingledine realized Hoffman was serious, he beat him to the punch. He did not want Steelman anywhere near this trial, and more specifically in front of a jury, so he decided to get the matter out of the way quickly. Although Pima County had filed a motion days earlier to prevent the defense from calling Steelman, it was David Dingledine who got the warrant to bring Willie Steelman to Prescott.

Willie came in late Tuesday morning. Again it was Jack Bowman who flew witnesses back and forth from Tucson, while Rex Angeli again drove his motorhome up to Prescott to shuttle them to and from the airport outside of town. Along with both Angeli and Hust, Bowman too was considered quite a character, and it seemed as if he and Angeli took turns playing practical jokes on each other. Bowman had spent some time with Willie while flying him to St. Johns, and now to Tucson, and while he had no mercy for Steelman, he had to admit he enjoyed their conversation. He got a good laugh when he heard about the homemade knife and what Willie had planned for him back in St. Johns.

Angeli watched while Willie was pulled out of the plane and readied for the trip into town. Bowman found Angeli and took him aside. "Rex, when we get to the RV, put this in. "He handed Angeli an eight-track tape.

"What in the hell's this?"

"Just put it in. It'll be as funny as shit," he promised.

Steelman, the deputies, Bowman and Angeli stepped up inside the RV and Rex did as he had been told. He turned on the stereo and blaring out from speakers came Tom Jones singing, 'The Green, Green Grass of Home'.

Bowman busted out laughing, as did Angeli, who finally got the joke. They both looked over at Willie, who was slow to crack a smile.

"That's a good one, Jack," Steelman admitted. "Weird thing is, I actually like that song."

With the joke over, Bowman told Rex he could turn it off. "No, leave it in" Willie asked. "I mean it. I really like it."

So the motorhome rolled into town with the three of them trying to remember the words and singing about the man getting ready to hang, and how wonderful it was going to be in the Promised Land on the other side.

"Your Honor," Dingledine began, "the State, in support of our previous motion, has asked that Willie Luther Steelman be brought here to court to show that, as his attorney has indicated, that he will not testify at this trial."

Steelman was taken to the witness chair, where it was Brenda's responsibility to swear him in. He slumped down into his seat and Druke told him to stand up. Willie ignored him as Brenda approached.

He glared down, his eyes burning right through her. She hesitated, terrified. To Brenda he looked like a trapped animal, and if he could break free, he would do to her what he did to those poor people down in Tucson. She wanted to turn and run.

"Do you. . .swear to. . .tell the. . .truth. . ." she stammered.

Willie's eyes burned right through her.

". . .the whole truth. . ."

He wasn't listening.

". . .and nothing but the truth. . ."

Steelman's mouth opened slightly, his eyes opened wider.

". . .so help you God?"

He uttered not a sound. His eyes continued to cut right through her. She turned away from his stare and looked to Judge Druke for help.

"Are you Willie Luther Steelman?" he asked.

Silence.

"Are you willing to answer any of our questions?"

"Might answer some," he spit. "Might not answer others."

Druke cut it short. "It does appear that a decision on this matter is not proper at this time.

Willie stepped down and looked at Brenda as he walked away. She swore, even if she lived to be a hundred years old, she would never forget those eyes. The look he gave her was one of shear hatred, like this whole thing was her idea.

"I might answer some of their questions," he repeated moments later when a reporter quizzed him outside the courtroom. "Might not answer others."

That was all Willie would give them this day. During that brief moment, with Steelman on the stand, and his partner sitting a few feet away, Brenda changed her mind about people like those two. Until today she was willing to try and find the best in everyone. Now she was convinced some people were just plain evil.

The potential jurors, one hundred citizens in all, were called from all over Yavapai County and asked to report to the Federal Building in Prescott. As they cluttered the tiny hall off the second floor courtroom, it was immediately clear this was going to be a long drawn-out process.

Last month in Tucson, both sides had submitted their list of questions for the potential jurors, and while Dingledine's list approached one hundred, Hoffman went a step further. He had created one hundred and sixty eight questions, and he intended to ask to ask every juror every one.

Question #27: "Are you a member of the American Independent Party or John Birch Society?"

Question #80: "Have you ever seen a dead body?"

And after filling page upon page, Hoffman finally presented to most bizarre.

Question #97: "There's a Perry Mason Syndrome in the country which Perry Mason, at the last minute, always finds the person who actually did the killing and it's never his client. He takes on the burden of finding and presenting the guilty person and pulls the rabbit out of the hat. I have never seen anyone of his pictures or books that failed in this regard. Do you understand that?"

No one ever found out if they did or not. Druke would not allow it. And while most of these questions were denied, eighty-four of them eventually comprised the list that was submitted to each of the potential jurors.

In addition, Hoffman filed a motion yesterday to allow him a full-blown voir dire examination of the jury panel. In other words, he wanted unlimited access and unlimited time interrogating each and every potential juror. Before the jury questioning even began, he filed a motion requesting additional challenges – even more than the ten state law allowed. If granted, David Hoffman would be allowed to strike any potential juror, regardless of his reasons, regardless of how many he many had already refused, and regardless of how few jurors might remain.

Druke knew what counsel was up to and denied both motions. He also knew there was no way they would have a jury in two days, and he had David Hoffman to thank for that.

Doug Gretzler's cell was one of a dozen buried in the basement of the Yavapai County Courthouse. The entrance to the jail was at the rear of the structure, looking slightly uphill to the Federal Building standing on an adjacent corner. Since its construction in 1917, the jail had played host to a wide array of lawbreakers – from common drunks to notorious bank robbers – but no one quite like the accused murderer who had just checked in.

The jailers were well aware of his crimes, including the nine people he murdered in California. The newcomer was neither friendly nor talkative, nor did he make any unreasonable demands. If it were not for the savagery of his crimes he was now on trial for, his presence in the Prescott jail might have gone completely unnoticed.

Certainly, Gretzler was much more presentable these days, although he remained terribly gaunt. Still, two years of incarceration (and its limited access to drugs), along with three meals a day, had managed to remove somewhat the hollow dead look from his face. While his eyes still set back deep into his long thin face, they now peered out through new glasses courtesy of David Hoffman. Gretzler's dark blond hair was purposely kept neatly trimmed up over the ears and parted to one side. On occasion, such as when he leaned over to help the guards cuff him, a long thick strand would fall over his forehead, making it necessary for him to snap his head back to get the hair out of his eyes. A stylish mustache drooped slightly over the corners of his mouth, but other than that he stayed clean-shaven. His wardrobe was basic; slacks and shirt (he preferred long sleeves) in pastel colors chosen by Hoffman himself. Jail protocol allowed the prisoner neither a belt nor a tie.

In conversation, Gretzler's response was certain to include a "yes sir" and "no mam", in a voice so quiet and meek he was often asked to speak up.

And yet, despite the mild impression he gave, there remained a strict procedure Yavapai County followed in his daily preparation for court. Two guards were required to be present anytime there was contact made with the prisoner.

Only after he was sufficiently secured was he removed from his cell, where an elevator took him upstairs. Although once outside he could easily see the Federal Building not more than a hundred yards away, the same two deputies drove him the short distance to the courthouse.

At the rear of the Federal Building was the loading area for the first floor post office. Stairs leading to the second floor were used almost exclusively for prisoners. Once upstairs, Gretzler was moved to an office adjoining the judges' chambers. If the wait was expected to be longer than even just a few minutes, extra precaution was taken and he was placed in the small holding cell in the U.S. Marshall's Office in an adjacent room. Regardless of how brief the wait might be, he remained handcuffed and in leg irons at all times when outside of the courtroom. During his time in court each day, Gretzler's cell was stripped and checked for contraband. A daily log was provided for any such unusual observations. The logbook remained clean for the course of the trial.

At a few minutes before nine each morning, Gretzler was taken into the courtroom and seated between Hoffman and his partner Michael Brown. During the frequent recesses and meetings held in Druke's chamber, Gretzler was escorted back into the office and recuffed. During lunch he was locked back in the holding cell and his noon meal was served to him there.

Gretzler was present for the entire trial, including the many days of jury selection, which continued today. Druke had revised his original estimate of two days, and was now hoping he could somehow seat a jury by the end of the week.

Naturally, Brenda was anxious to talk about what was happening during the trial, but by Druke's instruction, was careful to reveal only the very basics to her parents each evening. The trial was a big event in little Prescott and Brenda couldn't help but be excited about being right in the very middle of it. Still, she thought it funny that during the day she was involved in one of the biggest murder trials in Arizona history, and at night she scurried out of the house after dinner to coach girl's volleyball at the high school.

There was, in fact, very little discussion of the case any where in town. Out of one hundred potential jurors called, only a handful had ever heard the names Steelman and Gretzler, let alone know anything about what they did in Tucson. Fewer still knew about California. Yesterday, for the first time, the story of Steelman and Gretzler began filtering through town, across the counters in the bars along Whiskey Row, and over breakfast at The Talk of the Town Coffee Shop.

The Gretzler trial would make the newspaper, however, and each day's events found themselves on the front page of the *Courier's* early afternoon edition. The reporter jotted down notes of the morning session, then at the lunch recess, raced down Cortez Street to the newspaper office where he quickly punched out the story just before the presses rolled. Both Tucson papers reported on the trial, and a stringer for the *Arizona Republic* in Phoenix was present as well, but coverage of Gretzler's trial was just like that of Steelman's before him; sparse and low key. Television and radio was limited to whatever came across the newswire, and again, cameras were prohibited in the courtroom.

It was late Wednesday afternoon, October 15th, before the first name was called from the people who remained in the hallway. Druke had placed a blackboard at the front of the courtroom and on it he wrote the names of several people involved in the upcoming case. Steelman's name was one of them, along with names of the victims, police detectives, even some of psychiatrists. His idea was to ask the potential jurors as they entered the courtroom if they recognized any of the names. If so, chances were that they probably knew more than either side cared they did.

Much to everyone's surprise, the first man was brought in and said none of the names looked familiar. He was quizzed by Druke, Hoffman and Dingledine, and then quickly okayed by all. The process was definitely looking up.

However, out of the next eight people called, Hoffman challenged six, demanding they be excluded, and while Druke overruled two of them, he let the other four stand. Those, along with two others deemed unfit to hear the case, were excused. That left them with only 4 of the 36 jurors needed before final selection could begin. It was well after 5 o'clock when Druke told Brenda to send the rest of them home for the day.

Court began Thursday morning promptly at nine, and like yesterday, David Hoffman played a major role in bogging down the process. Over the course of the day, 24 more people were interviewed and Hoffman challenged over half of them. While Judge Druke denied several of the challenges, a large number of potential jurors were excused. Adding to the list the hardship cases, and the ones who were clearly unable to be impartial, the list of 36 needed was growing at a snail's pace. By quitting time Thursday, only eight additional names were added. And while they were still a long way off, Druke hoped to give a positive twist to the day by pointing out that eight was twice as many as they had selected yesterday.

It had been an exhausting two days for everyone, and so after work on Thursday, many of those in the courthouse walked the short distance to the saloons on Prescott's Whiskey Row. There they would have a cold one, listen to some music, try to unwind, maybe even forget for a moment the seriousness of the task ahead. It was not uncommon to see a court reporter or a bailiff talking with an off duty cop or city councilman. There was always some dime store cowboy kicking up his heels with a pretty young secretary from the county offices across the street.

Even a few of those potential jurors stopped by. David Hoffman and Michael Brown were there, sitting in the rear of the darkened Bird Cage Saloon, viewing the developing scene with keen interest. Only a few tables away, Dingledine and Hust nursed their beer and talked shop, certain Hoffman and Brown were listening in.

To everyone's surprise, Druke showed up too, looking almost normal out of his robes. It wasn't long before, with beverage in hand, he was with the rest of them, trying his best to sing along with Freddy Fender on the jukebox. In fact, he was doing a pretty good job of minding his own business, until one of the women from a nearby group came over and asked him to dance. Failing to recognize her, he agreed. With keen interest, David Hoffman sat back in the corner and watched the whole episode unfold, because unfortunately for Druke, the woman was one of the potential jurors.

Soon advised of his blunder, Druke excused himself and hurried out of the bar, with Hoffman just steps behind. Both went back to their motel rooms, but while Druke fretted over how he was going to address the situation at tomorrow's court session, Hoffman penciled out a motion for mistrial, based on Druke's last dance.

Hoffman confronted Druke before court began Friday morning and told him bluntly what he intended to do. Fearful a mistrial was a real possibility, Druke called the Superior Court in Tucson, hoping someone could advise him on how he should approach this recent twist. While his colleagues gave him a good ribbing, they also assured him there was little harm done as long as the woman in question was not selected to serve on the jury.

In the end, she was not. Still, Druke stayed clear of Whiskey Row while in Prescott. And although he loudly threatened, Hoffman did not bring his motion up during the trial and the episode remained out of the official court record.

The pace picked up considerably Friday, and by the end of the day another twelve names had been added, doubling the combined total from the previous two days. Druke hoped that with any luck the final selection of sixteen, including the four alternates, would be finished by Monday.

David Hoffman remained busy this day as well with his relentless attack on each of the potential jurors. While questioning one of the prospects, the woman let slip that a rumor had been circulating out in the hall about how Doug Gretzler had been extradited from California after a murder trial there. Hoffman demanded Druke allow him to challenge every person who had appeared after 2:30 that afternoon, an action threatening to wipe out the entire day's work.

Hoffman said such talk reinforced his claim that his client was not going to receive a fair trial in Prescott.

But Druke denied the motion, while promising Hoffman he would vigorously question any future prospect about whether they had heard such a remark. It was nearly six o'clock by the time court was recessed. Druke returned to Tucson for a much needed weekend break, while Dingeldine looked forward to his family coming up for a visit.

Doug Gretzler, on the other hand, was chained back up, then taken on a thirty second car ride to his basement cell across the street.

24

Monday, October 20, 1975 | 9:00 am.

When court began again this morning, Judge Druke promised himself one thing. The selection of the initial 36 jurors would be completed before the day was done. It did not matter how late they stayed, or how many people they called, it would be done. He had revised his timetable once already, but he vowed the State would present its opening arguments on Wednesday, and not one day later.

The selection crawled on, and the procedure was repeated for the umpteenth time. Brenda Harris would usher in a potential juror, after which both sides would review their completed questionnaires, and then begin their lengthy examination. Druke would ask a few questions and scribble a few notes. Hoffman would challenge half of the candidates, prompting Druke to either grant or deny the challenge, thus setting into motion still more arguments, resulting in more lost time.

The original one hundred names called came from the voter rolls. It was a selection system that often brought with it a multitude of shortcomings, all of which David Hoffman was doing his best to expose. According to the County Registrar's Office this year, Yavapai County was nearly 90% white, fewer than two hundred were black, less than six thousand residents were of Mexican-American decent, and not even one thousand were American Indian In fact, of the one hundred people called to the Gretzler trial, only two could be even considered a member of a racial minority. It also appeared that the age of those called appeared to be much older than the median age listed by the registrar.

So with that, would it be possible then for Douglas Gretzler to receive a trial heard by a jury of his peers? David Hoffman did not think so.

Throughout Monday's session he complained vigorously about the make up of the potential jurors. More than once he threatened action designed to throw out the whole lot of them. He argued and complained as much as Druke would allow, challenging as many candidates as he could get away with. Druke gave him plenty of leeway, but they were quickly running out of people and time. And yet somehow, just before 5 p.m., the final juror in the cast of thirty-six was selected. True to form, it was done over Hoffman's protest and not a moment too soon. Out of the original one hundred candidates, only seven remained seated in the hall

Druke set aside Tuesday for the preemptory challenges that would reduce the jury panel to the necessary sixteen. But Hoffman again announced he would move to quash the chosen thirty six, and the original one hundred from which they came, complaining loudly about the age and the jury's lack of racial diversity.

Tuesday afternoon David Hoffman was back in fine form. He had decided early on the defense of Doug Gretzler would have little to do with his guilt or innocence, because Gretzler had already confessed his involvement several times over, many of which were on tape. He said he was there at the Sandberg home. He admitted pulling the trigger. He was as good as convicted. So Hoffman decided to test the system instead – to see how far he could stretch it – and to what limits he would be allowed to ruffle judicial feathers. Knowing the twelve jurors would not be asked to make any landmark decisions, his goal would be only to raise enough doubt in their minds to get a Second Degree conviction, which would at least spare his client's life.

So Hoffman decided to test the patience and the wisdom of Judge Druke's court, realizing it would ultimately be the higher courts that would one day decide the fate of his client. He knew the final decision in the case against Douglas Gretzler would be made in the appeals courts much later down the road. Whatever was to be decided in Prescott, at least when it came to Doug Gretzler, would be of little consequence. From the moment he agreed to take the case, he realized there was only one way to save Gretzler from the executioner, so each step was aimed directly at the appeals process guaranteed to follow the trial. With each boisterous objection, with every question asked, with every motion filed, with every demand, with every complaint, he worked only to create opportunities down the road.

David Dingeldine knew his opponent was a tenacious attorney, with a very successful practice and an impressive track record. Unlike some court appointed public defender with little to gain, Hoffman took pride in his work, and his ability to push the system. Every case he took, every man he defended, he put his name on it, and in 1975 David Hoffman was fast becoming a very big name in the Tucson legal circles. But Dingeldine also had a plan. One much easier than Hoffman's. It was simple. Don't screw up. He had Gretzler dead to rights. Had him by the balls. He had his weapon, his motive, his fingerprints, he even had his confession. Had it more than once. All he had to do was to lay it all out very carefully, do his homework, and make sure he didn't give Hoffman any openings. Keep to the basics. Stay focused.

There had been no public mention of it prior to the trial date, but Hoffman had hinted around about the possibility of a plea bargain. Nothing formal, just a casual testing of the waters. Two months earlier, he presented the idea to Dingeldine for the County Attorney's Office to consider. It mattered little how Dingeldine felt about it, as Chief Prosecutor it was his duty to discuss the matter with his boss. Several days later he and Randy Stevens met with Dennis Deconcini to review the proposal.

There was little to discuss. The mood of the department, the law enforcement officials who had worked the case, as well as the entire Tucson community for that matter, was that there would be no deals. Period. "If there was ever a case that called for the death penalty," Dingeldine repeated, "this is it." As far as he was concerned, the matter was closed.

At 3:45 Tuesday afternoon, the jury of sixteen had fianlly been selected, and ten women and six men would hear the case against Douglas Gretzler. But before they were excused for the day, Judge Druke made good an earlier promise to Hoffman regarding sequestration of the jury. "One of the ways in which a court can insure that jurors don't hear or read anything about the case is to sequester them," Druke said. "Which means to put them in a hotel and not let them go home to their families and go about their daily affairs. But it is not the intention of the court to do that in this particular case," he continued. "However, if the court finds that it loses one or two jurors because they aren't following the admonitions by not talking about the case, or hearing about it, or discussing it, it may be that admonition won't be sufficient. It may be the jurors who remain would have to be sequestered."

It was a relieved jury panel that left the courtroom. They were told to return at one thirty the following afternoon.

As the last one exited the courtroom, Hoffman started in. He immediately objected to Druke's warning to the jury. "The court has cast a chilling effect on the jury," he cried out. "I move for a mistrial! Your instructions to the jury were little more than a threat. They have been intimidated in a manner that they would dare not revel to the court if they had heard prejudicial statements or not! It is impossible for my client to receive a fair trial when the jury panel has been so threatened."

Druke denied the motion, but Hoffman wasn't finished. He again moved for a mistrial, contending that because Druke had warned them not to read or listen to news reports about the case, he had prejudiced the jury as to the sensationalism of the upcoming trial. Earlier Druke had said he would allow them to read selected newspapers, with stories concerning the case carefully removed, of course, and newspapers could be saved and read after the trial was concluded, if they so chose. In both instances Hoffman argued Druke had created an effect on the jury that would prejudice his client and prevent him from receiving a fair trial.

Again, Judge Druke denied the motion. Again, Hoffman wasn't finished.

For whatever reason, he decided now was the tiime to mention the plea bargain offered earlier to the prosecution. There were only a handful of spectators and only a few reporters remaining in the room, but Dingeldine cut him off before the discussion could be heard in open court. Druke agreed and said the terms of the proposed bargain could be disclosed only in chambers, and that is where he and both attorneys adjourned. Hoffman explained to Druke the repeated attempts to plead his client guilty before the trial began, but all offers had been ignored by the prosecution without discussion or consideration.

It was later learned Hoffman had offered to plead his client guilty, with a sentence of 125 years without parole, if the State would give up it's death penalty demand. While Gretzler was on trial for only two murders in Arizona, he had been charged with killing Robbins and Hacohen in Maricopa County and the death of Sierra in Pima. The murder charges of Steve Loughran were on hold, as were those of Ken Unrein and Michael Adshade in California. Hoffman said his client would agree to plead guilty to all five murders if the state would agree to a 25-year minimum sentence for each one. Served consecutively, Douglas Gretzler would serve 125 years, in essence agreeing to live, and die, in prison.

Hoffman told the media later that Gretzler understood the gravity of his actions and was willing to accept his punishment. "My client does not expect, nor wants to be released from prison," he told reporters. "He is probably more content with himself behind bars. That is where he is willing to stay."

Dingeldine realized such an offer could look mighty attractive to money-conscious taxpayers, but there would be no deal. He also knew that to deny such a bargain would portray the state as bloodthirsty. But he claimed to know his opponent's true motives. "David Hoffman is talking only for the press," he told reporters. " He's just waiting for a mistrial."

Hoffman's disclosure of the plea bargain was recorded into the transcripts, but the contents of his offer never made the minute entries of the trial. *The Arizona Republic* ran a story about it the following day and *The Daily Star* in Tucson passed over it in one sentence in it's Wednesday edition. That was the last time the plea bargain was ever discussed.

25

Wednesday, October 22, 1975 | 10 am.

It had taken David Dingledine and his staff over a year to get to this point; nearly two years after the bodies of Michael and Patricia Sandberg were discovered, and today he would bring his first witness in the case against Douglas Gretzler.

Vince Armstrong's testimony was potentially the most damaging, because unlike Mike Marsh, Joanne McPeak, and Donald Scott, whose background and questionable lifestyles limited their credibility, Armstrong was a believable witness. Gretzler was on trial for his kidnapping, as well as the double murder of the Sandbergs, and Dingeldine was confident Armstrong's convincing testimony in St. Johns played a key role in Willie Steelman's conviction there.

Late Tuesday afternoon, Jack Bowman flew Armstrong into Prescott, and again, Hust and Angeli were there to meet the plane. On the way into town, the conversation got around to the very reason Armstrong was there.

"I imagine Gretzler looks different now," Armstrong acknowledged.

"He's been cleaned up," came Hust's reply.

Armstrong got the message. He had not seen Gretzler in almost two years and wondered if he could still recognize him. Dingledine wondered too, so at an early morning meeting on Wednesday to go over his testimony, he asked him two basic questions. Could he remember in detail the route taken during the kidnapping? And could he positively identify Douglas Gretzler? He knew Hoffman would attack Armstrong's memory, unlike Norgren, who was surprisingly easy on him in St. Johns.

But just to be sure, Dingeldine planned a slight diversion Wednesday morning. It was customary for Gretzler to be removed to the small hallway just off the courtroom during the many delays in the pretrial jury selection, and there was no way anyone could enter the courtroom without walking down that same hallway. Dingeldine guessed Gretzler would likely be sent out at sometime during the morning to wait, so when Armstrong was brought in, he was taken down the hall, through the double doors and into the courtroom. In doing so, he passed within a few feet of Douglas Gretzler, giving him a fresh look at the man he hadn't seen in two years.

The Dessureault Hearing to determine if Vince Armstrong would even be allowed to testify was the first order of business. David Dingeldine carefully walked him through the events of November 3, 1973 and asked him to retrace his path after picking up the two hitchhikers, making sure he mentioned what a good look he got at both.

Q: "Okay. Now, as far as the passenger is concerned, do you see that particular man in the courtroom today?"

A: "Yes I do."

Q: "Could you identify him for the record, please?"

A: "He's the gentleman at the table in the blue shirt."

Q: "Does he appear any different today than he did on November third, nineteen seventy three?"

A: "Yes sir."

Q: "Would you tell the court what difference?"

A: "His hair is darker and much shorter, and he has a moustache."

Q: "Is there any doubt in your mind that this is the man who was the passenger in your car on November third, nineteen seventy three?"

A: "No doubt."

It was now Hoffman's turn and he wasted no time getting to the point on cross-examination.

Q: "Are you the same Vincent Armstrong who gave a statement to the Tucson Police sometime after this incident allegedly occurred?"

A: "That's correct."

Q: "And after you gave your statement you were subjected to a polygraph examination by Tucson Police. Is that correct?"

Dingledine objected, but was overruled. Hoffman said nothing more about the lie detector test, nor did he demand the witness answer the question. Instead he moved to the areas he most wanted to focus on. The first was Armstrong's worth as a witness. If the defense could bring out a character flaw, like the real reason why he left the police force, his truthfulness could be questioned by the jury, and his potentially damaging story of that Saturday in Tucson would be greatly diminished. Secondly, Hoffman wanted Armstrong to admit he was so concerned with the man in the back seat pointing the gun at him, it was all he could do to drive, and therefore had little time to look at Gretzler sitting right next to him. Because of that, the witness was in no position to identify the suspect. The third area was Hoffman's contention that the prosecution team, which included Angeli and Hust, had shown Armstrong police photos to aid his memory. On at least six occasions during his cross examination of Armstrong at the Dessureault hearing, Hoffman suggested the witness had viewed photos supplied by the County Attorney, or had conversations about how Gretzler might look years later.

Each time Armstrong held firm, saying there was no doubt he could recognize his kidnapper. He assured Hoffman he didn't need any help from anyone to remember Doug Gretzler, but of course said nothing about his side trip down the hall before court began.

However, identifying the defendant was the easiest thing Armstrong would have to do. The hard part was withstanding Hoffman's bombardment. He was well known for his ability to ask the same question over and over, twisting his words, and those of the witness, to trip them up. Even in his Desseauralt hearing, Hoffman was merciless.

Q: "How many times would you say that you've glanced at Mr. Gretzler during the course of your trip. . .your ride on November third?"

A: "I would say quite a few. I wasn't counting."

Q: "Well sir, can you tell me how many quite a few is? Apparently you spent much of your time watching the road in front of you. Is that correct?"

A: "Yes."

Q: "The majority of your time glancing in the rear view mirror at Mr. Steelman and responding to his orders."

A: "I wouldn't say I was looking at him a majority of the time."

Q: "Where were you looking?"

A: "The majority of the time I was looking at the road."

Armstrong was getting rattled, trying to outguess Hoffman, backtracking to remember how he had answered the previous question. Hoffman reached over and picked up a notebook from the table and read from it.". . .'spent quite a bit of time looking at Mr. Steelman.' That is what you testified to earlier!"

Before Armstrong could respond, Dingeldine interrupted. "Object to this line of cross examination! I think the Desseauralt is designed to see if there is any tainted pre-trial identification. Mr. Hoffman is really cross examining, which is proper at the trial, but certainly not here!"

He was again overruled.

The fourth and final area of Hoffman's attack was the composite drawing. He held the drawing quizzed the witness.

Q: "Sir, you provided information to the Tucson Police Department on the day in question, is that correct?"

A: "Correct."

Q: "And as a result of your information, a composite drawing was made depicting Mr. Steelman, and the other person that was in the car, correct?"

A: "Correct."

Q: "And this (the drawing) is an accurate representation that was formed from your information?"

A: "Yes."

Q: "Would you describe the man as you saw him then. . .what he he was wearing, sir."

A: "He was wearing a dirty greenish type of t-shirt, black jeans, sunglasses. And he was wearing a knife on his left hand side."

Q: "Would you describe the sunglasses?"

A: "To the best of my recollection they were dark tinted, black plastic framed, thin-framed glasses."

Q: "And you say that at the time his hair was darker then?"

A: "No, it was. . .it is darker. . .now than it was then."

Q: "Shorter now?"

A: "Yes."

Q: "Shoulder length?"

A: "Yes."

Q: "Can you tell me sir, how much time did you spend looking at the street? How much time you spent looking at Mr. Steelman. . .either in minutes or percentages."

Hoffman was clearly trying to trip Armstrong on the composite drawing he helped create, as well as the amount of time he had to look at Gretzler during the ride. Moments later, when Hoffman questioned the shape of the man's face in the drawing, Armstrong stumbled for a moment, then admitted he had protested many of the features used on the composite that day, agreeing that he wasn't totally satisfied with its outcome. But Hoffman abruptly cut him off, telling him only to answer the questions asked, because he wasn't interested in his opinions.

Armstrong was asked to step outside for a moment, but Hoffman remained standing, anxious to let his thoughts be known. "Your Honor, I would object to the identification made of the defendant by this man on the grounds that the time in which he had to observe him, or says he observed him, was apparently small by comparison with the times he has observed him here this morning. He has been told what to expect by the County Attorney's office."

Druke did not respond. Hoffman moved to the composite drawing. "He talks about recognizing Mr. Gretzler's eyes, but admits Mr. Gretzler was wearing dark sunglasses. I think the man is trying to identify Mr. Gretzler, but he's doing it improperly. It's tainted by both out of court exposure and by the comments of, possibly Mr. Dingeldine and Mr. Rollman, and certainly by Investigator Hust." Druke said he didn't see why Armstrong's identification should not be used in open court.

"Your Honor," Hoffman replied while glaring at Dingledine, "I move in limine that he (Armstrong) not be allowed to talk about Mr. Gretzler having long hair at the time. That's not important. But if he says that's the man. . .then that's the identification."

Druke took little time in announcing his decision. "The court finds that there's clear and convincing evidence the identification was based upon the incident and (the witnesses) recollection, and not anything else. And as to your motion in limine, Mr. Hoffman, that too would be denied."

Without pause, Judge Druke looked at Dingeldine. "Now, who is your next witness that we can cover in this regard?"

Donald Scott was called and Dingeldine guided him through the basics, saying he knew the two guys only as Bill and Doug, and he had met them about a week or so before the day in question. Dingeldine asked Scott if he had seen photos of the either man. Scott admitted he had, but could not remember really when it was, or who showed them to him.

If Scott's identification of Gretzler had been based on something other than the few days he was with he and Steelman, then Hoffman might be able to persuade the court to disallow Scott's testimony.

But Donald Scott had a difficult time remembering much of anything over past few years, let alone specifics surrounding that week in November. Years of drug abuse hung on him like the long straggly, dirty blond hair on his head. His answers were laden with, "I'm not sure", and "I can't really remember", or, "I don't know exactly", with long, torturous pauses in between. Hoffman realized quickly the guy might be more of an asset than a liability. He was having a difficult time remembering if the trial in St. Johns was last month, last summer, or two years ago, admitting he had no idea what month, or even what year it was when he met Bill and Doug, and that it was Mr. Dingeldine who had to remind him that it all happened in November of 1973.

It was clear Hoffman wasn't too concerned about the jury seeing or hearing from Donald Scott. It was, however, difficult to get anything of substance from him on the stand. When asked about the photos, his answers and lack of a direct response created more confusion. Finally, when it became obvious neither lawyer was gaining any ground, Judge Druke stepped in.

Q: "You say you saw the photographs at the trial in St. Johns. When during the trial did you see them? At the beginning, at the end. . .in the middle?"

A: "I think at the beginning. I'm not really sure."

Q: "Was it Larry Hust who showed you the photos?"

A: "Could have been."

Q: "You're not sure now?"

A: "I'm not really positive, no."

Q: "Did whoever showed you the photographs say anything?"

A: "I can't really remember what was said too much. That was a couple of months ago, and there's been a lot on my mind with work and everything since".

Q: "Sure."

Hoffman and Dingeldine watched as Druke took over the questioning. He wasn't getting any further than they did. The judge was patient, but frustrated.

Q: "Let's narrow it down. Was it Rex Angeli?"

A: "Might have been. He was there."

Q: "Was it Mr. Dingeldine or Mr. Rollman?"

A: "Yes sir."

Q: "Do you recall them?"

A: "Yes."

Q: "OK, now you say they were mug shots. Side views, like on a wanted poster in the post office?"

Scott nodded yes, and Druke felt like maybe he was making some progress. He had narrowed it down to four people who could have offered the photographs in question to Scott. Both counsels watched as Druke continued.

Q: "Did they have numbers on them?"

A: "I don't remember."

Hoffman stood and interrupted. "Can we approach the bench?"

Druke shrugged his consent and motioned him forward.

"I realize the court has a duty and the right to ask its own questions, but I have to object to the court doing an extensive examination of the witness before I have the opportunity."

"I was just trying to find out about the photographs," Druke replied, realizing his efforts had gotten carried away.

"Right. Fine," Hoffman said, taking the opportunity to scold the court. "I just don't want get into a position where I have the second cross exam."

"I understand," Druke shrugged.

After lunch Scott retook the stand. Dingeldine apparently had cleared up the mystery of the photographs. He took several from his table and offered them to Scott, who finally agreed they were probably the photos he had seen earlier. It all came down, however, to two questions again posed by Judge Druke. "Did you expect to see any photos of Mr. Gretzler when you were browsing in that folder?

"No sir, not of him."

"Did you have any trouble recognizing him when you saw him?"

"No sir."

"OK then, you may step down," Druke said, retaking control. He looked over at Hoffman and Dingeldine. "Either counsel wish to argue the matter? No? Then the court finds the testimony is not tainted. Call in the jury, Brenda. Mr. Dingeldine, you get Mr. Armstrong in here and let's get started."

It was mid afternoon before the sixteen jurors took their seats. They had been sitting outside since nine that morning. The soft autumn sun filtered through the large windows open to the southern exposure. The sealed courtroom was exceptionally warm and very stuffy. Several jurors fanned themselves with accordianed notepaper to try and catch a breeze.

"Members of the jury," Druke apologized, "there is air conditioning in this building, but there is difficulty in hearing witnesses when it's on, so I've turned it off because it makes it easier to hear. If anyone gets unduly warm, let me know, and we'll turn it back on. Mr. Dingeldine, you may begin with your opening statement."

There was little difference between this one and his opening made in St. Johns. Steelman became Gretzler, but the story was the same. "It was a Saturday," he began. "And on that day, a path of terror and murder swept through that city."

He paused and let his words sink in. "It started about eleven a.m., when a young man, Vincent Armstrong, a student at the University of Arizona, was heading down to the school to do some work. Two men were hitchhiking. . ."

Dingeldine turned away from the jury as he continued, leading each of them through the streets of Tucson, describing the harrowing events of the day. Vincent at the wheel, a gun at his head. He relived Armstrong's daring escape, and how the blue Firebird eventually found its way to Villa Parasio apartment complex on Fort Lowell Road. He introduced the names of Michael and Patricia Sandberg, James Nelson, and Donald Scott. "You're not going to like Donald Scott," he warned. "But he will tell you about the drugs, and the crash pad and motels they stayed in."

Dingledine spoke of stolen cars and credit cards, bullets and ballistics, a camera and a California capture. When he finally got around to the Sandberg's murder – mentioning for the first time the name Larry Hust – he advised the jury that it will be Hust who will describe, in vivid detail…"the deliberate, premeditated, cold-blooded, cruel, brutal, execution-type murders committed on Pat and Michael Sandberg."

He told the jury about the two tapes and the conversations recorded between Gretzler and authorities in a California jail. He forewarned them that it was on the second tape where they would hear for themselves Gretzler's own confession…"that will implicate him in the terrifying events which went on in the Sandberg's apartment. And at the conclusion of this case, the state is going to ask you for a guilty verdict on all counts against Douglas Gretzler. But especially a guilty verdict of First Degree Murder on Michael Sandberg, and, a guilty verdict of First Degree Murder on Pat Sandberg."

Dingledine sat down. David Hoffman said he would reserve his opening remarks for later. At which time the State called Vincent Armstrong.

During the remainder of that warm fall afternoon, the jury listened as Armstrong described what happened that day two Novembers ago. Surprisingly, Hoffman seemed to go easy on him, offering not even one objection during the testimony.

It was now Scott's turn, and even though he had been cleaned up for the trial, Scott's appearance was still quite alarming to the jury. And yes, he was wearing the cape.

But when Dingeldine tried to connect him with Steelman and Gretzler in Tucson, Hoffman finally protested, making it clear he didn't want this witness and his client associated in the slightest. One could hardly blame him. From appearance alone, it could be reasoned that Scott was the man on trial, and the clean cut Gretzler the witness against him.

"How was your relationship with Douglas Gretzler and Willie Steelman?" Dingledine asked.

"I object!" Hoffman interrupted. "That's not material."

"Overruled," Druke replied. "He may answer the question."

Scott looked at Dingeldine, and then to the judge. "I felt close to them as a fellow street person."

That was all Hoffman needed to hear. "Your honor, may we approach the bench? Mr. Dingeldine has sandpapered this witness frequently," Hoffman argued, "trying to get an illusion to Gretzler and Steelman being street persons. I think it is extremely prejudicial to the defendant to be characterized as such!"

"What's your point," Druke asked sarcastically, "just to make an objection?"

"No sir. I move for a mistrial on that basis."

"Denied. Okay?"

It appeared Hoffman was willing to represent an accused murderer, just as long as he wasn't confused with being a hippie. Truth be told, Hoffman was perfectly content with his motions being denied. It was the ones Druke granted that he feared. He kept track of the denials, making notes as he went, especially his motions of mistrial that were so quickly brushed aside by the court. Motions granted would need to be dealt with immediately, but motions denied would become ammunition later, and Hoffman counted as their numbers grew rapidly. Within ten minutes time, Hoffman would again interrupt the proceedings, arguing for a mistrial in response to statement made by Donald Scott. Again Druke denied the motion, and once again Hoffman silently kept score.

Hoffman objected one more time that afternoon. When Dingledine asked Scott why he got out of the car in Pine Valley, and if something had happened just before that to help him make his decision, Hoffman interrupted. He had heard about Scott crying when he told the story in St. Johns. He wanted no part of that here.

"We both know what the answer is going to be," Hoffman complained after Druke motioned them both to the bench. "That there was an older couple along the side of the road, and he thought about his grandparents. . ."

"No, I wasn't going to ask that," Dingeldine snapped.

". . .and thought they were going to knock off the older couple, "Hoffman sing-songed, ignoring Dingeldine's response. "There's nothing of probative value in the question because nothing was done to the older couple. I move for a mistrial."

While Judge Druke denied the motion, he did agree with the defense and sustained the objection to where the prosecution's line of questioning was headed. Druke knew about the St. Johns incident as well, and like Hoffman, did not want it duplicated in his courtroom.

Dingeldine wrapped up his questioning a few minutes later. Druke, anxious to get a full day in, told Hoffman to begin his cross-examination. Hoffman said he would rather wait until morning. Druke told him to get started anyway and he would let him know when it was time to quit.

Q: "Mr. Scott, I've noticed that you've got a problem with your teeth. Is that from drug use?"

A: "Yes it is."

Q: "That from heavy use of amphetamines and speed?"

A: "Yes sir."

Q: "Would you tell the jury what speed is?"

Scott answered the question as best he could, mentioning that even students have used it to keep them awake. It was not the answer that Hoffman was looking for.

Q: "Gets people out of control? Weird?" Hoffman asked.

A: "Not out of control."

Q: "You've seen a number of people out of control on speed, haven't you sir?"

A: "Well, no. Not very many."

Q: "And violent. People violent?"

A: "Yes sir."

Q: "You were taking speed at the time surrounding November third, is that correct?"

A: "Yes sir."

Q: "Taking about as much as you could get?"

A: "No sir, I wouldn't say that."

Q: "Frequently though."

A: "Yes."

Q: "And Douglas Gretzler was taking it with you?"

A: "Yes sir."

Q: "And cocaine?"

A: "Yes sir."

Q: "And marijuana?"

A: "Yes sir."

Q: "And alcohol?"

A: "Yes sir."

Q: Hoffman turned and looked at Scott. "You've made a deal with the prosecutor in this case, haven't you sir? For your own benefit."

A: "Yes sir."

Q: "And the prosecutor has told you that you would have immunity from the use of drugs up until today, didn't he, sir?"

A: "Yes sir."

Q: "Just so you would come and testify?"

A: "Yes sir."

He asked Scott about his testimony in St. Johns, and Scott confessed he had used drugs up until a few days before he took the stand that summer. Scott admitted the prosecution said they would ignore it in trade for his testimony.

Q: "You're getting what, thirty dollars a day diem while you're here?" Hoffman asked.

A: "Yes sir."

Q: "Paid by the County Attorney's office?"

A: "I believe so."

Q: Hoffman stopped, letting Scott's answers sink in, allowing the jury to see what kind of witness was on the stand against his client. "Sir, with regards to the use of drugs, Doug seemed to be somebody who enjoyed getting high and partying?"

A: "Yeah."

Q: "And he was using drugs a little bit more heavily than you were at the time?"

A: "I don't know."

Q: "Well, was he using speed and cocaine as frequently as you were, at least to your knowledge?"

A: "As far as I know, Mr. Gretzler was using drugs just like any other street hippie."

Q: "Okay, he was using drugs. In fact, this walk you took, drugs were used on that walk you took to the gas station."

A: "I'm not positive."

Q: "But you talked about drugs being used?"

A: "Yes."

Q: "And that was on the walk on November third?"

A: "Yes."

Q: "And they had been using drugs the night before?"

A: "Yes sir."

Q: "With regard to Mr. Steelman, he seemed to be kind of a pushy guy, kind of a man prone to violence?"

"Objection!" Dingledine interrupted.

Druke had heard enough for one day as well. He told Hoffman he could pick it up in the morning, and announced a recess.

But David Hoffman had made his point. Donald Scott was not a witness any member of the jury would want to associate with. Nor should anything he said be mistaken for the truth. His implication was clear. Scott's testimony, as feeble and disjointed as it was, had simply been bought and paid for by the State of Arizona.

26

Thursday, October 23, 1975 | 9:30 am.

David Hoffman would not again speak to Donald Scott. But what he had achieved during his cross-examination yesterday would prove to be an extremely critical part of Douglas Gretzler's defense. Even Hoffman himself could not have begun to comprehend its significance at this point, for he was more than likely just being sarcastic and flip when he quizzed Scott about the effects of using speed on that Saturday in November.

But before the defense of Gretzler was complete, an appeal would be filed based on these very questions, using medical terminology unheard of in 1975. The appeal would be a deciding factor on whether or not Douglas Gretzler would be executed for the murders of Michael and Patricia Sandberg. The testimony by Scott, and later by Michael Marsh, Joanne McPeak, along with several doctors and psychiatrists, would play a pivotal role in whether Gretzler would keep an appointment with Arizona's executioner.

So already the case against Doug Gretzler was taking the turn of most capital cases, moving away from the actual guilt or innocence of the accused and the merits of the crime itself, and more towards the weaknesses and fine lines of the American legal system. For example, not once yesterday was there any testimony given as to whether Gretzler was even in the Sandberg's apartment. Not one word spoken about the crime itself, only legal maneuvers to determine who could, and could not speak about their involvement or association with the defendant. Vince Armstrong's brief stay with the Tucson Police, and the manner in which he left, was seemingly more important than whether he could identify his attacker. Donald Scott's drug abuse and less than extemporary lifestyle was given more attention than the obvious fact that he could identify photographs of

Sandberg's stolen Datsun in which he was a passenger.

Maybe that's why David Hoffman was becoming such a talented defense attorney. He may not have been the most polished of litigators, or the sharpest member of his graduating class – and maybe he was more lucky than good – but he understood, probably before any of the others, where this case was heading and what his role needed to be.

James Nelson took the stand, recalling that he saw Michael Sandberg twice on the morning of November 3rd; once with Pat Sandberg at about nine a.m. carrying groceries from their car, and again a couple of hours later in the company of two men, neither whom he had seen before. In between those two occasions was when he first remembered seeing the blue Firebird.

He claimed to have known the Sandberg's reasonably well, a statement Hoffman objected to and asked to be stricken. Druke disagreed, stating Nelson's familiarity with the couple was important because it would allow him to notice the change in Mr. Sandberg between the first and second meetings. Nelson said it was the usual happy and talkative Michael on the first occasion, but it was a quiet and stand-offish Sandberg later when seen accompanied by the two strangers.

Nelson testified that about two hours after first seeing Mr. Sandberg was when he saw the Firebird driving slowly down Ft. Lowell Road and turn into the condominium parking lot. He also claimed the two men in the car asked him for directions to the Sandberg's apartment, a statement that would be hotly disputed at a later date. Thirty minutes later, Nelson said he came out of his office to see the same two men walking down the sidewalk directly behind Michael Sandberg.

Dingeldine had placed a large aerial photograph of the Villa Parasio condominiums on an easel near the witness stand. He gave Nelson several large Magic Markers, and asked him to retrace his steps of that morning. Red was for his house several blocks from the complex, green for the route of the Firebird, and later black and yellow were used, until lines, squares and circles covered the photograph. He had evidently confused even Judge Druke, who wondered out loud why the witness was changing colors, a comment that drew snickering from the jury.

Nelson returned to the stand and Dingeldine asked about the second meeting with Mr. Sandberg.

"They came down the sidewalk and I walked right up to the curb, and as they passed me, I spoke to them. I remember greeting Michael and he didn't respond to me."

Q: "Was that unusual?"

A: "Yes it was unusual! It bothered me because he was not the type of person that would not respond. We always had a very friendly attitude between us."

Q: "Did the other two individuals that you described behind Michael, did they respond in any way?"

A: "I greeted them also, and as I recall, they did respond, either by a nod of the head, or "Hi", or something like that."

Q: "Where did Michael and the two males proceed to?"

A: "They continued down the sidewalk, up the stairs and went into the apartment."

Q: "After they went into the apartment, did you ever see Michael Sandberg after that again?"

A: "No, I have not."

Q: "Pat Sandberg?"

A: "No, I have not."

Q: Dingeldine walked back towards the photograph and turned towards Nelson. "On the next day, did you return to the office?"

A: "Yes, I did. I opened the office up approximately at noon on Sunday the fourth."

Q: "Did you see the blue Firebird?"

A: "Yes. It was still parked in the same position in the corner of the carport."

Q: "Did you see Michael's Datsun?"

A: "No I did not."

Q: "What did you do about the Firebird?"

A: "Well, I reported the car to the police."

Oddly enough, Dingeldine never asked Nelson to identify Doug Gretzler in the courtroom. The closest he came was when he asked if the two individuals on the sidewalk were the same two men he saw driving the blue Firebird. Nelson admitted he could not positively make that connection.

Druke told the defense that it was their turn, but Hoffman had other ideas. "I move that this testimony be stricken!" he bellowed.

Druke waved him forward. "Do not make motions to strike in front of the jury!" he lectured.

"I move his testimony be stricken," he repeated loudly, ignoring the warning. "And I move for a mistrial! This is nothing but prejudice. There's nothing to connect it with the defendant!"

Druke rolled his eyes.

"That's mistrialable!" Hoffman roared, making up new legal jargon as went. "And I move for a mistrial!"

"Motion will be denied."

"Both motions? Motion to strike also?"

"Yes. Both of them."

"Then I ask leave to file a special action."

"We're not going to stop the trial for that purpose. The testimony shows materiality as to the Datsun and the fact he saw the deceased alive." Druke was firm and ready to do battle, almost eager to take Hoffman's challenge head on.

But just as quickly as Hoffman had roared in protest, he broke into a big grin. "Okay. I'll cross examine." One could almost see the wheels spinning in his head.

Q: "Mr. Nelson, are you comfortable?"

A: "Yes, very."

Q: "Like a drink of water before I start to cross-examining you?"

A: "No," Nelson replied. "I'm fine."

Q: "Sir, my question to you is, did Mr. Dingeldine ask you to make an identification in this courtroom of anyone?" Hoffman's question confused Nelson, and he had to rephrase it several times. Nelson finally replied he had not been asked to do that. Several of the questions seemed rambling and confusing. He was asked more than once to repeat himself, until Nelson acted like he finally understood, or could at least answer the question. Hoffmann, the other hand, acted like he was talking to the village idiot.

Q: "You paid an awful lot of attention to this Firebird. You watched it for a block and a half."

A: "That's correct."

Q: "Must have made an impression on you...for some reason."

A: "I think what impressed me most was the way the two individuals were acting."

Q: "Yes sir!" Hoffman roared sarcastically. "You observed that? It really made an impression on you, didn't it sir?"

A: "I thought perhaps they were looking for a residence..."

Hoffman wheeled and roared, catching Nelson off guard. "I'm not asking what you thought!"

He turned away, acting as if he was trying to calm himself down. He walked to his table and looked over his notes. His next question seemed odd He wanted to know about distances and square footage of the apartments. When Nelson admitted he really didn't know too much about the size of each unit, or exactly how many feet away the Firebird was parked, Hoffman insinuated that if the sales manager of the development didn't know answers to the simplest of questions, how in the world could he be expected to know the important ones.

Q: "You said I was five feet six inches tall," Hoffman stated.

A: "Yes."

Q: "When you stood up to me, did your opinion about my height change?"

A: "I think so, yes sir."

Q: "Now, how tall would you approximate my height?"

A: "Maybe five feet eight."

"Thank you."

That was it. Hoffman changed the subject. But almost an hour later he pulled the question back out of thin air and asked it again.

Q: "Have you identified a man known to you as Willie Steelman as the taller of the two individuals you observed on November third?"

A: "Yes I have."

Q: "You stood next to these men for a moment, is that correct?"

A: "Yes I did."

Q: "And you described the shorter individual as being five feet five to five feet six inches tall?"

A: "Yes I have."

Q: "I ask Mr. Gretzler to stand next to me for a moment." Doug Gretzler stood up, appearing almost a half-foot taller than his lawyer.

A: "Would you describe Mr. Gretzler's height?"

Q: "Well, at this moment, Mr. Gretzler appears to be six feet tall," Nelson answered sheepishly.

There was one other area Hoffman wished to cover. Why did the witness wait well over a year before he described the events of that Saturday to police officers? Even on the following Sunday, when he called to report the Firebird, he never said a word about the stranger in the complex, or his unsettling hello with Michael Sandberg the previous day. Even five days later, when they pulled the bodies out of the upstairs apartment, Nelson still remained silent. Hoffman wondered why.

Q: "The first time you ever told the story you told in this courtroom sir, was on January seventh, nineteen seventy-five?"

A: "That is correct."

Q: "And the reason you never told it to the police was that you didn't want to 'muddy the waters'?"

Dingeldine objected and Druke asked Hoffman to rephrase his question. He asked it again and again and Nelson acted as if he didn't understand. Hoffman was perfectly clear, much more forceful and much louder the third time he asked.

Q: "I'm asking you if that's the reason you didn't tell anyone before this, before January seventh, nineteen seventy-five, because you didn't want to muddy the waters?"

A: Nelson fidgeted. "I do not recall using that term."

But Hoffman wasn't satisfied with the answer.

Q: "You didn't want to MUDDY THE WATERS with this information until January seventh, nineteen seventy-five! Is that correct?"

"Objection! Asked and answered!" Dingeldine shouted.

Hoffman let everyone know of his disgust. "I don't have any more questions for you, Mr. Nelson."

David Dingledine stood for his re-direct.

Q: "When the bodies were found on November ninth, how did you feel?"

A: "I was practically in a state of shock."

Q: "And where did you go the next day?"

A: "I went to the mountains for a week."

Q: "Did you have a lot of time to think about it?"

A: "I certainly did."

Hoffman's indignation had not diminished. His re-cross pounded away where he had left off moments earlier.

Q: "You left on November tenth for the mountains, is that correct?

A: "Yes it was. . .the morning of November tenth."

Q: "Nineteen seventy three?"

A: "That's correct."

Q: "And you returned from the mountains – after having all this time to think on November the seventeenth, nineteen seventy three. Is that correct?"

A: "I was gone approximately five to six days, yes."

Q: "And the first time this story ever emerged was January seventh, nineteen seventy five?"

Dingledine objected, but Druke let the question stand. Hoffman asked it again, but by now it was a statement of indignation. "The first time you told this story was January seventh, nineteen seventy five!"

A: "Correct."

Hoffman turned and walked away as Judge Druke dismissed the witness. The court record shows that Hoffman asked Druke if he could be excused from the courtroom for a moment, and the request was granted. Dingledine, however, had not heard the exchange. To him it appeared as if Hoffman was simply trying to show off. He watched as the burly Hoffman disappeared through the courtroom doors, only a few steps behind Nelson.

"I want the record to show that Mr. Hoffman deliberately left this courtroom after Mr. Nelson got off the stand. All I can say is that it looks like a bit of 'Hoffman Showmanship', and I object to it strenuously!"

Hoffman, who had already returned to the courtroom, joined the discussion. "I went out there to compose myself," he said.

"Let the record show that the witness has identified the defendant as Douglas Edward Gretzler."

"So ordered."

Larry Bunting had taken the stand, and when asked, pointed to Gretzler as the man he had interviewed in the Stockton jail. As was the case in St. Johns, Bunting was an important member of the prosecution team because of the extensive work he performed for the prior twenty-three months they had worked on the case. Bunting had been there from the beginning. He often told people about entering the Sandberg's apartment; with one hand covering his face from the stench, the other swatting away flies buzzing around his head. He viewed this case as every bit his, and was determined to see it to the very end.

Earlier in the day, Dingledine introduced more than two dozen photos into evidence and Donald Scott identified two of them as being the Datsun he had been in. The other 24 were painfully morbid, all taken inside the apartment before the bodies had been removed. Hoffman protested vigorously their inclusion, and there was one in particular he was adamant the jury not see. It was the Sandberg's wedding photo – the one that bothered Randy Stevens so much – and Hoffman successfully managed to have the court agree it did not have any evidentiary value. It was excluded, although most of the other gruesome black and white shots of the bodies were allowed. Hoffman felt that images of corpses so decayed as to be almost unrecognizable were one thing, but in no way should the jury see the victims as the once attractive young couple they had been.

Ironically, the prosecution managed to sneak in the wedding picture after all. One of the snapshots was of a spare bedroom in the apartment, and in the corner of the photograph was the wedding picture sitting on a small dresser. The jury members, if they looked closely, could clearly see the photo Hoffman argued so desperately to keep from them.

Scott had also identified the camera as the one he remembered Steelman having with them when they left for California. There were other items from the Sandberg's including a bottle of Clairol hair color, a ball of twine, Mrs. Sandberg's purse, and a bloodstained blanket and pillow.

But the most important piece of evidence introduced Thursday morning, was a cassette recording of Doug Gretzler discussing the crimes.

There were two tapes actually, but the first one - the tape introduced this morning - was the more damaging of the two. Dingeldine wanted it played early, because on it Gretzler made statements about his innocence and ignorance of the crime, statements that Dingledine would have no trouble disputing. The tape could prove Gretzler was a liar.

That is exactly why Bunting was on the stand, to explain what had taken place during the weekend in Stockton when he first met the defendant.

Dingeldine offered the tape into evidence. Hoffman protested. Druke agreed and said he wanted to listen to it before allowing a jury to do so. He called for a lunch recess and took the cassette into his chambers.

David Hoffman's argument against the photographs continued after lunch. Druke decided to allow 15 of them, but dismissed Mrs. Sandberg's purse and its contents after Hoffman protested their value. The blanket that covered Patricia, and bloodied pillow remained, as did the ball of twine found on the coffee table – twine Dingeldine said matched the bindings removed from the victim's wrists and ankles. Druke announced the cassette tape could also be heard.

Larry Bunting retook the stand and said the defendant voluntarily made the statements they were about to listen to. "We explained to him that we could not talk to him unless he waived his rights to an attorney. He explained his attorney advised him not to speak to anybody. He said he would like to talk unofficially if he could, but we explained we could not talk unofficially; that anything he said would be used against him."

"We also explained he had certain rights that we would have to advise him of, and he told us he had been advised many times of his rights, and that's all he had heard since he was arrested was his rights and that he was completely aware of them. After I was satisfied in my mind he knew his rights, we went ahead and spoke with him about it, but we explained it would be used against him."

The recording was not the first conversation between Bunting and Gretzler. They had spoken for about an hour the night before, but the session was not recorded. When they were finished, Gretzler told Bunting that he might be willing to make a tape recording the next day. "Sounded to me like he wanted time to think about it," Bunting surmised.

The recording was of poor quality and somewhat lengthy. For most of the jurors it was the first time they had heard Gretzler's voice although he had sat but a few feet from them for several days. The tape began with Bunting introducing himself, Michael Tucker, and the defendant. That, along with the time, date and place were just about the only true statements made.

Gretzler began by describing, somewhat accurately, how the kidnapping of Armstrong went down. But he was adamant that it was Steelman who held the gun to Armstrong's head. When Armstrong became too nervous to drive, Gretzler said he took the wheel, until Armstrong jumped out of the car only a few seconds later.

"Bill and I both got paranoid. We thought we should get rid of the car," Gretzler remembered, "so we pulled into the parking lot of an apartment building. We saw a guy washing his Datsun – the car we used to go to California – and Bill threw down on him."

It was the last of Gretzler's honesty. "He told me to wait by the car while he went inside with the guy. I waited by the car for three to four hours, then Bill came from the apartment. He had a suitcase, camera case, and some clothes for me. He said 'Come on, we got a car'. So we picked up this other guy and drove to California."

Gretzler went on to say that he had no idea what had happened in the apartment because Willie said nothing about harming the Sandbergs. When cross-examined by Hoffman, Bunting admitted Gretzler insisted throughout the recording that he had no idea they had been killed until after he had been arrested and the police told him.

Hoffman objected again to the tape, but Druke allowed it to be admitted as evidence.

Dingeldine next called Larry Hust, who laid the foundation for the second tape, the recording made by Hust on November 19, 1973, when he traveled to Stockton to serve Steelman and Gretzler with the Pima County murder warrants. Dingeldine said he was going to wait until later on to play the tape, but Hoffman objected to Hust as a witness, arguing that he should be allowed to voir dire the witness as to the second tape in question. Druke said he would wait until the tape was actually introduced before ruling on Hoffman's request. With that, Druke told the jury their work was finished for the day. In fact, the Federal courtroom was reserved for other business on Friday and they would have a three-day weekend from the trial.

Before they left the courtroom, David Hoffman had one last announcement to make.

"Your honor, I would like to instruct the court that we plan on calling Willie Steelman next Wednesday when we open our defense."

27

Monday, October 27, 1975 | 9:30 am.

Brenda Harris had spent the long weekend away from the trial doing what most of the others, including the sixteen jurors, attempted to do. She tried to relax.

Although there was no court seesion Friday, she reported back to her regular job at the county offices, and her workload was light, so she spent most of the day going over her notes of the week, preparing them for her supervisor's approval. This trial was the most important assignment ever and she wanted it perfect, so Brenda was on cloud nine when her boss complimented her on such fine detail.

But the work was demanding, especially for the twenty year old, and so it seemed like everybody else got to take a break or a recess during the trial, but she was always scrambling between the courtroom and judges chambers, flipping the pages of her shorthand book, writing as fast as she could, hoping she hadn't missed anything, so by the end of the day she was exhausted. That, and being so worried about what terrible thing might happen next – fearful that at any minute someone was going to pull a gun – all helped wear her down. She felt like she had to have one eye on her work, and the other on the constant lookout for trouble.

But there was more to it. No one knew yet, but Brenda was expecting her first child, and the emotional roller coaster that came with pregnancy only added to her anxious behavior. One minute she would be fine, the next, flushed with anger. She could, at times, be unbelievably fearful of her surroundings, and at others feel overwhelming compassion and unexplained sorrow over the sadness in the lives of people she had never met. At one point, when a concerned Judge Druke asked if everything was all right, she broke down and told him about her pregnancy. From there on Druke doted on her, fatherly and protective, quick to offer kind words and compliments on her excellent work, insisting she take a break when the opportunity presented itself. From then on she pledged to keep it all inside and retain her composure, regardless of what was swirling on around her.

But today, however, she was unable to keep her emotions in check. And all because Doug Gretzler smiled at her.

Her fear of him was actually short lived. After the first day or so, he became just another fixture in the courtroom: hustled in and out at will, always guarded, never smiling, never talking, staring into space, as if daydreaming about something or somewhere. What, she could only imagine. Occasionally she found herself sneaking a peak at him, wondering what was going on in his head. Every so often, he would catch her stare and she would quickly turn away, embarrassed, as if her trusted position with the court forbade such contact. And yet, as horrible as the things he was accused of doing – guilty of doing, Brenda was already certain – he was one of the few people in the courtroom her age. Like many others who had crossed Gretzler's path over the past few years, she too wondered, how in God's name, he had come to do what he did?

And with her confusion came condemnation. While she worried about what he might try, she was also a bit fascinated by him. Not in any physical or sexual way, but a connection she could not begin to explain. She knew very little about him, other than the few words she had heard about his crimes, so it bothered her that she had been so quick to judge him. At times she pitied him. It seemed so confusing to her. There he set, between guards and prosecutors who bragged about wanting him dead. She wondered how that made him feel. He never looked mad. Sad? Yeah, sometimes, but she couldn't tell if he even cared, or if he was even sorry, or if he would do it again if given the chance. Brenda felt like maybe she cared more about all those poor people than he did. Or anyone did. He would die one day for what he had done – Brenda was certain of that – and she wondered if he thought about that as much as she did. Although watching him sit there, trance like, starring into space, flipping the hair out of his face, it was hard for her to imagine him dead. She hated him for being so stupid, for denying himself the simple pleasures of life, of denying them all – the people he killed, their family, his family, everyone. She hated him for dragging her into this, and the next minute thanked him, secretly, for the opportunity to be here.

This swirling mix of compassion and hatred was an emotion she could not wrap her arms around, and it was this contrast of feelings that made her terribly uncomfortable. Brenda wanted so much to understand this weird wavelength between them, a connection she could only guess was their closeness in age, as feeble as that sounded. She sometimes wondered if he felt it too. She hoped so. God, she hoped not! Here she was, soon to be a new mother, ready to bring an innocent life into this world (one that seemed so mixed up and ugly these days) and with each moment she went from being anxious about the birth of some little person she did not know yet, to how Douglas Gretzler did not deserve to even live. It all would be much easier – her life, everyone's life – if he was dead.

She did not like herself for feeling that way, but decided there was only Doug Gretzler to blame.

Last Thursday morning, Brenda was waiting in the hall near the elevator. She was alone, waiting for court to begin, when the elevator doors opened. Standing directly in front of her was Doug Gretzler. What followed seemed the simplest of human reactions. Maybe it was something more. Maybe he just saw someone his own age, someone who, out of all of these people, might understand how his life, and the lives of others of their generation, could sink so low. Maybe he thought, that because she was young, she was a friend. Maybe what he did required no thinking at all. Maybe it was everything, and maybe it was nothing, but when the elevator doors slid open, and they found each other face to face, inches apart, their eyes met and Doug did the most natural, the easiest, the only thing he knew to do. He smiled.

It was the slightest of expressions. A blink. A tiny sliver of acknowledgement. His lips barely moved. His gray eyes never brightened. Their connection was made, awkward, and so thankfully brief. Guards hustled him past her, weaving in and out of those mingling in the hallway, and he was gone, disappearing through the nearest open door.

Brenda fought for her breath, hating him all over again for the horrible things he had done, loathing him now for his simple smile. She ran to the woman's room and let the tears flow uncontrollably.

Monday morning. Everyone was back. Everyone was ready. Everyone, that is, except for one very important witness.

FBI agent Charles Richardson was expected to arrive in Prescott over the weekend, and take the stand Monday afternoon. His testimony would tie fingerprints found inside the Sandberg apartment to the defendant, thus disputing Gretzler's claim that he never set foot inside. Without Richardson, the string of evidence Dingleldine was preparing would have a very large gap in it. He informed the court the witness was being held up by a civil rights case in Mississippi, and while it was expected to last another day, the FBI had promised to send another fingerprint expert to Prescott, if necessary.

Richardson never arrived Monday, or any other day of the trial, for that matter. The backup was apparently on his way, although it would be several days before he could get there.

With the jury sent home again, courtroom discussion focused on Hoffman's decision to bring Willie Steelman to trial on Wednesday, the day defense arguments were scheduled to begin. Over Dingeldine's continued objections, Druke said, like it or not, Steelman was coming.

The F.B.I. experts might not have arrived Monday, but other important items did, namely the bullets Dr. Brucker had removed from the skulls of the Sandbergs. California had refused to release to Arizona the revolver taken from Steelman upon his arrest, so Dingeldine had little choice but to send the bullets there for analysis, certain the small revolver was the weapon used on the Sandbergs. Tests conducted in Sacramento proved the bullets and the weapon were a match, so when court resumed Tuesday morning, the bullets were back on the prosecution's table. Marked Plaintiff Exhibit 53 was a box containing the handful of unused .22 shells found on Gretzler when he was arrested at the Clunie Hotel. Bullets found in the victims during the autopsies were labeled Exhibits 53 A through F.

Dr. Edward Brucker, the Coroner's Pathologist, was the same doctor who had also examined the body of Gilbert Sierra. Along with Brucker, the list of witnesses scheduled this morning included Tucson Police Detective Condiss, one of the first officers on the scene at the Sandberg home. Hoffman, concerned he might present a less than desirable picture of the crime scene to the jury, motioned to limit his testimony to simply the facts, and not to embellish on what he saw. Dingeldine's assurance to the court allowed Judge Druke to deny the motion.

However, Detective Condiss was not called, but Dr. Brucker was, and took the stand for the prosecution. The doctor had a bad cold and spoke with a sniffle. He received little sympathy, but managed a few laughs when he confessed having caught it the previous week while vacationing in Hawaii. Under the questioning from Dingeldine, Brucker read from his own autopsy reports. The male had a single wound, the bullet in front of the left ear and was found on the opposite of the skull. The female had much greater damage, including multiple facial fractures. Pieces of bone were found in several areas; damage caused by blunt trauma, not gunshot wounds. Five bullet wounds were noted; four entrance and one exit. They had entered in a circular pattern, beginning in the middle of the forehead, with the final wound at an angle to the right side of the jaw. When he removed the gag during the autopsy, Brucker reported that the bullet fell out and was discovered lying in the wound. The doctor, who graduated from Loyola University in Illinois, was very crisp and precise in his answers, giving the faint impression he was a bit above all of this perverse drama. He confirmed both bodies were brought to him with bindings and gags intact and were badly decomposed. He took this opportunity to school the court how brain tissue deteriorates rapidly, and there was little of it remaining, not even enough to trace the bullet's paths. His report estimated they had been dead about seven days and probable cause of death to both victims were gunshot wounds to the head.

When Hoffman had his turn with Dr. Brucker, there was little discussion regarding the cause of death or how the victims were tied up, but he did attempt to paint a less than perfect portrait of the Sandbergs. In St. Johns, Steelman rambled on about how Michael Sandberg got what he deserved, boasting the ex-Marine wasn't the big hero everyone pictured him as, going so far as to insinuate both of the victims were addicts themselves, and even did drugs during the time he and Gretzler were in the apartment.

At the bottom of the autopsy reports, Brucker had listed the toxicology of each victim. The words "ethyl alcohol" were noted, and next to it the amount found; 08%. Thinking this might be an indicator Steelman was on to something, Hoffman asked Brucker to explain why each victim had the same amount of alcohol in their system as found in a person who was legally intoxicated.

Brucker brushed him off. He knew what Hoffman was getting at and he didn't care for it. It isn't the same type of alcohol, he snapped, and has nothing to do with being intoxicated. When a body decomposes as much as these had, he lectured, it produces an alcohol that shows up in the system.

Hoffman sat back down and Dr. Brucker was excused. Now that Brucker had mentioned the bullets, Dingeldine was free to introduce them with the jury present. With the bullets now matched to the gun taken from Steelman and Gretzler in Sacramento, and to the victims through Brucker's testimony, the bullet trail was complete.

Next was to place Gretzler inside the apartment, something the defendant claimed never happened. Brought to the court's attention only minutes earlier, along with the bullets were panel cards containing latent fingerprints, subsequently marked Exhibits 54 through 57. Latent prints are prints taken from items and surfaces. The very type of prints Doug Gretzler spent much of his time trying to wipe away.

Don Rees, the Tucson Police ID technician who handled the crime scene, was brought in and Dingeldine showed him the cards.

Q: "Where did you obtain these prints?"

A: "Three of them were lifted from a mayonnaise jar and one from a water glass in the Sandberg kitchen."

But Hoffman again objected to the testimony, claiming the fingerprint evidence Rees was referring to was inadmissible due to lack of foundation, insisting Rees could not be certain who lifted what prints from where. But Rees was adamant about his work, making it crystal clear he alone pulled each and every print, describing in detail how his work was accomplished. Druke overruled Hoffman's objection and allowed the prints and the officer's testimony to stand.

Larry Hust was recalled and the matter of the second tape recording was about to begin.

As soon as Dingeldine mentioned the cassette tape and offered it into evidence, Druke sent the jury from the courtroom. Only then did he allow Hust to turn on the machine. The court, counsel and those remaining in the gallery heard the ten-minute conversation. Its contents were clear, but told a much different story than the first tape heard last Thursday. This confession to the Sandberg murder's made by Gretzler on the tape contained many references to the death penalty in Arizona. Dingledine did not want the jury to hear anything about such a penalty, claiming it was strictly up to the court to decide the punishment for a capital crime. Druke agreed, and ordered the portion of the tape referring to California be omitted when played for the jury.

Again Hoffman protested, claiming it was obvious the only reason his client confessed at all was because of the continued threat being made of the death penalty. His objection was overruled, and the decision stood. This ruling too would turn out to be an important one later.

But even Gretzler, despite his attorney's remarks, appeared to have little concern one way or another about the argument. During the hearing on the above matter, Druke asked Gretzler about the tape recording and more specifically about when Detective Hust mentioned the death penalty.

Q: "The nineteenth was the day you gave the statement to Mr. Hust? You remember giving the statement to him?"

A: "Yeah."

Q: "Prior to that, did you know that life imprisonment was the maximum penalty for the charges against you in California?"

A: "I guess I figured it was, but I wasn't sure."

Q: "Between the eighth, when arrested, and the nineteenth, (the date of this recording) did you ever know what the penalty for the Arizona charges were?"

A: "The Arizona charges?"

Q: "Yes. What was the maximum for those charges?"

A: "No, not for sure."

Q: "What did you think? If you thought about it at all."

A: "I figured probably. . .I don't know. . .twenty years? I don't know."

Q: "Did you even think about it?"

A: "No, not really."

While it appeared that Gretzler was simply being honest in his answers, his nonchalant attitude was working against him. But clearly, from the moment of his capture until he finally spilled his guts to Hust about his involvement, he gave little thought to what the consequences might be for his actions. And by his response to Druke's questioning, he wasn't giving it much thought today either.

The jury, having been wandering the hallway for over a half hour, was brought back in. Druke had the tape recorder turned back on, and the voices of Larry Hust and Douglas Gretzler were heard once more.

"We killed them," Gretzler was heard to say.

"Who killed them?" Hust asked. "Who pulled the trigger?"

"Myself and Bill," came the reply.

Everett Justice. The perfect name for an FBI agent.

Richardson couldn't make it, so Justice, being the back-up fingerprint agent assigned to the case, got the call and arrived in Prescott on Wednesday. Dingeldine hoped to wrap up the prosecution's case yesterday, but even late last evening, he had no idea if Washington was going to get anyone to the trial. Justice, however, arrived in the nick of time.

According to testimony from Officer Rees earlier, 26 prints were taken from inside the Sandberg residence. Of those, 8 were sent to the FBI lab in Washington D.C., along with ink prints from Gretzler's booking into Pima County jail. Once again, the cards containing the latent prints, and the photos of Gretzler's ink prints were brought out. The later set, being introduced for the first time, were marked for identification and offered for exhibit. Over a Hoffman objection, the prints were admitted and handed to the witness. Under questioning from Dingeldine, Agent Justice indicated the match was identical and there was no doubt in his mind that both sets came from the same individual.

Under cross-examination, David Hoffman played the only card he had. "Can you be equally sure, Mr. Justice, the prints found on these two items were made inside the Sandberg apartment?"

"No, I can't be sure of that," Justice admitted.

"I have no further questions of this witness," Hoffman snapped.

After Druke had ordered the jury from the courtroom, Hoffman stood and moved for a direct mistrial. Denied.

He then moved for a judgment of acquittal to both the murder charges and the Armstrong kidnapping. It too was denied. Then a motion was made to dismiss only one of the charges.

Denied.

Finally, Hoffman renewed his motion for a mistrial, again stressing that his client was being denied a fair and impartial trial because he could not give his opening statement at the proper time. Hoffman complained that the court would not allow a continuance in the trial when he first made the request over two weeks earlier.

Once more, denied.

Druke called for a recess until 3 o'clock. The time Willie Steelman was expected to arrive.

Willie certainly didn't mind coming back to Prescott, anything to bust the monotony of the prison walls at Florence. He had been transferred from his death row cell to the Pima County Jail on Tuesday, then flown early Wednesday to the trial. Angeli took the RV out to meet the plane. There was no joking around with him on this trip and Rex was surprised how quiet Willie was, seemingly content to stare out the window. Two sheriff guards escorted Steelman up the back elevator to the second floor. Separated by a single wall, Gretzler was held in one office, Willie Steelman under heavy guard next door.

At 3:10 p.m., Druke assembled the courtroom again, minus the jury. At David Hoffman's request, the court called Willie Luther Steelman. He shuffled in; his lean, long frame swimming in his prison issued jump suit. Shoulders hunched low, eyes glaring, chains rattling on the wooden floor with his every short step.

Brenda watched him with her lookout eye, just to see if he was staring back. He wasn't. She looked over at Doug Gretzler. His head was bowed. Brenda was relieved to hear the witness did not need to be sworn in again, although she still had to sit right next to him.

But it did not matter if he had been sworn or not, Willie wasn't talking. Hoffman attempted to find out whether the witness would respond his questions, or plead the Fifth, but there came not a single worded. After several tries, Judge Druke interrupted. "You are Willie Luther Steelman?"

Steelman stared straight ahead, saying nothing.

"Could you give us your name, sir?" Hoffman asked again.

Silence.

Robert Norgren had again accompanied him to Prescott. "Your Honor. My client has no intention of answering any questions. It has already been determined that he would be violating his rights under the Fifth Amendment by doing so."

Hoffman, who was still standing, interrupted before Druke could even speak. "We argue, Your Honor, that Mr. Steelman waived his rights to protection when he testified at his own trial."

"My client is not competent to testify as to the incidents that took place in the Sandberg's," Norgren replied.

"Then the defense will ask the court for a competency hearing for Mr. Steelman," Hoffman declared.

Druke finally managed to squeeze into the argument. "That will be denied. The witness is excused."

Dingeldine's motion to preclude Steelman from testifying for the defense was granted. Having no idea what he might say if Steelman ever opened his mouth, he was relieved to watch Willie walk from the courtroom for what would be the last time.

With Steelman out of the way, Dingeldine directed his attention to Willie's partner, making a motion in limine regarding the scope of his possible cross examination if Doug Gretzler took the stand in his defense. Specifically, Dingeldine made it clear he intended to ask about the killings in California and the nine life sentences Gretzler received for them. Hoffman clearly wanted no part of that. "We ask the court to preclude questioning of my client in that area," he said. "That evidence alone would tend to convict Mr. Gretzler."

But Dingeldine countered he has the right, if not the obligation, to discredit Gretzler's testimony if he speaks in his own defense. "He now has the veil of constitutional rights which he will lose if he takes the stand."

Druke agreed. "Motion by the plaintiff is granted. Counsel for the plaintiff may be permitted to inquire of the defendant as to whether he has been previously convicted of any offense, specifically the convictions in California. And, if the defendant answers in the affirmative, counsel for the plaintiff may inquire at to the names of the offenses and the dates and places only."

So David Hoffman faced another tough decision. How to get the jury to hear from his client without putting him on the stand?

He had two basic areas of defense. The first being Gretzler's claim, despite his taped confessions to the contrary, that he was never inside the Sandberg's apartment, but only waited outside while Steelman murdered the couple. With the evidence presented by the prosecution, that would be extremely difficult, if not impossible, to support.

The second approach was Gretzler's drug use, and the contention that being under the influence prevented him from 'pre-thinking' intent. The 'intent' was the difference between First and Second Degree murder. If Hoffman, by showing his client's long period of drug abuse, could convince the jury Gretzler never really intended to hurt the victims – that it was actually all Willie Steelman's idea – then he might be able to avoid the First Degree conviction and keep Doug Gretzler alive.

But the real problem with this defense was two fold. Arizona law prohibited an expert, like the psychiatrists who examined Gretzler, from giving an opinion based on facts that were not in evidence. In order to lay such groundwork, Hoffman almost certainly would have to put Gretzler on the stand so he could back track and explain the events that led to his drug use, and thereby try and excuse his weakness in blindly following Willie Steelman.

Dingeldine promised if Gretzler got on the stand, there would be nothing he wouldn't ask, including every other crime and every other murder he was charged with or linked to. These 'Bad Acts', as the trial court would refer to them, were the last thing Hoffman wanted the jury to hear. Therefore, despite his dilemma, Hoffman realized there was no way he could ever put his client on the stand. He had struggled with this issue since first agreeing to take the case. Then one day it dawned on him how to let Gretzler say all he wanted, and never have to worry about the prosecution asking incriminating questions. Hoffman congratulated himself on such a brilliant idea, but had a difficult time convincing his client to go along. He told Doug, that under his plan, he could give whatever story he chose and could leave out any parts he wanted. He could ask for forgiveness, plead for mercy, and relive his tortured childhood, all while omitting California and the rest of the bodies he scattered about. He could take only a few minutes, or go on for hours; it would be entirely up to him. What's more, Hoffman assured him, Dingeldine wouldn't be able to touch him, question him, or dispute anything he said.

It was a novel idea indeed, and it took almost a year to finally convince him to do it. But David Hoffman had finally talked Gretzler into giving his own opening statement, after he had tactfully postponed it at the beginning of the trial.

28

Thursday, October 30, 1975 | 9:30 am.

Between the wasps and the wrangling, the murder trial now entered its 13th day. The cumbersome delays finally became too much for even Judge Druke, who, as court began this morning began by apologizing to the jury for the repeated interruptions and inconveniences. He might as well have been pointing his finger directly at Hoffman and Dingledine, who battled each other every step of the way. With each argument came a recess designed to clear the jury, and the air as well. The room was stuffy, and Hoffman's boisterous voice seemed even louder when the jury was present. Quarrels over witnesses and their testimony, points of procedure, even the law itself, led to a repeated sidebars, and on many occasions, conference in closed chambers.

The clashes between Hoffman and Dingledine, and the delays they created, were to be expected. The wasps, on the other hand, were not. The old courtroom had been ignored for many years, and was now home to a large pesky swarm. For the third time this week, they wrecked havoc with the proceedings, flustering the jury, and playing no favorites with counsel as well. The sporadic swat of a legal document against the table indicated to all there would be at least one less flying nuisance to deal with. At least for the moment. Druke waved his arms wildly, shooing them away while doing his best to focus on what was being said. Without fail, the distraction became too much and he would halt the trial, pleading with the bailiff to see if there was anything that could be done about the problem.

Brenda had cringed earlier in the week, when after an especially annoying round of attacks, Druke once again asked his staff for help. The bailiff however, was as exasperated as everyone else. Nothing had seemed to stop the wasps;

not sprays, or traps, nor even leaving the windows open during breaks would rid them from the courtroom. Finally, in a show of complete desperation, the bailiff yanked his revolver from its holster and waved it in the air, as if to shoot every last miserable annoyance right out of the sky, one by one, if need be. His comical approach brought a chuckle from the courtroom. All, that is except Brenda, who, already jumpy and terribly gun shy, didn't find it very funny at all.

"I see there's another attacker up there," Druke offered.

"I think the record should indicate the attacker is a wasp," Hoffman added, making sure it was he who got the last laugh. Even Druke found the humor in Hoffman's quick wit. "Yes, that's correct, it should so reflect, in the event someone reads this later."

In the summer of 1974, when George Dedekam was preparing Gretzler's presentencing reports on the California conviction, he asked Doug's father to write a few words about his son. "Put in there something about his childhood," Dedekam requested. "Something interesting about him when he was young and growing up."

So the father wrote;

"Doug has always been fascinated by animals of all kinds. At various times during his childhood, he had pet alligators, a guinea pig, even an iguana. He also had far more vivid imagination than most children. Doug claimed to have an invisible squirrel that he would blame in situations when discipline would be in order. While Doug would accept credit for achievements, the squirrel would be blamed for accidents or failures."

"It has been our opinion that Doug could not, or would not, accept responsibility or face reality."

This morning his son stood slouched at the podium, his head held low, strands of hair dangling across his forehead. He paused for a moment, then looked up, and in timid, hesitant voice, read to the court from a script Hoffman had prepared the night before.

"Ladies and gentlemen of the jury, I'm the person you have heard so much about. I ask you to reserve judgment of my guilt until you have all the evidence. That is as important as life...or death. Throughout my life, prior to meeting Willie Luther Steelman, I had a reputation of being a peaceful, law-abiding citizen."

Gretzler then explained how he first started using drugs in 1969; LSD, speed, cocaine, offering reasons on how they changed him, how they altered his judgment and reason. "I have always been a follower, and throughout my life I have been led by others. Then I met Willie Luther Steelman and began to blindly follow him in disregard of my own feelings. Those days made me extremely paranoid, and I was afraid of Mr. Steelman. I will not attempt to hide behind the shield of an insanity defense. The evidence will show that I helped the California authorities capture Mr. Steelman."

Turning his attention to the kidnapping charge, he admitted being with Steelman that day when they took Armstrong and his car. "But at no time did I harm him, threaten him or intimidate him. The evidence will also show I did not enter the Sandberg apartment on November 3, 1973, although you have heard a tape to the contrary. But because of my participation in the horrible and tragic events of that day, I ask you to find me guilty of two counts of murder in the second degree. Thank you."

Gretzler had kept his father's word; accepting credit for his achievement, blaming the invisible squirrel for everything else. And yet it was the first time trial observers could recall a defendant replacing his attorney in delivering the opening statement to the jury, although there was additional discussion later on how well it came off. They did agree on one thing. David Hoffman had brilliantly managed to sideswipe any damaging cross-examination of his client. Gretzler came across as a remorseful, if not a somewhat tragic figure, explained away his years of drug abuse, and therefore, had, within just a few minutes transformed himself from a cold-blooded murderer to a helpless victim. More importantly, Dingeldine couldn't touch him on anything he had offered.

"Next witness, Mr. Hoffman."

"We call Janet Gretzler."

David Dingledine had attempted to remove Mrs. Gretzler as a defense witness early that morning, or at least prevent her from saying anything about her son's drug use, and in particular, an episode that occurred in 1968.

Gretzler and some friends had been driving to the lake, when Doug, who was unbelievably stoned, got sick and vomited all over himself. They pulled over to the side of the road to clean him up, but soon a state trooper pulled up to find out what was going on. Doug explained to the officer that he was a frog and had merely stopped for a swim. Before the cop could sit him back down, Doug ran over to a nearby river and dove in, head first. Problem was, the riverbed was dry, and Doug spent the next few days in the hospital; one day to close the huge gash on the top of his head, and two days for observation.

Dingeldine complained to the court that allowing Mrs. Gretzler to discuss this episode would open an insanity defense, regardless of what Doug Gretzler promised in his opening statement minutes earlier. Druke disagreed and permitted Hoffman to ask the question, while reserving the right to disallow any testimony about Gretzler's short stay in the mental ward of a New York Hospital for impersonating a frog.

Mrs. Gretzler, and her daughter arrived in Prescott late Wednesday night, too late to visit Doug at the jail, so Druke allowed them a few minutes together in his chambers this morning while he attended to business in the courtroom. Their visit was an emotional and terribly difficult one for Mrs.Gretzler, although Doug tried to assure her he was doing all right and not to worry. "It's all going to work out," he said. Not once did she ask him about the crimes he was accused of.

Brenda swore in Mrs. Gretzler, feeling pity for the small woman who, even before the first question was posed, appeared on a constant verge of tears.

David Hoffman asked her to talk a little bit about her son.

"Doug was always a gentle person," she began. "He never got into trouble with the law until he left home on Christmas 1972. That was the last time I saw him."

"Mrs. Gretzler, did anything unusual occur in March of 1969?"

She hesitated, gathered her words, and answered. "Yes. I rode to the hospital with Doug. . .and he was in a straitjacket. . ."

And with that, she burst into tears. Druke looked at Hoffman, who indicated he had no further questions, and allowed her to step down. She walked directly to her son and wrapped her arms around him. The guards tensed, but kept their distance. Brenda could hardly bare to watch.

"We'll take fifteen minutes, ladies and gentlemen," Druke announced. "Mr. Dingeldine, you can cross when we return, if you like."

Janet Gretzler was still hanging on to her son as the last of the jurors walked past, their heads turned away, as if shamed by their intrusion of such a tender moment.

The reason for Doug Gretzler's hospital stay was never asked, nor did his mother say anything about his drug use. Hoffman avoided both areas prior to the recess. But when court resumed twenty minutes later, Dingeldine had Rich Rollman, handle the cross-examination. She had composed herself by this time, but Dingeldine didn't want to play the heavy.

"Mrs. Gretzler, how long was your son in the hospital at the time you mentioned in 1969?"

" Only about three days, I remember. Long enough to allow the wounds on his head to start to heal."

"Was he ever in the hospital again?"

"Not that I know of."

"Thank you," Rollman concluded. "That will be all."

It was enough to at least have the jury believe it was three days for medical reasons and not mental ones.

The next witness was Joanne, Doug's younger sister. Hoffman began. "Joanne, were you close to your brother?"

"Yes. He was like my best friend. But he started using drugs while in high school and our relationship was never the same. He'd take speed for a couple of weeks, then take LSD for a while, then go back to speed. It got to the point where we couldn't tell whether he was on drugs or not – he was always spaced out and confused. I remember seeing him on Christmas Day 1972. He was married and living with his wife and child, and then he was gone."

Lt. Harold O'Kane had been brought to Prescott from the Sacramento Police Department. As the arresting officer at the Clunie Hotel, he was an interesting choice as a witness for the defense.

"Tell the court what the defendant said when you arrested him on November 9th, 1973." Hoffman asked.

"He said he did not want to see any more killing. . .that Steelman was dangerous. He showed us where Steelman could be found, and we arrested him on that information."

O'Kane said that the defendant had nine .22 caliber bullets on him when he was arrested, but no weapon. Hoffman wanted it clear the revolver used on Michael and Patricia Sandberg was not in Gretzler's possession when he was taken into custody. When O'Kane left the witness stand he walked past Gretzler who raised his hand to give him the "OK" sign.

The detective glared down at him in disbelief. You stupid sack of shit, he muttered to himself, you don't get it do you? You think I'm here because I'm on your side? O'Kane told Dingledine later what Gretzler had done. "You tell him when you see him that I'd pay good money to be the one to pull the switch on him, the sonafabitch!"

"It's kinda like shock. If you've ever seen somebody shot up real close, now that'll throw you into shock. When you actually realize you're the one doin' it, it puts you into some heavy shock. But after that, you do whatever you were gonna do – you finish doin' it – kinda without thinkin'. You just start shakin'. But the way I figure it is, there's nothin' I can do about it now. I can't bring 'em back."

"Shit yeah, I wouldn't do it again for the world. You see them later in your head – the way they looked when they were dead, and you keep seein' 'em again and again. What it looks like after a bullet goes through somebody's head and the blood spurts out. . .the blood shoots, splatters, hits the wall on one side and geysered on the other, and you just made a mess on the rug. It's just like. . .say you're a mechanic and all you do is work on American cars and they're just a blur. . .you know what to do with them. Then you work on an MGB or a Rolls Royce or something foreign, you look at them that night, and you see it again, and again. You see it clearly, exactly like it was. I mean, you know where the oil spots were on the valve cover. It's the same way with the blood from all of them."

"I can't analyze my feelings and stuff like that. When you're running around like that, you don't have time to think about your feelings or figure out how you feel."

Douglas Gretzler
November 10, 1973
Stockton, California

"This subject appears to have little, if any, remorse over what has happened. A review of his work history and past history suggests a minimum of victories, as it were, and it is clear that this patient uses even minute events for ego trips. He spent a considerable period of time describing how he shot heroin two weeks ago. Indeed, his description made me wonder if he ever really had shot at all."

"There was a superficiality to his thought process that suggests a very poor set of lifestyles, poor defense mechanisms, and an inadequacy in dealing with pressure and stresses in life."

Robert G. Austin, M.D.
November 12, 1973
Stockton, California

Dr. Austin was in the courtroom Friday morning, brought to Prescott by the defense. His psychiatric report of Douglas Gretzler was exactly what David Hoffman was looking for.

But Dingeldine was opposed to the doctor making any observations about the defendant's drug use, and the effects it may, or may not, have had, or on his state of mind at the time of the murders. Dingeldine argued that Austin could not accurately say what the impact of drugs would be on Gretzler because he had not observed him in a drug-intoxicated state, and he asked the court to preclude Austin from such testimony.

But Hoffman pointed to Dr. Austin's lengthy and honored record of service to the medical community and his list of qualifications in this field of psychiatric study.

So Druke found a middle ground. He refused to allow Austin to make an opinion on Gretzler's personality defects other than how it related to McNaughton or incompetence, and he prohibited Austin from testifying about the defendant's drug abuse, agreeing with the prosecution that the doctor had no first hand knowledge of such activity.

While the jury waited outside, Druke called Austin and allowed him to testify in their absence. Satisfied in what he heard, Druke reminded the doctor what he could and could not say in open court, and then asked for the jurors to return.

Dr. Austin said the he met with the defendant for about an hour on the day he was arrested in California, and then again two days later. When Hoffman asked him if he had formed an opinion of Gretzler during the examinations, Austin said the man he interviewed has a character disorder that showed him to be weak and a follower, mimicking, almost word for word, Gretzler's opening statement. Austin claimed Gretzler told him he had not used drugs from November 3rd, the day the Sandberg's were killed, until the day he was captured.

Hoffman asked if someone was in an advanced state of drug intoxication – using lots of drugs for an extended length of time – would his memory be impaired? Austin said it probably would be.

During cross-examination, Dingeldine asked if a person under the influence of amphetamines, such as speed, would still be able to drive a car, or even shoot a gun? Austin said they could.

Detective Bill Miller was also called. Hoffman asked him if the defendant told him he hadn't gone in the Sandberg apartment, but instead waited outside for several hours while Steelman went inside. Miller replied he had. Both knew Gretzler had been lying, but the detective was required to answer the question directly, which he did.

On cross, Dingeldine asked, "Mr. Miller, did Mr. Gretzler say anything about a mayonnaise jar or a water glass being outside the Sandberg apartment?"

"No, he didn't. But of course I didn't think to ask him that question," Miller replied.

"A reasonable doubt for reasonable fee."

It is a phrase known to defense lawyers and members of the psychiatric community alike. If you have the money and the need, there is no shortage of doctors who can give you the answer you are looking for, and testify to them in court.

In late 1974, Dr. Allan Beigel and Dr. David Gurland examined Douglas Gretzler. During their haggling over the lack of a Rule 11 filing, each side was allowed to choose one doctor to make their independent psychiatric findings pertinent to the McNaughton insanity defense. Gurland, it was said, had a reputation for being very sympathetic to the defense, so Hoffman selected him to examine his client.

Dr. Beigel, being well known around Tucson for his work as well, was chosen by Dingledine to do the same. Both sessions with the defendant were very brief; Gurland's an hour and a half, Beigel's less than 25 minutes.

Several days later, each submitted their findings. To Hoffman's dismay, Gurland's opinion was, that on November 3, 1973, Douglas Gretzler was not under any drug intoxication, and very much in control of his mental state. He was not frightened of his partner, as he insinuated, and was certainly capable of knowing what was going on around him. The doctor stated emphatically that Gretzler was not insane, neither at the time of the incident, or during the interview in December of 1974.

Dr. Beigel was more to the point in his report, saying although Gretzler was suffering from an "acute paranoid state", he was not insane by any definition, and could stand trial. On the surface, his findings were slightly more helpful to Hoffman because they showed the defendant somewhat less than capable of thinking rationally on the day in question. In a sly twist, Hoffman turned around and called Biegel as a witness for the defense.

On the stand, the doctor said that paranoia could distort Gretzler's intent, or lack thereof, as it pertained to harming the Sandbergs. But he also believed, much to Hoffman's dismay, such paranoia associated with long term drug abuse was not relevant to Hoffman's primitive concept of drug intoxication. Again, because Arizona law prohibited Beigel from offering any of his conclusions about Gretzler's ability to form intent, Druke was forced to dramatically limit what the doctor could say.

Hoffman, who was already seething about the lack of money the state had set aside for psychiatric studies, erupted. He dismissed Beigel as a defense witness, and then demanded a mistrial on the grounds the doctor's original examination lasted only twenty-five minutes. "Insufficient time to make any kind of evaluation about a person's state of mind!" he stormed, which was exactly what the prosecution had claimed just minutes earlier.

Hoffman continued. "I think the record should also indicate that as a result of the court's denial of my motion, neither doctor examined him with regard to his state of mind other than the MacNaughton rule, or as far as competency to stand trial is concerned!"

"Let the minutes reflect the motion was made for additional psychiatric examination, and denied," Druke answered.

And what about Dr. Gurland, then? Druke inquired of the defense counsel.

"I have spoken with Dr. Gurland again," Hoffman responded. "He is unable to say, to a reasonable medical certainty, that is was the drugs that caused Mr. Gretzler to follow Mr. Steelman, or say that it was drugs, rather than Mr. Gretzler's personality, that may have been affected by the long term use of drugs."

Druke took no time in his response. "Given those facts, the court would find there is insufficient foundation for the testimony of said doctor."

In his written opinion, presented to the court through David Hoffman, Gurland said he could easily testify the defendant was a follower and may not have been able to form his own intent. But Gurland was more apt to believe Gretzler merely chose the easiest path, and that was simply to act out Steelman's intent. In other words, he just went along for the ride. He admitted he could not say for sure it was the drug use that made him this follower, and because of this admission, Druke decided there was insufficient foundation for his testimony and it could not be used.

It was a Catch-22 for Hoffman. Both doctors could have offered something to a drug intoxication defense, but only if Gretzler would get on the stand to talk about his drug use. And if he did, the prosecution could dredge up every other crime he was involved with. And yet, without such an admission by the defendant, there would be no foundation for either doctor's opinion.

So the jury never heard what Dr. Beigel had to say, and Gurland never even came to Prescott. This jury would not hear about Doug Gretzler's state of mind when they examined him, or what role his years of drug abuse played. That, along with his excuse that he was just a follower of the true bad guy, Willie Steelman, and any medical testimony that could help support such a claim, would not be heard.

It was a tremendous setback for the defense, and Hoffman protested vigorously to the court the awkward position he had been placed in. But to no avail. He complained that Druke did nothing to study Gretzler's mental state prior to the trial. But Hoffman did not sway the court, and this issue would remain a hotly debated topic for years to come.

Weeks later, Beigel, who was admittedly no fan of David Hoffman, sent a letter to Judge Druke complimenting him on how he handled the trial overall, and that day, November 3rd, in particular. "Overseeing a proceeding like this," he wrote, "had to be one of the most agonizing, if not depressing, ways to make a living. My lay impression was that, if anything, you were more than fair to the defense, whose flamboyance and talents sporadically gave way to book-slamming and various theatrics."

They had found Joanne McPeak. She was living in a halfway house for convicted drug users in Norfolk, Virginia and by now was but a small, burnt out shell of a woman with bad teeth, scraggly hair, and a voice that was all but gone.

Q: "You will have to speak up so the jury can hear you," Druke requested.

A: "Joanne McPeak"

Q: "They can't hear you, ma'am. You will have to speak right up and tell us what you have to say. All right? As loudly as I'm speaking now. Think you can do that?"

A: "I think so...Joanne McPeak."

Q: "A little louder if you could...Mr. Tucker, can you come over here and help us with the microphone...if you could talk right into the microphone..."

Joanne leaned forward and began talking.

They finally managed to get out of the witness that she had seen Doug Gretzler with Willie Steelman, and she had been with them off and on for a week or so up to the day they left, which she was told later by David Hoffman, was November 3, 1973.

They had done some crystal together, she said. She saw Doug do some heroin. Maybe it was heroin, she added, she wasn't sure, but that's what he said it was. She saw a .22 Willie had, but never saw him point it at Doug, or threaten him with it. Hoffman kept pulling out of her the continuing drug use by the four of them in the little house on Mabel Street.

Q: "How was Doug using it…injecting it?"

Q:"How many times a day did he use it?"

Q:"How long had he been shooting crystal?"

Q:"How many days?"

Q:"How was it determined that Doug would shoot it?"

A: Joanne thought for a moment, and then gave Hoffman the answer he had been fishing for. "It was whatever Bill wanted to do, we did."

Q: "You say that whenever Bill wanted to do some, you all did it?"

A: "Yes."

Q: "Did you ever hear Doug make any suggestions as to what he and Bill should do?"

A: "No."

Q: "Did you ever hear Bill make suggestions as to what he and Doug should do?"

A: "Yes. He was like the main person, whenever he wanted to do something it was always done."

David Hoffman announced he now rested his defense of Douglas Gretzler, but after Druke dismissed the jury, he continued his demand for more psychiatric observations of his client.

"Let the record show" he declared "that previous to this hearing, and in chambers, that we have requested psychiatric examinations and additional examinations for my client-let the record so reflect this."

"The motion is denied," Druke answered. "And the record will so reflect."

Dingledine never hid his contempt for what David Hoffman brought to the courtroom. He felt he was above Hoffman's showboat style, and believed the legal system deserved better, but he was also the first to admit the dangers in taking David Hoffman too lightly. The professional relationship between two remained on rocky ground for most of their stay in Prescott, and yet one evening, Hoffman found Dingeldine in their Whiskey Row hangout having a beer. They had just waged battle over the psychiatrist's testimony and Dingeldine was still in a fighting mood. Hoffman, who had just returned from a visit with his client, walked over to Dingeldine's table and pulled up a chair

"I don't want to talk to your ass!" Dingeldine snorted.

"No, no wait," Hoffman pleaded. "I just got some information I thought you should know about."

Dingeldine didn't say a word, although couldn't help but be a tad bit curious.

"I just spoke to Gretzler a little bit ago," Hoffman continued, noticing he had finally got his opponent's attention. "I told him I had some good news, and I had some bad news.

Hoffman seemed very serious, and Dingeldine turned towards him to hear more.

Hoffman said, "The good news is, I told him, you're not crazy."

Dingledine took a sip of his beer and nodded in agreement.

"The bad news," Hoffman deadpanned, "is they're gonna kill you 'cause you're not!"

Dingeldine spit his beer all over the table. Hoffman was one sick man, he thought, but he still could crack him up. Hoffman ordered a couple more beers. The ice was broken. At least until the next court date.

29

Wednesday, November 5, 1975 | 9:40 am.

"It was a trail of kidnapping, robbery, burglary, and the ultimate crime of murder," David Dingeldine began. "November third, nineteen seventy three, the day a two man gang of terror swept through Tucson."

In dramatic fashion, so began the final day in the trial of Doug Gretzler, as the prosecution addressed the jury with its closing arguments. He led them back to that Saturday morning kidnapping of Vince Armstrong, and later, his daring escape. Knowing the police would soon be on their heels, the pair decided to find another car, Dingledine added.

"Who would be next on this parade of terror?" he asked, knowing very well whom.

He described Gretzler and Steelman as "seeking and stalking", when they went to the Sandberg's condominium complex. "And what happened inside that apartment? Only four people really know, and two of them are dead."

He reminded the jurors again of the physical evidence. "Five bullet holes in the pillow. The pillow used to muffle the sound of the shots fired into the couple's head, Gretzler's fingerprints on the water glass and mayonnaise jar in the Sandberg's kitchen, proving beyond any doubt that he was inside, and not outside by the car as he claimed. And his own taped confession that he shot both the Sandbergs."

Richard Rollman was given the task, as he had all through the trial, to watch each juror closely to see if he could detect one that might be trouble later when the panel would decide on their verdict. He saw nothing.

"Douglas Gretzler is a liar!" Dingledine roared. "He has tried to put everything on Willie Steelman! But Douglas Gretzler is guilty of First Degree murder. You have no doubt about that in this case."

Dingeldine's close lasted less than an hour. Druke told the jury Mr. Hoffman would give his closing arguments for the defense after a brief recess.

Brenda also managed to sneak a glimpse of the jury members as Mr. Dingeldine spoke, wondering what was going through the minds. Brenda had known many of them all of her life, but now she felt a sorry for them. The trial had been lengthy and the delays made it seem even longer. Time and time again, the jury was asked to wait outside the courtroom while the two lawyers argued, and the interruptions became tedious. Brenda noticed how several of them had a habit of rolling their eyes when they saw another delay coming.

They were simple people, and Brenda was angry about having to put all of them through this. They didn't ask for it. They didn't ask to have Doug Gretzler's horrible crimes dragged through their lives, with his fate heaped upon them. Most of them were older – old enough to have a son Doug's age –and maybe that thought went through their minds, as well, after hearing what he had done. She watched them as Mrs. Gretzler talked about her son, then break down, and Brenda knew the sight of her sobbing in the arms of her son weighed upon them all.

"All of you probably think Douglas Gretzler is guilty," Hoffman began when his turn came later that afternoon. "But let me remind you of your individual promises. . .to keep an open mind. But we know you can't do that, don't we? Mr. Gretzler has only one chance and you're it."

He asked them to consider both sides of the evidence when they retired to deliberate. Then, with what could only be considered an odd choice of words, he challenged them. "Play the devil's advocate," he said. "You have heard about the terrible and vicious crime. You have heard about people whose minds work differently than yours, but Douglas Gretzler's limited participation in those crimes only make him guilty of Second Degree murder."

He reintroduced evidence and disputed its importance. He recalled witnesses brought by the state, repeated word for word their testimony, then simply charged that it was untrue, unconvincing, or both. The two confession tapes made by the defendant, both telling a different story, were explained away by merely saying the detectives confused his client when he was weak and at his most vulnerable time, and that Douglas Gretzler was under such drug intoxication at the time, he was not capable of the deliberation and premeditation required for a First Degree murder conviction the state was asking for. It was Steelman who was the mastermind, Hoffman alleged. He was the one ultimately responsible for the Sandbergs' deaths.

"Willie Luther Steelman was the man who terrorized the victims, and Douglas Gretzler as well," Hoffman bellowed, making it clear his client was afraid of Steelman and he could have easily would up dead if he didn't go along with him.

Two hours later, David Hoffman was finally finished. Dingeldine was allowed a final rebuttal close. Knowing that his opponent had either worn down, if not worn out, the jury, he was brief and to the point.

"Ladies and gentlemen, Mr. Hoffman has tried to filibuster you into Second Degree murder verdicts. The facts are not that complicated. We are talking about vicious, execution-style murders! Let me remind all of you, reasonable doubt is not created by two hours of oratory. It is created by the facts as shown in this courtroom."

Judge Druke thanked both counsel, and the jury for their diligence and patience, but it took him the better part of an hour to instruct the jury on every count of the indictments against the defendant. When he was finished, and was confident they understood, he asked Bailiff Tucker to draw four names from the sixteen, and those four, after all they went through, were designated as alternates and dismissed.

The remaining jurors, seven women and five men, were led to the jury room at the rear of the courtroom. The bailiff closed the door and stood nearby in the event they needed assistance or had a question for Judge Druke. It was 3:30 in the afternoon. Druke retired to chambers and Gretzler was led back to the room next door. He would wait there, at least for an hour or so, and if the deliberations lasted longer, he would be taken back across the street.

Brenda finished up her notes and left. Judge Druke told her to go home and rest, offering to call her when the time came. She had an odd feeling about what was happening, although she couldn't really put her finger on the sensation. She decided not to go home, but to her parent's house instead. There she thought about the trial; how exciting, and at the same time, how heartbreaking it had been. She sat at the kitchen table and for the first time told her dad all that had gone on, but she had not been there very long, when the phone rang. The jury was ready. Brenda asked her father to go back with her to the courthouse. There would be a time when she would laugh at how frightened she was.

Back in the courthouse, Doug Gretzler was brought in. His skin was flushed, as pale as the courtroom walls, and he was visibly nervous and animated, unlike at any other time during the trial. He had every right to be. The jury had been out just over two hours.

Judge Druke. "Ladies and gentlemen, it appears you have reached a verdict in this case. Will the foreman please hand the verdict to the bailiff and the defendant remain standing?"

Bailiff Tucker handed it to Druke, who opened it, then handed it back to Tucker for him to read out loud to the crowded courtroom. He wasted no time in doing so.

"As to the murder of Michael Sandberg? Guilty in the First Degree."

"As to the murder of Patricia Sandberg? Guilty in the First Degree."

"As to the kidnapping and robbery charges? Guilty."

Gretzler's knees buckled and there was a gasp of air as Hoffman grabbed his arm to steady him.

"We'll set the date for sentencing on Monday in Tucson," Druke announced as those in the room began to bustle about. "This court is dismissed," he announced over the din.

Hoffman could also be heard telling his client not to worry; they still have a chance of winning on appeal. "It is Mr. Gretzler's wish to be confined in solitary confinement in Santa Cruz County Jail," Hoffman barked over the growing clammer in the courtroom, as his client was lead out of the room for the final time. He would be returned to Tucson that evening.

Judge Druke attempted to soothe some of the jury members who appeared shaken. He acknowledged how difficult the decision was to make and how proud he was of them, how well they performed their task. Brenda looked over to find several of the jurors weeping, their emotions finally allowed to surface.

She gathered her few belongings and left the courtroom with her father. Neither spoke. They walked from the old Federal Building, across the courthouse plaza, and into the downtown. The cold night air snapped at her face and her eyes burned with the tears she too was finally allowed to shed. Autumn had taken its grip. Winter would come much too soon. She looked down the streets of Prescott. This was her home. She had to remind herself of that, because tonight it seemed so foreign, so strange, so cold and uninviting. There was nothing warm, nothing familiar, nothing comforting. She felt a million miles removed from the Prescott she had grown up in.

There was a sadness that blanketed Brenda that night, and yes, part of it was for Doug Gretzler. But she also couldn't help but blame him for how he had come to Prescott and ruined everything.

Book 3

THE AFTERMATH.

1
Nogales.

In the summer of 1975, less than three weeks before Willie Steelman's trial was to begin, and at least three months before Gretzler's case would be heard, Pima County transferred Doug Gretzler to the Santa Cruz County Jail at Nogales, citing improved security the new facility would offer. David Hoffman had vigorously protested the move, claiming client conferences would be nearly impossible with him being housed an hour away.

But Doug enjoyed his new surroundings far more than his small, dank, solitary confinement cell in Tucson. Nogales was new, bright, and laid back. No one knew who he was, or seemed to care what he had done when they did. He was allowed out in the general population and was given the same limited privileges of most other inmates. Seemingly resigned to his eventual fate, he told Hoffman he wished he could just stick it out here in Nogales forever, if forever was what his punishment was to be. He could live with that, he said.

But on Sunday, July 27th, a mere six weeks after he had arrived, Santa Cruz County Jail authorities said they had caught Douglas Gretzler trying to escape. Undersheriff Raul Parada reported Gretzler had pulled the bed loose from the anchor in the wall and had started to enlarge the hole it left. "A blatant attempt to escape," he claimed. But Doug protested, arguing the bed was already loose and it only got worse every time he sat on it. He wasn't trying to go anywhere, he said, but there was no place else to sit.

Several days later, with Gretzler now in solitary, five inmates did escape from Nogales, using a smuggled hacksaw to cut through a single steel bar in a skylight above their cell.

"It's more like a motel here than a jail," Sheriff Zeke Berjarano was quoted in a Tucson newspaper. "It's hard to keep prisoners in here."

After learning of the escape, Pima County Attorney Dennis DeConcini hurried to Nogales to see for himself how secure his prize prisoner really was. But now Bejarano changed his tune and assured him that Gretzler wasn't going anywhere, downplaying the shortcomings of the jail and highlighting what steps were in progress to correct them. Still, Bejarano admitted he never cared for the new facility, but when the plans were being drawn, no one would listen to his opinion.

Unconvinced, DeConcini returned to Tucson, and on Friday, August 1st, David Dingledine asked Judge Mary Anne Richey for permission to bring Gretzler back to Pima County for obvious security reasons. When Hoffman heard about the move, he went to Richey and got an injunction to halt the transfer – the same transfer he was so adamantly against only weeks before. A hearing was held to decide once and for all where Douglas Gretzler would be housed. Dingledine argued Santa Cruz wasn't safe enough, while Hoffman countered his client was content and secure there, and that it was simply proposterous to believe he would even consider trying to escape.

Richey listened. Hoffman won. Gretzler stayed.

So after the trial in Prescott, Hoffman assumed his client would be returned to Nogales. He wasn't. He was taken to Pima County to await sentencing. On November 10th, Hoffman repeated his request to Judge Druke to have Gretzler housed in Nogales. Druke refused.

On December 29th, hoping to begin hearings shortly after the new year, Druke sent Gretzler to the Diagnostic Facility at the Arizona State Prison in Florence for a routine pre-sentence evaluation. One week later, he gave Hoffman twenty days to provide the court a list of mitigating circumstances in his client's defense, but the request date was not met. At a hearing on March 3rd, 1976, Hoffman ignored Druke's second request for the list, then asked for money to travel to California to interview several Stockton psychiatrists. Necessary, Hoffman explained, because they play such a critical role in his mitigation defense. Druke asked why he couldn't just talk to the doctors on the phone, but Hoffman changed the subject.

What he really needed, Hoffman countered, was the necessary funds to go to Denver to find out whether the Smaldone Family really existed. If they did, as he believed, it would be crucial for the court to know more about them before sentencing Douglas Gretzler. If there was such an organization, and Willie Steelman had indeed crossed them, then there would be every reason for Douglas Gretzler to believe his partner, and therefore fear for his life if he didn't do exactly what Steelman told him to.

Druke had heard the story before. It had nothing to do with the proceedings, he said, and denied both monetary requests. Still managing to circumvent the court, Hoffman somehow pushed the pre-sentence hearings well into spring. On April 15, 1976, he again requested additional psychiatric studies on his client, adding that even Dr. Komisaruk, who had examined Gretzler earlier, said time spent with the prisoner had been woefully inadequate. "In depth analysis is what is needed," Hoffman quoted the doctor as saying. "Four hours, at the very minimum."

Dingledine objected, arguing this was nothing more than another Hoffman tactic to delay the process. The sentencing hearings have been put off long enough, he scowled, insinuating Druke himself was to blame for allowing the defense to drag its feet.

Hoffman bounced back. What about neurological exams? Steelman has had several. Why couldn't his client be afforded the same attention? Dingledine shook his head.

But Druke agreed if Steelman had one, then Gretzler should have one too. Hoffman could schedule an EEG for his client, paid for at court expense. But there would be no more money given for psychiatric studies. None. If the defense insisted they were so necessary, Druke ruled, then they could pay for it themselves.

Hoffman continued the attack, bantering about how absolutely imperative it was for the Gretzler family to be at the upcoming hearings to testify, and therefore he would need the appropriate funds be set aside for their travel to Arizona. Somewhat surprisingly, Druke agreed to consider the request.

And phone calls. "I'm making a lot of phone calls," Hoffman whined. He asked the court to help pay his long distance bill, complaining, "It's coming out of my own pocket now."

The hearing resumed on Tuesday, April 20, 1976. David Dingledine, fearing he had not driven home what a savage crime Douglas Gretzler committed when murdering the Sandbergs, asked Druke to allow the photographs omitted at trial be included during the sentencing hearings. Crimes of a cruel and heinous nature are one of the aggravation factors the court would need to consider, Dingledine argued.

Druke denied the request. Nor did he feel it necessary to have the Gretzler family present during the sentencing hearings and refused Hoffman funds for their travel. However, he did give him $200 for phone calls, and then asked about the progress of the EEG test, which he had already approved.

Hoffman ignored him, saying something about lack of transcripts from the trial, then changed the subject again, insisting a jury be impaneled to decide what Douglas Gretzler's sentence should be.

This was Judge Druke's chance to turn a deaf ear. He said that he felt all the basics had been covered and both sides could offer their aggravation and mitigation arguments on May 5, 1976.

But just two days later, David Hoffman motioned the State for a stay of that date, arguing not all information was in place, including the neurological exams approved by the court. His request was approved, once again delaying the start of the hearing.

Then, on May 4th, the Court of Appeals vacated the order, allowing the hearing to proceed on schedule. Druke told both sides that he fully expected them both to be in court the following morning.

Hoffman said he couldn't make it. When he filed for the stay, and thinking it would not be acted upon so quickly, he made vacation plans. He would not be back in town until the end of the month. Exasperated, Druke rescheduled again, this time for June 2nd.

But on that first Wednesday morning in June, Hoffman came to court and asked for another continuation, claiming that since he had not been given the money for the Gretzlers to attend the hearing in person, he had asked the family to write letters to the court explaining their son's many virtues. As of yet he still had not received any of the letters. And because of several unforeseen complications, Doug Gretzler's EEG had not been arranged for either.

Druke fumed, yet gave Hoffman two weeks to obtain the letters and get the exam completed. Gretzler's EEG was finally performed on June 10th.

Back in court on the morning of June 15th, Hoffman called to the stand Santa Cruz County Jail Administrator Jere Lee Brenner. When asked what he thought of Gretzler while he was in Nogales, Brenner replied that he was a model prisoner, and as far as he was concerned, would remain so if given life. Hoffman then asked about the alleged escape. Brenner replied that he did not believe there was any attempt made at all. "He just sat there," Brenner said. "He didn't look like he ever wanted to go anywhere."

Hoffman concluded by inquiring if there was anything else that the court should know before handing down their sentence. Brenner smiled. He said the crew at the jail had found a copy of a detective magazine with a story in it about the killings in California, and after that they started making fun of their prisoner. "We started calling him Baby Face Gretzler," he said.

Surprisingly, just two days later, Hoffman threw a wrench into the proceedings and filed a motion to withdraw as counsel for Douglas Gretzler. In an attached memorandum, Hoffman wrote:

> *This court has denied virtually all of the defendant's motions for funds with which to produce mitigating circumstances necessary to prevent the imposition of the death penalty. This Court has denied defendant's motion for funds for Dr. Richard Komisaruk to continue his examination, after the initial examination was paid for in whole by the appointed counsel, even after receipt of a letter (from Komisaruk) indicating further examination by him was necessary. This Court has effectively denied Mr. Gretzler his right to effective assistance of counsel under the Sixth Amendment, and due process under the Fourteenth Amendment, and equal protection under the Fifth and Fourteenth Amendment of the Constitution of the United States. Because counsel has an ethical duty to competently represent Mr. Gretzler, and because the court has deprived counsel of all ability to do so, counsel must respectively withdraw (representation) and request this Court appoint counsel who feels he can adequately represent the defendant within the bounds set by this Court.*

Judge Druke denied this motion as well.

Hoffman wasn't going anywhere.

In San Francisco, Roderick Mays had made every attempt to follow what was happening in Tucson. With absolutely no news coverage locally, his only hope of staying informed was through the Pima County Attorney's Office. On a regular basis he called and spoke with either Randy Stevens or Dave Dingledine regarding the progress, or lack thereof. He could not believe that more than six months after he had been found guilty, his daughter's killer had not been sentenced for his crimes. It was becoming clear, that as summer approached, Mays was becoming more and more frustrated with the delays. Still, Dingledine always tried to keep a positive outlook on their conversations, once even hedging a guess that a sentence would be handed down before summer, at the very latest.

But on July 5, 1976, Roderick Mays made another anxious call to Tucson. Dingledine tactfully tried to tell him that, because of summer vacations and short staffs in the courts, delays were inevitable. Even he would be out of the office until the first part of August. Until then Randy Stevens would be handling the case. Mays, although disappointed with the lack of progress, was noticeably pleased to hear Stevens would be in charge. Stevens had pulled no punches with how he felt about Gretzler, or what he would do to him if given half a chance, and Dingledine assured Mays that Randy would keep him abreast of how things were progressing. During the same call, Dingledine got around to talking about the race for County Attorney was starting to heat up and that William Risner was running on the Democratic ticket. He then told Mays about the letter Risner wrote to his office shortly after the murders were committed, and that Risner had very strong feelings against the death penalty.

Mays was flabbergasted. He had no idea any changes were under way that could further delay Gretzler's sentencing. No one had ever mentioned to him anything about the possibility of some new county attorney putting a halt to what little hope he had left of resolution to his daughter's murder. He asked that a copy of Risner's letter be sent to him immediately, deciding it was time to get personally involved.

2

July 1976.

Although the mitigation hearings resumed the following Wednesday, July 7th, David Hoffman managed to create the necessary roadblocks to postpone them once again.

His main focus was now on Druke's denial of funds to bring out of state witnesses; primarily the Gretzler family, to Arizona to testify on Doug's behalf. At a follow up hearing on July 13th, he repeated his objections, and while there was some progress made that day, Hoffman closed the session by moving the proceedings be terminated and a new trial ordered.

His reasoning? Pima County's prosecution team had seemingly unlimited money – taxpayer money – available for witness expenses, while the defense was not being afforded the same consideration. Plus, because the county was picking up the tab for mileage, meals and hotel rooms – "a vacation in the desert", he claimed – their witnesses could not help but feel indebted to those who were paying their way. Therefore, Hoffman alleged, their testimony would most certainly slant in favor of the prosecution. In addition, the County Attorney's Office was showing their witnesses graphic photos of the crime scene immediately prior to them taking the stand, an act specifically designed to escalate their hostility towards his client.

Druke brushed aside both charges, and the defense motion as well. Still, Hoffman had managed to further delay the hearings.

While the next day's session actually contained some usable testimony, (six witnesses took the stand – four doctors, Larry Hust, and a surprise showing by Joanne McPeek) the ground covered was largely uneventful. Dingledine was now on vacation, and although a well-prepared Randy Stevens was in charge, the hearing felt lackluster. McPeek had to be coached every step of the way and was asked to speak up continuously. When she was finally asked to step down, Druke decided enough was enough and rescheduled the next hearing in exactly seven days.

But on July 21st, Hoffman began by complaining that McPeek's transcripts of the previous week were not ready and he could not continue without them. Directing his question to the court reporter, Druke asked for a reason for the delay. With a shrug, the response was that with all the vacations being taken by other reporters and stenographers, he was already working extra sessions and extra hours. He was hopelessly behind, he admitted, and it could be as much three weeks before the transcripts in question were completed. Several other excuses were offered, but regardless, Druke had no choice but to put everything off for another six full weeks. The next hearing would not be until August 31st, and by then the minor problem of timely transcripts would be the least of Judge Druke's concerns.

With the nation's Bicentennial holiday festivities now behind them, the American people were hearing more and more about the upcoming elections. While the national contest between Carter and Ford was more entertaining, the local battle for County Attorney was already promising to be far more boisterous. Earlier in the year, Dennis DeConcini had decided to leave his top post at Pima to take a run at the U.S. Senate, but not before attempting to hand pick his successor by recommending a devoted member of his staff, Democrat Steven Neely, to the post.

With the September 7th primary just six weeks away, the Republican candidate, Ann Bowen, was running unopposed. But on the Democratic side. Neely's opponent, it was learned, would be William Risner.

These were not new combatants. Both Neely and Risner had competed years earlier, beginning in the classrooms at the University of Arizona. Upon graduation in 1969, Neely went directly to work for the County Attorney, while Riser went into private practice. In 1970 and 1971, the student turmoil that plagued campuses across the country found its way to Tucson as well. Students and non-students alike were arrested over the months and months of civil disobedience that flowed off the university grounds and onto the adjacent streets of Tucson. Instantly, Steven Neely became the eager, energetic young prosecutor, and his courtroom nemesis was none other than William Risner, who ably defended the accused against the hard line establishment.

Their battle lines were clearly drawn. Neely thrived and learned the lessons DeConcini taught daily in his "tough on crime" atmosphere of the county prosecutor's office. Risner, on the other hand, remained openly critical of the tactics DeConcini and his staff used, saying at one time that office would better serve the citizens if it was more of a "people's law firm", working with its residents instead of suppressing them and their ideals.

By 1976 Risner was well know in Tucson for his enthusiastic support of a variety of causes, most notably his stance against the nearby copper mines and their decades of environmental abuses. In addition, the justice system in Pima County had had more than its share of scandal and criticism over the past decade. Not everyone was convinced that the current approach was the best approach, and Risner used that as his campaign theme.

After several weeks of phone calls, Mays finally reached Randy Stevens on Monday, August 2nd. He asked for an update on the Pima County Attorney's race, and specifically what ad agency was handling Steven Neely's campaign. Having just retired from a career in advertising, he was confident he had the stuff to help insure Neely's survival, and along with it, seal Steelman and Gretzler's fate once and for all. During their conversation, most of which was centered on the capital punishment issue, Stevens mentioned that Charles Manson would be eligible for parole in two short years, and if serving time in California, the two punks who murdered his daughter would be up for parole in 1982.

The very idea infuriated Roderick Mays, and he began making plans to go to Tucson. Gathering his indignation and disgust, he also composed a letter to Asa Bushnell, an editor with the Tucson Daily Citizen who had earlier wrote a piece sympathetic to Mays' feelings and frustration. In the letter Mays wrote he was, *"appalled to think a person dead-set against the full imposition of justice should be seeking the law enforcement post of Pima County attorney. His questioning of the costs of extradition and prosecution of these two murderers bespeaks a type of mind for which I find an enormous amount of disgust, but I further recognize the danger to the residents of Pima County of electing a person whose mental inclination is to be soft on criminals."*

On August 9th, Mays followed up his letter with a phone call to Bushnell and told him he was coming to Tucson to campaign against William Risner. It was also during that first week in August when Steven Neely was informed about Roderick Mays' determination to help in his campaign. Although he had not spoken to Mays directly, Randy Stevens had advised Neely about potential problems with such an association. Neely decided to contact Judge Druke to get his opinion on the matter.

The question posed was specifically about the possibility of running radio or TV commercials, even newspaper ads, focusing on the crimes committed by Steelman and Gretzler and the positive legal action Pima County had taken against them. Druke replied the matter was out of the trial phase so the gag order had been lifted, and because a guilty verdict had been handed down, he saw no conflict with advertising centered on those themes. He personally did not care for the idea, and wondered out loud why Neely would go along with it, but stated there was nothing legally wrong with making a commercial about the crime, or showing the pictures of the man who had been found guilty in his courtroom.

On August 12th, the Neely campaign produced the first draft of the Steelman/Gretzler TV commercial. While consensus was that it had real possibilities, most agreed it lacked the magnitude or impact of the horrific murders discussed within it. Something, it was agreed by all involved, was missing.

The following Monday, Roderick Mays called Tucson again. This time he was directed to Richard Moret, the advertising manager for Neely's campaign. Mays told him he was interested in doing whatever he could to help the cause. Remembering the less than spectacular reviews the commercial had gathered,

Moret suggested Mays write a television spot for the Neely campaign. Mays was ecstatic.

The next afternoon he called Moret again and read to him the copy from his proposed commercial. The hook, he explained, would be his daughter's wedding picture and how lovely and innocent she looked. Then flash to mug shots of the killers, and how cold and evil they were. Mays promised the contrast would be heart wrenching. He advised Moret on how to get his hands on a copy of the wedding picture. The mug shots, of course, would be easy to obtain. The concept excited Moret and he asked Mays how much it might cost to produce the spot in California where Mays could oversee its development. Mays said it would be much too expensive to do the commercial in San Francisco and instead suggested he travel to Tucson to supervise the production. While he was there he could make the rounds of the radio and television stations to promote the finished product.

Again Moret was enthusiastic, offering to trade out a free hotel room for Mays during his stay, and to pick up some of his expenses, "as a fellow ad man, of course". Mays said he could be in Arizona the day after tomorrow, so Moret got busy and set up interviews at two televisions stations.

Mays made a few phone calls himself, the first being to Randy Stevens to advise him of his plans and to ask if the County Attorney's office had any objections to his visit. Other than his concern about the hotel trade out, and the Neely campaign picking up his travel expenses directly, Stevens said there was nothing to prevent Mays from coming to Tucson to speak his mind.

Moret also called the Attorney's office and spoke to Neely, who sounded equally excited about Mays' arrival. He did, however, instruct Moret to stay close to Mays and make sure he didn't do or say anything that could be embarrassing to the campaign.

Mays arrived on Thursday, August 19th, and after checking in to his motel, he called Stevens once again and asked specifically what he could say and how far he could go without opening himself up to a libel issue. Stevens gave him his best advice, then called Moret to say he was beginning to think it wasn't such a good idea after all to get the County Attorney's office involved in what Roderick Mays had to say while in Tucson. But Stevens had not made his concern known to Steven Neely. That night, at a candidates gathering, Neely told Ann Bowen that the victim's father was in town to take on Risner and his open opposition to the killer's extradition from California. "He's going to raise hell," Neely promised, "You wait and see."

David Hoffman was also clued into Mays' arrival. In fact, before the weekend was over, anyone who watched TV knew the dead woman's father was in town. Mays was all over the local radio and television, but ironically it was Neely's side first to be blindsided by what he had to say.

Mays insinuated in his interviews that the Neely people had requested he come to Tucson on their behalf, and at their expense, a claim that made Stevens cringe. Plus, Mays appeared extremely vengeful, even suggesting at times the County Attorney's Office was somehow responsible for allowing the case to drag out for almost three years. Hoffman kept a keen eye on the weekend's events as

Mays spread his message across the local media. Seizing what he determined as yet another opportunity, Hoffman decided such adverse publicity could not be favorable to his client, especially just before the sentencing hearings were to begin.

On Tuesday, August 24th, worried Mays might leave town prematurely, Hoffman filed a motion in Superior Court asking for sanctions against all parties involved in the recent media barrage. Subpoenas to appear at the hearing were served late Tuesday morning on Mays, and then the next day on David Dingledine, Steven Neely, Randy Stevens, and most of the television station managers in town as well. Judge Druke was on vacation that week, and his subpoena was waiting for him upon his return. Over the prosecution's written objections, Hoffman's request for a hearing was scheduled for the following Monday.

On the day Mays received his subpoena, his picture and a story about his visit to Tucson was bannered across the *Arizona Daily Star*:

"GRETZLER VICTIM'S FATHER FIGHTING RISNER"

The article quoted both Mays and Risner, each proclaiming their frustration with the position they had been placed in. Mays, with his anger with how long the process has taken, and Risner with accusations of dirty politics. "They brought him (Mays) over here and lied to him," Risner was quoted. "I'm terribly sympathetic with the man. They told Mays that I objected to extradition. They told him that, if elected, I was going to fire the people who handled the Gretzler case. There is no truth to this."

Risner admitted writing the letter to Stevens, but simply because he felt the Steelman and Gretzler cases would be little more than tests on Arizona's new capital punishment laws; laws he also admitted not being in agreement with, and that he was merely "curious as to the cost."

Coincidentally, on Wednesday, the crosstown *Daily Citizen* ran an editorial backing Steven Neely for County Attorney. Somewhat contrary to recent media events, there was not a single word mentioned about the murder case that had found its way back into the news in a big way this past week. On Thursday, the *Daily Star* ran yet another piece on Mays' bid to block Risner's race to the County Attorney post. Needless to say, the article did not put the candidate in a very favorable light.

On Friday, at a press conference featuring the two Democratic candidates, Risner and Neely took turns accusing each other of misrepresenting the truth. Risner charged his opponent with preying on "the natural grief of a father who lost his daughter in a brutal and shocking murder," and in doing so had jeopardized the outcome of the trial. Fully aware of Hoffman's current actions, Risner said he was very concerned about all the publicity Mays had received. "Mr. Neely had handed the defense attorney, on a silver platter, enough ammunition to fuel appeals for years." In doing so, Risner warned, he may have paved the way for the conviction to be overturned.

Neely scoffed at such an idea, insisting Mays came to Tucson on his own free will. While acknowledging the commercial accused Risner of being against extradition for Steelman and Gretzler, it was prompted only after Risner publicly criticized his office for spending $200,000 for the trial, even though court records indicate that barely $34,000 had been spent thus far. After Risner claimed it would be highly unlikely either would have ever been released from California prison, Neely went to great pains to point out that no judge's recommendation was ever binding, nor was he willing to take the chance that either Steelman or Gretzler could be paroled as early as 1981.

On the morning of August 31st, announcing he wanted the court to determine whether there had been "intentional misconduct" by the County Attorney's Office, David Hoffman opened the hearing by claiming Roderick Mays knew much too much about the case against Douglas Gretzler. Plus, the media frenzy of this past week had, "created an atmosphere of political pressure under which there is grave danger that no court can sentence Mr. Gretzler solely upon the evidence presented." His finger was pointed directly at Judge Druke, who despite declaring shortly after the hearing began that he had not been influenced by the publicity, removed himself from presiding over the hearing, and Superior Court Judge Harry Gin was called in as his replacement. To support his accusations, Hoffman asked that several newspaper articles and videotapes of television commercials be entered as evidence. While the editors and program directors responsible for running the ads and articles were in the courtroom, the main focus of the hearing quickly moved to Steven Neely, Randy Stevens, and Roderick Mays.

As a courtesy, and at Stevens' request, Gretzler, who was present at the hearing, was removed from the courtroom prior to Mays taking the stand. Mays admitted his expenses while in Tucson might be paid by the campaign, but denied he had been encouraged by any member of the County Attorney's Office to get involved. He came only because he believed William Risner was too lenient with criminals, and specifically because of Risner's open opposition to the death penalty. "Such a man should not be elected to the office of County Attorney," he declared.

Both David Dingledine and Randy Stevens stated also they had not invited Mays to Tucson, nor had they encouraged him to campaign or did they furnish him with sensitive material about the case. When asked about a comment Mays had made earlier about a rumor that Risner was going to fire anyone associated with the Gretzler case if he was elected, neither indicated they had heard of any such plan, although both announced that they would resign their positions immediately if Risner became their boss.

When the hearing resumed the following day, Judge Druke was summoned to clarify his involvement, if any, in the recent media campaign. He admitted speaking with Steven Neely about using Gretzler's photo in his campaign. He told him the trial's gag order had been lifted, therefore there was no legal reason why he could not use the photo. But after heated accusations from Hoffman, Druke emphatically denied he had been influenced in any way with what had transpired the past week. In fact, he had been out of town the entire time and hadn't even seen any of the materials in evidence. At one point he even walked into a room where a TV announcer was talking about the case, only to walk right back out so he would not hear what was being said.

When Neely took the stand, he accused Hoffman of putting on this show solely because of his support of Risner for County Attorney, a claim Hoffman quickly agreed with. "I have been neutral in this campaign," he stormed, "but not anymore!"

The two-day session was concluded Wednesday afternoon. Judge Gin was not required to rule on any of the testimony, his task merely to hear Hoffman's contention of misconduct by the County Attorney's office, and therefore Judge Druke's inability to sentence his client fairly. Asked afterwards about the problems created by getting a free motel room, Roderick Mays harrumphed and said he had decided to pay his own way. He was on the first plane back to San Francisco Thursday morning.

Coincidently, six weeks later, on October 15th, Mays filed a claim with Pima County requesting that because he had been summoned to appear in court beyond his scheduled stay, he deserved to be paid for at least those extra expenses. Upon hearing this news, David Hoffman, ever the hard nose, filed an affidavit, claiming that because the witness had been in Arizona voluntarily, he wasn't entitled to anything. Not one cent. Zero.

But Hoffman lost again. Mays eventually got his money.

At the hearing held two weeks earlier, Judge Druke admitted Steven Neely had informed him he intended to use the Risner letter as a political issue. While Druke added he believed such a move to be politically unwise, he had no grounds to prohibit Neely from going ahead with his plan.

Naturally, Hoffman disagreed. Within a new motion filed this morning, he claimed "just as it is improper for a prosecuting attorney to disseminate news about a trial, so is it improper for a judge in charge of a case to advise that such dissemination is permissible." He asked that Judge Druke be removed from the case and to not be part of the sentencing phase.

So Judge Gin agreed to hear Hoffman at nine a.m. the following morning. He denied the motion before the day was over.

The aggravation/mitigation hearings continued off and on for the next six weeks. There was little provided by either side that could be considered new or valuable information. Hoffman continued to provide the excuses for delays; missing transcripts, scheduling conflicts, and always the lack of money.

Two months lapsed with little activity. On November 6th, Steven Neely was elected County Attorney by a wide margin, while William Druke defeated Joe Jacobson for one of the four Superior Court judgeships up for grabs. The *Daily Star* reported he spent $5,007 in doing so, far more than any other candidate.

By now David Dingledine had turned over the sentencing phase to Deputy Attorney Randy Stevens, who had argued passionately the State's case these past several weeks, attacking David Hoffman head on with every word he spoke. Stevens had never camouflaged his disgust for his opponent, and so his enthusiasm poured new life into Pima County's quest to insure the death penalty be implemented.

"This is a case that does not call for leniency," Stevens proclaimed, "It calls for death!

And so with these words delivered Friday afternoon, November 12th, the final arguments from both sides were presented. There was nothing new. Stevens called the crimes "heinous, cruel and depraved". Hoffman countered, reminding the court how his client had showed compassion towards his victims when he padded their wrists so the bindings would not cut into their skin. "We are not here to decide whether Doug should be excused for the murders of Pat and Mike Sandberg," he pointed out. "We're here to decide whether he should spend every day of his life in a prison in Florence or he be put in a gas chamber and killed." But before taking his seat, Hoffman took one final swing at Judge Druke and told him the easiest thing for the court to do was go along with public opinion and impose the penalty of death, as if daring him to do so.

The following Monday afternoon, Druke requested both sides be back in the courtroom. His voice was noticeably subdued. Within one minute of opening the session, Druke informed the prosecution, with the exception of the nine counts of first-degree murder the defendant had brought from California, he had found no additional aggravating circumstances required in a capital punishment sentence. Stevens was stunned, but said nothing.

Without missing a beat, he claimed that neither had any mitigating circumstances been offered to alter his decision.

Hoffman was allowed to reiterate his position, and he reminded the court the psychiatrist's testimony alone showed that Mr. Gretzler's ability to follow the law was significantly impaired. If not that, then the noticeable absence of funds necessary to defend his client was certainly enough to prove mitigating circumstances.

Stevens then took his turn, suggesting the court had erred in not finding these murders cruel, heinous and depraved. If nothing else, he said, he wanted the prosecution's protest noted for the appeals guaranteed to follow.

Judge Druke then spoke. "Mr. Hoffman, if you and your client will stand before the Court at this time. Mr. Gretzler, as a matter of law, you have the right to say anything that you would like to the Court, at this time, on your own behalf."

Gretzler tossed his hair out of his eyes and answered he had nothing to say.

Druke waited for a moment, and then asked if either side had any other legal issues to add. Each replied that they did not.

Druke paused, as if gathering strength. "Then it is the judgment of the Court, Mr. Gretzler, that you be sentenced to death for the crimes of first degree murder – two counts – committed on three, November, nineteen seventy three."

Druke paused. Doug Gretzler did not move. After adding twenty five to fifty years for the robbery, burglary and kidnapping, Druke said David S. Hoffman Esquire would handle the appeal.

Judge Druke, whose voice and presence had not one time wavered during the past twenty-four months, was now low and halting. "Mr. Gretzler, Mr. Hoffman argued to the Court on Friday, as I recall, that it would be easy for the Court to impose a sentence of death."

Another pause. He found his voice again and continued. "Mr. Hoffman was woefully and sadly mistaken. The Court will stand at recess at this time."

And with that, Druke lowered his eyes, swung his chair around and hurried out of the room.

3

The Business of Execution: 1976-1998.

It has been argued by some in Tucson, at least those who were directly involved in the case of Douglas Gretzler, and most certainly by those close to Judge Druke, that the twelve minutes in court that day were the most difficult in his professional life. Some will even swear they saw tears in his eyes as he exited the room.

True to the words he promised the defendant, it was not, despite the volumes of gruesome testimony offered and the dozens of horrific photographs presented, an easy decision for him to make. It would be his first such sentence, and his last, and while he remained active on the bench in Tucson for another twenty-five plus years, he has never spoke publicly about the case, or his feelings so visible that day.

The death penalty debate had been an emotional issue long before Druke became personally and professionally involved, and perhaps it is somewhat ironic it would be Doug Gretzler who would be the most affected by the turmoil the capital punishment argument created in Arizona and throughout the United States.

While the issue had been debated for years, modern day arguments really surfaced on June 29, 1972, when the United States Supreme Court ruled on the case of Furman vs. Georgia. The court said Georgia's death penalty was unconstitutional for the basic reason, that while the jurors determined the punishment, they were given no standards by which to make their decision. And because nearly every state in the union had essentially the same procedure, the ruling invalidated every death penalty law on the books across the land. Therefore, all prisoners awaiting death had to be resentenced, and eventually were, most to life. At the time, Arizona statute provided the trial judge impose the death penalty in first degree murder cases if the state could prove at least one of six aggravating circumstances. That too would be ruled unconstitutional by the high court.

A small story buried in the Tucson papers on July 2, 1976, in essence, reinforced a newly created Arizona death penalty law developed specifically to address the above issues. In the meantime, The U.S. Supreme Court ruled the punishment of death was not cruel and unusual, and upheld existing death penalty statutes in Georgia, Texas, and Florida. Because Arizona's new laws were very similar, on December 20, 1976, just over a month after Gretzler was sentenced, the Arizona Supreme Court upheld the current death penalty, deciding it was indeed constitutional, although the merits of the aggravation and mitigation process were still being argued. The final outcome however, especially on how it would affect Doug Gretzler, was far from over.

By the time Gretzler was transferred to Florence to take his place on death row, Willie Steelman had been there for over a year. He had not wasted any time in making his presence known. His record was full of fighting and insubordination. He threatened guards and fellow inmates alike, receiving days, even weeks, in isolation as punishment. In his cell they found homemade knives and other weapons, even a crude still which, with fruit cocktail, hot dog buns, and sugar from his meal trays, he made some very nasty spirits.

Association between these former partners was limited. They conversed only when their cells were within shouting distance, although Doug made no secret that he still thought of Willie as his superior, if not his savior. Being no apparent shortage of drugs, both continued their usage. Guards would turn a blind eye to such activity as long as it kept the inmates quiet and comatose. Anything was better than being pelted with food, feces, and urine.

While probably not to the degree of Willie, Doug was also viewed as a disciplinary problem, although the naivety he had to his situation was alarming. After the prison banned guitars in June of 1977, (the garroting capability of a guitar string apparently had been overlooked until then) Doug wrote a letter to Department of Corrections politely asking they rethink their decision while offering an idea he was sure they would jump on. He suggested a one-for-one string replacement to keep track of all potential weapons. "I'm getting pretty good on mine," he added, as if his untapped talent on the guitar might change their collective minds. While he was at it, he told them a weight machine and group exercise would be a good idea as well. There would come a time when he would even suggest a blood drive on his cellblock for the soldiers in the Gulf War. "There's so little we can do," he argued, visibly disappointed when this idea too was turned down.

On April 21, 1978, Judge Carl Muecke once again held the Arizona death penalty statute unconstitutional because of the limits it placed on mitigation factors presented by the defendants. Because so many were affected by his decision, Muecke made this a class action representing all death row inmates, thereby staying all pending executions and placing all current litigation on hold while his decision was reviewed by the higher courts. The judge was proved correct when, on July 3, 1978, the United States Supreme Court voided

Ohio's death penalty for the very same reasoning. The Arizona Supreme Court responded quickly to change the state's mitigation ruling once more to satisfy Muecke's concerns. Subsequently the U.S. Supreme Court, along with the Ninth Circuit, agreed, and by November of that year the state of Arizona was back in the execution business.

One year later, on December 15, 1979, Willie Steelman was re-sentenced to death. On April 21st of the following year, Doug Gretzler's conviction was reaffirmed as well, although neither was given a firm execution date.

So for the next three years they sat. Willie used his time causing trouble and renewing an apparent interest in religion, while Doug began surfacing out of his self-inflicted exile from reality and started thinking about what he had done. The ascent was a slow one, for he still felt lost without Willie to guide him. Nor could he really talk to anyone about what he was feeling, or come to grips with the crimes he was accused of. He began to get angry, knowing he had turned his life over to this guy he hardly knew. The more he thought about it, the more he hated himself. Of course, the more self-loathing he piled on himself, the more he tried to suppress his memories of what he had done. Without the help necessary to sort out his emotions, the circle remained unbroken.

Willie, on the other hand, flourished. While Doug refused all contact from the outside, including any with family, Willie relished it. The attention only made him stronger, and it was during this time when the first curiosity seekers began to trickle in. A woman working in the legal system in Pima County, who of course had a front row seat to Willie and Doug's exploits over the years, befriended Willie in hopes of convincing him to tell his story. Flattered by the attention, and remembering his claim long ago of how he would be remembered along the likes of Charles Manson, he granted her the rights. He began making lengthy and unbelievably inaccurate tape recordings for her, recounting his life and the crimes he had committed. What he hadn't done, he made up. What was weak and uninteresting, he embellished. Wild tales came forth, and because his new confidant had made known to him her Christian beliefs, most of what Willie confessed to her followed that path. Once he told Gretzler he was born Jewish, but raised in a Japanese family, and Doug believed him. She would as well.

The Christian angle worked like magic and soon Willie found himself immersed in the subject. He hit the books to learn more about what he was professing, and as he did, his woman friend brought new people to the party. Outreach groups who specialized in prisoner connections began contacting Willie, asking he tell his transformation to their congregation. Lonely women, who upon hearing his sad tales, flocked to him, offering their love and support, opening their abundant hearts and meager pocketbooks to prove he was not alone, and more importantly, that he had been forgiven. Willie studied hard, and was soon sucked into his own deception, once again blurring the line between blatant lies, and his version of the truth.

As part of her plan to tell his story, the woman who started all of this brought in a noted author who specialized in true crime to write about Willie. She also made contact with a magazine writer from Phoenix who had taken an interest in the inmates on Arizona's death row. Careful to protect her position, she set up barriers between Willie and these writers, in essence telling them how she saw the story being told. Willie had handed over all access to her, so therefore any contact with him went through her, and all materials related to his story were dispersed only with her written approval.

After being told his book must have the angle of his Christian rebirth, and having read through Willie's distortion and self-promotion, the crime author packed his bags and headed home. He was a *true* crime writer, he reminded her, and there was nothing remotely close to the truth with anything Willie Steelman was spouting. Likewise, the local author battled endlessly the roadblocks set up between her and Willie before she too decided it wasn't worth it. In the meantime, she had discovered the most interesting of the duo was not Steelman, but the man hiding in his shadows, Doug Gretzler, and her later impact on both of their lives would be staggering.

Church women came and heard Willie's tales, falling at his feet, falling in love with the man society had turned their collective backs on years earlier. They believed him, all of him. They allowed his words to be published in church newsletters. They believed him when he sent them his old Jewish prayer book from his days in Viet Nam – a book torn by shrapnel and stained in blood, he claimed. They believed him when he said he had a witness who would say they saw him outside the Sandberg apartment that entire day in November. They believed him when he said the Sandbergs were dealing heroin and the Parkins were trafficking drugs, and both needed to be killed to stop this madness. He said he was studying to be a minister. He said he had saved the lives of three prison guards and was a hated man because of it. He said he had given away all his earthly possessions to benefit others on the inside. He said he didn't know where he was going to get the $300 he needed to pay off a debt to a prison gang; a debt he had taken on to save the life of a young prisoner who had incurred it. The Lord would find a way to help him, he said, and he loved and trusted the Lord. He said he was sick. He said he was not afraid of death. He said he wanted to be an example to others. He said he was sorry. So very, very sorry.

They in turn wrote him letters. They sent him Bibles. They sent him money to help his missionary crusade inside prison. They sent him the $300. They sent him tape recorders, which he sold. They sent him pictures of themselves and their children, which he saved, passed around, and gloated over. They sent along their hopes and prayers. They sent their unwavering devotion. Some sent their undying love.

In January 1983, Willie and Doug were among twenty-five inmates waiting on Arizona's death row. Although its constitutionality was still being debated, the state continued ahead with its timetable. On January 6th, Doug Gretzler's sentence was reaffirmed and his execution set for February 23rd. In March, Steelman was also given his date, June 1st, although their respective appeals attorneys managed to stay both executions. And while Gretzler would eventually face years and years of courtroom battles, Willie's struggles to stay alive soon took a different turn.

In the fall of 1983, gaining well over a hundred pounds and experiencing constant sickness, prison doctors determined Steelman was suffering from severe, possibly even terminal, liver damage.

For the next two and a half years, even with help from Phoenix area doctors and hospitals, his condition failed to improve. He was transferred to another cellblock and lost contact with his partner, but not before having a falling out over a $500 typewriter belonging to Doug. Willie tried to talk him into selling it for $40 worth of drugs, and this became the final straw. With all the confusion and turmoil swirling around in his head over who he was and what he had done, and with the realization that he had already turned his pathetic life over to this man years ago, the very idea that Willie still wanted more sickened him. Doug refused, and in doing so, removed himself, once and for all, from Willie Steelman's grip.

In April of 1986, and now extremely ill, Steelman's lawyers asked the State of Arizona to provide an experimental operation that could extend, possibly even save, their client's life. While doctors argued the merits of such a procedure, Willie's health deteriorated rapidly.

"It's hard to justify the expense of caring for me when I'm condemned to death," Willie was quoted. "When they told me it was terminal, they had guards outside the door. They didn't know I was going to react. It's the one way (Governor) Babbitt can't get me. I beat the state."

But the state disagreed, arguing the delay was less about money and more about the danger and uncertainty of the operation known as a Leveen shunt. A 2-foot long tube would be placed in his abdomen and inserted into veins behind his collarbone, thus re-circulating the deadly toxins building up inside him. Hopefully the shunt would give his now damaged kidneys the opportunity to reprocess the fluids. The twenty-minute operation was estimated to cost $4,000 to $6,000, but it could buy him some time.

"I don't like knowing that I have to be sick," Willie said, angry he had no say in the operation. "And I don't like the idea of them gassing another Jew. My faith keeps me strong, but when it's time for me to go, then it's time."

Willie had already made out his will, leaving photographs and cassette tapes to a woman he had met through a church in California, a woman he claimed to love, a women he had promised to marry when he got out. He left what else he had accumulated, including ten percent of whatever proceeds might come from the publication of his story, to the Temple Beth Israel in Phoenix.

And finally he wrote. "I have intentionally made no provision for my brother, Gary Steelman. He wanted no part of me in life and shall get no part of me in death."

The operation did not come. Willie was in and out of the prison hospital ward, even transferred to the Maricopa Medical Center in Phoenix when his condition became too much for them to handle.

On July 17, 1986, a guard noticed Steelman's noon meal had not been touched. He entered the cell and discovered Willie slumped over on his bunk. Willie was rushed to an outside facility where he was stabilized, only to return to CB1 at Florence a few days later.

On August 7th, after his condition again worsened, he was again taken to the Maricopa County Hospital where he was pronounced dead at 2:28 that afternoon.

Upon learning of this news, Roderick Mays said he was annoyed that Steelman died of natural causes before he could be executed, lamenting, "He had been condemned to death at every level, and I believe he should have been executed long before this."

Frances learned of her brother's death the following morning. She hastily made plans to attend his services to be held several days later at the Temple Beth Israel cemetery in Phoenix. The man who had once boasted that he was bigger than Manson, the condemned killer who had devised a plan to sell tickets to his execution at $2,500 a pop, was dead. Gone with barely a whimper, remembered with little more than a few paragraphs in the Tucson newspapers. A gassy, toxic, blimp of a man, found slumped over in his cell, clad only in his underwear, his trousers crumpled at his feet.

For the past several years, both Steelman and Gretzler, as well as all others on death row, were intentionally held in limbo while the courts continued to argue the constitutionality of the law. In December 1988, after reviewing another prisoner's appeal, the Ninth Circuit court decided Arizona's death penalty was invalid, not simply because of the ongoing battles over mitigation, but primarily because of the aggravation criteria of what determined a cruel, depraved and heinous act. It was too vague, they said, and if their decision was upheld, it would mean all death sentences in Arizona would have to be voided.

To make sure that didn't happen, the state ceased all activity against those condemned to die, merely to keep them from being included in this action.

It was during this time when Douglas Gretzler had the opportunity to examine where his life had led. The magazine reporter from Phoenix, who originally was invited to write about Willie, found herself drawn to the quiet and totally withdrawn Gretzler. It was this woman, Laura Greenberg, who through her countless hours of conversations with him over the coming years, forced him to open up and face who he was, what he had done, and the reasons why he allowed himself to sink to such a pathetic and disgusting low. Despite the years and years of suppression, Greenberg, without mincing words or catering to his fragile psyche, faced him down, asking him point blank, time and time again, how anyone could do the horrible things he had done? How could anyone pull the trigger on a child?

At first Doug could not answer her. He did not really know how he had gotten to this place. "If I could do these things," came the excuse, "then anyone is capable of doing them."

"You don't have a conscience, do you?" Greenberg snapped.

"I don't know. How do you get one?" came his honest reply.

Year after year, Greenberg continued her dissection of a very willing Douglas Gretzler. She saw first hand his slow journey from the years he had lost. He cried. She cried. He talked. She listened. She watched as the transcriptions of the tapes he made for her uncovered a man far removed from the callous and uncaring murderer he entered prison as.

He got a job in the prison waxing floors, spending hours to himself, thinking, remembering, long after lights out. He gained the respect of guards and fellow prisoners alike. He began taking responsibility for his actions, ending the years of blame he had heaped upon his father and family. In 1991 he found the courage to apologize to them for what he had put them through. The following year he looked me in the eye and did the same, asking if my grandmother, Richard's mother, would want to be invited to his certain execution? It was the only way he knew to prove how sorry he was.

In June of 1992, his attorneys filed yet another appeal, citing 26 reasons why his sentence should be remanded. Two weeks later, without comment, U.S. District Judge Richard Bilby denied 15 of them, but agreed to hear arguments on the claim David Hoffman had provided ineffective counsel during the trial, a claim that began with Hoffman himself.

The hearing was postponed several times, until August 1995, when all parties gathered in a Tucson courtroom to rehash the entire story once more. It seemed odd to hear David Hoffman admit he had done such a second rate job as defense counsel, arguing his many inadequacies, even though his client was still very much alive almost two decades after his death sentence was handed down. Doug Gretzler was not in the courtroom that afternoon, deciding that he did not care to attend any more hearings held on his behalf.

The one final appeal was heard, and on September 26, 1995, Bilby denied the petition, reluctantly, but with much thought and concern. As a footnote to his decision, the judge wrote:

> *This case represents everything that is wrong with death penalty litigation - an inexperienced lawyer (only three years experience with no death penalty cases); a parsimonious criminal system that would not grant the defendant sufficient funds to adequately defend himself and an over-zealous prosecutor who did his best, successfully to deprive the defendant of needed funds for an adequate defense. Were it not for the overwhelming evidence of his guilt, this Court would have granted the Writ. No one can take any solace from this case - the victims' families who have had to wait too long, and even more so, the criminal justice system. The end does not justify the means, and if it does, we are just one step away from anarchy.*

In the spring of 1998, Doug Gretzler met with his family, spoke with the daughter he had left almost a quarter century earlier, as well as the grandchildren she had given him in the years since. He told his appeals attorney he was not interested in continuing with the attempts to keep him alive. He put his affairs in order, said goodbye to the woman who had helped him come to terms with who he was and what he had done, and waited.

On June 3, 1998, the State of Arizona finally did what they had set out to do decades earlier. At 3:08, on a bright and magnificent afternoon, they carried out the execution of Douglas Edward Gretzler for his role in the murders of Patricia and Michael Sandberg.

EPILOGUE

Death. And Everything After.

"We are most like beasts when we kill,
most like men when we judge,
and most like God when we forgive."

~ Henry Ward Beecher

I have just one more story to tell. Two stories, actually, that tie together. I'll try and be brief.

Of all my years, 1998 will turn out to be the most difficult, the most hectic, the most revealing, and in the end, one of the most satisfying. I had just sold my business; a business that had consumed me – in a way, destroyed me – and while I had been married for almost thirty years, that too had come to an end. I was starting a new job, living in a tiny $300 a month apartment, writing this book, trying to figure out who I was, where I had been, and where I was going. Even though I had two grown kids out on their own, I was now the father to a new baby girl, and I struggled with how I was going to handle starting all over again at forty-seven years of age.

In March, I learned Doug Gretzler's appeals had run their course. He told his attorneys it was time to let it rest, and so after over twenty years there would be no more arguments made on his behalf. His execution was imminent. He certainly did not want to die, but on the other hand, he was tired. It was as if he wanted to prove to all how sorry he was for what he had done. Allowing the State to complete its agenda seemed the best way, maybe the only way, to achieve that end. His execution was set for June 3rd. I had not planned on attending, but as the date approached I was told Doug expected me to be there. I decided I had come too far not to finish my journey, so I notified Arizona Department of Corrections of my intentions, received my invitation, and made plans.

Here's the other story.

There was a guy who worked for me for several years; I'll call him John, who had not only become a good employee, but a good friend as well. John had, without question, the toughest life I had ever known. He had little family; a mother in Southern California he hardly spoke to, a sister somewhere, and all he knew of his real father was that he was killed in a motorcycle accident when John was a baby. He was about as alone as a person could be. Needless to say, John was a very fragile guy; extremely insecure and unbelievably sensitive. The closer we became, the worse I felt about his situation. I, at the time, had everything, and he had nothing. It didn't seem fair. He worked so hard at the shop to please me, and yet the tiniest bit of criticism, even looking the wrong way at him, would crush him. I learned early on how to walk that fine line.

One day, about the time I began this book, and about the time my world was starting to spin off its axis, John did something to hurt me. I know now he didn't mean to, and at the very least, wasn't even thinking about how it would affect me. It was, however, about the worst thing a guy could do to a friend. I'll leave it at that.

I fired him. But what apparently troubled him more was how badly he had hurt me, and how it had ended our relationship. We didn't see each other for over a year, until one day I decided enough was enough, that his friendship was more important than what had happened, so I called and asked him to have a beer. He agreed.

We talked about nothing for awhile before we eventually got around to us, and what had taken place. He asked how I could forgive him for what he had done, and I said that I didn't know why, I just did. It wasn't anything I thought much about, or worried about, or grieved over, I just did. John could not believe how I could just let it go that easy. He couldn't do that, he told me. He didn't have it in him to forgive and forget. He said he couldn't even forgive his mom for how she had treated him when he was little. Nor could he forgive his current girlfriend for the things she had done years earlier; things that happened long before she had even met John. He said he did not have the ability to forgive, and he begged me to tell him how to do it; how to find, in himself, that trait.

I told John I just couldn't go around carrying the load of hating someone forever. I just did not have the energy or the strength, so I decided to forgive him. It was just that easy. Forgiveness. I didn't even have to struggle with it, it just came upon me. I didn't think of it as some remarkable feat on my part. Truth be told, I looked at it as more of a weakness. I had often wondered why I wasn't man enough to stand up to someone who had crossed me, or in this case, taken from me something that I had cherished for so many years. I drank my beer in sudden silence and began to question what kind of man I really was.

But none of this was good enough for John. He still felt so bad about what he had done that he told me he wanted me to take him outside and hit him. Right in the face, he told me. Hit him hard. Just beat the ever lovin' shit out of him, he said, because, damn it, he deserved it. I laughed and told him I wasn't going to hit him, that he was my friend, and that was what was important to me now, and what he had done wasn't anymore. But that only made him more upset. He wanted, even expected, to be punished for what he had done.

I didn't hit him. We got over it. We had another beer. Our friendship continued, although I'm sorry to say John never found the ability to forgive. He lost a wonderful woman who really loved him because he could not let go of what she had done years and years earlier. Unimportant things, really, and John knew that. But his insecurity and uncertainty always reined heavy over him, robbing him of what little chance he had to be happy. More importantly, it stole from him the opportunity to have a real family and the love of another person, the feeling of being wanted and needed, and the comfort of place and purpose, a feeling he never had growing up.

Fast-forward a few years. It was now only days before Doug's execution. I had agreed to do an interview with the local newspaper about my writing project and my date with an executioner. Just minutes before meeting with her, I got a phone call. John had killed himself. Put a shotgun in his mouth and pulled the trigger.

I was devastated. I'm sure my heartache spilled over into the interview, because I said things I had never even thought about. Feelings and emotions poured out of me. I remember sitting in that coffee shop, weeping, trying to hide my tears from the reporter. Not knowing I had just lost my dear friend, she most certainly thought I was real head case, crying over some guy who had murdered my family twenty-five years earlier.

A few days later I carried my emotions with me to Arizona. The story in the local paper had traveled far and wide and by now I had given interviews to many other newspapers, from Lodi to Tucson, and in each I spilled my guts, and spoke from my heart. I said I had forgiven Doug Gretzler for what he had done. He didn't ask me to, I just did. I wrote to Doug about this one time and he answered back that he was shocked. He said that after all he had done to our family, he didn't deserve to be forgiven. Maybe he didn't, I don't know, but I just woke up one morning and that was it. I told the newspapers that I was going to his execution, not to find closure, not to demand retribution, not to protest his killing or make light of the awful, disgusting things he had brought to so many people. I was going because he expected me to be there, maybe so he could show me how sorry he was. It was his way, probably the only way he had left, to apologize. I couldn't speak for anyone else, I said. Nor did I fault others for continuing to hate him. In a way I admired their resolve, their strength in holding on to what they believed to be right and true and just. That Doug Gretzler must die.

I drove from Phoenix to the prison in Florence the morning of the execution. All the way over I held on to a picture of Richard, Wanda, Debbie and Rick, and prayed that somehow they could forgive me for what I had done, what I felt, and what I was about to do. I must say there was no overwhelming sense of relief that morning, no heavenly pronouncement they understood and were there with me. I entered the prison with that photo clutched in my hand, and a knot tightening in my stomach. I saw others arrive; witnesses, victim's family, like me, I was certain, and I hoped maybe by talking to them, we could find a common strength, share our stories and the events that had lead us all to this place and time. I knew I would feel better if we could just talk this all out.

Instead I was moved to a small office and kept there, away from all the others. Through the glass and across into the other rooms, I watched them gather. I felt the stares directed my way. As Doug's time came closer, their numbers grew. They mingled and talked, interspersed between the awkward hugs and hesitant handshakes. I recognized several, although there were many unfamiliar faces, and I had no idea who was who, only that I was being kept away from them for a reason, and it hurt. I sunk deeper.

We were escorted from the waiting rooms to the small theater used for the executions. It was a brief walk, taken on the most wonderfully warm Arizona summer day, across the courtyard of the old part of the prison; an oasis purposely kept green for visitors such as us, with its lush lawns and bountiful flowerbeds. I was kept twenty to thirty feet way from all the others during our walk, and was asked politely by my escort to keep to myself at all times. I was told not to speak to anyone. They heard what I had said, and my words had upset them, even angered them.

After the execution I was pulled aside and asked if I wanted to make any comments to the media. I still don't know why I agreed. Maybe it was my way to apologize. I do remember trying to gather my wits, making small talk with those who chose not to ignore me, being introduced to the media people I had spoken with by phone days earlier. Dave Dingledine was there and I watched as he addressed the cameras, still arguing Gretzler's insincerity and lack of remorse; as if the man was still alive. I was amazed at how much passion and anger he could still muster after all these years. I envied him, and pitied him at the same time. He had done such a thorough and professional job years earlier, but it was as if he couldn't let go of the intensity, the rage he felt all those years ago. Today he had finally won, the victory of death he fought so hard to obtain, but you wouldn't know it by listening to him. He saw me. He knew who I was. He spoke his mind to all the others, but didn't say a word to me.

I was called before the group, shaking on the inside, hoping it didn't show on the outside. I knew why I had been kept separated and I felt shame. I had no business expressing my feelings at the expense of others. These were good people; regular folk, who had lost as much or more than I had, and here I was telling everyone how I had forgiven the man who had murdered their sons, brothers, daughters, sisters.

I remember standing there in front of the cameras, trembling, sweating, hanging on to that photograph for dear life, apologizing profusely if my remarks had caused them pain. I answered a few questions, biting my lip, afraid I was going to come undone at any moment. Later, someone sent me a tape of that press conference. To this day I haven't had the guts to watch it.

It might have appeared to those in that room, knowing I had just come from watching a man die, that my emotions were because of Douglas Gretzler. That wasn't true. In fact, just minutes after they closed the curtain on him, I gave his death little thought at all. It was a non-event, actually, and far more peaceful and humane than any of the killings he was responsible for. No, I remember standing there and thinking of all the others affected by what he had done; the Sandbergs, the Sierras, the Parkins, and yes, the Earls. Even the Gretzlers.

I remember thinking about my friend John.

And I remember thinking about the pain we pile upon ourselves and others, and the ability we have to hate and to hurt, without even knowing why. I"ve now have come to understand we are born with this human flaw and cannot shake it on our own. Our society so easily demands punishment and retribution, yet shuns forgiveness and understanding – labeling it a weakness – without a single moment of consideration. I thought about how we have become our own worst enemy. I thought about Gary Steelman Jr., and the story I heard in my travels. They said he was never the same after that night he got the gun for his uncle. They said he just shriveled up after that. They said he started drinking and using drugs, while his name became shit on the bottom of Lodi's shoes. His name! They said even the school principal came right out and told him it would be better for everyone if he didn't attend his graduation ceremonies because, "the Steelman name stills angers a lot of people", and that Gary and his family would be disruptive if they were there. I was told Gary spent the next dozen years living in a camp trailer in his father's backyard and eventually drank himself to death. A doctor had warned him. He told the doctor he didn't care. It astonished me how we all could be so cruel.

Of all the people I spoke with during my writing, hundreds probably, the one person I could not bring myself to call was Roderick Mays. I knew where I could find him. I had his number. I picked up the phone a dozen times, but I could not bring myself to interrupt his grief. I had read the eloquent words he had spoken over the years about the love he held for his dear, sweet daughter, as well as the bile he felt in his throat for the men who had ended her life. How could I push my way into the middle of that? Who was I to tell him what I thought and felt? In the grand scope of things, I was nobody. Yet here I was at Doug Gretzler's execution, proclaiming my forgiveness, while Mr. Mays did not have the opportunity to live long enough to witness the one final act that might help unload the burden he had carried in his heart for far too long. Yes, I remembered Roderick Mays.

I left the prison, alone, and drove back across the desert in the twilight of a perfect summer's eve. And I cried. I sobbed in a way I had never done before, or since. I guess I cried about what I had witnessed, and probably about the pain I had imposed on others. I thought about John, and Doug. About how different they were, and yet how similar was the hurt they both carried. One whose life's struggles were self inflicted, the other who had nothing whatsoever to do with the life he was thrust into.

Neither wanted to die. I'm certain of that much. Yet they were both gone. Both struggled with what was inside them; Doug fought to find his conscience, John battled his inability to forgive. In the end, neither could forgive themselves.

Let me just end with this. To the people whose lives I have trespassed upon with this book, and for those wounds I have reopened, I'm sorry. I'm so sorry if I've caused any additional pain. That was never my intent. What I hoped for by telling this story was that maybe I could make people aware of the anger, and even the sadness, in the souls of those who wander in and out of our lives. Hopefully this story might awaken us all to the desperate acts such struggles often lead to. Maybe with this knowledge we might come to understand our neighbors, our family, yes, even our children, a little better. Maybe we can rekindle that compassion all of us are capable of; that love Our Father has asked us to show one another. Maybe we can offer only a kind word, or a sympathetic ear. Maybe it's just a dollar, or a friendly hello that could make all the difference in their world. Would it have made a difference to Doug or Willie? I don't know. Maybe not. I guess it didn't seem to make much difference to John. But I know I'm still willing to try.

I also know I can never forget what Willie and Doug did to my family and to all the people whose lives they crossed during that autumn so many years ago. I've never asked anyone to forget, I only ask that we consider the power of forgiveness. It is the easiest, and at the same time, the most difficult gift one human being can offer another.

> For God will bring every deed into judgment, including every hidden thing, whether it be good or evil.
>
> Ecclesiastes 12:14

ACKNOWLEDGEMENTS.

During my years of research I had the opportunity to meet many people whose lives had been affected as much as mine by this story. Most were like me. They knew part of it – their part – but never the whole story, so each was anxious to help fill in the blanks of how they became involved, but at the same time they often pelted me with questions about what I had learned. I often joked that I spent more time explaining this sad but interesting tale, as I did asking questions to uncover more about it.

Because of the many years that have passed since I first began this book, sadly some of the people listed have passed away, and I've tried to note that where possible.

Let me begin by first thanking my sister, Marilee Cross, who was instrumental in getting me started. She collected the very first Arizona police reports in late 1991 and showed them to me, figuring I might be interested. She certainly had no way to comprehend at the time how much they moved me, let alone how those first few pages would set off an odessey that would continue over the next two decades. Thank you, Marilee.

In California.

My family members, Dave and Donna Christy, John and Debbie Oldenhage, and Bill Reynolds. In addition, Sam Libicki, Mike Brown, Debbie and Ed Brammer, Dan Walters, Lt. MacFarren, Sgt. Steven Mello, Norm Parkin, Mr. and Mrs. Leon Machell, Carol (Jenkins) Mettler, Charles Shipley, Kathy Stone, JoAnne Porter, Jim Fulkerson, Lonnie Rueb, Dana Sparks, Jack Billingsley, Steve McFadden, Cindy Benning, Harold O'Kane , Peter Saiers, Mrs. Leonard Chaotain, John Barbieri, Doug Barr, Lt. Marlene Kinser, Sgt. Robert Nelson, along with countless others from the law enforcement and legal communities in Stockton, Lodi, Sacramento, Santa Rosa, and Modesto areas.

In Arizona.

A special thank you to Dave Arrelanes, who sadly is no longer with us, for sharing his time and memories with me. Also to his one time partner, Bill Miller, for the same reason. I would also like to single out Martha Hernandez in Tucson, whose kindness, enthusiasm, and many extra hours she spent helping in my research will never be forgotten. Thanks as well to Mark Stanoch, David Hoffman, Robert Norgren, David Dingledine, Rex Angeli, Joe Godoy, Larry Hust, Chris Nanos, Weaver Barkman, Brenda (Harris) Parkin, Crane McClennan, Phil McCurry, Cary Sandman, Willian Randolph Stevens,{deceased) The Honorable Richard Greer, (deceased), C. Art Lee, and his staff, Bob Gilchrist, Gladys Jaramillo, and all the people of St. Johns, along with the cooperative staffs at both the Tempe and Tucson Public Library.

I will forever be indebted to Laura Greenberg, who was so gracious, enthusiastic, and helpful with this project from the very beginning. Our's has been a friendship that continues to this day, and I've said in all seriousness that she knows me better than any woman on the face of this earth. Her twenty years of constant encouragement has finally gotten me to this place. Thanks Laura. You are the definition of a true friend.

Elsewhere.

In Denver, my thanks to Marsha Renslow, her mother, Mary, and brother Jake, as well as Francis Bender and her family who openly shared so much of this painful family saga with me. Thanks also to Jack Cantwell.

In Oregon, Ken Lindbloom (deceased), Sharon (Lang) Woods, who decided after so many years to break the family code of silence and tell me the intimate details of her family's heartbreak. Thanks also the Gail Hanson for her invaluable help in formatting this book, as well as her encouragement and support in getting it published. Thanks to Caroline Gober for taking this idea I had in my head and making a perfect cover.

I can't begin to thank enough the woman who was with me on this story from that very first night 39 years ago. Her support and patience went far beyond what was returned to her by me. From the bottom of my heart I thank Sue Deaton and her selfless role in helping me get this story told.

Lastly, to Annie Bell, whose actions over the Summer of 2012 became the catalyst for me finally getting off the dime and getting this book published. For that, I thank you.

I am certain there are so many who I have overlooked and I apologize for any omissions. For those who are not listed here, you know who you are, and how you greatly contributed to the book you now hold in your hands.

Jack Earl
Roseburg, Oregon
November 2012

Made in the USA
Lexington, KY
14 February 2019